OUR TIMES
VOLUME II

William Jennings Bryan

WILLIAM JENNINGS BRYAN

MARK SULLIVAN

OUR TIMES

1900-1925

Introduction by Dewey W. Grantham

II
America Finding Herself

New York

CHARLES SCRIBNER'S SONS

INTRODUCTION TO VOLUME II

AMERICA FINDING HERSELF

In the first volume of his six-volume popular history, Mark Sullivan concentrated on the 1890's and the early years of the twentieth century.* In this second volume the chronological coverage is more sweeping, extending in its examination of cultural and economic trends as far back as the Civil War. The first part of the book focuses on the American mind. A second part discusses some of the major industrial tendencies of the late nineteenth and early twentieth centuries, while a third deals with Theodore Roosevelt and the politics of his early years in office. The last section is made up of several unrelated chapters on other developments. The amount of space devoted to social and cultural matters—almost two-thirds of the text—is one of the volume's most prominent features.

In searching for the sources of the American mind (the average man's "stock of ideas"), Sullivan is preoccupied with the role of the common school from the 1870's to the end of the century. Although he neglects such influences on the American mind as newspapers and magazines, universities, religious institutions, and the Chautauqua, he is very effective in his use of textbooks as a source of information about the American mentality. His leisurely exploration of nineteenth-century readers, histories, geographies, spellers, and grammars suggests the importance he attaches to schoolbooks as a means of perpetuating basic

---

* A more comprehensive discussion of Mark Sullivan and the writing of *Our Times* is contained in the general introduction to Volume I of this edition.

American cultural traits. Sullivan describes the common schools as workshops of democracy and patriotism. He strongly approves of the homilies they inculcated, though he is somewhat ambivalent on the question of how well they prepared children for the realities of modern life. Commenting on the schools' penchant for moral didacticism, he observes that the practice of requiring children "to pretend to believe what they knew wasn't so, was food for the iconoclastic rebellion of youth that came into full flower many years later."

This volume contains one of the few sustained efforts in the series to describe the main economic trends of the era. Although the treatment is quite selective and restricted in scope, it throws light on the transformation of the industrial economy, the role of the railroads, the rise of big business, the contribution of the industrial and financial entrepreneurs, and the problem of the trusts. The case studies the author uses to illustrate these developments are familiar to all students of United States history, but they are still dramatic and revealing. Sullivan also tries to present a balanced view of such captains of industry as Carnegie and Rockefeller. On the positive side, he points to their "stupendous benefactions," certain "enrichments of the average man which came partially as an accompaniment of the organization of industry into large units," and the greater appreciation of their role that came with the "economic well-being" of the 1920's.

Many years ago Louis Filler, in his *Crusaders for American Liberalism*, referred to the early Mark Sullivan as "part muckraker and part cultist." By "cultist," he meant a votary of the Roosevelt enthusiasts, and he asserted that in *Our Times* the former muckraker had tenderly woven "the best tribute that all the factions together could have prepared for T.R." There was much truth in what Filler wrote, for Roosevelt was the great political hero of Sullivan's history, the leader used as a standard of comparison for all other politicians. The manner in which the writer introduces T.R. is instructive. He devotes the opening chapter of Part II of the book to an account of Roosevelt's entry into politics and his opposition to the Old Guard in the Republican party. He then shifts abruptly to the story of Edwin Markham's protest poem, "The Man with the Hoe," which he calls "the average man's symbol for the political and economic mood of the time." At this point Sullivan begins his consideration of the transformation of industry and the increasing threat of monopoly in American economic life. Following this section, the narrative turns to the Roosevelt administration. It is apparent from Sullivan's spirited account of several episodes in the Roosevelt era that he regards the ebullient T.R.'s leadership as an effective response to the challenge of big business. Under the tutelage of the youthful President, America was "finding herself."

Sullivan makes no pretense of presenting a comprehensive treatment of national politics during this period, and his failure to deal with Roosevelt's foreign policies is glaringly apparent. He is successful, however, in recapturing the mood of early twentieth-century politics as many ordinary Americans must have experienced it, and, despite his adulation of Roosevelt, he is frequently penetrating in his understanding of the man. He points out, for example, that Roosevelt appreciated the role of public opinion, that he was "the first public man to realize and adapt himself to the relative ebbing of the power of the editorial compared to the news despatch and the cartoon, the first to have a technic for getting the advantage of the head-line." He notes T.R.'s preference for the middle of the road and his addiction to the "balanced sentence." Yet, he declares, the twenty-sixth President was, essentially, "the most forthright public character of his time."

Sullivan understood that Roosevelt was in many respects the political extension of the average American's personality. His political genius was grounded in the many-faceted symbol he projected to his contemporaries, for he symbolized many of their fears, frustrations, and aspirations.

"The Crusade for Pure Food" was a part of the politics of the Roosevelt administration, but Sullivan's chapter on the movement is not narrowly political. Indeed, his account is filled with interesting material on food habits, food and drug adulteration, and medical quackery. Sullivan had played a part in the campaign he describes. It was Sullivan, in fact, who discovered that Lydia E. Pinkham was not "in her laboratory at Lynn, Massachusetts," as a well-known advertisement implied, but was in her grave in the Pine Grove Cemetery near that city, and had been there, according to the date on her tombstone, for twenty years!

Why Sullivan decided to end the narrative of this volume with a chapter on aviation—"The Airplane Emerges"—is not clear. Perhaps he wanted it to balance the account of the emergence of the automobile with which he completed the narrative of his first volume. In any case, the development of the airplane was a topic that he could not ignore, and the story he tells of Orville and Wilbur Wright and the men with whom they competed is one of the most diverting parts of *Our Times*.

Dewey W. Grantham
Vanderbilt University

CONTENTS

ILLUSTRATIONS

ILLUSTRATIONS

ILLUSTRATIONS xxi

America Finding Herself

THE AMERICAN MIND

Channels through Which a People Receives Its Culture.
One Channel Which in America Had Special Importance.
Education. The Schooling of the Average American. Some
Living Links between Our Times and Old Times.

THE aim of Part I of this volume is to survey the average
American's stock of ideas, so far as those ideas came to
him through his early education. What is commonly
called, loosely, a nation's culture includes the points of
view every one has about individual conduct and social
relations; his attitude toward government and toward
other peoples; his habit of mind about the family, the
duty of parents to children and children to parents; his
standards of taste and of morals, his store of accepted
wisdom which he expresses in proverbs and aphorisms;
his venerations and loyalties, his prejudices and biases,
his canons of conventionality; the whole group of ideas
held in common by most of the people. This body of culture comes to every individual mainly through well-
recognized channels, through parents and elders who hand
it down by oral tradition, through religion, through
schools, and through reading, both of books and of newspapers and periodicals. These composed the principal
mediums of American culture as of 1900.[1]

[1] About the turn of the century, new mediums arose and old ones changed in
their relative influence. The stage was always a medium of culture, but in America up to about 1900 had comparatively little contact with the predominantly
rural part of the population, or with the considerable body of people who held the
stage under a taboo. After 1900 the influence of the stage spread and there was
added to it a new and potent source of manners and points of view, the motion-
picture. About 1900 also, part of one of the older sources of culture, reading
matter, in so far as it appeared in newspapers and periodicals, came to be occupied
in increasing degree by persons having wares to sell, was devoted mainly to causing people to want more goods, was called advertising, was highly organized and
became extremely potent as an influence on American habits of mind.

Without undertaking to assign relative importance to the various channels, education is treated at this point merely because of convenience in the arrangement of these volumes. It is tenable to say, however, that schools provided a larger proportion of the average American's stock of ideas than was the case with other nationalities. Education in America was much emphasized and practically universal. Wherever education is general, it tends to modify or supplant oral tradition, it overlaps[1] religion, and is apt to be more potent than reading, because education has a sanction of authoritativeness, and comes when the mind is plastic.

For an obvious reason education is treated, not as it was during the period with which this history mainly deals, but as it was during the generation immediately antecedent. The average mature American of 1900-1925 had gone to school during the decades preceding. To a large extent the ideas he held as an adult, which he expressed through the public men whom he elected to office, through the leaders he chose or accepted in all lines of thought, and the principles and issues he supported or opposed, had been formed, or at least the foundation for them had been acquired, in the American schools as they were during the generation in which he was a child.

The period when the average American of 1900-1925 received his education, the time when his mind was stored with the ideas that largely determined his political and other convictions and biases, is obvious. Consider that the average adult American of 1900-1925 was of the same age, roughly, as some Presidents for whom he voted, and some other typical leaders to whom he gave allegiance. Roosevelt was 43 when he became President in 1901;

---

[1] "Overlaps" is insufficient. Education, in its origin, was closely associated with religion, was indeed an instrumentality of the church; this conception endured, with some diminution, to the present. See Chapter 5.

Wilson was 57 when he became President in 1913; Bryan was 50 when he last ran for the Presidency in 1908. Calvin Coolidge was 51 when he became President in 1923. These leaders had received their schooling within a period running from about 1865 to about 1895. The average American who voted for them obviously had received his schooling during approximately the same period or a little

A country school in up-state New York, about 1870.

later, in many cases as late as 1910. In the American public school, therefore, of the 1860's, '70's, '80's, '90's and early 1900's, we shall discover the sources of whatever it was that education did to form the minds of the American generation who were adult between 1900 and 1925. For the great majority, the vast majority, of the average, formal education ended with what they got from the common schools.

The survey that follows has made use of the obvious sources, including a large number of the text-books.

These springs have been supplemented by personal recollections from a large number of persons who were school
children at one time or another during the decades from
1860 to 1900, and who were still living during the years
when these chapters were composed. Those who have
made these personal contributions — at once to the fruit-
fulness of the author's work and to the accuracy, scope,
and richness of history — came from all sections of
America and from a wide variety of occupations. Many
were persons whose mature careers had given them unique
equipment for expressing judgment about the value of
their educational experiences. The names of some appear
from place to place in the text, in connection with quotations from them, or otherwise. The value of this collabora-
tion by living, personal sources of information and judgment is unique and incalculable. Much of the material in
the following pages had its existence solely in their minds.
Some, who knew of education in the 1890's and 1880's,
were, in 1927, in the prime of life. But many were elderly,
and some old. With their passing, some of the details they
knew about education in earlier America would have
passed from the knowledge of man. The author, in his
contacts with them, thought of them as Daniel Webster
thought of the Revolutionary veterans at Bunker Hill,
venerable men who had come down from an earlier America. They, in their kindly willingness to help, and their
pleasure in recalling their youth, had a corresponding
attitude, of handing on something that to them was both
valuable and, in a different sense, dear; something they
were sadly reluctant to see lost to their sons and daughters,
and happy to help perpetuate. Association with some of
the more elderly, when they were in a mood of living over
their school days, was an experience spiritually enriching,
emotionally exalting. One was able, almost literally, to
live for a few hours from time to time, in the America

of forty to sixty years ago; to feel as new and pristine, things which the later generation of Americans have only known as familiar and commonplace. Some of their letters were completely modern, dictated and typed in important offices where virile age still holds its sway; but

Charles Evans Hughes
at the age of eight.

William Howard Taft
as a schoolboy of fifteen.

many came on old-fashioned blue-lined paper, the economy learned in McGuffey's Readers still expressing itself in use of both sides of the sheet, the handwriting a wavering line of a battle between Spencerian flourish and age's quaver, the phraseology quaint alike in its idioms and its gentle courtesy. The quality of these letters, at once very enriching and a little poignant, was typified by one from an old-time school-teacher living his retirement in a rural village in central New York, who, in sequence, apologized for writing, supplied priceless information about an old-time American institution, analyzed shrewdly and profoundly the causes of the passing of New England's supremacy in pedagogy, told of a rear-guard resistance he

From "Harper's Young People," an illustrated weekly.
Cold morning in a country school.

was still making against the recent standardization of education, and closed with a few words of appreciation (their brevity was part of their distinction) for the author's interest in older American schools, ending: "We who are about to die, salute you!"

2

THE AMERICAN MIND: EDUCATION

The "Readers," Which Were the Backbone of Instruction in Common Schools. The Source of Much of the Average American's Stock of Ideas about Conduct, His Mental Attitude, His Aphorisms, His Familiar Phrases, His Knowledge of Books. An Itinerant Clergyman-Schoolmaster, by a Good Deed, Sets in Motion a Stream Which Shapes Much of American Culture for Nearly a Century.

THE backbone of education in the common schools of America — so far as it aimed to impart ideas, standards of individual and social conduct, and the like — was the "Readers." They were to the last two-thirds of the nineteenth century what the New England Primer had been to the eighteenth. The Readers were the only textbooks used in all schools that bore directly and positively upon the formation of character, or that provided ethical guidance. History and Geography dealt mainly with facts; Arithmetic and Spelling were designed for mental discipline. "The Readers were the proper and indispensable texts for teaching

integrity, honesty, industry, temperance, true patriotism, courage, politeness, and all other moral and intellectual virtues. Readers which have been recognized as formers of good habits of action, thought, and speech for three-quarters of a century; which have taught a sound morality to millions of children without giving offense to the most violent sectarian, are surely worthy of study as to their origin, their successive changes, and their subsequent career.[1]

The Readers came in series, usually six, graduated to meet the needs of pupils of all ages — the First Reader

[1] Quoted from Henry H. Vail, an official of the American Book Company and of predecessor firms engaged in publishing school text-books. The passage is from a booklet he wrote about the principal series of Readers used in American schools.

dealing with the alphabet and words of one syllable, the Sixth adapted to pupils of fifteen and older. They were, in one of their aspects, an amplification of the New England Primer, and, like it, had, in the beginning, a semi-religious as well as educational rôle.

Blanche Bates, aged fourteen, when she was a schoolgirl in San Francisco.

It is possible to set down a rough statement of the order of succession[1] in American school books. The New England Primer was the principal one, often the only one, until well toward the opening of the nineteenth century. Because the schools were closely associated with the churches, the New England Primer aimed definitely and almost exclusively at religious and ethical teaching. Then came a comparatively brief supremacy of "Spellers," beginning with Noah Webster's in 1782. These were more than Spellers. Catering to the tradition which thought of education as a means of teaching religion and conduct, the Spellers included ethical maxims, stories with morals, aphorisms of right living. About the 1820's came the Readers, which, accepting the general conception that schools were places for moral teaching, included the same kind of stories and maxims as the New England Primer, and more of them. About that time education became more general; a conception of schools arose containing the seed of what we now know as common schools. With that, the Readers were much expanded in size, and began to

[1] For a more complete statement of this sequence, see page 10.

include material less strictly confined to ethical teaching. The beginning of the Readers was more or less simultaneous with the beginning of public education at the expense of the State. The Readers reflected, as this conception of education did, a liberalizing spirit, a tendency to teach more than religion and ethics. As we shall see, the tendency did not become extravagant, judged by modern standards.

The preparation of the earlier Readers engaged men who had standing in the church and in public affairs, as well as in scholarship. At that time, thoughtful persons were conscious of the importance of school textbooks, the key[1] position they occupy in the formation of the national spirit — a point of view quite lost sight of in a later generation when the manufacture and sale of

Mrs. Herbert Hoover as a schoolgirl in Waterloo, Iowa.

text-books became an organized industry, and hardly anybody paid any attention to who was hired to write them. The compiler of an early series of Readers, 1799, was

[1] When people could not read, who wrote the ballads of a nation may have been more important than who made the laws. After literacy and schools became general, the authorship of school text-books became important.

Lindley Murray, accepted during four generations as the standard authority on English grammar. "Peter Parley's" Readers, issued in 1839, were prepared by S. G. Goodrich; Goodrich was a relative of the founder of the New England orthographic dynasty, Noah Webster, famous during a hundred years for his dictionary and his "Blue-Back" Speller. Another early compiler of Readers, about 1825, was a New England scholar and clergyman named John Pierpont; he was destined to pass from the knowledge of man, as respects his own rôle; but his name was destined to have immense prestige sixty to a hundred years later, when two of his namesakes and descendants, grandson and great-grandson, respectively, were heads of the principal private banking-house in America, John Pierpont Morgan, Senior (1837-1913) and John Pierpont Morgan, Junior[1] (1867-   ).

Pierpont's Readers were published in the 1820's;[2] "Peter Parley's" in 1839. About this time the adoption, by the States, of the system of free and universal public schools, began to have momentum. With that came increased demand for Readers. To meet it came a new series, eclipsing all others, past or later — the Reader of Readers.

II

A historian, if asked who was the most popular American of the second half of the nineteenth century, might answer incorrectly, if his researches had been confined to

---

[1] In the year in which this is written, 1927, John Pierpont Morgan, Junior, had become Senior, and there was another John Pierpont Morgan, Junior.

[2] The exact sequence of the series of Readers was: Murray's, 1799; Abner Allen's, used about 1804–1810; Pierpont's, about 1825; Samuel Wood's, 1828; Warren Colburn's, 1833. The Angell Readers were published in the early 1830's, the Mount Vernon Readers in 1836, and "Peter Parley's" in 1839. Then came McGuffey's. (The information in this foot-note was given me by Albert Mordell, of Philadelphia, and George A. Plimpton, of the publishing firm of Ginn and Company, leading authority on American school books, and owner of a unique collection of them.)

the more usual fields of investigation. He might, bearing in mind the regard of old soldiers for a military hero, answer Grant; or recalling the martyr of the Civil War, say Lincoln. Probably he would not think at all of the one who was really most popular, in the sense of being most affectionately remembered, who was named McGuffey. Schoolboys did not know him as that, but as "McGuffey's," as if he were an institution, which in fact he was. Such was the modesty of the man, or such his assurance of the permanence of his fame, that on the title-pages of the later editions of his Readers he did not give his first name; and in the specimens preserved in the Congressional Library, his full name is supplied, in pencil, at the bottom of the title-page, "William Holmes McGuffey." He, or his publishers, tried to minimize his personality by calling his Readers the "Eclectic" series, failing to anticipate that such an abstraction could never, in the minds of schoolboys, displace the more familiar and affectionately held "McGuffey's."

From "A History of the McGuffey Readers," by Henry H. Vail.

William H. McGuffey

McGuffey is not mentioned in the conventional histories of America. His name is not in the index of the pretentious (and also worthy) "Main Currents in American Thought" of Vernon Louis Parrington; nor in the two-volume "Rise of American Civilization," by Charles A. and Mary R. Beard. "Nelson's Encyclopedia" gives him fifteen lines; the "Encyclopædia Britannica" none at all.

For this the obvious explanation is that McGuffey did not function in any of the fields which are conventionally credited with making important contributions to history; he was not an author, in the accepted sense, nor a military man, nor a politician, nor a judge. One is moved to reflect that too faithful fidelity to the accepted may be a limitation of historians, both as to their omissions and as to their inclusions; that we are too complacent in taking it for granted that a people's history is made, and their thoughts formed or led, exclusively by those who function in the traditional forums, those who write or fight, orate, or rule. However that may be, the suggestion that McGuffey had a large influence in determining the thoughts and ideals of the American people is ventured on the testimony of witnesses who at least are convinced and earnest. From an abundance of them a few are here set down.

David Swing[1] said that the books which most influenced his mind and character were "The Bible, Calvin's Institutes, Fox's Book of Martyrs, and the McGuffey Readers." On the last Doctor Swing expanded in a sermon:

Much as you may have studied the languages or the sciences, that which most affected you was the moral lessons in the series of McGuffey. . . . Up out of the far-off years come all the blessed lessons in virtue and righteousness which those reading books taught. I cannot but wish the teachers had made us bound the States less and solve fewer puzzles in cube root, and made us commit to memory the whole series of the McGuffey Eclectic Readers. The memory that comes from these far-away pages is full of the best wisdom of time. In these books we were led from beautiful maxims for children up to the best thoughts of a long line of sages and poets. There we all first learned the awful weakness of the duel that took away a Hamilton; there we saw the grandeur of the Blind Preacher of William Wirt; there we saw the emptiness of the ambition of

---

[1] A Presbyterian clergyman who wrote "Truths for Today" and "Motives of Life." The passage quoted here is condensed.

Alexander, and there we heard even the infidel say: "Socrates died like a philosopher, but Jesus Christ like a God."[1]

That final note exalting religion had a dominance in McGuffey's Readers proportionate to the impress it left on Doctor Swing's memory. The same passage, about Christ and Socrates, was vivid in the recollection of ex-Governor Lowden, of Illinois, when he wrote in 1927:

The Readers we used were McGuffey's. The selections I now recall are "Thanatopsis," the "Battle of Waterloo," Webster's "Reply to Hayne," and another "piece" which concluded, as I now recall it, something like this: "Socrates died like a philosopher; Jesus Christ like a God."

Will Owen Jones, of the *Nebraska State Journal*, wrote:

I received more inspiration from McGuffey's Readers than from any other books in my experience. I can still quote pages from their selections. I asked the people around a dinner table last night what books had influenced them most in early life. A majority declared for McGuffey's Reader, the Fifth.

John H. Clarke, as a Justice of the Supreme Court of the United States, 1916-1922, handed down decisions colored by the McGuffey's Readers he had studied in Lisbon (then New Lisbon), Ohio, fifty years before:

The selections in these Readers were for the most part serious and of real worth. Oftentimes expressions, even yet, come into my mind, which very certainly are derived from them.[2]

[1] Throughout this volume, for the purpose of reducing quotations to the briefest space consistent with keeping the integrity of their authors' thoughts, and also for the purpose of clarity, use has been made of three dots, thus . . . , to denote elision of words or phrases not essential to the meaning in the present connection, or otherwise redundant. Sometimes, more than one elision is made in a quotation. In such cases, in order to avoid awkwardness of typographical appearance and impediment to the reader's quickness of grasp, only one set of dots is used. In this book, therefore, the appearance of three dots . . . in the body of a quotation signifies that one or more words or phrases have been deleted, always, of course, with care not to alter the meaning. Occasionally, to achieve clarity, the order of the sentences in a quotation is changed. In such cases attention is called to the fact in a foot-note.

[2] Among others who in letters to the author recalled McGuffey's were Ida M. Tarbell, Senator Simeon D. Fess, Senator Frank L. Greene, ex-Senator Albert J.

One of the best minds of his generation in the United States Senate, Thomas J. Walsh, wrote in 1927:

McGuffey's was the standard Reader in our schools in my boyhood days. I still have a copy of the Sixth which is at the foundation of what I know of literature. I think I can still recite all of "Rienzi's Address to the Romans," most of Patrick Henry's speech, considerable of Webster's "Reply to Hayne," and snatches from excerpts from Milton and Shakespeare.

Nowhere has any one pictured the life of an average American better than Herbert Quick, in the period in which he lived, 1861-1926. Quick, in his "One Man's Life," devotes a whole chapter to paying tribute to "My Debt to the McGuffey Brothers": "I had," he says of his childhood in rural Iowa, "a burning thirst for books. On those farms a boy or girl with my appetite for literature was a frog in a desert." The thirst was satisfied and, more important, was stimulated to aspiration for further satisfaction, by "an old dog-eared volume of McGuffey's, the standard school Readers of my day. My mastery of the First and Second Readers — just the opening of the marvels of the printed page — was a poignant delight, gave me a sort of ecstasy. These text-books constitute the most influential volumes ever published in America."

To say Quick's broad assertion is more inspired by affection than dictated by exactness, to answer him by

Beveridge. The most tangible sign of the affection in which McGuffey's was held came from Henry Ford, who, in 1925, had the entire series (the revised series used when Ford was a schoolboy) reproduced, and distributed them widely. It is an odd fact that Ford came into one kind of fame in 1919 by saying "history is bunk," meaning history as written; and a few years later became, in a true sense, the most authentic historian in America, and also the most effective. To this appellation he is entitled by his reproduction and circulation of McGuffey's, his purchase and restoration of an old American inn, the "Wayside," made famous by Longfellow, and an old American one-room schoolhouse; his revival of old American dances and songs, and his effort to make them familiar to modern America, by dancing them himself and by giving painstaking public instruction in them through his weekly paper, the Dearborn *Independent;* his museum of old American implements of transportation and other utensils. If America should experience a renaissance of interest in its own past, affection for its own institutions, and pride in its own traditions, Henry Ford would be entitled to much of the credit.

pointing out that McGuffey was merely the compiler of the selections so fondly remembered, and that only the authors of them, Shakespeare and Milton and the others, are important — all that is easy. But is it safe to underestimate the man who, for millions of Americans, just at the right moment in their fleeting adolescence, opened the gate to literature? To open the gate in just the right way, to lead the child in, to cause him to want to go in; to point the way and to make it seem alluring, calls for inspiration and understanding little short of authorship itself. How many of us would have learned to know any of the English poets if we had been left to begin at the first page and try to find our own discouraged ways to the passages that would thrill us? Quick, and the others whose testimony to McGuffey is quoted, were unusual men; with the texture native to their minds it is probable they would have found some road or other leading to good books. We cannot be sure; in any event, it was McGuffey's compilations that reached the mind of young America.

But the certain importance of McGuffey is seen less by considering the cases of eminent men than by reflecting on men of more nearly average circumstances. To millions of others, to probably nine out of ten average Americans, what taste of literature they got from McGuffey's was all they ever had; what literature the children brought into the home in McGuffey's Readers was all that ever came. Broad classical reading was decidedly not general. McGuffey, in short, because of the leverage of his Readers, had a large part in forming the mind of America. A compiler who selects, from the entire body of English literature, enough to fill six small books, may put into the process as much personality as many an author of original works. McGuffey, his compilations reveal, had a very definite mind and a temperament, which he expressed in what he selected, and in what he omitted. The principles,

ideals, and rules of conduct that McGuffey held are clearly
revealed in the stories and passages he selected to illustrate them and drive them home.

However, the part McGuffey had in influencing the
mind of America is to be understood not by analyzing
it but by feeling it — seeing it glow in the affectionate
memories of those who were school children during the
second half of the nineteenth century. "McGuffey's,"
wrote Charles F. Buck, of Lacon, Illinois,

hangs as the brightest picture in the halls of memory, recalling
the springtime of youth, the plastic clay of development that
fashions a human soul. . . . The school Readers were about
the only reading matter in the home, aside from the Bible and
"Pilgrim's Progress."

"Great indeed were the old McGuffey's Readers,"
wrote John B. Dennis, of Ottumwa, Iowa, adding a super-
lativeness of judgment that may be based partly on affection: "This whole country is literally full of their ardent
admirers. Nothing like them ever existed in any age, anywhere in the world. They did more in shaping American
character than all the Presidents combined."

III

The history of McGuffey and the origin of the Readers
he compiled provide one of those occasions when it is
possible to go one remove back of the man and identify,
with reasonable accuracy, his inspiration; or at least identify an incident that was indispensable in enabling the
man to do what he did. The story is such a one as McGuffey himself might have included in his Readers to teach
the value of good deeds — indeed, who can doubt that
much which McGuffey put into his Readers was inspired
by recollections of the beginning of his own education?

In the year 1802, in the part of Pennsylvania that was
then the American frontier, a Presbyterian clergyman

named Thomas Hughes erected a building known for a long time as the "Old Stone Academy." To solicit funds for the school, Hughes travelled about the country on horse-back. One day in the summer of 1818, riding through Trumbull County, Ohio, in dust so deep it deadened the sound of his horse's feet, Hughes passed a log cabin, half-hidden from the road by bushes, in the garden of which the traveller overheard a woman praying. Her prayer was an appeal that God might send some means by which her children could get an education. Hughes, riding on, asked at the next cabin who the woman was, learned the name and was told the circumstances of the family. He turned back, sought the distressed mother, and took the oldest son, William Holmes McGuffey, into the "Old Stone Academy." [1]

To the knowledge of the writer of this page, the influences thus casually set in motion were flowing in broad streams through the life of America more than a hundred years later.

The McGuffey family, and McGuffey himself, had had an origin and experiences which made him of the essence

[1] This story, long told and widely accepted, is printed in the account of the McGuffey Readers written by H. H. Vail, an official of the company that published the later editions of the Readers. But alas for legend, and alas also for the difficulty of getting history accurate. After the present chapter was in type, it was sent for verification to many persons who had knowledge of the subject, among them Reverend Edward H. McGuffey, Rector of St. James Church, Elmhurst, New York (a son of Alexander H. McGuffey and nephew of William H.), who, among other valuable corrections, wrote:

"I note you repeat Vail's story [about the way William H. McGuffey got his education]. That is pure fiction. Nothing like it ever occurred."

Doctor McGuffey also said, concerning an imputation on page 41, not meant to be taken too literally:

"Your assumption that the McGuffeys were pacifists, because of the poem 'What Made Alexander Great?' is entirely superfluous. The McGuffeys never declined a conflict. Their father was an Indian-fighter, and both his sons were always ready to put on the gloves. William H. McGuffey was always in active contention with those who disagreed with him. Both of these brothers were hard-headed sons of Scotch immigrants, born on the frontier, and accustomed to its hardships and Indian warfare. That either of them should now be classed as a 'pacifist' is quite absurd. They were pacifists, so long as all things were going right. Otherwise,——!"

of average America — at least, of the essence of that part
of America that did not come through New England.
One finds in the text-books used by American public
schools two springs of influence: In New England, Noah
Webster wrote a Dictionary, a Speller, and a History;
and S. G. Goodrich, "Peter Parley" (nephew of Chauncey
A. Goodrich who was a son-in-law of Webster), wrote a
Geography, a Primer, Histories, and text-books on other
subjects. That composed a New England dynasty in
American text-book history. More or less simultaneously, William and Alexander Hamilton McGuffey,
brothers, wrote the series of Readers that became practically universal throughout America except New England[1] and part of the Pacific Coast. This distinction between the New England dynasty and the McGuffey one
is more geographical than spiritual. Spiritually, the origins of the two were no more different, than Puritan
England (which settled New England and founded Harvard and Yale) differs from Presbyterian Scotland (which
was a main stream in the settlement of the rest of the
country, founded Princeton, and otherwise provided intellectual and spiritual leadership to portions of the
country not influenced by New England). That difference is small.

McGuffey's grandparents,[2] coming from Scotland the
year before the Revolutionary War opened, 1774, landed
in Philadelphia and followed what was then the frontier
to York County, Pennsylvania; to Washington County,
Pennsylvania, and thence to Trumbull County, Ohio.
His father was a frontiersman living in a log cabin, a
"settler," a seeker of free land, and a soldier and scout

---

[1] In a rather painstaking survey to determine the area of McGuffey's influence,
I found that apparently it had never reached any of New England except the one
small southwestern corner close to New York City. Elsewhere, McGuffey's was
almost universal.

[2] There is a curious similarity in time, place, character, and background between the McGuffey family and Woodrow Wilson's forebears.

in wars against the Indians in Southern Ohio under General Anthony Wayne. William Holmes McGuffey, the eldest son in the large family, was born September 28, 1800, on the southern border of Washington County, Pennsylvania, attended the "Old Stone Academy" when his father could spare him from reclaiming the family farm from the wilderness, graduated at Washington College, taught school at Paris, Ky., in 1824; served as Professor of Ancient Languages at Miami University from 1826 to 1832; became president of Cincinnati College in 1836; president of the Ohio University at Athens, Ohio, in 1839; helped in the passage of the General School Law under which the common schools of Ohio were organized; and became Professor of Natural and Moral Philosophy in the University of Virginia in 1845. To give orthodox authenticity to the services he conducted when he was at Miami University, he secured a license as a preacher in the Presbyterian Church, and preached more than three thousand sermons. He died on May 4, 1873, three years before the centennial of American Independence, and one year before his family had concluded a hundred years of American residence.

In 1836 McGuffey compiled, for a firm of publishers[1] in Cincinnati, a First and Second Reader; and in 1837 a Third and Fourth.[2] In 1841, with the assistance of his brother, he compiled the Fifth, first known as "McGuffey's Rhetorical Guide." In 1851 the five Readers were

[1] McGuffey received a royalty of ten per cent until $1,000 was reached, after which the Readers became the absolute property of the publishers. The contract was mutually satisfactory and remained so. For his work in the various revisions McGuffey was paid a fee. After the Civil War the publishers gave McGuffey a voluntary annuity until he died.

[2] "The Fourth Reader was probably the work of the younger brother, Alexander H. McGuffey, as I have reason to believe. The Rhetorical Guide was entirely the work of Alexander H. McGuffey."—Reverend Edward M. McGuffey, in a letter to the author.

made into six. The series was revised five times. The
last revision was copyrighted in 1901. They were still
being sold in 1927. Their vogue endured from the Presidency of Martin Van Buren to that of Theodore Roosevelt. Children studied McGuffey's, grew up, had children
who in turn studied McGuffey's; these again had children
who read McGuffey's sixty years after their grandparents
had begun with them. In a country prone to change, Mc-
Guffey's had permanence for a strikingly long time.

The compilation and publication of McGuffey's Readers
coincided with the time when the idea of free common
schools was getting into swing. By that, and by the
energy of the publishers,[1] but more by the merit of the
compiler, the McGuffey Readers "attained the largest
sales that have as yet been accorded by the public to a
single series of books." Of the earlier editions there are
no records, but of one revised edition more than eight
million copies of the First Reader were used. Of the Sixth
Reader, which, being for mature pupils, had the least sale,
over a million copies were distributed. One feels justified
in estimating that, taking into account all the editions, as
many as seventy or eighty millions[2] of McGuffey's Readers
must have been used by American school children. This

---

[1] McGuffey's publishers had an energy and aggressiveness that caused them to
be called, during the '60's, '70's, and '80's, the "octopus" and "monopoly" of the
school-book business. In a long and bitter fight between the McGuffey Readers
and the Appleton Readers, "every device known to the agency managers of the
houses engaged was employed. . . . It was war." The name of the firm, as it was
in 1877, after various mutations, was Van Antwerp, Bragg & Company, a title
which its rivals translated into "Van Anteup, Grabb & Company." The firm continued until 1890, when the copyrights and plates were sold to the American
Book Company. (The authority for the facts in this foot-note is Henry H. Vail,
a member of the firm that published McGuffey's.)

[2] After this was in type, a letter from Louis M. Dillman, President of the
American Book Company, informed me the estimate is too low. Mr. Dillman
estimates the combined sales of McGuffey's Readers, Primers, and Spelling-book,
between 1836 and 1920, at 122,000,000. He has exact figures for two years in
the late eighties:

1888 2,082,624
1889 2,172,413

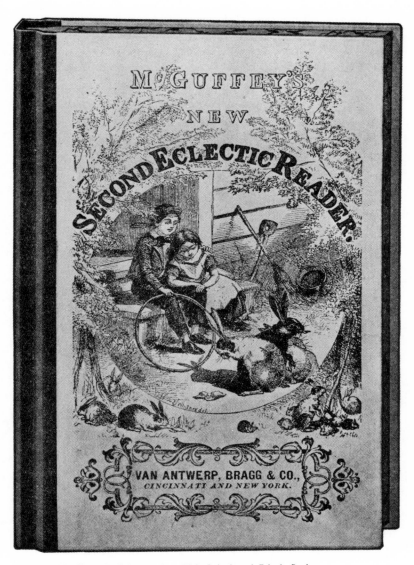

Reprinted by Henry Ford in 1925 from McGuffey's Second Eclectic Reader.

should be qualified by remembering that some children used more than one Reader, depending on how long they remained at school. Taking everything into account, it would not be surprising if at least half the school children of America, from 1836 to 1900, drew inspiration from McGuffey's Readers. When America sent expeditions of school-teachers to carry American culture to the Philippines and Porto Rico, McGuffey's Readers were translated into Spanish; when Japan felt an urge to experiment with American ways, McGuffey's was translated and carried its democratic point of view into the background of a crystallized feudalism centuries old.

IV

The comprehensive purpose of McGuffey's Readers is to be found in sentences from the Prefaces:[1]

. . . to obtain as wide a range of leading authors as possible, to present the best specimens of style, to insure interest in the subjects, to impart valuable information, and to exert a decided and healthful moral influence.

These purposes corresponded with the effects McGuffey's had on four generations of American life. McGuffey's was the source of America's taste in reading — for many average Americans, the only reading of poetry or classic prose they ever had. Along with that, McGuffey's was the source of that stock of points of view and tastes held in common, which constituted much of America's culture, its codes of morals and conduct, its standards of propriety, its homely aphorisms, its "horse-sense" axioms. In this field McGuffey's embodied, of course, some points of view common to civilization everywhere; but McGuffey's also taught and accounted for mental attitudes and ethical concepts which differentiated America from other peoples,

[1] 1879 revised editions of the Fifth and Sixth Readers.

or were more emphasized in America than elsewhere. In this respect, McGuffey was a kind of American Confucius, the latter, like the former, taking his sayings from the accumulated lore of the race. McGuffey's had the effect of having combed the whole folk-lore of the human species, as well as its printed literature, for stories and fables conveying the race's familiar wisdom. Some fables came from as far back as Æsop; others retold bits of homely truth that had been crystallized generations before by British people — many of the scenes of the McGuffey's stories had a British setting. Yet others of McGuffey's stories and aphorisms were indigenous to America, lessons learned by pioneer contact with the frontier of a new country, experiences with Indians and wild animals. At all times and in every respect, McGuffey's Readers had a strong flavor of religion; much of its contents was Puritan and evangelical, none was inconsistent with the religion of Calvin and Knox.

Most of the direct teaching of morals, the formal *haec fabula docet*, was in the Readers designed for younger pupils with more impressionable minds, the Primer and the First to Fourth Readers. These books were, to the average American, the storehouse of the fables, stories, mottoes, proverbs, adages, and aphorisms which constituted the largest body of ethical teaching he had, excepting the Bible, and the teaching of the Bible was overlapped by that of the Readers. In these books many a mature reader will find phrases, words associated in familiar couplets and passages, that have become standardized parts of his personal vocabulary. It was from McGuffey's that Roosevelt got the devastating epithet he once hurled at some self-starting proponents of plans alternative to his own, "Meddlesome Matties." Because allusions to characters in McGuffey's were as quickly grasped, or quicker, than allusions to Biblical characters, everybody recalled the little girl in McGuffey's who, overcome by an over-mastering intellectual curiosity, could not obey the ban put upon opening her grandmother's snuff-box, and suffered a retribution described in the couplet:

> In vain she ran about for ease;
> She could do nothing else but sneeze.

Many another reader will find in McGuffey's, to his surprise, the origin not only of phrases but of sentiments, tastes, standards of conduct, and inhibitions which in his pride he supposed were indigenous to himself, the native evidences of his own superiority of inner grace.

The Primer and First Reader were in words of one syllable, so far as this simplicity could be achieved. The lessons they taught, all the lessons in all the Readers, were moral, orthodox, religious, and put emphasis on the common virtues, industry, mercy, self-control. Industry was inculcated by the "How doth the little busy bee"; and also by an exhortation to a little girl named Lucy to get up early in the morning. The incentive held out to the little lie-abed was emulation, which does not seem the most wisely chosen motive. "Mary was up at six," said the Primer. "Up, up, Lucy, and go out to Mary!" (Scoffers abbreviated that to "Double up, Lucy!") The wholesome psychological effect of good associations and good examples was illustrated in "The Idle Boy Reformed," a story of a boy who asked a dog to play with him. The dog replied: "No, I must not be idle; I must catch a hare for my master's dinner." In turn, the boy solicited to truancy a bird and a horse, each of whom replied, with a reiteration of phraseology designed to make the lesson indelible: "No, I must not be idle." The closing paragraph put the moral in words not to be missed by the most youthful intelligence:

"What! is nobody idle? Then little boys must not be idle."
So he made haste, and went to school, and learned his lesson
very well, and the master said he was a very good boy.

That small children should not scare their playmates
was driven home by the tragic tale of a boy who played
ghost and made another boy insane. The unforeseen and
tragically retaliatory consequences of mischievousness
were illustrated in "The Boys Who Did Mischief for Fun,"
a story of two brothers who tied the grass across the path
and thus upset the milkmaid, which was their mirthful
intention; but upset also the messenger running for a
doctor to come to their father. "Oh, father will die,
what must we do?" cried the repentant boys. Whereupon the author of the narrative gravely sets down the
moral, tempering it with a diluted hope that the experience had not been as tragic as it might.

I do not know whether their papa died or not; I believe he
got well again; but I am sure of one thing, that Edward and
William never tied the grass to throw people down again as
long as they lived.

A moral lesson even more direct was conveyed by a fable
about two quarrelsome cocks; the defeated one, in his
malice, admitted to the barnyard a fox — who promptly
slew both victor and vanquished. Direct retribution for
evil was depicted so frequently that children taking
McGuffey's on faith must have thought it a universal law
of life. A vividly prompt form of retribution came to
"The Passionate Boy" who "would strike and throw
things at his brothers and sisters if they offended him."
One day he picked up a flat-iron for use in a purpose of
anger toward his sister, but the iron, being hot, "burnt
his hand so that the skin came off and he suffered much
pain." Therefore, said the moral: "When you are at
play with your little companions you should be very
careful and not get angry with them."

Kindness to animals[1] was taught by

> I love my dear puss,
> Her fur is so warm;
> And if I don't hurt her,
> She'll do me no harm.

Incitement to consideration for animals was taught also by a story about a lame dog who, when cured, brought

From McGuffey's First Eclectic Reader.

"George is kind to Jack and Jack loves him, be-cause he is kind. The kind and good are al-ways loved."

another lame dog to be doctored. That story, incidentally, imputed to dogs a mutual helpfulness, a so-to-speak philanthropic caninitarianism that calls for a good deal of proof. McGuffey, when bent on teaching a moral lesson, was conspicuously indifferent to details of natural history. He attributed human traits to animals; caused them to reason, if the lesson demanded it; even put wordy morals

---

[1] Is this a distinctive American trait? If so, did McGuffey's inspire it or pass it on? That Americans are more kind to animals than some other peoples, is a common generalization, whether or not it is based on a sufficient number of examples to support generalizations about whole peoples. A European was surprised to learn of an American "Society for the Prevention of Cruelty to Animals"—why should anybody bother about cruelty to beasts?

into their mouths. A later generation, more literal and more meticulous, would have classified McGuffey with the "nature-fakers."

Frequently McGuffey imputed to animals codes of conduct superior to those of human beings. This romantic attribution to animals of such functions as reasoning, and such qualities as kindness, and the tacit acceptance of the idea by teachers, or their insistence that the children must accept it, led to a state of mind on the part of some pupils, in which we shall find the first of several clews to the spirit of iconoclasm, of reaction to stark realism, even of rebellion, that arose some decades later. Gene Stratton Porter, in her autobiographical story, "Laddie," describes her first day in school. The teacher told her to read:

"Birds in their little nests agree,
And why can't we?"

"B-i-r-d-s, birds, i-n, in, t-h-e-i-r, their, l-i-t-t-l-e, little, n-e-s-t-s, nests, a-g-r-e-e, agree" . . . I followed the point of her pencil, while, a letter at a time, I spelled aloud my first sentence. . . .

As I repeated the line, Miss Amelia . . . sprang to her feet, tripped a few steps toward the centre of the platform, and cried: "Classes, attention! Our Youngest Pupil has just completed her first sentence. This sentence contains a Thought. It is a wonderfully beautiful Thought. A Thought that suggests a great moral lesson for each of us. 'Birrrds — in their little nests — agreeee.' There is a lesson in this for all of us. We are here in our schoolroom like little birds in their nests. Now how charming it would be if all of us would follow the example of the birds, and at our work, and in our play, agreeee — be kind, loving, and considerate of each other. Let us all remember always this wonderful truth: 'Birrrrds — in their little nests — agreeeee.'"

In three steps I laid hold of her apron. . . ."Ho but they don't!" I cried. "They fight like anything! Every day they make the feathers fly!"

In a backward stroke Miss Amelia's fingers, big and bony, struck my cheek a blow that nearly upset me. A red wave crossed her face, and her eyes snapped. I never had been so

surprised in all my life. I was only going to tell her the truth.
What she had said was altogether false. Ever since I could
remember I had watched courting male birds fight all over the
farm. . . . If a young bird failed to get the bite it wanted, it
sometimes grabbed one of its nestmates by the bill, or the eye
even. Always the oldest and strongest climbed on top of the
youngest and fooled his mammy into feeding him most by having his head highest, his mouth widest, and begging loudest.
There could be no mistake. I was so amazed I forgot the blow,
as I stared at the fool woman.

"I don't see why you slap me!" I cried. "It's the truth!
Lots of times old birds pull out bunches of feathers fighting,
and young ones in the nests bite each other until they squeal."

Miss Amelia caught my shoulders and shook me.

"Take your seat!" she cried. "You are a rude, untrained
child!"

"They do fight!" I insisted, as I held my head high and
walked to my desk.

Requiring children to pretend to believe what they
knew wasn't so, was food for the iconoclastic rebellion of
youth that came into full flower many years later.

A McGuffey's story entitled "Little Henry," about
three boys each of whom had a large cake, compressed
into three brief sentences a trinity of fundamental morals,
retribution for greediness, dust and ashes for miserliness,
and approval for generosity:

James ate so much that it made him sick. George kept his so
long that it got dry and was not fit to eat. But John gave some
of his cake to each of his schoolmates, and then took a piece
himself and gave the rest to an old blind man.

The moral of "The Truant" pictured the sin of that
delinquency in terms of the sad effect on parents:

Wretched are the parents of such a son! Grief and shame
are theirs. His name shall be stamped with the mark of infamy
when their poor broken hearts shall moulder in the grave.

Paired with this was a contrasting picture of the
parents of "The Diligent Scholar":

Happy are the parents of such a son! Gladness and triumph are theirs. His name shall be crowned with honor by the virtuous and the good, when the pious counsels of his father and mother are heard no more.

That virtue will be rewarded was taught by a story about a chimney-sweep who, under strong temptation, stole a gold watch, but under a subsequent impulse of contrition brought it back, and thereupon was educated by the owner. In "The Righteous Never Forsaken," a widow living in a cottage shared her last smoked herring with a strange traveller, who revealed himself as her long-lost son, returning rich from the Indies.

In McGuffey's Second Reader was the story of George Washington and the mutilated cherry-tree, ending:

"George," said his father, "do you know who killed that fine cherry-tree yonder in the garden?" This was a hard question; George was silent for a moment; and then, looking at his father, his young face bright with conscious love of truth, he bravely cried out: "I can't tell a lie, father; you know, I can't tell a lie. I did cut it with my hatchet."

"Come to my arms, my dearest boy!" cried his father, in transports; "come to my arms! you killed my cherry-tree, George, but you have now paid me for it a thousandfold. Such proof of heroic truth in my son is of more value than a thousand trees, though they were all of the purest gold."

A questioning of the authenticity of that story, a doubt whether any father and son in real life ever talked as McGuffey's said they did, was one of the major points of controversy in the phenomenon of iconoclasm that came to America in the 1920's. Youth doubted whether that story accorded with what they — or their fathers — would have done under similar circumstances, decided it was inconsistent with their own observations of life — and passed on to raise doubts about some other orthodox statements of history and rules of conduct.

Napoleon was used by McGuffey to convey a lesson of a different sort. The Third Reader engaged the imagination of boys by a picture on the cover showing Bonaparte seated on a gloriously rearing charger; and then insinuated a lesson of daring, determination, and sententiousness with Scott's "Bonaparte Crossing the Alps," beginning:

"Is the route practicable?" said Bonaparte.
"It is barely possible to pass," replied the engineer.
"Let us set forward, then," said Napoleon.

McGuffey's story of "The Peacock" admitted that "this is the most beautiful bird in the world." But, in consequence, it is "haughty and proud and loves to display its fine colors, . . . like those little boys and girls who are proud of their fine clothes." Consequently, ran the moral in the closing paragraph:

Little boys and girls, be not like the peacock, proud and vain, on account of your beauty and fine clothes, for humility and goodness are always to be preferred to beauty.

The sin of vanity, or at least the vanity of adornment of the body, was driven home, rather grewsomely in "Death at the Toilet," the story of a girl who was stricken dead while in the very act of artificially beautifying herself — her family found her in her room before the looking-glass, the implements of deplorable decoration in her hands:

Grasping a pair of curling-irons, various paraphernalia of the toilet lay about — pins, broaches, ribbons, gloves, etc. Each of her wrists was encircled by a showy gilt bracelet. . . . The glass reflected with frightful fidelity the clammy, fixed features, daubed with rouge and carmine, the traces of a smirk of conceit which even the palsying touch of death could not wholly obliterate. Poor creature! Struck dead in the very act of sacrificing at the altar of female vanity! Never have I seen so startling a satire upon human vanity, so repulsive, unsightly, and loathsome a spectacle, as a *corpse dressed for a ball*.[1] The

---

[1] Italics are McGuffey's

ghastly visage of death thus leering through the tinselry of fashion — the "vain show" of artificial joy — was a horrible mockery of the fooleries of life.

The "mockeries of the fooleries of life" was a note frequently emphasized in these old Readers. Did the commanded simplicity, the prohibitions and inhibitions of that period in America, have any relation, as a cause of the reaction, to the defiantly exuberant personal decoration of a later generation?

So far as the Readers gave a noticeable proportion of space to any particular mood, one sensed a greater emphasis on melancholy than was characteristic of the more light-minded generation that followed. That, however, was no more a trait of the compilers of Readers than of the spirit of the times. It was a part of decorum and piety, even of propriety, to be a little melancholy. That went with a philosophy common to McGuffey's dour Scotch Presbyterian ancestors and to the Puritan forebears of New England as well. From the two, expressing themselves in education and religion, it infected nearly all America. The "hair shirt" was a hardship physically, but because of that, a luxury spiritually. Sheer enjoyment, of poetry or anything else, was not to be indulged except with the accompaniment of the recalling of death.[1]

Newton D. Baker, who in the cabinet of President Woodrow Wilson was the director of America's military participation in the Great War, recalled:

In McGuffey's there is a poem called "Ginevra" which has to do with a very brilliant and beautiful girl who roguishly hid herself in a chest without knowing of its spring lock. Years later her skeleton was discovered, to account for her mysterious

[1] In the *Literary Digest* for April 25, 1903, a symposium about the books read in childhood by a number of English men of letters showed that in fifty books published for children, from the years 1830 to 1850, most of the stories were written for the purpose of producing in the child's mind a thought of death.

disappearance. There is also a poem in that Reader called "Lord Ullin's Daughter." Both of these poems made an impression which still remains, perhaps because of the tragic note which fitted into a mood of persistent melancholy which I did not outgrow until about my twentieth year.

Practically every series of school Readers included "Mortality," almost always with a preface saying, at some length and with moral admonitions, that it was Lincoln's favorite poem. The following presentation was in a text-book[1] compiled in 1892:

(This was President Lincoln's favorite poem. He knew every word and line of it, and it is said that he often took great pleasure in his meditative moods in repeating the poem. The words in themselves are well worth any one's attention, but since having been the favorite poem of our martyred President it finds a warmer spot in all our hearts.)

> Oh, why should the spirit of mortal be proud?
> Like a fast-flitting meteor, a fast-flying cloud,
> A flash of the lightning, a break of the wave,
> He passes from life to his rest in the grave. . . .

Equally common was Bryant's

> The melancholy days are come,
>   The saddest of the year,
> Of wailing winds, and naked woods,
>   And meadows, brown and sear . . .
> And then I think of one, who in
>   Her youthful beauty died,
> The fair, meek blossom that grew up
>   And faded by my side. . . .

In those days, wherever American life was touched by either the school or the church, it heard a note of "Hark from the tombs a doleful cry." With a curious combina-

---

[1] All the selections mentioned on the preceding pages of this chapter are from McGuffey's. Some of those that follow were not in the copies of McGuffey's that I found, and I have taken them from other text-books used in the schools, including Lippincott's Readers, the National Readers, and several others. There were many revised editions of McGuffey's and I should be very much surprised if the ones after 1860 did not include "Mortality."

tion of consistency and inconsistency, there was equal assertion that death was a happy state. A frequent inclusion in the Readers was:

"Weeping may endure for a night, but joy cometh in the morning."—Psalm XXX. 5.

From McGuffey's First Eclectic Reader.

Sad fate of a boy who stopped to play in a pond on his way to school, and was drowned.

After the shower, the tranquil sun;
Silver stars when the day is done. . . .

After the bud, the radiant rose;
After our weeping, sweet repose. . . .

After the flight, the downy nest;
Beyond the shadowy river — rest.

Space proportionate to melancholy, and having the effect of balancing it, but only of balancing it, was given to passages having the note of joy in nature, usually accompanied by a prudent reminder that joy is fleeting and death certain. A bit of verse that gave my own boyish imagination a lift, and has stayed with me to this day, began:

> I hear a sound below me,
> A twitter of delight.
> It is my friend the swallow,
> Come Northward over-night.

That is all I can remember. I suspect the remainder contained some moral lesson or other, which a self-protective memory has sloughed off. It was the way of many of the selections to hold out, in the first few lines, the bait of joy, in order to get in, at the conclusion, the castor oil of pious admonition — enjoyment as bait for enjoinment. For example, Lucy Larcom's "The Brown Thrush" began with an opening stanza calculated to make children dance with pleasure:

> There's a merry brown thrush sitting up in the tree,
> He's singing to me! He's singing to me!
> And what does he say, little girl, little boy?
> "Oh, the world's running over with joy!
> 　Don't you hear? Don't you see?
> 　Hush! Look! In my tree,
> I'm as happy as happy can be!"

But inevitably came the pious admonition, including, in this case, an injunction to restraint particularly unpalatable to birds'-nesting boys:

> And the brown thrush keeps singing: "A nest do you see,
> And five eggs hid by me in the juniper-tree?
> Don't meddle! don't touch! little girl, little boy,
> Or the world will lose some of its joy!
> 　Now I'm glad! now I'm free!
> 　And I always shall be
> If you never bring sorrow to me."

Imagine a boy required by his teacher to memorize that, and stand up and recite it, in front of thirty or forty other boys, every one of whom knew the hypocritical renegade on the platform had been particeps criminis with them in scores of birds'-nesting expeditions — nearly every schoolboy had collections of birds' eggs. "The

Brown Thrush" was not content with the specific admonition not to rob birds' nests. The closing stanza had a wholesale admonition to universal goodness, put in the specific words that every boy felt were hateful to hear:

> And he sings all the day, little girl, little boy,
> "Oh, the world's running over with joy;
>   But long it won't be,
>   Don't you know? don't you see?
> Unless we are as good as can be?"

Even Lowell's lovely "The First Snow-Fall," after four joyous stanzas of delight in nature, could not refrain from getting around to melancholy in the fifth. Allusions to the joy of nature could never be permitted to be wholly undiluted; could not be wholly unaccompanied by the suggestion of a moral lesson, such as obedience to the parental precept that "Mother knows best," as in Tennyson's "Little Birdie":

> What does little birdie say,
>   In her nest at peep of day?
> "Let me fly," says little birdie,
>   "Mother, let me fly away."
>
> "Birdie, rest a little longer,
> Till the little wings are stronger."

A prose poem of Spring began:

> Spring is here. The shad, at once a harbinger
> Of Spring and Plenty, comes up the River.

The impression that made on a lad who went to school as far away from the Atlantic Ocean as Lansing, Michigan, was recalled in 1927 somewhat iconoclastically: "Few of us," F. L. Smith wrote, "could do more than guess at what a shad might be; nobody ever knew what a harbinger was, and to this day I am uncertain as to the hard or soft quality of the 'g'."

"Which?" in McGuffey's Fourth Reader began:

> Which shall it be? Which shall it be?
> I looked at John — John looked at me.

The parents, being poor, had received a letter from a wealthy relative who offered:

> "I will give
> A house and land while you shall live,
> If, in return, from out your seven,
> One child to me for aye is given."

The parents are inclined to accept:

> I thought of seven mouths to feed,
> Of seven little children's need. . . .
> "Come John," said I,
> "We'll choose among them as they lie asleep."

They stopped first at the cradle.

> Softly the father stooped to lay
> His rough hand down in loving way,
>
> When dream or whisper made her stir,
> And huskily he said: "Not her!"

Then they moved to the trundle-bed.

> I saw on Jamie's rough, red cheek,
> A tear undried. Ere John could speak,
> "He's but a baby, too," said I,
> And kissed him as we hurried by.

They also found they couldn't part with "pale, patient Robbie's angel face"; nor with "Poor Dick! bad Dick, our wayward son" —

> Only a mother's heart can be
> Patient enough for such as he.

There were two more, but after gazing upon them the parents found they could not let them go.

> And so we wrote in courteous way
> We could not drive one child away. . . .
> Thankful to work for all the seven,
> Trusting the rest to One in heaven!

"Somebody's Mother" began:

> The woman was old and ragged and gray, . . .
> She stood at the crossing and waited long,
> Alone, uncared for, amid the throng.

Scores passed her without offering to help. Boys out of school ran by, careless of her. At last, however, came one youth, "gayest laddie of all the group," who did not need to have had the instruction, later available to Boy Scouts, that he should do one good deed a day:

> He paused beside her and whispered low,
> "I'll help you cross if you wish to go."

The youth, like his later prototype of the Boy Scouts, believed not only in doing good but in reporting it:

> Then back again to his friends he went,
> His young heart happy and well content.
> "She's somebody's mother, boys, you know,
> For all she's aged and poor and slow."

Frequently, the pious lesson was presented without placebo or sweetening. To be resigned to what was called "God's will" was part of the philosophy of the age. "Little Victories," in McGuffey's Fifth Reader, was the story of a boy who had lost his limb. "Limb" was the word — no polite little boy would have spoken of his "leg" in that generation. And the baddest boy would not have been equal to the diabolical audacity of standing in front of a mixed company of boys and girls, and using the word "leg."[1] A thunderbolt would have been expected from the heavens, and if that source were inat-

---

[1] In Maria Edgeworth's "The Parent's Assistant," Patty, aged six, fell downstairs. "She did not cry, but writhed in pain. 'Where are you hurt, my love?' asked her father, who came on hearing the noise of the fall. 'Here, papa,' said the little girl, touching her ankle, which she had decently covered with her gown."

tentive, the teacher would have supplied one. "Little
Victories" began with the boy saying: "Oh Mother, now
that I have lost my limb, I can never be a soldier or a

Published by Van Antwerp, Bragg & Co.

sailor!" The mother, in a long dialogue, reminded the
child that Beethoven had gone deaf, and Huber, the student of bees, had gone blind. The lesson was that a
Heavenly Parent had given these geniuses

" — something better to do than they had planned for themselves. . . . They very soon found God's will to be wiser than
their wishes. They found, if they bore their trial well, that
there was work for their hearts to do far nobler than any the
head could do through the eye or the ear. They soon felt a
new and delicious pleasure which none but the bitterly disappointed can feel."

"What is that?" asked the boy.

"The pleasure of rousing the soul to bear pain, and of agreeing with God silently. There is no pleasure like that of exercising one's soul in bearing pain, and of finding one's heart
glow with the hope that one is pleasing God."

"Shall I feel that Pleasure?"

"Often and often. Every time you willingly give up anything you have set your mind upon. You will be more beloved by us all, and you yourself will love God more for having given you something to bear for His sake."

Possibly, speculation by youthful minds as to whether everything their elders called "God's will" was really the will of a benevolent deity, or whether a more accurate bookkeeping should charge some of it against something less benign and hardly Divine — possibly that may have had a part in causing some of the questioning doubt that was characteristic of that generation when it grew up, and of a later generation. The expectations aroused by the lessons in the Readers may not have been borne out in later experience.

McGuffey's Fourth Reader contained "Dare to Do Right!" by Thomas Hughes, adapted from "School Days at Rugby," in which a brave boy kneeling beside his bed in the dormitory to say his prayers is ridiculed by the others. However, one of the boys took the scene to heart; recalling a promise he had made his mother which he had been afraid to keep, he was tormented by his conscience.

Several times he faltered, for the Devil showed him first, all his old friends calling him "Saint" and "Squaretoes" . . . and whispered to him that his motives would be misunderstood. However, his good angel was too strong. Next morning, in the face of the whole room, he knelt down to pray. Two other boys followed his example, and he went down to the great school with a glimmering of another lesson in his heart — the lesson that he who has conquered his own coward spirit has conquered the whole outward world. For a few nights there was a sneer or a laugh when he knelt down, but this passed off soon, and one by one all the other boys but three or four followed the lead.

In its efforts to "exert a decided and healthful moral influence" McGuffey's Readers included many selections designed to inculcate an appreciation of water as superior to intoxicating liquors. One was the passage in which Nathaniel Hawthorne exalted water by picturing the Town Pump making a speech about its own virtues.

That, being written by Nathaniel Hawthorne, was literary and mild. McGuffey's deeper emotion about rum expressed itself with language more like a club. That he detested the thought the State should license any one to sell liquor is sufficiently clear from

> Licensed — to do thy neighbor harm;
> Licensed — to kindle hate and strife,
> Licensed — to nerve the robber's arm;
> Licensed — to whet the murderer's knife.
>
> Licensed — like spider for a fly,
> To spread thy nets for man, thy prey;
> To mock his struggles, crush his soul,
> Then cast his worthless form away.[1]

Patriotism was inculcated — adequately, surely — by selections in the spirit of "The American Eagle."

> Our Eagle shall rise 'mid the whirlwinds of war —
> Shall spread his wide wings o'er the tempest afar . . .
> And still 'mid the smoke of the battle shall soar
> Our Eagle — till scattered and fled be the foe.

And Phillips's "America," ending:

Happy, Proud America! The lightenings [sic] of heaven yielded to your philosophy! The temptations of earth could not seduce your patriotism!

Then there was Webster's speech in which from his own eloquent imagination he caused John Adams to say: "Sink or swim, live or die, survive or perish; I give my

---

[1] I have quoted only this one selection about temperance, because later, in describing the "Speakers," I quote more. Both the Readers and the Speakers gave much space to pieces about temperance and laid strong emphasis on it. Persons who thought that the coming of national Prohibition to America in 1918 was a war-time accident, should acquaint themselves with the amount of teaching of temperance in the schools a generation before, and learn that Prohibition came as the fruit of long and zealous education.

hand and my heart to this vote"; and at its close: "it is
my living sentiment, and, by the blessing of God, it shall
be my dying sentiment; independence now, and independence forever." There was also Webster's speech on the
"Importance of the Union," with its conclusion: "Liberty
and Union, one and inseparable, now and forever."[1]

McGuffey, we can infer, was a pacifist. In a later generation, any time between about 1917 and 1924, he would
have brought upon himself the attention of the courts;
and a selection he included in his Fourth Reader would
have been hounded out of any schoolbook as pacifist
propaganda, leading the young to look too logically upon
war. "The Child's Inquiry" was a rhymed dialogue in
which the son asks:

> "How big was Alexander, Pa,
> That people called him great?
> Was he, like old Goliath, tall ——"

The father explains:

> " 'Twas not his *stature*[2] made him great,
> But greatness of his *name*. . . .
> I mean, my child, his *actions* were
> So great, he got a name
> That everybody speaks with praise."

The child, pertinacious in his search for light, inquired:

> "Well, what actions did he do?
> I want to know it all."

The father recited Alexander's battles:

> ". . . A hundred conquered cities shone
> With midnight burnings red;
> And, strewed o'er many a battle-ground,
> A thousand soldiers bled."

[1] I quote but a few of the se'ections designed to inspire patriotism, because in
describing the "Speakers" I quote many.
[2] The italics and capitals in these quotations are McGuffey's.

Thereupon, the too unsophisticated son:

> "Did *killing people* make him great?
> Then why was Abdel Young,
> Who killed his neighbor, training day,
> Put into jail and hung?
> I never heard them call him great."

After the father's somewhat labored explanation of the distinction between killing one and killing many, the too logical son concluded:

> "Well, then, if I should kill a man,
> I'd kill a HUNDRED more;
> I should be *great* and not hung."

McGuffey, apparently, not only had his individual view about war, but departed from the ordinary American attitude toward the race they were edging off the soil. McGuffey knew. He had grown up on the frontier. Herbert Quick thought that much of the sentiment of a later generation of Americans favoring justice to the Indians came from reading the "Speech of Logan," beginning:

I appeal to any white man to say if he ever entered Logan's cabin hungry, and he gave him not meat; if ever he came cold and naked, and he clothed him not. During the course of the last long and bloody war, Logan remained in his cabin, an advocate for peace. Such was my love for the whites, that my countrymen pointed as they passed and said: "Logan is the friend of white men." But Colonel Cresap, in cold blood and unprovoked, murdered all the relations of Logan, not sparing even my women and children. There runs not a drop of my blood in the veins of any living creature. This called on me for revenge. I have sought it. I have killed many. I have fully glutted my vengeance. . . . Logan never felt fear! He will not turn on his heel to save his life. Who is there to mourn for Logan? Not one!

Pieces like the "Speech of Logan" and "How Big Was Alexander, Pa?" were permitted to insinuate their own lessons. The great majority of the selections in the First

and Second Readers, designed for younger pupils, refrained
from putting upon immature minds any burden of deduction; at the close of each story, the moral was clearly
stated in didactic words. The pill was never sugared.
Sometimes the reasoning powers of the child might con-
ceivably have arrived at a conclusion different from the
one McGuffey wrote out in the moral. For example, at
the end of a story narrating the results of disobedience,
McGuffey pictured three little girls as talking about "how
happy it made them to keep the Fifth Commandment."

Even the familiar "Casabanca" (spelled thus in early
editions):

> The boy stood on the burning deck

could not be allowed to tell its own story, but was introduced by eight numbered paragraphs of moral lessons
entitled "The Obedient Casabanca":

> Still this noble-hearted boy would not disobey his father.
> In the face of blood, and balls, and fire, he stood firm and
> *obedient*. "Father, may I go?" the boy cried out. But no
> voice of permission could come from the mangled body of his
> lifeless father; and the boy, not knowing that he was dead,
> would rather die than disobey. And there that boy stood at
> his post . . . and perished in the flames. Oh, what a boy was
> that! Everybody who ever heard of him thinks that he was
> one of the noblest boys that was ever born. Rather than diso-
> bey his father he would die in the flames.

And so on, and on. Here was the fountain-head of
America's instruction in familiar virtues. "Stick-to-it"
was taught in the poem "Never Give Up" and in the
story about "Self-Reliance." Decorousness of language in
"Profanity is a *brutal* vice. "Look Before You Leap."
"Advantages of Industry." "The Importance of Well-
Spent Youth." "Procrastination":

> Of man's miraculous mistakes, this
> Bears the palm.

"Sublime Virtues Inconsistent with Infidelity," and "Religion the Only Basis of Society." "The Boaster." "The Danger of Riches"— this was taught, incidentally, to children who, when they grew up, found their elders didn't really believe it, and who, by that experience of disillusionment, more powerful than the schoolbook precept, had a lasting lesson in hypocrisy. "Politeness." "Effects of Gambling." "Temperance (or prohibition) taught in "Touch not! Taste not! Handle not!" Beecher's "The Necessity of Education,"[1] beginning:

We must educate! We must educate! Or we perish. . . .

That sentiment at once reflected and inspired one of America's most characteristic zeals.

v

Much of this teaching of moral principles, especially in the earlier editions of McGuffey's Readers, was in direct terms of "thou shalt" and "thou shalt not"; or in the form of "morals" labelled as such. In later revisions, *haec fabula docet* was omitted, and the pupil left to make his own deduction. That the child made it, and that it remained with him throughout life, was the experience of many a mature American, whose life was enlarged by some of these early precepts, inhibited by others. Many persons, mature in 1925, were able, if they had sufficient capacity for self-analysis, to put their fingers on the early springs of their mature traits.

Clem Shaver, of West Virginia, Chairman of the Democratic National Committee, 1924-1928, had read in the Third Reader a story of a boy whose bow-string broke at a critical moment as he was about to shoot his arrow; the boy, having an economical trait, happened to have in his

---

[1] Emphasis on education was clearly a distinctive American trait.

pocket a piece of whipcord, with which he was able to mend his bow and win his prize. That story so gripped Shaver that when he was in his fifties, a man of comparative wealth, he found it a literal, physical impossibility to pass a piece of string on the pavement or floor without picking it up. Another adage that Shaver learned in his youth was "never throw away anything any animal can eat." In the summer of 1926, just before leaving his home in West Virginia for a trip to New York, he took some ears of corn to toss to his cattle and chickens. Next morning, putting on his coat at the Waldorf-Astoria Hotel in New York, he found in his pocket five grains of corn. Though he remained in New York six weeks, he was never able to throw those grains of corn into a wastebasket; they accompanied him back to West Virginia, and to the chickens who could eat them.

VI

The moral precepts in McGuffey's First to Fourth Readers left their record in the ideals of conduct held, and to some extent lived up to, by several American generations. McGuffey's other purpose, accomplished mainly in his Fifth and Sixth Readers, for older pupils, was to provide good reading matter and to elevate reading as an art. "In schools," McGuffey wrote,

It ought to be a leading object to teach the art of reading. It ought to occupy *threefold more time* than it does. . . . It is better that a girl should return from school a first-rate *reader*, than a first-rate performer on the pianoforte. The voice of song is not sweeter than the voice of *speakers*. Let us see years devoted to this accomplishment.

Teachers, carrying out McGuffey's purpose, had classes in reading aloud, which led to "reading schools, contests between rival districts, in which judges decided who did the best reading."[1]

The method of instruction was recalled by ex-Senator Thomas, of Colorado, who went to school in Georgia:

> We were taught in classes. In reading, each pupil would, beginning at the head of the class, read a verse or stanza or paragraph, the next taking up the succeeding verse, and so on.

In making the selections for reading, in the Readers designed for more mature pupils, McGuffey lived up adequately to the ideal of President Eliot, of Harvard:

> When we teach a child to read our primary aim is not to enable it to decipher a way-bill or a receipt, but to kindle its imagination, enlarge its vision, and open for it the avenues of knowledge.

By the selections McGuffey took from the best literature, he imparted a love of good reading to multitudes of Americans, at least to such happy souls as could take it in. In 1927 James M. Cox wrote recalling his school days. He had been, in the meantime, a Congressman, candidate of the Democratic party for President, publisher of three newspapers, and business man of large affairs. That McGuffey's Readers had been able to give him an affection for literature, and a grounding in it that remained with him for forty years, is proved by his ability to say, in an off-hand dictated letter:

> No set of Readers has ever brought together the literature that was found in McGuffey's. The outstanding things which come to my mind, particularly from the old McGuffey's Sixth, are "Dawn," by Edward Everett; "Description of a Storm," Benjamin Disraeli; "Death of Little Nell," Charles Dickens; "Elegy in a Country Churchyard," Gray; Speech before the Virginia Convention, Patrick Henry; "The Snow Shower," William Cullen Bryant; Speech of Walpole in reproof of Mr. Pitt; Pitt's reply to Sir Robert Walpole; "The

---

[1] From a letter written by E. Davenport, Professor, University of Illinois.

Soldier's Rest," Sir Walter Scott; The church scene from "Evangeline," Longfellow; Antony over Cæsar's dead body.

The complete contents of McGuffey's Sixth Reader consisted of 138 selections from 111 different authors. From Shakespeare were more than from any other author, nine, including "Hamlet's Soliloquy and "Fall of Cardinal Wolsey." Sir Walter Scott and Henry Wadsworth Longfellow stood next, with four each. Two of Scott's were "Marmion and Douglas," and "Lochinvar." The Longfellow selections included the church scene from "Evangeline," and "A Psalm of Life." There were three each from the Bible, Bryant, Washington Irving, and Daniel Webster. Two each from Whittier, Dickens, Samuel Johnson, and Oliver Wendell Holmes. Thomas Gray was represented with the "Elegy in a Country Churchyard"; Felicia Dorothea Hemans with "The Landing of the Pilgrims"; Milton with "The Death of Samson"; Bulwer-Lytton with "The Surrender of Granada"; Tennyson with "Enoch Arden at the Window"; Macaulay with "The Impeachment of Warren Hastings"; Poe with "The Raven"; Emerson with "Value of the Present."

It is this aspect of McGuffey's, as a collection of well-chosen selections from the best English and American literature, that inspires the most affectionate recollections of it. Rev. Joseph Fort Newton[1] wrote that,

for many a boy of the older West, McGuffey's varied and wise selections from the best English authors were the very gates of literature ajar.

This simile of McGuffey's as "the gates of literature ajar" is, as respects its appealing truth, duplicated by a charming passage in which Herbert Quick describes one of the effects of McGuffey's that returned to him as a joy in later life. McGuffey's did not pretend to give him

[1] A Universalist clergyman, author, and lecturer.

extensive familiarity with the English classics, but they did give him a taste and an introduction, so that

when I did come to read the English classics, I felt as one who meets in after years a charming person with whom he has had a chance encounter on the train. I had already met the gentlemen. I could say as I opened my Shakespeare, my Milton, or my Byron: "Why, don't you remember our meeting away back on the farm in that old book with the front cover torn off? Here's this passage in which the little prince appeals to Hubert de Burgh not to burn out his eyes with those hot irons! I haven't read it yet, but I'll just repeat it from memory. You're no stranger to me. I don't know much of you, but what I do know I know well!"

The tie that McGuffey's made between American schoolboys and Shakespeare, Milton, and Byron, was stronger than Quick suggests. It accounted, in part, for the rôle America played in the Great War. The racial and national psychologies attending that conflict gave rise to much intellectual controversy, and are not to be disentangled with temerity. One can readily believe that millions of Americans must have been moved subconsciously by the feeling, not always identified by themselves, that they were one with the race of Shakespeare and Milton. Every little prairie schoolhouse in America was an outpost of English literature, hardly less potent to inspire recruits when the time came than the British drum-beat itself. Had American school children been brought up on Goethe and Heine, as they were on Shakespeare and Milton, is it certain America's rôle in the Great War would have been the same?[1]

[1] I realize this argument runs counter to another, on page 61, but I think both are correct.

3

THE AMERICAN MIND: INHERITED IDEALS

Origin of Certain National Traits, Including a, So-to-Speak, Aggressive Complacency; and of Some Individual Traits, Notably "Resistance to Something." Together with the Condition That Made It Profitable for Politicians to "Twist the Lion's Tail." Persistence of the Spirit of the Revolution. Explanation of the Attitude of America toward Some International Questions. Patriotic Emphasis on National Heroes.

NEXT to the Readers, which aimed directly at implanting principles, the subject that did most to give American school children ideas about their relation to the universe was History. As taught in American common schools during the 1870's and 1880's, it meant American history, and American history meant chiefly the Revolutionary War, the Declaration of Independence, the founding of our government, and other events associated with our separation from Great Britain. History, as such, had not been taught at all until about 1850; when the need for textbooks arose, they were built largely on Revolutionary War legends, handed down, many of them, by oral tradition; and on the laudatory narratives and biographies of Revolutionary War events and heroes. Through this material, and consequently through the History textbooks, ran one clear thread.

Although the education of Henry Adams[1] was far distant from that of the average American, the schooling of both had at least one common characteristic, which led to one common quality in the generation from 1900 to 1925, especially in the political standpoint of that generation. "Resistance to something," Adams wrote,

[1] See chapter 11.

"was the law of New England nature; the boy looked out on the world with the instinct of resistance."

It seems startling to say, but is easily provable, that the American schoolboy of the 1870's and 1880's lived in an atmosphere as close to the Revolutionary War as if it had taken place a decade before, instead of a century. Our American resistance to economic and political oppression by Great Britain was the one great epic of our history, our one great adventure as a nation in its relation to other nations; and the writers of schoolbooks gave it proportionate emphasis. Many of the writers of the text-books had had the story of the Revolution direct from the lips of fathers or grandfathers who had fought in it. Traditions passed on by word of mouth endure for incredibly long periods. A politician who was powerful in Congress and in Massachusetts politics as late as 1890, Benjamin F. Butler, used to describe a scene that he said was the most formative influence in his life. To his father's home on winter nights would come two old Revolutionary soldiers. The father and the guests would go to the cellar and draw a big pitcher of cider, which they would set in the hot ashes of the fireplace. To give further heat to the beverage they would add to it dried peppers from a string hanging above the fireplace. Fortified with this stimulus to patriotic memories, they would fix their eyes on the old musket that hung above the mantelpiece, and would rehearse the times they beat the British tyrants, to the ears of a small boy in whose mature life that story was to be a dominating influence. Many of the American authors whose writings were quoted in the schoolbooks and memorized by the pupils had their principal inspiration out of memories like that. Theodore Parker (1810-1860), described by one of his biographers as the "best working-plan of an American yet produced," who probably reflected some of the major influences of his time more completely than any other American, who was the outstanding "embodiment and epitome of the New England renaissance" of the 1850's, described some of his inspiration:

I do not like fighting. . . . But what could I do? I was born in the little town where the first bloodshed of the Revolution began. The men who first fell in that war were my kindred. My grandfather drew the first sword in the Revolution; my fathers fired the first shot; the blood which flowed there was kindred to this which courses in my veins to-day. When I write in my library at home, on one side of me hangs the fire-lock my grandfather zealously used at the battle of Lexington, and beside it is another trophy of that war, the first gun taken in the Revolution, taken also by my grandfather.

Among the text-books on American history surviving in the memories of those who went to school in the 70's and 80's, one of the most frequently mentioned was John Clark Ridpath's[1] "History of the United States, Prepared Especially for Schools," published in 1879. In that the outstanding chapter begins:

The American Revolution was an event of vast importance. . . . The result has been the grandest Republican government in the world.

Statements indisputably accurate, yet capable of leaving a disproportionate sense of cosmic values in the mind of youths whose study of history ended with this one book. Literally, many an American boy knew every battle and detail of the American Revolution, who never heard or read the phrase "French Revolution," or, if he heard it, regarded it as an ungallant appropriation by a

[1] Among those who in 1927 recalled using Ridpath's History were ex-Governor Lowden, of Illinois, John McCutcheon, and Miss Ida M. Tarbell. Ridpath's, like all the Histories, was used for many years after its publication in 1879. Other Histories used in various parts of the country were: Barnes's, 1874, A. S. Barnes & Co., New York; Venable's, 1879, Van Antwerp, Bragg & Co., Cincinnati; Swinton's, 1874, Ivison, Blakeman & Co.; Anderson's, 1865, Clark & Maynard, New York; Thomas Wentworth Higginson's, 1884, Lee & Shephard, Boston.

foreign people of a word whose true brand was American. Many an American youth knew what the "Stamp Act" was, but never knew the part the "Salt tax" played in the history of Europe; knew all about the Boston Tea Party, but never heard of the ultimatum of the barons at

From Quackenbos's "American History for Schools."   Appleton.

Jefferson reading the Declaration in committee.

Runnymede. Many an American youth thrilled at the mention of Faneuil Hall, and in his maturity made patriotic pilgrimages to see it, but went to his grave without ever seeing a picture of the Acropolis, or knowing the part it played in the history of civilization. An American schoolboy of the 1880's, if asked to name the eighteen decisive battles of history and left to the resources of his common-school education, might possibly have included Waterloo; aside from that, he probably would have named half a dozen from the Revolution, half a dozen more from the Civil War; would have thrown in one or two each from the War of 1812 and the Mexican War,[1] and would have stopped, patriotically, at his own shores.

Always, in the Histories, the emphasis was on liberty, freedom, independence. Ridpath's account of the American nation began:

[1] Charles R. Lingley, who in 1927 was Professor of History in Dartmouth College, wrote me: "In American history, the book I most remember is Montgomery's 'Leading Facts of American History.' The things I most remember are chiefly foot-notes about Indians who scalped early colonists, and various prominent men and women who did remarkable things in the Revolution, the War of 1812, and the Mexican War."

The cause of the Revolution was the passage by Parliament of laws destructive of colonial liberty. . . . In 1765 the English parliament passed the Stamp Act. The news of the hateful act created great wrath in America. The bells of Philadelphia and Boston rung a funeral peal. In New York a copy of the Stamp Act was carried through the streets with a death's head nailed to it. The Sons of Liberty was organized. The colonists were few and feeble but they were men of iron wills who had made up their minds to die for liberty.

At Boston the authorities would not permit the tea to be landed. On the 16th of December there was a great town meeting at which seven thousand people were present. Adams and Quincy spoke to the multitudes. Evening came on, and the meeting was about to adjourn when a war-whoop was heard and fifty men disguised as Indians emerged. The disguised men quickly boarded the vessels and emptied 340 chests of tea into the bay. Such was the BOSTON TEA PARTY.

In nearly all the Histories, the great seal of Virginia was an essential illustration. Since no schoolboy was sufficiently equipped with education in the classics to understand the symbolism of the figures in the seal — and since, for that matter, few teachers in American schools could have explained them — it followed that the pupil saw the picture as merely that of an indignant and successfully belligerent lady standing with one foot on the neck of a presumably undesirable man. That the lady was insufficiently clothed according to the standards of the 1890's[1] made the picture a little embarrassing to look at; however, the schoolboy charitably assumed her negligée was not wanton, but was an accident of recent combat. The suggestion of combat was further borne out by the sword held triumphantly in the lady's hand; the defeated party, one could presume clearly, was the man who now lay beneath the victress's foot. The identity of the villain was conveyed by one word in the Latin inscription; "tyrannis" was sufficiently close to the English equivalent to enable the schoolboy to associate

[1] Though not according to the standards of 1927.

it with the word his text-books commonly used as a synonym for the British. Accounts of battles between Americans and British usually described the enemy as "tyrants" and "red-coats"; accounts of battles with Indians pictured the enemy as "redskins," and "savages." Children could readily associate the qualities implied by all the epithets with both enemies interchangeably, and thought of America always as the heroic defender of freedom. "Liberty" or "Independence," or equivalents of them, in Latin or in English, in word or in picture, appear in a majority of the seals of the original thirteen States and the ten earliest admitted.

The Great Seal of Virginia.

The Histories gave to minor episodes of the Revolutionary War a loftiness of treatment to which authorities on military science would have hesitated to assent. Battles and skirmishes were described in phrases which one might explain, perhaps, on the quite worthy theory that the writer of text-books had to compete with the dime-novels which the boys sometimes read surreptitiously behind the camouflaging covers of the text-books. The authors of the text-books could not leave a monopoly of dramatic interest to Mr. Beadle, Captain Collier, Mr. Nick Carter, and other literary outlaws.

In every History, the Patrick Henry episode was a high spot. The youth of that Virginia hero, his scorn of the hesitancy of his elders, must have had much to do with forming the spirit of the generation that read about him a hundred years later. As Ridpath told it:

Patrick Henry, the youngest member of the House, waited for some older delegate to lead in opposition to Parliament. But the older members hesitated or went home. Offended at this lukewarmness, Henry snatched a blank leaf out of an old law book and drew up a series of resolutions. . . . The eloquent Henry bore down all opposition. "Cæsar had his Brutus," said the orator; "Charles I had his Cromwell, and George III !——"

"Treason !" shouted the Speaker.

"Treason ! Treason !" exclaimed the loyalists, springing to their feet.

"—And George III may profit by their example," continued Henry; and then added: "If that be treason, make the most of it !"

No less dramatic was Ridpath's picture of the battle of Lexington:

The British, under command of Pitcairn, came in sight. . . . Pitcairn rode up and exclaimed: "Disperse, ye villains ! Throw down your arms !" The minute-men stood still, and Pitcairn cried, "Fire !" The first volley of the Revolution whistled through the air, and sixteen of the patriots fell.

He described the capture of Fort Ticonderoga by the Vermont patriot, Ethan Allen:

With this mere handful, Allen made a dash and gained the gateway of the fort. The sentinel was driven in, closely followed by the patriot mountaineers. Allen rushed to the quarters of the commandant, and cried out: "Surrender this fort instantly !"

"By what authority ?" inquired the officer.

"In the name of the great Jehovah and the Continental Congress," said Allen, flourishing his sword.[1]

[1] This episode and the words attributed to Ethan Allen by the Histories were used as a hateful example by hard-headed old Professor William Graham Sumner at Yale, in a famous lecture he delivered on the expurgation of history. Professor Sumner's desire was to expurgate from history, not its profanities but its sentimentalities. More definitely, he wanted to expurgate the sentimentalities by including the profanities that the characters of history actually used. He was confident that what Ethan Allen really said to the British general was "Open up here, you —— ———!" Dashes were not resorted to by Professor Sumner in his oral lecture— that would have been to defeat the very purpose he had in mind. Nor are dashes resorted to by Mr. Thomas Beer, in his "Mauve Decade," in which he prints his recollection of hearing the lecture. The present history, however, being more timorous, prefers to use the typographical euphemism. The esoteric, and those whose paths have occasionally led them into places where strong feeling finds outlet in rough-barked words, may be able to divine the actual phrase—though I do

Quackenbos's History characterized a British officer:

The British major, at a tavern in Concord, had boastfully remarked, as he stirred a glass of brandy with his finger: "I mean to stir the Yankee blood before night, as I stir this." He had indeed stirred it to its depths. Connecticut and Rhode Island promptly sent aid to their sister-colony. The men of New Hampshire, under the veteran Stark, hastened across the Merrimac. Putnam, true as steel, left the stone wall that he was building, and without waiting to change his check shirt spurred his horse to the camp at Cambridge.

not ask them to. It was that very familiar American epithet, which, in six short words, achieves a condensation of disapproval such as, when translated into printable language, necessitates ten long words, "Heaven condemned offspring of doubtful paternity and most undesirable maternity." The literal epithet was America's most guarded taboo, like "bloody" in England. Each of the words standing alone, or in another connection, could be used freely. The most doubtful of the six was printed as a matter of course in newspaper accounts of dog shows, or of canine pedigrees. A political tirader could call a man "a dog" with impunity; a jury-lawyer shocked no one when he called the defendant a yellow dog. (Why was "yellow" more opprobrious than black or red, or spotted or piebald?) Probably it was the inferential assigning of a woman and a mother to the canine species that made the epithet objectionable, running counter to a strongly cherished convention of sentiment and chivalry. About 1926, the year the "Mauve Decade" was published, the printableness of this epithet constituted one of the sharpest battles in a war of taste between old-fashioned American reticence and a truculent frankness advocated, and practised, by the younger generation, then in defiant rebellion against a good many former standards of conventionality. The battle resulted, as respects Laurence Stallings's play of the Great War, "What Price Glory?" not in a compromise but in a division of victory. The version on the speaking stage used the forbidden word; the motion-picture version substituted an emasculated word that resulted in extreme violence to the rhyme of a familiar soldier ditty:

> You're in the army now,
> You're in the army now.
> You'll never get rich,
> You son of a gun,
> "You're in the army now.

Professor Sumner's theory, that Ethan Allen used the rougher form of address to the British general, is supported by the fact that Allen was the sort of man who would have used that sort of language. After Allen had been captured by the British and was a prisoner in England, Sparks's biography says,

"Persons who had heard him represented as a giant in stature, and scarcely short of a cannibal in habits and disposition, came to see him and gazed at him with mingled wonder and disgust. It is said that, on one occasion, a tenpenny nail was thrown in to him, as if he were a wild animal. He is reported to have picked it up and, in his vexation, to have bitten it in two. It is in allusion to this that Doctor Hopkins wrote:

> 'Lo, Allen 'scaped from British jails,
> His tushes broke by biting nails.'"

Escape of Putnam.

Old State House in Philadelphia.

First cheer for the Stars and Stripes (1777).

57

Some of the students of these History text-books of the '80's felt, when they grew up, that this rather narrow teaching left much to be wished for. W. D. Howe, long a teacher at the University of Indiana, and compiler of school Readers, wrote:

What a farce the teaching of American history was; for to-morrow take four pages, and we sat down and learned those pages over and over until we could answer how many men were shot in such and such a battle, and how many miles they marched and whether Antietam came before Gettysburg or after — what a waste of time. But there were two things that we got from it; first, the hatred of the British. . . .

The second thing Doctor Howe mentioned is emphasis on the Civil War. He, studying history in southern Indiana, "got the feeling that right across the Ohio River they were not only a wicked but a very perverted lot." Undoubtedly, the teaching in some parts of the country gave a biassed impression of the Civil War. Until the present study was made, the author supposed there was more of this than it now seems there was. Doctor Howe is the only one of many informants who has mentioned it; and his case may be accounted for by his having gone to school where sectional feeling was particularly strong, close to the scene where Confederate raiders had come, and in a State where tension between Unionist Republicans and "Copperhead" Democrats was strongest.

Histories printed soon after the Civil War, for use in the North, treated the Confederates in a spirit far from historical or judicial. The "History of the United States of America; for the use of Schools,"[1] seemed to gloat in dragging in such words as "rebel" and "treason":

The rebellious States seized the forts, arsenals, mints, ships, and national property of whatever description within their boundaries. In Washington but little was done to stem the

[1] By Charles A. Goodrich, revised and brought-down to the present time by William H. Seavey. Published by Brewer and Tileston, Boston, 1867.

tide of treason. . . . Most of the members of Congress from the seceding States resigned their seats, and, defiantly exulting in their treason, would listen to no terms of accommodations. [Cabinet members] resigned from sympathy with secession, and were permitted, like the rebel delegations in Congress, to leave Washington and return to their own States, to plot treason there. Robert E. Lee took command of the State Forces of Virginia, in opposition to the nation which had educated and honored him, and which he had sworn to support.

This note of violence toward the South[1] soon softened, and in a comparatively short time disappeared. But the treatment of the British as the stock villains of American history continued to be a fundamental theme of our text-books until more than a century and a quarter after the Revolution. The effect on generation after generation of American youth was unescapable. John McCutcheon, cartoonist of the Chicago *Tribune*, wrote in 1927: "I have no very clear recollection of my history studies, except that the Redcoats were held up as tyrants, and the heroes of the American War of Independence were glorified."

Niles Carpenter, of the University of Buffalo, sending suggestions for this chapter, said:

I think considerable attention might be given to American history. How much of it was "trumpet and drum" history? How biassed and distorted was it, on the Revolution, the "bloody" British, the Civil War, etc.? Are our present-day Histories more or less chauvinistic and biassed?[2]

[1] While it lasted, the South adopted text-books of its own.

[2] However, the recollection of his study of history which came to Mr. Carpenter's mind when he was writing his letter to me were, not the anti-British sentiment but two schoolboy commentaries on Barnes's History: "Don't you remember the jingle which used to be chanted furtively on school playgrounds:

> In fourteen hundred and ninety-two,
> Columbus sailed the sea-ee.
> He sailed across, and he sailed afar,
> In a Barnes's History-ee.

> He landed at San Salvador,
> And all the dusky maidens wore
> Was U-m-m-m-m-m-m! (Very, *very* wicked to a schoolboy

in those days of mid-Victorian smugness.)"

B. L. Eddy, of Roseburg, Oregon, comparing his own school days with the present ones, was moved to say:

It seems to me that the United States History and other books that told us about our country gave us the impression that it had been founded and led by men of virtue and wisdom — and that no other country could compare with ours in liberty, enlightenment, or progress. I am mighty sure there was no "internationalism" taught in those old books. We have much taught in the schools nowadays [1927] in the way of patriotism, but it seems to me, as I look back, that patriotism was just our native atmosphere then; whereas now we have to use a ventilator fan to force it in. The country has too many highbrows writing text-books and holding university chairs who haven't much use for the Constitution or the flag or our great statesmen. Such chaps hadn't been pupped in the '70's!

From Quackenbos's "American History for Schools." *Appleton.*

Mount Vernon.

E. E. Smith, who went to school in Minnesota, wrote:

There was much more of patriotism fifty years ago than now. At least it was talked more. We were strongly American. No other country could compare with the U. S. A.

In what is here written, there is a running implication that the spirit of resisting tyranny, of fighting for liberty, in the education of the generation that went to school in the '70's and '80's, accounted for the fight the same generation made, when they became mature men and voters, against economic oppression. The American trait of resistance was not patriotic or military merely. The British oppression in its beginning was economic chiefly, having to do with tea, ships, and taxes; America acquired a tradition of resistance to oppression, whether political or economic.

However, assigning specific causes to national traits is perilous.[1] Some historians, and other authors, do it with a manner in which debonair assurance is substituted for logical proof. Each reader had best do it for himself, using such insight as he has and such information as comes to him. But probably one indisputable assertion can be made: The treatment of the British in American schoolbooks accounted for the sympathy Americans had for the Boers in 1899; for much of the sympathy Americans always had for the Irish in their struggle for independence; and accounted generally for a prevailing anti-British strain in American thought and feeling.[2] As late as 1927, Mayor William H. Thompson, of Chicago, found it politically profitable to denounce King George — not the Third, but the Fifth.

[1] In fact, assigning traits to nations is perilous. Are all British stolid? Or all Frenchmen like Chanticleer?

[2] The reasons for a partial change that came with the Great War are discussed on page 48.

4

THE AMERICAN MIND: OUTLOOK

Explanation of an International Point of View Leading to
Insularity. An Attitude Due in Part to Insufficiency of the
Information about Cosmos in Some Schoolbooks. Preoc-
cupation with His Own Time, Place, and Kind. Nearness to
Pioneer Conditions. Naïveté. "Singing Geography."

PRIDE of country, dominant strain in the Histories,
characterized the Geographies as well. The Primary
Geography, compiled by James Cruikshank, LL.D.,[1] in
1867, and current for a decade after, assured young
America that

There are now more than 30,000,000 of people and the United
States are the freest, most enlightened, and powerful government on earth.

Toward peoples other than American, Cruikshank had
the spirit of generous tolerance that can only accompany
assured superiority:

France is celebrated for its manufactures; especially of silks.
. . . Education is not universal, but the better classes are refined and cultivated.

This teaching, that America was "God's country," may
have accounted for a certain air of condescension, not
always tolerant, which American doughboys carried with

---

[1] Editor of the *New York Teacher* and assistant superintendent of schools, Brooklyn, N. Y. Cruikshank's Geography was published in 1867, by William Wood and
Company, New York. It, like all the Geographies, was in use for many years after
the date of its publication. J. H. Colton's Geography was published in 1863, by
Ivison, Phinney & Co., New York; G. W. Colton's Geography in 1877, by Sheldon
& Co., New York; Guyot's, 1868, Charles Scribner & Co., New York; Monteith's,
1885, A. S. Barnes & Co., New York and Chicago; Cornell's, 1867, D. Appleton
and Co., New York; Swinton's, 1875, Ivison, Blakeman, Taylor and Co., New
York and Chicago; Warren's, 1877, Cowperthwait & Co., Philadelphia.

them through the Great War, to the puzzlement of some
of their Allies who had not learned relative values of nations from the same schoolbooks. The same cause may
lie behind America's attitude of self-sufficiency in international relations, its unwillingness to join the League of
Nations, the readiness
with which American
politicians can stir the
people into insistence
upon isolation.

Toward Prussia (then
a separate country)
Cruikshank was in-
clined to be gracious:

Prussia is a large and
powerful kingdom . . .
one of the first powers in
the world. It is more than

*From "A Primary Geography," by James Cruikshank.
Wm. Wood & Co.*

A log cabin.

twice as large as the State of New York. Every child is compelled to attend school. The people are intelligent.

Toward some other outlander nations, Cruikshank was
definite in the assertion of their inferiority:

Half-civilized peoples, like the Chinese and Mexicans, have
towns and cities, cultivate the soil, and exchange products;
but have few arts[1] and little intelligence.

Colton's conceded a little more to China, though it
found some grave defects:

The Chinese are ingenious, industrious, and peaceful; but
miserably conceited. They cling to the customs of their ancestors.

[1] It would be interesting to compare, as of the decade (1867–77) when this
Geography provided instruction to American youth, the relative amounts of art
in China and in the United States.

The Geographies, in a way different from the Histories, but having the same effect, recalled to the child of the '80's the youthfulness of his country, how near its beginnings in pioneer life and Indian wars. Many included in their illustrations pictures of wigwams, palisades for

defense against Indians, log cabins, and maps showing Indians and buffaloes on territory which, to many school children of the '70's, was next door. The West was usually called the "Far West." It was pictured by Guyot's[1] Elementary Geography:

From Warren's "Common School Geography." Cowperthwait & Co.
Travelling among the Andes.

Nearly all parts of the East are occupied by a busy people. The larger part of the West has few inhabitants, except Indians. [In] Kansas, Nebraska, and Texas, the people . . . employ themselves chiefly in raising cattle and horses. Great herds of these animals roam wild over the plains of Texas. When they are wanted by their owners, men go out on very swift horses and surround them.

Standard Geographies published between 1867 and 1877, and studied during one or two decades later, said of the West that "large herds of buffalo roam over the prairies. . . ." "Most of the Indians within the United States inhabit this section; several tribes maintain almost

---

[1] Published in 1868.

constant hostilities against the whites. . . ." "Santa Fé
is the principal point in the wagon-train route from North
to South. . . ." "The wild horses, known as mustangs,
are commonly taken with the lasso." Colton's Geography,
published twenty years before the discovery of the rela-

From Cornell's "Intermediate Geography." Appleton & Co.
Miners at work.

tion between disease and mosquitoes, said that "in
nearly all parts of the West intermittent chills with fevers
are more or less common; the air is rendered malarious by
the frequent disturbance of the rich virgin soil." Of the
territories then still existing Cruikshank said:

They are very thinly settled by whites, and contain many
Indian tribes. They are divided into sections, called, Indian
Territory, New Mexico, Dakotah, Montana, Idaho, Washing-
ton, Utah, and Arizona.

The Geographies, unable to keep step as fast as Congress conferred statehood, were always several years be
hind. It was difficult, indeed, for text-books or anything else to keep pace with the swiftness of the changes
that were taking place. Men like William E. Borah, of
Idaho, and Thomas J. Walsh, of Montana, when they

were schoolboys, studied Geographies in which the States
they were destined to represent in the Senate were described, in the words of Guyot's Geography, as having
"few inhabitants except Indians."

Of the South, Cruikshank's said:

Atlanta is a new and flourishing city, made famous by General Sherman's campaign in the late war.

Cruikshank had not heard of Miami, nor Jacksonville.
He had not heard, indeed, and could not dream, of a race
of Americans so prosperous that they would give rise to
a Palm Beach. All he had to say to the school children
of the '70's about Florida was:

Tallahassee is the capital. Key West is the largest and most
important city. Many vessels are wrecked here. Much salt
is made by evaporation of sea water, and exported.

III

To the children who studied those old Geographies,
doubtless the information seemed as permanently dependable as everything else they learned. But in the
nature of things, many of the facts of geography are
bound to be ephemeral, and the transiency of the picture
of the earth's political divisions was greater during the
past fifty years than at any time before. Beginning in
1870, something like three-fourths of the earth's surface,
and about two-thirds of its population, slid out from
under kings and emperors, becoming republics of one
kind or another. All in all, possibly it was just as well
that the memories of pupils of the 1870's held the solemn
facts less tenaciously than various whimsical impressions,
picked out and stored away by the not-to-be-guessed
selectiveness of childish minds. The residuum left with

From "A Complete Course in Geography," by Wm. Swinton. Ivison, Blakeman, Taylor Co.

Scene in Polynesia.

A village scene in Europe.   Travelling in Russia.

From "Elementary Geography for Primary Classes," by A. H. Guyot. Charles Scribner & Co.

Ostrich-hunting on the Sahara.

Newton D. Baker was probably similar to that retained by many another youth:

I am not certain that my mind has not always been defaced with the notion, which I got out of Mitchell's Geography, that the various countries were yellow, pink, green, or red splotches on a piebald globe.

Charles W. Hobbs, who studied Warren's[1] Geography, recalled chiefly certain vivid pictures.

The cover was of pasteboard with an overdress of bluish-green paper bearing a wonderful picture of Columbus landing at San Salvador, with priests, soldiers, and awe-struck natives looking on. I also remember a picture of a fight between a grizzly bear and an Indian on the tip-top of a mountain.

E. Davenport recalls that in Monteith's[2] Geography,

The Atlas spoke unblushingly of the Great American Desert which began, as I remember, not far west of Omaha. Cincinnati was called Porkopolis from the porcine contribution of the Miami Valley where the Poland China hog was being invented.

F. L. Smith, of Detroit, who studied Colton's during the 1880's, remembered

California, as the State wherein one stands on huge fallen trees and shoots with an archaic fowling-piece lordly stags as they bound under the trees. . . . Michigan was noted for its vast forests of pine and its wealth of copper and iron. Also for its fisheries and furs. All gone now with the snows of yesterday, except the iron.

Unsatisfactory though this might be, as a basis for knowledge of the world of 1927, Mr. Smith found one reason for recalling Colton's with affection and gratitude, as having a specific usefulness:

Colton's Geography was an understandable book, admirably conceived as to size. Behind its ample pages one could read

[1] Published in 1877.   [2] Published in 1885.

the *Fireside Companion* with its never ended tales of blood and romance, or the *Nickel Library* or *Ole Cap Collier*, without fear of detection.

V

In teaching the facts of geography, an almost universal practice was to take advantage of rhyme and harmony, to sing them. Apparently this was a folk-method, begun by some one so long ago that it is impossible to identify him, and passed by word of mouth from one generation to the next, and from one part of the country to another. The chants and rhymes that were evolved constituted one of America's very small number of oral[1] traditions. The simplest version of it — there were difficulties of metre and rhyme in achieving simplicity — consisted of the name of the State, the name of the capital city, and the name of the river on which it was located.[2] This, as sung, was repeated for each State, with no change in the words, but with a rising inflection at the end of the first line, and falling at the end of the second. On this, which presumably was the original form, were built scores of variations, many of them reflecting the inventiveness of teachers or others musically or poetically endowed. The names of

[1] At the time I wrote this, I believed none of the many examples of rhymed geography had ever been printed; but upon publishing an appeal for help in some sixty newspapers, I learned (through H. W. Conrad, of Guthrie, Okla.) that a song about the States, different from the chants, giving details about climate, population, characteristics, crops, and other products, to be sung to the tune of "Auld Lang Syne," was printed in a text-book published by Sowers and Barnes, Philadelphia, in 1851. The same text-book contained compilations of the oceans, bays, mountains, political divisions, etc., arranged in verse form and set to the music of songs popular at that time. Examining this old text-book, Pelton's "Hemispheres," I was unable to determine whether it originated the institution of "singing geography," or, what seemed more probable, gathered together and amplified the materials of a custom already general. This information came to me after the present chapter was written. All the versions given here, which I collected in 1927, came from the memories of living persons, who were taught them a generation or more before; those who knew the chants composed a picturesque tie to the America that was, a link between our times and old times.

[2] Before the coming of the railroad, a navigable river was an important element in the location and growth of a city.

the rivers in the first two States happened to approximate
a rhyme:

> Maine, Augusta, on the Kennebec.
> New Hampshire, Concord, on the Merrimac.

With this start, many tried to introduce rhyme, as well
as metre, throughout — an ambition made sadly difficult

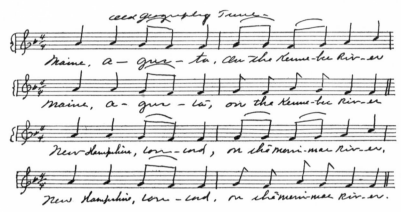

The old chant to which Geography was sung.   Sent by Mrs. J. N. Allen,
Muskogee, Okla.

or wholly balked by disinclination of the names of rivers
to agree with each other euphonically, by an equally
arbitrary refusal of geographical names to have the same
numbers of syllables, and by other recalcitrancies of
geographical facts. In the version [1] most commonly used,
the third line was

> Vermont, Montpelier, on the Onion River.

[1] That the reader may have a complete version before him, I print the following,
which conforms most nearly to the largest number of the variations I received:

> State of Maine, Augusta, on the Kennebec River.
> (*Repeat each line*)
> New Hampshire, Concord, on the Merrimac River
> Vermont, Montpelier, on the Onion River.
> Massachusetts, Boston, on the Boston Harbor.

At this point is one of the many variations. Most of the versions located the capital of Vermont as this does, "on the Onion[1] River." The versions do not all put it so baldly as this. One of the rhymed variations gives a fine touch of poetic movement:

> Vermont, Montpelier, there we see,
> On an Onion rolling free.

Some doubt seems to have existed about the name of the river — if it is a river — on which the capital of

---

Rhode Island, whose capitals are Providence and Newport.
Connecticut, its capitals are Hartford and New Haven.
New York, Albany, on the Hudson River.
New Jersey, Trenton, on the Delaware River.
Delaware, Dover, on the Jones Creek.
Pennsylvania, Harrisburg, on the Susquehanna.
Maryland, Annapolis, on the Severn River.
Virginia, Richmond, on the James River.
North Carolina, Raleigh, on the Neuse River.
South Carolina, Columbia, on the Congaree River.
Georgia, Milledgeville, on the Oconee River.
Florida, Tallahassee, inland.
Alabama, Montgomery, on the Alabama River.
Mississippi, Jackson, on the Pearl River.
Tennessee, Nashville, on the Cumberland River.
Kentucky, Frankfort, on the Kentucky River.
Louisiana, Baton Rouge, on the Mississippi River.
Ohio, Columbus, on the Scioto River.
Indiana, Indianapolis, on west fork of White River.
Illinois, Springfield, on the Sangamon River.
Wisconsin, Madison, on the Fourth Lake.
Michigan, Lansing, on the Grand River.
Minnesota, St. Paul, on the Mississippi River.
Iowa, Des Moines, on the Des Moines River.
Texas, Austin, on the Colorado River.
Kansas, Topeka, on the Kansas River.
California, Sacramento, on the Sacramento River.
Oregon, Salem, on the Willamette River.
Arkansas, Little Rock, on the Arkansas River.

[1] The Indians called the river Winooski, their name for the wild onions that grew along the stream. The early white settlers translated the word, naming the river, in early Geographies, "Winooski or Onion River." A later generation, having sensitiveness to the æsthetic aspects of the situation, dropped the "Onion" and restored "Winooski." This explanation was given me by an elderly lady in Knoxville, Iowa, Anna McDuffee, who had been brought up in Maine when "most of New England was forest, Indian guides were a common sight, and afoot or horse-back a usual means of travel."

Vermont stands. Some elderly memories recall the line as

Vermont, Montpelier, on the Winooski River.

Yet others seem to concede doubt whether there is any river whatever. In one version[1] the author of the chant (one wonders who he was and where he lived, and how long ago) departs completely from pretense that every State capital must necessarily be on a river:

> Vermont, Montpelier, Montpelier, Montpelier,
> Vermont, Montpelier, the capital Montpelier.

The next line, "Connecticut, its capitals are Hartford and New Haven," fixes the date of the original composition of this version as of the time when Rhode Island and Connecticut, with an un-New England extravagance, each maintained two capitals, holding alternate sessions of the legislatures at each. The existence of two capitals causes the chant to depart from naming the bodies of water[2] on which they are located. To insist that every State capital was on some kind of water, preferably a river, was an underlying tenet of the institution, causing the composers some embarrassment, as we shall see.

Yet another version adheres faithfully, if awkwardly, to rhyme, at the expense of going some distance afield into extraneous characteristics of the capitals; and unnecessarily reducing the location of the capital of Massachusetts to the standing of mere rumor:

> Massachusetts, so they say,
> Has Boston East upon its bay.

[1] Sent me by Mr. L. M. Brock, of Mackinaw, Illinois.

[2] The version recalled by Mrs. A. J. Thompson, of El Dorado, Kan., gave, as to most of the States, the counties in which the capitals were located. Part of it ran:

> Delaware, Dover, in the County of Kent,
> North Carolina, Raleigh, in the county of Wake,
> Georgia, Atlanta, in the county of Fulton,
> Florida, Tallahassee, in the county of Leon.

This version took equal pains to keep to poetry[1] in
locating the capital of New Jersey:

> New Jersey, with its fruits so fair,
> Has Trenton on the Delaware,

but fell away from rhyme rather sadly, and interjected a
needless doubt in

> New York, so they say,
> Has on the Hudson, Albany.

When the chant reached Delaware, it ran into the
necessity of a humiliating confession. Delaware has no
river, and the poet — if he was a poet — was obliged to
descend to

> Delaware, Dover, on Jones's Creek, Sir!

The "Sir!" one suspects was a gesture of defiance,[2]
aiming to eke out the attenuated dignity of the stream,
on the Freudian theory of an inferiority complex taking
on a self-protective aggressiveness, as a man of small
stature frequently carries a chip on his shoulder.

Probably a similar sense of the insufficiency of the body
of water accounts for the roundabout rhyme[3] in which
the capital of North Carolina is located:

> North Carolina, famous for tar and turpentine and gold,
> Its capital is Raleigh, by River Neuse controlled.

[1] Another version, sent me by Mr. D. R. McIver, of Jonesboro, N. C., began:

HOW GRANDFATHER JINGLED HIS GEOGRAPHY

> I can't sing much but I can learn,
> To sing of the States as they come in their turn,
> The United States—may they live forever,
> The capital is Washington on Potomac River.

> Maine has Augusta on the Kennebec. . . .

Mr. McIver added that he had been a school-teacher in four States, between
1880 and 1892, but had heard geography sung only in North Carolina.

[2] An elderly gentleman who has read the proof of this chapter says I am wrong
about this; the "Sir" was thrown in to eke out the brevity of the other words in
the line, and try to approximate the beat of the tune.

[3] This was sent me by Mr. A. Van Valkenburg, of La Porte City, Iowa.

Another embarrassment, due to the failure of a State capital to locate itself on water, existed in the case of Tallahassee. The chant sent me from Fargo, N. D., admitting defeat by an arid fact, says:

Florida, Tallahassee, upon an elevated plain, sir.

While this saves the rhythm and admits that one State capital was not on water, is not truth sacrificed in another respect? Can any spot in Florida be described truthfully as elevated?

Most of the versions of the chant began with Maine, came down the Atlantic Coast, went along the Gulf of Mexico, then through the central States, and as far west as there were States at the time the version was sung. A version[1] ending with California wound up with a flourish:

California, Sacramento (la-si-la-sol-la-si-do),
And this comprises all, sir (la-si-do-si-re-do-do).

On any school-day morning,[2] in schoolhouses all over America, hundreds of thousands of children were sending out one variation or another of that old chant in waves which, in the aggregate, reached from the Atlantic to the Pacific, a kind of radio by relays, long before the world had heard of aerials or heterodynes. While it might almost be said that there were hours when practically all the childish voices in America were singing it in unison, the methods were as various as the versions of the words. The system[3] followed in Brooklyn, N. Y., was:

The teacher would start off with pointer in hand, standing in front of a large map, and the boys in a sing-song or chant.

[1] Sent by John J. Ackerman, of Paterson, N. J.
[2] Not invariably in the morning. Sometimes at the close of the day, sometimes at a lesson period in the usual routine. Occasionally a teacher used the chant at any time to stir up the spirits of a drowsy schoolroom.
[3] Recalled by Mr. Sydney Fisher.

. . . I don't believe it was ever set to music, but scholars were appointed from the schools of New York at that time as monitors at $50 a year and brought the chanty with them.

But an old gentleman who went to school in Illinois in the late 1860's, and in Missouri during the early 1870's, thought one reason for this method was lack of maps:

The old jingle furnished a cheerful method of fixing, *memoriter* (no maps in sight), a list of geographical facts.

"We children loved it," wrote Mr. L. M. Brock, of Mackinaw, Illinois; and Mr. John B. Dennis, of Ottumwa, Iowa, added:

The poetry of it is rather awkward, but when a schoolroom full of young, childlike voices rang out, all in good, harmonious tones, it was really catchy and sounded well.

Equally with affection goes insistence that it was a good way to learn geography:

It was hard for some of us youngsters to make the words and metre harmonize — but we learned geography. I recall the words yet and frequently sing them for the children of this community. . . . To this very day when I wish to ascertain what river a capital is located on, I immediately run over in my mind the old chant till I reach the one I want.

That the method was not only useful, but also enjoyable, was the testimony of an old gentleman[1] who went to school at Bloomville, Seneca County, Ohio, between 1860 and 1865: "We certainly enjoyed it; it was claimed that singing would help pupils to remember better." A lady who spent her school days in New York City recalled the early scene: "When the order was given by teacher, forty children started right in and gave out the same 'sing-song' and rhythm, no one knowing where it came from, or thinking about it, for that matter."

[1] Mr. F. P. Klahr, of Algona, Iowa.

As to where[1] it came from, and when, there is no dependable light, except glints that strongly suggest an age as great as that of the country itself. Mr. Frank B. Shutts, who in 1927 was publisher of the Miami *Florida Herald*, recalled his father, in Indiana, teaching him the version that began not as most of the others did, with Maine, but more patriotically with the capital of the whole country:

United States, Washington, on the Pot-o-mack River

with the accent on the first syllable, "Pot." That spelling and pronunciation runs back to the time when the earliest pioneers took the word by ear from the Indians.

By the number of capitals named in any one version, it is possible to fix the time when it was current. The longest, and therefore the latest, mentioned thirty-one capitals. Lines were added, however, as Congress added States. Probably the institution began to ebb from its status of universal use some time in the 1870's; but it was common in the 1880's and not infrequent in the 1890's. The place where it lingered longest, and finally passed away, was the rural schools of some counties in northern New Jersey.[2]

---

[1] Madame L. Demorest, French by birth and wife of the professor of French at Miami University, Oxford, Ohio, recalled that in France her mother used to sing the capitals of Europe, beginning:

> "Quel est notre pays natal?
> C'est la France, petits amis.
> Quel en est la capital?
> Chacun sait bien que c'est Paris."

> ("What is your native country?
> It is France, little ones,
> What is its capital?
> Everybody knows it is Paris.")

And so for the different countries.

[2] In 1927, Mr. John J. Ackerman, of Paterson, N. J., who had taught for thirty-eight years in Bergen and Passaic counties, New Jersey, and Rockland county, New York, wrote me that up to 1922, when he retired, he had been using this method of teaching the State capitals, and also the counties of New Jersey.

Mrs. Ann E. Ray Cook, of Stephenville, Texas, wrote that she taught the chant in Texas schools until 1919.

As to the tune, in many places the air of "Yankee Doodle" was conscripted; elsewhere the tune was borrowed from an old-time song known variously as "Go Tell Aunt Rhody," or "Aunt Lucy," or "Aunt Martha," or "Aunt Sallie," or "Aunt Abbie," or "Aunt Nancy."

"Go Tell Aunt Rhody"[1] was familiar practically everywhere:

Go tell Aunt Sallie.

Go tell Aunt Rhody,
Go tell Aunt Rhody,
Go tell Aunt Rhody,
The old gray goose is dead.

The one she was saving,
The one she was saving,
The one she was saving,
To make a feather bed.

[1] Mrs. J. L. Blake, of Perry, Iowa, said "Go Tell Aunt Rhody" was a parody, built by impish children on a hymn that was popular in those days, "Greenville," composed by Jean Jacques Rousseau, words written by Walter Shirley:

Lord, dismiss us with thy blessing,
Fill our hearts with joy and peace . . .

"Mother would never," Mrs. Blake writes, "allow us to sing 'Aunt Rhody' because it seemed disrespectful to our elders, who loved the old hymn."

Mrs. F. L. Newkirk, of Brooklyn, Iowa, who went to school at Bear Creek, adds another bit of lore about the "Aunty Rhody" tune. She remembers the following words sung to it, but "not," she adds, "in school":

Saw, saw my leg off,
Saw, saw my leg off,
Saw, saw my leg off,
Clear up to my knee.

> She died easy,
> She died easy,
> She died easy,
> Out behind the shed.
>
> The gander is grieving,
> The gander is grieving,
> The gander is grieving,
> For the old gray goose that's dead.

In many places, however, the chant of State capitals had the dignity of a tune of its own. In Boonesboro, Iowa, the air was called the "India-rubber tune,"[1] because of the elasticity enforced by failure of the names of States and capitals to have uniform numbers of syllables. That name was apt for another reason, the many variations the air assumed in different parts of the country. Mrs. S. Bell Tilton, of Marysville, Washington, said: "It was much more musical than a chant; I never saw notes to it — our teacher just seemed to improvise the music, which was very catchy." A man who went to a "six-sided" schoolhouse in Harford County, Maryland, in 1860, recalled the chant as "a jolly, rollicking tune":

> State of Maine, Augusta,
> Tol-le, rol-le, rol-le.
> New Hampshire, Concord,
> Tol-le, rol-le, rol-le.

In communities less merry than Maryland, or where schools were more touched with the Puritan notion of life, the tune was trimmed down to "a drawling sing-song manner," as it is recalled by a resident of Springfield, Mass. In Iowa, it was "a sing-song droning tune, repeated ad finitum." A lady living in El Dorado, Kan., says the tune, having served a scholastic purpose during the day, was used in the evening as a lulling song for sleepy children; "the tune was about as sen-

[1] My authority for this is Miss Nellie M. Northrup.

sible as 'Old John Brown Had One Little Nigger Boy.'"

At all events, in all its variations, the melody was unique. "The tune was very simple," said a resident of Dubuque, Iowa, "but I cannot connect it with any other words I ever heard, nor can anybody else to whom I have whistled it." Another Iowa lady[1] said:

I never saw any music printed for it, but think it must have been handed down by word of mouth, like Indian traditions.

She added:

The rhythm was kept not only by the voices but by the gently swaying little bodies standing in a line.

"O, have you heard geography sung?" ran one[2] of the school chants. Practically every schoolboy of the early days heard geography sung, and participated in the singing. The song of the State capitals was the most familiar, but practically every detail of geography was put into rhyme of a sort. Probably a journeyman poet would say that of all possible combinations of facts and words, the least hospitable to rhyme would be the boundaries of the United States. But in the schools of New York State it was managed:

> The United States boundary to you we proclaim.
> Say on the North lies Britain's domain,
> The Atlantic East, the farthest bound shore,
> To the South the Gulf and old Mexico.
> On the West the Pacific is found
> And this completes the United States bound.[3]

In the same schools, the prodigiously difficult boundaries of New York State were made to lend themselves to versification:

[1] Mrs. F. W. Robertson, of Waterloo.
[2] Recalled by Thomas E. Will, who went to school in Missouri.
[3] This and the rhymed boundaries of New York were sent me by Mrs. J. H. Albright, of Petersburg. Ohio, who in her youth was a teacher in Michigan, and who had some of her lore from her mother, also a teacher.

> To bound New York, this Empire State,
> Say on the North lies Erie Lake,
> Ontario and St. Lawrence too,
> Canada, there, we also view. . . .

An old lady in Mahoning County, Ohio, recalled singing the peninsulas, to the tune of "Old Grimes Is Dead":

> Now the peninsulas we sing,
> Alaska leads the rhyme.
> Then Melville, Nova Scotia,
> A-comes, all in the Northern clime.
> In Southern regions, Florida,
> With Yucatan, we meet,
> Then California follows next,
> To make the list complete.

A song[1] of the mountains of South America limped as to rhyme, but nevertheless achieved a spirit of majestic grandeur appropriate to the theme:

> The mountains are before us,
> Their snowy tops rise o'er us,
> And now in lively chorus
> With Andes we'll commence. . . .
>
> Illimani next in order
> Stands upon Bolivia's border,
> Like a bold, gigantic warder
> Then Sorata's heights ascend.
> Cotopaxi next we mention,
> Give Pichincha some attention,
> And, with a steep ascension,
> With Chimborazo end.

An outstanding achievement in reducing geographical names to metre and music was a "Song of the Rivers of Europe," sent me by the Director of Music in Central College, Conway, Arkansas. "My mother," he said, "who was brought up in western New York, used to 'bring down the house,' performing it in her elder years":

---

[1] Recalled by Mrs. C. T. Hillman, of New York City, and by several others.

Volga, Danube, Dnieper, Dniester,
Don, Duero, Minuho, Nemann,
Drina, Dwina, Tagus, Ebro, Elbe

Gaudiana, Gaudelquiver,
Garonne, Vistula, Shannon, Severn,
Thames, Olga, Perth.

Bog, Save, Oder, Drave,
Seine, Saone, Rhine, Rhone,
Tiber, Po!

Not all the songs were so stark as that; many tried to weave a rhymed story about the names:

At Henlopen he stopped, and then
He saw two boys called Charles and Hen(ry)
He shouted out with all his might
Gracias, Gracias, stop that fight.

Chorus sung after each stanza:

So round and round each bay and sound
Each mountain, cape, and river,
So round and round the world we bound
In concert all together.

An ingenious adaptation of this plan aimed to interest the vagrant minds of youth in the lakes of the world by introducing what the modern "movies" would call "a strong heart-interest":

O, Winnipeg, dear Winnipeg, if you will be my bride,
We'll live at Athabasca, and I'll be your Slave, he said,
But Winnipeg was much incensed; she called him a Great Bear,
And at the Slave she threw the Tules, the Salt and all 'twas there.
She drove him to Chapala Lake, way down in Mexico,
And all because the fellow wished that he might be her beau.[1]

Even the statistics of area were made to rhyme:

North America millions eight,
Europe three and a half we state,
South America millions seven
Asia sixteen, and Africa eleven.[1]

[1] Sent me by Mrs. Florence Bunce, of Omaha, Neb.

208.   A "TEA-PARTY" SONG.   W. B. B.

From "The Singing Bird, or Progressive Music Reader," by William B. Bradbury. Iveson, Blakeman, Taylor & Co.

Singing the counties was common in each State. A chant of the New Jersey counties had a manner of Walt Whitman:

> We will sing of the counties
> We will sing of the counties
> We will sing of the counties
> Of our New Jersey State.
> Atlantic, Bergen, Burlington, . . .

Not only geography. The alphabet and the multiplication[1] table were quite generally sung. Mr. Charles P.

---

[1] Ed Bass, of Batesville, Ark., recalled singing the multiplication tables to the tune of "Weevily Wheat." This old-time song is printed in Chapter 12.

Tuttle, of New York City, who grew up in New England, recalled that

In the middle of the morning, if the teacher wanted to air the room, we would all march up and down the aisles singing (to the tune of Yankee Doodle) "five times five is twenty-five and five times six is thirty;" and so on up. This was in 1893.

A quite dignified bit of verse is recalled by an old gentleman in Poland, Ohio,[1] who, writing in 1927, said he had learned it sixty years before, but was able to repeat it from memory:

> Men, women, children live on land
> With birds and beasts on every hand.
> On the land are mountains high,
> Almost mingling with the sky.
> On the land are hills so green,
> With quiet valleys all between.
> On the land is many a town,
> And many a city up and down,
> And people on the roads do go,
> In cart or carriage, fast or slow.
> And thus while people, girls, and boys,
> Are busy with their carts and toys,
> Cows, sheep and horses, dogs and cats,
> Great elephants and little rats,
> Flies in the air, worms in the ground,
> Insects in plants and all around,
> These, these are seen on every hand,
> Living and happy on the land.

[1] Mr. John F. Case.

5

THE AMERICAN MIND: ORTHODOXY

Strength of the Spirit of Religion in Schools. Religious
Tradition More Powerful than Secular Form. The Best
Process by Which to Gain Understanding of the American
Mind. From the "Hornbook," through the "New England
Primer," to "McGuffey's Readers." The Spirit of Religion
Continues into Text-Books about Physiology, Chemistry,
Botany, and Physical Geography. Some Results of it.

DURING a period ending about 1912, and ranging backward more than sixty years, a wave of amendments[1]
to State constitutions throughout America inserted into
the fundamental law statutes of religious freedom, providing for universal education at the expense of the State,
aiming to insure complete and rigid separation of church
and State, and forbidding the use of State funds for sectarian religious teaching. In a common interpretation of
these phrases, it is customary to say, but as misleading as
many familiar sayings, that the constitutional provisions

---

[1] The dates of amendments to State constitutions providing there should be
no sectarian religious teaching in the State-supported schools, were:

1897 Delaware	1876 North Carolina	1868 Mississippi
1885 Florida	1875 Missouri	1857 Iowa
1879 Louisiana	1875 Alabama	1855 Massachusetts
1879 California	1872 Pennsylvania	1851 Indiana
1877 Georgia	1870 Illinois	1851 Ohio
1877 Minnesota	1868 Arkansas	1850 Michigan
1876 Texas	1868 South Carolina	1844 New Jersey

Similar provisions were incorporated into the original constitution of the following States when admitted to the Union:

1912 Arizona	1889 Washington	1867 Nebraska
1912 New Mexico	1889 Montana	1864 Nevada
1907 Oklahoma	1889 South Dakota	1859 Kansas
1896 Utah	1889 North Dakota	1857 Oregon
1890 Wyoming	1876 Colorado	1848 Wisconsin
1890 Idaho	1872 West Virginia	

ended the connection between the schools and religion, that thereafter the public schools of America were secular. That is far from true. The religious spirit and tradition were more powerful than the secular form. In practice, all that was ended or prevented by the constitutional amendments was any sectarian or religious teaching that should run counter to the dogmas or practices of any important[1] sect or creed. Religion remained in the schools to practically as great an extent as immediately before the amendments. What happened was that the States carried on a system of education in which practically all the traditions and most of the influences were religious. The spirit of the schools was religious and continued so. So deeply embedded was the spirit of religion in the common schools of America that nothing short of a revolution, or a trend immensely long, could have uprooted it. Through study of the history of education in America, especially the elementary schools,[2] more than by any other process, will understanding be gained of the American mind, of the reasons an American was American.

From the earliest beginning, in every section of America, education started as a religious conception, was regarded as a part of religion almost as much as baptism, or any other sacrament; the schools were instrumentalities of religion, wholly, their sole purpose to enable the child to read the Bible; that continued to be the sole purpose for

---

[1] The religious teaching that continued in the schools often ran counter to the tenets of denominations relatively unimportant in numbers, such as Unitarians and Mormons.

[2] It would probably be safe to go further, and say that more insight into the history of the United States will be gained by adequate study of the history of education, than by study of any of the formal histories which devote most of their bulk to politics. Any one who wishes to study the history of education cannot do better than read "Public Education in the United States: A Study and Interpretation of American Educational History," by Ellwood P. Cubberley, Professor of Education, Leland Stanford Junior University, California.

approximately half the entire history of education[1] in America; it remained a chief purpose for some generations later, and religion continued to be the dominant note in education until the period with which this chapter deals, the last quarter of the nineteenth century.

In the colonial South, as well as to some degree in New York and New Jersey, substantially all public education was carried on by an auxiliary of the Church of England, or Protestant Episcopal Church, called "The Society for the Propagation of the Faith . . .," whose purpose was "to train children in the tenets and worship of the church through schools." The church charity schools of this society furnished the nearest approach to a free school system there was in the South; their traditions color education in that section to this day, and some of the old church charity schools were still in existence in 1927.

---

[1] "The most prominent characteristic of all the early colonial schooling was the predominance of the religious purpose in instruction. One learned to read chiefly the Catechism and the Bible, and to know the will of the Heavenly Father. There was scarcely any other purpose in the maintenance of elementary schools. In Connecticut colony the law required that the pupils were to be made 'in some competent measure to understand the main grounds and principles of Christian Religion necessary to salvation,' and 'to learn some orthodox catechism. . . .' Such studies as history, geography, science, music, drawing, secular literature, and physical training were unknown. Children were constantly surrounded, week-days and Sundays, by the sombre Calvinistic religious atmosphere in New England, and by the careful religious oversight of the pastors and elders in the colonies where the parochial school system was the ruling plan for education. Schoolmasters were required 'to catechise their scholars in the principles of the Christian religion,' and it was made 'a chief part of the schoolmaster's religious care to commend his scholars and his labors amongst them unto God by prayer morning and evening, taking care that his scholars do reverently attend during the same.' Religious matter constituted the only reading matter. The Catechism was taught and the Bible was read and expounded. Church attendance was required, and grammar-school pupils were obliged to report each week on the Sunday sermon. This insistence on the religious element was more prominent in Calvinistic New England than in the colonies to the south, but everywhere the religious purpose was dominant. The church parochial and charity schools were essentially schools for instilling the church practices and the beliefs of the churches maintaining them. This state of affairs continued well toward the beginning of our national period."—Cubberly, "Public Education in the United States."

In the colleges, uniformly, the ecclesiastical spirit was equally dominant. "The greater number of their students were preparing for the ministry in some one of the branches of the Protestant Church."—Encyclopædia Britannica.

In Maryland, Pennsylvania, and to some extent elsewhere, education was carried on through parochial or church schools of the Lutheran, Catholic, Dutch Reformed, Moravian, Presbyterian, Quaker, Baptist, and other churches; their conception of education was dominated by church purposes only, and the teaching was done by ministers or other formal representatives of the churches.

In New England, education was wholly in the hands of the Puritans. Their chief concern, elevated above the State, was religion and education, and they regarded education as merely an instrument with which to teach religion. Their fundamental dogma included two tenets: that the individual is solely responsible for his salvation, and that the sole guide and source of authority is the Bible; hence it followed that everybody should be able to read the Bible. That conception, shared by the Puritans and other sects that arose in Europe during the sixteenth century, is the ultimate parent, from which a direct lineage leads to the modern vernacular elementary school in America. It was the Puritans who, "more than any others, gave direction to the future development of education in our American States . . . established in practice the principles which have finally been generally adopted by our different States."[1]

With the Puritans, the State was the servant of the church. In time, the Puritan church turned over to the civil organization, as its agent, the work of conducting education. More accurately, the church turned over to the State the business of collecting taxes for the schools and enforcing penalties for failure to maintain them; the church maintained its hold on the teaching, and the purpose was still the one expressed in the Massachusetts statutes of 1642 and 1647, that children be able "to read

[1] "Public Education in the United States," by Ellwood P. Cubberley.

and understand the principles of religion and the capital laws of the country," so as to defeat the "one chief point of that old deluder, Satan, to keep men from a knowledge of the Scriptures." Later, the Puritan church and the Puritan civil organization became separate entities.

Still later, at a period ranging from quite early up to 1912, throughout America, education came to be conceived as solely the concern of the State, and as its responsibility; and statutes or constitutional amendments were adopted carrying that conception into effect. But this was not regarded as entailing, and did not entail, any change in the nature of the teaching. The traditions of the schools, and their influence, continued to be religious.

Another way to show this is to state the sequence of text-books and subjects studied in the schools. The first text-book was the "Hornbook," generally used in the seventeenth century, a thin board on which was pasted a printed leaf,

> Neatly secured from being soiled or torn,
> Beneath a pane of thin transparent horn.

The hornbook usually contained nothing more than the alphabet, and a prayer —

> "the prayer the Saviour designed to teach,
> which children use, and parsons, when they preach."

Next, beginning about 1700 and lasting in some places until after 1800, came the New England Primer,[1] as a rule the only text-book of any kind in the schools, not only in New England, but elsewhere; "for a century and a quarter [to about 1810] it was the chief school and reading book in use among the Dissenters and Lutherans

---

[1] During the latter portion of this period, in some places the New England Primer was supplemented by the Psalter, the Testaments, and the Bible. The last edition of the New England Primer I have found was published in 1840.

in America."[1] "It taught millons to read, and not one
to sin." Every home had copies of it, it was for sale
everywhere. Its total sales have been estimated at more
than three million copies, at a time when the whole population of the country was not that much. The chief purpose of the New England Primer is shown by one of its
lessons:

PRAISE TO GOD FOR LEARNING TO READ

The praises of my tongue
    I offer to the Lord
That I was taught and learned so young
    To read His Holy Word.

The New England Primer was succeeded by Noah
Webster's Spelling Book. That, written in 1782, was the
first widely used text-book that included material exclusively secular; but Webster conformed to the universal
religious tradition about school text-books, by including
among the lessons in spelling, fables and stories with
religious and ethical morals. Webster's Speller lasted
more than a hundred years, was in very wide-spread use
as late as 1890, and in some use after 1900. When the
scope of education was broadened by the adoption of
Readers, they, like the Spellers, conformed to the religious
tradition by making up much of their contents of stories
with religious or ethical morals. As education broadened,
with the addition (in about the following order) of arithmetic, grammar, geography and history, the religious
tradition was carried on in all the text-books in which
it could be included appropriately.

The introduction to "Fourteen Weeks of Chemistry"[2]
began with a direct affirmation:

Each tiny atom is . . . watched by the Eternal Eye and
guided by the Eternal Hand, all obey immutable law. When

[1] "Public Education in the United States," Ellwood Cubberley.
[2] J. D. Steele, Ph.D. A. S. Barnes & Co., 1873.

Christ declared the very hairs of our head to be numbered, he intimated a chemical truth which we can now know in full to be that the very atoms of which each hair is composed are numbered by that same watchful Providence.

"Chemical Physics"[1] said that "no science furnishes more . . . convincing proofs of the existence of God" [than Chemistry]. Peter Mark Roget[2] put the orthodox affirmation into the title of his "Animal and Vegetable Physiology, as Exhibiting the Power, Wisdom, and Goodness of God." The great American botanist, Asa Gray, in his "Botany for Young People and Common Schools"[3] introduced a quotation from the Bible as the opening passage of his book; and, for himself, began:

This book is intended to teach Young People how to begin to read, with pleasure and advantage, one large and easy chapter in the open Book of Nature; namely, that in which the wisdom and goodness of the Creator are plainly written in the Vegetable Kingdom.

II

In the American public schools during the period from about 1865 to 1900 and later, the Geographies contained all that was then taught about the origin of man, and the other subjects which in the later schools of a more complex age came to be called geology, zoology, and biology; so far as these subjects were differentiated from ordinary geography, it was sometimes called "physical geography."[4] In this field the Geographies had the orthodox fundamentalism natural to an age in which the ideas later to be called "modernism" and "higher criticism"

[1] Thomas Ruggles Pynchon, 1877.
[2] Author, also, of the familiar "Thesaurus of English Words and Phrases."
[3] American Book Company, 1858.
[4] The text-book from which I have quoted passages here was described by the title-page as: "J. H. COLTON'S *AMERICAN SCHOOL GEOGRAPHY;* Comprising Separate Treatises on Astronomical, Physical, and Civil Geography. 1863.

were utterly unknown. Darwin's "Origin of Species" had been published in 1859; but its influence had not yet reached the authors of text-books, much less the students of them—the controversy he inspired did not seriously trouble the common schools until more than sixty years later, at Dayton, Tenn., in 1925. "Higher criticism," a euphemism for a gentle and qualified questioning of the orthodox explanation of the origin of man, and man's relation to the universe, did not come until the '90's; "Modernism" about 1920.

In the comfortable fundamentalism of the common schools of the '70's and '80's, text-books were not only 100 per cent orthodox, they were even a little complacent about man's place in cosmos. To the youth of that period they taught a comforting philosophy; as respects the universe, it was "God's in His Heaven; all's right with the world"; as respects the United States, the philosophy was, in effect, an abbreviation of Decatur's famous saying, amounting to "My Country! Always right!" Cruikshank's Primary Geography gave complacent assurance:

God made the world for man to live on, and has fitted it for man's convenience and comfort; giving the food that is best for him to eat; the air to breathe; and making storms and tempests to purify the air.

Colton's Geography admitted that "a certain relation exists between climate and the 'tendency of Nature to produce this or that animal form'"; but

Climate by no means controls their origin. The resemblance, in corresponding climates, must be traced to an agency above that of known natural laws; and since it relates, in a great measure, to peculiarities which fit them for kindred abodes, this agency must be ascribed to a Being of superior wisdom and beneficence; or, in other words, to the Creator himself.

The author . . . has endeavored to exhibit the various divisions of the earth's surface, in such relations as would best enable the scholar to view them as parts of a comprehensive whole, created and governed by DIVINE POWER.

III

From the prevailingly religious tradition of the textbooks, it followed that the Geographies of the 1870's, and on to later than 1900, were serenely confident about the inferiority of religions other than Christian. This note may have accounted in part for the zeal for missionary work in foreign fields that was characteristic of America. Colton's Geography said that

> Mohammedanism or Islamism is the religion taught by Mohammed, an imposter who recorded his doctrines in a book called the Koran. It consists of a confused mixture of grossly false ideas and precepts with Judaism and Christianity. . . . Most systems of religion, while professing to cultivate virtue, often encourage vice; and thus injure both spiritual and worldly interests. Christianity is the only system which elevates man to a true sense of his moral relations, and adds to his happiness.

Warren's Common School Geography conveyed confidence that man in general has a right to feel quite well satisfied about himself: "The Earth was made for man."

> . . . Christian nations are more powerful, and much more advanced in knowledge than any others. Their power also is continually increasing. They have colonies in many Pagan countries. They send missionaries to the remotest parts of the earth. There is little doubt that in the course of a few generations the Christian religion will be spread over the greater part of the earth.

To the child of the '70's and '80's, the spirit of religion in the schools gave a sense of definite relation to the universe, of eternity of personality; caused his mind to dwell frequently on things of the spirit, and gave him a personal sense of spirituality; caused him to have reverence. Most important of all, it provided him with comfort-bringing definiteness of rules in the otherwise difficult area of right and wrong — in short, supplied him with standards. The unsettlement of standards, the uncertainty about moral anchorages, the weakening of authoritative criterions of ethics and taste, were the unhappiest of the consequences that attended the decline of religion that came during the nineteen-twenties, in the schools and elsewhere. Every people is bound to have, in one degree or another, standards held in common. They are a necessary implication of organized society. Human nature demands them. Very few individuals wish for themselves the privilege of living according to standards separately evolved each for himself, or wish for a condition in which that shall be the rule — or, more accurately, the chaos. No such experiment[1] has ever been made. If it were made it would be anarchy. Human nature instinctively looks about for common standards, gropes for them, seeks them in custom or civil authority, leadership or religion. Even the qualities regarded as most individual — conscience, taste, the bases of self-respect — probably consist, in most cases, of a selection made from the common standards of the place and time. Without falling into the complacence of some of the schoolbooks of the 1880's, we may say as a minimum affirmation that the standards set up by the Christian religion have, at least, satisfied as many people as any others ever attempted.

[1] The reasons why the author does not regard the Bolshevik régime in Russia as such an experiment are too long to set down here. However, it may be said that the codes of personal conduct based on the Christian religion, which the Bolsheviks abrogated, allowed more latitude of individual freedom than the one they substituted.

6

THE AMERICAN MIND: ELOQUENCE, OR AT LEAST ELOCUTION

Part of the Training by Which the Necessary Recruits Were Provided for a Nation Uncommonly Endowed with Legislatures, City Councils, Town Meetings, Religious Organizations, and Other Forms and Occasions Calling for Public Speakers, and Persons Competent to Instruct and Entertain. Some American Traits Reflected in the "Pieces" Printed in the "Speakers" and "Readers" for Exercise in Public Recitation. A National Preoccupation with Forensics.

AMERICANS, as individuals, were not, in their personal relations, a histrionic people, hardly even a declamatory one; were inclined, indeed, to the suppression of personal emotion. Reticence about emotions went hand in hand with taciturnity as a prized intellectual trait. In business and in social relations, loquacity, and especially discursiveness, marked a man as probably not of the highest dependability for the weighty affairs of life. That "silence is golden" was a maxim more approved in America than in almost any other nation. The arts of conversation had little chance to develop, or to be esteemed, in a community in which the major occupation called for long hours of hard work, usually solitary, in the fields, with the homes far apart.

Yet this same people, in their schools, put emphasis on elocution. For the explanation we must consider, therefore, conditions of American life. The United States, with a Congress, forty or more State legislatures and thousands of town and city councils, had more forums for law-making, and hence for public speaking, than other nations. Public life was the most prized career, until close to the end of the nineteenth century, when the service of corporations became extravagantly remunerative. "Young men were encouraged on all hands to aspire to a public career; it was not thought well of a youth if he evinced no public concern; so as soon as a young man showed he was something more or better than the rest of us, the rest of us made much of him."[1]

Political campaigns were frequent and the people took interest in public debate. When there were no motion-pictures and the theatre was taboo to a considerable portion of the people, political debate was at once public business and also entertainment; an attractive political orator had some of the glamour that heroes of the stage and the movie came to have later. When neither mechanical music nor celluloid reels were shipped from cities, smaller communities created their own amusements, in which the lyceum and the "literary society," with local speakers and reciters, were the principal feature.

Among the professions, the two respected most were law, which involved mainly court-room forensics (until the "office-lawyer" came, with aggregations of organized wealth); and the pulpit, which still held some of the authority that attended the Puritan clergyman of the eighteenth century. Some religious sects made much use of lay speakers; Quakers, having no official clergy, were addressed only by members, who spoke when "the spirit moved" them; some other sects heard the official "circuit-rider" only once in so often — for the most part, the congregations were led by members. To be able to expound a gospel at one of the Sunday or mid-week religious services — at least three a week were the usual routine — or to take charge of the Sunday-school or prayer-meeting, or to say the prayer at a funeral, was a duty that might come to almost anybody.

<hr>

[1] Quoted in "Understanding America," by Langdon Mitchell.

To equip youth for a function, at once a public duty and an opportunity to stand out, which might come to any one, either as career, avocation, or emergency, the schools gave formal training at least once a week, many schools oftener. The pupils as a rule made their own selections, though frequently the teacher directed students to memorize and recite specific "pieces."[1] The universal source of the selections was either the text-book formally called a "Speaker," or the other text-book called "Reader." In the earlier days, the Readers were relied upon chiefly. In the 1880's and 1890's, a tendency to expand the number of text-books for specific subjects, accompanying a tendency toward specialization in all fields of life, expressed itself in books designed exclusively for elocution. Among the earlier ones were McGuffey's "New Juvenile Speaker,"[2] 1860; "Young America Speaker,"[3] 1870; "Young Folks Speaker,"[4] 1882; the "Manual of Elocution and Reading,"[5] 1882. In the nineties came the "Star Speaker,"[6] 1892; "Uncle Herbert's Speaker,"[7] 1896, and the "Delsarte Speaker,"[8] 1896. The last was named after a French singer and teacher, who evolved and made popular an intricate philosophy of "correspondence" of the parts of the body, which came to be widely known in America as the system of "Delsarte gestures." If the "Delsarte System,"[9] as practised by school children and other amateurs, gave occasion sometimes for critical amusement, the fact remains that Delsarte was

---

[1] "Piece" was the universal term for selections to recite or read.

[2] Winthrop B. Smith & Co., Cincinnati; J. B. Lippincott & Co., Philadelphia; Clark & Austin, New York.

[3] Porter and Coates, Philadelphia.

[4] Arranged by Grace Adelaide Cook.   D. Lothrop & Co., Boston.

[5] Edward Brooks, Ph.D.   Eldredge and Brother, Philadelphia.

[6] Arranged by Flora N. Kightlinger.   Star Publishing Co., Jersey City, N. J.

[7] J. A. Ruth & Co., Philadelphia and Chicago.

[8] National Publishing Co., Philadelphia.

[9] The "Delsarte System" was not only for elocution, but for carriage and bearing, while walking, sitting, or standing. So general was it in the nineties that

a pioneer in analyzing the movements of the body that accompany various emotions. The "law of correspondence" he based on nature — a mother desiring to show affection for a child presses it to her breast, not to her head. According to other laws, a gesture of mentality

From the "Delsarte Speaker," edited by Henry Davenport Northrop. National Publishing Company, Philadelphia.

Fig. 20.—Remorse.   Fig. 4.—Denying—rejecting.   Fig. 15.—Repulsion.

Oh, wretched state! Oh, bosom black as death!   A proposition so infamous should instantly be voted down.   Avaunt! Richard's himself again.

takes the point of departure from the head, one of moral value from the chest. All this, the "Delsarte Speaker" illustrated with pictures. There were full-page drawings showing appropriate poses and gestures for "Accusation" — "Thou art the man"; "Remorse" — "Oh, wretched state! Oh, bosom black as death"; and so on through the gamut, "Meditation," "Defiance," "Easy Repose," "Exaltation," "Horror," "Invocation."

Joseph Newman wrote a popular song, which did not take Delsarte as seriously as many did, "Since Birdie Commenced Her Delsarte":

"Her right hand goes this way, her left one goes that,
   And she flings them high into the air,
To show her improvement she gives the "wave" movement
   And impersonates Hate and Despair. . . .
There's lots of sleep-walking, also dumb talking,
   Since Birdie's commenced her Delsarte."

Another text-book was:

THE STAR SPEAKER

A COMPLETE AND CHOICE COLLECTION OF

The Best Productions by the Best Authors.
With an Exhaustive Treatise on the
Subject of Vocal and Physical
Culture and Gesturing . . .

The "Star Speaker," in its preface, recommended itself as an improvement on previous text-books, lamenting that

The subjects of Vocal and Physical Culture and Gesturing, as heretofore given, have been wanting that clearness to make them easily understood. Our idea will open an avenue of graceful and pleasing carriage and delivery for all occasions.

The "appropriate and numerous illustrations" began with one giving the amateur elocutionist the proper pose for opening, because the "Star Speaker" thought, correctly, that every declamation, whatever the mood it might later develop into, should begin with a negative gesture of gentleness, as in the illustration. Thereafter, the pose should be changed to accord with whatever might be the dominant mood of the selection. "Fear" was to be expressed, or, as the modern movies would put it, to be "registered" by an explicit pose;
"Anger" by another,
"Sorrow" by a peculiarly tear-compelling attitude,
'Joy," "Patriotism" and "Disdain" by yet other poses.
The "Star Speaker," being explicit, did not leave the pupil to depend on the illustration, vivid though it seems; but gave specific instructions for just the mobilization of legs, feet, arms, and eyes best adapted to convince the audience that the reciter was in a mood of loving his country:

PATRIOTISM. DESCRIPTION OF FIGURE

The right foot a slight space in advance; the form elevated to full height; the right arm extended, and the hand just raised to a level with the eyes; the left arm extended, so that the wrist is on a level with the waist; the hand open, the palm horizontal.

Such an attitude, the "Star Speaker" suggested as an example, would be suitable while delivering:

Breathes there the man with soul so dead,
Who never to himself hath said,
This is my own, my native land !

Gesture for beginning recitation.

For the pose of "Cursing," also, there was specific and minute instruction about the disposition of feet, arms, fingers, and palms, including

shoulders well back; head erect; lips wearing a fierce expression, eyes glancing malignantly.

Patriotism.

The Speakers and Readers had formal lessons on "Articulation, Pronunciation, Inflection, Accent and Emphasis, Pitch and Compass of the Voice"; including "faults to be remedied," such as to avoid saying "par-ticlar" for "par-tic-u-lar." McGuffey, quoting an authority even greater than himself, advised the pupil that words

should be delivered out from the lips, as beautiful coins, newly issued from the mint; neatly struck by the proper organs.

For the attainment of this elegance, Brooks's "Manual of Elocution and

Cursing.
From the "Star Speaker."

Reading" provided "Exercises for Elocutionary Practice," gymnastic exercises for the lips and tongue, and also the mind:[1]

The sun shines on the shop signs.
She sells sea shells. Shall he sell sea shells?
Six gray geese and eight gray ganders.[2]

Round the rough and rugged rocks the ragged rascal ran.

Some shun sunshine; do you shun sunshine?

The old cold scold sold a school coal-scuttle.

The laurel-crowned clown crouched cowering into the closed corner of the cupboard.

When loud surges lash the sounding shore,
The hoarse, rough verse should like a torrent roar.

Peter Prangle, the prickly prangly pear-picker, picked three pecks of prickly prangly pears from the prangly pear-trees on the pretty pleasant prairies.

The stripling stranger strayed straight towards the struggling stream.

Amidst the mists, with angry boasts,
He thrust his fists against the posts,
And still insists he sees the ghosts.

Theophilus Thistle, the successful thistle-sifter, in sifting a sieve full of unsifted thistles, thrust three thousand thistles through the thick of his thumb. Now, if Theophilus Thistle, the successful thistle-sifter, in sifting a sieve full of unsifted thistles, thrust three thousand thistles through the thick of his thumb, see that *thou*, in sifting a sieve full of unsifted thistles, thrust not three thousand thistles through the thick of *thy* thumb. Success to the successful thistle-sifter.[3]

---

[1] A predecessor—and one may suggest—a worth-while successor, to the "Cross-Word Puzzle," the "Limerick" and "Ask Me Another."

[2] Another version of this was "Six gray geese in a green field grazing."

[3] Some earlier schools had used the old "Peter Piper's Practical Principles of Plain and Perfect Pronunciation," designed "to Please the Palates of Pretty Prattling Playfellows"—in which the antic Peter:

"Prays Parents to Purchase this Playful Performance, Partly to Pay him for

The "pieces" in the "Star Speaker," its preface said,

are pure in language, lofty in sentiment, pithy, bright, and sparkling.

For boys the favored selections were those through which they could give expression to the patriotic sentiments about America, the spirit of heroic resistance they had learned from the Histories. Practically every boy declaimed at least once, and certainly every pupil heard many times, the speech of Patrick Henry[1] ending:

There is no retreat but in submission and slavery! . . . The war is inevitable; and, let it come! I repeat, let it come! Gentlemen may cry peace, peace; but there is no peace. The war is actually begun. Our brethren are already in the field! Why stand we here idle? What is it that gentlemen wish? What would they have? Is life so dear, or peace so sweet, as to be purchased at the price of chains and slavery? Forbid it, Almighty God! I know not what course others may take; but as for me, give me liberty, or give me death.

A favorite into which a youth particularly inclined toward elocution could put several varieties of emotion, all coming to a patriotic climax, was the description of an incident in the Revolutionary War.[2] It began by picturing the impact of war upon the peaceful colonies.

his Patience and Pains; Partly to Provide for the Printers and Publishers; but Principally to Prevent the Pernicious Prevalence of Perverse Pronunciation."

Some of Peter's lingual acrobatics were familiar to school children as late as 1900, especially:

Peter Piper picked a peck of pickled peppers;
Did Peter Piper pick a peck of pickled peppers?
If Peter Piper picked a peck of pickled peppers,
Where's the peck of pickled peppers Peter Piper picked?

[1] In a biography of William Jennings Bryan, written by Mrs. Bryan, entitled "The First Battle," there is an indication of the extent to which recitations figured in education in the old-time schools: "A prize contest always fired William's ambition. . . . During his first year at the Academy he declaimed Patrick Henry's masterpiece. The second year he entered with 'The Palmetto and the Pine.' Later he declaimed 'Bernardo del Carpio' and gained the second prize. Finally, with an essay on Labor, he achieved first prize.

[2] Part of Thomas Buchanan Read's "The Wagoner of the Alleghanies."

> Out of the North the wild news came,
> Far flashing on its wings of flame, . . .
> And through the wide land everywhere
> The answering tread of hurrying feet,
> While the first oath of Freedom's gun
> Came on the blast from Lexington. . . .

The subsequent several stanzas were devoted to the scene of the particular episode, a lovely bit of pastoral verse containing some lines often quoted:

> Within its shade of elm and oak . . .
> . . . Sunday found the rural folk . . .
> . . . their feet with loitering tread
> Passed 'mid the graves where rank is naught:
> All could not read the lesson taught
> In that republic of the dead.

With this elegiac background, the heroic part of the poem began; at this point a reciter with variety of talent stiffened himself into impersonation of the hero:

> The pastor rose: the prayer was strong;
> The psalm was warrior David's song;
> The text, a few short words of might —
> "The Lord of hosts shall arm the right!"
>
> He spoke of wrongs too long endured,
> Of sacred rights to be secured;
> Then from his patriot tongue of flame
> The startling words for Freedom came. . . .
> And grasping in his nervous hand
> The imaginary battle-brand
> In face of death he dared to fling
> Defiance to a tyrant king. . . .
> Then swept his kindling glance of fire
> From startled pew to breathless choir;
> When suddenly his mantle wide
> His hands impatient flung aside,
> And, lo! he met their wondering eyes
> Complete in all a warrior's guise.

At this startling transformation of the cloth from clerical to military, the Lord of the Manor, who was in the congregation, and who, of course, was a Tory and a royalist, arose. With a startling capacity to improvise rhyme when in a state of excitement on a Sunday morning, the Tory cried:

> "Cease, traitor! cease!
> God's temple is the house of peace!"

But — and here was one of the several climactic opportunities for elocutionary energy:

> The other shouted, "Nay, not so,
> When God is with our righteous cause:
> His holiest places then are ours.
> His temples are our forts and towers. . . .
> In this the dawn of Freedom's day
> There is a time to fight and pray!" . . .

Now the reciter's voice and posture could fall back a little, into the mood of one of the most remarkable recruiting scenes in either poetry or history, a bit of dramatic stage-management which the clergyman had provided for his coup:

> And now before the open door —
> The warrior priest had ordered so —
> The enlisting trumpet's sudden roar
> Rang through the chapel, o'er and o'er.
>
> While overhead with wild increase,
> Forgetting its ancient toll of peace,
> The great bell swung as ne'er before: . . .
> And every word its ardor flung
> From off its jubilant iron tongue
> Was, "WAR! WAR! WAR!"[1]

That was recited by many of the schoolboys of the '70's; it was heard by all of them, over and over. That it, and others like it, together with a similar influence

[1] That passage, more than any other the author can recall except Mrs. Leslie Carter in "The Heart of Maryland," provided energetic elocutionists with the opportunity literally to make the welkin ring, and good elocutionists did.

from the Histories and Geographies, molded an American attitude of mind, is hardly to be doubted.[1]

Heroic verse about American history was supplemented with "pieces" having the same spirit wherever it could be found in English literature. Many Readers had:

> "Make way for Liberty," he cried;
> Made way for Liberty, and died. . . .

In letters to the author "Marco Bozzaris" is recalled by ex-Governor Chase S. Osborn, of Michigan, who went to school in Indiana; Arthur Ruhl,[2] who went to school at Rockford, Illinois; E. E. Smith, of Minneapolis, who went to school in Minnesota; and so many others who went to school in so many different States, that I conclude Greece's triumph over the Turk must have resounded in practically every schoolhouse in the country:

> At midnight, in his guarded tent,
> The Turk was dreaming of the hour
> When Greece, her knees[3] in suppliance bent,
> Should tremble at his power.

[1] "Patriotic recitations and songs always thrilled me," wrote Mrs. Frank Allen Whitten, née Street, who with her brother, Julian Street, went to the Oakland School in Chicago. "I think they had great influence in schools." United States Senator Simeon D. Fess, of Ohio, wrote me in 1927:

"In that one-room school of all grades I have noted the entire school at a pause listening to the reading of one of those stirring addresses. I am quite sure that my taste for public utterance found its origin there."

[2] Arthur Ruhl wrote: "One got a great kick out of these more romantic poems, especially those which brought back a Europe so different from the town in which we were living. And these bits of verse have the capacity to give one great pleasure afterward. Only last year, visiting Munich for the first time, I was enchanted to run across the Isar there, and to find that it *was* flowing rapidly! I kept adding 'And Isar rolling rapidly' to everything I saw in Munich."

[3] On April 12, 1897, at a time when Theodore Roosevelt was in much demand as a speechmaker, the New York *Sun* printed a story which it said had been told by one of Roosevelt's schoolboy companions. Roosevelt had been called on to recite, had chosen "Marco Bozzaris," and had got off the first two lines successfully, but stumbled on the third. After reciting "Greece, her knees—" he strove desperately to recall what followed, but failed, and repeated again in a louder voice: "Greece, her knees —." Again he stopped. A second or two passed and the silence was broken by the teacher, who remarked encouragingly: "Grease her knees once more, Theodore; perhaps she'll go then."

While this was told of Roosevelt, I suspect it was told of many others, too.

Ex-Secretary of the Navy Josephus Daniels recalled "going into the garden to practise 'Friends, Romans, Countrymen, lend me your ears.'" Other patriotic, military, horse-back, or otherwise heroic "pieces" were: "The Sword of Bunker Hill," "The Boston Massacre," "The Polish Boy," "Mazeppa," "The Battle of Waterloo," "The Charge of the Light Brigade," "How Sleep the Brave," "The Old Continental":

> In their ragged regimentals,
> Stood the old continentals,

"Barbara Frietchie," "Sheridan's Ride," "Lincoln's Gettysburg Address," "The Debate Between Hayne and Webster," "Thou, too, sail on, O Ship of State," William Cullen Bryant's poem of the Revolutionary War, "Song of Marion's Men," beg'nning:

> Our band is few, but true and tried,
> Our leader frank and bold;
> The British soldier trembles
> When Marion's name is told. . . .

Familiarity with tnese old selections, universal among school children and public alike until the early 1890's, began, about 1900, to be supplanted by the popularity of some of Rudyard Kipling's poetry, such as "Tommy Atkins," "Danny Deever," "Gunga Dinh," "Fuzzy Wuzzy," "Mandalay," "The Recessional."

In the earlier "Speakers" was no humor; they were still under the preoccupation that education is an incident of religion. By the 1880's, however, they began to include selections which at once expressed the particular sense of humor called "American," and, by impressing it on school children, perpetuated it — Mark Twain's account of his experiences as a farmer, his tale of an ambitious dog which overestimated its capacity to catch

up with a confident coyote, and his "Funeral of Buck
Fanshaw." Other humorous selections were: "Samantha
at Saratoga," by the American humorist who was immensely popular during the 1880's as "Josiah Allen's
Wife"; Oliver Wendell Holmes's "Height of the Ridiculous," and "One-Hoss Shay," and his "Katydid," in
which some of the humor depended frankly on a pun

> Oh tell me where did Katy live,
> And what did Katy do?

and contained a familiar quotation:

> Thou sayest such an undisputed thing
> In such a solemn way.

Some of the more simple humorous selections, designed
for younger children, were direct enough to be looked
down upon a little by a later generation, which would
call them "slap-stick." In the "Delsarte Speaker,"
pages 197 to 290 are formally labelled "Humorous Recitations." One feels the categorical designation was an
unnecessary tribute to exactness; one could not have
confused it with the next grouping, which was "Pathetic
Recitations." Some of the pieces were humorous and are
funny. I use both the past and the present tenses because of a vague feeling that, as to some of these pieces,
the reasons for which they seemed humorous in 1896,
when the "Delsarte Speaker" was published, are not the
same reasons for which the generation of 1927 will concede they are funny. "Uncle Herbert's Speaker" gave
text and minute directions for what modern comedians
would call "putting over the 'laugh line' ":

A LITTLE BOY'S LECTURE

Ladies and gentlemen: Nearly four hundred years ago the
mighty mind of Columbus, traversing unknown seas, clasped
this new continent in its embrace. A few centuries later arose

one here who now lives in all our hearts as the Father of his Country. Christopher Columbus was *great*. George Washington was *great*. But here, my friends, in this glorious nineteenth century is — a *grater!* (Exhibiting a large, bright

From the "Delsarte Speaker." National Publishing Company, Philadelphia.

A humorous recitation.

tin grater. The large kind used for horseradish could be most easily distinguished by the audience.)

A faintly beginning willingness to look with lack of completely awed respect on father — but as yet far short of the unfilial irreverence of the "Everybody Works but Father" of about 1910 — was:

We all look on with anxious eyes
    When Father carves the duck,
And mother almost always sighs,
    When Father carves the duck;
Then all of us prepare to rise,
And hold our bibs before our eyes,
And be prepared for some surprise,
    When Father carves the duck.

One recitation, standard at the time, told a familiar story, which may be inferred from the first line:

Grandpapa's spectacles cannot be found.

After six stanzas of description of search, the closing two lines told the dènouement:

You may leave off your looking, both Harry and Ned,
For there are the glasses on grandpapa's head.

Sometimes the boys supplied humor themselves, at points where the compilers of the Speakers had not intended it. Their inventiveness frequently took the form of parodies, the subtle means by which suppressed youth expressed its feeling that some sentiments, presented by their tyrant elders as heroic, were in reality ridiculous. The parodies of "Curfew Shall Not Ring To-Night" would fill a hundred pages of this book. Some, regrettably, were ribald. "Casabianca,"

The boy stood on the burning deck,
Whence all but him had fled,

was printed in practically every Speaker, but the boys remembered it less in its original form than in the innumerable parodies it provoked, of which one began:

The boy stood on the burning deck,
Eating peanuts by the peck.

A more subtle sense of humor was pleased by "The Aged Stranger," in which Bret Harte satirized the poetical heroics of the battle-field:

> "I was with Grant" — the stranger said;
> Said the farmer, "Say no more, . . .

> "I was with Grant" — the stranger said;
> Said the farmer, "Nay, no more —
> I prithee sit at my frugal board,
> And eat of my humble store.

The farmer's hospitality had a purpose, not only patriotic but personal. He wanted to know:

> "How fares my boy — my soldier boy,
> Of the old Ninth Army Corps?
> I warrant he bore him gallantly
> In the smoke and the battle's roar!"

After several verses of this, the stranger concluded the poem, and also his welcome, by saying:

> "I cannot tell," said the aged man,
> "And should have remarked before,
> That I was with Grant — in Illinois —
> Some three years before the war."

The "Pathetic Recitations" usually included Dickens's "Death of Little Nell." An expression of this aspect of popular taste was "Nobody's Child," published in the *Schoolday Magazine*, and "noticed and copied and sung and spoken almost everywhere":

> Alone in the dreary, pitiless street,
> With my torn old dress, and bare, cold feet,
> All day I have wandered to and fro,
> Hungry and shivering, and nowhere to go;
> The night's coming on in darkness and dread,
> And the chill sleet beating upon my bare head.
> Oh! why does the wind blow upon me so wild?
> Is it because I am nobody's child?

All the six stanzas were sheer gloom. There was no story; nothing happened; and no comfort for the child was suggested except in the concluding three lines a hope of a future "home above."

Tragedies of the sea were favorites:

> *Old Ironsides* at anchor lay, . . .
> A dead calm rested on the bay, . . .
> When little Hal, the captain's son,
>   A lad both brave and good,
> In sport, up shroud and rigging ran,
>   And on the main-truck stood!

With the boy in this dangerous situation — he could not climb down again, for some reason not explained — the father took a heroic measure. Doubtless this was designed to convey a lesson, also — that a boy should do what his father tells him, without question; and that a father is justified in enforcing his measures:

> The father came on deck. — He gasped,
>   "O God! thy will be done!"
> Then suddenly a rifle grasped,
>   And aimed it at his son:
> "Jump — far out, boy, into the wave!
>   Jump, or I fire!" he said;
> "That only chance your life can save!
>   Jump! jump, boy!" He obeyed.

This had a happy ending, unusual among the maritime adventures in the "Star Speaker":

> He sank — he rose — he lived — he moved —
>   And for the ship struck out:
> On board we hailed the lad beloved,
>   With many a manly shout.
> His father drew, in silent joy,
>   Those wet arms round his neck,
> And folded to his heart his boy —
>   Then fainted on the deck.

A sea tragedy with the familiar moral lesson:

> We were crowded in the cabin,
>   Not a soul would dare to sleep,
> It was midnight on the waters,
>   And a storm was on the deep. . . .
>
> As thus we sat in darkness,
>   Each one busy with his prayers,
> "We are lost!" the captain shouted,
>   As he staggered down the stairs.

Irvin Cobb questioned the wisdom of this captain; questioned, indeed, the whole incident as lacking fidelity to truth and human nature:

> If ever there was a time when those in authority should avoid spreading alarm this was the time. By all the traditions of the maritime service it devolved upon the skipper to remain calm, cool, and collected. But what does the poet reveal to a lot of trusting school children?
>
> > "We are lost!" the captain shouted,
> >   As he staggered down the stair.
>
> He didn't whisper it; he didn't tell it to a friend in confidence; he bellowed it out at the top of his voice so all the passengers could hear him. The only possible excuse which can be offered for that captain's behavior is that his staggering was due not to the motion of the ship but to alcoholic stimulant.

There is more than humor in Cobb's indictment. Many of the stories in those old Speakers and Readers pictured men doing what the children, with their instinctive insight, knew men would not do, or should not do; pictured as heroes and as heroic, men and actions that the children felt were not heroic, nor natural under the circumstances. The children of that generation were not permitted to speak their minds openly, were required to act as if they believed. The children of a later generation, affected by the vogue of a new literature of realism, frankly questioned whatever did not seem to them true;

and that was a chief part of a change in the manners of the young, much talked about in the 1920's.

Most favored, as the true type of sea tragedy,[1] with deep gloom and a fatal ending, was Longfellow's:

> It was the schooner *Hesperus*,
>   That sailed the wintry sea;
> And the skipper had taken his little daughter,
>   To bear him company. . . .
>
> Down came the storm, and smote amain
>   The vessel in its strength; . . .

The skipper sought to comfort his child:

> He wrapped her warm in his seaman's coat,
>   Against the stinging blast;
> He cut a rope from a broken spar,
>   And bound her to the mast. . . .
>
> "O father! I see a gleaming light,
>   O say, what may it be?"
> But the father answered never a word,
>   A frozen corpse was he. . . .
>
> At daybreak, on the bleak sea-beach,
>   A fisherman stood aghast,

[1] Other favorite poems of the sea were Southey's "Inchcape Rock," and "The Gray Swan." The latter begins with a mother seeking her boy who had run away to sea twenty years before.

> "Oh! tell me, sailor, tell me true,
>   Is my little lad, my Elihu,
>   A-sailing with your ship? . . .
>   My Elihu, that took to the sea
>   The moment I put him off my knee!
>   It was just the other day
>   The *Gray Swan* sailed away! . . ."

For a wonder, this had a happy ending. The mother, having mentioned a kerchief the boy had when he left:

> The sailor twitched his shirt so blue,
>   And from within his bosom drew
>   The kerchief. She was wild.
> "O God, my Father! is it true?
>   My little lad, my Elihu!"

> To see the form of a maiden fair
> Lashed close to a drifting mast.

Ex-Governor Chase Osborn, of Michigan, sending suggestions for this chapter, wrote:

> Of course you won't forget the temperance movements . . . the echo of Neal Dow and others. The red ribbon and blue ribbon movements went so far that Michigan became a Prohibition State from 1856 to 1875.

No schoolboy of the '80's can forget, and no accurate historian should; though it is forgotten by those who claim the National Prohibition Amendment of 1919 was an emotional incident of the Great War, a war-time submissiveness to propaganda, war-time acceptance of regulation and restraint. Actually, the roots of the movement ran back more than half a century, and included the organized and practically universal inculcation in school children of detestation for the liquor traffic. It included the recruiting of children to "sign the pledge"; the wearing of a blue ribbon, through which total abstainers proclaimed their convictions on the lapels of their coats; and recitations without number. One that ex-Governor Osborn recalls was presumably for little girls:

> No matter what any one says;
> No matter what any one thinks;
> If you want to be happy the rest of your life
> Don't marry a man if he drinks.

There was conscious effort by the zealous temperance leaders to organize the schoolgirls into crusading bands, using pressure — or wile — to convert the boys. "Blue Bows" was a dialogue between two persuasive girls and a temporizing youth. It began:

CHARLES: Whew! Making so many blue bows. What are they for?
ELLICE: Temperance badges. Will you wear one? . . .

The missionary determination of girls was expressed
in a ditty that was often parodied, sometimes ribaldly:

> The lips that touch liquor
> Shall never touch mine.

A similar appeal was "Come, Sign the Pledge":

> Young man, why will you not sign the pledge,
>   And stand with the true and the brave?
> How dare you lean over the dangerous ledge
>   Above the inebriate's grave?

"The Price of a Drink" had an agreeable rhythm, easy
to learn and fluent to recite:

> Five cents a glass, does any one think
> That that is really the price of a drink? . . .
> The price of a drink, let him decide
> Who has lost his courage and his pride,
> And who lies a grovelling heap of clay,
> Not far removed from a beast to-day.

Another, often recited in the '80's and '90's, began:

> There stood two glasses filled to the brim,
> On a rich man's table, rim to rim.[1]

During the eighties, some schools made use of a booklet put out by the National Temperance Society and
Publication House, called "Exercises and Dialogues for
use of Sunday-Schools, Bands of Hope, and other Juvenile
and Religious Temperance Organizations." The opening
piece was called "The Alcohol Fiend: A Temperance
Dialogue for Lodges, Divisions, Lyceums . . ."

---

[1] I have forgotten the rest, though I once won a prize for reciting it with excellence of conviction. I know, however, the poem dealt with the desirability of
taking one of the glasses only, and the right one, the one that contained water;
and with the rewards that would follow continuity in always making the same
choice. One of the impressions conveyed by the poem, but not borne out in later
experience in circles far removed from that old one-room school, was that the
drinking of liquor was prevailingly a defect of the rich, rather than of the poor.

In the mood of prophecy of fulfilment, was a temperance song often sung by fresh young voices in schoolrooms:

There is a happy time, not far away,
When Temp'rance truth shall shine bright, bright as day;
O, then we'll sweetly sing, make the hills and valleys ring,
Earth shall her tribute bring — God speed the day.

In some of the Speakers were sections marked off as "Selections for Missionary Exercises." The selections were sufficiently numerous to suggest that they either reflected, or accounted for, the extent to which missionary work in foreign countries was taken up by American young folks. America had more zeal than any other nation for evangelization among the heathen. "Missionary work" had almost the status of a career, and enlisted enough youths to be almost a recognized occupation.

From "The Sunday-School Concert." National Temperance Society and Publication House.

Pieces formally marked off in the Speakers as "Selections for Boys and Girls" had the note that in a later generation came to be called "inspirational." A more than commonly good one was the Carey sisters' (Alice and Phœbe):

We get back our meet as we measure;
We cannot do wrong and feel right
Nor can we give pain and gain pleasure,
For Justice avenges each slight:
The air for the wing of the sparrow,
The bush for the robin and wren,

But always the path that is narrow and straight,
For the children of men.

The "Star Speaker" provided children with some mediums for artificially naïve expression. "A Little Boy's Speech" recalls two words now gone from the common tongue:

> I am a little boy, you see,
>   Not higher much than pappy's knee;
> Some of the big boys said that I
>   To make a speech ought not to try.
> This raised my spunk.

Admonitions to right conduct were put directly:

> Don't go to the theatre, grange, or ball,
>   But stay in your room to-night; . . .
> Write to the sad old folks at home,
>   Who sit when the day is done,
> With folded hands and downcast eyes,
>   And think of the absent one.

One of the characteristics of the generation that succeeded this period was frankness — young folk of the 1920's said what they thought and felt. Certainly the youth of the seventies and eighties were taught, to some extent, to say what they didn't think. To require a child to memorize and deliver the following "Presentation Speech" was a lesson in artificiality, smugness, hypocrisy:

Dear Teacher: I have been requested by the pupils of this school (or institution), to ask your acceptance of this little token of their respect and affection. We wished in some way to show our appreciation of your ability as a preceptor, and of your patience and kindness in dealing with [our] faults . . . and concluded that the most befitting exponent of our feelings would be a memento to which we could all contribute, and which, however insignificant its value might be when measured by the magnitude of our obligations, would agreeably remind you that we are not ungrateful. When we go into the world, we shall not forget to whom we owe our acquirements, but shall remember you ever with almost filial regard. Whenever memory recalls our school days, our hearts will warm toward you as they do to-day.[1]

The sentiments the pupils actually felt were probably more accurately expressed in a closing-day ditty:

No more school, no more books,
No more cross-eyed teacher's looks.

Some passages were so uniformly included in Speakers and Readers that they were, for this purpose, almost as standardized as a Ford car: "Paul Revere's Ride," "Elegy Written in a Country Churchyard," "'Twas the Night Before Christmas," "Twinkle, Twinkle, Little Star," James Whitcomb Riley's "Little Orphant Annie," "The Destruction of Sennacherib," of which the first line ran

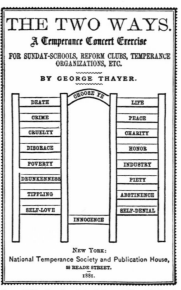

THE TWO WAYS.
A Temperance Concert Exercise
FOR SUNDAY-SCHOOLS, REFORM CLUBS, TEMPERANCE ORGANIZATIONS, ETC.

BY GEORGE THAYER.

CHOOSE YE

DEATH		LIFE
CRIME		PEACE
CRUELTY		CHARITY
DISGRACE		HONOR
POVERTY		INDUSTRY
DRUNKENNESS		PIETY
TIPPLING		ABSTINENCE
SELF-LOVE		SELF-DENIAL

INNOCENCE

NEW YORK:
National Temperance Society and Publication House,
58 READE STREET.
1881.

From "The Sunday School Concert." National Temperance Society & Publication House, N.Y.

"The Assyrian came down, like a wolf on the fold"

"Excelsior," "Bingen on the Rhine," "The Battle of Blenheim," "Abou Ben Adhem," "The Village Blacksmith," "Woodman, Spare that Tree," "The Pied Piper," "'Ostler Joe," "The Sleeping Sentinel," "John Burns of Gettysburg," "The Barefoot Boy," "The Skeleton in Armor," "The Lady of Shalott," Trowbridge's "Vagabonds," always a favorite with boys for its picture of the affection between boy and dog. "Thanatopsis," "Hia-

---

[1] Parts of two forms of "Presentation Speech," provided by the "Star Speaker."

watha," "Evangeline," "Maud Muller," George Mc-
Donald's lovely "Baby":

> "Where did you come from, baby dear?"
> "Out of the everywhere into here."
> "Where did you get those eyes so blue?"
> "Out of the sky as I came through."

Thomas Bailey Aldrich's "Face Against the Pane" (girls
named Mabel had to endure a lot of quoting and parody-
ing of that); Longfellow's "The Children's Hour":

> Between the dark and the daylight,
> When the night is beginning to lower.

Tennyson's "You must wake and call me early, call me
early, mother dear," "Annabel Lee" — satisfying for a
lover when he was in a mournful mood:

> It was many and many a year ago,
>   In a kingdom by the sea,
> That a maiden lived whom you may know
>   By the name of Annabel Lee;
> And this maiden she lived with no other thought
>   Than to love and be loved by me.

"Grandpa's Soliloquy," which deprecated slang — the
expressions mentioned as new and deplorable included
"the light fantastic toe" for dancing, "passing in his
checks" for dying, and "just the cheese" as a description
of perfection, like the "bee's knees" of 1924. "Rock Me
to Sleep":

> Backward, turn backward, O time! in your flight.

Mellow affection for the old, without acrimony for the
new, was in

> O Good painter, tell me true,
>   Has your hand the cunning to draw
>   Shapes of things that you never saw?
> Ay? Well, here is an order for you.

> Woods and cornfields, a little brown —
>> The picture must not be over-bright,
>> Yet all in the golden and gracious light
> Of a cloud, when the summer sun is down.

As well as Oliver Wendell Holmes's

There is no time like the old time, when you and I were young,
When the buds of April blossomed and the birds of springtime
    sung!

The "Blue and the Gray," universal for Memorial
Day:

> By the flow of the inland river,
>> Whence the fleets of iron have fled,
> Where the blades of the grave-grass quiver,
>> Asleep are the ranks of the dead;
>>> Under the sod and the dew,
>>>> Waiting the judgment-day;
>>> Under the one, the Blue;
>>>> Under the other, the Gray.

7

THE AMERICAN MIND: DISCIPLINE

Studies Meant to Impart Mental Discipline. Endorse-
ments of — and Some Dissents from — the Theory that the
Studies Were Happily Chosen for That Effect. The "Blue-
Back Speller." "Spelling-Down." "Spelling-Bees." Arith-
metic and Grammar. The Discipline of Chores, and of
Poverty. Together with Some Surprising—and Dismaying—
Records of the Corporal Punishment Practised Generally in
American Schools as Late as the Eighteen-Nineties.

"My recollection," wrote John H. Clarke, in 1927, "is
that the drill was very thorough in what was then called
'mental arithmetic'; I have found the capacity derived
from it — to solve problems without resorting to pen or
pencil — very valuable; especially in the hurry of trials
of cases." Mental Arithmetic was real drill — to stand
on your feet and think fast and accurately, before the
eye of a minatory teacher, and under the gaze of the whole
school, and to answer such problems[1] as:

How many square inches in a piece of paper six inches long
and four inches wide?

Reduce to their lowest terms: $\dfrac{12}{16}, \dfrac{24}{36}, \dfrac{16}{28}, \dfrac{28}{49}, \dfrac{32}{36}$.

Henry paid ¼ of all his money for a knife, ⅛ for a ball, and ⅙
for a necktie: what part of his money had he left?

A harness was sold for ¾ of ⅘ of what it cost. What was the
loss per cent?

"The tests of rapidity in addition, multiplication, and
division," wrote James M. Cox in 1927, "gave spur to

---

[1] The first two problems are from "Ray's New Elementary Arithmetic," Van
Antwerp, Bragg & Co., Cincinnati, 1879; the last two from the "Oral Exam-
ples" in "Robinson's Intermediate Arithmetic," Ivison, Blakeman, Taylor &
Co., New York, 1874.

the mind and were a good form of mental gymnastics.[1] The average country boy in those days went through Ray's Higher Arithmetic, a wonderful text-book, a real challenge to the young mathematician. If I remember correctly, and I haven't seen one of these books for thirty-five years, the last problem in it runs something like this: If you set a globe 10 inches in diameter in the corner of a room, what is the diameter of the small globe that can be set underneath and behind it, its surface touching the floor and the two walls and the larger globe?"

This problem that Governor Cox could recall offhand was, of course, in written arithmetic, not mental. Many of the examples in written arithmetic would be stiff to the average adult with a college education:

The fore wheel of a carriage is 9 feet, and the hind wheel 10½ feet in circumference; how many times will each turn round in running from Boston to Andover, 20½ miles?

The salary of the President of the United States is $25,000 per annum; what sum may he expend daily and yet save $41,560 in one term of office, viz., 4 years?

Those problems are from Eaton's[2] Common School Arithmetic, the contents of which included:

Compound Interest; Discount; Banking and Bank Discount; Insurance; Stocks; Commission and Brokerage; Taxes; Custom House Business; Exchange; Equation of Payments; Profit and Loss; Partnership; Compound Proportion; Alligation Medial; Involution; Evolution; Arithmetical Progression; Annuities; Permutation; Tare and Tret.

Charles W. Hobbs, who in 1927 was an official of the Massachusetts Department of Education, thought some

---

[1] Mr. Tom Finty, of Dallas, Texas, recalls that in his school days in Illinois, an element of competition was introduced in the form of "ciphering matches." "A number of the boys and girls learned to add six rows of figures as they were called out; the winner was the pupil who could write the total the quickest."

[2] By James S. Eaton, M.A. Taggard and Thompson, Boston, 1867.

of the subjects in Eaton's Arithmetic were of dubious
value, and that the text-book itself was

a book of torture. In those days education was expected to
provide mental discipline, and mathematical authors seemed to
comb their field for subjects that would produce the greatest
amount of drudgery. . . .   The mathematics book of to-day
[1927], designed for grammar-school pupils, would omit most
of the topics listed in Eaton's Arithmetic. It has been found
that a working knowledge of the four fundamental operations
(addition, subtraction, multiplication, division) and an understanding of percentage and interest are sufficient for most
people. I have not been able to find an engineer in this department who can tell what 'alligation medial' means, and
the head of the Massachusetts Department of Education,
himself a mathematician of no mean achievement, has entirely forgotten how to do cube root and isn't ashamed to say so.

Problems in arithmetic were "figured out" on slates,
the pupils using pencils of soft stone sharpened at one
end. The slate has given way almost everywhere before
the scratch pad, but in the '70's, '80's, and '90's it was the
commonest article in a school child's equipment. Slates
were fragile and liable to break if let fall, but with care
could be made to last several years, being passed down,
in that economical age, from older brother to younger.
The cheapest, selling for ten cents, were about the size
of this page, were made of poor material, with smooth
places where no pencil could make a mark; they were
framed in a plain wooden border, poorly mortised, forever coming apart. Better grades of slates were almost
as large as a tabloid newspaper, had double panels hinged
in the back, and about their borders a protective strip
of bright red or blue flannel.

The strongest argument against slates was hygienic and
was doubtless one reason why they lost their former ubiquity. Fastidious teachers showed their pupils how to
erase writing by wiping it off with a damp cloth or a

sponge; but to school children this seemed a long-way-around method for achieving results that could just as efficaciously be attained by saliva and a brisk rubbing with the coat-sleeve. This was the custom among boys; girls were neater, whether because they lacked coat-sleeves, or because the sleeves of their dresses were of bright colors and not to be soiled.

The slate is gone,[1] and with it has gone the gleeful practice of the mischievous youth of forty years ago, of drawing caricatures of the teacher or the girl with pig-tails across the aisle — caricatures that, when danger of approaching authority threatened, could be deftly swept into oblivion by the stroke of a moistened thumb.

II

"Spelling," wrote E. Davenport in 1927, then Dean and Professor Emeritus of the College of Agriculture, University of Illinois, "was the *pièce de resistance* and test of scholarship in the district school." In Ohio, Senator Simeon D. Fess recalled, "much emphasis was placed on spelling." "We all began life on Webster's spelling-book," wrote a resident of Buffalo, N. Y. In North Carolina, Ex-Secretary of the Navy Josephus Daniels, making a comparison between an early triumph in spelling and a later one in a different field, to the greater glory of the first, recalled that:

The schools elevated spelling to a very high place. I remember when I was 14 receiving the greatest honor of my life. Our teacher required every pupil from the highest to the lowest — and there were 188 of us — to attend the spelling class every day at noon. In those days they had the "cut down and cut up" system and competition was keen. I received the dictionary as a prize for the best speller in the school. I felt I

[1] Not quite: An inquiry made in 1927, of a firm that had made school slates for more than forty years, revealed that the peak of production was between 1895 and 1900, when about twenty-five million slates were made. In 1913 the production was six million; in 1926 two million.

was "some pumpkins." A little job like the Secretary of the
Navy never seemed half so great as that dictionary.

The methods of conducting the spelling class varied.
As recalled by Professor Davenport:

The class stood in a row with toes on the same crack of the
floor, as the last "exercise" of every school day. Beginning
at the "head" the teacher pronounced from the lesson to
each in turn. If any one missed, the next tried and the next,
down the line until some one, either through superior knowledge, or profiting by the trial and error of his less fortunate
fellows, or else by hasty application of the principle of reductio
ad absurdum, hit on the correct spelling, whereat he took his
place up the line just above the one who first missed, horning
everybody down one notch accordingly.

Many teachers introduced an element of group competition. Senator Fess recalled:

The teacher would select a leader on each side, and proceed
to divide the entire school into two divisions. Each leader
would choose a captain, whose function was to note errors on
the opposite side and trap the speller the moment the error
was made. After a time, during which each pupil took his
turn in spelling, the sides contested in a match of "spelling
down."[1] When any pupil misspelled a word, he took his seat.
This was continued until all were seated, if that could be done.

---

[1] The place the spelling-match had in the schools is celebrated in Whittier's
"In School Days," which pictures a boy and a girl on their way home after school:

> He saw her lift her eyes; he felt
>   The soft hand's light caressing,
> And heard the tremble of her voice,
>   As if a fault confessing.
>
> "I'm sorry that I spelt the word;
>   I hate to go above you,
> Because,"—the brown eyes lower fell—
>   "Because, you see, I love you!"
>
> Still memory to a gray-haired man
>   That sweet child-face is showing.
> Dear girl! the grasses on her grave
>   Have forty years been growing!
>
> He lives to learn, in life's hard school,
>   How few who pass above him
> Lament their triumph and his loss,
>   Like her—because they love him.

Neighboring schools were pitted against each other. Often whole communities took part. Senator Fess recalls some so heated that they lasted beyond midnight. Usually, in spelling-bees,[1] the first step was to select two captains. To determine which should have first choice in making up the sides, one captain tossed a stick to the other, who held it fast just where he happened to catch it. Then the first placed his hand above the second, and so the hands were alternately changed to the top. The one who held the stick last[2] without room for the other to take hold had the first choice and picked for his side the person who had gained the reputation of being the best speller in previous matches.

The mute umpire of these matches was a book, one of the most widely known ever printed in America. "The Blue-Back Speller" or "Webster's Blue-Back Speller," was a universal text-book in the schools, but was more than that, the master-book on spelling everywhere, a standard article of commerce, like sugar and salt, kept in the stores, alongside the gingham and calico. Every one was familiar with its vivid blue covers, and had a curious affection for it. In 1912 a speaker[3] before the Oklahoma Legislature, to prove a point he was making, held up a book, and heard from the older men in the room an audible whisper of pleased recognition: "My God, it's an old blue-back speller."

More than five generations of Americans learned from it. The first studied it before there was any United States, as early as 1787; and it was still being used in schools as

---

[1] The best description of a spelling-bee with which the author is familiar is in Edward Eggleston's "The Hoosier School Master." Their function was broader than a mere exercise in orthography. "There was," Eggleston wrote, "laughing and talking, giggling and simpering, ogling and flirting and courting. . . . It is an occasion metaphorically inscribed with the legend, 'choose your partners.'"

[2] This advantage was called the "last holt."

[3] It was William H. ("Coin") Harvey, of Monte Ne, Ark.

late as the early 1900's. Boys learned from the Blue-Back Speller, grew up, became Presidents of the United States, died, and were relatively forgotten, while the presses of D. Appleton & Company ground out new editions for second, third, and fourth generations. The first edition was printed on a hand-press, the last on the most modern Hoe; the first antedated the Presidency of Washington, the last was contemporary with Roosevelt.

The compiler was Noah Webster, who called the earliest one, printed in 1783, "First Part of a Grammatical Institute of the English Language." That too ponderous title, destined to be simplified by five generations of school children into "The Blue-Back Speller," must have struck old Noah Webster himself as cumbersome, for by 1789 apparently he was calling it a "Spelling-Book."

For nearly half a century, Noah Webster lived upon the profits of his Speller. As it was his only means of livelihood and he needed protection from piracy, Webster visited many States and secured the enactment of copyright statutes, "so that," says Grant Overton, "he may be the instigator of American copyright protection." Webster, using the profits of his Speller as his means of livelihood, devoted himself to compiling his dictionary, which yielded him no profit at all, although it has been a valuable estate to his family.

In 1855, the plates of the Speller were taken over by D. Appleton & Company. The Speller was then seventy-two years old, a longer life than any other text-book had ever had. But the Appletons took it up with as much enthusiasm as if it were the newest and most up-to-date manuscript. By 1880, William H. Appleton was able to reply[1] to an interviewer who asked him what was the best selling book published by his firm:

[1] Quoted in the *Youth's Companion*, May 27, 1880.

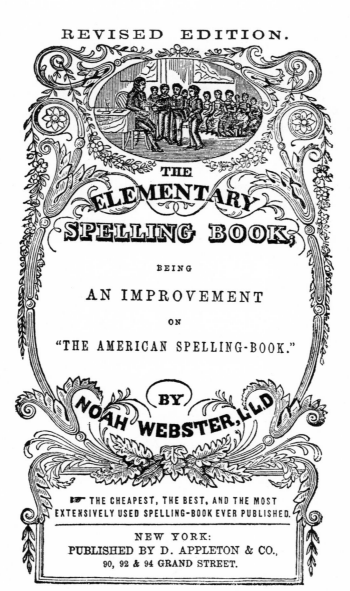

REVISED EDITION.

THE ELEMENTARY SPELLING BOOK,

BEING

AN IMPROVEMENT

ON

"THE AMERICAN SPELLING-BOOK."

BY

NOAH WEBSTER, L.L.D

☞ THE CHEAPEST, THE BEST, AND THE MOST
EXTENSIVELY USED SPELLING-BOOK EVER PUBLISHED.

NEW YORK:
PUBLISHED BY D. APPLETON & CO.,
90, 92 & 94 GRAND STREET.

This spelling-book was in common use during the 1890's, and
still used in schools after 1900.

Webster's Speller; and it has the largest sale of any book in the world except the Bible. We sell a million copies a year. Yes, and we have been selling it at that rate for forty years. The year following the emancipation of the slaves we sold one million five hundred thousand, because every negro in the South thought it only necessary to have a Webster's Speller to read. After that year it fell back to the original million, and has never varied. We sell them in cases of seventy-two dozen, and they are bought by all the large dry-goods houses and supply stores, and furnished by them to every cross-roads store.

One of the largest presses in the Appleton plant ran day after day, on this one book, until it was completely worn out. By 1890 the sales of "old Blue-Back" had reached the astonishing total of over 35,000,000 copies, in which some five generations of American youths adventured among the mysteries of English orthography.

Neither the Speller nor any other schoolbook of the early days of the nineteenth century could confine itself to the branch of learning it taught. It had to be semi-religious. The Blue-Back Speller had its quota of moral lessons of the usual type, one of which was the "Fable of the Boy that Stole Apples," followed by the formal:

Moral: If good words and gentle means will not reclaim the wicked, they must be dealt with in a more severe manner.

The moral of "The Country Maid and Her Milk-Pail" was:

When men suffer their imagination to amuse them with the prospect of distant and uncertain improvements of their condition, they frequently sustain real losses, by their inattention to those affairs in which they are immediately concerned.

This country maid was carrying a pail of milk on her head as she walked along, thinking how she would sell it and with the money buy eggs. She then counted the number of chickens that would hatch from the eggs, which in turn she would sell and with the money she would buy a new dress. "Green! — let me consider — yes, green becomes my complexion best, and green it shall be." She then pictured herself at the fair with all the young fellows trying to secure her for a partner. Her

From "*Webster's Elementary Spelling-Book.*" *D. Appleton & Co.*
The country maid and her milk-pail.

intentions were not matrimonial, however, or rather they were only ultimately matrimonial, and included a period when, having reduced the swains to a condition of abject idolatry, she visualized herself haughtily tossing her head. "Transported with this triumphant thought, she could not forbear acting with her head what thus passed in her imagination, when down came the pail of milk, and with it all her imaginary happiness." This fable, far from impressing at least one pupil who learned it with the wisdom of its moral, had the effect of arousing sympathy for the unfortunate maid whose iridescent dreams came tumbling down with her spilled pail of milk.

In the teaching of spelling, a difficulty lay in the fact that before the teachers had time to give sufficient drill in spelling, the pupils, as they took up other subjects, were obliged to make daily use of some words that to them were new and very formidable. There would be regrettable lack of balance in having pupils studying, for example, arithmetic but not knowing how to spell the word. To give young minds a short cut to the spelling of polysyllabic words, there was an ingenious device with which one learned to spell the word "Arithmetic" by memorizing a sentence "A rat in the house may eat the ice cream." The initial letters of the words in the sentence spell "Arithmetic." Similar expedients were:

G E O G R A P H Y
George Eliot's Old Grandmother Rode a Pig Home Yesterday And

P R E F A C E
Paul Rice Eats Fish and Catches Eagles

To give the device an additional gymnastic twist, it was sometimes operated backward, thus for "Preface":

E C A F E R P
Eagles Catch Alligators; Father Eats Raw Potatoes

A device intended to bridge over the difficulty of very long words was to spell them one syllable at a time, each syllable being repeated as the spelling of it was completed:

c–o–n con, s–t–a–n stan, constan, t–i, ti, constanti, n–o no, constantino, p–l–e, ple — CONSTANTINOPLE.

The "American Advanced Speller"[1] included several "Dictation and Language Exercises," designed to give students practice with different forms of the past tense, and in words pronounced the same but having different meanings and different spellings. One was:

The general saw the mangled *corpse* of the bravest officer of his *corps*. He asked him if he would as *lief* pluck a *leaf* from the

[1] By Lucius Osgood, published by A. H. English & Co., Pittsburgh, Pa.

tree. Is there *need* for you to *knead dough?* The hunter shot a *doe.* The soldier had a *martial mien.* The *marshal* had a *mean* fellow in his company. He met a *peer* upon the *pier.*

Osgood's Speller stood up bravely for the desirability of learning to spell long words, saying in the Preface:

More long words (which some have *derisively* styled *sesqui-pedalian*) have been introduced, perhaps, than many might think necessary; but it will be readily admitted, that the pupils ought to be made familiar with the methods of combining letters and syllables in long, difficult words.

In that spirit, Osgood's began at Lesson 1 with "a-m am" and by easy stages led up to

lat i tu di na ri an	su per nat u ral i ty
pu sil la nim i ty	in com mu ni ca bil i ty

Nearly all who have sent me their recollections of their school days have shown pride and affectionate approval for the proficiency in spelling that the old schools developed; have had the air of saying: "Those were the days when boys and girls could *spell*" — with a manner of confidently inviting comparison with the modern generation. "In those days," Josephus Daniels wrote:

The pupils really learned how to spell. At recess they would try to stump each other with hard words, so that spelling became a sort of recreation at playtime.

And Senator Fess, of Ohio:

The result was a superior ability to spell, over the present day. . . . The practical value in insuring correct spelling was immensely important in after-life. The same may be said of the study of grammar, as an insurance against embarrassment in incorrect use of English.

The same conviction, that school children of the 1880's and 1890's were better spellers than the generation that

followed, and the same emphasis on the value of spelling
as intellectual discipline, were expressed by James M. Cox:

There was great pride then in knowing something about
history, civil government, and being able to take good rank
as a speller and as a rapid calculator in figures. The spelling-
match was held every Friday afternoon. During the winter
months there was a competition between different schools.
There was one or more located in each township. It's amazing,
when one stops to think of it, how the youngsters could spell
then as compared to those of the present day. . . . Arithmetic
gave spur to the mind and was good mental gymnastics.

Arithmetic really produced exactness of the processes
of thinking. Spelling could only produce, at best, exactness of memory. Spelling was a kind of memory mara-
thon, the mental equivalent of six-day bicycle races, or
endurance contests in dancing. Arithmetic led to intellectual skill. No one could speak of such a thing as skill
in spelling. You either remembered how the word was
spelled, or you did not. If memory training were the object, it would be better accomplished by the memorizing
of good poetry, which would give rise to worthy and
agreeable emotions in the process, and leave in the mind
a valuable residue, which spelling did not.

This doubt about spelling for spelling's sake is held by
a few whose recollections have contributed to this survey. Professor Davenport wrote:

We seemingly inherited the passion from our fathers and
mothers, as they had been in their day, mighty men and women
of valor in respect to the gynmastics of English orthography.
With them, words were made to be spelled, their meaning and
use being purely incidental to their construction, and the worse
the construction, the better the word. My mother never went
to school after she was twelve but I never knew her to misspell
a word. She had learned by main strength how to spell, not
only all kinds of common and uncommon words, but also a
choice collection of "catch-words" of which Kamtchatka, as
it was then spelled, was one of the easy ones, and such as seraglio

nothing at all. We used regularly Sanders's New Speller, Definer, and Analyzer — they used pretentious titles those days. Beginning with words of two letters, it gradually increased in difficulty to incomprehensibility, transubstantiation, and the like, never omitting a single "jaw-breaker," as the tough ones were expressively called. One found such useful and self-explanatory terms — to a child — as parsimoniousness, advantageousness, penuriousness. Yet it was a good book, especially in its definitions, for it was our only dictionary — no school possessed a dictionary, even a small one — I never saw a dictionary during my district-school days — and the teachers then knew the meaning of very few words, one venturing the opinion that luncheon, being a light meal between breakfast and dinner, must occur around ten o'clock.

III

Ranking with Spelling and Arithmetic, as studies good for mental discipline, was Grammar; and ranking with McGuffey's Readers and Noah Webster's Speller in ubiquity and venerableness was Murray's "Grammar of the English Language," first issued by Lindley Murray in 1795, regarded as the standard text-book on its subject throughout England and America for nearly a hundred years, and still studied in some American schools as late as the seventies. Another familiar Grammar was Greenough's,[1] of which John H. Clarke wrote:

My chief recollection was a very thorough drill in parsing, in analyzing of sentences, and especially in memorizing prepositions and irregular verbs. I could amuse you by repeating a list of prepositions as I learned it approximately fifty years ago.

Greene's Grammar[2] contained a record of, and reflection upon, some familiar American locutions:

The following are actual expressions collected from a large number of schools. They should be carefully corrected.

[1] Other Grammars were: "The Institutes of English Grammar Methodically Arranged," by Goold Brown; "The Child's Grammar," by E. M. Murch; "An Introduction to the Study of English Grammar," by Samuel S. Greene.
[2] Cowperthwait and Co., Philadelphia, 1868.

'Taint no good. I hain't got no writin' pen. I've got some on t'other side of me slate. You said 'twas yourn. Mine was writ better'n hisn, only he writ more nor I did. You be's telling on him. He done it, too, marm. I can't git it no way. Be them two right? I cotched the ball. Hullo, teacher!

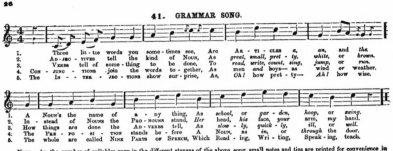

Note.—As the number of syllables vary in the different stanzas of the above song, small notes and ties are printed for convenience in adapting them to the music. This mode of adapting different stanzas to music is frequently resorted to. The necessity of such an arrangement will appear on reading the poetry.

From " The Singing Bird, or Progressive Music Reader," by William B. Bradbury. Ivison, Blakeman, Taylor & Co., New York.

Florie and me went out and drove hoop. She jawed her mother.

Grammar, especially parsing, was regarded by Albert Mordell as an unhappy denaturing device for taking the poetry out of poems. "We would be given selections from poems and told to find the subject, which might be half a dozen lines away from the predicate, with dependent clauses strung all around. Prose was not used for parsing because the subject was before the predicate where it belonged, and therefore provided no puzzle to sharpen our wits — or confuse them. In the opening lines from 'Snowbound,' often used as an exercise,

> A chill no coat however stout
> Of homespun stuff could quite shut out,
> A dark, dull bitterness of cold
> That checked, mid-vein, the circling race
> Of life-blood in the sharpened face,
> The coming of the snow-storm told.

how could I see that in parsing, the object 'chill' belonged
after the verb 'told'?" Time spent trying to determine
whether "President" is nominative or accusative, in the
sentence, "He was elected President," caused a boy who
later became President, James A. Garfield, to say:

> The time spent on grammar attempted at too early an age is
> wasted; to me it is a perpetual wonder that any child's love of
> knowledge survives the outrages of the schoolroom.

"Grammar," said Clarence Darrow, "was a hideous
nightmare. I tried and tried, but even now I can hardly
tell an adverb from an adjective, and I do not know that
I care." This doubt about Grammar[1] was shared by a
New Hampshire Commissioner of Education who, as
early as 1870, wrote: "How vague and unsatisfactory the
ideas which our pupils gain from such terms as auxiliary,
antecedent, correlative, co-ordinate, proposition, passive,
impersonal, infinitive, logical, synopsis."

Important as discipline were the chores, outside the
school, the farm and household tasks concerned with
food and heat and light, in the days before "press the
button"; when heat meant, for the boys, chopping wood
and carrying it in and filling the wood-box; and light
meant, for the girls, filling the lamps; water meant pump-
ing, and carrying in buckets; milk meant milking the cows;
butter meant churning. The countless other chores: rising early to help feed the animals, cleaning the stables
and providing fresh straw in the evening, turning the
grindstone, supplying muscle-power for the corn-sheller

---

[1] The author prefers not to let these condemnations of grammar pass without
some qualification. If the teaching of it was badly done, that may have been
because many of the instructors, not having clarity of thought themselves, tried
to teach grammar by rule, or by memory. To parse is to analyze writing; to
analyze writing is to analyze thought, to analyze thought successfully is to arrive at clarity—for the purposes both of understanding others and of expressing
one's self. Clarity of thinking is one of the least usual of mental attributes, and
one of the most useful.

and the grain-fan. Many a boy was led to give thought
to the value of school by being taken from it in the early
spring to help with the plowing and planting.

Most important of all in imparting the discipline of
foregoing the unattainable, was poverty. A story told
of Calvin Coolidge as a schoolboy at Plymouth, Vermont,
in the fall of 1880, said he requested a penny of his
father, a country-store keeper and farmer, a "man of
means" according to the standards of that time and
place; the father replied: "Well, if the Democrats win,
we'll have hard times, but if the Republicans win, times
will be good; come back after the election."[1]

IV

No aspect of those early schools will surprise, and probably dismay, the America of 1927 so much as the extent
to which teachers expressed their disapproval by physical
means. Apparently it was not merely frequent, but almost
universal, and wholly accepted as a thing to be taken for
granted. Charles S. Thomas, United States Senator from
Colorado from 1913 to 1921, whose school days were
spent near Macon, in central Georgia, described "a
teacher who might well be considered a type of his day
and generation; he was a strict disciplinarian." The
phrase, "a strict disciplinarian," would be inferred by
moderns to be a euphemism, in the light of what Senator
Thomas went on to say. Apparently this teacher did
not confine his whippings to punishment for misconduct.
Indeed, punishment for misconduct was so much a matter of course that Senator Thomas had the air of merely
mentioning that category of whippings in passing:

Those who were inclined to be dull and stupid had hard rows
to hoe, for they were required, regardless of capacity, to make

---

[1] May this have been parental propaganda, designed to make young Coolidge
the kind of conservative Republican he became?

a minimum standard of progress or take the consequences. These consequences consisted, for the most part, of physical punishment, generally administered with long hickory switches, applied with a vigor commensurate with the teacher's state of mind on each particular occasion. . . . To misspell was to go to the foot of the class. Be at the foot for three days and

"What has he done? He laughs and talks in school. He loves to be idle. Does he not look bad?"

the pupil got an indefinite number of credit marks across the back. . . .

Whipping was administered even for lateness at morning roll-call — and lateness under a schedule of hours which in 1927 would be regarded as sweat-shop education:

In that section of the country our terms began in March, with two weeks vacation in July, and ended in December. Sessions began at seven o'clock A. M., in the summer, and half-past seven in the early spring and late fall. Some pupils lived from three to three-and-a-half miles from the schoolhouse, and since they walked to school, they were required to be through breakfast and on the way by half-past five to six o'clock. Whippings for tardiness, therefore, formed one of the permanent ceremonials of every session.

There was lack of a distinction that would have been expected in the South most of all.

Rules of behavior prescribed by the teacher were enforced impartially against all pupils, no distinction to speak of being made between boys and girls. Infractions, and especially those involving disobedience or truancy, were inevitably followed by severe whalings, and if the pupil complained to his parents the dose was apt to be readministered [by the parents].

Edward N. Hurley, of Chicago, who went to a private school at Galesburg, Illinois, recalled in 1927:

When we were disobedient, no matter how trifling the offense, we were told to put out our hands, and received the usual number of strokes of the standard school-ruler. I should like to be able to send you this ruler, as I am sure you would find my finger-prints imbedded on parts of it. The teacher was about six feet three inches tall, with a long flowing beard, and in his boyhood had had both of his hands burnt. His fingers and thumbs were deformed and stiff, and his writing pen had to be inserted between the first and second finger. The reason I remember so many details in connection with his hands is the fact that when he lost his temper over some infraction of the rules, and the ruler was not handy, he would give me a cuff with his stiff hands. I can still feel the imprints of those bony finger tips on the back of my neck.

In Lansing, Michigan, F. L. Smith recalled:

It is hard to believe now that in a first-class high school, in the capital of the great State of Michigan, not only corporal punishment existed into the late '80's anyway, but other punishments, cruel and unusual (hence unconstitutional had we but known it), such as holding a book on the palm of the hand with arm extended vertically for minutes of torture. The teachers wielded a wicked rawhide, and for due offenses one visited the superintendent himself and tasted the bitter medicine we all knew as "strap-oil."

Of Lisbon, Ohio, John H. Clarke, ex-Justice of the United States Supreme Court, wrote:

One of my school-teachers (he was widely known, and is remembered to this day as "Old Davey," although he probably was by no means an old man when we began giving him the title), believed very thoroughly in corporal punishment. I can see him to this day, obviously enraged, as he would go across the room with his heavy switch in hand to administer what he thought was necessary discipline, but which would be thought "cruel and unusual punishment" in any school to-day and would probably expose the teacher attempting it to arrest and fine for assault and battery.

Of Iowa durng the 1880's, Jay N. Darling wrote:

Discipline was enforced by a leather strap and ruler. The culprit was led out of the room into the hall and there the punishment was administered. We were not permitted to be eye-witnesses, but care was taken, evidently, not to remove the scene of activity far away from the student body that the re-sounding whacks did not reach our ears. It was a dull hour when from some room or other a culprit was not dragged out into the hall and physically admonished.

Of Georgia in the 70's, William G. McAdoo recalled:

The earliest school of which I have a recollection was con-ducted by a short, stout man, who sat in a very high chair so that he could overlook the whole room. He was very severe. . . . He administered corporal punishment with unusual liberality and I never heard of any objection from parents, who seemed to take it as a matter of necessary discipline.

Clem Shaver wrote that in West Virginia the instru-ment of punishment was a stiff stick, which the teacher constantly carried over his shoulder, as, so to speak, his mace of authority. It was called a "gad," a local con-traction of "goad." Martin Gillen, who went to a Cath-olic parochial school at Racine, Wisconsin, from 1878 to 1884, recalls that Sister Corona was thorough in her teaching:

A mispronounced word meant repetition of it correctly thirty times, slowly, with care as to articulation. You never mispronounced it again during your after life. There was on her desk at all times a long green rawhide whip, which she did not hesitate to use, but in a just manner.

This view is shared by some of the pupils who in their mature years contributed these recollections. If they felt that conduct called for some kind of punishment, they did not seem to object because it was physical. Some concede that there was frequently a spirit which called for physical forcefulness in the teacher. F. L. Smith admitted:

Honest reflection causes me to state that moral suasion would not have ensured order in the schoolrooms of the '80's. I have seen the principal engaged in a lively wrestling-match with one of the big boys (in long pants) and getting the worst of it so obviously that those nearest the blackboard pegged the wrestlers with chalk or "erasers," while those of us less happily situated, having not the wherewithal to hurl, quietly projected ourselves out of the rear windows, where an eight-foot drop was easily negotiated.

Alfred Holman, long editor of the San Francisco *Argonaut*, wrote of a school in Oregon:

In our own school, and pretty much every other, there was a new teacher at the beginning of each school term, and it was necessary for him to establish himself in authority as against the two or three big boys who were found in every such school. I recall that one of our teachers, a frail young chap, summoned our prize bully to the platform. When he refused to come, the teacher gathered him by the collar and dragged him the whole length of the room. Thereafter the bully ate out of his hand, so to speak. This was a common experience and it explains, in part, why it was necessary that the pioneer schools should be taught by men rather than women.

Even where overt rebelliousness was lacking, pupils seem to have looked upon whipping as part of the accepted order. Senator Thomas expressed his philosophy:

Whether these methods of treatment were justified I cannot say. Speaking from my own experiences I know that whippings were so constant with me that I became somewhat indifferent to them. Indeed, if a day elapsed without one I had a sort of lonesome feeling that something was lacking. Yet I hasten to add that practically all the fundamentals of my education were received from this teacher. Perhaps a less harsh disciplinarian would have been equally successful, but I knew of no such animal in those days.

Not all of Senator Thomas's fellow students seem to

From *"Old-Time Schools and School Books," by Clifton Johnson.   The Macmillan Company.*
At work.

have shared his urbanity about whippings, for he added:

Needless to say, with youths of spirit, and young girls in their early teens, this treatment provoked many rebellions, some of them with serious consequences, although that made no impression upon their rigid enforcement. I recall that two boy friends of mine, believing their treatment to be no longer bearable, solved the problem by burning up the schoolhouse, an act which brought dire punishment to them but unlimited joy to the rest of us, since it meant an indefinite vacation. . . .

Doctor W. D. Howe, who went to school in Southern Indiana in the 1880's, dissented strenuously from tolerance about corporal punishment:

I think nothing has left such an impression on me as the floggings which we youngsters in our seats in the next room could hear going on, given to certain boys who had to have them regularly and who were of an inferior mental calibre. I am sure that others had the same impression that I had — a sort of sickening disgust after the teacher took the big switch from over his desk and went into the next room to give the beating. You can talk all you please about the value of such punishment; as I remember it, it didn't mean anything; indeed, I hardly know of a boy who was constantly whipped that way who ever amounted to anything later in life.

About the change[1] — from the things here described to the modern condition, in which a teacher who "lays hands" on a pupil is liable to find himself in the criminal courts — there could be more discussion than there is space for in this history. One reflection about the newer order was printed in the *Literary Digest:*[2]

Then, again, when one observes certain types of the new and perky generation, one is moved to repeat with the poet the line: "Oh, for the smack of a vanished hand on the place where the spank ought to be."

[1] Friedrich Froebel, father of the Kindergarten, did much to take the prison atmosphere out of the infant classroom. The seventy-fifth anniversary of his death was noted in the New York *Times* on June 26, 1927, by L. H. R.:

> "Frederic Froebel was queer in the brow.
> A switch in the schoolroom he wouldn't allow.
> He started the fad
> Of not using the gad,
> And look at the young people now!"

[2] April 30, 1927.

8

THE AMERICAN MIND: ORNAMENT

So far as I could discover, the last American[1] who used a quill pen regularly died in 1913. In 1927 they were still placed regularly on the tables before the bench of the Supreme Court of the United States, but that was a routine perpetuation of tradition. While many venerable persons clung to the quill as late as the 1890's, it had gone from general use as early as 1866, when the Spencer family recorded its passing in a book;[2] not merely recorded it — gloated over it, quoted poetry about it:

> In days of yore, the poet's pen
>   From wing of bird was plunder'd,
> Perhaps of goose, but now and then,
>   From Jove's own eagle sunder'd;
> But now metallic pens disclose . . .
> In iron, inspiration glows. . . .

That the Spencers should have printed that seems a little out of taste — it was as if Henry Ford should gloat over the eclipse of the horse.[3]

The founder of the Spencer dynasty, and originator of the "Spencerian Style and System of Penmanship," was Platt Rogers Spencer, a school-teacher in New York State and Ashtabula County, Ohio, who, in the language of his biographer and relative, "made the sublime resolution to rescue from its undeserved obscurity the practical Art of Writing."

[1] He was an old North Carolina gentleman, father of William Hand Browne, Jr., of the State College of Agriculture and Engineering, Raleigh.

[2] "Spencerian Key to Practical Penmanship; Ivison, Blakeman & Co.

[3] This comparison of the Spencer name to the Ford name will be utterly unintelligible to the younger reader of 1927; but older persons who went to school in the '70's, '80's, and '90's will remember the time when "Spencer" and "Spencerian" meant pens and penmanship, as generally as "Ford" in 1927 meant automobile.

The quality of his personality, suggested by the ornateness of his penmanship, is confirmed by the encomium his biographer-relative wrote:

His temperament was strongly poetic, his love for the beautiful . . . amounted to an ecstatic passion, and his whole nature was emotional and sympathetic. There existed in the

From "*Spencerian Key to Practical Penmanship.*"   *Ivison, Phinney, Blakeman & Co.*
Penmanship as taught in the days of the Spencerian hand.

magnetic brain of this unassuming but enthusiastic youth an idea of graceful lines, and curves, and characters, which, combined with a proper regard to symmetry, utility, and general beauty, would at once embody his darling idea and glorify the art which he so devoutly desired to serve.

By the appeal Spencer's "graceful curves" made to a people then rather starved for opportunity for artistic expression in the ordinary sense, it resulted that "Spencerian flourish" became the model of handwriting for three generations of Americans. To promoting the favor his system met, Spencer gave exuberant enthusiasm. His appreciation of the profession he had made for himself was such as could be adequately expressed only in poetry; and since apparently the other poets of the day performed inadequately, or failed sufficiently to notice the new and exquisite art that had been brought into the world, Spencer wrote his own celebrations:

> There is beauty in that letter
>   Which my sister wrote to me; . . .
> With rose-leaf curves — her capitals
>   Are shaped of graceful lines,
> And every speaking image blent
>   With undulating vines.

Spencer proselyted, solicited apostles to carry his teaching up and down the land. "A profession so honorable," he said to teachers, "should win to its ranks the noblest and the best." He commended the career to "young ladies of refined tastes who wish to earn their own support," urging them:

If possible, place yourself under the tuition of a recognized master of the art; one, also, who is a true *gentleman*. With the penman, as with the painter and the sculptor, there must ever be a definite ideal. . . . The art of penmanship presents a wide field for the exercise of woman's refined taste and skill. . . . The essential qualities in Ladies' Hand are legibility, neatness, grace, and beauty.

Penmanship was the especial study, the particular aspect of the schools, in which pupils with latent capacities for the ornate, the artistic, and the elegant could exercise their aspirations — the nearest to pictorial art they were permitted to come, the only outlet for artistic expression. Penmanship had the virtue of being useful, as well as ornamental — the accomplishment had a value in the market-places. Teachers and parents thought "drawing"[1] was a waste of time, but admired the "har-

---

[1] A movement for school instruction in drawing was stimulated by the Centennial Exposition at Philadelphia in 1876. That, with other effects of the Centennial, was responsible, to a considerable degree, for the subsequent trend to-

mony of curve and slope" in the penmanship flourishes
portraying birds and flowers. The "Manual of Penmanship"[1] set out the summons to beauty, didactically:

If the work in hand be business writing only, where the prime
requisite is a plain, neat record of transactions which must be

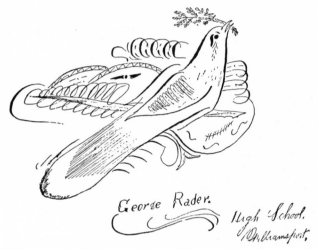

This is a sample of the work of an assiduous student of penmanship.

penned in the briefest time, then it may be said emphatically,
dispense with all shading. . . . But if the chief object is to
write something attractive and beautiful, to catch the eye or
please a refined and cultivated taste, and if time is not a consideration, then by all means let shading come in.

The teacher of penmanship was the centre round which
grew up a vogue of "business colleges," Spencerian
schools, commercial schools. Several in different parts
of the country were conducted by members of the Spencer
family; others by Pierce, Eastman, Bryant and Stratton.

ward greater gracefulness of design in many industrial arts. A second result of
the Centennial was the beginning of manual training in American schools. The
Centennial and the Chicago World's Fair of 1893 were the two, out of many such
expositions, that had a definite and worthy effect on America.

[1] H. W. Shaylor.   Harper and Brothers, 1887.

These were the "schools of business" until after 1900, when Harvard University appropriated the term for a more pretentious treatment of the subject.

The emphasis which the common schools of the 1870's, 1880's, and 1890's put upon handwriting, and allied subjects, reflected a social point of view and an economic condition. Parents, farmers or others, who toiled with their hands, wanted their children to have "white-collar" jobs. To be a bookkeeper in a business house, or a clerk in a government office, was at once genteel and more remunerative than what was called "labor." Many who achieved the ambition lived to see the overalls-worker pass far above them in remuneration and economic standing. About 1890, a dollar and a quarter a day was good wages for workers in steel-mills, while bookkeepers could make $15 a week. By 1925 bookkeepers and clerks could make $20 to $35 a week, while carpenters, bricklayers, and plasterers made $10 to $15 a day.

Virtue has its own reward.

In every schoolbook, emphasis was placed on the moral lesson. The copy-book did not escape, for what better way could a maxim be impressed on the mind than by writing it over and over on the twenty ruled lines on the page? The maxim here reproduced is from Potter & Hammond's "Synthetical, Analytical and Progressive System of Penmanship." Other copy-book maxims were: "It is never too late to mend." "Judge not at first sight." "Quit not a certainty for hope." "Being upright in all things, we gain a reputation." "Pleasant words with pleasant tones will accomplish much."

Alas for the Spencerian system. Just as Spencer had played Henry Ford to the quill pen, so in due course came another, who played Henry Ford to Spencer. The invention of the typewriter doomed the Spencerian glory.

9

THE AMERICAN MIND: SENTIMENT

THE autograph albums appeared toward the end of the term, a seasonal accompaniment of school life as regular as snowballing in winter or marbles in spring. They were brought by the girls as a rule; the boys, most of them, though they really shared the emotion that was conscious of early parting, felt that passing an autograph album around was a little effeminate, "sissy." When boys brought autograph albums at all, they did it rather furtively, waiting for opportune moments and seeking secluded spots to ask friends of both sexes: "Won't you write in my album?" The girls, all shy, expressed their shyness in opposite ways; some blushing with lowered eyes as they passed an album across the desk with a whispered request; others putting on a defensive armor of pretended "forwardness" as they gaily called out: "Come and write in my album!" The collections of friends' signatures were invariably saved (the schoolbooks rarely were) as mementoes. At first they were kept in daily sight, on top of the bureau, along with framed "cabinet" photographs of friends. A little later, as other interests edged in, the albums went into bureau drawers, among the lavender-scented handkerchiefs and the dance programmes. Later yet, they were pushed still farther back in the owners' interests; to-day, in many an American garret is the sad impermanence of eternal friendship recorded by ancient autograph albums containing:

> When the name that I write here is dim on the page,
> And the leaves of your album are yellow with age;
> Still think of me kindly, and do not forget
> That, wherever I am, I remember you yet.

The albums usually had padded covers, often with the word "Autographs" in gilded or silvered script. The pages for the signatures were sometimes plain, sometimes ornamented with forget-me-nots, roses, lovers'-knots, or similarly appropriate decorations. The pages themselves

For the Album!

When'er, perchance, you turn this page,
Your eyes may meet the words I've traced,
And woo remembrance back when age
Has all except these lines effaced

From "Knowlton's Copy Book." C. B. Knowlton, Buffalo, N. Y.

were in delicate tints of pink, blue, and faint green. The minimum expectation was that friends should write their names and the dates; to stop at that, however, was little short of rudeness; the tacit expectation was that you should include something described as a "sentiment." This requirement was a hardship on those of reserved temperaments, and also on those who were not shy in temperament at all, but were deplorably ungifted in expression. For the relief of those who shrank from demands on assertive originality, sentiments ready-made were supplied by printed books of "autograph verses"; or else a few pages at the back of the collections of "pieces for speaking" were devoted to this purpose. One such was "Uncle Herbert's Speaker and Autograph Album Verses."[1] In this was provided a variety that met every shading of emotion and every degree of commitment. Just what sentiment to choose from the "Uncle Herbert" collection presented a problem to the youth whose impulse was to make a strong affirmation of devotion, but

[1] Published by J. A. Ruth and Company, Philadelphia and Chicago.

who was obliged to reflect that an autograph album was a
semi-public place, open to the possibly jeering eyes of
others whose signatures were asked, and likely to be
shown to friends for some time afterward. Occasionally
this impediment to privacy was overcome by agreement
between the signer and the owner of the album; the
friend or lover, shy or cautious, wrote his sentiment on
one page; then, with a home-made paste of flour and
water, the edges of the opposite page were fastened down
upon the page containing the record of devotion. As a
rule, there was but one such closed page in each album;
more would have been evidence indicting the owner of
lack of singleness of affection.

It was not for expressions of affection between boy and
girl that the albums were mainly meant; girls wrote in
girls' albums, and boys in boys'. It was not Moore's:

> When other lips and other hearts,
> Their tales of love shall tell . . .
> Then you'll remember me,

but rather the Moore songs of absent friendship, like:

> Go where glory waits thee,
> But while fame elates thee,
>   Oh ! still remember me . . .
> When around thee dying
> Autumn leaves are lying,
>   Oh ! then remember me.

The sentiment associated with the autograph album as
an institution, the note dictated by the circumstances,
was remembrance; consciousness of present happiness and
the wish to have mementoes of it, a wish that suggested as
much uncertainty as youth is ever apt to have about happiness enduring; the high spirits of youth just faintly
touched, as with an impalpable aura, by the sense of
parting; wonder where the years would take them, and

how far apart, a wonder, however, that was forbidden to be too serious; the wish of the one to have a memento, of the other to be remembered. They were destined, those American school children of the 1880's and 1890's, to go, in the furious social and economic ferment that America was becoming, farther apart — both horizontally and vertically—than similar groups of children in any other country at any other time. Some were fated to follow the same trail as the Covered Wagon to the West; some to go to Cuba and the Philippines, many of the boys to go to France, and some to stay there; a poor farmer's boy in a Michigan country school to become the richest man in the world, a peaked little Vermont boy to become President of the United States.

A selection presenting most directly the simplest purpose of the autograph album was:

> A place in thy memory, dearest,
> Is all that I claim;
> To pause and look back when thou hearest
> The sound of my name.

The same mood, more gloomfully put, was in:

> As over the cold sepulchral stone
> Some name arrests the passer-by,
> Thus, when thou view'st this page alone,
> May mine attract thy pensive eye!

Or, less pretentiously:

> Passing through life's field of action,
> Lest we part before its end,
> Take within your modest volume,
> This memento from a friend.

The mood intended to be attained, the arresting of memory, and then reconstruction of the past, was in:

> When on this page you chance to look,
> Just think of me and close the book.

A quite frequent inclusion, reflecting an American trait of independence and self-reliance more common then than later, was:

> Voyager upon life's sea,
>   To yourself be true;
> And where'er your lot may be,
>   Paddle your own canoe. . . .

A frequent favorite was:

> Roses are red, violets are blue,
> Sugar is sweet and so are you!

"Uncle Herbert's Speaker and Autograph Album Verses" was careful to classify the sentiments with which it accommodated varying needs, as:

Dedicatory   Humorous   Remembrance
Sentiment   Love   Miscellaneous

Children who, even at so early an age, had had experiences so tragical to their minds as to have given them an unhappy skepticism whether the eternal friendships of youth really are eternal, could use:

> Remember me, is all I ask,
> And, if remembrance is a task,
>   Forget me.

Often they made a selection that sounded "pretty," without caring much what the message conveyed. For those who, because of temperament or circumstances, desired the clearest affirmation of a strictly non-committal relation, "Uncle Herbert's" collection provided:

> Round went the album; hither it came,
> For me to write in; so here's my name.

Mere good wishes, without any claim to intimacy, could be expressed in

May you always be happy,
  And live at your ease;
Get a kind husband,
  And do as you please.

From "Real Pen Work—Self-Instruction in Penmanship."
Knowles & Maxim, Pittsfield, Mass.

An expression of good wishes similarly practical was:

In the storms of life,
  When you need an umbrella,
May you have to -uphold it
  A handsome young fellow.

The picture of the future that was in every child's mind
as he wrote in an autograph album, and also the smile
with which youth often tempers its sentiment, was in:

Methinks long years have flown,
  And, sitting in her old arm-chair,
—— has older grown.
  With silver sprinkled in her hair . . .
As o'er these pages thus she runs,
  With many a sigh and kiss,
Then suddenly she stops and says:
  "Who could have written this?"

10

THE AMERICAN MIND: DIVERSION

Games Played in the School Yards. Some Childhood Be-
liefs about Grasshoppers, Snakes, Eels, and Hair from a
Horse's Tail; Together with Maxims about Luck, Affirming
an Empiric Relation between Cause and Effect. Songs
through Which Adolescents, as well as Elders, Expressed
Sentiment, Pathos, and Satire. Dance Tunes Heard by
Boys and Girls, Though Not in the Schools, Where Such
Music Was Banned.

"WE had no athletic coach," wrote Tom Finty,[1] with
what was meant to be a "dirty look" at modern innovations; "but we managed to have a lot of fun playing
marbles, mumblety-peg, town ball, shinny, making snow
men, skating on the mill-ponds, building dams in the
creek in Squire Paine's pasture, and visiting the flour-
mill."

What was meant to be a diligent search into the origins
of school-yard diversions was ended suddenly — and with
a sense of disappointment, even though it foreclosed
much labor — by the discovery that a great majority of
the games played by American school children are written
down, with complete directions, in "The Boy's Handy
Book," published more than fifty years ago, in England.
Apparently no accretion was made to American boys'
games by any of the successive waves of immigrants'
children, that passed through our schools. The English
book describes, as traditional in that country: "Prisoner's
Base," "Leap-Frog," "Blind Man's Buff," "I Spy,"
"Follow My Leader," "Hare and Hounds," "Paper
Chase," "Hide and Seek," "Hop Scotch," "Hop, Step,

[1] Of Dallas, Texas. He went to school at Xenia, Illinois.

and Jump," "Puss in the Corner," "Rounders," "Ring Taw," "Kite Flying," "Tops," "Fox and Geese," "Jack Straws," "Consequences," "I Love My Love With an A."

Some American games are indigenous, in their evolution at least, baseball notably; one feels that some others must have been derived from our changed conditions, or

From "Youth's Companion," May 27, 1880.
The greased pig.

taken from the Indians — did the English have "Post-Office" too; and "Drop the Handkerchief," "Pom Pom Pullaway," "Snap the Whip"?

II

In the minds of teachers and schoolbook compilers, a main purpose was to impress children with precepts, adages, maxims, "this fable teaches," concentrated bits of wisdom about morals, as "be good and you'll be happy"; "do unto others as you would be done by"; "always remember the Golden Rule"; or economics, as "a stitch in time saves nine"; or, "wilful waste brings woeful want." The children may have had their own suspicions that these were adult and utilitarian slogans; nevertheless, the testimony is universal that the lessons stuck and had an influence in later life, almost amounting to psychological bents and inhibitions. But while the children remained children, those precepts handed down from above had less validity in their own little world than certain rules-of-thumb for given situations, which the children held among themselves; private bits of magic, not taught by the teachers, nor even sanctioned by them, but held more firmly in the minds of boys and girls than any that rested merely on the authority of the text-books, such as "Step on a crack, you'll break your mother's back." Or the standardized answer for insult when the circumstances were such as to cause one to prefer not to try to hit back in kind:

> Sticks and stones may break my bones,
> But names will never hurt me.

A theory in the world of biology, having to do with the origin of species, not included in Darwin but accepted as more orthodox, was to the effect that a hair from a horse's tail, placed in water, will turn into an eel. Equally unknown to Darwin, but held no less valid, was the spectacle, never actually seen by any smaller child, but vouched for by older ones as a repeated personal experience, of the snake that could take his tail in his mouth, make himself into a hoop, and with incredible rapidity roll on indefinitely, unless he struck a tree, in which event he shattered into glassy fragments. Frequently tested, and always believed, however the experiments turned out, was the theory that no matter how early in the day a snake was killed, his tail would remain alive until sundown. A theory that touching a toad would cause warts, and another about commanding a grasshopper to "spit tobacco." Empiric wisdom, more valid to the child than science:

> See a pin and pick it up,
> All the day you'll have good luck.

Together with

> Sing before breakfast
> You'll cry before night.

And a device of safety, partaking of the nature of primitive religion, "knock wood."

III

"Even if I had been a Caruso," wrote Charles W. Hobbs,[1] who was brought up in New England,

> I doubt if I should have received very much encouragement in the Puritanical community in which I was brought up. The boys and girls practically never really sang, either in school or out. . . . We were brought up not to laugh at our meals. The example of Sodom and Gomorrah was kept constantly before us. The only music that seemed to have any approval at neighborhood "sings" which occasionally took place, were psalm tunes, started with the aid of a tuning-fork.

This attitude was not quite universal, even in New England; Boston[2] had authorized the teaching of music in the city schools as early as 1838, and by the 70's, a tiny trickle of secular music had edged itself in by paying the price of teaching a moral lesson, or inculcating love of nature. Throughout America, as a rule, music was only tolerated in the schools if it was religious or patriotic, or when it could be made to serve a scholastic purpose, as in "singing geography." In practically no school anywhere were the type of songs called "popular,"[3] sung; in

---

[1] Mr. Hobbs, in 1927, was an official of the Massachusetts State Department of Education. The only songs he could remember, as associated with school, were "Up-i-dee-i-dah" and "Sucking Cider Through a Straw"; and at the neighborhood "sings," "Listen to the Mocking Bird" and "Where Have You Been, Billy Boy?" together with some Civil War songs.

[2] The first song ever sung in unison by the pupils of a public school in Boston, and probably in America, was "Flowers, Wildwood Flowers."

[3] As late as 1922, at a country school reunion in an Eastern State, the singing of "Annie Laurie" was interdicted on the ground it would not be in keeping with the spirit of the school as the old folks remembered it, and was of doubtful taste at a school event.

none were dancing tunes heard; that had to be for the school yard, if even there, and for neighborhood gatherings in the evening. In the South and Southwest, wrote J. B. Cranfill, of Dallas, Texas:

There was a great prejudice among the religious people against the traditional dances in which the fiddle was used, but

there was not such a strong prejudice against dancing the old-time reel to singing. The old-timers who were deeply religious thought the devil was in the fiddle.[1] None of the country churches in the early days tolerated dancing, but there was a rather benignant attitude toward the reel as compared with the square and round dances.

To take advantage of the distinction between dancing to the banned fiddle, and to tunes sung by the dancers, the young folks had songs in which the metre lent itself to the reel,

Mrs. Dorothy Canfield Fisher as a schoolgirl in 1895.

which, with other "square dances," was tolerated in places where the polka and schottische were disapproved, and the waltz regarded as the latest device of Satan. One popular reel-song, recalled by ex-Governor Chase S. Osborn, of Michigan, who went to school in northern Indiana, and by several others in widely separated parts of the country, which was never reduced to print, so far as is known by those familiar with this field, was "Weevily Wheat":

> We don't want none of your weevily wheat,
> And we don't want none of your barley;
> Nothing but the best of wheat,
> To make a cake for Charley.

[1] Chase S. Osborn says the fiddle was banned in Northern Indiana, also.

Additional lines are recalled by M. C. S. Noble, Professor of Pedagogy at the University of North Carolina:

> I'll have some flour in half an hour,
> To bake a cake for Charley.
>
> Oh Charley, he's a fine young man,
> Oh Charley, he's a dandy;
> Charley is a fine young man,
> For he buys the girls some candy.
>
> Hand me down your high-heel boots,
> Made of Spanish leather;
> Hand me down your little white hand
> And we'll unite forever.

Researches made by Professor Noble among his neighbors led him to believe this song came from Great Britain and that as time went on, some lines were added, others forgotten:

The verse about "boots of Spanish leather" tells us it was written at a time when to have boots of that material was a mark of being "high-toned." (I can remember when it was French calfskin that was the real thing.) The verses I send come from localities around here where the original stock is still to be found.

Songs glorifying any one named Charley lead one to wonder if they go back to the eighteenth century in England and Scotland, and if the hero was the Stuart heir to the British throne, the "Bonnie Prince Charley" of whom the Scots sang so much, and loved better than he deserved. That explanation would not seem to have relevance to one of the stanzas of "Weevily Wheat":

> Charley is a handsome boy,
> Charley is a dandy,
> Charley is the very boy
> That stole old Abram's brandy.

In any event, it is certain Charley was a popular youth, especially where dancing was restricted to music

provided by the voices of the dancers; and that over a
period of many years in many sections of America there
was a wide-spread and persistent wish that he should be
provided with a cake.

Where the fiddle was not banned, some of the tunes for
square dances were "Miss McLeod's Reel," "Fiddler's
Reel," "Haste to the Wedding," "The Irish Washer-
woman," "Money Musk," "Pop Goes the Weasel,"
"Green Grow the Rushes, O"; and "Turkey in the
Straw," of which an earlier incarnation was "Old Zip
Coon." "Home, Sweet Home" could always be made to
serve for a plain quadrille.

A faint suggestion of invitation to a thing forbidden,
natural under the circumstances, is in the words of a
dance-song recalled by J. B. Cranfill and several others,
including ex-Governor Osborn:

> Oh, Buffalo gals, am you coming out to-night,
> Am you coming out to-night . . .
> To dance by the light of the moon ?[1]

Apparently "Buffalo gals" were the ones generally
complimented, though in other parts of the country ingenuity on the part of the singing swains made the invitation local and personal, as "Louisiana gals." Some
of the stanzas were:

> As I was lumb'ring down de street,
> A handsome gal I chanced to meet,
> Oh, she was fair to view.
> I axed her would she hab some talk;
> Her feet covered up de whole sidewalk,
> As she stood close by me.

---

[1] In this, and in quotations from other songs, lines repeating phrases are
omitted. Repetition of lines, and lines made up of conventional syllables, such as
"Hie Ho, fernint, fernaddy," "Rissity, Rossity," were frequent in the old songs.

An additional stanza recalled by ex-Governor Osborn, believed by other informants to have been added to the original, was:

> And I danced with a girl with a hole in her stocking,
> And her heels kept a rocking,
> And her knees kept a knocking,
> The prettiest girl of all.

From "Heart Songs," published by the National Magazine World Syndicate Co., New York.
"Buffalo Gals."

"Buffalo Gals" is believed by Professor Noble to have been a "darky song," in which the phrase was "yaller gals." (There are cases of songs of Caucasian origin being adapted by the slaves, and then adopted by the whites in the negro vernacular.) Professor Noble wrote in 1927:

I am carried back to a long-gone time when the old "nigger fiddler," sitting up on a table, knocked on the back of his fiddle and called out, in commanding tones that all loved to obey: "Git yur pardners fur the nex' set." Then he struck his bow across the fiddle strings and the inspiring tune, "Oh yaller gals, won't you come out to-night," flew from his fiddle to the couples ready for the dance, and heels went high in the air and toes kept time to the music. . . . These old-time tunes might have come from Great Britain with our pre-revolutionary ancestors. I have heard it sung "Oh, pretty girls." I have danced to the music and my feet can right now "knock the back step" quite vigorously if I hear the tune from the right kind of a fiddle in the hands of the right kind of an old-time nigger fiddler. You will notice I say "nigger fiddler" rather than negro violinist; it was the former who could bring the music in moving strains from his fiddle with irresistible power over a fellow's feet.

Dance tunes, to which often there were no words, or as to which the words, if any, did not matter; and other familiar tunes included: "Heel-and-Toe Polka," "Rochester Schottische," "Danish Polka," "The Lancers," "Fisher's Hornpipe," "Sailor's Hornpipe," "Shufflin' Feet," "Fiddler's Reel," "Devil's Dream," "The Wind That Shakes the Barley," "The Red Bird," "Up the Road to Lancaster," "Rocky Road to Dublin," "The Wind That Blew the Herring Up," "Stack of Barley," "Great Big Taters in Sandy Land," "Green Fields of America," "Can't You Dance the Hog-and-Eye," "Hell Among the Yearlings," "Swallow in the Swamp," "Chicken Crow," "Picking the Devil's Eyes," and "Fine Times at Our House," also known as "George Booker" and "Joe Booker."

The "Arkansas Traveller" was combined folk-story and folk-music, more the former than the latter. The dialogue was prefaced by a detailed description of the setting — an Eastern man, travelling through Arkansas in the days not only pre-automobile but pre-railroad, came one evening at dusk of a very rainy day, across a woe-begone log cabin, in the door of which sat a man playing a scrap of a tune over and over on the fiddle, while his wife sat on the step and his daughter was preparing a rude supper. The traveller, eager for even so unpromising a shelter, tried to negotiate it diplomatically:

How do you do?

The old man replied: "I do as I please," and played his scrap of a tune once more.

From "The Arkansas Traveller," by Mose Case.

After another attempt, equally unsuccessful, to get the conversation on an ingratiating basis, the traveller asked:

Can I stay here to-night?

To which the old man replied: "No, ye can't stay here," and played again his scrap of a tune. The dialogue continued, the old man giving his brief answer and repeating his four-measure bit of tune:

"How far do you call it to the next tavern?"
"I reckon it's upwards of some distance."
"How do they cross this river ahead?"
"The ducks all swim across."
"Where does this road go to?"
"Well, it hain't moved a step since I've been here."

At this point came the passage in the dialogue that became a part of every American's stock of stories, repeated on every occasion when confusion between logic and common sense made it apt:

"Why don't you cover your house? It leaks."
"'Cause it's raining."
"Then why don't you cover it when it's not raining?"
"'Cause it don't leak then."

The traveller, impressed by the repetition of the same scrap of tune, and by a quality it had of seeming to end up in the air, asked:

Why don't you play the second part of that tune?

Upon which, for the first time, the old man showed interest, an interest in which, however, inhospitable truculence was still dominant:

If you're a better player than I am, you can play it yourself. I'll bring the fiddle out to you. I don't want you in here.

The old man passed the fiddle over the fence, the traveller took it and played:

From "The Arkansas Traveller," by Mose Case.

The old man melted — more accurately, exploded — into hospitality:

Git over the fence and come in and set down. You can board here if you want to; kick that dog off that stool and set down and play that over.

The traveller played his contribution once more, and the remainder of the relations between traveller and host were in the key of the old man's next remark:

Our supper is ready now; won't you have some with us? What will you take, tea or coffee?

After the traveller said "Tea, if you please," the old man gave a direction to his daughter, cryptic to the generation which does not know a frontier substitute for tea:

Sall, git the grubbin' hoe and go dig some sassafras, quick.

Almost as familiar a character as the old man in the "Arkansas Traveller" was "Old Dan Tucker." Because the song that celebrated Old Dan was written by a "nigger minstrel"[1] — that is, a white man blacked up — it is frequently assumed that Old Dan Tucker was a negro character, and printed versions of the song are usually in negro dialect. "Old Dan Tucker" is no more a negro song than the other of Emmett's creations, "Dixie"; and I am sure that white folks usually thought of Old Dan as one of their own race. The rôle they gave him, as the hero of many a party, was not one they would have assigned to a negro.

Old Dan began in early life
To play the banjo and the fife. . . .

Except as to music — in which he had industry, pertinacity, and conscience — Old Dan was, in all his personal relations to the universe, rather shiftless, as shiftless — and as independent, and also as likable — as the old man in the "Arkansas Traveller":

Old Dan Tucker was a funny old man,
He ate his dinner in an old tin pan;
The pan had a hole and the dinner ran through,
And what was old man Tucker going to do?

Because of the spirit inherent in the notes of the music, one felt that while Old Dan was carefree about his meals,

[1] It was Dan Emmett, earliest of the minstrels, author also of "Dixie," "Boatman's Daughter," "Walk Along, John," "Early in the Morning."

and about all the aspects of life that make a steady-going citizen, he was, as respects the search for pleasure, exceptionally up-and-coming; indeed, gaiety, in Old Dan's philosophy, was the real purpose of existence, and he pursued it with unfailing high spirits. This trait, sensed by those who danced to the tune, led to a feature of the old-time dances that was a precursor of "cutting-in." When there was an odd man, he was called "Tucker"; and the fiddler, or the caller of the figures, when he saw an opportunity for the odd man to get a partner, would shout "Go in, Tucker," whereupon the odd man would take the unattached girl.[1] The chorus of "Old Dan Tucker," which raised the spirits and heels of probably more Americans than any other one tune, had an air of recognizing that Old Dan was the life of the party. The dancers visualized Dan as coming to the party, either rushing in with a whoop, or possibly galloping up on a nag; and by his coming giving the occasion a lift of the spirits which the dancers expressed with a shout:

Get out the way, for old Dan Tucker.[2]

The stanzas were numerous; all described Old Dan as a man of merriment, and therefore of importance:

I come to town the other night,
I heard the noise and saw the fight;
The watchman was a-running round,
Crying "Old Dan Tucker's come to town."

The carelessness of Old Dan, about everything except music and dancing, together with a Gargantuan quality he had in the minds of the people, and his whimsical ir-

[1] This ancestor of "cutting-in" was sometimes called the "tag-dance." For this detail of the old-time "gatherings" I am indebted to E. E. Smith, of Minneapolis, whose youth was spent in rural Minnesota.

[2] Printed versions frequently say "Get out the way, old Dan Tucker." That does not accurately portray the spirit of the song. Nobody wanted Old Dan to get out the way; all wanted him with them.

relevancy to what steady-going folks call normal and usual, was expressed in:

> Old Dan Tucker was a fine old man,
> He washed his face in the frying-pan;
> He combed his hair with a wagon wheel,
> And died with a toothache in his heel.

The full chorus, as commonly printed, runs: "So

get out de way, Ole Dan Tuck-er, get out de way, Ole Dan Tuck-er get out de way, Ole Dan Tuck-er, You're too late to come to sup-per.

From "Heart Songs," published by the National Magazine World Syndicate Co., New York.
"Old Dan Tucker."

The closing stanza assigned to Dan an exit from this world appropriate to the exhilarating part he had played in it. As printed in negro dialect:

> Ole Dan Tucker he got drunk,
> He fell in de fire an' kicked up a chunk;
> A red hot coal popped in his shoe,
> An' bless you, honey, how de ashes flew.
>
> And now Ole Dan is a gone sucker,
> And nebber can go home to supper;
> Old Dan he has had his last ride,
> And de banjo's buried by his side.

In American songs that became universally familiar were five male characters loved by everybody. Two were

negroes. Of these, one, "Old Black Joe," was a figure of
sadness, the sentiment associated with death. The other
negro character, "Old Uncle Ned," was also associated
with death, though less sombrely:

> There was an old darkey and his name was Uncle Ned,
> And he lived long ago, long ago;
> He had no wool on the top of his head,
> In the place where the wool ought to grow.
>
>> Then lay down the shovel and the hoe,
>> Hang up the fiddle and the bow;
>> For there's no more work for poor old Ned,
>> He's gone where the good darkies go.

The outstanding white characters of American song
were Old Dan Tucker, the old man in the "Arkansas
Traveller," and Yankee Doodle. Of the latter, all that
was known about his personality and appearance suggested the same spirit of defiance, impish or truculent,
toward the accepted rules of conduct laid down by the
respectable, that Old Dan Tucker and the old fiddler in the
"Arkansas Traveller" showed:

> Yankee Doodle came to town,
> Riding on a pony;
> He stuck a feather in his cap
> And called it macaroni.

Is it possible to infer anything about the American
spirit, as exhibited in the males of the species, from the
qualities common to these three heroes of song, universally loved and, one feels, furtively admired or envied?
All three ignored conventionality, or scorned it; they
evaded the tax-collector, the clergyman, the teacher,
every agency of organized society; they did not take life
as they found it — they made life what they wanted it.
They recognized no such compulsion as duty or service
or co-operation; by no conceivable exertion of the imagi-

nation could one think of them as members of Rotary or Kiwanis. They were, in short, the antithesis of all that the average American, in the gradual crystallization of organized society, was coming to be. They were the opposites of the ideals set up in the schoolbooks. Modern psychologists, who make much of certain laws of opposites, might say that average Americans loved these characters as what they themselves were not able to be, loved them for continuing to live the lives they chose in a time when the average man increasingly deferred to his neighbors and submitted to authority. The delight in songs about them may have been a reaction from the repressive respectability taught in the churches and enforced in the schools. In any event, those characters were only possible in the pioneer times, when a bit of land could be had for squatting on it; when life was easy and free, when a man could safely wait till four o'clock in the afternoon before taking his musket to the woods to get the meat for his supper. They lived in the cabins along the creeks where the fishing was good, a contrast to their conforming neighbors who dutifully ploughed, and sowed, and reaped, and improved their houses, and went to church and sent their children to school. With the crowding of more people and the slow settling down of organized society, the Dan Tuckers, the Arkansas settlers, and the Yankee Doodles were edged from the face of the earth, and came to have their being solely in song and legend.

A song recalled by J. N. Darling, of Des Moines, Iowa ("Ding," the cartoonist), seemed to give reproof to the shiftless type, reflects gradual conquest of spontaneity by thrift and prudence:

> There was an old man and he had a wooden leg,
> He had no tobacco, no tobacco could he beg;
> He blew in his nickels and he blew in his rocks,
> And he never had tobacco in his old tin box.

There was another old codger as sly as a fox . . .
He saved up his nickels and he piled up his rocks,
So he always had tobacco in his old tobacco box.

Says the first old man: "Will you give us a chew?"
Says the second old man! "I'll be damned if I do.
Save up your money and pile up your rocks,
And you'll always have tobacco in your own tin box."

J. N. Darling ("Ding," the cartoonist) at the age of thirteen.

Similar to the joyously unconventional spirit of "Old Dan Tucker" and the "Arkansas Traveller" was "Old Rosin the Bow,"[1] though by one spelling of his name, "beau," and by other circumstances, he had his being in a more sophisticated social level:

I have travelled this wide world all over,
And now to another I'll go . . .

The gay round of delights I have travelled,
Nor will I behind leave a woe,
For while my companions are jovial
They'll drink to Old Rosin the Bow.

And when through the streets my friends bear me,
And the ladies are filled with deep woe,
They'll come to the doors and the windows
And sigh for Old Rosin the Bow.

No boy was denied the privilege of going to the circus, on moral grounds, though many were subjected to economic pressure to accumulate the price of admission. The circus, among other delectations, was an agency[2]

[1] What is the origin of the name? Is it supposed to express personification of the fiddle, and the "resin" used on the bow?
[2] Other agencies were "nigger minstrels," free-lance troupes of strolling banjo

which, in the days before mechanical music, brought the newest songs from the cities. "Circus Songs" became a familiar classification. One was:

> He flew through the air, with the greatest of ease,
> The daring young man on the flying trapeze;
> His movements so graceful, all girls he could please
> And my love he purloined away.

Another, preserved in collections of college songs, was the familiar "Van Amburg:"[1]

> He sticks his head in the lion's mouth,
> And holds it there awhile,
> And when he takes it out again
> He greets you with a smile.
>
> Oh, the elephant, he goes round.
> The band begins to play,
> And the boys around the monkey's cage
> Had better keep away.

A consequence of the circus coming to town was:

> My love has joined the circus,
> And I don't know what to do,
> She feeds the elephant crackers and cheese,
> And she plays with the kangaroo.

Youths of that generation, nor elders, did not lay so much stress on knowing the "latest hit," did not have the characteristic of a later day, a breathless anxiety to have the newest, accompanied, necessarily, by lack of self-confidence about the virtues of what one already had. Singers took pride in being able to render a few of the old songs well; hearers got their pleasure more out of repeti-

players; also "patent-medicine shows" — singers and banjo players to collect the crowds on the street corners, and a barker or salesman to sell the miracle-working oil. A famous one, that had standing as legitimate musicians, was "The Hamlin Wizard Oil Company." It was, writes E. E. Smith, of Minneapolis, "a large concern, considered reliable, with high-class, genteel salesmen, not fakers. I have listened to their concerts many times."

[1] From Van Amburg's, a famous circus.

tion of the tested, than out of novelty. Every community had some one who, because of voice and well-memorized words, had almost a semi-official status as singer of the Irish and Scotch ballads of Tom Moore and Robert Burns, was called on at every appropriate gathering, and expected to be called on, to give "The Last Rose of Summer," "Believe Me If All Those Endearing Young Charms," "Blue-Eyed Mary," together with "Kathleen Mavourneen," "John Anderson, My Jo," "Annie Laurie," "Loch Lomond," and "Comin' Thro' the Rye."

Civil War songs were not only permitted in the schools, but encouraged, especially on "exhibition day," when the local head of the Grand Army of the Republic often participated in the ceremonies, or sat in an honored place. The Civil War gave rise to a greater number of patriotic songs, and better ones, than any other war in history. They reflected the spirit of solemn dedication in which the war was fought, quite different from the lighter songs that accompanied the Great War. The splendid "We Are Coming, Father Abraham, Three Hundred Thousand More," was written in response to Lincoln's call, by a Quaker. Mrs. Julia Ward Howe wrote "Battle Hymn of the Republic" at the request of her old pastor, to the air of a religious camp-meeting tune. "John Brown's Body" was written to the same Sunday-school tune, appropriately enough, for the old fanatic abolitionist was a Puritan of Puritans, looked it and acted it — "he was simply a belated Covenanter," wrote Thomas Wentworth Higginson. "We Are Tenting To-Night on the Old Camp Ground," both words and music, were written by a young volunteer in a few minutes of inspiration just before he left for the front. On the Southern side, a romantic young school-teacher, stirred by a moment of wavering on the part of his native state, wrote "Maryland, My

Maryland," justly described as "the Marseillaise of the Confederacy." "The Battle Cry of Freedom" and "Rally Round the Flag" were written by a Northern organist and composer; "Marching Through Georgia," by Henry Clay Work[1] who combined the occupations of songwriter and inventor. Other songs associated with the Civil War were: "The Years Creep Slowly By, Lorena," "Bonny Eloise — the Belle of the Mohawk Vale," and "Massa's in the Cold, Cold Ground;" and on the Southern side, "The Bonnie Blue Flag." The light-spirited, gaily defiant, "Shoo, Fly, Don't Bother Me," together with "When Johnny Comes Marching Home," were the Civil War equivalents of what in the Great War was the dominant note of the music.

In the well-recognized classification of "darkey songs," one of the most familiar came down from ante-bellum, dealing with a feature of slave life, the patrol, called by the negroes "pateroller," sent out to intercept runaways:

> Run, nigger, run, the pateroller ketch you,
> Run, nigger, run, it's almost day.
> Dat nigger run, dat nigger flew,
> Dat nigger tore his shirt in two. . . .
>
> Dis nigger run, he run his best,
> Stuck his head in a hornet's nest,
> Jumped de fence and run fru de paster;[2]
> White man run, but nigger run faster.

Another negro dancing song, recalling a distinction between "meal" and "bran," familiar in the days of gristmills, but now almost as unknown as slavery, was:[3]

> Sif' dat meal and save de bran,
> Gwine to de weddin' with Sally Ann.
> O, shake dat wooden leg, Dinah, Oh. . . .

---

[1] Some of Work's other songs, all popular, were: "Grandfather's Clock," "Kingdom Coming," and "Father, Dear Father, Come Home with Me Now."

[2] Pasture.   [3] Recalled by J. B. Cranfill, Dallas, Texas.

Other negro songs were "O, Dem Golden Slippers,"
"Carry Me Back to Ole Virginny," and of course, "Old
Folks at Home" ("Suwanee River").

The American spirit obviously had a furtive affection
for characters of daring, even outlaws, the latter often
extolled in proportion to the number of their captors they
shot down. "Bold Jack Donahoo," beginning,

> Come, all you bold, undaunted men,
> You outlaws of the day,

told the story of an Irishman exiled, apparently unjustly
(as may well have been) to the penal colonies of Australia,
who there "became a real highwayman," escaped, defied
"the horse police from Sydney":

> "To surrender to such cowardly dogs
> Is more than I will do,
> This day I'll fight if I lose my life,"
> Says bold Jack Donahoo.

and shot down six police

> Before the fatal ball,
> Did pierce the heart of Donahoo
> And cause bold Jack to fall.

The "Boston Burglar" was a doleful sentimentality
that had wide-spread favor. When a diamond-studded,
curly-haired, shoddy Falstaff of Wall Street, Jim Fisk, a
supreme mountebank of the 1870's, was murdered by a
rival in finance and love, a good many Americans sang:

> We all know he loved both women and wine,
> But his heart it was right, I am sure;
> Though he lived like a prince in a palace so fine,
> Yet he never went back on the poor!

> If a man was in trouble Fisk helped him along
> To drive the grim wolf from the door;

He strove to do right, though he may have done wrong,
But he never went back on the poor!

The death of three hundred people in an excursion boat
on Lake Michigan was described in "Lost on the Lady
Elgin." A holocaust in a Brooklyn theatre led to "We
Ne'er Shall Forget the Two Orphans."

A sentimental song "dedicated to Miss Astor," at a
time when that was one of the two exalted New York
names in what was then called "the upper crust," was
written by Reginald de Koven.[1]

> We part to meet again, love,
> If on this earth no more,
> Surely our souls shall meet, love,
> On that eternal shore. . . .
> My heart cannot refrain
> From thinking, love, we soon shall meet,
> Never to part again.

Another song by De Koven, "Oh, Promise Me"
(originally in "Robin Hood"), became almost as familiar
a part of wedding ceremonies as the "wedding march"
itself. De Koven had much influence in popularizing
good music in America. So had Gilbert and Sullivan,
whose light operas, "Mikado," "Patience," "Pinafore,"
and others, were brought from England to America during
the eighties, and set nearly everybody singing: "The
Flowers That Bloom in the Spring, Tra-la," "Little But-
tercup," "Wandering Minstrel," "A Beautiful Maid,"
"He Never Will Be Missed."

A sentimental song widely familiar in the 1880's was:

> Over the garden wall, the sweetest girl of all . . .
> And you may bet, I'll never forget
> The night our lips in kisses met,
> Over the garden wall.

[1] Later famous as the author of "Robin Hood" with its "Brown October
Ale," and of others of the best light operas ever written by Americans.

Oh prom-ise me; that some day you and I Will

take our love to - geth - er to some sky.

"Oh, Promise Me."

The adolescent youths were countless who sang:

> Wild roved an Indian girl, bright Alfarata,
> Where sweep the waters of the blue Juniata.

And "Juanita":

Soft o'er the fountain, ling'ring falls the southern moon;
Far o'er the mountain, breaks the day too soon!
In thy dark eyes' splendor, where the warm light loves to dwell,
Weary looks, yet tender, speak their fond farewell!

Nita! Juanita! Ask thy soul if we should part!
Nita! Juanita! Lean thou on my heart.

"Only a Pansy Blossom," both words and music, was
written by a man who had standing as a poet, writer of
short stories, musician, and professional cultivator of
flowers, Eben E. Rexford,[1] who played the organ and

---

[1] Author also of "Silver Threads Among the Gold."

sang in the choir of the Congregational Church at Shioc-
ton, Wisconsin.

> 'Tis only a pansy blossom,
> Only a withered flow'r . . .
> Bringing me back the June-time
> Of a summer long ago,
> The fairest, sunniest summer,
> That I shall ever know.

"Kiss, but Never Tell," similar to "Kiss Me Quick
and Go," "was considered," writes E. E. Smith, of Minneapolis, "not proper to sing in the presence of ladies in that
Victorian period, but rebellious boys sang it for hours
after dark":

> A starry night for a ramble,
> In the flowery dell,
> Through the bush and bramble,
> Kiss, but never tell!
> Kiss, but never tell to any —
> Telling breaks the spell.

Other songs of sentiment were "When the Robins Nest
Again," and "Pretty Pond Lilies." There was a song
called "Love Among the Daisies," though it was not the
source of the familiar lines:

> One I love, two I love, three I love I say,
> Four I love with all my heart,
> And five I cast away.

"Wait for the Wagon" was known for its chorus:

> It's every Sunday morning, when I am by your side,
> We'll jump into the wagon and all take a ride. . . .
> Wait for the wagon, . . . and we'll all take a ride.

"What Could the Poor Girl Do?" reflected the time
when sight of a girl's ankle on the street was something
to write a song about:

While walking down a busy thoroughfare,
You see a pretty girl with golden hair,
Tripping along, humming a song, . . .
When suddenly the rain it patters down, . . .
Her dress holds high to keep it dry,
And the men stare as she toddles thro' the town.

But what could the poor girl do?
Boys, what could the poor girl do?
She'd a pretty little shoe and she liked to show it too,
So I couldn't blame the girl, could you?

One of the earliest satires on sentiment and chivalry, a theme not so often attempted then, was Dan Lewis's:

I took my girl to a fancy ball,
It was a social hop. . . .
Then to a restaurant we went,
The best one on the street.
She said she wasn't hungry,
And this is what she eat:
A dozen raw, a plate of slaw,
A chicken, and a roast.
Some sparrow grass with apple sass
And soft-shell crabs on toast.
A big box stew with crackers, too;
Her hunger was immense.
When she called for pie, I thought I'd die,
For I had but fifty cents.

The tune of "Oh, My Darling Clementine," was the very essence of sad sentiment; but the words had a quality of jeering less completely realized from the first and familiar stanza:

In a cavern, in a canyon, excavating for a mine,
Dwelt a miner, forty-niner, and his daughter Clementine.
Oh, my darling, oh, my darling, oh, my darling Clementine,
You are lost and gone forever; drefful sorry, Clementine.

than in some of the subsequent stanzas giving particulars of the lady's fate:

Drove she ducklings to the water,
Ev'ry morning just at nine,
Hit her foot against a splinter,
Fell into the foaming brine.

In the churchyard, near the canyon,
Where the myrtle doth entwine,
There grow roses, and other posies,
Fertilized by Clementine.

Oh, My Darling Clementine

P. MONTROSE

From "*The Book of a Thousand Songs.*" *Muncie Publishing Company.*

"Oh, My Darling Clementine."

"Good-bye, My Lover, Good-bye" began:

The ship goes sailing down the bay,
Good-bye, my lover, good-bye!

From "*The Book of a Thousand Songs.*" *Muncie Publishing Company.*

"Good-bye, My Lover, Good-bye."

> We may not meet for many a day,
> Good-bye, my lover, good-bye!

It was even better known by the innumerable parodies:

> I saw Jim Smith go down the street,
> Good-bye, my lover, good-bye!
> Both his shoes were filled with feet, . . .

Songs of home, mother, and children, often emphasizing death, were as general then as later, though with the more simple directness of sentiment. "What Is Home Without a Mother?" "A Flower from Mother's Grave"; "That Little Old Red Shawl My Mother Used to Wear," "Granny Has Only Left Me Her Old Arm Chair"; "All Bound Round with a Woollen String," sung — and most quaintly danced — in every one of the innumerable performances of Denman Thompson's "Old Homestead"; "Old Oaken Bucket"; "Do They Think of Me at Home?" "Empty Is the Cradle" recited that:

> Baby left her cradle, for the golden shore,
> O'er the silv'ry waters she has flown,
> Gone to join the angels, peaceful evermore;
> Empty is the cradle, baby's gone.

Another pathetic song about a child was:

> Mother dear, come bathe my forehead,
> For I'm growing very weak, . . .
> Tell my loving little schoolmates,
> That I never more will play.
> Give them all my toys; but Mother,
> Put my little shoes away.

A home song of a unique sort, remembered by J. N. Darling, went by word of mouth for at least two generations, and in 1927 was rescued for print by John A. Lomax in his "Cowboy Songs and Other Ballads." It is a faithful picture of a phase of life common in the West for fully fifty years:

I am looking rather seedy now while holding down my claim,
And my victuals are not always served the best;
And the mice play shyly round me as I nestle down to rest
In my little old sod shanty on my claim.

The hinges are of leather and the windows have no glass,
While the board roof lets the howling blizzards in; . . .

But I'm happy as a clam on the land of Uncle Sam
In the little old sod shanty on my claim.

A song to a prospective son-in-law was:

> Treat my daughter kindly,
> And say you'll do no harm,
> And when I die, I'll leave you
> This little home and farm,
> The house, the cow, the shed, the plow,
> The horses, stock and barn,
> And all the little chickens in the garden.

Other songs, affectionately popular for one human appeal or another — of various periods, some of them timeless

From "The Book of a Thousand Songs." Muncie Publishing Company, New York.
"Wait Till the Clouds Roll By."

— were: "Wait Till the Clouds Roll By, Jennie," "Mollie Darling," "Love Among the Roses," "My Bonnie Lies Over the Ocean," "Must We Then Meet as Strangers?" "Take Back the Heart Thou Gavest," "Maid of Athens," "Darling Nellie Gray," "In the Gloaming."

"The Little Brown Church in the Vale" had a literal

existence at Nashua, Iowa, to which, in the summer of
1927, came over ten thousand visitors who signed the
register in memory of having sung, as children:

> How sweet on a bright Sabbath morning,
> To list to the clear ringing bell . . .

"Dear Evalina," "Cottage by the Sea," "Oh, Susanna,
Don't You Cry for Me" (revived in the "Covered Wagon"
motion-picture), "Whoa, Emma"; the lively

> Oh, I went down South for to see my Sal,
> Sing Pol-ly — wol-ly — doo-dle all the day.
> My Sally am a spunky gal . . .
> Fare thee well, my fairy fay.

"Bingo," "Dandy Jim of Caroline," "Billy Boy,"
"Hannah's at the Window Binding Shoes," "Castles in
the Air," "Billy Grimes, the Drover," "Tombigbee
River," "Old Dog Tray," "The Captain with His
Whiskers," "Down in the Coal Mine," "Grey Eagle,"
"Forked Deer," "Billy in the Low Ground," "Joe
Bowers," "Here Come the Natchez and the Robert E.
Lee," "You Never Miss the Water Till the Well Runs
Dry," "Little Brown Jug." An old English song about
the "Brave Old Duke of York" was, in America, abbrevi-
ated to a nonsense verse, expressing some indisputable
truths of levitation:

> When you're up, you're up,
> And when you're down, you're down;
> And when you're half way up
> You're neither up nor down.

Mark Mason wrote three — how shall we characterize
them ? — they had hardly substance enough to be called
songs — but they were on everybody's lips: "Let Her
Go, Gallagher," "Three Little Injuns," and "Johnny Get
Your Hair Cut."

"Johnny Get Your Hair Cut."

A song, of which the name seems to have descended into oblivion, is remembered for two lines:

I am a roving journeyman,[1]
I travel from town to town.

"When the Swallows Homeward Fly," "Darling Chloe," "Mollie, Put the Kettle On," "Oh, Dear, What Can the Matter Be?" "Black-Eyed Susan," "Yellow Rose of Texas," "Blue Alsatian Mountains," "Love's Old Sweet Song," "When You and I Were Young, Maggie," "Good Night, Ladies," "For Everything Is Lovely and the Goose Hangs High"; Helene Mora's famous song success, "Bright Happy Days"; "You're Not the Only Pebble on the Beach," introduced and sung by Lottie Gilson; "Oh! Uncle John," sung by Kittie Gilmore; "Where Was Moses?"

[1] This word, it may be desirable to explain to a later generation, had no relation to travel.

11

THE AMERICAN COMMON SCHOOL

Its Fundamental Ideal, Which Was Democratic, Rather
Than Scholastic. The Simplicity of the Curriculum. The
Lacks in It. Science. "The Education of Henry Adams."

THE nature of American education was always a subject
of earnest attention from thoughtful persons. The books
written about it compose a considerable library; the
speeches were innumerable. Of the books, one, published
in 1906 and again in 1918, by an American historian and
philosopher, Henry Adams (1838–1918), was adjudged by
some exalted authorities to be the most important work
published in America during so much of the twentieth
century as had then passed. Some of the erudite compared it to the indisputable classics of Jean Jacques
Rousseau, Saint Augustine, and Thomas Aquinas. This
estimate, like the contemporary valuations of many new
books, contained surprise at a new point of view, in
proportions greater than this quality counts in the more
seasoned verdicts of time, time being a judge that takes
no account of novelty. Time has shown "The Education
of Henry Adams" was overrated — it belongs in that
considerable library of books which were the "greatest of
the century" for six months after they appeared. Nevertheless, it is a genuinely worth-while effort in a field where
many have labored but few multiplied their talents.
The theme was formidable: what should be the educational equipment for "man as a unit in a unified universe?" The treatment, while recondite enough, was
sufficiently human and personal to rescue the work from
excessive abstractness. Adams devised an ingenious and
piquant literary mechanism. By writing his autobiography, not in terms of "I" but in terms of "he," not in

the first person but in the third, he made a book which is about the author, but in which the author is able to achieve frankness without the appearance of so much self-consciousness as would disturb the reader, or cause critics to allude to egotism; a book in which the author writes about himself with as much detachment as if he were a calmly impartial biographer[1] telling the story of a man to whom he had no personal relation.

The readers Adams aimed especially to reach with his appeal for a new approach to the training of youth were educators. With his "Education of Henry Adams," and a smaller companion volume, "A Letter to American Teachers," he measurably stirred the higher circles of the academic profession to new and concentrated thought on education as it affects the individual and consequently as it affects the collective individual, the society in which the individual spends his mature years.

Adams's purpose was to review his own education, both that which he had received from schools and universities, and that which came to him from other sources and other experiences, with the purpose of determining what part of it turned out, "in his personal experience, to be useful, and what not"; to what degree his education had equipped him to function "as a consciously assenting member in full partnership with the society of his age." Adams's conclusion, as to his own education, was seriously adverse; the training he had received, he said, had equipped him better to live in the time of Julius Cæsar than in the time of Theodore Roosevelt:

Pondering on the needs of the Twentieth Century . . . in the essentials like religion, ethics, philosophy; in history, litera-

---

[1] This method, among other effects Henry Adams had on his contemporaries, supplied a pleasingly welcomed model for other men, who were moved to write about themselves, but feared that the truth as they saw it might seem unduly self-complacent if put in the first person. One familiar book having the same form as Adams's was "The Americanization of Edward Bok."

ture, art; in the concepts of all science except, perhaps, mathematics, the American boy of 1854 stood nearer the year 1, than the year 1900. The education he had received bore little relation to the education he needed. Speaking as an American of 1900 he had no education at all.

In this complaint, Adams was not quite fair to his teachers. He was able to "ponder on the needs of the twentieth century" after that century had arrived; his teachers were not. We cannot expect teachers to be prophets, or demand that they give education for conditions not yet in sight. And of all the requirements ever put upon prophets anywhere, one of the most extreme would have been to expect teachers during the last half of the nineteenth century to anticipate the kind of world their pupils would live in during the first quarter of the twentieth. In all time, no such colossal changes had occurred in so brief a period. Moreover, we cannot grant Adams any exemption from the rule that what a youth or a man gets from the agencies of formal education is affected by what he brings to them, by his temperament and his other qualities of personality. If it were true that Adams's deprecatory estimate of what education did for him was applicable to everybody, we should be obliged to be more than a little appalled. For the education that Adams received was, according to standards commonly accepted, the best the world afforded. Certainly it was the most elaborate that pains had devised or money could purchase. If that kind of education did nothing for Adams, if it failed to equip him for the world of 1900 in which he lived, then we should be obliged to suffer from disquiet when we think of the more ordinary and casual education available to average men who lacked Adams's advantages of fortune and background. The education of Henry Adams was as distant from that of the average American as, let us say, the term "education" is from "schooling," or even "larnin'," the latter being a by-no-means uncommon word in the period in which Henry Adams lived — though it was uncommon in the particular circle in which Adams grew up, and in the schools from which he got his education. Adams was a great-grandson of one President of the United States, grandson of another, and son of an American Minister to Great Britain; his education was received at a Boston private school, at Harvard College, at the University of Berlin and elsewhere abroad. It was a de luxe education. For the less pretentious educational influences that determined the spirit and point of view of persons less favored, for the education received by the average American of the period of this history, we must search, obviously, in much humbler quarters, quarters as distant as "the little red schoolhouse" on an Ohio hill is from the elm-shaded walls of Harvard Hall.

The superficial inference from this comparison would be disquieting to accept without giving as much weight as we justly can to a possible qualification. Perhaps we shall be more comfortable if we concede that Adams was a very unusual personality, and that his failure to derive satisfaction from his education was due not wholly to the nature of the education he received, but partly to his own unusualness.[1] Probably by this assumption we shall be more accurate also, for the clear fact is that the ordinary education which America provided for average men gave satisfaction and enjoyment to great numbers of

---

[1] This passage has a manner of jeering at Adams, which is wrong. To be accurate, and to be fair to Adams, he was a superior person; and it is a fact that superior persons sometimes get less from schools than ordinary persons. Superior persons are farther advanced than other pupils of the same age; frequently they feel irked at being made to go over things they already know. Sometimes they have just cause to feel the school is trying to make them accept things they know are not so. Newton D. Baker, Secretary of War in Wilson's cabinet, writing in 1927 about a portion of his own schoolboy experiences, said:

"I think I ought to be fair enough to admit that I was by no means a usual or average schoolboy. And it was probably wholly my fault that I got less than I

them; and produced from among them many who are fairly to be described as able to cope with the conditions in which they spent their mature lives; not only to cope with them, but to master them.

Let us then, for the purpose of the present history, confine what we accept of Adams's book to merely one of his underlying theses, namely, that the spirit of any era, such as the one from 1900 to 1925, is determined largely by the education which the persons who were adults during that period had received some five to forty or more years before: Let us by no means deny Adams's main conclusion. It is possible the early education of the American generation that was adult between 1900 and 1925 was utterly distant from an ideal education for the kind of world in which they were destined to live.[1] The present purpose is merely to survey the education they actually had.

II

The common schools, that provided the average American with education, must be judged as what they were. The one outstanding ideal they had was less in the world of education than in the world of democracy. They were founded and maintained on the principle that all the people should have some learning, that the entire nation should be literate.

should have gotten out of my school days prior to college. The difficulty, as I look back upon it now, was that my father matured my mind with his conversation so early that I was impatient of the childish learning which the school tried to give me, and which it would have been very well for me to have. The consequence has been that I have always known how to spell complicated words and been uncertain about simple ones; fairly fluent with trigonometry and conic sections but amazingly stupid about addition and subtraction."

[1] It is equally possible the education of the present generation of children, those who will be adults from, say, 1935 to 1975, is far from ideal for the conditions of the world in which they will find themselves.

Schools dedicated to so high and difficult a purpose of democracy, necessarily, could not have pretentious curriculums. So far as their teaching had direct purposes, they aimed to make their pupils good men and women, and to equip them with some facility in indispensable fundamentals, reading, writing, and arithmetic.

The great bulk of education in the United States was provided by the common schools. High schools were late in coming and slow in growing. The map above (adapted from Cubberley's "History of Education," and based on figures from the United States Department of Education) shows approximately the only high schools existing in America in 1860. There had been about thirty more than are here shown, chiefly in the Southern States, where education was interrupted by the Civil War. The total number was only 321, of which more than half were in three States, Massachusetts (78), New York (41), and Ohio (48).

Possibly, even with so titanic a burden as giving some education to all, the schools might have done more. Some earnest persons thought they could, and worked diligently to enlarge their scope.

In a few high schools during the latter part of the nineteenth century, drawing had made a timorous beginning, but as a rule the schools of the seventies and eighties continued the earlier tradition described by Horace Mann:[1]

With all our senses glowing and receptive, how little were we taught; or rather, how much obstruction was thrust between us and nature's teachings. Our eyes were never trained to distinguish forms or colors. Our ears were strangers to music. So far from being taught the art of drawing, I well remember when the impulse to express in pictures what I could not express in words was so strong that it tingled down to my fingers; then my knuckles were rapped with the heavy ruler of the teacher or cut with his rod, so that an artificial tingling soon drove away the natural one.

Pitiable was the neglect to take advantage of the Nature that lay all about the country school, causing Gene Stratton Porter to write:

I began debating whether it was a big enough thing to bother the Lord with, this being penned up in the schoolhouse droning over spelling and numbers, when you could smell tree bloom, flower bloom, dozens of birds were nesting, and everything was beginning to hum with life. I couldn't think, for

All the birds are on the wing;
Little maiden, now is spring.

I made up my mind that it was of enough importance to call for the biggest prayer I could think of. I was nearly to the point where one more killdeer crying across the sky would have sent me headlong from the schoolhouse, anywhere that my feet were on earth.

Physical training was unknown in the common schools though some normal schools and colleges were beginning to experiment with it as "calisthenics," "physical culture," "Swedish movements," in which a principal means was dumb-bells. The photograph on page 191, of two girls fencing against a background of Indian clubs, taken

[1] American educator; from 1853 to 1859, President of Antioch College, Ohio; previously Secretary of the Massachusetts Board of Education, where he brought about a revolution in the common schools which ultimately affected the common schools of other States.

at the University of Nebraska in 1892, represented a bold invasion, due to the fact that Chancellor Canfield had been a lifelong feminist, ever taking steps toward opening new fields to women and girls, and regarded, therefore, as radical. He brought a gymnasium instructor to

The figure on the right is Mrs. Dorothy Canfield Fisher at the age of thirteen, wearing
what was considered in 1892 a very daring gymnasium costume.

the university, and required gymnasium dress, because, as one of his students wrote, "with corsets and long skirts and petticoats, nobody could move faster than a walk, let alone stoop over." At the beginning of each term, when the new girls, fresh from the standards of propriety in their Nebraska homes, first came on the gymnasium floor with the garments shown in the photograph, "they were overcome with shame, although no man, not even the janitor, was allowed to enter while the girls were there; most of the new girls were so shy, even before others of their own sex and age, that they could not take a step, but sank down in a heap on the gymnasium floor, huddling together and refusing, almost to tears, to take part. Within a week, however, under the urging of older girls to 'get over their foolishness,' they exulted in their new freedom."[1]

III

The one conspicuous lack in the schools[2] of 1865–1895 was Science.[3] In that field the only subject generally taught was physiology; and that was taught not as science, and not in the scientific method, but for a reason apart from science, for a moral purpose. The method was memory-work wholly; the pupils learned by heart the names, in Latin, of the bones, arteries, veins, viscera, valves of the heart. Of the two hundred and fifty paragraphs of summary at the ends of the chapters in one widely used text-book, Blaisdell's "Our Bodies and How We Live," fifty dealt with the injurious effect of alcohol and tobacco on the organs and processes of the body. The Preface had a foot-note saying the work had been revised by an official of the Women's Christian Temperance Union. To Albert Mordell, who went to school in Philadelphia in the 1890's, "it seemed as if the reason for studying about the organs and skin was to learn the effects of alcohol and tobacco on them."

The absence of Science teaching in the schools would have justified, if anything would, Henry Adams's complaint of ill-equipment for life in the twentieth century. The schoolboy of the 1880's was destined to spend his

[1] The girl in the photograph who is parrying was the Chancellor's daughter, in 1927 well known in literature as Mrs. Dorothy Canfield Fisher. The military instructor at the University of Nebraska was Lieutenant John J. Pershing, a modernist who abetted the Chancellor in introducing athletics for girls.

[2] And even, at that time, the universities.

[3] Even in the high schools, little science was taught, and this as late as the nineties was available to only an insignificant proportion of children of school age. In 1890, there were in the whole country only 2,256 public high schools, with 202,968 pupils. In 1922 the corresponding figures were 14,056 and 2,319,407. In 1890, less than one-third of one per cent of the country's population were enrolled in high schools; in 1922, the percentage was 2.04, a sevenfold increase.

mature life in a world in which science and its applications affected his existence vitally, but the common schools taught him not even the elementary facts of physics[1] and chemistry. He was destined to see the automobile substituted for the horse; to see electricity take the place of his former means of providing himself with light, and become a large source of his supply of heat and power; to have daily familiarity with the telephone and radio, to come in contact with the laws of refraction as expressed in the camera, to see the X-ray and radium in the hands of his doctor; to see chemistry, by the devising of rayon and other products, flout one of the most infallible maxims in his schoolbooks: "You cannot make a silk-purse out of a sow's ear."

For all that transformation, the schoolboy of the seventies and eighties had no preparation — for the very good reason that the scientists themselves did not anticipate it. Had the children studied "Natural Philosophy," written by William G. Peck in 1881, they would have learned, about electric power, that

Attempts have been made, and with partial success, to employ electro-magnetism as a motor for the propulsion of machinery, but in all cases the expense has been so great as to preclude its economical use.[2]

Perhaps it is just as well the school-children did not learn much of what science thought it knew in the seventies and eighties. Not only would they have had to get rid of it; they would have been worse handicapped than if they had known nothing of science, except as respects what they learned of science's methods and standards. They would have known a good deal that was not so;

[1] There was no physics; but two young men whose education stopped with the high school in Dayton, Ohio, invented the airplane.

[2] By 1925 electricity was generated and used in the United States to the extent of 31,500,000 horse-power. The industry represented an investment of over $7,000,000,000.

would have had their minds set against the amazing revelations that science was bringing about. It was difficult enough for some who followed science as a career to adjust their minds to the changes.

Had the school children of the 1880's been taught what science then thought it knew, they would have learned the principle of the immutability of the chemical elements — and would have lived to see it overturned by the discovery of radio-activity. They would have learned the principle of the conservation of mass — and would have lived to see that principle vanish with the experimental discovery of the increase in mass of the electron with speed as the velocity of light is approached. They would have learned the principle of the conservation of energy — and would have lived to see that principle suffer a material change "when both experimental and theoretical evidence came forward that energy and mass are interconvertible terms related by the Einstein equation $Mc^2 = E$, since in that discovery the ideas of energy and of mass became completely scrambled."[1] They would have learned the principle of conservation of momentum, and would have seen it denied universality by the subsequent formulation of the quantum theory.

In short, what science a student could have learned, even as late as 1895, was to be subjected to revolutionary changes such as had never before taken place and were at that time inconceivable. The changes were summarized by Doctor R. A. Milliken in 1926:

The historian of the future will estimate the past thirty years as the most extraordinary in the history of the world up to the present, in the number and the fundamental character of the discoveries in physics to which it has given birth; and in the

---

[1] Quoted from Doctor R. A. Milliken's paper read to the American Philosophical Society in 1926.   All the changes in science summarized above rest on the authority of this paper.

changes brought about by these discoveries in man's conception as to the nature of the physical world in which he lives.
. . . Of the six basic principles which at the end of the nineteenth century acted as the police officers to keep the physical
world running in orderly fashion, there is not one the *universal*
validity of which has not been recently questioned by serious
and competent physicists, while most
of them have been definitely proved
to be subject to exceptions.

A reader of the books on science of the past fifty years will
be struck by an atmosphere that
is like a recurring refrain. One
reads the science books of 1870
and finds them having a manner
of saying: "It was once thought
. . . but we now know." One
passes on to the books of science
of 1880, and again one finds: "It
was once thought . . . but we
now know." Doubtless the process is not ended. One is tempted
to think a scientific law is a hy-
pothesis that works for a while.

H. L. Mencken at the age of
eight, a student at F. Knapp's
Institute, an old-time private
school in Baltimore.

This did not deter the devo-
tees of science from accepting
for their branch of learning an authoritativeness above
all others. "Indeed," said Beard's "Rise of American
Civilization" in 1927, "science was now so enthroned in
America that it became a kind of dogmatic religion itself, whose votaries often behaved in the manner of the-
ologians, pretending to possess the one true key to the
riddle of the universe."

Possibly there was soundness in the instinct that led
McGuffey to put his emphasis on Shakespeare and Milton, and the other literary storehouses of the accepted

wisdom of the race. They were as nearly changeless as anything. Throughout all the furious ferment, the undermining and overthrowing of old standards, that began with the emergence of science about 1860, art and letters kept their standing secure. No work of letters or

From "The Life of John W. Davis," by Theodore Huntley.   *From "The Life of Calvin Coolidge," by Horace Green.*

John W. Davis at the age of seven.   Calvin Coolidge at the age of seven.

Some American minds at the time they were in the making.

of art, accepted as valid in 1860, was any less valid in 1927. There was a race of critics, conscientious about the obligation put upon them by their superiority, who insisted on reading the race's accepted books in the light of the discoveries of modern science, in a spirit which, in the lengths to which it sometimes went, would have translated Shakespeare's "my kingdom for a horse" into "my kingdom for a spare tire." But the average man had no difficulty in grasping the truth in his accepted books, regardless of how obsolescence may have overtaken the imageries in which they were expressed.

12

"THE YEARS THAT THE LOCUST HATH EATEN"

THE changes that came were due less to new conceptions of education than to economic causes, and political conditions that accompanied them. When Guyot's Geography described the United States of 1868 it pictured a pastoral people:

Tilling the soil, called farming, or agriculture, is the principal business of the people in nearly all the States.

In that condition of the seventies, the farmer was a political majority. He could have held his power if he had consulted the economic interest of his class with intelligent political foresight. But the farmers of the North, thinking at that time of the Republican party in terms of moral leadership, crediting it with saving the Union and abolishing slavery, voted for it and its candidates too much out of memory, too little out of anticipation. The men who controlled the Republican party, who sat in its centres of power, had taken on an added view-point immediately after the Civil War. The leaders made the Republican party an instrument for getting and keeping a high protective tariff on manufactured goods. The farmers voted to endow and nourish "infant industries"; quickly the infant industries became, as regarded agriculture, a Frankenstein. Decade by decade, the proportion of farmers in the population diminished. By 1925, they were a definite minority, subordinated politically and economically. In that year, some of the farmers' friends saw what had happened, tried to arrest it and reverse it. They were late. The farmer, his point of view, his way of life, his institutions, including the country school, were being crowded out, superseded.[1] Frank O. Lowden, former Governor of Illinois, chief of those who in 1927 were trying to rescue the farmer, wrote in that year:

A healthy rural community life is essential to any continuing civilization. Is the rural community breaking down in the

Courtesy of the United States Bureau of Education.

Modern high school serving thirty-six square miles at Sullivan, Maine.

United States? Many think so. The country school of my early days was the centre of a genuine community life. The country school-teacher was a very important person, a leader

[1] The diminishing numerical importance of the farmer, in relation to the rest of the population, is shown in the following table:

Year	Urban	Rural	Total	Percentage of Rural to Total
1880	14,358,167	35,797,616	50,155,783	71.4
1890	22,298,359	40,649,355	62,947,714	64.6
1900	30,380,433	45,614,142	75,994,575	60.0
1910	42,166,120	49,806,146	91,972,266	54.2
1920	54,304,603	51,406,017	105,710,620	48.6

The rural totals of the above table take in the populations of all incorporated places of 2500 inhabitants or over, and consequently include a not inconsiderable proportion who were not strictly a part of the farm population. The first census to gather statistics of the actual farm population, that of 1920, showed that in that year the percentage of farm residents to the total population had dwindled to 29.9 per cent.

in the intellectual and social life of the community. The school-house was something more than a mere educational centre. How changed the country school of to-day! The population of the school district . . . has steadily declined. A few years ago, Iowa enacted a law by which, when the number of pupils in any school district was reduced to five, the school should be closed and provision made for carrying those pupils to another. Under that law five hundred schools in Iowa alone have been closed. The country school has lost its old vitality and its old importance in the life of the people. For the most part, the little schoolhouse, once so dynamic a thing in the life of the community, has fallen into neglect. It remains upon the hill-top as of yore, too often [with] an appearance of decrepitude, a melancholy memorial of better days.

In every respect, the old-time school was tied close to the community and to the home. There was little of system, and of standardization nothing. The teacher was often an ambitious young man bound upward toward some other career, giving a few years of his life to a folk-service, as, so to speak, a liaison between the older generation and the new, passing on the accumulated wisdom, traditions, and precepts of the race.

The old-time country school[1] was a folk-institution. A farmer donated an acre of ground, often a corner of wood lot, which took nothing from the crop land. In the older days, the neighbors came together for a "rais-ing," at which they put the timbers in place, or carried and laid the brick, while their women-folk brought food. The desks and seats were made of plain boards by the local carpenter, often of pine — agreeably soft for whit-

---

[1] There will never be a better picture, of course, than Whittier's:

"Still sits the schoolhouse by the road,
   A ragged beggar, sunning;
Around it still the sumachs grow,
   And blackberry vines are running.

Within, the master's desk is seen,
   Deep scarred by raps official;
The warping floor, the battered seats,
   The jack-knife's carved initial."

tling with Barlow knives — though by the eighties and
nineties salesmen began to persuade school directors to
buy machine-made desks and seats of iron and hard
wood, very ugly and often uncomfortable. As a rule
desks and seats took no account of the varying ages and
sizes of the pupils, and many an adult of 1900–1925 carried his right shoulder higher or lower than the left as a
permanent relic of school desks too high or too low.
Heat was provided to the whole room by one big stove
in the centre or in a corner. The water came in a wooden
bucket filled twice a day by two boys, who carried it from
a near-by spring, or the pump of the nearest neighbor.
Teachers shrewd in psychology turned the service into
a highly prized privilege, the reward of good conduct.
One tin dipper accommodated everybody — the germ
theory had not come to make man fastidious.   Girl
pupils helped sweep out the school, and clean up the chalk-
dust. Schoolbooks, as a rule, had to be paid for by the
pupils' parents, and money was hard to get. "Sometimes," wrote William G. McAdoo, "two boys who could
live at peace with each other studied from the same book."

In every aspect, the old-time school was a product of
self-reliance, community and individual; was tied intimately to the home life, reflected the self-sufficient traits
of the time. Mothers made the children's clothes, knitted
the heavy mufflers and mittens for the boys and the
"stocking-caps" for the little girls, crocheted the bright-
colored "fascinators" for the older ones, buttoned the
girls' dresses up the back and plaited the universal "pig-
tails" as a morning rite. The dresses were calico in summer, with sun-bonnets; in winter, woollen, with gingham
aprons. Alpaca, merino and cashmere were materials to
make "Sunday-best" dresses, not seen at school, as a
rule, except on exhibition day; a dress of plush was a
prized elegance, a fur tippet an ostentatious luxury. All

One-room schoolhouse in Berks County, Pennsylvania.

Types of old-time one-room schoolhouses. This one was in the town of Peru, Mass.

clothes, for children and adults alike, were chosen for durability, not style. As a rule the children's clothes were made of materials that had already seen one or more successive services with the elders of the family. While there was a smiling deprecation of "hand-me-downs," the deeper

The old district schoolhouse, Moravia, Cayuga County, N. Y., where John D. Rockefeller went to school.

feeling was one of pride in buying for durability, and in the thrift that got the greatest service out of the goods, to the limit of the last patch. That led purveyors to make goods to last; the point of view was the opposite of the one that came with mass production by machinery — to make for a season only, to change the model for the quickly succeeding season, and by advertising cause the consumer to feel "out of style" if he had not the latest.

II

The decay of the country school began about 1900. Not only did the rural population become too small to support them. Families who remained on the farms felt the instruction in the near-by town schools was better — at least it conformed to the modern idea. Farmers who were prosperous enough, and ambitious for their children, sent them to the town schools, paying a

A little boy who went to school in Minnesota in 1871.

A little girl in Wisconsin, afterward the wife of Senator Irvine L. Lenroot.

fee the towns exacted from outsiders, and continuing to pay the usual tax to support the rural schools they did not patronize.

Then came the incitement, universal in American life, to centralization, consolidation, "bigger and better." Rural school boards, infected by the vogue of statistics, estimated that five separate schools with thirty pupils each, and one teacher to each school, was more expensive than one central school. Also, the central school would be more efficient — that was another word that came into vogue. The process was hurried by the automobile and improved roads. Consolidated schoolhouses were built near the centre of the district. Busses, provided by the school board, went about the district, gathering up the children each morning and returning them each evening. With that innovation went a subtle psychological change — the difference between going to school, or being sent by parents; and on the other hand, being picked up by the State-owned bus and carried. In 1927 a publication of the University of North Carolina recorded, with pride, that the State had 2317 school busses, carrying an average of 87,000 children daily to 814 consolidated schools, a use of the new system exceeded only by Indiana and Ohio.

That was less than one lifetime after the conditions that Bernard M. Baruch pictured in the neighboring State of South Carolina during the 1870's. The letter he wrote in answer to a request for recollections is a vivid picture not only of school days, but of life and ideals. It conveys, also, suggestions of the immense contrasts that came to America. To understand one of America's outstanding characteristics, opportunity for the individual, the reader should know that within twenty years after the conditions pictured in this letter, the writer of it was an important figure in the New York financial district, and became later a vital instrumentality in public life.

The school I went to was a private[1] one next to an Episcopal church in Camden, South Carolina. The older boys went to the school, but I, being the youngest, went to the wife of the teacher. I have the most distinct picture in my mind of sitting on the floor deciphering "I see the cat" and "I see the dog," while she had her baby on her knee feeding it porridge. After a year or two I went to school with the schoolmaster. There

[1] Private schools were the prevailing means of education in the South. The idea of schools supported by the State had not taken hold before the Civil War. After the Civil War, for many years, the South was too impoverished to support public schools.

A generation ago children walked long distances to school.

In the 1920's motor-busses collected and carried children to consolidated schools. This bus served a school in Hopewell Township, New Jersey.

all the pupils sat in one room, with the teacher in front, and behind him, a lot of long switches, which he used when necessary. Also he had a long rule with which he would hit you over the palm of the hand, which you had to stretch out to him if you misbehaved yourself or did not know your lessons.

Boys used to come to school on horseback, or would walk. I did not think much of walking from my house to the school and back again, something like a mile and a half by the road and about a mile across lots and a couple of creeks. School books were rather scarce and were passed on from one child to another, just as the clothes of the father were altered for the eldest son and passed on down the line. In the village in which I was born no child wore shoes or stockings for about four or five months in the year. We carried our lunch to school. We played such games as baseball, shinny, and marbles. Boys made collections of old knives and hickory nuts and walnuts, and used to spend any spare time they had picking up various pieces of junk, like brass and lead, which they would sell for a few pennies. As soon as a boy was old enough, in cotton-picking time, he would put a bag around his neck and pick cotton in the afternoon, to get a few pennies with which to buy powder and shot. The guns were all muzzle-loaders. The powder was carried in a horn and the shot in a little leather bag. The horn was generally a cow's horn, and the thinner you made it by filing it with sand-paper the better it was.

Every boy had to recite a piece. We all commenced with "Mary had a little lamb." Everybody knew the one starting:

> You can hardly expect one of my age
> To speak in public on the stage.

We had a summer vacation. There was the swimming-pool, the factory pond, and the race where smaller boys went in swimming and where negroes were baptized. Those were the days of the country circus, where they had peanuts, lemonade, and pink candy. At Christmas time if you got some figs, dates, oranges, raisins, and an apple, you thought you were getting something; it was not necessary to give a boy a Rolls-Royce, a thousand-dollar bond, or a gun.

The country teacher occupied a place in the community somewhat on a par with the minister and the doctor. The whole community looked up to them. Teachers then (and doubtless now) had a greater effect upon the people than perhaps any other single influence. They taught the boys and girls fine ideals. The poetry and pieces we spoke were inspiring and ennobling.

Nobody knew much about money, because nobody had any, and it didn't mean so much. For amusement the people had a Shakespearean reading; they discussed authors; when somebody would get a magazine from New York or something from Europe, they would have long discussions about them. They were simple, character-developing amusements; now it is a nerve-racking jumping from one thing to another.

The letter Chase Osborn[1] wrote about his school days was singularly convincing. His recollections poured out in just the disorder in which school-day influences are apt to remain, with a fragmentary quality, like a jumble in an old attic — the whimsical inferences, the queer questionings that children make from bits of knowledge. Not only do his memories have the convincing effect of truth; his observations reflect candor, the more so because some of them run counter to the note common in comparisons of then and now. He wrote:

Boyhood photograph of former Governor Chase S. Osborn, of Michigan.

I went to the common schools, good ones, at LaFayette, Indiana, from 1866 to 1880. The first schoolbook I ever saw was a Speller. It had a picture of good dog Tray getting a beating because he was caught in the company of bad dogs. "Evil communications corrupt good manners" was the lesson. On another page was a wood-cut of a boy up in an apple-tree and an old man pelting him with clods. The boy laughed and the old gentleman took stones and brought him down. The interpretation was "If sticks will not do, take clubs (stones)."

[1] Governor of Michigan 1911–1912.

That's where Roosevelt got his "big stick" phrase. He got
many of his other maxims and aphorisms out of McGuffey's
Third Reader, too. That is one thing that made him and his
precepts popular — they recalled things everybody had learned
at school and believed. They had almost the standing of the
Ten Commandments. There was another maxim, illustrated
by a wood-cut showing four mastiffs beating a lion. There and
then I made up my mind to get four mastiffs as soon as I had
accumulated one dollar and sixty-five cents. The moral was
supposed to be co-operation, or in union there is strength. I
recall both McGuffey's Readers and Monroe's. The latter had
"The Burial of Moses":

> By Nebo's lonely Mountain
> On this side Jordan's wave.

What appealed to me most about that was the idea of the
Heavenly Father being an undertaker, although I had not heard
the word "undertaker." Then there was the boy who stood on
the burning deck. That was Casabianca, which I know now
means "Whitehouse"; but at that time I could only grasp as
much of it as was possible to a boy who lived on the Wabash
and had never seen a deck. So I was determined to get a deck
of cards and burn them and stand on them, which I did, in
company with John Godfrey, the son of a Methodist preacher,
who was the best bass fisherman in the riffles below the paper-
mill at LaFayette, Indiana, more than fifty years ago. We had
Day's English Composition and Harvey's Grammar. Lord,
how I hated them! Later there was Wells's Geology and Dal-
ton's Physiology. Biology had not been born.

We had a song book called the "Forest Choir," and believe me
we were a lot of birds as we tried to sing from it. At examination Katie Stockton passed me slips of paper or I would have
been disgraced in music. As it was I passed a wonderful exam.
and have known nothing about music ever since, except that a
lyricist is not necessarily a liar. There were such songs as:

> The strawberries grow in the mowing field, May,
> And a sweet afternoon I shall pass,

which is all I remember, for I ran away to do it. Another song
was something like this (very sad and philosophical):

> Summer's going; summer's going:
> See the leaves are falling fast;
> Winter's coming; winter's coming:
> All the beauty gone at last.

This and the fact I had no stockings made me hate winter. I think attached to the same song were other words which I recall brokenly as something like:

John T. McCutcheon drew many pictures of school days as he recalled them.
"Dog-gone the Luck, Any Way," was published during the early 1900's.

> The winds from the blossoming orchards
>   Bring up the low hum of bees,
> And shouts of the bareheaded children,
>   At play in the shade of the trees.

I remember wondering if the bees would sting the children and turn their shouts to cries. We were taught to pronounce "winds" as if spelled "wyndes," which gave me a sort of shamed feeling, as if "putting on airs" or "dog." Another part went:

> Then play whilst you can, little children,
>   For childhood and summer are sweet;

Then play whilst you can, little children,
For childhood and summer are fleet.

That made a vast and persistent etching in my mind. And
it is true. There was a song describing the first snow of winter:

Softly like down on the breast of the river.

I could not see to save my life how a river could have a
"breast" and it was years before I knew that the "down" was
goose fur.

Very early we got to the "dime novels." (They were better
done, I think, for ten cents than the average novel of to-day,
many of which sell for two dollars but are still dime novels.)
These would fire our imaginations and we would run away and
go rafting down the Mississippi. Every river town had its
Huck Finn and Tom Sawyer. Mark Twain wrote true life
in those classics.

Very few boys had money, and fewer spent it. We picked up
old iron and rags and sold them to the rag man. When a circus
came we went to the Wildcat Creek to meet the elephant and
see him "test" the old wooden bridge and then solemnly go
down the bank and wade through. That made a deep impression upon all of us. We had guns hid out as soon as we could
carry a musket, and we shot any bird that would sit still long
enough. Sometimes we peppered each other across the Wabash. Some of us could shoot a sling-shot better than a gun.
If our parents would not allow us to join the gang at night we
peacefully retired and then climbed down and out over the
back shed.

In Governor Osborn is a trait of realism that causes
him to be more fair than is the usual custom in comparisons of the youth of that day with those of 1927.

We played games and kissed like the dickens. Modern
"petting" had nothing on us. And the girls were more shy
but they were out to do anything that any flapper will do now
and the boys were not afraid of them. One of the games was,
of course, "London Bridge," and another "Drop the Handkerchief." The violin (fiddle) was taboo, but we sang songs and
danced to them and hugged the girls until they would often
grunt as we swung them clean off the floor or ground, in the
barn or house or on the green. One of the tunes was:

Oh, Buffalo gals, ain't you comin' out to-night,
Ain't you comin' out to-night, ain't you comin' out to-night;
Oh, Buffalo gals, ain't you comin' out to-night,
To dance by the light of the moon?

Other lines went:

Oh, Buffalo gals, am you comin' out to-night
To dance by the side of me?

Then it went on, with the girls' response to assure the Buffalo boys that they were going to be right there. And they were:

And I danced with a gal with a hole in her stockin'
    An' her knees kep' a knockin'
    An' her toes kep' a rockin',
    The purtiest gal that roams.

And:

Higher up the cherry trees the sweeter grows the cherry,
The more ye hug an' kiss the gals the sooner they will marry.

And "Billy Boy"—"She's a young thing and cannot leave her mother!" It was the time of "Captain Jinks of the Horse Marines," and "Down in a Coal Mine"; "To Blackwell's Isle I'll Go." Rich in mirroring the times. And "Round and Round the Meadow We Go." And "Round and Round the Mulberry Bush."

In the afternoons we played shinny, a real hockey with hickory clubs, and roughed it. That was in winter. In the spring, along with agate shooting and marbles, and "playing for keeps," came "crack the whip."

In the summer we ran away and went to the Ole Sycamore, to swim in the Wabash. In the autumn there was war. Clans of boys from the Protestant wards would assemble and do battle with the Micks from the Plank Road. When the crowds were evenly divided we sent out a David against a Goliath. First we would search the opponent for brass knucks, or a key that, held between the fingers, could gouge out an eye. Niggers were usually barred because they could bite a bigger piece out of a feller than a white boy could. At that I have a good many nigger-bite scars.

When it was cool enough we built fires at the curbs and told bad stories. And we knew, as small boys, all the tough talk of the town and all the interdicted programmes. My parents were doctors and I lectured to the kids about sex-diseases and child-birth that I read about surreptitiously in the home library. So they called me "Doc." There was printed a scurrilous scandal sheet in Chicago. I got this in a keg three or four miles out of town where the baggage-man was subsidized to throw it off.

Old fellows and others of their kidney have a manner of saying the kids of this era are going to the devil in all sorts of hand-baskets. I mentioned how tough all of us were in my low set when I was young but older than I am now. There was a song all of us sang in the dark that had a depth of analysis we did not realize. It showed how eager and coarse sex was compared to now. It seems to me more than passing strange that I can recall it, but when I was thinking for you it buzzed into my mind with never a shock. To indicate the tenacity of that damned stuff, I am a pretty good Presbyterian and yet it clings to my memory like the stench of a glue factory, and somehow, as I said before, it does not shock me as it ought. It is for this reason and others that I believe things are getting better all the time. My children are twice as good as I was and more. Again I say Mazzini and his congeners were right; there is an amethystine thread of the Divine that ties things together as they should be huddled; and whilst men cannot be as the follower of Mahomet and leave it all to Allah, they have darn little to do with the thing in the long run.

There was not much actual stealing except for watermelons, and apples, and grapes, and such, and I do not believe the boys of to-day are inclined to be thieves. As I see it, we were tougher than the boys and girls of to-day; but we did go to Sunday-school and learned "Now I Lay Me" and the Lord's Prayer, and had a genuine feeling that God was a friend, and prayer merely talking to him; sort of "speaking to Him on the street" as it were.

I was not much of a "scollard" and it is strange to the degree of being uncanny how little I remember about school, and how much I remember about the myths and the nigger-boys and the scraps I had; and going nutting, and hiding out a gun almost before I could hold one up.

PART II

13

A DUDE ENTERS POLITICS

He Is Called a "Young Squirt," a "Weakling," a "Punkin-
Lily," a "Goo-Goo," a "Jane Dandy," an "Oscar Wilde,"
and Various Other Epithets of Deprecation; and Is Accused
of "Insufferable Conceit," of "Banging" His Hair, and of
Uttering His "*r's*" in a Manner Regarded by Chicago as
Effeminate. But He Remains in Politics, and Presently
Finds Himself Called "Strenuous," a "Fighter with Two-
Ounce Gloves," a "Fire-Eater," a "Rough Rider," a Sinner
Against Elegant Manners; and Is Judged by the Highest
Authorities to Be an Outstanding American. Including
Two Episodes of Controversy, in Which the Same Men
Were Principals, but with Their Rôles Reversed and the
Conditions Changed by the Passage of Twenty-three Years.
Together with Some Allusions to the Republican Party, the
Standard Oil Company, the Art of Cartooning Public Men,
and the Processes of Newspaper-Making. All Composing
What Might Be Called The Times and a Man.

IN eighteen hundred and eighty-four, Joseph Benson
Foraker pasted some newspaper clippings in his scrap-
book. A rising, but still minor, political figure of his
time, he had just enjoyed a happy experience of political
advancement and personal triumph (impaired only by
one infinitesimal dissonance); had been initiated into fraternity with the "Old Guard" that composed the leadership of the Republican party. That was a time when almost any degree of rank in the Republican national organization was a prized distinction; delegates to national
conventions sometimes had their official badges cast in
gold and disposed of them in their wills as precious relics.
The party was at an apex of strength and prestige — the
Republican National Convention of 1884 has been described as the ablest body of men that ever came together

in America since the original Constitutional Convention.[1]
The group who dominated it included, on one hand, the
old soldiers of the Grand Army of the Republic who had
been present at the party's birth and had shed their blood

for its early ideals; and, on the
other hand, the newcomers in
leadership, the rising generation
of captains of industry, typified
by Mark Hanna, with their corporation lawyers, typified by
Chauncey M. Depew. In that
commingling of leaders was a
symbol of the party itself as it
then was, thirty years after its
birth — idealism waning, mate-
rialism crescent; midway between the Civil War it fought to
abolish slavery, and the Arma-
geddon, it fought in 1912 to re-
pel the "social justice" programme of the Progressives.

Foraker, at that 1884 national
convention, had been chosen to
make the speech proposing John
Sherman for the Presidential
nomination. His oration had
been successful, according to the
rather florid standards of political oratory then current. "The
friends of the eloquent young

Roosevelt, as he figured in a cartoon in *Puck*, November 10,
1886, during his early participation in politics when he was
universally pictured as a dude.

leader," said the Cincinnati *Commercial*,[2] "may safely
congratulate him upon his effort; he made his mark upon

---

[1] This judgment was expressed as late as 1927 by Nicholas Murray Butler,
President of Columbia University. It is open to question, but is also tenable.
[2] Reproduced in "Notes of a Busy Life," J. B. Foraker.

the convention. . . . . Foraker's speech was the best that was made."

But in the triumph thus agreeably lauded was one faint blemish, as slight as a withering curl on the edge of one leaf of the orator's laurels. Among the newspaper accounts he saved were some that recorded an annoyingly incomplete appreciation on the part of one of his auditors — an auditor then relatively unimportant in the hierarchy of the Republican party, one who was new in politics and young in life, whose very presence in that convention, among the Forakers, the Shermans, and the Hannas, reflected a disdaining deference by the Old Guard leaders to what they called "the younger element."

Roosevelt as the cartoonists saw him nineteen years later. This cartoon, "To the Bride," was made by Briggs on the occasion of the marriage of Roosevelt's daughter Alice to Nicholas Longworth.

The clippings that caused a slight compression of Foraker's lips as he pasted them among the encomiums of his oration, recited that:

Theodore Roosevelt, who is a rather dudish-looking boy with eye-glasses and a scowlet-for-a-cent, applauded with the tips of his fingers; he had his hair parted in the middle, banged in front, rolled [1] [sic] his r's and pronounced the word *either* with the *i* sound instead of the *e*. He may have ability but he has also an inexhaustible supply of insufferable dudism and conceit, that will some day be fittingly rebuked.[2]

[1] The reporter's meaning is clear, though his choice of words was inept. Cultivated New York and Boston did pronounce their r's in a manner that would strike a Chicago reporter as unusual, but they did not "roll" them.

[2] This description of Theodore Roosevelt at the Republican National Convention at Chicago in 1884 is detached from two different clippings reprinted at

Foraker, as the admiring reporter said, "made his mark upon the convention," the mark of a coming man. With the Old Guard, Roosevelt made his mark, also. To them, Roosevelt was a weakling dude, a "goo-goo,"[1] a mugwump. If the future was to see anything of him, it was to see him "fittingly rebuked."

Twenty-three years later, on January 27, 1907, Foraker, making another speech, again had Roosevelt for an auditor, and again pasted clippings in his scrap-book. Both men, meantime, had travelled far. Roosevelt was now President of the United States; Foraker had arrived in the Senate and was the outstanding "railroad Senator." Roosevelt had forced on the unwilling Senate a

length in Joseph B. Foraker's "Notes of a Busy Life." A similar tone characterized allusions to Roosevelt in many other newspaper accounts. A skit published by the Chicago *News* spoke of Roosevelt as a "young squirt of a dude," and the New York *Press* said Roosevelt's hostility to the Convention's nominee for Vice-President was due to the fact that Roosevelt had once detected him "in the act of eating pie with a knife."

This deprecation of Roosevelt's demeanor was to some extent spiteful exaggeration. That there was another view of him, even this early, is shown by a sentence from a despatch to the New York *Journal*:

"Theodore Roosevelt, the Cyclone Assemblyman from New York, stood upon his chair, and, as the chairman announced his name, a thunder of applause greeted [him]."

There is one clear and convincing statement of the impression Roosevelt made on impartial observers at this time, June 1, 1884, when he was twenty-six years old and making his début in national policies. After the convention, he did not return to New York but went West, to spend the summer on a ranch he had bought in Dakota Territory, and to reflect on whether he should bolt the Republican presidential nominee, Blaine, or remain a regular Republican. At St. Paul, he was interviewed by a reporter of *The Pioneer Press*. At that time, St. Paul was real West; if Roosevelt's manner suggested superciliousness, St. Paul would have been the first to recognize it and jeer it. The *Pioneer Press* reporter wrote, June 8, 1884:

"He is short and slight and with rather an ordinary appearance, although his frame is wiry and his flashing eyes and rapid nervous gestures betoken a hidden strength. He is not at all an ideal Harvard alumnus. for he lacks that ingrained conceit and grace of manner that a residence at Cambridge insures. Although of the old Knickerbocker stock, his manner and carriage is awkward, and not at all impressive."

[1] This epithet, by 1927, had become obsolete; during the 1880's and 1890's it conveyed rich meaning as a derisive diminutive for persons charged with thinking themselves better than ordinary politicians. Its derivation probably was from reform associations having the phrase "good government" in their titles.

Theodore Roosevelt in 1916.

Theodore Roosevelt when New York City Police
Commissioner.

railroad rate regulation bill and similar measures; Foraker had resisted to the last ditch,[1] and had assailed most of Roosevelt's policies, including his discipline of a battalion of negro soldiers at Brownsville, Texas. The tenseness of the atmosphere when the two men came face to face as guests at the dinner of the Gridiron Club at Washington on January 27, 1907, was happily described by the club historian:[2] "There passed down the spines of those around the tables that tingle of excitement which one feels when something seems about to happen which you hope will not happen, but which you would not miss for the world if it should happen."

That the encounter should have become public is unique evidence of its sensational quality, for the binding rule of the Gridiron Club, broken only this once since the Club was founded in 1885, is that the speeches of guests are never reported[3] outside. But no club rule could prevent public notice of "perhaps the only time in the history of our government when a President and a Senator, or anybody else for that matter, have engaged in a public debate."[4] As the Washington *Post* put it:

SENSATIONAL ENCOUNTER

WAR OF THE STRONG

The tilt between the President and Senator Foraker at the Gridiron dinner on Saturday night cannot be ignored or silenced by club etiquette. It was sensational in the extreme. . . .

[1] Foraker made eighty-seven speeches against the railroad rate bill of 1906 (Hepburn Act), and, at the end, cast the solitary Republican vote against it, when all the others had either succumbed to Roosevelt's advocacy, or, as in the case of Aldrich, of Rhode Island, refrained from voting.

[2] Arthur Wallace Dunn, in "Gridiron Nights."

[3] The Gridiron Club, composed solely of newspaper men, expresses its only two rules in phrases which, though paradoxical, are serious and binding. The rules are formally recited by the president of the Club as part of the ritual at the opening of each dinner: "Reporters are never present; ladies, always."

[4] This characterization is Foraker's, written in a long letter to his son immediately after the incident, as a record of his version of the encounter.

Mr. Roosevelt was forceful — more than strenuous — and cuttingly incisive. It [was] a speech of biting sarcasm, interlarded with a vigorous vocabulary delivered in a high, strident pitch, and sandwiched with gestures more than emphatic. It was taken by all who heard it as a direct challenge to Senator Foraker. More, indeed. It was taken as a lecture to him as an individual and the Senate as a whole, reprobating both. He was striking at Senator Foraker then. Afterward he rapped J. Pierpont Morgan and Henry H. Rogers, the vice-president of the Standard Oil Company. Looking squarely at them, he sounded what was intended to be a warning that they and other men, representative of Wall Street, should not undertake to block the reforms he had set in motion and still had in contemplation. Morgan and Rogers flushed deeply.

I can best describe the incident by likening it to a battle in the prize ring. In the first round, Mr. Roosevelt entered the arena, wearing regulation boxing-gloves. He made a long speech — a very long speech. Toward the close Mr. Roosevelt laid aside his soft gloves and put on a pair of the two-ounce kind. . . .

When the President concluded, Mr. Blythe, the toastmaster, called on Senator Foraker for a reply. When Foraker arose he was ashen white. I did not look at his hands, but I think he had on one-ounce gloves. His blows were hard. He hurled back the flings at himself and the Senate. He declared with great dramatic effect that his oath of office was as sacred to him as was the President's to him, and that no preachments from the White House were essential to the proper performance of his duty.

When Foraker finished Roosevelt jumped to his feet and struck back. He was mad clean through . . . teeth clinched. . . . It was a battle royal.[1]

---

[1] This account is condensed from the Washington *Post*, January 29, 1907. The order of the sentences is here rearranged. *The Post's* story reflects accurately the atmosphere during and after the incident, which on the whole was unsympathetic to Roosevelt. It was felt that Roosevelt was the aggressor. Also, the atmosphere of every gathering of politicians, and of Washington generally at that time, was prevailingly on the "stand-pat," Foraker side. Some of the excited discussion criticized Roosevelt on the ground that he had initiated a political and personal debate at a private dinner. There was little in that. Gridiron dinners are political, and characterized by extreme frankness of personal allusion. Moreover, Roosevelt did not regard politics as a gentleman's sport, to be played in the spirit of a private duello, with a meticulous code about choice of time and place. Roosevelt had a trait of ruthless righteousness; once he had made up his mind that Foraker was an undesirable Senator, he would say so, on the first occasion, and every occasion, that offered.

Once again, in 1908, the fundamental antipathy between the two men, and the ideas they represented, erupted into open conflict, bursting, finally, the restraints

Thomas Nast, in "Harper's Weekly" for April 19, 1884.

Roosevelt as the cartoonists saw him during the 1880's, when he first entered politics. The figure on the right is Grover Cleveland, then Governor of New York.

both of social decorum and of party solidarity. In this final encounter, the arena was not a private dinner, nor a political convention, but the whole broad stage of national politics, with the entire public as excited spectators; an encounter in which the expression of the combatants' emotion was not limited to ironic applause with the finger-tips, nor their blows softened by gloves; an encounter predestined to be conclusive. Both combatants had come to the mood of finality; the situation called for finality. Roosevelt, writing to a friend about the state of the Republican party, had said: "If they split off Foraker they split off a splinter; but if they split off me, they would split the party nearly in two."

Into this tension, the agency of precipitation came from an outsider. During the presidential campaign of 1908, a Democrat, William Randolph Hearst, in the course of a country-wide speech-making tour, read at public meetings a series of letters written by the vice-president of the Standard Oil Company to Foraker, containing such expressions as

It gives me pleasure to hand you herewith certificate of deposit for [various sums were mentioned in different letters: $50,000, $14,500, and $15,000] in accordance with our understanding.

And:

Again, my dear Senator, I venture to write you regarding the bill to amend the act against unlawful monopolies. It really seems as though this bill is very unnecessarily severe, and even vicious. I will be greatly pleased to have a word from you on the subject. The bill is, I believe, still in committee. . . . Here is still another very objectionable bill. It is so outrageous as to be ridiculous. But it needs to be looked after and I hope there will be no difficulty in killing it.[1]

The authenticity of the letters was admitted by Foraker; he explained, however, that the $50,000 had not been for himself, but was a loan he had arranged for a friend who wished to buy a newspaper, *The Ohio State Journal*, then for sale. As to other sums, he explained they were retainers — for his private services as a lawyer, not

[1] Condensed from two of the letters sent to Foraker by John D. Archbold, vice-president of the Standard Oil Company.

his public services as a Senator. But the public, in its angry state of feeling about the trusts, was unable to ratiocinate as meticulously as Foraker claimed he could, between fees for legal services, and requests for action on legislation; the public, in short, accepted the inference that Foraker had received money to influence legislation, and drowned his protestations in a roar of outrage.[1]

Roosevelt from a picture supposed to have been made about 1886.

Roosevelt, accepting the common assumption that the money Foraker received from the Standard Oil Company was quid pro quo for senatorial services, and seeing in the incident an opportunity for a knock-out blow, characterized[2] the transaction as "the purchase of a United States Senator to do the will of the Standard Oil Company," denounced Foraker as "the attorney of the corporations, their hired representative in public life," and told Taft (whose campaign for the Presidency Roosevelt was directing) to "decline to appear on the platform with Foraker." On December 29, 1908, when Foraker was

[1] The letters had been taken from the files of the Standard Oil Company by an employee and delivered to Mr. Hearst, who, refraining from prior publication in his own newspapers, read them at public meetings and released them to the entire press of the country. Foraker's explanation of one of the sums he received, $50,000, was true. But the explanation left him in the position of a go-between for the purchase of a newspaper in which the Standard Oil Company was to have a large interest. As to the other sums he received, his explanation was sufficiently characterized by the *World's Work*, a magazine not unfriendly to the Standard Oil Company: "There has never been any code of ethics, commercial or political, approved by American public sentiment, which excused a man who sat as a Senator of the United States while he received money from any client who wrote him to 'look after' proposed legislation."

[2] In a letter to William H. Taft, Sept. 19, 1908.

a candidate for re-election, Roosevelt inspired a newspaper dispatch telling the people of Ohio that in "the opinion of President Roosevelt, to support Foraker is AN ACT OF TREASON against the Republican Party."[1] Foraker, dashed on the rocks of public odium, was defeated and carried into a backwater of retirement, where he spent his remaining years writing two volumes which he called "Notes of a Busy Life,"[2] a political parallel to Cardinal Newman's *Apologia Pro Vita Sua.*

From "Puck," March 26, 1884.

Roosevelt as the cartoonists pictured him during the early 1880's. The figure on the right is Grover Cleveland, then Governor of New York.

The America of the 1880's saw the Forakers of the Old Guard secure in their seats of power, and saw Roosevelt as an ineffectual amateur trying to introduce ideas so far in advance of the time as to seem Utopian.

But the alarmed America of 1908 saw the Forakers of the Old Guard as the agents of a system that had grown to seem monstrous, saw the ideas of Roosevelt as

---

[1] The capital letters are Foraker's, as he repeated the passage in his book. The original article appeared as a dispatch from Washington in the Cincinnati *Times-Star*, December 29, 1908, under a headline saying: "Roosevelt Believes to Support Foraker Is Party Treason."

[2] Eight years later, Roosevelt and Foraker exchanged friendly letters, Roosevelt withdrawing much of what he had charged, and saying ". . . I admire your entire courage. I grew steadily more and more to realize your absolute Americanism." Foraker wrote that he had always been "an ardent admirer of your great intellectual power, fervent patriotism, and fearless courage." When Elihu Root read the letter Roosevelt had sent Foraker he described it as "thoroughly characteristic of a nature combative, always ready to fight, but never sulky or cher-

the people's salvation, and Roosevelt himself as St. George fighting the dragon.

II

The Roosevelt of the Republican national convention of 1884, a "dude" daintily applauding "with his finger-tips," a reforming young Mugwump barely tolerated by the Old Guard leaders, gave little promise of becoming the invincible personality that dominated the party twenty years later.

The newspaper writers and cartoonists of the early 1880's, complacently or cynically reflecting the spirit of that period, estimated Roosevelt as an impetuous boy beating puny fists against the impregnable walls of what is. They dressed him in a high hat, a coat of the smart style called "cutaway," and the skin-tight trousers that were the fad of the day. His teeth they did not notice, concealing them under a rather too carefully tended moustache. Altogether, they gave him that mien and manner of the up-to-date eighties which Gilbert's "Patience" satirized as a "je ne sais quoi young man," but which the average American of the period understood rather better in the slang translation, "lah-de-dah." They completed their pictures with labels usually synonomous with "dude reformer."

Roosevelt making his maiden speech as an office-holder[1] was pictured by the New York *Sun:* "Young Mr. Roosevelt of New York, a blond young man with eye-glasses, English side-whiskers and a Dundreary drawl in his speech." The drawl was illustrated by eccen-

---

ishing revenge." Those who were familiar with the reconciliation felt there was an additional reason. At the time it took place, July, 1916, all Republicans were composing their feuds with each other for the purpose of uniting in a common and strong hostility to the then Democratic President, Woodrow Wilson, who was running for re-election on a slogan "He kept us out of war."

[1] In the New York Assembly, January 24, 1882.

tric typographical treatment of a phrase from the speech
— "r-a-w-t-h-e-r r-e-l-i-e-v-e-d."   Equal belittlement,
coupled with a hint of advice to Roosevelt's constituency,
was expressed, after another of Roosevelt's speeches, by

Roosevelt as the cartoonists saw him during the 1900's.

another New York paper: "The popular voice of New
York will probably leave this weakling at home hereafter." One newspaper called him "Oscar Wilde,"[1] and
others repeated the epithet. The Albany correspondent
of *The Observer* in his despatches customarily referred to
Roosevelt as "the little man" and "His Lordship," and
pictured him as strutting about with his nose in the air,
and comporting himself with more than a touch of condescending superiority toward his rustic and East Side

[1] The original of the name was then at the height of his æsthetic vogue.

colleagues. The most tireless among the newspaper detractors of Roosevelt was the New York *World*.[1] Throughout Roosevelt's three terms in the Assembly, whenever he made a speech or gave out an interview or otherwise came into public notice, *The World* aimed at him barbs dipped in poison. His youth, his wealth, his appearance, his speech, his associates — all served as pretexts for ridicule. One day, *The World* dispatch from Albany began: "Young Mr. Roosevelt, having recovered from his recent attack of the croup . . ." Another time the jeering took the form of verse:

> His strong point is his bank account,
> His weak point is his head.

For a political meeting organized and addressed by Roosevelt, *The World* invented the name "The Dudes' Reform Club," and thus described the proceedings:

THE DUDES' REFORM CLUB

MR. ROOSEVELT UPBRAIDS THEM FOR NOT KNOWING WHETHER
HE IS AN ALDERMAN OR A LEGISLATOR

. . . The chief of the dudes bowed his acknowledgments. His trousers were so tight that in making gyrations he only bent the joints above the belt. He certainly must have used

---

[1] Throughout this book, many newspapers are quoted and mentioned. The reader should bear in mind that there may be very little relation between the character, political complexion, and standing of a newspaper as of the year in which the quotation appeared, and as of the year in which this history is read. For example, the New York *World*, at the time it printed these jeers at Roosevelt, was owned by a New York promoter, a sensational stock-market operator. Soon afterward it was bought by Joseph Pulitzer, and became one of the most independent papers in the country (though it continued to oppose Roosevelt, in a different way and for different reasons). A newspaper, as respects its fundamental character, is one of the least permanent of institutions, although the popular psychology thinks of it otherwise. A newspaper can change ownership overnight, after which little may be left of it except its name. Even though it remain in the same ownership, its character, point of view, and policy may be altered by a change in the owner's interests, by his necessity for borrowing money, or otherwise.

a shoe-horn in getting them over his heels. When Mr. Roosevelt finished, the other dudes took the tops of their canes out of their mouths and tapped the floor with the other end, and then they lighted cigarettes.[1]

Homer Davenport in the New York "Evening Mail."

Roosevelt as the cartoonists saw him during the 1900's.

Roosevelt was not the sort to take *The World's* abuse lying down. Even this early he had a well-stocked vocabulary of scorching invective. Nothing *The World* ever printed about Roosevelt was half so devastating in brutal

---

Or the character of a newspaper may undergo transition with a change of editors, or even with a change in the post of managing-editor, where, commonly, the contents of each day's issue, and the relative emphasis on subjects of news, is determined.

[1] "And then they lighted cigarettes"! To the America of 1927, consuming 90,000,000,000 cigarettes annually, the force of this jeer may not be apparent. In the eighties, cigarettes were regarded as the apotheosis of insipidity, indulged in only by dudes and weaklings. The 1880 equivalent of "he" men smoked cigars, or pipes; or they chewed. Roosevelt never used tobacco at all.

directness, or so pungent with innuendo as the characterization he delivered on the floor of the Assembly:

> The New York *World*, a local stock-jobbing sheet of limited
> circulation, of voluble scurrility and versatile mendacity —
> owned by the arch-thief of Wall Street and edited by a rancor-
> ous kleptomaniac with a penchant for trousers.

Some of the deprecation of Roosevelt was a reflection
of partisanship among the New York papers — *The
World's* was a direct expression of the interests that then
owned it, Jay Gould and his associates, railroad and
public utility promoters, and monopolists. But the same
note is to be found in newspapers published outside New
York State. The Boston *Herald*, with an air of artistic
objectivity, gave this portrayal of the young Roosevelt:

> He has a very light colored, slight mustache, wears jaunty
> clothes, and his head is topped by a small straw hat with a
> straight rim dyed blue on the under side. . . . He looks for
> all the world like a young college graduate hunting for a place
> on the editorial staff of some newspaper.

Even as late as 1890 newspapers used such phrases as
"a Jane dandy," "punkin-lily," "scion of a diluted an-
cestry," "Terrapin Teddy," "descendant of the wayback
Roosevelts from Rooseveltville," "Rosy Roosy," "Tin-
tinnabulating Ted," and a strange epithet, mysterious as
to its derivation, and cryptic as to meaning, but clearly
devised to convey derogation, "Mr. Theossehos Roosevelt."[1]

Even such newspapers as wished to be friendly to
Roosevelt gave him, so to speak, discouraged encouragement; spoke of him in terms of giving a pat on the back
to a well-meaning young man who one hopes will stay in

---

[1] One can visualize these editorial contemners, searching strange vocabularies
for a word to describe their notion of the youthful Roosevelt; and can feel regret,
for the sake of their convenience, that "boy scout" had not yet come into the
language—how they would have rung the changes on that!

politics, but who one expects hardly will. An oasis of not too hopeful approval was published on the editorial page of the New York *Times :*[1]

Mr. Roosevelt has a most refreshing habit of calling men and things by their right names, and in these days of judicial, ecclesiastical, and jour- nalistic subserviency to the robber barons of the Street, it needs some lit- tle courage in any public man to characterize them and their acts in fitting terms. There is a splen- did career open for a young man of position, character, and indepen- dence like Mr. Roosevelt.

"He has been called a swell," said a New England journal, "but it would be well if every State had just such swells." "Let them all come to the front and take part in the government," added a Western paper encouragingly.

Roosevelt as the cartoonists saw him after he had attacked the trusts.

Doubtless Roosevelt, wearing the clothes a young man of his background would naturally receive from his tailor, stood out from the older members of the New York As- sembly, and from the rural type as well as the usual city type. His energetic forthrightness set him apart also, as well as his spontaneousness, his lack of youth's ordinary disposition toward self-effacement in the presence of elders. Roosevelt was not a dude, either in meticulousness

[1] April 6, 1882.

of dress, or in vacuity of mind, or in indolence. Neither at that time, nor at any time was he self-conscious about dress or manner. As a youth at Harvard, he paid considerably less than the normal young man's attention to clothes. His mother, with presumably accurate knowledge, used to speak of him as her "young berserker." The newspapers assumed that a young man who came from a wealthy old family and had been educated at Harvard must have the characteristics that newspapers commonly attributed to that caste. Or they seized upon foppishness as the most convenient trait with which to identify a new and conspicuous figure in public life. Or they used this means of expressing the contemptuous superiority of the "hard-boiled," among both newspapermen and politicians, toward the young and the idealistic. Or they thought of "dude" as a symbol for the futility of attacking the accepted order. All motives combined to fasten upon Roosevelt the tag that became practically universal during the early years of his public life.

From the New York "World."

Roosevelt as the cartoonists saw him during his Presidency.

By the rule that usually governs, that early conception of Roosevelt should have remained to the end. The public's initial impression, the rôle the newspapers give a man when he first appears in the news, almost always sticks. To alter the public's first conception of a man is almost more difficult than to alter personality itself. There is a fatality about it: A person is introduced to the public as having certain characteristics, is tagged with certain adjectives. That first characterization has, in the popular mind, the tenacity of all first impressions. In the mechanism of newspaper work, there is a process that perpetuates it. The first items about any one newly emerged into public notice are clipped, indexed, and filed away in that repository of personal information which newspapers call their "morgue" or "obituary department." Upon the subsequent appearance of the man in the news, reporters and editors turn to the morgue. Unconsciously they absorb, indolently they accept, automatically they repeat, the early adjectives. For newspaper writers and cartoonists, and consequently for the public, a character's personality is commonly fixed forever by the initial impression he makes. He is put into a mold; to wrench himself out of it, to take on a new rôle in the public eye, is almost impossible.[1]

Nevertheless, Roosevelt changed that picture. More accurately, the times changed, the mood of the people changed, and the newspapers reflected the transition. In the early 1880's, the forces Roosevelt attacked were seen as those that had fought the Civil War, abolished

---

[1] This point is amplified in a letter written to the author in 1927 by Jay N. Darling ("Ding"), one of the leading American cartoonists:

"When a new figure appears the cartoonist begins with rather an accurate portrayal of his countenance and figure. This picture soon takes on, by a process of accretion, characteristics which portray the personality and activities of the man, his eccentricities and hobbies—until much of the original portraiture is lost. This evolved figure becomes the accepted symbol of the man in the minds of the public. I had drawn a great many cartoons of Bryan before I ever saw him, using the popular conception of Bryan which I in turn had gleaned from the cartoons of the day; and I was shocked, when I first met Bryan, to find that in reality the cartoon portraits looked very little like him. I was equally surprised when, upon a complete revision of my picture of Bryan, I found that the public refused to accept it as satisfactory. It was a long time after John D. Rockefeller added a wig

slavery, preserved the Union; that were resisting the economic heresies of greenbackism and free silver; and, as business leaders and railroad builders, were opening up the country. By the early 1900's, "opening up the country" was called "stealing the public land," and in all respects the forces Roosevelt opposed were seen in a very different light. The writers and cartoonists of the 1900's portrayed Roosevelt at the height of his Presidency as the fighting champion of the people, a combination of Rough Rider and fireeater, fists clenched, chin thrust forward, hair bristling, eyes glaring, and — final touch of belligerency — teeth made to symbolize a steam-shovel biting into an ogre labelled "The Trusts," teeth gnashing defiance at

Macauley in the New York "World."
Roosevelt as the cartoonists saw him during the 1900's.

to his make-up before the cartoonists could revise the formula which had been accepted in the public mind as a picture of Rockefeller. The cartoonist's formula for Theodore Roosevelt pictured him with a square head and a square jaw, undoubtedly reflecting the common impression of his virility. Roosevelt's head was from every aspect round, but once the public has become acquainted with the synthetic formula, it is a bold cartoonist who will venture to alter materially the conception. Farmers no longer wear whiskers, but for so many years did cartoonists picture the farmer according to that old familiar formula, that to make a cartoon in which a farmer appears and give that farmer the modern contours which he deserves, would certainly require a signboard on which should be 'This is a farmer.' Since cartoonists convey their message by the most direct route possible, they are very loath to change the formula of any particular figure when once it has been accepted by the public. Exceptions have been very rare."

Wall Street, or gloating in triumph over it — the outstanding, incomparable symbol of virility in his time.[1] Of the elements that entered nto the transformation, com-

Roosevelt when he was elected President—as seen by Bernard Partridge, the cartoonist of *Punch*.

paratively little is to be ascribed to change in Roosevelt's personality. Much more potent was a change that came in the conditions of the times and the mood of the people.

[1] "Mr. Dooley," describing Roosevelt's arrival at a meeting during the 1900 presidential campaign, said: "And thin along came Teddy Rosenfeldt and bit his way to the platform."

14

A PICTURE, A POEM, AND THE TIMES

A School-Teacher Sees the Picture and Writes the Poem; Whereupon Many People Realize He Has Expressed Their Thoughts, and the Country Becomes Excited. It is called "The Cry of the Zeitgeist." A University President Delivers a Series of Lectures on It, a Railroad President Offers a Prize for an Answer to It, and Bryan Writes an Exegesis of It. Together with Some Other Expressions from Exalted Persons about the State of the Nation.

DURING Christmas week of the year 1898, a California school-teacher, Edwin Markham, living on the heights back of Oakland, in a cottage that looked down upon the bay and city of San Francisco and the Golden Gate, utilized his vacation to complete a poem. For years he had been haunted by the memory of a painting he had seen reproduced in *Scribner's Magazine* in 1886, "The Man With the Hoe," by the French peasant-artist Millet. Then he had the great joy of seeing the original painting in San Francisco. He described the experience subsequently:[1]

I sat for an hour before the painting and all the time the terror and power of the picture was growing upon me. I saw that this creation of the painter was no mere peasant, no chance man of the fields, but he was rather a type, a symbol of the toiler, brutalized through long ages of industrial oppression. I saw in this peasant the slow but awful degradation of man through endless, hopeless, and joyless labor.

The poem was first published in the San Francisco *Examiner*, January 15, 1899.

[1] In an article by Markham in *The Saturday Evening Post*, December 16, 1899.

This reproduction of Millet's painting is printed through the courtesy of William H. Crocker, of San Francisco, owner of the original.

The Man With the Hoe.

THE MAN WITH THE HOE

By Edwin Markham

(Written after Seeing Millet's World-Famous Painting)

"God made man in His own image,
in the image of God made He him."—Genesis.

Bowed by the weight of centuries he leans
Upon his hoe and gazes on the ground,
The emptiness of ages in his face,
And on his back the burden of the world.
Who made him dead to rapture and despair,
A thing that grieves not and that never hopes,
Stolid and stunned, a brother to the ox?
Who loosened and let down this brutal jaw?
Whose was the hand that slanted back this brow?
Whose breath blew out the light within this brain?

Is this the Thing the Lord God made and gave
To have dominion over sea and land;
To trace the stars and search the heavens for power;
To feel the passion of Eternity?
Is this the dream He dreamed who shaped the suns

"The Man With the Hoe."

Written After Seeing Millet's World-Famous Painting
Now in This City.

BY EDWIN MARKHAM.

BOWED by the weight of centuries he leans
Upon his hoe and gazes on the ground.
The emptiness of ages in his face.
And on his back the burden of the world.
Who made him dead to rapture and despair.
A thing that grieves not and that never hopes.
Stolid and stunned. a brother to the ox?
Who loosened and let down this brutal jaw?
Whose hand that slanted back this brow?
Whose light within this brain?

Reproduced from the original publication of "The Man With the Hoe," in the San
Francisco *Examiner*, January 15, 1899.

And pillared the blue firmament with light?
Down all the stretch of Hell to its last gulf
There is no shape more terrible than this —
More tongued with censure of the world's blind greed —
More filled with signs and portents for the soul —
More fraught with menace to the universe.

What gulfs between him and the seraphim!
Slave of the wheel of labor, what to him
Are Plato and the swing of Pleiades?
What the long reaches of the peaks of song,
The rift of dawn, the reddening of the rose?
Through this dread shape the suffering ages look;
Time's tragedy is in that aching stoop;

Through this dread shape humanity betrayed,
Plundered, profaned and disinherited,
Cries protest to the Judges of the World,
A protest that is also prophecy.

O masters, lords and rulers in all lands,
Is this the handiwork you give to God,
This monstrous thing distorted and soul-quenched?
How will you ever straighten up this shape;
Touch it again with immortality;
Give back the upward looking and the light;
Rebuild in it the music and the dream;
Make right the immemorial infamies
Perfidious wrongs, immedicable woes?

O masters, lords and rulers in all lands,
How will the Future reckon with this Man?
How answer his brute question in that hour
When whirlwinds and rebellion shake the world?
How will it be with kingdoms and with kings —
With those who shaped him to the thing he is —
When this dumb Terror shall reply to God
After the silence of the centuries?

The poem flew eastward across the continent, like a contagion. As fast as the mails carried it, newspapers printed it as a fresh focus of infection, first California and the Pacific Coast, then the Mississippi Valley, on into New York and New England, over the line into Canada. Within a week, phrases and couplets from it were on every lip. Newspaper editions containing it were exhausted and publishers reprinted it, together with editorials about it, and the hundreds of manuscripts of comment received from the public. The newspapers, a historian of the day remarked, as a unique phenomenon, "gave as much space to 'The Man With the Hoe' as to prize-fights and police stories. The clergy made the poem their text, platform orators dilated upon it, college professors lectured upon it, debating societies discussed it, schools took it up for study. . . . The president of Leland Stanford Univer-

sity, Doctor David Starr Jordan, used it seriously and intelligently as the theme of a lecture delivered in many
places"; "and," said *The Arena Magazine* six months
after the poem's publication, "there is not yet an end."

Not only did the poem become general as the average
man's symbol for the political and economic mood of the
time.[1] Within the narrower world of literature, critics
hurried to place an estimate on the newly arrived poet.
Up to this time they had not noticed him, although for
years he had been sending verse to Eastern magazines and
had won some slight recognition as a poet with a bent for
esthetic themes.

Among critics who looked to the effect of "The Man
With the Hoe" on the social ferment of the day, it "was
hailed by many as 'the battle cry of the next thousand
years.' "[2] The New York *Herald* asked: "Has a great
poet arisen in the teeming West? Is . . . a revolution
impending in America — a bloodless revolution this time,
fought not with bullets but with ballots? If so, Edwin
Markham will prove to be at once its despised prophet
and its accepted high priest."[3] Another newspaper said:

---

[1] In addition to the poem's quality of jeremiad protest, it carries the suggestion
of "thunder on the left," the Roman warning of impending menace. Read
aloud, each line, or each couplet, has the auditory effect of near-by cannonading.

[2] This estimate is reproduced in the biography of the poet in "Who's Who."

[3] In order to compare these prophecies about the Markham on 1899 with the
Markham of 1927, I consulted, in the latter year, Nicholas Vachel Lindsay.
Lindsay makes the convincing point that the early encomiums of Markham looked
upon him not primarily as a poet, but as a reformer. Consequently, they, in Mr.
Lindsay's phrase, "thrust upon him an inflated political expectation." This
worked a disadvantage to Markham as a poet, of whom Mr. Lindsay writes:
"Markham's standing to-day is as good as Longfellow's ever was. . . . It is a
real victory to outlive a vague political ascendancy and to build up a literary
one that is solid." Mr. Lindsay's enthusiasm for Markham's poetry is stronger
than is conveyed by this quotation from him. He endorses the judgment of Benjamin de Casseres: "'The Man With the Hoe' is technically a great poem.
There are vastness, power, and passion in it. It is Markham on his soap-box,
but his soap-box is a star. . . . [Markham] is an artist . . . a real poet, sometimes
a great poet. [He is] steeped in the ecstasy of eternals. There is a touch of crazy
beauty in him, and he has caught the wild music of the Angel Israfel." Markham
clearly is not to be classified with those authors who produce one striking work in

"This poem comes as the cry of the zeitgeist." Equal elevation of tone appeared in all the comment that looked primarily at the relation of the poem to the common

"Jingle bells, jingle bells, jingle all the day !
Oh, what fun it is to ride in a one-horse open sleigh !"

F. Opper, in the New York "American," January 10, 1910.

During the trust era, Frederick Opper, in a forceful series of cartoons, pictured the average American in a rôle he labelled "The Common People," a figure harassed, unhappy, driven, always oppressed or "put upon" by immense, obese figures labelled "The Trusts."

---

a lifetime, literary century plants of a single blooming. The judgment of his fellow poets is suggested by their keeping him Honorary President of the Poetry Society of America during the greater part of its history. In 1922, he was chosen by a committee headed by Chief Justice William H. Taft, to read, at the dedication of the Lincoln Memorial at Washington, a poem of his own that had been selected from among two hundred and fifty. Markham's only important later activity as a leader of a cause occurred in 1907, when he took part in the early crusade against child labor, writing a series of magazine articles called "The Hoe-man in the Making," later published as a book called "Children in Bondage." In these later years, at his public appearances, he seemed not at all the rabble-rousing crusader that "The Man With the Hoe" would suggest, but rather a benignant old gentleman who found the world kindly and good. The contrast between the fiery poem of 1898 and the gentle author of 1927 may have been caused partly by added years, partly by the emollient of personal success—but probably much more by the immense change that had taken place in America.

mood of the day. Applause of the poem and its author included such expressions as: "One of the greatest thinkers of the world." ". . . touches the high-water mark of American achievement in verse." "The foremost name in poetical literature since Tennyson and Browning." The San Jose (Calif.) *Mercury*, moved, perhaps, by local California pride, assured all doubters that " 'The Man With the Hoe' is the strongest, most meaningful, and most striking poem, with the single exception, perhaps, of Kipling's Recessional, that has been written in any country in the last quarter of a century." Many quite temperate persons compared "The Man With the Hoe" with Thomas Hood's similar appeal to a similar zeitgeist, "The Song of the Shirt":

> With fingers weary and worn,
>   With eyelids heavy and red,
> A woman sat, in unwomanly rags,
>   Plying her needle and thread. . . .
>
> "O men with sisters dear!
>   O men with mothers and wives!
> It is not linen you're wearing out,
>   But human creatures' lives!
> Stitch - stitch - stitch!
>   In poverty, hunger, and dirt —
> Sewing at once, with a double thread,
>   A shroud as well as a shirt!"

To Americans of a later generation, it may seem fantastic that the average man of 1900 should have taken Markham's poem as meaning him; that he should have seen in "The Man With the Hoe" a mirroring of himself; that he should have read "slave of the wheel of labor," and thought of himself; that he should have regarded "masters, lords, and rulers in all lands," as something that might oppress him, here in America; that he should have looked upon himself as "plundered, pro-

faned, and disinherited," and as the victim of "perfidious
wrongs, immedicable woes." Yet that is precisely what
did happen, and that is why the poem had such an
enormous vogue.

Sociologists, editors, political leaders, all who were close
to the heart of the crowd or concerned with it, seized
upon "The Man With the Hoe" as an expression of the
prevailing mood of the American people. William Randolph Hearst, with true journalistic instinct, realizing that
William J. Bryan was the outstanding spokesman of the
sort of protest the poem expressed and appealed to,
asked Bryan to write about it for the New York *Journal*.
Bryan made the poem the text for a characteristic summing up of the complaints of the times. Ominously, he
quoted Victor Hugo's description of the mob as "the
human race in misery." On his own account Bryan said:

It is not strange that "The Man With the Hoe" created a
profound sensation. It is a sermon addressed to the heart.
It voices humanity's protest against inhuman greed. There is
a majestic sweep to the argument; some of the lines pierce like
arrows. How feeble in comparison have been the answers to it.
The extremes of society are being driven further and further
apart. Wealth is being concentrated in the hands of a few.
At one end of the scale luxury and idleness breed effeminacy;
at the other end, want and destitution breed desperation. . . .

Markham himself had not anticipated the kind of
acclaim that came to his poem, and certainly not the
volume of it. He had looked upon Millet's powerful
painting, he had been moved to an ecstacy, and had
written a poem. Apparently it took time for him to find
just the significance that the country saw in the poem
instantly, its direct relation to concrete conditions in
America. Asked by a magazine editor to tell how he came
to write it, he said: [1]

[1] *The Saturday Evening Post*, December 16. 1899.

THE NEW ROBINSON CRUSOE.

He Meets His Man Friday.

F. Opper, in the New York "American," January 2, 1904.

The "Man With the Hoe" harmonized with the cartoonist's conception of "The Common People."

I was born a man with a hoe. I am a child of the furrow. All my youth was passed on a farm and cattle ranch, among the hard, severe conditions that go with that life. Of course I do not mean to say that there are not happy phases of farm life. I enjoyed as a boy the horseback rides on the long ranges of hills. The smell of the furrow was pleasant to me. I knew and loved animals, the horses and cattle. But with all this I felt, too, the privations and scraping poverty that are the frequent accompaniment of the farm boy's life.[1]

[1] Elsewhere Markham added: "From boyhood to this hour I have wondered over the hoary problem that has been passed on to us from Job: Why should some be ground and broken? Why should so many go down under the wheels of the world to hopeless ruin as far as human eyes can see?"

Merely to see "The Man With the Hoe" as the poetic assertion of an analogy between a French peasant and an American farmer was sentimentalism and fallacy. Nevertheless, supporters of the established order saw, or affected to see, only this limited application, and wrote ready answers. To reply by the device of giving a true picture of the American farmer, in contrast with the French peasant, was obvious and frequent. One critic said:

> Markham's "Man With the Hoe" is an insult to every farmer and every farmer's son in America. It draws a picture that has no foundation in fact. It is utterly vicious in that it degrades honorable labor and promotes contempt for work, and dissatisfaction, unrest, and despair where there should be hope, happiness, and courage. It and all similar woeful wailings are worse than worthless trash.

A more honest criticism was written by E. P. Powell, author of "Our Heredity from God," who said:[1]

> Mr. Markham shows us the workman of civilization, not going up from the animal, but going down from what God made him. . . . Such an interpretation of man and labor, especially of agricultural labor, at this time, puts the poem in alignment with that pessimism and explosive arraignment of social order in which sentimentalism strikes hands with brute force.

Powell, reversing Markham's point of view, rewrote the poem as he thought it should be:

> Lifted by toil of centuries, he leans
> Upon his hoe and gazes on the heavens,
> The glorious light of ages on his face . . .
> What gulfs between him and the anthropoid.[2]

---

[1] *The Coming Age*, November, 1899.

[2] There were many parodies. The Chicago *Times-Herald* published one, by S. E. Kiser, called "The Man With the Load":

> Bowed by a weight of fiery stuff, he leans
> Against the hitching-post and gazes 'round!
> Besotted emptiness is in his face,
> He bears a load that still may get him down.

Another parody was "The Man With the Lawn-Mower." Still another, "The

Herbert Johnson, in the Philadelphia "North American."

"Common People" determines to use the ballot as a grubbing-hoe to get rid of weeds
in the political garden.

But the true symbolism of "The Man With the Hoe,"
as applying to the average man — artisan, clerk, small
business man; and the effect the poem was having on the
social feeling of the time, was not missed by those who had

Woman Under the Heel of the Man With the Hoe," One of the earliest of that
class of writers who later became known as "colyumnists," Newt Newkirk, of the
Boston *Post*, used "The Man With the Hoe" as the model upon which to write
about the current fad of bicycling:

THE MAN WITH THE HUMP

Bowed by the drooping handle-bars he leans
Upon his bike and gazes at the ground;
His back is humped and crooked and his face
Is strained and agonizing in its look.
Who made him sit upon a wheel like this?

most reason to apprehend it. They sought ways to offset it. An anonymous donor — it was revealed to be Collis P. Huntington, a railroad multimillionaire, after he died in 1900 — offered a prize of $700[1] through the New York *Sun* for the best poetical answer to "The Man With the Hoe." In making the offer, Huntington affirmed, anonymously, that Markham's poem did injury to a great class of agricultural toilers who would resent the statement that they were "brothers to the ox." He said that this poem would add to the tendency, already too strong, of young Americans to look on field labor as distasteful.

The fallacy of this kind of reply, the insincerity of some who made it, angered those who felt Markham had made an unanswerable indictment. Bryan retorted:[2]

The literary sycophants who strew rhetorical flowers in the pathway of the successful . . . complacently throw the responsibility for failure in life upon God, or Nature, or upon the man himself.

It was Bryan, too, who tied Markham's poem directly to existing American conditions, translated Markham's generalizations into an indictment with specific counts. Some of Bryan's accusations were aimed at conditions already passed or passing; others pointed straight at the heart of conditions that were causing wide-spread discontent. When Bryan asked:

Is it the fault of God or Nature . . . that our tax laws are so made . . . that the poor man pays more than his share and the rich man less?

he was referring to the Supreme Court's invalidation, in 1895, of the attempt to have an income-tax law, an attempt that had to wait for success until 1913.

---

[1] Markham's compensation had been $40.

[2] Bryan's questions are taken from his article in Hearst's New York *Journal*.

But when Bryan asked:

Is it the fault of God or of Nature that children are driven into factories?

THE WAR CHANT

Every time I come to town
The boys keep a-kickin' my dawg aroun.
Makes no diff'rence if he *is* a houn'——
They gotta quit kickin' my dawg aroun'!

Herbert Johnson, in the Philadelphia "North American."

"Common People's" insurgency, after growing for many years, became acute during the Taft administration.

he was referring not only to child labor (then coming to be generally looked upon as deplorable), but, in a broader sense, to the increase of factory life in America, the economic condition what was increasingly taking American families from the farm to the factory — a transition which, in connection with what had previously been the ideal of life in America, was a principal cause of social fretfulness. And when Bryan asked:

Is God or Nature responsible for the . . . trust? Is God or Nature responsible for private monopolies?

he was putting his hand on the name for the particular institution which, in that year, and for fifteen years afterward, was the country's outstanding political issue, regarded as its outstanding social menace.

Indictment of the times was not confined to Markham's poetry or Bryan's exegesis. Men of different temperaments, from a variety of fields, described the condition in phrases no less strong. A message sent to Congress by one of the most solid of conservatives, Grover Cleveland, had asserted that

the gulf between employers and the employed is constantly widening, and classes are rapidly forming, one comprising the very rich and powerful, while in another are found the toiling poor. . . . The communism of combined wealth and capital, the outgrowth of overweening cupidity and selfishness, which insidiously undermine the justice and integrity of free institutions, is not less dangerous than the communism of oppressed poverty and toil, which, exasperated by injustice and discontent, attacks with wild disorder the citadel of rule.

Theodore Roosevelt, shortly before the presidential elections of 1904, in a conversation with a journalist,[1] painted a word-picture not less sombre than Markham's:

Corporation cunning has developed faster than the laws of nation and State. Corporations have found ways to steal long before we have found that they were susceptible of punishment for theft. Sooner or later, unless there is a readjustment, there will come a riotous, wicked, murderous day of atonement.

[1] Lindsay Denison, quoted in the New Haven *Register*, March 4, 1909.

There must come, in the proper growth of this nation, a readjustment. If it is not to come by sword and powder and blood, it must come by peaceful compromise. These fools in Wall Street think that they can go on forever! They can't!

I would like to be elected President of the United States to be the buffer between their foolishness and the wrath that is surely to come — unless they sober up.

Chief Justice Edward G. Ryan, of the Supreme Court of Wisconsin, addressing the University of Wisconsin as early as 1873, had foreseen an arrogance of corporate wealth which came promptly upon his prediction of it, and continued for more than thirty years:

There is looming up a new and dark power. I cannot dwell upon the signs and shocking omens of its advent. The accumulation of individual wealth seems to be greater than it ever has been since the downfall of the Roman Empire. The enterprises of the country are aggregating vast corporate combinations of unexampled capital, boldly marching, not for economic conquests only, but for political power. For the first time really in our politics money is taking the field as an organized power. . . . Already, here at home, one great corporation has trifled with the sovereign power, and insulted the State.[1] There is grave fear that it, and its great rival, have confederated to make partition of the State and share it as spoils. . . . The question will arise, and arise in your day, though perhaps not fully in mine: "Which shall rule — wealth or man; which shall lead — money or intellect; who shall fill public stations — educated and patriotic freemen, or the feudal serfs of corporate capital?"

President Schurman, of Cornell, in his June, 1906, commencement address, painted a picture of the America of the day, no less menacing than Markham's:

[1] This reference in Justice Ryan's speech was to the refusal of the C. M. & St. P. Ry. to obey a law of Wisconsin, in a letter written by the president of the road, Alexander Mitchell, to Governor Taylor, of Wisconsin: "Being fully conscious that the enforcement of this law will ruin the property of the company and feeling assured of the correctness of the opinions of the eminent counsel who have examined the question, the directors feel compelled to disregard the provisions of the law so far as it fixes a tariff of rates for the company, until the courts have finally passed upon the question of its validity."

A conception of organized society in America, visualized by Opper in the New York *Journal* during the McKinley administration.

To get and to have is the motto not only of the market, but of the altar and of the hearth. We are coming to measure man — man with his heart and mind and soul — in terms of mere acquisition and possession. A waning Christianity and a wax-

This cartoon by Herbert Johnson, in the Philadelphia *North American*, pictured "The Common People" being victimized by the power that "predatory wealth" had in politics, as symbolized by "Uncle Joe" Cannon, then Speaker of the House of Representatives. The series of cartoons in which "The Common People" figured as always downtrodden, always "put upon," ran for many years, and were especially trenchant about the time of the Insurgent Progressive Party movements.

ing Mammonism are the twin spectres of our age. The love of money and the reckless pursuit of it are undermining the National character.

The condition that caused those excited utterances and the condition that explained the furore over "The Man

With the Hoe" were one. The year of the publication of Markham's poem, 1899, and the following year, saw the publication of twenty-eight books about "Trusts," and more than 150 magazine articles, in addition to several of the nineteen volumes of the official report of the United States Industrial Commission which had spent many months hearing testimony about monopolies.[1]

"Is God or Nature," Bryan asked, "responsible for the trust ? Is God or Nature responsible for private monopolies ?" By implication, he answered, the trust was wholly man-made. (And to Bryan's way of thinking, wholly evil.) In this Bryan was only partly right. That simple believer that black is all black, and white all white, did not always understand those more complex fields of truth where black shades into white. The complete truth about the rise of the trusts was that some of the responsibility lay in one quarter, some in another. Concretely, the trusts were partly a phase of normal industrial evolution, partly a product of the greed of individual men. To understand the trust, we had best begin with the part industrial evolution had in it.

---

[1] So great was the outpouring that in 1900 there was compiled a "List of Books relating to Trusts (with References to Periodicals)" revised, with additions, in 1902. Among the books were: "The Trusts," W. M. Collier; "The Trust Problem," Jeremiah W. Jenks; "Trusts and Their Relation to Industrial Progress," H. Apthorp; "Trusts and the Public," G. Gunton; "The Mother of Trusts," J. Hardesty; "Trusts," S. C. T. Dodd; "Book of Trusts," H. L. Chaffee; three striking pamphlets, "To What Are the Trusts Leading," by J. B. Smiley, "The Coming Trust," by L. L. Hopkins, and "The Impending Crisis," by B. Bouroff; "Monopolies and the People," C. W. Baker; "Restraint of Trade," W. H. Harper; "Who Rules America," F. A. Adams.

15

FROM OLD TO NEW IN INDUSTRY

From Little One-Man Businesses to Big Corporations.
Fewer Men Answering the Call of Their Own Farm Dinner
Bell; More Obeying the Summons of a Factory Whistle.
A Picture of Old-Time Communities. The Significance of
"Off the Railroad." The Principal One of the Agencies That
Brought About Big Units of Industry in the United States.
An Adjustment of Man to Steam. Cities Growing.

THROUGHOUT America, during the latter half of the
nineteenth century, went on a process of little shops
closing down, big factories growing bigger; little one-man
businesses giving up, great corporations growing and expanding; rural communities becoming stagnant, big cities
pulsing forward; farm districts thinning out, cities growing denser; fewer shop-keepers able to buy where they
would, more compelled to take what a monopoly gave
them, and at a monopoly's price; fewer craftsmen, more
factory operatives; fewer workers known by name to their
employers, more carried on big factory payrolls as numbers identified by brass checks. The process was essentially an adjustment of man to Steam.

As soon as James Watt and others learned to apply the
force inherent in water when heated to steam, it became
probable[1] that individuals of exceptional initiative would

---

[1] I use the word "probable." Nearly everybody takes it for granted that the
economic and social developments following the application of steam to industry
were inevitable. I hesitate to use the conclusive word. Who can say any one turn
that civilization took was "inevitable"? that every other conceivable course was
impossible? (One of the commonest handicaps to clear thinking is acceptance
of the familiar, as if it were divinely ordained, or inevitable in nature.) In the
stage which this development ultimately reached, steam served man greatly,
but in some ways it seemed as if steam also dominated man. It is conceivable
man could have been more indisputably the master.

adapt the new-found power to the making and transport-
ing of man's goods, would organize it, capitalize it, exploit it. Before steam came, the principal agency man
relied upon for the production of goods was his own muscles, supplemented by the muscles of a few animals,

From a photograph by Brown Bros.
A shoemaker of the old-time type.

mainly horses and oxen harnessed to rude treadmills and
wagons, and a limited use of wind and running water. In
that period, manufacture still meant literally, "making by
hand." With the coming of steam, hand-work was at a
disadvantage as respects cost (though not in some other
respects). Industry and manufacture began to pass from

the home and the little shop where a skilled artisan and a few apprentices performed all the operations (from cowhide to finished shoe,[1] for example), to large factories where laborers were assembled in greater numbers with much of their work specialized.[2]

When steam was adapted to transportation, and the

Relic of an old-time business still in use. This sign was hung over George W. Hubbard's hardware store in Flint, Mich., in 1865, and still remains there. In the country about Flint, Mr. Hubbard in 1926 had signs saying: "I sold your grandfather ox yokes in 1865." This shop spanned transportation from oxen to internal combustion engines.

railroads came, the wider markets thereby opened up hastened the movement toward larger units of industry.

[1] Of this change, "Mr. Dooley" wrote: "Th' shoes that Corrigan th' cobbler wanst wurruked on f'r a week hammerin' away like a woodpecker, is now tossed out be th' dozens fr'm th' mouth iv a masheen. A cow goes lowin' softly in to Armours an' comes out glue, beef, gelatine, fertylizer, celooloid, joolry, sofy cushions, hair restorer, soap, lithrachoor and' bed springs so quick that while aft she's still cow, for'ard she may be anything fr'm buttons to Panny-ma hats."

[2] A comparison of the productiveness of the old order of industry with the new, published in 1925 by the American Telephone and Telegraph Company, stated that:

In 1781 One Man Working One Day Produced:	In 1925 One Man Working One Day Produces:
500 lbs. of iron	5,000 lbs. of iron
or 100 ft. of lumber	or 750 ft. of lumber
or 5 lbs. of nails	or 500 lbs. of nails
or ¼ pair of shoes	or 10 pairs of shoes
or ½ ton of coal	or 4 tons of coal
or 20 square feet of paper	or 200,000 square feet of paper

It was to be expected that the individual cobbler and spinner, for example, supplying a village, should be supplanted by a shoe-factory or spinning-mill supplying as large a territory as could be economically served by the new facility for shipping. It was natural, in short, that manufacture should gravitate into larger units.

Courtesy of the United States Bureau of Public Roads.

A relic of transportation as it was before the railroads came. This photograph of the old Lancaster Pike in southeastern Pennsylvania was taken in 1907.

The change was continuous, going on hand in hand with the growth of the railroads. In America, railroad building began with 23 miles in 1830, increased to a total existing mileage of 2818 in 1840, expanded rapidly, was interrupted by the Civil War, was resumed in 1865, and by 1880 had practically covered the then settled portions of the country will a total of 93,671 miles. Later this mileage reached a maximum of 254,251 in 1916; but these additions, as well as part of the earlier mileage, were built mainly to open up unsettled territory in the West and elsewhere. In the newer parts of America, the railroad came first; industrial organization came afterward, and was based on the railroad. What is described in these pages is the older phase, the adjustment of a settled, pre-

Courtesy of the United States Bureau of Public Roads.

Old-time Conestoga wagon that made the trip from Philadelphia to Pittsburgh in twenty days.

existing order to the coming of the railroads as a disruptive invasion.

To many an American community the arrival of two parallel lines of iron brought a change, momentous economically, and often poignant. The country was dotted with towns and "settlements" — this pioneer name for a village persisted in many sections. Their location had been determined by natural advantage, a ford across a river, a stream-site suitable for a mill, or the conjunction of two or more highways; and their size by the limits of pre-existing forms of transportation, each community serving as large a territory as could be conveniently covered by horses or oxen, or relays of them. Such transportation as reached beyond the immediate neighborhood was done at the gently ambling pace of mules harnessed tandem on the tow-paths of a few canals; on shallow steamboats on a few of the deeper rivers; or on rough "turnpikes," on which the "wagoner" [1] with his canvas-covered Conestoga wagon was the transportation king, his sceptre a leather whip long enough to reach two, three or four pairs of horses.

In each community were little industries conducted much as from time immemorial — a dusty flour-mill with huge, crudely fashioned stone grinding discs [2] turned by a creaking water-wheel; a wheelwright shop, perhaps; a chair factory, a pottery, a tinsmithy. There would be, practically always, the ubiquitous blacksmith, usually an imposing, heavily muscled figure in a black visorless cap and leather apron, majestically sure he was a changeless institution in an unchanging world, who varied the routine of shoeing the horses of the countryside with making tools for the farms and households. Often there would be a saddlery and, in some of the larger places, a tannery, the latter, usually situated in the outskirts, in deference

[1] For a poetic picture, read Thomas Buchanan Read's "Wagoner of the Alleghenies," published in 1856. The word "turnpike," abbreviated to the tempo of a more feverish time, survived here and there into the twentieth century, in the name of old streets in a few interior towns—"Pike Street." The inns that were the stations along these old turnpikes were named in a manner reaching back to the time when fewer travellers could read a signboard than could recognize a painting of an animal or of something else familiar—the "Red Lion," the "Black Boar," the "Green Tree," the "Seven Stars," the "Blue Ball," the "Turk's Head," the "Hammer and Trowel." With the coming of the railroads these old hotels passed into desuetude along with the highways upon which they were situated. After 1900, when the automobile caused some of the old pikes, after half a century of decay, to be revived as concrete roads, many of the old inns were revamped and enabled city motorists to grasp an hour of the glamour of America as it used to be, by taking a meal under one of the quaint old signs.

[2] By 1925, these old-time millstones from abandoned grist-mills came to be prized as "antiques," and were used as door-steps for households that now got their flour from Chicago or Minneapolis.

to a sentiment even then becoming critical about elemental smells. In the larger towns would be found a
bakery or two, beginning a slow invasion of the custom,
then almost universal, of home baking.

In that pre-railroad order of industry,[1] the owner of the
plant was also the master workman, employing either his

Courtesy of the United States Bureau of Public Roads.

Pre-railroad transportation. Stage-coach on the national pike at Cumberland, Md.

sons or an apprentice or two. (To one of the latter in
many cases he married his daughter.) He was his own
bookkeeper, posting the day's entries in his crude accounts by candle-light at night; was his own treasurer,
and as a bank used a leather bag attached to his person
by a belt; acted as his own salesman and either waited for
customers to come to his door or drove his own delivery
wagon, making periodic trips as far as his market ex-

[1] A picture of a pre-railroad iron forge in eastern Pennsylvania, and the community around it, is in Joseph Hergesheimer's "The Three Black Pennys."

tended, usually not farther than the distance a horse-drawn vehicle could travel comfortably in a day.

To many such an old-time manufacturer pursuing the leisurely routine of ancient ways, came one day the news that a new and curious form of transportation would come through the country near by, following the valleys and the lower grades, often some distance away from the turnpikes or waterways which were the sites of the older industries. Not at once, but with slow certainty, came realization by many a thriving old community of the portentousness of "off the railroad."[1] Even communities through which the railroads passed felt the disruptive effects of the new form of transportation, some taking an immense new growth, more put at a relative disadvantage, all brought to a new relation to trade.

Presently, to many an old-time local manufacturer came the day when a customer told him that the railroad train had dropped a passsenger who introduced himself as a travelling salesman, or "drummer,"[2] and who offered wares made in great quantities by machinery in distant cities, at prices no local manufacturer could meet.

In the towns left off the railroad, many an old-time individual manufacturer, and the whole community of which he was a part, came to recognize the railroad whistle, heard over the hills a few miles away, as a knell. Stagnation began. Schools and churches ceased to grow. Young men, seeking greater activity and higher pay, said good-by to sisters who stayed to tend the hollyhocks in

---

[1] While this illustration of the transition from small units of industry to large, and of one of the effects of the railroads, is typical, several qualifications should be borne in mind: Often the railroad was laid out to take in existing towns; and before the railroads came there were already, in some industries and in some sections, factories employing considerable numbers of workers.

[2] After "drummers" became an established institution, they took on a conspicuousness befitting the innovation in industry of which they were the herald. Their clothing was of the brightest, their jewelry of the flashiest, their speech of the loudest and most self-confident. They were missionaries not only of the goods they sold, but of new styles, new slang, new jokes, of the whole city spirit.

old-fashioned gardens and became "old maids," whose chief function, at once their diversion and their service, was occasional trips to the city to play the rôle of useful aunts to their brothers' growing families. Retail trade was the first to scent decay and set up new stores at new

Courtesy of the B. & O. Railroad.

A railroad engine of 1851, "The Cumberland Valley Pioneer."

centres on the railroads. The local manufacturer, more deeply rooted by his circumstances, frequently tried to carry on, relying on old loyalties of personal contact with his customers. Occasionally, he was able to hold his own,[1] but never more than that. To grow, to fit into the new order, was the prerogative of the competitor who had the advantage of favorable railroad location and favorable freight rates.

Even among the manufacturers on the railroad, the great majority were in no better fortune than those

The railroad transformed American industry. Modern coal train on the Baltimore and Ohio Railroad.

whom the railroad passed by; a few were destined to expand gigantically, many to become the food the giants fed upon.

The statistical picture of the change from small to large units of industry in America is in the accompanying table.[2] It shows that as late as 1850, a manufacturer of farm implements could have only five employees and yet be as large as the average. He could be an independent manufacturer and as rich as the aver-

[1] As late as 1925 one could still find an occasional old-time factory, protected by possession of an individual process or some other safeguard, doing business at the old stand, "off the railroad."

[2] From "The Trust Problem," Jeremiah Jenks and Walter E. Clark.

age, yet have only two thousand six hundred dollars as his capital. By 1910 it took four hundred thousand dollars to be an average manufacturer of agricultural implements. In 1850 there were 1333 factories making farm implements; by 1910 the number had shrunk to 640 — though the quantity of goods they turned out had grown from a value of six million dollars to one hundred forty-six million dollars:

	1850	1860	1870	1880	1890	1900	1910
FARM IMPLEMENTS							
No. of establishments	1,333	2,116	2,076	1,943	910	715	640
Average capital..........	$2,674	6,553	16,780	31,966	159,686	220,571	400,439
Average number workers..	5	8	12	20	43	65	79
Average value products...	$5,133	9,845	25,080	35,327	89,310	141,549	228,639
COTTON GOODS							
No. of establishments.....	1,094	1,091	956	1,005	905	1,055	1,324
Average capital..........	$68,100	90,362	147,182	218,412	391,183	442,882	621,025
Average number workers..	84	112	142	185	242	287	286
Average value products...	$56,553	106,033	185,659	209,901	296,112	321,517	474,616
IRON AND STEEL							
No. of establishments.....	468	542	726	699	699	668	654
Average capital..........	$46,716	82,283	161,523	294,692	591,085	858,371	2,281,828
Average number workers..	53	65	103	197	250	333	426
Average value products...	$43,650	97,341	274,878	418,583	683,124	1,203,545	2,105,737

In this gradual consolidation of industry into larger units, in the doom of the small local manufacturer[1] and the older order of industry of which he was the unit, the

[1] Some of these old-time businesses, by some miracle of adaptiveness in their owners, managed to adjust themselves and survive. They were few. In 1925, in the entire business world of America there were but eighty-nine businesses that had been in the same family descending from father to son for as much as a hundred years. This little band of heirs of the older order in America gathered into a club called the Centenary Association of America, which had annual dinners in Philadelphia. They composed a gallant group. Not only had their pride resisted the tendency that had wiped out many a family name, such as "Jones's Forge," or "Moore's Mills," replacing them with "Consolidated," or "Amalgamated," or "United." They had also had to survive wars, panics, changes in industry such as the substitution of steam for water-power, and electricity for steam; and changes in custom or style, often devastating to individual industries, such as the blight the automobiles brought to manufacturers of wagons and horse-shoes, the effect of bobbed hair for women on manufacturers of combs and hat-pins, and the effect of another change in women's styles on the manufacture of corsets.

Of the eighty-nine family firms that resisted the consolidations and other muta-

most potent cause was the railroad, and the use made of the railroads by those who controlled them. If the effect of the railroads on industry had been restricted to the necessary consequence of lower cost of railroad transportation compared to older forms, many a small local

This photograph of Henry Ford's first factory is typical of old-time industry.

manufacturer would have been doomed anyhow; but he would have submitted to his extinction as an economic inevitability, as something not to be averted, like the visitation of a storm or some other influence of nature.

tions of American business, the one best known is the DuPont company, founded as manufacturers of powder at Wilmington, Del., in 1802, and in 1927 a leader in many additional lines. Others well known were D. Landreth Seed Company, Bristol, Pa., founded in 1784; Schieffelin and Company, manufacturing chemists, New York City, founded in 1794; Alexander Brown and Sons, bankers, Baltimore, founded in 1800; Colgate and Company, manufacturers of soaps and cosmetics, New York City, founded in 1806; Samuel Kirk and Son Company, jewelers, Baltimore, founded in 1815; Browning, King and Company, New York, founded in 1821; Powers-Weighman-Rosengarten, chemists, Philadelphia, founded in 1823. Some of these family businesses that have shown sustained vitality and resistance to change for more than a hundred years are quite small. One is a country store, Jenkins's, at Gwynedd, Pa.; another is Hager and Brother, at Lancaster, Pa., now called a "department store," but doubtless known as grocers, or "drapers," when founded in 1821.

Without rancor, he might have decided to go himself to
the city, or to unite with another manufacturer, or otherwise to adjust himself as dictated by his years, his temperament, and the other circumstances. Neither he, nor
his neighbors, nor the public generally would have seen
the process as justification for a sense of outrage and
occasion for political protest.

But we cannot think of the railroads as if they came
by nature, like the phenomena of weather. The railroads
were made by men — were conceived and built for gain,
and managed for gain. The planning for gain took in
every possibility that self-interest could envisage. Had
the effort for gain been restricted to the normal profit on
carrying goods and passengers, those who were affected
would have had no justification for resentment. But in
the use made of the railroads by their owners and managers, the legitimate profit on transportation was often a
relatively unimportant motive.[1] The power to fix freight
rates carried opportunities compared to which reasonable
return for services rendered was inconsequential. It
opened the door to schemes and conspiracies. Frequently,

[1] Congressman Henry Allen Cooper, of Wisconsin, having read the proof of this
chapter, calls my attention to a message sent by Governor William H. Seward, of
New York, to the Legislature, as early as 1842, when there were only 2000 miles
of railroads in the entire country. Governor Seward foresaw the evils that would
come in the train of unrestricted and unregulated railroad building and operation,
and he believed they could be obviated. "It is not obvious why," he asserted,
"a system of supervision of railroads could not be adopted." He admitted
that such a course would "increase central influence"; nevertheless, he said,
"it is not clear that the influence of corporations would be more harmless." His
message concluded with this wise and statesmanlike suggestion: "I respectfully
recommend that all such improvements [further railroad construction] be henceforth regarded rather as parts of the general system of interior communications,
designed to promote the general welfare, than as mere investments for gain;
that a careful supervision of all such roads be established to ascertain the accommodations afforded to the public, the fares received, and profits realized; and that
the right of resumption [the taking over of the railroad by the State] stipulated
in charters, shall be as hitherto carefully preserved." Due to the political power
of the railroad owners and managers, it was forty-five years before regulation
became a national policy through the passage of the Interstate Commerce Act
in 1887; and sixty-four years before the policy was made fully effective by the
passage of the Hepburn Rate bill during Roosevelt's administration in 1906.

there was common ownership[1] of the railroads and of some industries, or community of interest between them. In such cases railroad rates were fixed to give advantage to the favored industry and to handicap its rivals. Often, low rates were given to the favored industry, and high rates imposed on its competitor, with the deliberate, specific purpose of driving the victim out of business, or compelling him to sell out to the favored rival. Sometimes the motive of the railroad managers for making low rates was competition of railroad against railroad. In such cases, all the manufacturers had the rôle of pawns, sometimes elevated to temporary advantage, sometimes de-

Reece's Mills in Ohio, built in the early years of the nineteenth century. A good type of the old-time "off-the-railroad" industry.

stroyed. Occasionally there was competition of community against community, with the railroad manager giving the advantage of low freight rates to the community with which his personal interest was identified, and fatally high ones to the rival.

[1] The coal lands in eastern Pennsylvania were owned by the same interests as the coal-carrying railroads, and each was made to serve the other.

The power to fix freight rates was the power of life and death over industries, and often over whole communities. The individuals possessing that power were unrestrained (there was no Interstate Commerce Com-

Akron, Ohio, a city whose phenomenal growth was made possible by the revolution in industry and transportation brought by the railroad. The upper photograph shows the city as it was in 1865, when much of its commerce was carried in canal-boats. The lower view is of a busy Akron street in 1925.

mission or other regulation until 1887, and no effective regulation until 1906), and they used it ruthlessly.

It was not merely that they destroyed individual businesses and bankrupted individual business men; by their arbitrary exercise of uncurbed power, bodies of workmen were forced out of employment, families dislocated, whole communities laid prostrate and disrupted.[1] The average man came to think of the power of the railroads as a malevolent influence manipulated secretly by persons distant and mysterious. He came to think of the railroad as having a more essential power over his happiness than the government, and to feel that the equality guaranteed to him by the Constitution was a small thing, if he had not equality before the railroads.

There were other agencies in the transition from small to large units of business. The same improvements in the use of steam that made larger locomotives possible, made larger stationary engines possible, and therefore a greater concentration of industry. Of this and other agencies the present chapter takes no account; it deals wholly with the part the railroads had. That was the largest cause. "No one thing," said the Interstate Commerce Commission,[2] "does so much to force out the small operator, and to build up those trusts and monopolies against which law and public opinion alike beat in vain, as discrimination in freight rates."

One "reflex of the prevalent railway methods," wrote Gilbert Holland Montague,[3] was the oil business in its early phase."

---

[1] Several novels of the early 1900's dealt with the effect of railroad discrimination, and trusts, on communities and individuals; among them "The Octopus" and "The Pit," by Frank Norris; "Calumet K," by Samuel Merwin and Henry Kitchell Webster, and "Coniston," by Winston Churchill.

[2] In their report to Congress, January 9, 1899.

[3] "The Rise and Progress of the Standard Oil Company," 1904. The statement quoted was based on the report of the Hepburn Committee appointed by the New York Legislature in 1879 to investigate railroad abuses.

16

OIL

The History, Brief in Years but Very Crowded, of Man's
Contact with It. From a Detested Nuisance to an Immense
Benefaction. From the Status of a Patent Medicine to That
of the Country's Sixth Industry. John D. Rockefeller Makes
His Start — and Grows Fast. The South Improvement
Company. The Ingenious Device of a Pennsylvania Lawyer
Named Dodd. He Takes a Word out of the Bible and an
Institution out of the Law, and Puts Both into the Service
of Big Business — to the Great Scandal of Courts, Clergy-
men, Legislatures, the Press, and Little Business.

NEARLY all the varieties of attempts to achieve monopoly
in the modern sense are illustrated, many in the extreme
degree, in the career of one American industry, oil. Men
still living in 1927 had witnessed the whole history of that
industry, from its birth just before the Civil War to its
position in 1927. As this is written there still lived the
man who, watching the industry's spectacular beginning,
had dreamed its useful developments and participated in
them; had devised or shared in some of its practices that
the courts called iniquitous; had come to dominate it and
to be known throughout the world as the symbol of it;
had become, through it, the richest individual of all time.[1]

[1] And also, let it be said, the most generous donor of useful gifts to humanity,
in the shape of endowments for education and health. The money amassed by
John D. Rockefeller has been more wisely used, for the benefit of man, than any
other large amount of money ever brought together. Rockefeller spent a smaller
percentage of his money on nimself than probably any other man of his generation,
rich or poor. (To speak of Rockefeller's "generation" is inexact; he lived
through three.) He never bought any of the usual luxuries with which men commonly mark their acquisition of wealth. He never had a yacht, nor a "stable"—
in the eighties and nineties race-horses were one of a rich man's earliest ostenta-
tions; nor a box at the opera, nor a house on Fifth Avenue—that was another

270

It is as though the entire story of man's age-long contact with an element, such as iron, or even fire, were compressed within the lifetime of one generation — actually,
that epic can be read, by analogy, in the history of oil
between the years 1850 and 1925.

Man first regarded oil as a nuisance, as worse than a

In the early 1850's, oil had one commercial use—as a patent medicine. This is a
facsimile photograph of a label used by S. M. Kier in advertising "rock oil."

nuisance, a pest. He was annoyed by it, probably almost
to the same degree as were his primitive forebears by early
manifestations of fire, conflagrations started by lightning
sweeping over forests and plains. Oil, seeping out of the
rocks, flowed over the surfaces of brooks, making the
water unfit for the cattle to drink. Carried on to the
grazing lands by streams in flood, it ruined them — hardly
a weed could grow on soil defiled by "rock oil."

Man's first taking hold of it was as an accessory of
chicanery. He imputed to it a magic, impressed his fellows with it to his own profit, just as perhaps did the

favored feather of wealth; nor a private art gallery; nor did he ever speculate in
stocks or gamble in the casinos of Palm Beach or Monte Carlo. He never maintained more than one residence until in his old age he felt justified need for
seasonal change of climate. The enormous wealth Rockefeller brought together
went to two destinations, both beneficent to man: re-investment in industry, and
organized philanthropy.

first man bold enough to subject fire to his control. Samuel M. Kier and others skimmed oil from the surface of streams in Northwestern Pennsylvania or soaked it up with woollen blankets. They changed the common local name of "rock oil" to "Seneca Oil," thereby adding the mysterious virtue supposed to reside in Indian medicines to the other virtue supposed, with no greater relevancy, to attach to the evil smell of the substance. As the "great American medicine" of the 1840's, it was put up in eight-ounce bottles, wrapped in gaudy circulars which recited miraculous — though anonymous — cures of "cholera morbus, liver complaint, bronchitis and consumption," and was peddled the length and breadth of the then settled portions of the country; sold, as were the other "Indian medicines," as "good for man or beast, for the lungs, liver, and lights."[1]

[1] The word "lights" in my manuscript is queried by my assistant, William E. Shea, who, though old enough to have graduated from Harvard College in 1914, was still too remote from the era of the itinerant "Indian doctor" ever to have heard one of that gentry sonorously roll out this listing of the human anatomy from a stand on a village street or at a county fair. "Lights" is safely within the covers of the dictionary, though in recent editions it has been demeaned by the qualifications "now obsolete, vulgar, as used of a human being." "Lights" really means lungs—"so called from their lightness," says Webster's. It has not entirely gone out of use, I imagine, and is probably still a familiar term in some of the less changeable parts of the country. As late as the early 1900's, it was used by Alice Hegan Rice in her novel "Mrs. Wiggs of the Cabbage Patch," one of the characters in which described a sign of the approaching demise of the family horse by saying, "His lights has riz."

Some of the Indian doctors (most of whom were white men—use of the word "Indian" was an early instance of therapeutic psychology) must have said "Lights, liver, and guts." But my memory is clear about the "Kickapoo Indian doctor" who came through Pennsylvania in the early 1880's—for weeks after he had gone the youth of the vicinage declaimed his alluring slogan with delight. He, having the soul of an artist, accepted the disadvantage of duplicating the name of one organ for the sake of the alliteration, rolled out in a thrilling crescendo, at once staccato and andante, "the lungs! the liver!! the lights!!!" Gilbert Holland Montague tells me that the "Kickapoo Indian doctor" he heard in Massachusetts in the 80's did not pretend to use petroleum—indeed, claimed a virtue for not using it. As Mr. Montague recalls, this "Indian doctor's" ballyhoo included a cry that "We don't dig down to the bowels of the earth; we use nature's own remedy, herbs! leaves!! barks!!!" Mr. Montague also suggests, as a whimsical fact if correct, that the street flares burned by the "Indian doctors" to light their booths were one of the earliest uses of gasoline.

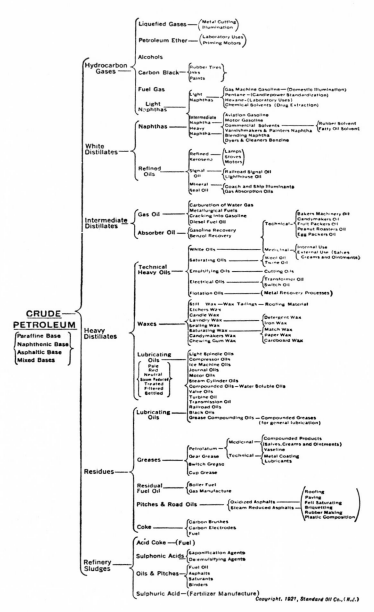

By 1927 oil had more than two hundred commercial uses. The more important ones are mentioned in this compilation made by the Standard Oil Company of New Jersey.

273

That, as late as the 1840's, was substantially all the use man knew how to make of a substance which by 1925 was to enable him to move about on the surface of the earth at more than fifty miles an hour; to go above the clouds and beneath the waters and direct his movements there at will; to cross the Atlantic ocean either through the air above, or in a submarine; which was to drive twenty million automobiles, thousands of railroad

From "The History of the Standard Oil Company," by Ida M. Tarbell. Courtesy of the author.

Crude tank cars of 1863.

engines, and hundreds of ships. By 1925 the raw material of the leering little patent-medicine business of 1840 was to be the sixth of the country's industries and indispensable to the first, the automobile business; was to be the basis of an industry which, in the aggregate, expressed as the total value of oil and its products in 1925, was more than two billions of dollars. Who can overstate the romance of its beginnings, a gift of nature urging itself upon the world, pressing out of cracks in rocks, clamoring for the attention of man — who responded by cursing it as a nuisance! Who can exaggerate the drama of its growth, which is the story of what man did about a great new natural resource, of how he refined it, adapted it, and how he arranged the division of it among those who could use it or had need of it!

II

Individuals here and there, men of exceptional initiative, used rock oil to soften leather or quiet the squeak of wooden axles. A few others made torches of it. In 1854 a graduate of Dartmouth College, George H. Bissell, leased some land from which rock oil was seeping, sent a specimen to Professor Silliman, of Yale, for analysis, and was informed: "You have a raw material from which by simple and not expensive process [you] may manufacture very valuable products."

The following year, 1855, a young farmer boy whose

Roby Frank, cabinet maker, bds 17 Johnson
ROBY E. W. & CO. (Edward W. Roby and William H. Keith), wood and coal, C. & P. R. R. Coal Pier, and Merwin n Columbus St. Bridge
Rochert Conrad, h 175 St Clair.
Rock John, bar keeper. bds 11 Public Square
ROCKAFELLOW JOHN J., coal, C. & P. R. R. Coal Pier, h 183 Prospect
Rockefeller John D., book-keeper, h 35 Cedar
Rockefeller William, physician, h 35 Cedar av
Rockett Morris, rectifier, h 182 St Clair
Rockwell Edward, Sec. C. & P. R. R., bds Weddell House

From "The History of the Standard Oil Company," by Ida M. Tarbell. Courtesy of the author.

John D. Rockefeller in the rôle in which he appeared in the Cleveland city directory in the 1850's.

family had shortly before moved from New York State began work as a bookkeeper in Cleveland. Out of his $25 a month he saved enough to become partner in a produce commission firm; out of that he saved enough to be able, in 1862, when he was twenty-three years old, to invest, with his partner and a daring young mechanical engineer, $4,000 in a business that people were beginning to speak of as "oil-refining." There, with his bookkeeper training, with his instinct for system that made him probably the first man in America deserving to be called an expert accountant, with his repugnance to gambling and his habit of orderly ways that expressed itself in regularly conducting a Sunday-school class, with his prudent, frugal temperament — he now found himself engaged in the least organized and most chaotic industry in the world, for which the only precedent — and that an inadequate one — was the California gold rush of thirteen years before; an industry characterized by a lack of orderliness which to Rockefeller's mind was akin to lack of Godliness; a prince-to-day-and-pauper-to-morrow industry, for which the popular personification was a character known as "Coal-Oil Johnny," familiar for a generation as the symbol of splurging wealth alternating with utter poverty; an industry in which chance was the largest element, in which calamity was forever just around the corner and did not always keep itself there; an industry whose susceptibility to fire seemed symbolic of its fundamental characteristics — "When the fire-bell rang," said Rockefeller, "we would all rush to the refinery and help put it out, and while the blaze was still burning, I would have my pencil out,

WM. ROCKEFELLER & CO.—The co-partnership heretofore existing between Wm Rockefeller, John D Rockefeller and Samuel Andrews, under the firm name of Wm Rockefeller & Co., is this day dissolved by mutual consent, having sold our entire interest in the Refining business to Messrs Rockefeller, Andrews & Flagler.
Cleveland, February 28, 1867.

THE UNDERSIGNED DO HEREBY certify that they have form d a special partnership under the act of the General Assembly of the State of Ohio, entitled "an act to authorize and regulate limited partnerships," passed January 24th, 1846; that said partnership is to be conducted, and its business done under the name of Rockefeller, Andrews & Flagler; that Stephen V. Harkness, of East Cleveland, in the County of Cuyahoga, and State of Ohio, is the special partner, and has contributed seventy thousand ($70,000) dollars in money as capital to the stock of said partnership, and that John D. Rockefeller, Henry M Flagler and Samuel Andrews, of Cleveland, in the County of Cuyahoga and State of Ohio, and Wm. Rockefeller, of the city, county and State of New York, are the general partners; that the business to be transacted is the manufacture of and dealing in crude Petroleum and its products; That the principal place of Business of said firm is to be at the said city of Cleveland and that said partnership is to commence on the twenty-eighth day of February, 1867, and terminate on the first day of March, 1872.

JOHN D. ROCKEFELLER, [L S]
WILLIAM ROCKEFELLER, [L. S.]
SAMUeL ANDREWS, [L. S.]
HENRY M. FLAGLER, [L, S.]
STEPHEN V. HARKNESS. [L S]
CLEVELAND, February 28, 1867.

State of Ohio, } ss
County of Cuyahoga. }
Before me George Hester, a Justice of the Peace, appeared John D. Rockefeller, William Rockefeller, Samuel Andrews, Henry M. Flagler, and Stephen V. Harkness, who acknowledged the signing and sealing the foregoing instrument to be their own free act and deed.
In witness I have hereunto subscribed my name this 28th day of February, A D 1867.
GEORGE HESTER,
Justice of the Peace.

feb 0 406

Partnership notices about Rockefeller's first firm, published in Cleveland newspapers in 1867.

ways keep itself there; an industry whose susceptibility to fire seemed symbolic of its fundamental characteristics — "When the fire-bell rang," said Rockefeller, "we would all rush to the refinery and help put it out, and while the blaze was still burning, I would have my pencil out, making plans for rebuilding"; an industry half at the economic mercy of wells that ran dry with a suddenness whimsical and disastrous, and half at the mercy of new wells and new fields; an industry in which, in 1859, the raw material, crude oil, sold at $20 a barrel, and in 1861 at fifty-two cents. To every fundamental trait in Rockefeller's character, the instability was abhorrent.

But while he had a strong distaste for mere chance such as the gambling nature of many of the other oil men loved for its own sake, while he had extreme aversion to being at the mercy of circumstances, at the same time his nature rose and expanded to the prospect of adventure of a different kind, had marked boldness for enterprise when it was predicated on careful thinking by himself and plans thoroughly prepared. With his intellectual sure-footedness he had studied the industry carefully, had not entered it until he had acquired confidence that in time it would be world-wide, would be carried on on a big scale, would ultimately be like steel or copper. Once in it, he brought to his own unit (Rockefeller, Andrews, and Clark) his qualities of careful planning, system, order, his instinct for economies, and also a high degree of intent devotion. The day he married, he celebrated in his refinery, with a dinner to the twenty-six employees, after which, on departing, he called the foreman aside and directed him: "Keep them all at work. Keep them all busy. But don't ask anybody to do anything for nothing." Rockefeller's sister, Mrs. William C. Rudd, of Cleveland, recalled in 1917:

I remember well when John went into the oil business. He was full of it. Not that there was any excitement about him, but he seemed to be always thinking about it. He was always making plans for extending the business, plans for the future. He and Will [William G. Rockefeller] slept together. I've heard them tell sometimes at breakfast that in the middle of the night John would nudge Will in the ribs and wake him up and say: "I've been thinking of a plan. Now, what do you think of this scheme?"

But before he could go on Will would say: "Oh, let me be!
Keep your schemes till morning. I want to sleep!"

John's partners, Maurice Clark and Samuel Andrews, used
to call for him mornings on the way to business. They did not
seem to want to go without him. They would come up to the
side door of the house, and walk in and visit in the dining-room

From "The History of the Standard Oil Company," by Ida M. Tarbell.

The offices of Rockefeller & Andrews in Cleveland, in 1865.

while John was at breakfast, and then they would walk to the
office together.

They were talking oil all the time. It was all foreign to me,
and I got sick of it and wished morning after morning that they
would talk of something else; but they didn't seem to care for
anything else. Breakfast was at half-past six. Father used to
tell the boys: "If you want your business to succeed, be there
early and start it yourself." So they were always at the office
or the refinery by seven in the morning.

By January, 1870, Rockefeller was the leading figure
in the Cleveland oil trade, doing, with his partners, about
a fifth of all the business. In that month, he and his

brother William, with some associates, organized the Standard Oil Company,[1] consisting of two refineries at Cleveland and a selling agency at New York. The capital was $1,000,000, divided into 10,000 shares at $100 each. The original stockholdings were:

John D. Rockefeller............................2667 shares
Henry M. Flagler...............................1333
Samuel Andrews.................................1333
William Rockefeller............................1333
S. D. Harkness.................................1334
O. B. Jennings.................................1000
The firm of Rockefeller, Andrews and Flagler.....1000

Rockefeller had done well in his own unit of the oil industry, but deplored the state of the industry as a whole, its ups and downs, its waste, the recurrent periods of opulence and distress, the overproduction alternating with underproduction, the violent fluctuations in price. Much of this Rockefeller attributed to the competition the oil men practised against each other, the throat-cutting competition of virile, rather reckless men struggling for advantage in a new and not yet organized industry.

Rockefeller abhorred competition, not only abhorred it in the industry in which he was engaged, but abhorred it as a principle of business. In a private conversation during his later years, he once spoke of the old-time competition as entailing "idiotic, senseless destruction," and explained:

Competition had existed for generations. In all lines of industry, history had repeated itself over and over, in cycles

---

[1] Less than four months before Rockefeller organized the Standard Oil Company, he went to New York with a letter dated September 20, 1869, written by the president of the Commercial National Bank of Cleveland, introducing Rockefeller and his associates to Henry F. Vail, of the National Bank of Commerce, and commending them as being very able and having the highest credit. The New York bank declined to accept their account, feeling that no conservative bank should handle the account of anybody engaged in a business which the bank regarded as wild-cat gambling. The Rockefeller family and their associates came in time to be the dominant shareholders in some of the greatest New York banks.

every ten or twelve years. Excessive production, followed by loss with failure and bankruptcy to the weaker concerns. The strong ones, the survivors, finding themselves in control of the trade, remembering the losses they had suffered, took advantage of the opportunity to recoup themselves by charging higher prices, and also picked up the wrecks along the shore, buying out the ruined competitors. For a while, business was good and profitable. Presently, outsiders, seeing the prosperity, set up new competition, and once more the experience was repeated, with consequent loss and bankruptcy.

From " The History of the Standard Oil Company," by Ida M. Tarbell.

William Smith, who drilled the first oil-well for Colonel Drake, in 1850.

The competition thus described by Rockefeller, from his point of view, was the universal order in industry. No one conceived any other. Economists regarded it as the underlying principle of trade; business men accepted it as that. When Rockefeller proposed an alternative system to a Cleveland business man, the latter said, in conservative puzzlement: "It looks all right on paper, but it's too 'scope-y.'" Rockefeller called his plan "co-operation and conservation"; a variation of it practised later in Germany was called the "cartel" system; by 1927 it came to be advocated by many American business leaders as "stabilization." At all times opponents of the idea and believers in competition called it monopoly, or the equivalent of monopoly.

Rockefeller's wish was to bring all the units of the industry into a group under one leadership, to eliminate less economical plants, to use combined strength for bringing about improvements and economies, to curtail production and hold oil off the market when there was over-supply, and to stabilize prices. His frank and sincere purpose was, in short, to end competition, to end the free working of the law of supply and demand, and to substitute for it an artificial control. His ideal took forms of varying rigidity from time to time, and the methods he practised in pursuit of it led to a resistance and outcry which, during more than fifty years, consumed more of the time of legislatures and courts, and more of the space of newspapers, than any other controversy in American business. Rockefeller talked of his idea with associates and competing refiners, but took no definite step toward carrying it out until, in 1871, he was given the opportunity to introduce "co-operation and conservation" into the oil industry through the initiative of some promoters who proposed to him a device which they called the South Improvement Company.

As to who devised this scheme, and who was the prime mover in attempting to put it into operation, there is controversy. The enterprise quickly received a kind of fame that caused its sponsors to have no great eagerness to make their authorship easy for future historians to identify. Several histories of the Standard Oil Company, written when popular indignation against Rockefeller was vehement, impute to him both leadership in formulating the plans of the South Improvement Company and tenacity in adhering to it after most of the other organizers had run to cover. That Rockefeller participated in the South Improvement Company in an important way is clear; of the company's two thousand shares, nine hundred were owned by him and men associated with him in the Standard Oil Company, his brother William, Henry M. Flagler, Oliver H. Payne, and J. A. Bostwick. This, however, may readily be the measure of the primacy Rockefeller and his associates had in the oil business as a whole, rather than evidence of their primacy in initiating the South Improvement Company. Persons having first-hand knowledge told the writer in 1927 that Rockefeller had nothing to do with inventing or chartering the South Improvement Company; that the idea was brought to him by men so important in the oil

From "*The History of the Standard Oil Company,*" *by Ida M. Tarbell.*

The house in which Mr. Rockefeller was born, July 8, 1839. Built by his father, Mr. William Avery Rockefeller, in 1835, at Harford Mills, Cortland County, New York.

business and the railroad business that it would be imprudent for him to stay out; that he entered more than half reluctantly, because he expected it to fail; and that his chief motive in participating in the company at all was to maintain a relation with the other refiners which would make them hospitable to co-operating with him in later plans for a different kind of combination, if the South Improvement Company should fail. There is ignominy enough for all, without placing all the odium on one pair of shoulders.

The South Improvement Company is classic. The contract between it and the oil-carrying railroads is the

fundamental document in the history of big business as a
political issue in the United States. It contains several
of the characteristic devices by which monopoly is attempted, and the most flagrant form of them. It illustrates the practices which made attempts at monopoly
odious; and, when exposed, became the starting-point of
anti-trust and anti-"big business" as political issues.

The South Improvement Company contract stipulated:

> That the party of the second part [the Pennsylvania Rail-
> road [1]] will pay and allow to the party of the first part [the
> South Improvement Company] . . . *rebates*.[2]

The amount of the rebates, varying according to point
of shipment, and ranging between 25 and 50 per cent,
was set forth in an intricate schedule in the contract.

III

At this point, it is desirable to be technical for a few
paragraphs, in order to explain what rebates were, for
that device was the heart of the secret iniquities of the
railroads and favored corporations, and the word was
familiar in political, legal, and economic controversies
until about 1906. "Rebate," in the South Improvement
Company contract — and this was the universal use of
the word — meant that the railroads would charge the
South Improvement Company the same freight rate as
other shippers of oil — *and would then secretly return to
the South Improvement Company a portion of the freight
charge it had paid*. The advantage to the favored company, the heart-breaking handicap to its competitors, is
obvious. It is equally obvious that rebates came about,
usually, upon the initiative of the beneficiary of them, the

---

[1] The Erie and the New York Central signed the same form of contract.
[2] The italics are the author's.

shipper or corporation that was favored by them. Corporations powerful enough to bully the railroads almost invariably exacted rebates. Bullying sometimes alternated with a softer means of persuasion. Gifts of corporation stock were made to railroad officials, who were

From "The History of the Standard Oil Company," by Ida M. Tarbell.

John D. Rockefeller's home in Cleveland, Ohio.

thereby provided with a motive for favoring the donor, crucifying the rival shipper, and cheating the railroad the officials were paid to serve. Occasionally there was common ownership of the railroad and the favored corporation, or community of interest between them. Sometimes the railroad manager initiated the proposal to grant a rebate to a large shipper, with the purpose, defended as legitimate, of keeping the business from a rival road, or of "evening" the traffic, as the phrase was, avoiding extreme alternations of heavy traffic and light; sometimes also, the railroad manager granted rebates to the big, as against the little, on the principle that, in selling railroad service, as in selling ordinary commodities, the buyer of large lots was entitled to a lower price.

That rebates tended to enlarge the already big, and handicap or destroy the little, is obvious. As a Senate investigating committee put it in 1865:

The effect of the prevailing policy of railroad management is, by an elaborate system of secret special rates, rebates, drawbacks, and concessions, to foster monopoly, to enrich favorite shippers, to prevent free competition in many lines of trade.

That point of view, at the time it was uttered, in 1865, was just beginning to be heard. Even where the consequence of rebates was realized, there was comparatively little thought that anything could be done about it. In law, and as yet in public opinion, a railroad was private property and its operation private business, little different from a tailor-shop or a farm. With that conception of the railroad went general assent to the right of the manager or owner to make one rate to one shipper and a different rate to another. The purpose of keeping rebates secret was not fear of the law, for there was no law about it; the purpose was merely to avoid recrimination from the unfavored shippers. The business ethics of the time looked upon rebates as part of the game. If your competitor were powerful enough to exact rebates, or if there were a common financial interest between your competitor and the railroad manager, or if your competitor were a relative of a railroad official, or if, for whatever reason, he was able to get rebates, your feeling was merely that you were "out of luck"; some later turn of the wheel, you hoped, might make you the favored one, your competitor the victim.[1] "Pull" and "has a pull" were expressions com-

[1] This was the prevailing attitude. It should be said, however, that a not inconsiderable minority of business men, chiefly those whose standards of business conduct were modelled on the older pattern, and who had not become inoculated with

mon at the time, characteristic of the current philosophy; used to connote pride in those having an intimate relation to sources of advantage, and to connote explanation and excuse — and envy — by losers in competition.

In this state of business ethics of the time lies the chief justification of Rockefeller and his associates in the South Improvement Company. They were able to say, with reasonable truth, "everybody's doing it who has the chance to do it." In later life, Rockefeller, when discussing in retrospect his experiences as a refiner, frequently told, as illustrative of the current attitude of business men toward rebates, the story of an old Boston merchant who said: "I am opposed on principle to the whole system of rebates and drawbacks — without I am in it."

Rockefeller and his associates were neither better nor worse than most of their contemporaries, though with their intelligence and forcefulness they carried the devices of railroad discrimination to a perfection not before attained. As it was put by an early discussion[1] of the South Improvement Company:

They [the Rockefellers and their associates] found a system of secret rebates and discriminations in flourishing existence. Should they become participants of [them], or become the victims of them? . . . They naturally chose the second alternative. They employed the ready-made system, and made their competitors the victims. It was because they adapted themselves skilfully to the system that they became masters.

Which is a quite sincere definition of the business ethics of the time:

> The good old rule, the simple plan,
> That they shall take who have the power,
> And they shall keep who can.

the virus of expansion at any price that had come into trade, looked upon rebates as vicious, immoral, and subversive, and resolutely refrained, at whatever cost to themselves, from asking for or accepting them.

[1] J. M. Bonham, in "Railway Secrecy and Trusts," 1890.

IV

Had the South Improvement Company contract contained no more meretricious clause than the one granting rebates, it would not have been novel in 1872, nor have become classic by 1925. But the contract went far beyond. It read:

. . . and on all oil transported for others, *drawbacks*.

"Drawbacks" meant that on oil shipped by a competitor of the South Improvement Company, the regular freight rate would be charged, *and that thereafter the railroad would give to the South Improvement Company* a percentage, ranging from a *fourth to a half of what the competitor had paid*.

Readers who happen to be business men will understand that sentence at a glance; others may require a moment of reflection to take it in.

Then, in order, one assumes, to enable the South Improvement Company to make certain of its kill and to give the company further weapons against its competitors, the contract exacted that the railroad should "send daily to the office of the South Improvement Company" duplicates of the way-bills of shipments made by its competitors. Finally, lest anything should have been omitted, the railroad agreed that it would

at all times co-operate . . . to maintain the business of . . . [the South Improvement Company] against loss or injury by competition . . . and to that end shall *lower* or *raise* the gross *rates* of transportation . . . *for such times and to such extent as may be necessary to overcome such competition*.

In trying to make those passages clear one is conscious not only of the ordinary difficulty of making technical phrases of business and law understandable, but also of the difficulty of convincing the reader, after he has understood the passages, that any such thing ever really happened; that such a perfect mechanism for the strangulation of business competitors could have been put in effect; that such cold-blooded business murder could have been conceived and practised as late as 1872.

John D. Rockefeller in 1872.

However, the South Improvement Company contract, once understood, speaks for itself, eloquently. To paint that lily would be a waste of good soot.[1]

Organization of the South Improvement Company was completed January 2, 1872. On the day before, the Standard Oil Company increased its capital stock by $1,000,000, a doubling from the original $1,000,000 to $2,000,000. Obviously a preparation for swallowing something.

With the South Improvement Company device ready for operation, Rockefeller and his associates approached the owners of the twenty-six independent refineries in

---

[1] In 1926 the writer made inquiry of appropriate sources whether Mr. Rockefeller had ever made any reply to Miss Ida M. Tarbell's "History of the Standard Oil Company" (in which some of the facts here recited were set out in detail), and was referred to "The Rise and Progress of the Standard Oil Company," by Gilbert Holland Montague. Montague's book is not a defense, and does not purport to be. It tells the history from a different point of view, but it does not negative any important charge made by Miss Tarbell, or by her predecessor, Henry D. Lloyd, author of "Wealth Against Commonwealth." Montague elaborates and emphasizes the point, that railroad rebates were common and were often initiated by the railroads. In his allocation of blame between the railroads and the Standard Company, between the briber and the bribed, whichever was which, Montague bears with slightly greater weight on the railroads. But as to the South Improvement Company contract, Montague says: "The [South Improvement] Company has never since had an apologist."

Cleveland. What words he and his associates said to the independents is nowhere on record as of the time they were uttered. They are the basis of the earliest charges made against the Standard Oil Company, and, as such,

The Rockefellers, father and son, John D. and John D., Jr., in 1923.

are the subject of an enormous controversial literature, legal and lay. All the records of what was said are as it was recalled later — by the independents in a Congressional investigation and in lawsuits, by Rockefeller in investigations and in conversations years later. Comparison of the versions reveals that the differences are slight, the position of a clause, a more emphatic word, or one version putting into words what in the other version was a mere implication. In the versions given by the independents there is always a tinge of threat, compulsion on the part of Rockefeller and his associates; in Rockefeller's memory, the offers he made are pictured as generous undertakings to take over competitors facing ruin. In any event, twenty-one of the twenty-six independent refiners in Cleveland sold out to the Standard Oil Company.

The threat, the independents felt, hardly needed to be put in words. It was inherent in the situation that Rockefeller and his associates had brought about. The South Improvement Company's preferential contracts with the railroads were about to go into effect, the independents were not in the South Improvement Company; the Standard Oil Company was, and, as the biggest unit in it and in the oil business, would have the independents at its mercy.

As to the material substance of Rockefeller's proposal, the independents and he agree. The Standard Oil Company would buy out the independents at valuations to be fixed by two appraisers, one representing the independent and the other the Standard Oil Company. A valuation, even thus arrived at, would be far below the independent's investment and probably below the capitalization on its earnings over a period of years, for the negotiations took place at a time when the oil business was depressed and when the independents faced ruin through the South Improvement Company. Rockefeller's offer in each case was to pay either in cash or in stock of the Standard Oil Company, with the seller having the election to say which he would take. This detail of the offer was stressed by Rockefeller in his conversations in later years. He said that the sellers who took Standard Oil stock — as Rockefeller always urged they should — and held on to it — this, too, Rockefeller always urged strongly — ultimately

had many times their own most extravagant valuations
of their plants. For those who did not take stock but
preferred cash, Rockefeller had a manner of sad regret,
tinctured just a little with resentment, regarding them as
self-made victims of their own lack of faith in his company. It was these, Rockefeller said, who later raised
much of the outcry against him — they saw the Standard
Oil stock increase to undreamed values; with it they saw
the plants they had sold, now under Standard Oil ownership, go to values higher than they would have put upon
them. They thought of the plants in terms of the later
valuation, and thought of themselves as having been
gouged. As Rockefeller saw it, they were blaming him
for their own lack of faith.

Among others who described the spirit of Rockefeller's
offer to the independents was his brother Frank, who was
on bad terms with him. Frank Rockefeller told a Congressional investigating committee that the independents

were told that if they didn't sell their property to them [the
Standard Oil Company] it would be valueless, that there was a
combination of railroad and oil men, that they would buy all
they could, [but] that all they didn't buy would be valueless —
because they [the independent refiners] would be unable to
compete. . . . They [the officers of the Standard Oil Com-
pany] made no bones about it at all. They said "if you don't
sell your property to us it will be valueless, because we have
got advantages with the railroads." I have heard Rockefeller
and Flagler say so.

John D. Rockefeller's version of the negotiations pictured his action as one of unique generosity. As he once
put it in a private conversation:

Every refiner in the country was invited to become a member
of the Standard Oil Company, and to participate in every benefit which this most aggressive competitor could secure. That
had never happened before in the old system of competitive
struggle. The weakest competitors were contemplating step-
ping down and out; it was only a question of days or weeks;

they well knew their obligations at the banks could not be met. Their anxiety was very great. The Standard Company turned to them with confidence and said: "We will take your burdens, we will utilize your ability, we will give you representation; we will all unite together and build a substantial structure on the basis of co-operation."

Rockefeller, throughout his long life, at times when he was the most criticized man in the world, and his company the most subpœnaed, never thought of himself as having done wrong to any man; always thought of his critics among the general public as excusable because they were uninformed or misinformed; and of his enemies in the oil business as inspired by envy. Much of the criticism, he said,

came from those who having been offered their choice to take cash or stock in our company for their business, had not faith enough to take stock. They took the cash; when the stock became many times increased in value, they blamed us for their own bad choice. They had no spirit for the adventure.

This man, the subject of discussion and speculation to an extent hardly equalled in his generation,[1] can be understood by interpreting him in the spirit of the strain of New England religion he had through his mother. His mind was impregnated with the old doctrine of "election." To his competitors he gave the opportunity to be saved — they could elect to take stock in the Standard Oil Company. If they failed to elect that salvation, they were responsible for their own fate, and Rockefeller looked upon them as Jonathan Edwards would have looked upon a man who declined to accept spiritual salvation, with regretful disapproval, tempered with tolerant pity. Once, in his old age, he was asked, "What did you do with those who refused to come in with you?" and replied: "We left

---

[1] James Ford Rhodes quoted Herbert Spencer's "Practically, business has been substituted for war as the purpose of existence," and added: "Rockefeller . . . was to business what Napoleon was to war and to civil society."

them to the mercy of time; they could not hope to compete with us."

Rockefeller's own convicton that he was always fair and

Risks in the oil business when John D. Rockefeller entered it — a tank of stored oil on fire.

even generous with his competitors and that the methods he used to gain a monopoly in oil were ethical, is beyond dispute. The shrewd "Mr. Dooley" once said of him:

There's wan thing sure fr'm what I can see, an' that is that Jawn D. hasn't an idea that he iver did wrong to annywan.

John D. Rockefeller and William Jennings Bryan were in almost every respect the antithesis of each other. Of all the men who lived during their generation, no other pair, probably, would have so strongly resented any imputation of similarity. But they had one trait in common. Each was able, by prayer and contemplation, with utter sincerity, to convince himself that his purpose coincided with God's — to the contentment of his spirit and the strengthening of his convictions.

v

At this time, 1872, the heart of the oil industry was Oil City, in northwestern Pennsylvania. Being at the source of production, Oil City had an advantage, in the refining business, over the Rockefellers in Cleveland, in that the latter were obliged to transport their crude oil long distances. Another and greater resource of Oil City was the character of its inhabitants — resourceful, ingenious, daring men, most of them young. In a dozen years they had built up an almost fabulous industry. With the confidence of success they frankly boasted that Oil City would outrun all rivals as a refining centre. They were pioneers, close to the soil, decidedly not the men to run from a fight, to stand meekly aside while their business was lost to rivals who matched secret intrigue against their pioneering energy.

On February 19, 1872, the freight rate from Oil City to Buffalo, which had been forty-five cents a barrel, was raised to sixty-five. Other advances followed. On February 26 the newspapers of the oil regions charged that the instigator of the rate increases was a mysterious newcomer in the oil business, the South Improvement Company. Who the backers of the South Improvement Company were, and what its purposes, Oil City did not know but set to work to find out. A day or two later, the Oil City *Derrick*, "one of the most vigorous, witty, and daring newspapers in the country," published in large type under the caption "The Black List" the names

"FORE!"

Herbert Johnson, in the Philadelphia "North American."

Respective rôles of "The Common People" and John D. Rockefeller, as pictured during the early 1900's by Herbert Johnson.

of the directors of the South Improvement Company. The list, printed with a black border, bore the caption:

BEHOLD "THE ANACONDA" IN ALL HIS
HIDEOUS DEFORMITY

A few days later the charter of the South Improvement Company was unearthed and published. Public indignation flamed. A newspaper editor fumed: "They are landsmen granted perpetual letters of marque to prey."

A mass meeting was held. A complete embargo was placed on the sale of oil to the South Improvement Company. Committees bearing bitter denunciations of the South Improvement Company were hurried off to the head offices of the railroad companies in Philadelphia and New York; to the State legislature at Harrisburg; and to Washington. On March 15 a resolution to investigate was introduced in Congress.

Rarely has remedy followed so promptly on the heels of public indignation. The contract had been signed on January 18, 1872. On March 25 the railroads publicly withdrew from the contract and promised that "all arrangements for the transportation of oil after this date shall be upon a basis of perfect equality to all." On April 6 the Pennsylvania legislature summarily abrogated the South Improvement Company's charter.

In the literature of protest against "big business" there is a classic indictment of the immorality of rebates, an arraignment of the South Improvement Company contract almost as famous as the contract itself. It was delivered by an eloquent young Pennsylvania lawyer, Samuel C. T. Dodd, at a Pennsylvania State Constitutional Convention, brought about chiefly by the producers of oil, who hoped through publicity and legislation to curb the abuses of monopolistic control. In part, Dodd said:

We well know that almost every railroad in this State is today in the habit of granting special privileges to individuals, to companies in which the directors of such railroads are interested, to particular businesses, and to particular localities. We well know that it is their habit to break down certain localities, and to build up others; to monopolize certain businesses themselves by means of the numerous corporations which they own and control, and all this in spite of the law, and in defiance of the law. . . . The South Improvement Company's scheme would give that corporation the monopoly of the entire oil business of the State. Their scheme was contrary to law — a deadly blow at one of the great interests of the State. The oil business would have laid prostrate at their feet, had it not been prevented by an uprising of the people, by the threatenings of a mob. Had the companies not cancelled the contract, I venture to say there would not have been one mile of railroad track left in the county of Venango — the people had come to that pitch of desperation."

Reading that indictment by Dodd, one is conscious of a glow. The arraignment is passionate, the argument convincing. Here, one feels, is a true defender of the common man. Dodd cannot help but go far. No gift of the people should be beyond his reach. He is outstanding as an exponent of a cause, a cause that later made Theodore Roosevelt the most loved President of his generation. One lays aside Dodd's speech with the conviction that he is a man we shall hear of again.

VI

The South Improvement Company was dead. If Rockefeller and the Standard Oil Company were to have monopoly, they must seek it another way. They wanted monopoly ardently. They were determined to have monopoly. "You can't keep such men down," William H. Vanderbilt said of them seven years later. "They are very shrewd men. I don't believe that by any legislative enactment or anything else, through any of the States or all the States, you can keep such men down. You can't do it! They will be on top all the time. You see if they are not."

Within two weeks after the railroads had issued the sweeping public renunciation quoted above, the Standard group were again getting rebates.

To take the place of the ill-fated South Improvement Company, they formed a loosely knit organization, the Central Association of Refiners, spoken of colloquially as "the Alliance," with John D. Rockefeller as president.

Two homes of the Standard Oil Company. On the left, 44 Broadway, occupied by the company between 1882 and 1885, reproduced from "The History of the Standard Oil Company," by Ida M. Tarbell. On the right, 26 Broadway, in 1927, headquarters of Standard Oil.

Following its organization, in 1875, the component refineries, as the lawyer for the Standard Oil Company put it, "ceased to be competitive with one another."

But Rockefeller was not satisfied, did not feel secure. The too loosely binding cement of the Alliance was mere mutual understanding, personal agreement between the officers of the component refineries and the officers of the

Standard Oil Company. A tighter form of combination was wanted. "The men in control of that combination," sententiously wrote one of its officials many years later, "foresaw that a business which had thus far been disastrous would require co-operation on a large scale."[1] What they were seeking was, in short, an improvement on the South Improvement Company. And they found it.

By the eighties, it had become common knowledge that the Standard Oil Company controlled more than ninety per cent of the country's refining business. How this control had been secured, how it was exercised, and whether the mechanism of control was within the law, were mysteries. Long since, government had created checks on firms, partnerships, corporations, and other business organizations; it was evident the Standard Oil Company had found something entirely new, some novel form of compact, some mechanism for monopoly too elusive for the laws as they then existed to catch. What it was, where it was kept, by what authority it lived, nobody knew.

A committee of investigation from the New York State Senate sought in 1888 to find out. It put Rockefeller

[1] This defense of the Standard Oil Company on the ground that it rescued the industry from disaster is a characteristic point of view of beneficiaries of monopoly and believers in it. Opponents of monopoly would say the "disaster" from which Rockefeller wanted to save the oil industry was the undisturbed working out of its destiny under conditions of free competition. What Rockefeller did was, through secret arrangements with the railroads and other devices, to introduce an artificial element into the situation which itself brought disaster to practically every one in the industry except himself and those who united with him. Many accounts, possibly partisan, bear testimony to the desolation that fell upon the Oil Region once monopoly had fastened upon it. Its condition prior to then is pictured in H. D. Lloyd's "Wealth Against Commonwealth:"

"There was a free market for the oil as it came out of the wells and out of the refineries, and free competition between buyers and sellers, producers, and consumers, manufacturers and traders. Industries auxiliary to the main ones flourished. Everywhere the scene was of expanding prosperity, with, of course, the inevitable percentage of ill-luck and miscalculation, but with the balance, on the whole, of such happy growth as freedom and the bounty of nature have always yielded when in partnership."

on the stand. From testimony sometimes plausible, sometimes apparently willing, sometimes evasive, at all times subtle,[1] the committee learned that

thirty-nine corporations had turned over their affairs to an organization having no legal existence, independent of all authority, able to do anything it wanted anywhere; and to this point working in absolute darkness. Under their agreement, which was unrecognized by the State, a few men had united to do things which no incorporated company could do. It was a situation as puzzling as it was new.

"This," wrote the committee, "is the original *trust*." That word, as the name for combination aiming at monopoly, first came into the language about 1882, three years after the device had been adopted by the Standard Oil Company. Thereafter, both the word and the thing it stood for spread through the country.

I said, a few pages back, that we should hear again of that able young Pennsylvania lawyer who, speaking eloquently for an outraged people, uttered the impassioned denunciation of the South Improvement Company in the Pennsylvania Constitutional Convention of 1873. At this point we meet him once more. It was none other than Dodd who brought the word "trust" from its ancient biblical and legal setting, into a connotation of popular odium. He did it, not in his 1873 rôle of tribune of the

[1] Rockefeller had been instructed by his counsel, Joseph H. Choate, to confine his testimony to "yes" and "no," and to the otherwise briefest possible answers to the investigating committee's questions, leaving everything in the nature of explanation or defense to be cared for by his lawyer. Choate's policy was based on the ground that the investigating committee, as he claimed, was biassed. For Rockefeller, obedience to his lawyer's instruction had one unhappy result. His enemies and critics were able to characterize his testimony as, to put it mildly, lacking candor, and as otherwise subject to criticism that could be fairly expressed in rather harsh terms. Comparison of Rockefeller's testimony with answers he had given on another occasion, enabled his critics to say that on one point his testimony was false. Rockefeller's associates explain the discrepancy as due to the injunction to brevity, the refraining from explanation, imposed upon him by his counsel's instructions.

people, but in a very different 1882 rôle, a rôle of employee of John D. Rockefeller.

By the transition through which Dodd passed, he has the appearance — though in his case there are strong qualifications — of an illustration of that rule rather frequently and conspicuously exemplified in American politics and business, that one of the best ways of getting yourself invited into an organization and shown to its high places, is to attack it.

In another respect, Dodd, as the first American lawyer of prominence to enter the exclusive service of one client,[1] an innovation accompanying the period when corporations grew large enough to have "legal departments" and staffs of lawyers — Dodd seems, though here again there are emphatic qualifications, to illustrate the tendency of the country's best talent to become the servants of corporations. This was just the period when politics and public service, as the one most prized career in America for the ambitious and the able, began to give way before the greater remuneration and in some respects greater power attending service of large business combinations. This aspect of the trusts was one of the counts in the general indictment of them. Dodd and men like him may well have been in the mind of Senator Cushman K. Davis, of Minnesota (a thoroughgoing conservative), when in an address at the commencement of the University of Michigan, July 1, 1886, he said:

Feudalism, with its domains, its untaxed lords, their retainers, its exemptions and privileges, made war upon the aspiring spirit of humanity, and fell with all its grandeurs. Its spirit walks the earth and haunts the institutions of to-day, in the great corporations, with the control of the national highways, their occupation of great domains, their power to tax, their cynical contempt for the law, their sorcery to debase most gifted men to the capacity of splendid slaves, their

[1] Excepting a few railroad lawyers.

pollution of the ermine of the judge and the robe of the Senator, their aggregation, in one man, of wealth so enormous as to make Crœsus seem a pauper, their picked, paid, and skilled retainers who are summoned by the message of electricity and appear upon the wings of steam.

The first oil well, drilled by E. L. Drake near Titusville, Pennsylvania, in 1859, and called "Drake's Folly."

The truth is, Dodd, instead of being the arch-type of corporation lawyer, was one among them who tried to hold most straightly to the older standards of his profession, to avoid the implications that came to attend such positions. About the time he had risen to be the leading lawyer in interior Pennsylvania, his voice became impaired, handicapping him in a community in which the most prized work of a lawyer was in the court-room and before a jury, where the "office-lawyer" had comparatively little opportunity to function in a large way. When

A modern oil field in Bakersfield, California.

the Standard Oil Company asked him to move to New York and give all his time to them, he fixed his salary at an approximation of what had been his income before, and this comparatively small amount remained his pay until close to the end of his connection with the Standard Company, though he remained with them into a time when the salaries of general counsel for similar corporations went to fifty or a hundred thousand dollars. In the same spirit he tried to cling to the old-time austere ethics of a lawyer's relation to his client, refraining from taking personal part in the corporation's enormously profitable expansion, and dying with only a modest fortune, little

larger, if any, than he might have had if he had remained
in a small Pennsylvania city. Neither financially nor
otherwise did he take on the grandiosity that came to attend the rôle of "big corporation lawyer." With the rest

From "The Literary Digest," May 6, 1905.

This cartoon, widely reprinted in 1905, was based on a sentence in a speech by
John D. Rockefeller, Jr.

"The American Beauty rose can be produced in all its splendor only by sacrificing
the early buds that grow up around it."

of his professional code went the attitude that what was
not specifically forbidden by statute was legitimate to
attempt. The public outcry that arose against the Standard Oil Company and other similar trusts, the pursuit by
legislatures, press, and politicians, left him a little dazed.

An associate of his recalls the last time he called at Dodd's office, seeing the aging man with a pile of law-books on his desk, and hearing the querulous plaint of a relic of the passing order: "You see, we try to know the law here, and to keep within it; but I can't see that it helps us any."

The old South Improvement Company had been clearly outside the law and so flagrant a piracy that many producers of oil would have starved rather than accept its yoke; its successor, the Alliance, had depended on mere informal harmony among the members. Rockefeller, wanting something more secure, something that would have the binding effectiveness of the South Improvement Company and yet be immune against prosecuting attorneys, turned to Dodd as one who possessed the best knowledge of the legal obstructions which a successful monopoly must get over. Dodd managed it by an adaptation, a perversion rather, of the familiar legal "trust," through which courts impose a solemn obligation on the custodians of property belonging to others; through which they take care of the estates of children, wards, legatees, and all such dependents, by turning the property over to a "trustee" and putting upon him a peculiarly sacred "trust," the most exalted human relationship ever created by law, the legal substitute for parentage, a relation even more carefully safeguarded than natural parentage.

Under Dodd's guidance, the stockholders of the various Standard and associated companies delivered their stock, with permanent and irrevocable power of attorney, to nine trustees, of whom John D. Rockefeller and his brother William were two. The trustees, having complete control, managed all the companies as one, and distributed the profits pro rata to the stockholders.

Decidedly, Dodd must be given a place in history. It was he who opened the door of the room which courts maintain and guard as the sanctuary of those who most rely upon the good faith of others: of widows, orphans, and dependents; and softly pushed through it the humbly appreciative persons of John D. Rockefeller, William A. Rockefeller, and their associates of the Standard Oil Company. He took the word "trust" when, in the vocabulary of the common man, it still stood alongside its ancient derivations "true," "troth," the Danish and Swedish "trost," meaning comfort, consolation; when it was synonymous with "confidence, belief, truth, hope, expectation,"[1] when the average man's most frequent use of the word was in quotation of the 71st Psalm, "O Lord God, thou art my trust from my youth" — and he added to it a meaning which dictionaries subsequent to 1882 defined as a "combination formed for the purpose of controlling or monopolizing a trade, industry or business by doing acts in restraint of trade."[2]

[1] Webster's Dictionary, 1858.

[2] There is no question that Dodd was the inventor of the "trust" device for achieving monopoly. He himself, in a book written years afterward, "Combinations," described his creation as "the parent of the Trust System." Some other authorities hold that Dodd, after all, was only wet-nurse to a child of unnatural forces. Jesse Hardesty, in his book "The Mother of Trusts," gives railroad rebates as the maternal parent. Henry O. Havemeyer, when he appeared before the Industrial Commission in 1899, said: "The mother of all trusts is the customs tariff law."

17

TRUSTS

The People Become Aware of Them. Courts and Legislatures Take Notice of Them. The Vocabulary That Arose
About Them. Some Austere Legal Definitions, Some Popular Phrases, and Some Political Slogans That Arose About
Them. The Man Who Was Called "the Father of Trusts,"
and the State That Was Called the "Mother" of Them.

DODD having pointed the way, and oil having pioneered
the trust[1] path to monopoly, whiskey followed. "We
thought," said one of the distillers, "we could make better
profits and create a more stable business by organizing
into a trust. . . . A trust agreement was drawn up,
which was a copy of the Standard Oil trust agreement, but
changed to suit our business."[2] Eighty distilleries were
taken in and all but twelve closed down. The next was
sugar. The Sugar Refineries Company, known later as
the American Sugar Company, took in eighteen refineries, immediately closed down eleven, and raised the margin between crude and refined sugar from a competitive
.787 cents in 1887 to a monopolistic 1.258 cents in 1888.
  The whiskey and sugar combinations had the literal
trust form, Dodd model. By now (1887), however, the
word "trust"[3] had come into the popular vocabulary as

---

[1] "Its [the Standard Oil Company's] success," wrote the New York State
Senate Investigating Committee of 1888, "has been the incentive to the formation
of all other trusts or combinations; it is the type of a system which has spread
like a disease through the commercial system of the country."

[2] C. C. Clarke, distiller, before the Industrial Commission, May 13, 1899.

[3] The first legal article about trusts appeared in 1887, in the October number of
Volume I of the *Harvard Law Review*. It attracted wide-spread attention, both in
legal circles and in the popular press, on account of the newness of the subject
and of the word, which the author, Frederic J. Stimson, spelled, in the title of the
article, with quotation marks, "Trusts."

For an attempt at accurate definition of the vocabulary that rose up about
the trust movement, see pages 320–329.

the name for all kinds of combination. In this broader sense, by February, 1888, the following additional commodities were in one form or another of combination:

glass, copper, rubber, coal, reaping and binding and mowing machines, gas, lead, threshing machines, ploughs, steel rails, steel and iron beams, wrought-iron pipe, iron nuts, stoves, school slates, castor oil.[1]

A committee of Congress investigating trusts in 1889 decided not to include a list in its report "for the reason that new ones are constantly forming, and that old ones are constantly extending their relations so as to cover new branches of the business and invade new territories."

The country flamed into apprehension,[2] an apprehension that even sensed danger to the people's political liberty. In 1892 Henry D. Lloyd wrote his impassioned "Wealth Against Commonwealth." In the courts hundreds of individual business men and small corporations

---

[1] I have rearranged this list from "Monopolies and the People," by C. W. Baker. I think it is somewhat exaggerated—Baker himself speaks of his list as "long and somewhat jumbled." However, any errors are immaterial. Combination had "spread like a disease." By 1899, the year Markham's "Man With the Hoe" appeared, the following additional articles, according to Baker, had been taken into trusts: beef, watches and watch-cases, carpets, coffins and undertakers' supplies, wall paper, dental tools, flour, matches.

[2] Many persons, having one or another definite point of view about the trust question, say the point of view of the present work has demerits. Quite probably this may be correct. While the ambitions of this history do not include a point of view among its major aims, it is a fact that complete exclusion of point of view from any writing whatever is quite impossible. It enters into practically every choice of one word rather than other, every selection of one fact from among the masses of them, every quotation of one passage, every omission of another. The prevailing point of view attempted in the present history is that of the average American as he was during the early years of the century, and as he looked upon the events of his own time. The average American of that period thought of himself mainly as an individual, had the older American preoccupation with freedom, economic as well as political. In his relation to organized business he thought of himself as a consumer, or as a small business man actual or potential, or as a workman, in all cases much concerned about freedom of opportunity. For evidence, it is sufficient to say that more than ninety-seven per cent of the voters were either for Roosevelt, Wilson, or Bryan, all of whom were, in differing ways, strongly opposed to the trusts.

brought suits against the trusts on the ground that they
had been crippled or driven out of business by the monopolistic practices of their large competitors. Investigations
were conducted by the New York Legislature in 1883,
1888, and 1891; by the Ohio Legislature in 1889. Kansas

THE NEW ROBINSON CRUSOE.

The lot of the average man during the trust era, as visualized by F. Opper in the New
York *American*, January 5, 1905.

passed an anti-trust law — the first in any State — on
March 2, 1889. In order, during the same year, followed
North Carolina, Tennessee, and Michigan; in 1890, South
Dakota, Kentucky, and Mississippi; in 1891, North
Dakota, Oklahoma, Montana, Louisiana, Illinois, Minne-
sota, Missouri, and New Mexico. Wisconsin waited until
1893 to pass an anti-trust statute, a laggardliness on the

part of this State, then dominated by the railroads, which gives the key to why La Follette was able to get his start a few years later. For a time, after 1893, there was a subsiding of anti-trust legislation, due to a subsiding of trust forming after the panic of that year. But in 1895 the movement began again and between that year and 1898 anti-trust statutes were passed by Alabama, Arkansas, New York, Ohio, South Carolina, Texas, and Utah.[1]

In this list of States that passed anti-trust statutes, there are some omissions, historically more important than the inclusions. As will appear, New Jersey, Delaware, West Virginia, and, to some extent, Maine — but especially New Jersey — worked the other side of the street.

In 1888, the word "trust" appeared in party platforms. The Republicans said: "We declare our opposition to all combinations of capital, organized as Trusts or otherwise." The Democrats: "The interests of the people are betrayed when . . . Trusts and combinations are permitted to exist." In both these platforms the word was spelled with a capital T, reflecting, partly, the newness of the subject, and the importance attached to it. In 1889, on December 3, President Harrison, in his first message to Congress, said: "Earnest attention should be given to . . . those combinations of capital commonly called 'Trusts.' "

Congress acted. In March, 1890, John Sherman, of

---

[1] Many of the States, from the beginning, had anti-monopoly clauses in their constitutions, like the Maryland 1776 declaration "that monopolies are odious, contrary to the spirit of free government and the principles of commerce, and ought not to be suffered." It is to be borne in mind, however, that these early constitutional prohibitions were directed against the type of English government grants of monopoly by royal decree or legislative franchise, such as the grant of Maryland to Lord Baltimore, or of Pennsylvania to William Penn, or of Virginia to the Virginia Company. In the earlier years also, the anti-monopoly spirit had been invoked with reference to the National Bank, public lands, the issue of money, the control of railroads. But the new type of combination of manufacturers, and especially Dodd's 1882 creation of the trust device, raised a wholly new problem.

Ohio, introducing a bill[1] designed to end all trusts of whatever form, predicted an ominous alternative:

They had monopolies and mortmains of old, but never before such giants as in our day. You must heed their appeal [the

Herbert Johnson, in the Philadelphia "North American."

Sentiment against the trusts was sympathetic to almost any degree of pictorial violence. Herbert Johnson visualized the average man as a figure called "Common People," and his oppressor as "the Trusts."

people of the United States] or be ready for the socialist, the communist, and the nihilist. Society is now disturbed by forces never felt before. . . . Congress alone can deal with the trusts, and if we are unwilling or unable there will soon be a trust for every production and a master to fix the price for every necessity of life.

[1] Known familiarly ever since as the Sherman Act. In fact, Senator Hoar, of Massachusetts, and Senator Edmunds, of Vermont, had rather more to do with it.

In the debate, Senator George, of Mississippi, expressed the emotion that explains the public's reception of "The Man With the Hoe":

They regulate prices at their will, depress the price of what they buy and increase the price of what they sell. They aggregate to themselves great, enormous wealth by extortion. . . . They pursue unmolested, unrestrained by law, their ceaseless round of peculation under the law, till they are fast producing that condition in our people in which the great mass of them are the servitors of those who have this aggregated wealth at their command.[1]

Rarely has unanimous public opinion so clearly expressed itself in so unanimous action by its representatives. I say "unanimous," and the license is permissible when the variation is so slight. Of the members of both Houses of Congress, less than a fourth of one per cent voted against the Sherman Act. In the Lower House there was no vote against it, and no speech. In the long Senate discussion, there was one speech — querying the Act rather than opposing it — by Senator Stewart, of Nevada; and just one vote against it — cast, without any explanation, by a New Jersey Senator named Blodgett, described, accurately, as undistinguished and unimportant.

---

[1] In 1927, the proof of this chapter was read by Huston Thompson, who, as an appointee of Woodrow Wilson to the Federal Trade Commission, had just completed ten years of investigation of business practices in the United States, and attempts to regulate them. Opposite the passage from Senator George, Mr. Thompson wrote: "Ditto to-day."

There is obvious value in the method of writing history that includes submitting the proofs to persons who took part in the events, or are experts in the field covered. But there is also great inherent difficulty, and much turmoil for the author, whose pained person occasionally becomes a battle-ground over which partisans struggle with each other. Several others who have read these proofs, taking a view directly opposed to the one here quoted from Huston Thompson, say that by 1927 the big units of business had become beneficent economically, unobjectionable politically and socially. Yet others argued strenuously from a number of varying points of view. The reader will be helped if he will remember that these chapters merely treat the trusts and public opinion about them, *as of that time*, and that the history of the subsequent evolution of big units of business, and of the public attitude toward them, belongs in a later volume.

The passage of the Sherman Act was expected to end monopolies. Whether it would or not depended on whether the courts would find it constitutional, would read limitations into it. Before the Federal Courts had a chance to pass upon it, the first[1] real victory of the people against the trusts came in local State courts, and not through any new statute, but through the application of ancient principles of law.

In 1891 an ardent young attorney-general of Ohio summoned the Standard Oil Company into the Ohio courts, which a year later, May 2, 1892, not only decided that the act of the corporation in joining a trust was an exceeding of its powers — *ultra vires* is the legal phrase — but made a sortie into a statutorial no-man's-land by further declaring that

trust agreements . . . tending as they do to the creation of a monopoly, are also against public policy, and therefore contrary to law.[2]

That Ohio decision, with the New York one, ended the trust device that Dodd had invented ten years before. Accordingly, in 1892, the Standard Oil Trust was dissolved. With it went the Sugar Trust and all the other combinations built upon Dodd's model.

These two court decisions were hailed, prematurely, as decisive victories in the struggle of the people against predacious capital. As it turned out, they were merely the shadows of victories. For the decisions ended only the Dodd model for combination; they did not end combinations. They ended "trusts" in the strict legal sense, but not in the popular sense. The combinations did not cease

---

[1] Not literally the first. The New York courts handed down an earlier decision (1891), "People versus North River Sugar Refining Company," holding that a corporation which had joined a trust had exceeded its powers. This New York decision against the Sugar Trust was put on narrower grounds, and therefore was less important than the Ohio decision against the Standard Oil Trust.

[2] State ex rel v Standard Oil Company, 49 Ohio State.

to be combinations; they merely, as it was said, "changed their clothes."[1]

With the passing of Dodd's invention, other ingenious lawyers evolved another device for besting the law. It was successful. The trusts wriggled out of the courts' grasp and by a mere change in their method of organization, that obeyed the letter but not the spirit of the law, audaciously retained their entities and continued flagrantly the practices which all the anti-trust legislation had been intended to suppress. The trusts were still, in reality, above the law.

For their new attire, the dress was already awaiting them in the shape of a statute passed by New Jersey in 1889, authorizing "holding-corporations."

But for understanding the next phase of attempts at monopoly, and for clarifying the whole subject, some definitions will be useful.

II

Trust-forming, and allied enterprises for capitalizing and selling stocks, became for a time almost a trade, a career with a technic, a terminology, and its heroes, the gorgeous personalities of that era, known as *Promoters*. In their early aspect promoters were the inspiration and model of aspiring youth, the glass of fashion and the mold of form, the figures pointed out as they strode through public dining-rooms behind proudly obsequious head-

[1] To change the form of the monopoly was not at all times the only remedy the trusts found for an unfavorable court decision. A witticism reflecting both a corporation practice and a public cynicism was printed in the Chicago *Evening Post* in 1903:

"'If our combination is illegal,' said the capitalist, 'I suppose we will have to change it.'.

"'Wouldn't it be easier to change the law?' asked his associate."

The facility with which corporations got what they wanted from State legislatures, especially railroad corporations, by the use of passes universally and more substantial mechanisms of seduction occasionally, calls for separate and larger treatment elsewhere.

waiters, in a hush of awed admiration. As the public became familiar with their ostentation of new wealth and their prodigality with it, and saw a seaminess in the reverse of their ornate fronts, the term promoter became tarnished and took on some of the significance that in 1925 attached to "big butter-and-egg man." When that happened, the fraternity tried to borrow some of the purer gilt that went with *Captain of Industry*, a legitimate term for a man who actually managed a business; as a result, in time this, too, came to have an uncomplimentary connotation.

The trust in the oil industry was brought about by a man within the trade. That was the exception to the rule. Most of the trusts were organized by promoters not associated with the industries on which they conferred their attentions. The man who was called the "father of trusts," Charles R. Flint, said that this was indispensable, that a combination could not successfully be brought about by a man within the industry, that the promoter must be, in Flint's phrase, a "disinterested intermediary." (That phrase seems to imply a comment bearing on the argument, frequently made, that the trusts were natural consequences of economic evolution within the industries they dominated.) As a rule, the only industry with which the promoter was identified was the manufacture and sale of securities.

John D. Rockefeller is mentioned in connection with promoters, not to include him, but to make it clear he did not belong. In one phase of his career, Rockefeller could be called a captain of industry, but a promoter never. He never threw industrial lame-ducks together to make a holding-company, never carried on a stock-market campaign, probably never speculated in the ordinary sense. He never sold stock to the public — the only stock he was actively interested in was Standard Oil, and his attitude

toward that was one of such confidence that he wanted
to keep as much as he could for himself. Always he was
persuading his associates to hold what they had and buy
more; but if they wanted to sell he wanted to be the
buyer. Rockefeller's career was the organization of the
business of refining and selling oil; when he made more
money than could be absorbed by the expansion of oil, he
invested it in such properties as undeveloped iron ore,
there to remain and ripen. Rockefeller, in short, never
engaged in what Andrew Carnegie described as the business of some promoters: "They throw cats and dogs
together and call them elephants."

The promoters and captains of industry were so varied
in position and quality that one cannot speak of them as a
group — under no conceivable circumstances could one
think of John Pierpont Morgan belonging to the same
fraternity as John W. Gates. Morgan was one of the
earliest promoters, and remained secure in the plane of the
original elevation of the term, after the word itself slipped
downward. Morgan was in a class by himself, a class
apart and above. He was a bridge between two conceptions of banking, the older one which consisted solely of
extending credit on approved security, and the newer one
which reached out for direct control of industries, used
them as the basis for issuing stocks, and stimulated the sale
of the stocks to the public. Morgan carried the prestige
and dignity of the older order into the new. One thought
of Morgan as of the bank buildings in which he had his
several thrones — structures impressing the public (and
designed to impress it), solid granite and gold, marble and
mahogany in every detail. He presented no false façade
to the public; with many of the promoters a papier-
mâché front, tawdrily gilded, was an essential part of
their modus operandi. Morgan would take advantage of
the public's moods, to sell it the securities he manufac-

Charles M. Schwab

J. Pierpont Morgan

Andrew Carnegie

Wm. M. Rockefeller

Composite Photograph of Industrial Organizers

Charles R. Flint

Henry C. Frick

August Belmont

John W. Gates

The "Father of Trusts," Charles R. Flint, published his "Memories of an Active Life,"
in which he included a page of "industrial organizers," as seen singly and
as a composite group.

tured. Like many other business men, he regarded the
public as fish to be lured to his net, but among his associates, his word was more relied upon than an ordinary
man's bond. Doing business on a basis of bringing character to the transaction himself, and expecting character
in others; believing firmly in the future[1] of the United
States — and therefore in the future of the securities he
sometimes issued and sold a little faster than the country's anticipated growth could give value to them;[2] as
impressive a figure as American business, in its aspect of
enterprise and imagination, has ever produced.

Many of the promoters were picturesque. Charles R.
Flint, who wrote proudly in "Who's Who" that he was
"widely known as the 'father of trusts,'" started as a
merchant, became a banker, and then created a unique
profession for himself: he fitted out war vessels for South
American republics, sold cruisers to Japan in the Chinese
War of 1895, sold submarines and torpedo-boats to Russia; reorganized street-railways in New York State; and
was an organizer of consolidations in rubber, wool, coal,
shipping, and chewing-gum. He developed a technique
of the art, which he explained at length in his autobiography.

Some promoters were lawyers by original profession,
among them James B. Dill, who began a lecture at the
Harvard Law School with "I am the lawyer for a billion
dollars of invested capital." Another, William Nelson
Cromwell, who wore the hair and mustache of a Buffalo
Bill trimmed and tended by a Waldorf-Astoria barber;
who wrote that he made a "specialty of international and
corporation law," maintained an office in Paris, and had
ribbons from the Roumanian and other governments;

[1] One of Morgan's aphorisms was "never be a bear on the United States."
[2] Morgan once explained a stock-market depression as due to "undigested
securities"—many of them were the United States Steel and other shares Morgan
had put out.

who, in the twenty-six lines of condensed autobiography he prepared for "Who's Who," mentioned no lawsuits he had tried, no courts he argued before, no professional positions or honors he had received, but recited that he was an "officer or counsel of more than twenty of the largest corporations of the United States, and one of the organizers of the United States Steel Corporation," and had "reorganized Northern Pacific Railway and many others and put all on a paying basis." Cromwell was counsel for the French owners of the old Panama Canal when Roosevelt was taking it over and recognizing the independence of the Republic of Panama. To Roosevelt came Mark Hanna, in the rôle of fatherly adviser. "You want to be very careful, Theodore," he said, "this is very ticklish business. You had better be guided by Cromwell; he knows all about the subject and all about those people down there." Roosevelt replied that "the trouble with Cromwell is he overestimates his relation to Cosmos." "Cosmos?" said Hanna. "I don't know him — I don't know any of those South Americans; but Cromwell knows them all; you stick close to Cromwell."

From that level of the elite, the connotations of "promoter" reached downward through many gradations. Somewhere about the middle were John W. Gates and his son Charlie. The elder Gates began as a "drummer," selling wire-fence in the West, hastily threw together a trust, sold it at immense profit, descended upon Wall Street, bought control of the Louisville and Nashville Railroad in the open market under Morgan's eyes, and made Morgan pay him several millions profit to ransom it; plunged, splurged, became known as "Bet-cha-a-million" Gates.

The inferior extreme of the promoter species was a character that George Randolph Chester put into fiction for the *Saturday Evening Post* — the closing touch of tawdriness was put upon the word "promoter" by the wide and eager reading of the picaresque adventures of "Get-Rich-Quick Wallingford."

Monopoly in its literal sense means "exclusive control of the supply of any commodity . . . in a given market."[1] More broadly, it means "any such control . . . as enables the one having such control to raise the price . . . materially above the price fixed by free competition."[1] The very elasticity of the definition of what constitutes monopoly gave much trouble to lawmakers and courts. Just what percentage of control would enable an industrial combination to raise prices? Obviously the percentage varies with different commodities and with different conditions. Wm. J. Bryan, after this political issue had been agitated more than twenty years, arrived at a limitation which he inserted in the Democratic platform on which he made his last campaign for the Presidency, in 1908. Bryan's limitation aimed "to prohibit the control . . . of more than 50 per cent of the total amount of any product consumed in the United States." Courts and legislatures never found themselves quite able to be so confidently dogmatic as Bryan. From about 1900 onward, trusts, in seeking to arrive at a formula for the largest percentage they could safely grasp without stirring up public opinion or prosecuting attorneys, gravitated, in many industries, to between, roughly, 45 and 60 per cent. Before that, many combinations aimed at 100 per cent. The Standard Oil Company, the American Sugar Refining Company, and some others achieved, in their earlier phases, upward of 95 per cent. Occasionally, but only rarely (except, of course, in the case of public utilities), monopoly was literal, attained 100 per cent. Both courts and popular

[1] Webster's International Dictionary, 1913.

usage conceded application of the word to a wide latitude of degrees of control.

In the shape it took in American business life, monopoly may be defined as a union, or a unification, of the sellers against the buyers. Its real motive and effect is to give the seller the whip-hand in the trade. A monopoly enables the seller to say to the buyer: "Here are our goods, and this is our price." Before monopoly, the buyer could enjoy the pleasure of dickering, could make an offer and watch the seller's reaction, could play off one seller against another, could say: "I'll pay you so much; if you don't like that offer, I can buy from your competitor." As monopolies grew powerful and developed their technique, they reduced the retailer's status from the independence of a business man "on his own," to that of agent for the monopoly, a cowed agent, forbidden to buy from any but the monopoly, required, in a typical case, to sign a statement every four months, that he had not "bought, sold, carried in stock, disposed of directly or indirectly, any [products — in this case photographic material] other than those manufactured by the General Aristo Company's factories."

The antonym of monopoly is *competition*, meaning "the effort of two or more parties, acting independently, to secure the custom of a third party by the offer of the most favorable terms; an act of seeking, or endeavoring to gain, what another is endeavoring to gain at the same time."[1] To escape this curb on arbitrary profits was the aim of all attempts at monopoly.

Pools were what may be called the common or garden variety of combination, the early, obvious form that first occurred to men seeking to achieve monopoly. The sim-

---

[1] Webster's International Dictionary, 1913.

plest of the many varieties of pools consisted of a few men, heads of competing companies, meeting informally and agreeing on prices or on division of markets. "The steel-rail pools," said Charles M. Schwab, testifying before the Industrial Commission in 1901, "were simply agreements[1] among the managers of the various works to sell steel rails at the same price." The defect of this earliest and most usual form of combination was a weakness in human nature: the agreements, being illegal, were unenforceable. Members overendowed with the instinct of individual self-interest would break them, thereby not only wrecking the pool but giving occasion to their associates for sad reflections about human frailty. "It was no uncommon thing," writes Arundel Cotter,[2] "for a manufacturer to station a salesman outside the building, and, as soon as a price settlement was reached, to stroll casually over to a window and, by fingering the shade in a prearranged way, indicate to him the level agreed on, whereupon the salesman would proceed to undercut the price his employer was even then pledging himself to maintain." A story that illustrates the perfidy of pool-members, relates that on one occasion, following the organization of a pool, one of the participants, hurrying to the telegraph office to wire his own deviation from the agreed-upon price, was shown by mistake a message filed a few minutes before by a fellow member quoting customers a price even lower than the more virtuous one had contemplated offering. He immediately revised his own offer, downward.

From time immemorial pooling has been illegal in common law, even when not forbidden by specific statutes. It was less to avoid the ban of the law, however, than to offset mutual bad faith, that business men had

---

[1] Pools were often called, with such appropriateness as will suggest satire, "gentlemen's agreements."

[2] "United States Steel, A Corporation With a Soul."

their lawyers seek a more binding form of organization.

Trust in the beginning was the technical legal term for a specific form of combination, the device first adopted by men seeking to achieve a mechanism for monopoly that should be within the law. It was the first improvement — improvement, that is, from the monopolists' point of view — upon the loose and dangerously illegal pool. (The history of the first trust is told in preceding pages.) Though trusts, in the technical meaning of the term, were outlawed and ceased to exist before 1900, the word passed into the common tongue as the familiar name for every sort of combination whatever. As the opprobrious designation, the epithet, for every kind of large business, it became, in the eighties and nineties, as familiar as the word "business," itself, or "corporation." By the nineteen-hundreds it was accorded a secure standing in the dictionaries as a generic synonym for attempts at monopoly of whatever form. The progress of the word through successive editions of dictionaries provides an interesting example of the evolution of living words. Trusts, in the original and legal meaning of the word, disappeared about 1892. Nineteen years later the eleventh edition of the "Encyclopædia Britannica" said the word "includes all those aggregations of capital engaged in productive industry that, by virtue of their industrial strength, have or are supposed to have, some *monopolistic* power." Twelve years later "Nelson's Encyclopedia," in 1923, said: "The word 'Trust' is used to designate a variety of forms of business organization, the common feature of which is *combination* and *unitary* control of a number of establishments that are adaptable to independent ownership and operation — usually a majority of those producing a given commodity or performing a given service."

Integrated Trust, Vertical Trust, were names for a combination recognized as not formed for the primary purpose of eliminating competition; not a combination spreading out to take in competitors, but one which includes all the processes in a given product, thereby reducing the number of separate profits, and otherwise lowering costs. A vertical trust in the steel business, for example, would conduct all the operations, from mining ore to making the finest wire. Many persons opposed to monopoly in the ordinary sense were willing to admit economic justification for the vertical trust.

Trust-buster was used as the term for a political candidate making an anti-trust campaign. Occasionally it reached the elevation of legal patois, meaning a prosecuting-attorney who haled trusts into court. Of this use of the word, various beneficiaries at various times were: Philander C. Knox, Attorney-General under Roosevelt; Frank B. Kellogg, special prosecutor of the Standard Oil Company by appointment from Roosevelt, and Herbert Hadley, Attorney-General of Missouri, who harried the Standard Oil Company.

Holding-Company (also *Holding-Corporation*) was the device adopted by captains of industry and their legal advisers from about 1893[1] on, as a substitute for the trust form after the latter had been declared illegal by legislatures and courts. The holding-company was "a new legal expedient to facilitate industrial combination."[2] "To inventive promoters," wrote Gilbert Holland Montague,[3] "came the idea of a legal person — a giant 'holding-company' which should buy a voting majority of the stock of

---

[1] This form of combination had been used earlier in the field of railroads and other public utilities. For several reasons, including limitations of space, the present history confines the discussion of monopoly to the field of ordinary industry, omitting railroads and other public utilities.

[2] Nelson's Encyclopedia. [3] In "Trusts of To-Day," 1904.

several concerns and elect [common] directors." A holding-company is a super-corporation designed either (a) to buy the physical plants of competing companies; or (b) to buy a majority, or sufficient to control, of the shares of stock of competing companies; or (c) to buy all the shares of stock of competing companies; or (d) to give shares of the super-corporation in exchange for shares of the competing constituent corporations. In the holding-company device, the super-corporation was frequently called the "parent company," which was a curious inversion of the order of gestation, for in all cases it was the holding-company that came into existence last. A figure of speech fitting the facts more accurately was used by those defenders of the holding-company device who said that the disruption of holding-companies by law — "trust-busting" the terminology of politics called it — was like trying to "unscramble an omelet." *Interlocking Directorate*, common directors in different corporations, was a term for the mechanism by which holding-companies were conducted, or by which "community of interest" was maintained. *Underwriter* and *Syndicate* were financial terms applied to the bankers or financiers functioning in trust promotions.

Merger in the popular sense was a generic term for some varieties of holding-company.[1]

Public Utility came into use fairly early, accompanying a consciousness that there is a fundamental distinction

---

[1] The Boston *Globe* published a definition of "merger" not as enlightening technically, perhaps, as some other definitions, but serving the useful purpose of illustrating popular feeling toward combinations in the early 1900's: "Mergers are monsters of so frightful mien, that to be hated need but to be seen; but when they're seen, despairing of a cure, the public has to whistle—and endure."

In June, 1904, *Puck* took similarly witty advantage of the word:

"'I see in the paper that a widower with nine children out in Nebraska has married a widow with seven children.'

"'That was no marriage. That was a merger.'"

between monopoly in the railroad, street-railway, gas, electric, and telephone fields; and monopoly in the other sense. It came to be recognized as natural that the telephones of a city, or the street-railways or gas or electric services, should be a consolidated unit. In the whole railroad and public utility field, the evolution of common thought and of law took the form of permitting monopolies, but asserting over them a public control as to rates and in other respects, exercised, in the case of railroads by the national Interstate Commerce Commission, and in the case of local utilities by State public utility commissions. There was a steady tendency to enlarge the number of services that should be regarded as public utilities, and be subjected to public control. By 1927, there were occasional suggestions of adding the selling of milk and ice in cities to the list.

As respects ordinary industry, however, the theory of enforced competition continued, with some modification.

There were many minor terms. *Combination in restraint of trade* was a legal definition, an approximately exact synonym for monopoly. *Community of interest* was a term for, so to speak, a non-competitive state of mind in the owners of businesses nominally supposed, and also legally supposed, to compete with each other. *Joint agreement* was an approximately exact synonym for "pool." *Alliance* was a term used by the Standard Oil Company during the seventies. Gilbert Holland Montague has a gentle phrase for the Standard Oil combination as it was in the interregnum between trust and holding-company, from 1892 to 1899, "purely informal harmony." *Trade Association* was sometimes a pool, fixing prices under a euphemistic name; sometimes an organization of the members of a trade coming together for other purposes. The latter type was declared legal, as to some of its practices, by the Supreme Court in 1925. *Aggregated capital* was the euphemism of the general counsel of the Standard Oil Company, Samuel C. T. Dodd, for "trust." To "aggregated capital," Dodd, in a famous address at Syracuse University in 1893, credited most of the advances of the human race from the time when even

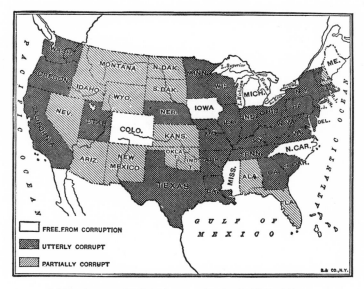

A French map of political corruption in the United States.

So great was the public discussion of political corruption in the United States, that it reached Europe, where a French publication made a map of it. The map was reproduced for the delectation of America in *The Literary Digest*, November 25, 1905.

"noblemen were destitute of comforts . . . [and] the coat-sleeve served the purpose of a handkerchief."

The System, spelled with a capital S, was a term invented by Lincoln Steffens when he found a super-community-of-interest between trusts — a fraternity including the banks that financed them and the politicians who served them. "Every time I attempted to trace to its

sources the political corruption of a city ring," he wrote,
"the stream of corruption branched off in the most un-
expected directions, and spread out in a network of veins
and arteries so complex that hardly any part of the body
politic seemed clear. It flowed out of politics into vice
and crime, out of politics into business, and back again
into politics. . . . Big, throbbing arteries ran out through
the country over the State to the nation and back. The
corruption of our American cities is political . . . but
financial and industrial too. . . . A system is in control
of the land." The term was adopted by Thomas W.
Lawson, who varied it with *Frenzied Finance*, in his con-
fessions about his own career as a stock-market handy-
man for some Standard Oil capitalists.

High Finance was meant as a jeering synonym for
Wall Street. *Graft* and *Boodle* were words that had come
up from the underworld to describe the means by which
corporations secured privileges from politicians.

The Octopus was synonymous with *The System* — the
first use of it may have been a visualization of the trusts
thrusting tentacles out over the country from Wall
Street. (Or was the word inspired by a map of the Standard Oil's pipe-lines criss-crossing the country? Or by a
map of the railroads? Or did Frank Norris, the novelist,
invent it, or appropriate it from general use?) *Tainted
Money* came into use when John D. Rockefeller began
to make donations to churches and colleges, and some
clergymen and educators questioned the propriety of accepting money acquired by Rockefeller's methods.

Special Privilege was the term commonly used by
Robert M. LaFollette, who had a more exact mind than
many other reformers, to describe those individuals and

corporations which enjoyed one kind or another of political advantage, public utility franchises, low tax rates, tariff and other subsidies. *Special Interests*, *Vested Interests*, and *The Interests* were looser variations.

III

Trusts: They Find a New Home

When the New York and Ohio court decisions of 1890 and 1892 ended the trust type of organization, the combinations found another form ready prepared on the statute books of New Jersey. Why New Jersey voluntarily assumed a rôle which made it a subject of jeering for twenty years,[1] just what were the circumstances, has been the occasion of much surmise. Lincoln Steffens's theory, that New Jersey, being the terminus of many great railroad systems, was responsive to corporation influence, may be a partial explanation. Nearness to Wall Street may have had an influence, as may also the fact that of the citizenry of New Jersey many of the ablest spent their working days in New York and had

---

[1] The anti-trust spirit of the rest of the country did not reach New Jersey until about 1908. When it finally came it expressed itself by taking Woodrow Wilson from the presidency of Princeton University and making him Governor. Much of Wilson's campaign for the governorship consisted of attacks on the New Jersey laws favoring trusts. He was elected Governor in 1910 but took no step toward repealing the old laws. Then, in 1912, he was nominated for the Presidency. In his campaign for the Presidency, again, he attacked the trusts. Whereupon a New York man, George W. Perkins, former partner in Morgan and Company, printed a series of advertisements in the principal newspapers of New York and New Jersey, calling attention to the fact that Wilson had been Governor of New Jersey nearly two years and had done nothing about trusts. The advertisements "got under Wilson's skin." After he was elected President, but while he still remained Governor, as one of his last official acts just before he was inaugurated President, Wilson had seven laws drawn up (the newspapers jeeringly called them the "Seven Sisters") which were designed to end New Jersey's statutory benevolerce to the trusts. They were passed on February 19, 1913. However, Wilson was hardly out of the State before the legislature began to whittle the new laws away; by 1920 the last recognizable vestige of them was obliterated, and New Jersey had restored, in substance, the old laws favoring trusts. New Jersey felt the "Seven Sisters" laws needlessly drove the trade in chartering corporations to other States.

slight civic interest in the State in which they slept. In
such a community it would be easy for politicians and
lawyers representing financial interests to take possession
of the machinery of the State and use it to the advantage
of the interests they represented. The revenue accruing
to the State from the fees it received for providing a home
for outside corporations lightened the burden of taxes on
New Jersey voters and their property.[1] Many New Jersey
people frankly and publicly justified the laws favoring
trusts on that ground. For whatever reason, New Jersey
maintained an attitude which officially said to the trusts,
"Come, all ye disconsolate"; which caused Woodrow
Wilson, who disapproved the policy, to speak of New Jersey in derogation, as the "mother of trusts"; which inspired cartoonists to picture the trusts harried in other
states, as calling "Help!" and New Jersey as an exceptionally full-bosomed matron, answering, "Come to
mother"; and other cartoonists to picture the trusts
crowded on a pier on the Wall Street side of the Hudson
River, and calling across to New Jersey: "Ferryman,
over."[2]

[1] Several well-informed persons who have read the proof of this chapter suggest
that investigation would probably show the author of the New Jersey practice to
be James B. Dill, a New Jersey lawyer who provided super-service to big corporations. This would be an interesting subject for historical research by a student
writing a thesis. It should be done soon, for much of the evidence is confined to
the minds of living men.

[2] Among many who have read the proofs of this section on the early New Jersey
laws favoring trusts, were: Chancellor Edwin R. Walker of New Jersey; George
L. Record, a New Jersey lawyer who for twenty-five years has been in the thick
of fights for many causes; William H. Speer, General Attorney of the Public Service Corporation of New Jersey; and Joseph P. Tumulty, formerly Secretary to
Woodrow Wilson when he was Governor and President. All took much pains and
gave unique help in avoiding errors of fact. Mr. Record felt strongly that I should
record the existence of a point of view, held by himself and others, that the Sherman Anti-Trust law and other anti-trust laws general in the States at that
time, "were based upon an entirely false economic principle," because, among
other reasons, they failed to draw a distinction between "corporations that have
a privilege [such as a patent or a natural monopoly], and corporations that have
no privilege." Mr. Record thinks that government ownership is the proper alternative for corporations having a natural monopoly, and that corporations having
no privilege need no regulating. Mr. Record thinks also, and justly, that I should

"Before 1889 the laws of no State authorized, the creation of a 'holding-corporation' [except as to railroad and public utility companies]; the purchase of stocks of other companies was not considered a desirable power, and, excepting private individuals, no legal entity could exist for the general purpose of owning property in other corporations. In 1889 New Jersey supplied the want."[1]

The New Jersey statute, designed directly to facilitate combinations, authorized directors of a corporation to purchase the stock of any other company "manufacturing and producing materials necessary to its business." In 1893, just a year after the Ohio courts had destroyed the trust form of organization and created the need of a new device, the New Jersey Legislature broadened its 1889

---

state that New Jersey has now, 1927, gone back to substantially its old position, with laws favoring holding-companies; and that many other States have followed New Jersey's example. Mr. Speer defends the old New Jersey laws as being of "sound theory in corporation law and development," thinks the substitution of the "Seven Sisters" anti-trust laws was a mistake; shows that the "Seven Sisters" experiment was abandoned within seven years, and that the old laws were in substance re-enacted and are now in force; points out that many other States have now followed the old New Jersey practice, and says the holding-company device "is now an accepted fact in the polity and jurisprudence of every advanced State in the United States."

The facts stated by Mr. Record and Mr. Speer are correct. As to their arguments, it is very important for the reader to bear in mind the distinction they make between corporations with a natural monopoly or other privilege, and ordinary manufacturing or other corporations without a privilege. To expand on this point here would be to enter a field about which hundreds of volumes have been written, and about which the conclusion is not yet.

Aside from this, the reader should understand that the present volume aims only to *picture the time* it covers. The later evolution of theory and practice about big units of business is one of the largest subjects in recent American history, and belongs in subsequent volumes covering the period in which the development took place.

[1] The quotations in this chapter—some of them abridged and paraphrased—are, except where otherwise noted, from Gilbert Holland Montague's "Trusts of To-Day," published in 1904. Mr. Montague was graduated from Harvard College in 1901 and from the Harvard Law School in 1904. While a student in the Law School he served as instructor in economics in the college. After 1904, he was a lawyer in New York City specializing in practice having to do with statutory restraints on combinations. His other books include: "The Rise and Progress of the Standard Oil Company," 1903; "Business Competition and the Law," 1917; and, as co-author, "Some Legal Phases of Corporate Financing, Reorganization, and Regulation," 1917.

statute to permit directors to "buy stocks of any other company which the directors might deem necessary."

This was as broad a license as could be desired by promoters or corporation lawyers seeking asylum for their clients. With it, quickly came the super-corporation, the holding-company. This had all the efficacy of the old "trust agreement," and resembled it in form, but there were sufficient points of difference to convince most lawyers that it was quite legal. The holding-company took two forms. In one, regarded as a little the safer, the holding-company bought outright all the physical property of the subordinate corporations. (The more specific term for this was "consolidation" or "merger.") While this was regarded as more secure against the assaults of prosecuting-attorneys, it had the disadvantage that under old laws the charters of many corporations forbade the sale of their entire property. Also, this kind of consolidation — complete absorption of all the physical assets of the subordinate companies by the holding-company — was expensive compared to the other form. Promoters who were more daring, therefore, would buy a majority of the stock — or enough for voting control — in two or more corporations and then elect common directors, who would manage the two as one. With $500,001, a promoter could buy control of a corporation which, if its physical assets were bought outright, would cost $1,000,000. By a process of pyramiding one holding-company atop another, the acquisition could be made even less expensive. Expense, however, was of less concern than technical legality; the common assumption was that monopoly, once achieved and safe from the law, would bear almost any amount of capitalization. Legality was now assured by the new New Jersey law, and, in accordance with "the comity among the several States guaranteed by the Constitution [so far as comity extended], this new legal entity could extend its operations throughout the whole United States. For a small franchise fee New Jersey offered to provide all comers with this convenient legal entity . . . every whit as effective as the 'trust agreement'; and after a narrow decision of the United States Supreme Court[1] generally regarded as immune from every law against combinations on both State and Federal statute-books. This form of combination promised shelter against ruinous competition within and hostile legislation without."

As other States continued to harry the combinations, New Jersey kept a jump ahead with its offers of sanctuary. In 1896, the New Jersey law became: "Any corporation may purchase, . . . the shares or any bonds . . . of any other corporation or corporations of this or any other State." When the New York State legislature sent a committee from Albany to New York City to investigage New Jersey trusts that were operating in New York, the Sugar Trust put its books on a boat and rushed them over to New Jersey; and New Jersey, to protect her own, hurried through the legislature a statute saying: "No action or proceeding shall be maintained in any court in this State against any stockholder, officer, or director of any domestic [New Jersey] corporation for the purpose of enforcing any personal liability . . . whether penal or contractual, if created by the statutes or laws of any other State."

"New Jersey," wrote Lincoln Steffens, "was regularly in the business of selling not only indulgences but absolution."

New Jersey, one reflects, might have charged each corporation heavily for the immunity it granted, but it

---

[1] In a case to test the applicability of the Sherman Anti-Trust Act to the American Sugar Refining Company.

adopted the economic principle of mass production —
large sales and small profits. For chartering corporations,
the New Jersey fee was only "twenty cents on each one
thousand dollars of capitalization — one-fifth the cost in
Illinois, and one-sixth the cost in New York and Penn-

Tillman "Cow Cartoon," one of the most widely circulated ever printed in America.

It was conceived by Senator Tillman, of South Carolina, and at his request drawn
by Tom Fleming. Millions of copies were circulated during the 1896 Bryan
campaign. Again in 1908, when Bryan ran on the anti-trust issue, Tillman had
the cartoon reproduced in *The Congressional Record* and circulated widely. This
conception, of New York milking the cow while the South and West fed her,
attended the whole trust agitation.

sylvania." The annual franchise tax in New Jersey was
similarly low compared to the tax in other States.

For the convenience of corporations having no interest
or existence in New Jersey, except as a legal domicile on
one day in the year when annual meetings were held,
and to look after more or less perfunctory details of
registration, local New Jersey trust companies made

themselves the "home offices" of hundreds of corporations. Providing homes for nominal head-offices of outside companies became an industry in itself, quite lucrative when the mass production of New Jersey corporations got under way. The Corporation Trust Company of New Jersey made itself — for a fee — the agent and the paternal home of seven hundred corporations with capital approximating $1,000,000,000. The New Jersey Corporation Guarantee and Trust Company represented five hundred companies with more than $500,000,000 capital; the New Jersey Registration and Trust Company, three hundred corporations with a capitalization of $400,000,-000. In accordance with the law, the New Jersey financial institutions engaged in this business displayed upon their buildings the name of each corporation on a sign. This was about the only demand on their space made by the trusts they represented, except that once a year each trust sent its officers over from New York, or from wherever it did business, to New Jersey to hold a cut-and-dried annual meeting in the State of its birth and legal domicile.

The increase of corporate industry which these easy devices stimulated was enormous. Most of the larger trusts incorporated under New Jersey laws, and a host of smaller combinations sought charters in one or another of the "charter-granting" States.[1]

"The Sugar Trust was among the first to avail itself

[1] The principal other States in the charter-granting business were Delaware, West Virginia, and to a less extent, Maine. Delaware and West Virginia were even more hospitable to fugitive corporations than New Jersey. Delaware did not even require stockholders' meetings to be held within its borders. West Virginia required neither stockholders' meetings nor a "home office" within the State—a promoter could charter his corporation in West Virginia, pay $50 a year as an annual license fee, and do as he pleased in every State of the Union, protected by the "comity of States" guaranteed by the Federal Constitution. These States, in spite of their more generous bid for the charter-granting trade, got less of the business. Possibly New Jersey was preferred for its greater nearness to Wall Street.

of the New Jersey law. On the dissolution of the Sugar
Refineries Company, caused by the decision of the New
York Courts, in 1891, its 'trust certificates' were exchanged, share for share, for the stock of the American
Sugar Refining Company. In 1899 the Standard Oil
combination, which had cautiously clung to the informal-
ity of community of interest since the 'trust agreement'
of its own contriving had gone awry, ventured to avail
itself of the New Jersey law. By 1901 a sufficient number
of combinations had been incorporated in the 'holding-
company' form to familiarize the public with their organization. In the opinion of the legal profession at
large, and among public prosecutors generally, the difficulties of the anti-trust laws had been surmounted. A
certain amount of doubt still attached to the principle of
combination by mere ownership of stock through a
'holding-corporation,' but there was no doubt about
combination through outright purchase of the subordinate
corporation. . . . A considerable body of judicial decision, particularly clear in New Jersey, where alone the
question was likely to arise, held in effect that combination through ownership of the properties was unassail-
able. The ease of changing, whenever convenience demanded, from a holding to a purchasing corporation
afforded, accordingly, a security which no attack on the
principle of merger seemed likely to threaten. As ninety-
five per cent of the trusts were incorporated in New Jersey
and Delaware, while outside their domicile-State the
question of their validity was unlikely to arise, these two
snug-harbors seemed sufficient."

"This New Jersey relaxation of corporation laws resulted in an immense increase in combination. In the
three years preceding 1901 — the year of high tide for
holding companies — 183 were organized, making in all
a total capitalization of over four billions of dollars —

one-twentieth of the total wealth of the United States, nearly twice the amount of money in circulation in the country, and more than four times the capitalization of all the manufacturing consolidations organized between 1860 and 1893."

Of these combinations, the biggest, then and yet, the largest unit of business in all time, was the United States Steel Corporation, organized by J. P. Morgan and Company in March, 1901, by outright acquisition of the stocks of ten corporations, many of which, each in its line, were already among the largest corporations in the world.

18

TITANS AT WAR

A Poor Little Scotch Boy, Following the Lure of Ambition, Comes to America. By Diligence and Thrift — Eked Out, Apparently, by Some Other Qualities—He Becomes the Greatest Iron Master in America. Mr. Carnegie Selects a Buyer for His Steel Works — Which, in a Way, Amounts to Vulcan Telling Jupiter What to Do. James J. Hill Finds in a Seattle Newspaper Reasons for Making a Hurried Journey to New York. Edward H. Harriman Has Occasion for Regret Because the Head of Kuhn, Loeb & Company Went to the Synagogue on a Certain Saturday Morning. Railroad Kings Fight a Battle, in Which Some Ordinary Folks Are Rather Severely Trampled. The Strange Ratiocinations of a Demented Pole, Which Had Effects, Later, on Matters of High Finance and Government.

STEEL, in America, meant Andrew Carnegie. As a child in Scotland Carnegie used to hear one of those westward-looking songs of ambition that had so much to do with the material making of America:

To the West, to the West, to the land of the free
Where the Mighty Missouri rolls down to the sea,
Where a man is a man even though he must toil
And the poorest may gather the fruits of the soil.[1]

The family, bitterly poor, came to Pittsburgh. The twelve-year-old lad went to work as bobbin-boy in a

[1] This assertion that Carnegie as a lad used to hear this song, I took from Carnegie's own words, in his autobiography: "My father's sweet voice sang often to mother, brother, and me, 'To the West,' . . ." But when a former associate of Carnegie, James Howard Bridge, looked over my proofs he noted on the margin, "Carnegie left Scotland before Henry Russell wrote this song!" I concluded to let the passage stand and make this explanation in a foot-note, thinking it would interest the reader to learn that in historical writing, autobiographies, instead of being the most dependable of sources, sometimes mislead. The reasons are many. In the present case, which is immaterial, Carnegie probably remembered the spirit in which his father in Scotland used to talk about bringing his family to America, remembered that his father was a singer, and remembered this song as identical with the feeling he and his father had about America.

cotton factory at $1.20 a week, became messenger-boy in a telegraph office at $2.50 a week, learned telegraphy and was getting $25 a month by the time he was seventeen. In 1853 he went to work as operator and clerk for Thomas A. Scott, division superintendent of the Pennsylvania Railroad, who called him, affectionately, "that little white-haired Scotch devil of mine," and paid him $35 a month. Six years later, at twenty-three, Carnegie was himself division superintendent at $1500 a year.

That, so far as Carnegie's "Autobiography" reveals, is the largest salary he received while with the railroad. Nevertheless, after six years he records: "My investments now began to require so much of my attention that I resolved to leave the service of the railway company." The investments consisted, among others, of interests in a locomotive works, a bridge-building company, a rail-making concern, and an iron mill.

The innocent-minded will conclude, too hastily, that a young railroad superintendent who acquired these interests and became a quite wealthy man,[1] at the age

---

[1] Just how rich Carnegie was when he left the railroad service at the age of thirty cannot be said; but a year later, in 1868, he wrote a private memorandum, of which the interest lies less in the facts it recites about his financial success than in the revelation it makes of curious conflicts in his inner personality:

"Thirty-three and an income of $50,000 per annum! By this time two years I can so arrange all my business as to secure at least $50,000 per annum. Beyond this never earn—make no effort to increase fortune, but spend the surplus each year for benevolent purposes. Cast aside business forever, except for others. Settle in Oxford and get a thorough education, making the acquaintance of literary men—this will take three years' active work—pay especial attention to speaking in public. Settle then in London and purchase a controlling interest in some newspaper or live review and give the general management of it attention, taking a part in public matters, especially those connected with . . . education and improvement of the poorer classes. Man must have an idol—the amassing of wealth is one of the worst species of idolatry—no idol more debasing than the worship of money. Whatever I engage in I must push inordinately; therefore should I be careful to choose that life which will be the most elevating in its character. To continue much longer overwhelmed by business cares and with most of my thoughts wholly upon the way to make more money in the shortest time, must degrade me beyond hope of permanent recovery."

of thirty, on a salary never greater than $125 a month, must be the outstanding example of Scotch saving in all history. Unhappily, the more sophisticated will be obliged, even though regretfully, to read into this picture an innuendo that the start of Carnegie's fortune was like the beginning of a very large number of American fortunes that grew up among the early railroad men — fortunes described in the phrase which said of an expensive horse bought by a minor official: "It was sired by the railroad and damned by the stockholders."

A railroad official is able to be of great service to a rail-making company, a locomotive company, a bridge-building company, and every sort of company along the lines. The nature of his serviceableness to purveyors of railroad supplies is obvious; to others his friendliness can take the form of providing cars promptly and otherwise facilitating shipments. Until as late as the nineties, even, the making of freight-rates was largely or wholly in the hands of subordinate officials — a situation that continued until the Interstate Commerce Commission acquired jurisdiction over this function.

The idea that Carnegie's early start toward fortune was seeded in this sort of practice rests, so far as this history is concerned, on inference from his circumstances and the conditions of the time. Everybody was doing it. Nobody thought of it as immoral. Moral standards vary with time, and also geographically. If Carnegie made money by taking advantage of his position with the railroad, no one at that time thought worse of him. Indeed, there is some evidence that Carnegie's business morals were rather above those of the day. The best informed critic of Carnegie, James Howard Bridge,[1] was not able

[1] Bridge was employed by Carnegie to help him write a book. Later, Bridge left Carnegie under unsympathetic circumstances, and on his own account wrote a book about Carnegie in which he treated his former employer with great detachment.

to find in this phase of Carnegie's career any occasion to be sardonic. Bridge merely wrote:[1] "Young Carnegie engaged in various outside enterprises, and through the aid of his chief, Mr. [Thomas] Scott, then superintendent of the Western division of the P. R. R., often made money in them." Bridge added what was a fact, and what accounted for as many American fortunes as any one industry: "It was no uncommon thing for the officials of a railroad to own shares in a corporation which obtained most of its business from such roads." Carnegie himself was quite naïve about it. Writing in 1906 (by which time these practices had come to be called by a name implying lack of perfection in business morals), Carnegie recited that having met a man with an idea, then novel, for building "cars for night-travelling," he introduced the patentee to his superior, Scott, with whom the patentee "contracted to place two of his cars upon the line." Whereupon, Carnegie recites:

Mr. Woodruff [the patentee] greatly to my surprise offered me an eighth interest in the venture. I promptly accepted his offer. The first considerable sum I made was from this source.

Again, of his bridge-building company Carnegie wrote:

I asked my friend, Mr. Scott, of the Pennsylvania Railroad, to go with us in the venture, which he did. Each of us paid for a fifth interest, or $1250. Looking back at it now, this sum seems very small, but "tall oaks from little acorns grow."

Very tall oaks indeed, for this bridge-works grew, with many important additions and transmutations, into the Carnegie Steel Company. In turn, the Carnegie Steel Company became the reason for organizing the United States Steel Corporation, and the keystone of it.

[1] "The History of the Carnegie Steel Company."

II

As Rockefeller became pre-eminent in oil, Carnegie became pre-eminent in steel. Rockefeller was the outstanding exponent of combination, Carnegie of ruthless competition. Rockefeller, thinking in terms similar to European "cartels," would go to other men in the oil business, would talk to them about the desirability of combination and stabilization; would argue against the wastes of competition, would ask his competitor to unite with him, would offer to give either cash or stock in the Standard Oil Company for his competitor's plant. If the competitor declined, he would be subject to the Standard's competition, and likely to find himself sooner or later a casualty.

Carnegie did nothing like that. He scorned co-operation with his competitors. Although he occasionally participated in pools, he disdained them. Of price-fixing agreements between competitors, he said: "artificial arrangements, strengthening the other fellow as much as they strengthen you . . . bad business." That is the key to Carnegie's point of view, an outstanding individualist in his era. To his board of managers of the Carnegie Steel Company, he wrote: "We should look with favor upon every combination of every kind upon the part of our competitors; the bigger they grow, the more vulnerable they become." Though he acquired two plants, Homestead and Duquesne, by purchase, Carnegie as a rule rarely tried to persuade or force a competitor to sell out to him, rarely entertained any notion of buying him out. Carnegie generally paid no attention to rivals except to gloat when his methods made them squirm, or succumb. Carnegie managed his business as an utterly ruthless individualist, and as the ablest manufacturer in his field. He made good steel, at a lower cost than anybody else, and sold it at such prices as, under the conditions, would give him the best advantages. When conditions called for the cutting of prices, Carnegie cut, murderously.[1] In the steel trade, Carnegie's methods, especially in times of depression, came to be called, with allusion to the way his Scotch ancestors harried their English neighbors, "Carnegie cattle-work along the border."

Andrew Carnegie.

By these methods Carnegie had become, by 1900, the greatest steel-maker in America. The entire steel and iron business of America in that year was composed of the Carnegie Company — and the others. "The others" consisted chiefly of seven fairly large companies, each less efficient than the Carnegie Company; all harried by Carnegie's hard-driving competition.

III

Carnegie, by 1900, had had his fill of business. For fifty years, from the age of thirteen, he had lived a life of ever-increasing pressure and strain. His dominance in steel had been achieved by unceasing battle, against his competitors, against his workmen, against all who got in his way. The pace he had maintained was a killing one, and he was tired. He wanted time to live up to the doctrine he had formulated: "The man who dies rich dies

[1] Of the methods of the two men, Rockefeller's were the more humane toward competitors; yet because of adventitious incidents it was Rockefeller who became the symbol of cruelty in business.

disgraced." He had interested himself in a large variety of avocations, including many philanthropies and some harmless, even laudable, social and literary vanities; and wished to devote himself to them exclusively.

But he feared merely to retire, leaving his capital in the business, and permitting it to be managed by others. No one of his partners was his equal in ruthlessness or resourcefulness, the two qualities which, as the steel business was at that time, were alone capable of keeping the Carnegie interests at the top. Steel then, as it had been from the discovery of the Bessemer Process, knew no such thing as stable prosperity. Carnegie feared that unless he himself were at the helm during the famine years, his companies would suffer. He was troubled, anxious, tired. His mind went back in his sixties to the memorandum for personal guidance he had jotted down one Christmas-time during his thirties, the longing to cast aside business, to become a figure in the world of education, literature, and public affairs. In spite of his pride in the company that bore his name, he was willing to sell out — "willing," indeed, is too weak a word.

To dispose of so huge a property as the Carnegie Steel Company and its allied interests, could not be a mere matter of offering it for sale. Probably — one need hardly say "probably" — there was only one possible purchaser, only one man in all America who combined the necessary requirements. To buy the Carnegie company meant, under the conditions of the time, to form a steel trust. There was only one man of such potent influence and ample financial backing as to command the confidence of investors in the plants to be combined and of the public generally; only one man who could "put over" the trust in the sense of buying the competing plants from their owners and also in the sense of getting the public to buy shares in the trust.

IV

The man thus fixed by conditions as the objective, the "prospect," of Carnegie's salesmanship was J. Pierpont Morgan. When Carnegie put out the tentacles of his business art to draw Morgan into a "dicker," he brought into temporary juxtaposition, though decidedly not into union in any sense, two of the greatest industrial Joves since Vulcan and Midas. By every aspect of their respective settings, they were fitted to have no relation to each other except that of rivalry. One difference between them was sufficiently suggested by the fact that when occasion brought them together, observers noticed Carnegie address Morgan as "Pierpont," and saw Morgan wince — there is no record that any one ever heard Morgan call Carnegie "Andy."

Morgan's title to eminence in what common talk of the day called "the upper crust" came by birth, education, and environment. He came of one of America's Colonial families, his father a banker, his grandfather a clergyman, teacher, and text-book compiler.[1] Morgan got his education at Harvard and at Göttingen in Germany; Carnegie got his by pitiful little devices of borrowed library books. Morgan entered the business world by way of inheritance of a great American private banking-house; Carnegie by way of the factory whistle that summoned a twelve-year-old boy at six a.m.

Let no one suppose this comparison pictures Morgan as the one of lesser force, nor imagine that only self-help can develop titanic qualities of personality. Of the two, Morgan was the greater Titan. Of the sort of man that Morgan was, the varied aspects of American life he dominated, there is a vivid picture in the words of Edward Page Mitchell, editor of the New York *Sun* at a time when Morgan had the relation of Maecenas to that paper:

[1] See Chapter 2.

What a whale of a man! was the measurement of every observer who, approaching that potent gentleman from any of his many fortified sides, got far enough through the barrier of brusque reserve and masterful demeanor to understand something of what lay behind the protective equipment. . . . Mr.

Morgan was dynamic both in intelligence and in will. There seemed to radiate something that forced the complex of inferiority, as the psychoanalysts delight in calling it, upon all around him, in spite of themselves. The boldest man was likely to become timid under his piercing gaze. The most impudent or recalcitrant were ground to humility as he chewed truculently at his huge black cigar. The lesser monarchs of finance, of insurance, of transportation, of individual enterprise, each in his own domain haughty as Lucifer,

J. P. Morgan leaving his Wall Street office, about 1910.

were glad to stand in the corridor waiting their turns like applicants for minor clerkships in the anteroom of a department official, while he sat at his desk in his library-room within.

There appears an unpublished photograph of J. Pierpont Morgan emerging from his office to be whirled up-town to the place where he perhaps best enjoyed being, the marble library in East Thirty-sixth Street. The central figure always gave me the impression of one who, by sheer force of will, might have stridden at need through a stone wall as readily as through these few flakes of snow.[1]

This judgment about Morgan was paralleled by that of James Ford Rhodes, the historian:

In the parlance of the street, his first name was Jupiter; this was properly bestowed, for his word was "I command."[2]

v

But Morgan could not say "I command" to Carnegie. To imply that Carnegie said "I command" to Morgan, would be too much; but Carnegie did make Morgan do what he wanted. Morgan's qualifications for the rôle to which Carnegie now proposed to assign him were not confined merely to his greater command of money than any other man or firm in America. As Carnegie was the leading exponent of competition, so was Morgan a leading exponent of combination — he had just concluded a decade devoted to the reorganization of the country's railroads into a group of systems, rescuing them from the rapidly recurrent bankruptcies that had accompanied their earlier phase. He had just combined a number of small steel companies, rescuing them from distress into which they had been driven chiefly by the ruthless competition of the Carnegie Company. In the Wall Street jargon of the day, to "reorganize" was to "re-Morganize."[3]

Carnegie now took a subtle advantage of his reputation for aggressiveness, the reputation that had made him

[1] "Memoirs of an Editor," Edward P. Mitchell. Mr. Mitchell said this estimate of Morgan was not only his own, but also that of his associate in the conduct of the New York *Sun* during its period of greatness, "after long and careful observation of him [Morgan] in action."

[2] I am told that "Jupiter" as a name for Morgan was originated by Thomas Hitchcock, who, under the pseudonym "Matthew Marshall," wrote financial articles for the New York *Sun*.

[3] Another pun of that day spoke of Morgan's office as the "morgue" of decrepit railroads needing to be combined with others.

feared in every quarter where his interests came into competitive relation with others. To Morgan in his New York offices came disturbing rumors from Pittsburgh, many in the form of newspaper headlines. The Carnegie press agent gave out a statement that "it has been determined by the Carnegie Company to establish an extensive pipe-and-tube manufacturing plant, representing an investment of $12,000,000, the most extensive and complete plant of the kind in existence." Morgan read that, and was obliged to be apprehensive about his own interest in the existing National Tube Works. Carnegie actually bought land, had plans drawn up, and began work on the foundations. Morgan felt half sure this was a bluff. Still he could not be comfortable, knowing that Carnegie was capable of carrying through any project he should undertake. For the time being, he "stood pat" and awaited further developments.

They were not long in coming. Almost daily, announcements left Carnegie's Pittsburgh offices of new enterprises on which Carnegie was about to embark. Carnegie, in the pressure he put on Morgan, was as characteristically ingenious and thorough as in his other arts of business. He started rumors that he was planning to set up competition to the Pennsylvania Railroad, a Morgan road, by building lines of his own between points of heavy traffic density, where he, as shipper, could influence business. He even began surveys for a Carnegie road from Pittsburgh to the Atlantic. Morgan, proud of the railroad stability he had brought about by ten years of effort, was given the opportunity to visualize the sort of competition that would be reintroduced into the railroad world by Carnegie, the rate-wars, bankruptcies, reorganizations, the renewal of competitive building. These announcements were irritating and unsettling to the whole financial world. Security values were upset and investors became timid.

The wide-flung "Morgan interests" suffered. Other bankers and industrial leaders pleaded with Morgan to "do something about this fellow Carnegie."

Fear of Carnegie provided Morgan with one motive for forming a steel trust which should at once take the Carnegie Company in and by the same act get Carnegie personally into private life. Another motive, the desirability, on the broadest grounds, of stabilizing the steel business, the general benefits which consolidation would bring to the steel industry and to the country's whole industrial structure, had already been urged upon Morgan by Elbert H. Gary. Steel had been, as Carnegie once expressed it, "always either prince or pauper"; violent expansion and high prices alternated with deep depressions and prices so low that only the unit most advantageously situated could survive; alternations of feast and famine distressed not only the owners but the workmen, whose customary characterization of dull times in the steel trade was "soup-house days"; values were periodically upset and investors made timid; consumers of steel could not count confidently on future prices. All this was recited to Morgan by Gary, but in vain, until Carnegie brought his kind of pressure.

Carnegie's salesmanship was a double art, in which threat was balanced with allurement. The whole of it was described in a picture taken from the field of religion: "In the conversion of the heathen, missionaries have found it useful to describe the condition of the damned before presenting a picture of the joys of the blessed. It was on some such principle that the threat of industrial war was thus made by Carnegie, before the blessings of the co-operation and consolidation were set out before the alarmed financier."[1]

Or one might say that Carnegie took his art of sales-

[1] "History of the Carnegie Steel Company." James Howard Bridge.

manship from his knowledge of the wonder-working powers of fire and air in the making of steel, in which the raw material is heated to melting, after which air is blown through it. Carnegie, having first built fires of threatened competition under Morgan, now sent to him one of the Carnegie salesmen, a young man named Charles

Charles Schwab.

Schwab, who, in the words of an entranced historian,[1] "had a veritable tongue of gold. To listen to him was to be converted to his views; he could talk the legs off the proverbial brass pot. . . ."

Carnegie told Schwab to concentrate on Morgan. He did. On the night of December 12, 1900, two close friends of Carnegie, Edward Simmons and Charles Stuart Smith, gave a dinner, ostensibly social, to which Morgan was invited. To Schwab was assigned the duty of making the speech of the evening. He chose for his subject the steel company of the future. "He played upon this theme as upon a harp. . . . He drew a word-picture of a company big enough to insure the greatest economies. He described such an organization as able to dominate the markets of the world and to set a pace that neither England nor Germany could follow. The ideal structure he painted was such a one as was well worth the attention of the greatest of bankers, an industrial enterprise for which even the great Morgan might well be proud to stand

---

[1] Arundel Cotter, author of the "United States Steel Corporation, a Corporation With a Soul."

sponsor. And the youthful Schwab swept the financier off his feet and along with him in the flood of his oratory. In that half-hour the United States Steel Corporation, to all intents and purposes, became an actual fact."[1] Thereafter, there began a series of interviews which eventually led to the founding of the United States Steel Corporation, to the realization of Carnegie's desire to retire.

"It was," says James Howard Bridge, a kind of literary secretary to Carnegie, "the most masterly piece of diplomacy in the history of American industry, and formed a fitting climax to Andrew Carnegie's romantic business career."

VI

The plan for organizing the United States Steel Corporation was made public March 3, 1901, through an advertisement signed by J. P. Morgan and Company. The reaction was instantaneous. Some of it was pride, a superficial national egotism inspired by the grandiosity of the biggest trust in the world. But much more of the spontaneous response was alarm, alarm of several different kinds, caused by contemplating different aspects of the trust. Much took the form of apprehension of socialism. Should the movement toward combination continue, the Boston *Herald* thought that

if a limited financial group shall come to represent the capitalistic end of industry, the perils of socialism, even if brought about by a somewhat rude, because forcible, taking of the instruments of industry, may be looked upon by even intelligent people as possibly the lesser of two evils.

Similarly, the Philadelphia *Evening Telegraph* considered that: "If a grasping and unrelenting monopoly is the outcome, there will be given an enormous impulse to the

[1] Condensed from "The United States Steel Corporation, a Corporation With a Soul," by Arundel Cotter. The order of some sentences is here rearranged.

growing antagonism to the concentration of capital, which may lead to one of the greatest social and political upheavals that has been witnessed in modern history." The New York *Evening Post* held that "if the raw materials of iron and steel are ever brought under monopoly control, society will find a way, under the law of eminent domain, or otherwise, to protect itself." [1]

Dr. Albert Shaw, in the *Review of Reviews*, expressed a fatalistic tolerance of coming socialism:

It is the belief among people — certainly of those who entertain Communistic or Socialistic ideals — that we are moving steadily toward the point where the economic and industrial community must become merged absolutely in the political community. . . . The disappearance of the old-fashioned competitive system must result in something like a great co-operative organization of workers.

Such placidity, however, was the exception. The contagion of alarm infected quarters so high and so ordinarily serene as the office of president of Yale University. Dr. Arthur T. Hadley's apprehension was apparently of something quite different from socialism. In an address entitled "The Development of Public Conscience," delivered before a church audience in Boston in March, 1901, he was reported as saying:

Trusts have got to be regulated by public sentiment, and that public sentiment is not merely the opinion of any particular part of the whole people, but is a readiness to accept, in behalf of the community, restrictions, independent of the question of whether you or I shall be personally harmed by these restrictions. You say the community will not be governed by this principle. We must expect that the community will, for the alternative is an emperor in Washington within twenty-five years.

[1] By 1927, it was easy to smile at these predictions. It is to be observed, however, that through them ran a tone seeming to "sense" vaguely the immense elevation business and economics were destined to have in politics and statesmanship.

Something of the same kind was predicted by John Brisben Walker, a unique and forceful person, genius of a sort, then editor of *The Cosmopolitan Magazine*, which

" An American syndicate has undertaken the construction of new and the reform of old lines of railway in London and its suburbs."

" Mr. Pierpont Morgan has purchased the Leyland line of steamships."

John Bull looks on and watches in dismay
His children by the ogre dragged away.
First he picked up the boy and then the girl—
One by the breeks, the other by the curl.
                    —From the *Daily Express* (London).

Reproduced in the "Review of Reviews," July, 1901.

at that time dealt largely with the discussion of public affairs and was influential, among other reasons, because of wide circulation at the popular price of ten cents. In the April, 1901, issue, Walker wrote:

The world, on the 3d day of March, 1901, ceased to be ruled by . . . so-called statesmen. True, there were marionettes still figuring in Congress and as kings. But they were in place simply to carry out the orders of the world's real rulers — those who control the concentrated portion of the money supply. Between the lines of this advertisement headed "Office of J. P. Morgan & Company" was to be read a proclamation thus: "Commercial metropolis of the world. The old competitive system, with its ruinous methods, its countless duplications, its wastefulness of human effort, and its relentless business warfare, is hereby abolished."

The New Orleans *Picayune* envisaged a gloomy future:

Governments will be operated, congresses and legislatures will be . . . continued for the express purpose of legislating for and settling the controversies of these mighty corporations, and individuals will cease to be considered. A man will then be designated merely according to his relations as an employee of some vast corporation and will be known only by a number. After that, what?

Arthur Brisbane's editorials in the Hearst newspapers, printed with the emphasis of big type and short paragraphs, were then new and much discussed. He thought that, as a result of the steel industry being brought into one organization, the "economic emperor" of the future would be not a trust magnate, but somebody quite different:

THE RULER OF THE STEEL TRUST IS THE MAN WHO CAN CONTROL THE . . . HUNDREDS OF THOUSANDS OF HUMAN BEINGS ENGAGED IN THE PRODUCTION OF STEEL.

The capable leader of that vast army of men may not be visible to-day. But he is bound to appear. [He will say] "I represent ALL THE MEN IN AMERICA CAPABLE OF MAKING STEEL. I am, therefore, the HEAD OF THE STEEL TRUST, and hereafter, YOU WILL PLEASE TAKE MY INSTRUCTIONS AS TO THE STEEL TRUST MANAGEMENT.

Great new problems confront the people in this trust age.

The greatest is the problem presented by the possibilities of a labor trust more dangerous and aggressive than any other.

A few papers, such as the Philadelphia *Times*, preserved the unfailing American humor. Even *The Commoner*, owned and edited by William Jennings Bryan, permitted itself a facetious interlude in its customary vociferation of alarm about trusts:

"America is good enough for me," remarked J. Pierpont Morgan a few days ago. Whenever he doesn't like it, he can give it back to us.

European countries had their own variety of apprehension. The Berlin *Kreuz-Zeitung* surmised that the organizer of the Steel Corporation would "Morganize" the world, would bring about consolidation of the iron and steel industries of Europe, which would be "the last humiliation of Europe by the young giant of the West." The London *Chronicle* declared: "It is little less than a menace to the commerce of the civilized world. It sets the seal to the triumph of the millionaire." In France, Paul de Rousiers wrote in *Le Correspondent* about "Le Trust de L'Acier" as a "trust of trusts," a "danger serious to European metallurgy."

All of which "Mr. Dooley" summed up:

Pierpont Morgan calls in wan iv his office boys, th' prisidint iv a naytional bank, an' says he, "James," he says, "take some change out iv th' damper an' r-run out an' buy Europe f'r me," he says. "I intind to re-organize it an' put it on a paying basis," he says. "Call up the Czar an' th' Pope an' th' Sultan an' th' Impror Willum, an' tell thim we won't need their sarvices afther nex' week," he says. "Give thim a year's salary in advance. An', James," he says, "Ye betther put that r-red headed book-keeper near th' dure in charge iv th' continent. He doesn't seem to be doin' much," he says.

Morgan having determined to form the merger, it was characteristic of his whole career that he entered into no argument about price with the owners of the merged

companies, but paid the first figures asked.[1] He capitalized
the new company at

Bonds $303,450,000
Preferred stock 550,000,000
Common stock .... 550,000,000[2]

In paying off the constituent companies Morgan
showed clearly his chief motive for organizing the combination. To all the smaller companies he gave stock, which
would permit them to have a proportionate voice in
management. But to the Carnegie Company he gave
chiefly bonds, the total bond issue of the new corporation, $303,450,000, plus $98,277,120 in preferred stock,
plus $90,279,040 in common stock. Carnegie's version of
this was that he insisted on having bonds because he regarded the stock as not merely water but air. Morgan's
version was that he wanted to get Carnegie out of the
management and out of the steel business, completely
out, with no leverage through which he could have a
hand in the management of the United States Steel Corporation, and no motive or excuse to de-stabilize Morgan's
stabilization.[3]

[1] Common legend said that in many cases Morgan paid, not the first figure
asked but much more. A story was told by nearly everybody and heard by all,
one of those stories not meant as literal, nor as applying to any specific incident,
but having the impressionistic quality of art, a detail in the picture of the time.
The story pictured two partners owning a Western steel mill that Morgan wanted
for his combination, their conversation with each other in which they agreed that
five million dollars would be a fair price, their decision—since they did not care
much to sell—to ask ten millions; their journey to New York and the conflict
in their minds between daring and timidity as they approached the great banker
—and, as the climax, Morgan's meeting them at the door of his office with the
forthright brusqueness, the "getting the jump" on the other party to a deal,
which was part of the Morgan legend: "Now, I don't want to hear any talk from
you men; I know all about your plant and exactly what it's worth; I haven't time
for any haggling; I'm going to give you twenty million dollars—now take it or
leave it."

[2] As against this total capitalization of $1,403,450,000, the physical value of the
plants was estimated, in a government report, by the United States Bureau of
Corporations, at $682,000,000.

[3] For some time afterward, Wall Street slang, when it wished to describe the
elimination of a man from a situation, especially if the removal was complete
and final, used "to Carnegie" as a verb.

Of the securities that went to the Carnegie Company, the lion's share went to Carnegie personally. It was commonly reckoned, and probably true, that Carnegie, as he retired, was worth $250,000,000, measured in cash. Carnegie went to Europe for a rest and shortly afterward began a career of giving, the magnificence of which was an ironic comment on those who thought one result of "big business" in America would be the setting up of a caste of hereditary plutocrats. (Carnegie retained so little of his fortune for his heirs that after he died in August, 1919, his widow found herself inconvenienced when the post-war period of high taxes continued.)

J. Pierpont Morgan.

Morgan, for himself and his associates in the underwriting syndicate, took 648,-988 shares of the preferred stock and 648,987 of the common, valued, at the lowest price at which the shares were sold in the ensuing stock-market campaign, at $77,987,-640.[1] This profit, however, was mere "paper," mere stock certificates, until the shares could be sold to the public.

To "make a market," Morgan employed a celebrated market manipulator of the day, James R. Keene. The time was propitious. Fundamental conditions were right, and with these right, the necessary superficial conditions, the atmosphere, could be made to order. The country had just finished a victorious war and acquired great over-seas possessions. "Empire" was in the air, and

[1] This estimate is given by James Ford Rhodes, who is dependable.

the psychology that went with it. Industrial enterprise, held back by the prolonged depression of the early nineties, had begun to pulse forward. Investors, who had been made timid by the threat of free silver, were reassured by the second defeat of Bryan in 1900 and the formal adoption of the gold standard by Congress in the same year. The discovery of a new gold supply, the Yukon, had at once stimulated the spirit of adventure and added more gold to the base of currency, causing wages to rise, as well as the prices of commodities. The creation of the trusts, the vogue of the promoters, their Monte Carlo prodigality and picturesqueness, the bigness of the extraordinary sums of money constantly mentioned in newspaper head-lines and the rapidity with which such profits were made, dazzled men's minds, so that they became drunk with the passion of money-getting, and blind to all other standards and ideals. Everybody thought and spoke in millions; and the Napoleons of finance "became, in a sense, heroes and demigods. Men and women and even children all over the country drank in thirstily every scrap of news that was printed in the press about these so-called 'captains of industry,' their successful 'deals,' the off-hand way in which they converted slips of worthless paper into guarantees of more than princely wealth, and all the details concerning their daily lives, their personal peculiarities, their virtues, and their vices. To the imagination of millions of Americans, the financial centres of the country seemed to be spouting streams of gold into which any one might dip at will; and every Wall Street gutter figured as a new Pactolus." All the conditions combined to compose an ideal time in which to "make a market" and unload stock on the public. Daily transactions on the New York Stock Exchange, many of them "wash" sales manipulated for psychological effect, reached totals never before approached — on one day over 3,000,000 shares changed hands, and in one week over 10,000,000. The public was kept advised, alluringly, of the winnings made in stocks by some of the spectacular figures of the new era. As a result, thousands of the public became ephemeral customers of the brokerage house. "The outburst of speculation during April, 1901, was something rarely paralleled in the history of speculative manias. . . . A stream of excited customers brought their money to New York and spent their days in offices near the Stock Exchange. The newspapers were full of stories of hotel waiters, clerks, even doorkeepers and dressmakers, who had won considerable fortunes in their speculations." [1] A stenographer, coming late in the morning, explained she had been to her broker to buy "a hundred Steel common." Barbers told customers of tips they had had from promoters they shaved, on which they had made thousands. A slogan ran through New York, not only down-town but in shops, on street-cars, on commuters' trains: "Buy A. O. T. — Any Old Thing." Everything was going up. No tip could fail.

The Steel Corporation's shares were put out as carrying dividends of four[2] per cent on the common and seven per cent on the preferred. Sales were started on the exchange at 38 for the common and 82¾ for the preferred; and were advanced to 55 and 101⅞ respectively.

Morgan, seeing this advance satisfactorily under way, in April, 1901, a little over a month after he had organized the Steel Corporation, took a trip to Europe for what the newspapers commonly designated as "a well-earned rest." It turned out, in a most adventitious and dramatic way, to have serious consequences.

---

[1] Condensed from "American Finance," by Alexander Dana Noyes.

[2] In 1903, the common dividend was suspended; the price of the common went down to 10, the preferred to 49.

A Struggle for a Railroad

One day late that month (April, 1901), when Morgan was refreshing himself at the baths in Germany, an incident occurred at a point nearly a third of the way around

J. P. Morgan's trip to Europe after completing the organization of the United States Steel Corporation, in 1901, led to this forecast by Donahey in the Cleveland *Plain-Dealer*.

the earth. It was as slight, relatively, as the imprint of a carefully light foot in the sand, and had the same suggestion of stealth. The man who noticed it was James J. Hill,[1] a close friend and associate of Morgan, partner with him in the control and management of the two great railroad systems of the Northwest — the Northern Pacific and the Great Northern. Hill, being in Seattle, Wash-

[1] Hill was called "the empire-builder of the Northwest."

ington, on an inspection trip, noticed in the scant reports of the New York Stock Market which local newspapers of that place and time carried, something that puzzled and disturbed him. The shares of one of his and Morgan's own railroads, the Northern Pacific, were being bought in enormous quantities. Hill knew the Northern Pacific as a chauffeur knows his taxicab. He could think of no reassuring explanation. It could hardly be a mere speculative flurry, he reasoned, because the operations were on too big a scale. Had Morgan been in New York, Hill would not have been seriously concerned; Morgan was more than competent to take care of their mutual interests. But Morgan, Hill knew, was in Europe.

Hill sensed menace. He ordered a special train,[1] had the rails cleared of all traffic east to St. Paul, and broke all records for fast travel between the Pacific Coast and the Mississippi River. While his special lurched and swayed eastward, Hill had time for concentrated thinking. One can picture him considering what the Stock Exchange activity in Northern Pacific might mean, reviewing certain incidents of recent railroad history in the Northwest that might provide the clue.

Hill's own domain was the two transcontinental lines of the Northwest — Northern Pacific and Great Northern; these were in control of himself and Morgan and their associates. At least Hill felt confident they had control, though the confidence was not quite complete — otherwise he would not be making his present trip.

To the far South lay the railroad empire of Hill's and Morgan's great rival, the Union Pacific and Southern Pacific, dominated by Edward H. Harriman and the banking-house of Kuhn, Loeb & Company.

Between the Hill-Morgan system on the north and the

[1] On the other of the two railroads he controlled, the Great Northern.

Harriman-Kuhn, Loeb & Company system in the south, and coveted gluttonously by both, lay the Burlington.[1]

That railroad map, three railroad systems roughly parallel, with the middle one a bone of contention between

The Hill lines on the north and the Harriman lines on the south were the contenders. The Burlington, between, was the prize for which they fought.

the other two, constituted the arena in which had been fought one of the greatest financial battles of our time. Hill and Morgan, on the one hand, and Harriman and Kuhn, Loeb, on the other, had fought for the Burlington, savagely in the open stock market, and by intrigue in

[1] To the public in the mood it was in at the time, when the facts became known about the historic Hill-Harriman struggle, it seemed like a performance in which Titans contended, using whole railroad systems as shuttlecocks, indifferent to millions of human beings whose destinies were vitally involved. Actually both Hill and Harriman had defensible motives for wishing to acquire the Burlington. Hill wanted it to provide him with an entrance to Chicago; to bring cotton from the South, coal from Illinois, and farm products from the Lower Mississippi Valley; to give him a market for lumber, the major product of the Northwest. Harriman wanted the Burlington to safeguard himself against some other ownership that might extend its western terminus to the Pacific Coast and thus compete with his Union Pacific.

the banking-house. But that fight, Hill reflected, had been fought and won — he and Morgan had won it. Or had they won it? Hill went over the circumstances.

The first move to grasp the Burlington had been made by Hill himself, four years before, in 1897. The attempt had failed because Hill at that time could not secure the necessary money. In 1900, Harriman had countered with a conference of his associates "for the purpose of considering the best means of preventing the Morgan and Hill interests from buying or controlling the Burlington system."[1] They had decided to buy 200,000 shares, had formed a pool, had begun to buy in the open market, but had stopped when they got 69,800 shares — they "found themselves up against a stone wall consisting of the great body of small shareholders,"[2] fifteen thousand or more, who did not wish to sell.

The next move had been made by Morgan and Hill. It had been bold, direct, and successful. The Hill lines, the Great Northern and Northern Pacific, had bought control (96.79 per cent of its stock) of the Burlington outright from the board of directors.

Harriman had not heard of their move until it was practically complete; he had then asked to be given a one-third interest in the purchase, but had been refused. The Burlington was safely in the joint ownership of the Northern Pacific and Great Northern — and Harriman was very angry.

Hill, arriving in New York, did a characteristic thing. He went not to his own bankers, Morgan & Company (J. P. Morgan was in Europe), but first and straight to the offices of his rival's bankers, Kuhn, Loeb & Company.

[1] "Edward H. Harriman, A Biography," George Kennan.
[2] "Life of James J. Hill," by Joseph G. Pyle.

There he talked with one of the partners, Jacob Schiff.
Hill asked a blunt question and received an equally blunt
reply.[1] Schiff told Hill that Kuhn, Loeb & Company was
buying all the Northern Pacific stock it could get hold of.
Hill asked why. At least, accounts from both sides say

James J. Hill, a railroad man, called
"the empire-builder."

Hill asked the question. If he
did, he was manœuvring for
time. Hill well knew the subtle
purpose, the only purpose Harriman could have, in buying
Northern Pacific stock. The
bone, the Burlington, was in
the treasury of Hill's road, the
Northern Pacific.[2] By buying
control of the Northern Pacific, Harriman could get the
bone — not only the bone but
also a part of Hill's own sinew.
The raid was a unique combination of daring and subtlety.
To put it in the plain words
used years later by Harriman's
biographer, "when Mr. Harriman discovered that the
Burlington had been captured and taken into the camp
of the enemy, he determined to make a sudden surprise
attack on that camp itself."[3]

Schiff talked to Hill with a frankness that can be explained only by confidence in the success of his plan. Hill
had invited trouble, Schiff said, by his action in getting

---

[1] There is another version. It says that Hill's strategy began with mere sleuthy
gossip about things in general, and that Schiff, in an expansive mood of success,
had volunteered the information that his banking-house had bought control of
one of his visitor's railroads. That could have happened. Schiff was tempera-
mental.

[2] Partly also in the treasury of the other Hill road, the Great Northern.

[3] "Edward H. Harriman: A Biography," George Kennan.

control, *sub rosa*, of the Burlington, thereby threatening the future prosperity of the Harriman-Kuhn, Loeb roads. Schiff added that he was confident of getting a majority of the shares of the Northern Pacific, after which this road, as well as its new subsidiary, the Burlington, would be added to the Harriman systems. Hill was thus invited to contemplate an unpalatable picture, the principal part of his and Morgan's railroad empire becoming an appanage to the domain of their rival.

"You can't get control," Hill told Schiff. "Morgan and my friends were recently holding $35,000,000 or $40,000,000 of Northern Pacific stock, and so far as I know none of it has been sold."

Actually, Hill was not so confident that Schiff and Harriman would not succeed in

E. H. Harriman, from a photograph on his last birthday.

carrying off the Northern Pacific. He left Schiff's office knowing a real battle was on. In that mood he went to his own bankers, J. P. Morgan & Company, and had the junior partners send a cable to the chief in Germany. That was on Saturday afternoon, May 4, after business hours.

Morgan's reply had the fighting magnificence of his nature. It came the following day, Sunday, and it instructed the firm to buy 150,000 shares of Northern Pacific at the market. On Monday morning the Morgan forces swarmed onto the floor of the Stock Exchange; they took all the common stock that was offered; paid prices that rose from 110 to 150; and by Tuesday afternoon had the 150,000 shares. These shares, with what Morgan and Hill already had, made 30,000 more than a majority of the common stock. Of the preferred, however, they had

Westerman, in the "Ohio State Journal."

"The Race for the Switch." The Hill-Harriman fight for the control of the Northern Pacific.

only a minority; and of the preferred and common combined, a slight minority.

Meantime, on the Harriman-Kuhn, Loeb side, Schiff on Friday night, May 3, after his talk with Hill, totalled what he had bought and found that he and Harriman had about 370,000 shares of the common and 420,000 shares of the preferred, for which he had paid $79,000,000. Schiff was confident this was sufficient for control. In the peace of a battle won, Schiff slept an easy night, and on the following day, Saturday, May 4, instead of going downtown to his banking house, went dutifully to his synagogue.

Harriman, however, always nervous, always half-sick with the burdens his spirit put upon his too frail body, did not pass a good night. He was uneasy about the sudden presence of his adversary, Hill, in New York, uneasy about the narrowness of the margin of control; and especially uneasy about a disturbing detail, the legal relation between the preferred stock, of which he had a majority, and the common stock, of which he had about 40,000 shares less than a majority — a fretful uncertainty whether, under the Northern Pacific charter, preferred stock had as much power for control as common stock. "On the morning of Saturday, May 4"—these are Harriman's own words as he told the story later —

I was at home, ill. . . . We had a majority of the entire capital stock, as represented by both the common and preferred shares, and I had been competently advised, and was convinced, that this holding was sufficient to enable us to control the Company. Nevertheless, the fact that the Northern Pacific could, on the 1st of January following, retire the preferred shares, of which we had a majority, bothered me somewhat; and I felt that we ought not to leave open to them any chance of retiring our preferred stock and leaving us with a minority interest in the common stock, or involving us in litigation about it. Some of our friends, however, felt that our position was secure enough, and that it would be foolish to go in and buy more Northern Pacific stock at the prices which then prevailed. Nevertheless, I made up my mind that we should have a majority of the common shares, and on that morning[1] I called up Heinsheimer [one of the junior partners in the firm of Kuhn, Loeb & Company] and gave him an order to buy 40,000 shares of Northern Pacific common for my account. He said: "All right"; and as dealings that day in Northern Pacific common shares continued to be very heavy, I felt that, come what might, I had control of Northern Pacific, common stock and all.

[1] This was Saturday, May 4, the same day Hill sent Morgan the cable that resulted in Morgan buying 150,000 shares.

On Monday, the 6th of May . . . I called Heinsheimer up and asked him why I had gotten no report of the execution of my order. He told me that before giving out the order he had to reach Schiff, who was at the synagogue. Schiff instructed him not to execute the order and said that he (Schiff) would be responsible. I then knew that matters were in a serious way and that the whole object of our work might be lost. Meanwhile, the day (Monday) had become so advanced and prices of Northern Pacific shares had gone so high that I realized the impossibility of buying, in such a market, 40,000 shares of stock.

The situation was made complex, and the outcome uncertain, by the figure played by outsiders — some of them destined to learn it is dangerous to get under the feet of giants when they are playing too roughly, and that whimsical visitations of fortune may attend such fights. The contenders had bought, nominally, shares; actually they had bought contracts to deliver shares. Whether all of those who contracted to deliver shares could do so constituted at once the unknown equation in the fight between Morgan and Harriman, and the quite certain tragedy of the outsiders. The outsiders were traders who, as Morgan and Harriman beat up the price, got into action. Seeing that the stock had gone much higher than it was intrinsically worth, the outside traders "sold short"; that is, they sold what they did not at the time possess, but which they expected to buy when they could do so at a price less than their selling figure. Under ordinary circumstances, the only danger in such a practice was that the stock might stay indefinitely at a higher figure than the one at which they had sold, in which event they would be compelled to pay this higher market price in order to make good their contracts. Such a development would mean a loss, of course, but not necessarily annihilation. In the Northern Pacific case, however, the men who "sold short" were taking a short cut to bankruptcy.

Harriman and Hill actually had purchased 78,000 more shares of stock in the Northern Pacific than were in existence. Those who had sold these shares were face to face with as bleak a situation as the imagination of a stock speculator can conjure up. They had contracted to deliver at prices ranging between 110 and 150 many thousands of shares of stock — and they now found that the only stand where they could purchase for delivery was that of the men who held their contracts. In other words, they were in the position of having to buy great quantities of a commodity at such prices as the sellers might choose to exact. The "shorts" were caught like

NEW YORK STOCK EXCHANGE.

Complete Transactions in Stocks—Thursday, May 9, 1901.

—Closing— Bid.	Asked	Sales		First	High	Low.	Last.	Net Change.
50	51	5,400	Norfolk & West......	50⅝	51⅝	47½	50	+7
78	86	800	North American	85	85	80	80	−5½
350	..	11,170	Northern Pacific	170	700	170	325	+165
..	..	8,700	Northern Pacific cash	190	1000	200	320	......
105½	106½	7,600	Northern Pacific pf..	106	106¾	104½	106	− ½
32½	35	8,250	Pacific Mail	38	36	30½	32	−6⅜
143⅞	144	72,400	Pennsylvania R. R...	145½	146	137½	144	− ⅞

Part of the financial page of the New York *Times*, May 10, 1901, showing the record "high" of Northern Pacific, caused by the battle between Morgan and Harriman for control.

rats in a trap. In their frantic grabbing for stock they forced the price at one time above $1,000 a share. In order to meet their obligations, they threw overboard their other holdings, with the effect that the rest of the market list dropped an average of 30 points in one day. As a result, on Thursday, May 9, Wall Street was visited with the "Northern Pacific panic," one of the worst in its history. It was ended by the banking interests, including Morgan and Kuhn, Loeb & Company, whose interest was not in money profits but in their own rivalry; they permitted the "shorts" to settle on the basis of

$150 a share, and the panic was stopped almost before it began.

The fight for control ended in a deadlock,[1] with one side holding a majority of the preferred and the other a majority of the common stock. Rather than face prolonged litigation, the protagonists decided to compromise. Harriman was given a place on the board of directors of the Northern Pacific; the Burlington was neutralized, so far as special favors to either the Hill or the Harriman roads was concerned; and it was agreed that the Burlington should not extend its lines from Denver to the Pacific Coast without the consent of Harriman.

To embody this compromise, Morgan, with Harriman, organized a new and gigantic holding-company with a capital of $400,000,000, the Northern Securities Company, taking in the three great railroad systems of the Northwest: the Great Northern, the Northern Pacific, and the Burlington.

To the sensational outcry that had attended Morgan's organization of the greatest industrial holding-company, the United States Steel Corporation, six months before — was now added a new explosion of clamor over his creation of the greatest railroad holding-company.

The negotiations for the Northern Securities merger lasted about six months, from May 9 to November 12, 1901, when the company received its charter from New Jersey.

Toward the end of this period, in September, 1901, an event occurred that was as remote from the calculations of railroad giants as imagination can conceive. A crazy

---

[1] Persons from both sides who have read this chapter, or discussed it with the author, have queried the word "deadlock," each claiming its faction was victorious. Who would have won depended on how the courts would act on the right of common stockholders to retire the preferred stock.

Pole named Czolgosz went into the tailor shop of a Chicago friend and said that after weighty reflection about the state of the world he had decided to kill a priest. "Why kill a priest?" asked the tailor. "There are so many priests; they are like flies — a hundred will come to his funeral." On considering this argument Czolgosz decided it was better to kill a President. He went to Buffalo, New York, and on September 6, shot and fatally wounded President McKinley.

By this utterly irrelevant, mad act, came to an end the Presidency of the man of whom Herbert Croly said:

When Mr. McKinley was re-elected, big business undoubtedly considered that it had received a license to do very much as it pleased.

That statement, very appropriately and authoritatively, was made in a biography of Mark Hanna.

19

THE TRUSTS AND THE GOVERNMENT

THE liaison between big business and the government was personified, in the popular mind, by Mark Hanna. The newspaper device of symbols — at once a convenience and a detriment to completeness of truth — which in cartoons and headlines personified Hanna as "Wall Street" and "The Trusts," was perfectly accurate in the sense that Hanna was the spokesman of big business in politics. That Hanna was the mentor of McKinley, his most intimate friend and his financial benefactor, everybody knew. That, during the McKinley administration, "big business . . . considered it had a license to do very much as it pleased" is attested by Hanna's biographer. That McKinley had allowed the Sherman anti-trust law practically to lapse[1] is a matter of record; during two years before his death no anti-trust prosecution had been brought, though it was a period when new combinations were being formed almost weekly — the United States Steel Corporation and the Northern Securities Corporation were merely the largest of scores.

As it happened — though the fact is immaterial — Hanna had never had anything to do with Wall Street

---

[1] "During the last few years of [McKinley's] administration, the Department of Justice was making hardly any attempt to enforce the Sherman law against anybody, or to apply it in any way to any combination whatever. Thousands of men who wanted to evade that law, and even to disobey it if necessary, for their own monopolistic purposes, took part in hundreds of organizations of holding-companies during a few years about . . . 1900 [in spite of the fact that] at the end of McKinley's administration the Sherman law stood with its original completeness and clearness unchanged by any amendment."—Albert H. Walker, "History of the Sherman Law."

until after he became powerful in politics; he was the head cf no trust and had never been a promoter — he scorned that quick path to wealth; the law of his nature made him take pleasure in starting an industry and building it up — at one time or another he was active in coal mines, iron ore, shipping, oil.

Not many men have ever functioned so directly toward a high destiny as had Hanna; still fewer ever attained their ambitions so completely. Nature had adapted him to power, for he was full-vigored; and to exercise power benignly, for he was generous, optimistic, loved to accept responsibility, and beamed when he carried it off brilliantly. From his earliest life, when he entered business and politics, he had prospered — prudently keeping politics subordinate until, in his forties, he had accumulated his fortune. By that time thousands of persons in Cleveland and Northern Ohio were the beneficiaries of one radiation or another of Hanna's high-powered ability. He had built up businesses, promoted community enterprises (including, for a time, a newspaper and a theatre). In politics he had taken part in local Cleveland fights, attended party conventions, collected campaign funds; and had become acquainted with a young lawyer and Congressman named William McKinley, in whom Hanna found an ideal at once of friendship and of politics. When McKinley, through unwise reliance on the miracle-working possibilities of the tariff, had endorsed the notes of an infant Ohio industry in steel, and had gone deep into bankruptcy, Hanna and some associates collected a fund that paid McKinley's debts and enabled him to remain in public life. Neither this nor any other aspect of the relation between the two men was sordid. That McKinley was an outstanding believer in the protective tariff made him satisfactory to all big business, but Hanna's relation to him was primarily that of a warm-hearted, expansive man who gets satisfaction out of promoting the career of a talented and, in the business sense, rather unworldly friend. Hanna devoted a year and a half, and more than a hundred thousand dollars of his own money, to getting

A forceful series of cartoons by F. Opper in the New York *Journal*, that had much influence, pictured President McKinley as the child of the trusts, and Mark Hanna as "Nursie." After Roosevelt was nominated for Vice-President he was introduced into the cartoons as a playmate of McKinley. The original caption for this cartoon read: "Yes, Willie, here is a nice little boy Nursie and I have found to play with you. Treat him kindly, as he is very timid and retiring."

the 1896 Republican presidential nomination for McKinley; and during another three months gave all his time to electing McKinley over Bryan, "frying the fat" out of the business interests of the country to the extent of more than four million dollars — the Standard Oil Company alone gave $250,000, and the banks everywhere were formally

assessed one-fourth of one per cent of their combined
capital and surplus.

March 4, 1897, found McKinley President, with Hanna
head of the Republican party. For Hanna, it was such a

F. Opper, in the New York "Journal."

When Roosevelt, as the candidate for Vice-President with McKinley, showed excessive initiative he was pictured as sat upon by "Nursie" Hanna while "Papa"
Trusts said: "Yes, Willie, Nursie has to sit on Teddy. He has been making
altogether too much noise lately."

position as fancy dreams. He was a king with two realms,
business and politics. The cartoons that pictured him
exploiting one of his kingdoms for the benefit of the other
were inaccurate; Hanna did not need to persuade McKinley to favor big business — to do that was McKinley's
political religion rather more than it was Hanna's. Hanna

was not a man to stultify either the friend he was proud of or the Presidency for which he had an old-fashioned sentiment that can be described by no less a term than awed respect. He was friendly to business, of course, but he liked business to come to him with its hat off, and when he transmitted the views of business to McKinley, it pleased him to take his own hat off. Frequently McKinley would not do what Hanna advised,[1] on which occasions it pleased Hanna to say, and honestly persuade himself to believe, that McKinley was wiser than he. Hanna would protest for an hour or so, and then embark on McKinley's alternative with as much enthusiasm as if it had been his own idea. On some occasions, Hanna would tell big business what to do — he made the coal operators and their Wall Street bankers grant an increase of wages to the miners on the eve of the 1900 election, though the sullen operators wanted earnestly to fight and believed confidently they could win. Hanna was always more sympathetic to organized labor than were most of his capitalist associates; he had had direct contact with his own workmen, had carried on his own negotiations with them, took a hearty pride in having a man-to-man footing with them, and called them by their first names until they numbered more than six thousand.

Hanna's relation to McKinley carried with it no direct material benefit. But in glory, in ornateness of position and power, in satisfying the spirit of such a nature as Hanna's, it was the kind of place that makes a man's throat choke when he tries to say: "My cup runneth over." When he came to Washington to represent McKinley in the Senate and as National Chairman of the Republican party, he had both the heart of power and its trappings to a degree rarely equalled, occupying, as

---

[1] Hanna was strongly opposed to the Spanish War; McKinley went into it under pressure from the press and from the "church people" who were shocked by the Cuban atrocities.

Roosevelt once put it, "a position of power and influence
. . . such as no other man in our history has had."

Hanna exulted in it with boyish enjoyment that caused
people to smile and like him. He wished everybody could
feel as buoyant as he, and not infrequently took pains to
bring about that state of happy confidence. Meeting
a friend, he said: "What are you looking so . serious
about?" and when the trouble turned out to be financial,
wrote out a check and said: "Pay your debts and look
cheerful." Walking into the room of a committee engaged
in a public enterprise, he sensed gloom, divined the cause
of it, and said: "I'll pay the deficit; now go on with your
work." In some men, that sort of thing might have been
largely vanity; in Hanna it was recognized as part of the
essential quality of a big and able man, a natural leader
— the fulfilment, in that place and day, of Carlyle's description of a true king, an "I can" man. To thousands
of acquaintances and much of the public, he was "Uncle
Mark." His cook, Maggie, was a public character; her
particular talent was to bring just the right tint of brown
and just the right degree of crackling crispness to the crust
of cornbeef hash. Senators, politicians, and newspaper
men invited to one of "Uncle Mark's breakfasts" ate
the sausage and waffles and afterwards retailed the experience as an insignia of their intimacy with power.

To Hanna, with McKinley in the Presidency, God was
in His Heaven, and the world was good. On the eve of
McKinley's second campaign, in 1899, Hanna expressed
not only his party's policy, but his own contentment in the
words: "All we need to do is 'stand pat.'" (Hanna was
proud of the phrase, and by repeating it often and
proudly, gave the Republican party a name that became
a permanent symbol.) The Republicans had stood pat,
and McKinley had been re-elected; but death had taken
a hand in the game.

Never was fulfilled ambition more utterly devastated than on the day when Hanna turned from McKinley in his grave to Roosevelt in the White House. Hanna did not dislike Roosevelt — it was not in his nature to dislike anybody, unless for a definite personal cause. But

F. Opper, in the New York "Journal."

After Roosevelt became Vice-President, President McKinley was pictured saying to "Papa" Trusts and "Nursie" Hanna: "We are playing Republican minstrels and Teddy wants to be the two end men and the middle man too."

he regarded Roosevelt as politically impossible and fundamentally dangerous — Roosevelt as a young Assistant Secretary of the Navy, at a Gridiron Dinner just before the Spanish War, had ground his teeth at the most powerful figure in the country, saying: "We will have this war for the liberation of Cuba, Senator Hanna, in spite of the timidity of the commercial classes."

For years, Hanna had sensed a magic in Roosevelt's star, and feared it. To him, Roosevelt was impetuous, altruistic, a foregatherer with reformers and high-brows — the epitome of what the business man means when he describes a public man as "unsafe." At the Philadelphia

F. *Opper, in the New York "Journal."*

The Trusts skinning the farmer and laborer, while Mark Hanna and President Mc-Kinley beam approval. "Papa doesn't kill them; he merely skins them and lets them go to grow more skins, and then he skins them again."

convention in 1900, Hanna had resisted the nomination of Roosevelt as Vice-President; had stormed peevishly when McKinley consented to it in order to appeal to the progressive Republicans of the West; had exploded to another Republican leader:

Do whatever you damn please! I'm through! Everybody's gone crazy! What's the matter with all of you? Here's this convention going headlong for Roosevelt for Vice-President.

Don't any of you realize there's only one life between that madman and the Presidency? [1]

and a few hours later, with his characteristic trait of accepting an inevitable programme, and putting his heart into making the best of it, had turned to the newspaper men, saying: "Boys, you can't stop it any more than you could Niagara."

Upon McKinley's death, Hanna's sorrow over the loss of his friend was mixed with rage at the trick Fate had played on him. And as sorrow's crown is self-reproach, he was filled with anger at his own part in his own un-doing. As he saw it, the Republican party had hatched this hybrid duckling, Roosevelt — and the Republican party was Hanna. He now found himself in the repug-nant rôle of political parent to Roosevelt; from father-hood to McKinley, a position lovable on both sides, he was now the uncomfortable stepfather of McKinley's successor. Leaving Buffalo on the McKinley funeral train, he sat beside H. H. Kohlsaat "in an intensely bitter state of mind. . . . He damned Roosevelt and said: 'I told William McKinley it was a mistake to nom-inate that wild man at Philadelphia. I asked him if he realized what would happen if he should die. Now look, that damned cowboy is President of the United States!' "[2]

[1] Arthur Wallace Dunn, in "From Harrison to Harding," says he heard Mark Hanna say this (and much more of the same kind) to another Republican Old Guard leader, Henry C. Payne, of Wisconsin, after a telephone conversation with McKinley at Washington.
[2] "From McKinley to Harding," H. H. Kohlsaat.

20

ROOSEVELT

I

A SEER of the 1860's, looking through the census roll for the one who forty to sixty years later would become the champion of the average American and lead him in a struggle against economic oppression, might readily have arrived last upon the name which in the census of 1860 figured as, Theodore Roosevelt, age 2. By his birth, because his father was a well-to-do New York City merchant of the oldest Dutch lineage and because his mother belonged to the "Southern aristocracy," Roosevelt's pre-ordained lot was to pass his life in the rather supercilious detachment of that stratum of American society for which the common term at that time was "the upper crust." By his inherited fortune — not large but yet substantial — he belonged, in Carlyle's famous classification, with the "haves," and not with the "have-nots"; and was destined to leisure, or to a career of further money-making in the family business. Through his education at Harvard, he might have shared the mental attitude known as "Harvard indifference." His puniness as a youth would have excused ease. His taste for writing books called for the cloister rather than the forum. The zest for outdoor life that he cultivated should have been satisfied, according to the standards of his class, by riding in a red coat after trained hounds across the sunny fields of Long Island. Had he ventured into anything so indecorous as politics, he should have had the rôle of the upper classes doing their duty, played in the costume with which the humorists of the early 1880's actually robed him, the typical "dude in politics." His intellectual endowment destined him, if he should enter politics at all, for the rôle then jeered at as "Mugwump";[1] forbade him to hope for leadership of a party, or even identity with it. He should have had no larger fellowship than as a "silk-stocking" in a little group of serious thinkers.

But why try to picture this contrast, between the Roosevelt that might have been and the Roosevelt that was, through the clumsiness of repetitive detail? It was put once by William Hard, in the obituary tribute he wrote, and it need never be put again:

> He might have been the greatest dilettante of his day. He might have been, in mind and body, its greatest dandy. He might have been the most promiscuous absorber of its offerings. He became the most girded pursuer of its activities.

II

Roosevelt, returning to his New York home after his graduation at Harvard in 1880, inquired of some of his family's associates — who were naturally "the men in the clubs of social pretension, men of cultivated tastes and easy life" — about the location of the district Republican Association and how to go about joining it.

> These men — and the big business men and lawyers also — laughed at me, and told me that politics were "low"; that the organizations were not controlled by "gentlemen"; that I would find them run by saloon-keepers, horse-car conductors, and the like, and not by men with any of whom I would come

---

[1] "Mugwump" was made familiar by frequent reiteration in the New York *Sun*, beginning March 23, 1884, as a description of Republicans who opposed James G. Blaine. Blaine said of the Mugwumps: "They are noisy but not numerous; pharasaical but not practical; ambitious but not wise; pretentious but not powerful." Actually, the Mugwumps included some of the most elevated men of their generation, William Everett, Carl Schurz, Henry Ward Beecher. While the New York *Sun* made the word familiar, its earliest use was by the Indianapolis *Sentinel*, in 1872. A modern phrase that would partially fulfil the meaning of mugwump is "high-brow."

in contact outside; and, moreover, they assured me that the men I met would be rough and brutal and unpleasant to deal with. I answered that if this were so it merely meant that the

Courtesy of the Roosevelt Memorial Association.

Roosevelt and his brother Eliot playing with Edith Carow, whom he later married, and his sister Corinne, later Mrs. Douglas Robinson. About 1875.

people I knew did not belong to the governing class, and that the other people did — and that I intended to be one of the governing class; that if they proved too hard-bit for me I supposed I would have to quit, but that I certainly would not quit until I had made the effort and found out whether I really was too weak to hold my own in the rough and tumble.[1]

[1] "Theodore Roosevelt: An Autobiography."

Roosevelt, joining the local Republican club, was noticed by one of the minor captains, "Joe" Murray, a party work-horse fitting in most respects the familiar type, but with more insight and character. Murray thought young Roosevelt, as a scion of wealth and social position, would be a good vote-getter in what the political argot of New York called the "diamond-back" district, the wealthiest in the city, with a constituency that included Columbia University and the principal "brownstone fronts"[1] of the city. Roosevelt accepted the suggestion that he run for the State Assembly, and he and Murray, following the customary practice, prepared a circular beginning:

We cordially recommend the voters of the Twenty-first Assembly District to cast their ballots for

THEODORE ROOSEVELT
for Member of Assembly,

and take much pleasure in testifying to our appreciation of his high character and standing in the community. He is conspicuous for his honesty and integrity, and eminently qualified to represent the District in the Assembly.
New York, November 1st, 1881.

For signatures to the circular, young Roosevelt and his mentor Murray called on some of the Roosevelt family's friends, the prominent men of the district. They, thinking the venture in politics as harmless a youthful altruism as missionary work in the slums, sponsored Roosevelt's beginning, and by that act equipped themselves to say years later "I knew him when — ," and to put an exceptional quality of emotion into the recollection. They composed a group whose names[2] looked like a combina-

---

[1] Meaning, in the early 1880's, the homes of wealth and social position.

[2] "They were all," Henry L. Stoddard wrote me in 1927, "reactionaries of a pronounced type. I am sure those signers who lived long enough must have been shocked at the thought they had urged Roosevelt to enter public life."

tion of the "Banker's Directory" and the "Social Register." They included Joseph H. Choate, already known as a leading lawyer with many corporation clients; Elihu Root, to whom the same description would apply; Morris K. Jesup, a New York merchant and banker; Elliott F. Shepherd and William H. Webb, both connections to the Vanderbilt family dominant in the New York Central Railroad. No "parlor socialists" there.

Courtesy of the Roosevelt Memorial Association.

Roosevelt on a vacation in the Maine woods in 1879.

III

In his early days in the Assembly Roosevelt "paid attention chiefly . . . to laws for the reformation of the Primaries and of the Civil Service,"[1] but quickly found that not all the corruption in politics consisted of ballot-box stuffing and getting offices for friends; or rather, found that these forms of political corruption were merely the small change which active politicians get from a bigger divide. He discovered for himself, in short, the existence of a superior force, symbolized later in a vivid appellation, "the man higher up."

[1] Roosevelt's own words, quoted by Charles G. Washburn.

This discovery Roosevelt blurted out, to the dismay of some who had promoted his entry into politics, in a speech in the Assembly attacking "the infernal thieves who have those railroads in charge . . . with their hired stock-jobbing newspaper, with their corruption of the judiciary, and with their corruption of this House." The passage ended with a phrase then new and seriously shocking, "the wealthy criminal class."

The phrase "was quoted again and again," often in connotations in which "a hundred prophets were ready to swear it would be Mr. Roosevelt's valedictory in politics."

The phrase did not end Roosevelt's political career; but — for reasons other than those the prophets had in mind — it marked the highest point his antagonism toward big business reached until two decades passed. From 1883 until 1902, Roosevelt measurably receded from that early impulse. His shock at the corruption of big business was overlaid by apprehension about the radicalism of some of the manifestations of social unrest, and the violence of some others. When Henry George, the single-tax advocate, ran for mayor of New York in 1886, Roosevelt ran against him. When members of the international anarchists' organization in Chicago, sentenced to death for throwing bombs that killed several policemen, were pardoned by Governor Altgeld, Roosevelt was shocked at the condoning of violence. When another anarchist tried to murder Henry C. Frick during the 1892 Homestead Riots, Roosevelt seriously feared the spirit of revolution might spread far enough to undermine the government. When Bryan ran for the Presidency on a platform demanding the so-called "free coinage of silver," Roosevelt felt that national honesty was on the defensive.

Roosevelt, believing these were a more fundamental menace than the corrupt practices of corporations, fell back from his early assault. During two decades, he not only "laid-off" the anti-big-business movements, but excoriated the leaders of them. Of Bryan he said in a

Roosevelt's home while a student at Harvard, from 1876 to 1880.

letter to his sister in September, 1896: "His utterances are as criminal as they are wildly silly. All the ugly forces that seethe beneath the social crust are behind him." Of the Populists he wrote in the same month:

Refinement and comfort they are apt to consider quite as objectionable as immorality. A taste for learning and cultivated friends, and a tendency to bathe frequently, cause them the deepest suspicion. . . . Senator Tillman, the great Populist, or Democratic, orator from South Carolina, possesses an untrammelled tongue. Tillman's brother has been frequently elected to Congress upon the issue that he never wore either an overcoat or an undershirt.[1]

By his recession from his early impulse to fight big business, Roosevelt for nearly twenty years was reduced to the rank of a political reformer of the ordinary type.

Courtesy of the Roosevelt Memorial Association.

Roosevelt on the round-up, 1885.

His instinct for better things he expressed, between 1889 and 1895, in a struggle for civil-service reform, a rôle pretty distant from high-rank warfare — fighting petty politicians, not big business — at that time civil-service reformers were looked upon as meddlesome cranks, more annoying than formidable. When the Republican National Chairman, James S. Clarkson, assailed Roosevelt for interfering with the accepted practice of rewarding faithful workers with party patronage, Roosevelt characterized the attack as a "loose diatribe equally com-

[1] Quoted by Charles G. Washburn in "Theodore Roosevelt."

pounded of rambling declamation and misstatement."
When a Democratic leader, Senator Arthur P. Gorman,
of Maryland, made a similar attack, Roosevelt wrote an
excoriating letter of sarcasm: "High-minded, sensitive
Mr. Gorman! Clinging, trustful Mr. Gorman!"

From 1895 to
1897 he threw his
vigor for decency
into service as Po-
lice Commissioner
of New York City,
where his forth-
rightness expressed
itself in giving the
precise names of
judges he criticized:
"When I speak of
inadequate sen-
tences I mean such
sentences as those
imposed by Judge
Cowing and his
associates." He
helped Jacob A.

Courtesy of the Roosevelt Memorial Association.
Roosevelt at Oyster Bay about the time he was
Police Commissioner.

Riis in his enterprise for improving the conditions of the
poor in New York. He wrote essays and made speeches
about purity in politics. But he was, during this period,
wholly a political reformer; in no sense an economic
reformer. Thomas B. Reed said to him ironically: "If
there is one thing more than another for which I admire
you, Theodore, it is your original discovery of the Ten
Commandments."

In 1897, as Assistant Secretary of the Navy, he made a
record of vigorous preparedness for the Spanish War.
In 1898, as lieutenant-colonel of the "Rough Riders"

regiment, he appealed romantically to the country. In 1900 and 1901, as Governor of New York, he managed the business of the State competently, enlisted popular

President Roosevelt on a bear hunt in April, 1905.

support of ideals of decency in politics, compelled the public service corporations to pay reasonable taxes, and resisted the State "boss," Thomas C. Platt, who, to get rid of him, "kicked him upstairs" into the Vice-Presidency.

Roosevelt's fame was great. It did not, however, include any general expectation that he would become a leader of the excited opposition stirred up by the trusts. The recollection of his early assault on "the criminal wealthy" was twenty years old and had become faint. People thought of him as personally independent, as cleanly and utterly free from the polluting alliance between politics and big business; but they did not commonly think of him as sharing the mood of "The Man With the Hoe," nor as among those who had a crusading conviction against "the world's real rulers, those who control the concentrated portion of the money supply." They did not think of him as a "trust-buster"; on the contrary, in the campaign of 1900, when he was the Republican candidate for Vice-President, he had spoken ironically of the attitude of Bryan and the Democrats about the trusts. One of Roosevelt's friends, Francis E. Leupp, writing a campaign biography, with every wish to give Roosevelt as many titles to distinction as his carer to that time warranted, described him as "that amiable and gifted author, legislator, field-sportsman, soldier, reformer, and executive." When McKinley's death elevated him into the Presidency and made him an object of world-wide curiosity, an English periodical, compressing his fame into rhymed similarities to the well-known, made no comparison with any economic St. George — only:

A smack of Lord Cromer, Jeff Davis a touch of him;
A little of Lincoln, but not very much of him;
Kitchener, Bismarck, and Germany's Will,
Jupiter, Chamberlain, Buffalo Bill.

21

INTERLUDE, WITH ACTION

Incidents, Some Important and Some Merely Interesting, Which Composed the Picture of a New Kind of Man in the White House. The President Admonishes a High-Rank Army Officer for Lacking Discretion, Causing Everybody to Understand Clearly Who Was Commander-in-Chief, and Leading "Mr. Dooley" to Foresee the Need of a First-Aid Station for Politicians on the White House Grounds.

ROOSEVELT, summoned from a vacation in the Adirondacks by McKinley's death, hurried to Buffalo; was advised by lawyers in the Cabinet to take the oath of office with as little delay as possible; replied: "I will call on Mrs. McKinley first — I do not wish to see her as the President when I am giving my condolences on her husband's death"; announced in a public statement: "It shall be my aim to continue absolutely unbroken the policy of President McKinley"; announced that he "would ask the Cabinet to retain their positions, at least for some months to come"; dismissed a troop of cavalry waiting to act as his escort, saying: "Go away, I don't want you"; sat for a while in the room with the dead President and tried to comfort McKinley's friend and mentor, Mark Hanna, by saying: "I hope you will be to me all that you have been to him" — a remark which Hanna no doubt interpreted as being in the nature of emotional consolation, rather than a solicitation of political guardianship; talked to a group of newspaper men, repeating his pledge to continue McKinley's policies and ending with a plea: "Everybody must be my friend, now"; took the train to Washington September 16, 1901, and went to his sister's home, not wishing to take up his residence at the White House until McKinley's widow should have an opportunity to have her own and her husband's effects removed; breakfasted the following morning, with his two sisters; went to the Capitol, where McKinley's body lay in state; held a short Cabinet meeting; went to Canton, Ohio, to attend McKinley's funeral; returned to Washington; received Cabinet members and Senators; went on Sunday to the Dutch Reformed Church, walking, the newspapers said, "with head erect and shoulders back."

On Sunday evening, September 22, 1901, he had his first dinner in the White House as President, with his two sisters as guests. All day, he told them, his thoughts had been of his father, whose birthday it was — he felt as if his father's hand were on his shoulder. At the close of dinner, according to White House custom, boutonnieres were passed about to the men and by chance the flower given the President was a yellow rose. His face flushed and he exclaimed: "Is it not strange! This is the rose we all connect with my father. I think there is a blessing connected with this."[1]

At the end of his first week as President, he wrote his friend, Henry Cabot Lodge, then in Europe: "It is a dreadful thing to come into the Presidency this way; but it would be a far worse thing to be morbid about it. . . . I believe you will approve of what I have done and of the way I have handled myself so far," and received a reply assuring him: "I cannot see that you have made a single mistake. You have done admirably, splendidly."

To some Southern Congressmen who asked his policy about appointments he said: "I am going to be President of the United States and not of any section; I don't care

[1] "My Brother, Theodore Roosevelt," Corinne Roosevelt Robinson.

that (snapping his fingers) for sections or sectional lines; if I cannot find Republicans I am going to appoint Democrats." He gave the New York Collectorship of the Port to an independent Republican, ignored the Republican organization in some other States, and restored to civil-

From a photograph by Brown Bros.

The cameraman here caught Colonel Roosevelt in a particularly energetic gesture. The occasion was a Decoration Day celebration at Grant's Tomb in New York shortly after Roosevelt had been elected President. The zeal of the speaker does not seem to be reflected in the faces of his auditors.

service protection 1500 employees of the War Department who had been taken out by a McKinley executive order in 1899. "Every day or two," observed the Detroit *News*, "he rattles the dry bones of precedent and causes sedate Senators and heads of departments to look over their spectacles in consternation."

He "saw more people during the first months he was in office, than any other President"; created an impression of receiving men, hearing them, getting their views, and disposing of them in the least possible time. To a caller who said something about advice, he exclaimed: "Advice! I have received more advice than any man living — mostly bad." To another caller, who warned him against going about unattended, he said: "I am amply able to protect myself," with a glance at his two fists. He took the delight of a truant boy in eluding the secret-service men, made nervous by the assassination of McKinley; went on horse-back rides in Rock Creek Park, or took rushing walks up and down the wooded hills, his head tipped upward to catch sight of birds, looking, in these expeditions, like a grotesquely burly Peter Pan. He played tennis — probably the first President who ever did; began a custom of ordering for the White House large numbers of books on a great variety of subjects; took notice of persons doing anything important in any line or in any part of the country,

One of the sketches of the kind Roosevelt used to draw between paragraphs of letters he wrote to children.

and invited them to visit the White House. To the young daughter of Nicholas Murray Butler, he wrote a "picture-letter" thanking her for birthday greetings she had sent him, and drawing a sketch, between paragraphs, of a bird that was one of the White House pets, as well as a hieroglyphic portrayal of a mishap his own little girl, Ethel, had suffered when she tried to ride the family pony without fully consulting the animal's wishes. When Senator Tillman, of South Carolina, engaged in a fist-fight on the Senate floor, Roosevelt took disapproving notice; to Tillman, he conveyed, through a Democratic Senator, an opportunity to withdraw his previous acceptance of an invitation to a White House dinner for Prince

Henry of Prussia. Tillman would not withdraw his acceptance, so Roosevelt withdrew the invitation.

He began an innovation of sending direct to bureau

From the painting by John Singer Sargent.

President Roosevelt.

chiefs or head clerks whenever he wanted information, short-circuiting the routine practice of sending through the Cabinet member having supervision of the depart-

ment;[1] wrote more public messages and letters than any
other President, striding up and down the room as he
dictated, "often stopping, recasting a sentence, striking
out and filling in, not disturbed by interruption, holding
stoutly to his purpose and producing finally a clear and
logical statement"; went to the Bicentennial of Yale
University to receive an honorary degree, and complained
bitterly at being forbidden to shake hands with the crowd
at the reception, because of fears remaining after the
assassination of McKinley; kept, for a while, a revolver
by his bedside at night, and carried one when travelling;
invited a negro educator, Booker Washington, to a meal
in the White House, and grinned through the ensuing
storm of criticism that raged in the South; went to a
Gridiron Club dinner and saw his Cabinet depicted as
Secretary of Mountain-Lion Hunting, Secretary of Horse-
back Riding, Secretary of Football.

When Senator Depew, calling in behalf of an applicant
for a diplomatic post, found the White House office
crowded, Roosevelt exclaimed: "We have no secrets
here; tell it right out" — and declined to make the appointment. On another occasion, Depew, entering Roosevelt's office as another Senator departed, was asked: "Do
you know that man?" and on replying "Yes, he is a
colleague of mine in the Senate," Roosevelt said: "Well,
he's a crook."

When the Naval Court of Inquiry in the Sampson-
Schley controversy reported its findings,[2] the senior commanding officer of the army, General Nelson A. Miles,
criticized it in a newspaper interview. Roosevelt, through
Secretary of War Root, publicly reprimanded the Gen-

---

[1] This departure was praised as a swift cutting of red tape; but Roosevelt was
obliged to abandon it when it became obviously subversive of discipline. It was
because of this practice, more than for any other reason, that Roosevelt had his
first resignation from the Cabinet, that of Secretary Gage of the Treasury.

[2] December 21, 1901.

eral. Miles called at the White House to protest. The
subsequent proceedings were the subject of widely dissonant newspaper accounts and comments, among which
the version of "Mr. Dooley" is no less valuable for its
wit than for the picture it gives of new ways in the White
House. Miles, said "Mr. Dooley," had been a mighty
fighter, of

th' Apachy, th' Sious, th' Arapahoo, th' Comanchee, th' Congressman, an' other savages iv th' plain. . . . Gin'ral Miles
was pursooin' th' thrue coorse iv a nachral warryor an' enlight-
enin' th' wurruld on th' things he happened to think iv. Wan
day, Gin'ral Miles pranced over to th' White House. Like a
sojer he wint on to th' east room where Mr. Rosenfelt shtud
in front iv th' fireplace. "I've come," says Gin'ral Miles, "to
pay me rayspicts to th' head iv th' naytion." "Thank ye," says
th' Prisidint, "I'll do th' same f'r th' head iv th' army," he says,
bouncin' a coal scuttle on th' vethran's helmet. "Gin-ral, I
don't like ye'er recent conduct," he says, sindin' th' right to th'
pint iv th' jaw. "Ye shud know that an officer who criticizes
his fellow officers is guilty iv I dinnaw what," he says, feelin'
him with his soord. "I am foorced to administher ye a severe reproof," he says. "I thought it was capital punishmint,"
says Gin'ral Miles as he wint out through th' window pursooed
be a chandelier.

Well, sir, they'll be great times down there f'r a few years.
A movement is on foot f'r to establish an emergency hospital
f'r office-holders an' politicians acrost th' sthreet fr'm th'
White House where they can be threated f'r infractions iv th'
Civil Sarvice law followed be pers'nal injuries. I'll be watchin'
th' pa-pers ivry mornin'. "Rayciption at the White House.
Among th' casualties was so-an'-so. Th' Prisidint was in a
happy mood. He administered a stingin' rebuke to th' Chief
Justice iv th' Supreme Coort, a left hook to th' eye. Th' afther-
noon was enlivened be th' appearance iv a Southern Congressman askin' f'r a foorth-class post-office. Th' Prisidint hardly
missed him be more thin a foot at th' gate, but th' Congressman bein' formerly wan iv Mosby's guerrillas escaped, to th'
gr-reat chagrin iv Mr. Rosenfelt, who remarked on his return
that life at th' White House was very confinin'.

22

WAITING

The Conservative Press Tells Itself That Roosevelt Is Going to Be the Kind of President It Wants Him to Be. Mark Hanna Agonizes in Apprehension. Wall Street Watches for a Sign of the New Administration's Policy about Trusts; but Roosevelt Does Not Give One, Yet.

I

ROOSEVELT'S first three months in the Presidency were interesting, even spectacular; the infectiousness of his exuberant vitality made the country realize there was a new man in the White House; indeed, a new kind of man. His high spirits, his enormous capacity for work, his tirelessness, his forthrightness, his many striking qualities, gave a lift of the spirits to millions of average men, stimulated them to higher use of their own powers, gave them a new zest for life. "He brought in," said Harry Thurston Peck, "a stream of fresh, pure, bracing air from the mountains, to clear the fetid atmosphere of the national capital."

But there was no light on what the new President would do about McKinley's essential policy, benevolence toward big business. Roosevelt's early assurance that he would "continue McKinley's policy,"[1] was believed — by Mark Hanna most of all — to be meant not as a pledge, but rather as a gesture of calm, appropriate to the circumstances, the natural impulse and act of any Vice-President on succeeding to power as an incident of national tragedy, designed to bring confidence to a country made nervous by an act of violence. The assassination of McKinley

---

[1] After Roosevelt got into his stride, cartoonists recalled this phrase, changed "continue" to "carry out," and drew pictures of the McKinley policy as the principal figure in a funeral, on a bier which Roosevelt, grinning, "carried out."

had caused, among other expressions of apprehension, a sharp drop in the stock market, followed by a stalemate, during which business watched for fulfilment — or disappointment — in its hope that Roosevelt would be a "pale copy of McKinley" (Roosevelt's own phrase for the

rôle many urged on him). The more important leaders of business, long dependent on Hanna as their friend in the high places of politics, besought him for light, but Hanna had no light. Roosevelt treated Hanna, whom he really liked, not only with sincere cordiality, but with the affectionate deference due an older man who for five years had been the most powerful political figure in the country, and had just been bereaved, at one blow, of his most intimate friend and of the leverage that had made his power secure. Roosevelt knew what Hanna's attitude toward him had been, but could

"To Mark Hanna, with McKinley in the Presidency, God was in His Heaven and the world was good." Hanna was shorn of his power when McKinley died and Roosevelt succeeded to the Presidency.

afford to be generous. His was the rising star; Hanna's the falling. He went out of his way to be cordial to the heart-broken Warwick, writing him a kindly letter asking for an early conference.

Hanna was touched. But it was characteristic of his impulsive optimism, which always expected the best, to take rather too much for granted. He replied:

There are many important matters to be considered from a political standpoint and I am sure we will agree upon a proper course to pursue. Meantime "go slow." You will be besieged from all sides and I fear in some cases will get the wrong impression. Hear them all patiently but RESERVE YOUR DECISION.

Hanna acted as if he thought Roosevelt's request for friendship and counsel called for a public gesture of appreciation; but with characteristic simplicity did it a little too bluntly, and in a way not best adapted to promote his purpose. To a correspondent of the New York *World* he gave an interview, meant to be eulogistic of Roosevelt to the last degree, intended to express what Hanna thought was the finest thing he could possibly say. Roosevelt must have grinned when he read:

> Mr. Roosevelt is an entirely different man to-day from what he was a few weeks since. He has now acquired all that is needed to round out his character — equipoise and conservatism. The new and great responsibilities so suddenly thrust upon him have brought about this change.

II

The tone of Hanna's interview was duplicated by the conservative press, as if moved by a strategy which says the way to make a child be what you want him to be, is to act as if he already is so, and praise him. The Washington *Star*, September 14,[1] 1901, spoke of the new President as "a man of unquestioned courage and of widespread popularity," and in the same breath reminded him that he was "thoroughly and conscientiously committed to the policies of the party in power as represented by Mr. McKinley." The New York *Tribune* felt no doubt that "President Roosevelt must be well aware that his temperament has been regarded as less cautious and conservative than that of his predecessor," but, fearful lest the reader should get a disquieting impression, added:

[1] The day of McKinley's death and Roosevelt's accession to the Presidency.

"Mr. Roosevelt has been in perfect sympathy with the triumphant policies of Mr. McKinley . . . whose beneficent administration he will assiduously endeavor to continue and perpetuate."

The New York *Times* made a transparent attempt to exorcise the spirit of disquiet by a variation of a device later familiar as "Coué-ism," by repeating the magic formula — the ogre before my eyes does not, cannot exist. "It will be in the minds of many," *The Times* put it, "that the temper of President Roosevelt's mind will incline him to seek for himself some more shining glory than that which has crowned the administration of his predecessor. That thought . . . should be dismissed before it takes shape."

The New York *Sun*, outstanding exponent of the conservative interests, and intimately close to J. P. Morgan, threw overboard every life-saver of caution that it might need later on; went out on the extreme end of the fragile limb of confident prophecy. On September 15, 1901, *The Sun* ended a column of almost fulsome tribute to the new Chief Executive with the words: "He is the most striking embodiment of contemporary Americanism; is of spotless honor and unconquerable fidelity to the loftiest and sternest ideals of public duty. . . . Theodore Roosevelt is a man on whom the American people can rely as a prudent and a safe and sagacious successor to William McKinley." On September 16 and 18 *The Sun* returned to the theme, asserting that "the great danger" attaching to the "succession of a Vice-President to the Presidency . . . is that the new Chief Magistrate will seek to distinguish his administration from the other for the mere sake of the distinction, for the sake of demonstrating that he is an independent and original force." But, *The Sun* assured the world — including Roosevelt — no such contingency was possible in the present case:

President Roosevelt is a man too large and too broad to be influenced by any such considerations of vanity or self-assertion. He knows that the preservation of the unexampled political repose in which the Republic was at the moment of the assassination of President McKinley is the first great duty

From the St. Paul "Pioneer Press," October, 1901.

The cartoonist has here portrayed the attitude of big business after Roosevelt succeeded to the Presidency, while it waited to see what he would do.

imposed on him. President Roosevelt starts out with the course for him exactly and precisely laid out. He represents the same political party and spirit and policies which were represented by Mr. McKinley; his political future, his whole reputation, depends on his fidelity to the sentiment of his party. President Roosevelt's career has been as a strict party man, happily for the public. His policy as President can be assumed from the policy of his party. It will not depend on the possible vagaries of an individual judgment.

That sort of thing, exhortation combined with assurance that no need for exhortation exists, was partly artless, partly very artful. For a wholly candid expression of the real feelings of conservatives, we may turn to the brilliant writer of an editorial in the Washington *Post* of September 15, 1901, a forthright person possessing at once a more self-respecting intellectual integrity, a greater candor toward the public, and a shrewder understanding of Roosevelt. This writer did not try to delude himself or his readers into believing that a man who has been one kind of person for forty-three years, can change his nature over-night, even under a stimulus so overwhelming as elevation to the Presidency; did not assume that by a flattering wheedling he could remodel the outstanding individual personality of the time into a rubber-stamp of William McKinley.

Instead, he placed Roosevelt on the dissecting-table and dispassionately analyzed him, much as a scientist studies a new and not very prepossessing insect, picking out, for warnings of pessimism and apprehension, precisely those qualities of Roosevelt for which the average man admired him:

In none of the fields of activity in which Mr. Roosevelt has hitherto figured do we find a single indication upon which we can build a satisfactory conclusion. . . . As a traveller, an explorer, a soldier, a cowboy, a litterateur, or an office-holder, he has been picturesque, often admirable, always interesting; yet nothing in his entire career supplies material for a forecast of the country's destiny with Roosevelt as Chief Magistrate. We need not tell our readers that up to this time we have discovered in Mr. Roosevelt very little cause for serious rejoicing. He has at all times been far too theatrical for our taste. He pranced too much in war. He vociferated too much in politics. We have not found him great in the uniform of a soldier or impressive as the superstructure of a bucking bronco. That he has amused us frequently and keenly we admit with becoming gratitude. That he has ever suggested to us the perfect model of a President we cannot truly say. His past contains no as-

surance of high adequacy; but who shall say that it forbids the
hope? History tells us of many men who made the worst and
even the most dangerous of subordinates, yet ruled with
strength and wisdom.

III

The earliest sign, the first occasion on which Roosevelt
must make official utterance of policies, would be his
message on the assembling of Congress, December 5, 1901.
The message was awaited with curiosity and, when published, was greeted with almost universal newspaper comment which said that apparently Roosevelt was not going
to break any big-business china. Some newspapers, having
hoped that Roosevelt would hit out in his characteristically vigorous fashion, were even a little disappointed:
"There are no fireworks in it"; "Anything but a sensational document"; and "Not exactly the kind of message
it was natural to expect from a man of Mr. Roosevelt's
temperament." From the conservative press generally,
came the relief which attends the ending of apprehension:
" 'The Rough Rider' and the 'Jingo,' the impetuous
youth of a year ago, has disappeared, and instead we have
in the White House a President who, to judge from his
first communication to Congress, might be a man of sixty,
trained in conservative habits." And: "The country will
draw a deep sigh of satisfaction."

Such passages as Roosevelt's message had about the
trusts were embedded in a mass of more than ten thousand words, dealing with more than twenty topics,
including international peace, the Monroe Doctrine,
civil service, conservation, game protection, and immigration. Such surroundings would have deadened almost
any utterance about the trusts, even had it been decisive.
But Roosevelt's allusions to the trusts were not decisive.
His mind was not decisive about them. He was still under

the spell of the influences[1] that for nearly twenty years had kept him away from this question; his mind was still under a momentum it had acquired in the campaigns of 1896 and 1900. In the first of these the issue had been currency; in the second, territorial expansion. As to both, Roosevelt had felt strongly that the Republicans were right, that Bryan and the Democrats were "utterly and hopelessly wrong." He had thrown himself so completely into those fights that when he became President he had not yet returned to equilibrium.

Moreover, Bryan and the Democrats were now making the trust question their chief issue; Roosevelt unconsciously tended to associate them with error on that question as he had on the previous ones; and tended also to be hesitant about taking up any position upon which Bryan and the Democrats had fixed their brand. Just the year before, in the campaign of 1900, he had jeered at the Democrats: "They have raved against trusts, they have foamed at the mouth, prating of impossible remedies they would like to adopt." Moreover, Roosevelt was a Republican, the Republicans were the business men's party, and reactionary business controlled it. Roosevelt, so long as he had been a subordinate, could conform or get out. Now he was chief and had to consider his responsibility.

As a result of all these influences, Roosevelt had never focussed his mind on the trust issue, had never been intellectually convinced or emotionally moved about it. Consequently, his treatment of the question in his first message to Congress was the sort that expresses itself inconclusively, tepidly, and in balanced sentences: "There have been abuses connected with the accumulation of great fortunes, *yet* it remains true that [such

[1] For a further statement of the reasons that kept Roosevelt from participating strongly in the movement against big business, see Chapter 20.

accumulations] confer . . . immense incidental benefits upon others." "It is not true that as the rich have grown richer, the poor have grown poorer; *on the contrary . . .*" Our "serious social problems" associated with great corporate fortunes are not due "to the tariff

From a photograph by Brown Bros.

Roosevelt's Cabinet. From left to right are Taft, Wilson, Straus, Root, Hitchcock, Cortelyou, Bonaparte, Metcalf, Roosevelt, Shaw.

nor to any other governmental action, *but* to natural causes in the business world. . . . Much of the antagonism to these fortunes is wholly without warrant." "The mechanism of modern business is so delicate that extreme care must be taken not to interfere with it in a spirit of rashness or ignorance."

In introducing such suggestions for remedy as he had to offer, he preserved the balanced form: "All this is true; and *yet* it is also true that there are real and grave evils." By a device that was frequent with him, he weighted one end of a sentence with reproof for business, the other with reproof for labor: "It should be as much the aim of those who seek for social betterment to rid the business world of crimes of cunning as to rid the entire body politic of crimes of violence." His specific recommendation said that "publicity is the only sure remedy which we can now invoke." Other than this he proposed that Congress, if it had the constitutional power, should provide for national "supervision and regulation over all corporations doing an interstate business"; and that "there should be created a Cabinet officer to be known as Secretary of Commerce and Industries."

Balanced and cushioned though this was, it contained substantially the whole of Roosevelt's philosophy about big organizations of business. To the end, even when his name was a world-wide symbol for belligerent attack against corporate power, he always maintained a distinction between the evil men who managed some trusts, and the good men who managed others. He never shared — indeed he deliberately and conspicuously avoided both the Bryan practice of denouncing all big business and the Wilson principle of insistence upon competition. Roosevelt would allow units of business to grow as large as economic conditions might permit — but would subject them to continuous supervision by the government. This last, that the government should have the right to regulate, and especially that the government should be recognized as above all business and above all business men, big or little — that was the heart of Roosevelt's doctrine, the point on which he fought his great controversies.

That Roosevelt's first message to Congress put its discussion of the trusts in the form of balanced sentences, was part of his conscious art of politics. The balanced sentence, used by a public man who never conspicuously uses anything else, may reflect a cautious "trimmer," or a man habitually verbose, or one temporarily tired. But Roosevelt essentially was the most forthright public character of his time — a man who could hurl, when the occasion demanded, such epithets as "malefactor of great wealth," and "out-patient of bedlam" was in no danger of being called timid. With Roosevelt, use of the balanced sentence was usually a precaution against misunderstanding; an insistence upon clearness; the reflection of a love of fair-dealing that will not leave a proposition half-stated; unwillingness to let one kind of evil escape censure while the public is stirred by another kind. When he condemned lynching, he did not fail to add wholesome denunciation of the crime for which lynching is commonly invoked. His approval of the right of labor to organize for its own protection was always coupled with a reminder that this right does not justify the commission of violence. When his trust policy exposed him to attack as an enemy of capital, his answer was: "We shall find it necessary to shackle cunning as in the past we have shackled force."

To be sure, when the balanced sentence had become an intellectual habit with him, it led him into some expressions that justified a smile. One learned to wait for it. It became a little boring in time, to hear him tell of appointing a Catholic to office, and add that he would have appointed a Protestant under similar circumstances. Composing a perfunctory message of consolation on the death of the Queen of England, he began: "In view of the sympathy shown by the late Queen Victoria with our loss in the death of President McKinley . . ." Describing an explosion of a Spanish shell among a group of his Rough Riders, he said it resulted in the death of "a singularly gallant young Harvard fellow" — and added: "An equally gallant young fellow from Yale had already been mortally wounded." That caused a witty newspaper man, Francis E. Leupp, to surmise that

Roosevelt's occasional coupling of labor-unions with the trusts, in his castigations, inspired this cartoon by Maybelle in the Brooklyn *Eagle*.

Roosevelt, if called on to repeat Grant's "Let no guilty man escape," would have added, "but guard equally the innocent"; and would have changed Cleveland's "Tell the truth" to "Tell both sides."

The country, especially the newspapers and critics, not yet familiar with the precise place the balanced sentence had in Roosevelt's use of language, interpreted his allusions to the trusts in his first message to Congress, as one of the class of his performances which *Blackwood's Magazine* characterized: "With splendid ingenuity he proved how [to] take both sides in any dispute at one and the same time; . . . [to] fight with the same hand for rich and poor." Or, as "Mr. Dooley" put it:

"Th' trusts," says he [Roosevelt], "are heejous monsthers built up be th' inlightened intherprise iv th' men that have done so much to advance progress in our beloved counthry," he says. "On wan hand I wud stamp thim undher fut; on th' other hand not so fast. What I want more thin th' bustin' iv th' thrusts is to see me fellow counthrymen happy an' continted. I wudden't have thim hate th' thrusts. Th' haggard face, th' droopin' eye, th' pallid complexion that marks th' inimy iv thrusts is not to me taste. Lave us be merry about it an' jovial an' affectionate. Lave us laugh an' sing th' octopus out iv existence."

That view of Roosevelt's first message to Congress was shared alike by those who were disappointed with it, and by those whom it relieved from anxiety. Wall Street slept well.

23

ROOSEVELT GOES INTO ACTION

Inspired by One of His Fundamental Traits, the Instinct
to Respond to Challenge, He Attacks the Legal Immunity
Enjoyed by Holding-Companies. Bad News Comes to J. P.
Morgan's Dinner-Table, and He Goes to Washington.

I

LESS than three months later, on the evening of February
18, 1902, J. P. Morgan, entertaining business associates
at dinner at his home on Madison Avenue, New York,
was summoned to the telephone by a friend in a newspaper office, who told him the press dispatches had just
brought from Washington an announcement given out by
the Attorney-General, which, in spite of the shock-absorb-
ing tortuousness of official phraseology, conveyed appall-
ingly the information that Morgan's latest merger, the
Northern Securities Company, was to be prosecuted by
the Government — with the implication inherent that the
action was the beginning of a policy of enforcing the
Sherman law against all trusts. The dispatch represented
Attorney-General Knox as saying:

> Some time ago the President requested an opinion as to the
> legality of [the Northern Securities] merger, and I have recently
> given him one to the effect that, in my judgment, it violates the
> provisions of the Sherman Act of 1890 [the Anti-Trust Act];
> whereupon he directed that suitable action should be taken to
> have the question judicially determined.

Morgan turned from the telephone to his associates
at the dinner-table, his countenance showing appalled
dismay, but little anger. In telling the news to his guests
he dwelt on what he felt was the unfairness of Roosevelt's

action. Roosevelt, he said, ought to have told[1] him, ought to have given him a chance to make over the

Reproduced by permission of the proprietors of "Punch." Cartoon by Bernard Partridge.

A famous cartoon, "The Soap-and-Water Cure," signalizing the beginning of Roosevelt's enforcement of the Sherman Anti-Trust Act.

PRESIDENT ROOSEVELT: "During the next sixteen months of my term of office this policy shall be persevered in unswervingly."

AMERICAN EAGLE: "Je-hosaphat!"

Northern Securities Company, if necessary, so as to conform to whatever Roosevelt thought was right. Or,

---

[1] Roosevelt, for whatever motive, had taken minute pains to keep his purpose secret. In his instructions to Attorney-General Knox, he warned the latter "this is not a Cabinet secret," and urged him to be careful lest other members of the Cabinet learn of it and incautiously reveal it.

if the company must be dissolved, Roosevelt ought to
have given him an opportunity to dissolve it voluntarily.
That alternative, Morgan felt, should have been afforded
him by any one, most of all by Roosevelt. He had regarded Roosevelt as a gentleman, reared in his own social

When Roosevelt began to enforce the Sherman Anti-Trust law, it was pictured as
the dead returned to life, by Bartholomew in the Minneapolis *Journal*.

setting; one of his partners, Robert Bacon, was a classmate of Roosevelt; another partner, George W. Perkins,
was close to Roosevelt — or thought he had been.

Morgan hurried to Washington. "If we have done
anything wrong," he said to Roosevelt, "send your
man [meaning Attorney-General Knox] to my man
[naming one of his lawyers] and they can fix it up."
"That can't be done," said the President. "We don't
want to fix it up," added Knox, who assisted at the interview, "we want to stop it." Morgan inquired: "Are

you going to attack my other interests, the Steel Trust and the others?" "Certainly not," replied the President, "unless we find out that in any case they have done something we regard as wrong." As Morgan went away Roosevelt remarked: "That is a most illuminating illustration of the Wall Street point of view. Mr. Morgan could not help regarding me as a big rival operator, who either intended to ruin all his interests or else could be induced to come to an agreement to ruin none."[1]

Meantime, on the day following announcement of the suit, "the security markets of New York, London, Paris, and Berlin," as the New York *Herald* put it, "were demoralized." "Not since the assassination of President McKinley," said the New York *Tribune*, "has the stock market had such a sudden and severe shock." These records of the technical financial consequences of the suit were varied by the Detroit *Free Press*, which undertook to epitomize the effect in terms of psychology: "Wall Street is paralyzed at the thought that a President of the United States would sink so low as to try to enforce the law." James J. Hill, writing privately to a friend, took a tone common with industrial magnates: "It really seems hard, when we look back on what we have done . . . in opening the country and carrying at the lowest rates, that we should be compelled to fight for our lives against the political adventurers who have never done anything but pose and draw a salary." Some New York corporation lawyers said that Roosevelt had shown lack of respect for the Supreme Court, since the legal device on which the Northern Securities Company was based had already been held valid, in a preceding case. Other New York lawyers, confident that the holding-company type of combination was secure against the law, said that Roosevelt had been led into an act of folly by "an unknown country lawyer

---

[1] "Theodore Roosevelt and His Time," Joseph Bucklin Bishop.

from Pennsylvania" — meaning Knox, who was from Pittsburgh — upon which Roosevelt's comment was: "They will know this country lawyer, before this suit is ended."[1]

II

The assumption was general among corporation lawyers, and others as well, that the holding-company form — in which all the recent trusts had taken refuge — was secure against the Anti-Trust law. The lawyers who made the Northern Securities Company and the other recent trusts thought they had found a device that was, to quote an old definition of a legal boundary fence, "horse-high, hog-tight, and bull-strong," a protection that could not be jumped over, squeezed through, or broken down. Roosevelt said later, and was substantially right, that Knox was the only prominent lawyer in the country who thought the Northern Securities Company could be overthrown.[2] The Supreme Court, in a decision in the Knight case, handed down in 1895, had held in effect that Congress was without constitutional power to forbid the holding-company type of trust. The essential fact in the Knight case was that the American Sugar Refining Company, having about sixty-five per cent of the business, bought up three other companies having about thirty-three per cent, making payment to the stockholders of the purchased companies with stock in the larger company. With ninety-eight per cent of the trade, the American Sugar Refining Company was as nearly complete a monopoly as often happens. But the Supreme Court did not look at the commodity in which substantial monopoly had been achieved; it looked

---

[1] The remark was made to Joseph Bucklin Bishop.

[2] The New York *Sun*, commenting on the initiation of the suit, said: "We believe that a serious mistake has been made somewhere, for the Northern Securities Company is the offspring of the ablest legal talent and conservative business sense that exist in the United States."

only at the act of acquiring stock. Seeing only that, the Court[1] declared, in substance, that (1) Congress's only power in the premises is derived from its constitutional authority to "regulate commerce"; and (2) combining corporations into a holding-company, by exchanging stock of the holding-company for the stocks of the constituent companies, is not "commerce." Under that decision, the stocks of any number of companies could be combined into a holding-company, and the holding-company could then have a monopoly of the substance in which it dealt, sugar or what not. It was a formidable decision and a formidable state of facts.

That immunity of the trusts from prosecution was the justification for a wide-spread cynicism and sullenness, which said there was one law for the corporations, another for the individual; one law for the rich, another for the poor. "The United States," said the New York *World*, years later, "was never closer to a social revolution than at the time Roosevelt became President."

The trusts, through the holding-company device, were above the law. They were more powerful than the people, more powerful than Congress, more powerful than the government.[2] That condition presented to Roosevelt

[1] The distinction here made is historically important. For several years following the Knight decision, it was the practically universal opinion of lawyers, and lay authorities as well, that the effect of the decision was to sanction monopoly when achieved through the holding-company device. But some of the lawyers who have read the manuscript of this chapter point out that the difficulty lay in the fact that the government's side of the Knight case was not well presented to the court. At that time, the prosecution of cases involving this kind of trust was comparatively new, and the technic had not been developed. The lawyers for the Government in the Knight case emphasized only the act of exchanging stock and did not sufficiently dwell upon the fact that this was followed by acts having to do with sugar as a commodity, and constituting restraint of trade.

[2] These sentences seem strong. They are supported by Roosevelt's own statement, written in retrospect twelve years after he instituted the suit against the Northern Securities Company. The passage is here condensed, and the order of some sentences rearranged:

"When I became President, the question of the *method* by which the United States Government was to control the corporations was not yet important. The absolutely vital question was whether the Government had power to control them

a challenge such as his nature would never ignore. The
dominant trait in his spirit was the urge to respond to
challenge; here was a challenge not merely to him personally, but to the government and people of the United
States, of whose power and dignity he was now the cus-
todian.

III

Roosevelt, having started the Northern Securities suit
on its slow way through the courts, took, during the summer of 1902, trips through the country, in the course of
which he explained what his policy about the trusts was
to be, always keeping the serenity of balanced sentences
and, as used by him, their forcefulness; always prefacing
statements of his determination to enforce the law with
assurances of his wish to preserve the economic good that
there might be in large units of business. At Cincinnati,[1]
he said: "The biggest corporation, like the humblest private citizen, must be held to strict compliance with the
will of the people." At Philadelphia, at a banquet of the
Union League Club, he said:

The question of the so-called trusts is but one of the questions we must meet in connection with our industrial system.

---

at all. . . . Holding-companies, the Supreme Court had decided, could not be
prohibited, controlled, or regulated, or even questioned, by the National Government. Such was the condition of our laws when I acceded to the Presidency. This
decision left the National Government, that is the people of the nation, practically
helpless to deal with the large combinations of modern business. The total absence of governmental control had led to a portentous growth in the financial and
industrial world. The power of the mighty industrial over-lords of the country
had increased with giant strides, while the method of controlling them, in check-
ing abuses by them, on the part of the people, through the Government, remained
archaic and therefore practically impotent. The big reactionaries of the business
world and their allies and instruments among politicians and newspaper editors
fought to keep matters absolutely unchanged. These men demanded for themselves an immunity from governmental control which, if granted, would be as
wicked and as foolish as immunity to the barons of the twelfth century. Of all
forms of tyranny the least attractive and the most vulgar is the tyranny of mere
wealth, the tyranny of plutocracy. . . ."

[1] September 20, 1902.

There are many of them and they are serious; but they can and will be met. Time may be needed for making the solution perfect; but it is idle to tell this people that we have not the power to solve such a problem as that of exercising adequate supervision over the great industrial combinations of to-day. We have the power and we shall find out the way. We shall not act hastily or recklessly, and a right solution shall be found, and found it will be.

From a photograph by Henry Miller.

Theodore Roosevelt and Niagara Falls were the two outstanding natural phenomena of America, observed John Morley after a visit to this country during Roosevelt's Presidency.

At which, as J. Hampton Moore noticed, some representatives of "large and prosperous public-utility companies shook their heads, as if to say 'that won't do.' They seemed to be sizing up the President, for throughout the country his critics were already beginning to get in their work, some of them going so far as to convey the impression that the President's mannerisms denoted a tendency toward the abnormal, and that because of this he was dangerous." [1]

Meantime, in another quarter, another form of capitalistic assumption of divine right had come to a head, in a form that constituted a challenge to Roosevelt — which asked him, as he saw it, whether any individual or group of individuals could be permitted to be more powerful than the government.

[1] "Roosevelt and the Old Guard," by J. Hampton Moore, ex-Congressman and ex-Mayor of Philadelphia.

24

ROOSEVELT SETTLES A STRIKE

By a Long and Complex Process, in the Course of Which, to the Dismay of "Intimate Friends of the Constitution," He Made Many Departures from Precedent. Also Some Enlargements of Executive Prerogative — Several of Them Deep-Reaching, Others Less Important — Including the Promotion of a Labor Leader to Be "an Eminent Sociologist."

I

THE[1] bituminous coal miners of the country had been brought into a union for the first time in 1890, and in 1899 had been joined by the anthracite miners, the two groups composing a nation-wide union, the United Mine Workers of America, destined to remain compact and successful, and to figure in a good deal of history under an able leader. John Mitchell, by studying in his spare hours, had risen from a laborer in the coal mines to a position of affectionate respect hardly attained by any other labor leader in America. His tact, intelligence, organizing ability, integrity, and personal charm had won for him the love and confidence of union men, and made him a popular figure with the public.

In 1900, the anthracite miners struck for a ten per cent increase in wages. Whether or not they chose their time with consciousness of the strategy of striking during a

[1] The coal strike of 1902 was attended by bitterly controversial attitudes. Many of the moves made by the parties involved, including Roosevelt, were secret, and many of the printed accounts are in error about fundamental details. For pains taken generously in an effort to make the present account complete and accurate, the author is indebted to Elihu Root and James R. Garfield, former members of Roosevelt's Cabinet; William Loeb, Jr., Roosevelt's secretary; William H. Truesdale, and Thomas H. Watkins, anthracite coal operators, who participated in the events; E. W. Parker, statistician of the anthracite coal industry; John L. Lewis, president of the United Mine Workers; William Green and Thomas Kennedy, labor-union officials; Edgar E. Clark, former chief of the Order of Rail-

political campaign, Mark Hanna quickly saw that aspect of it. He, as National Chairman of the Republican party, responsible for the success of McKinley, went to Wall Street, saw the operators and bankers of the industry, and told them they had better add ten per cent to the miners' wages, rather than run the risk of Bryan getting into the White House. The coal presidents and bankers shivered at the warmed-over scare of free silver and yielded.

John Mitchell, leader of the United Mine Workers of America.

The miners' union, soon after the campaign-year victory, began to press for further advantage. Its demands, as phrased in public announcements and discussions, were "for an increase in wages, a decrease in time, and payment . . . by weight [and not] by car."[1] But as the Anthracite Coal Strike Commission (appointed later) reported, with an understanding not common in official documents, "The cause lies deeper than the occasion, and is to be found in the desire for the

way Conductors and member of the commission that arbitrated the strike; James J. Davis, Secretary of Labor in President Coolidge's Cabinet; Ralph M. Easley, chairman of the National Civic Federation; ex-Senator Porter J. McCumber, of North Dakota; Professor Charles R. Lingley, of Dartmouth College; Professor John R. Commons, of the University of Wisconsin; Reverend J. J. Curran, of Wilkes-Barre, Pennsylvania; Joseph B. Bishop; John Cummings.

In making this acknowledgment of obligation, there is no intention to attribute to any of these men identification with all or any of the views set forth in the chapter.

[1] While this is an accurate epitome of the essential demands there were others which furnish striking evidence of practices then common that have since largely disappeared. They included: abolition of the company-store and company-doctor systems; compliance with the semimonthly pay law; and that pay should be in cash.

recognition by the operators of the miners' union." That was more repugnant to the operators and the bankers associated with them than almost any conceivable demand for wages. It involved treating the miners' union officials as equals, and carried with it the principle of collective bargaining. What now followed was an epochal step in the evolution of that system.

On February 15, 1901, the miners, through their president, John Mitchell, wired President Olyphant, of the Delaware and Hudson Company, asking him "if your company will participate in a joint conference with anthracite miners." Olyphant replied: "I . . . see no object in the conference you suggest even if that method of procedure were desirable, which seems doubtful."

February 26, 1901, Mitchell wrote Olyphant again, this time with a subtle variation of form, "for the purpose of inviting your company to be represented at a joint conference of mine workers and mine owners which has been called." To which Olyphant replied: "So far as regards conferences with its own employees . . . the officers of the company are and will be at all times ready and willing therefor."

The owners would deal with their own employees; they would not deal with officers of the national miners' union. That was the issue.

The following year, Mitchell repeated his invitation to "a joint conference of operators and miners." The invitation was sent to all the heads of mining companies and anthracite-carrying railroads. All replied; all declined. They would not put their feet under the same table with the officials of the national miners' union. Five weeks later, March 22, 1902, Mitchell repeated his invitation in a form whose completeness made the issue utterly clear:

I wire to ascertain if your company will join other anthracite coal companies in conference with committee representing anthracite mine workers for purpose of discussing and adjusting grievances which affect all companies and all employees alike.

The answers of the companies were typified in the letter and telegram sent by one who came to be pictured in the public mind as the personification of recalcitrant employer and capitalist, George F. Baer, head of the Reading Railroad. Baer became the spokesman of the operators; his attitude (modified, though very little, by J. P. Morgan, who had a rôle of speaking for the whole banking and business world) was representative of the operators generally. To the first of Mitchell's telegrams, Baer replied with a long letter:

George F. Baer, President of Philadelphia and Reading Railway, spokesman for the operators.

The proposition to unsettle all the labor conditions of the various anthracite districts each year by holding a conference between persons who are not interested in anthracite mining . . . is so unbusinesslike that no one charged with the grave responsibility of conducting industrial enterprises can safely give countenance to it. We will always receive and consider every application of the men in our employ. We will endeavor to correct every abuse, to right every wrong, to deal justly and fairly with them, and to give every man a fair compensation for the work he performs. Beyond this we cannot go. . . . There cannot be two masters in the management of business. . . . You cannot have discipline when the employee disregards and disobeys the reasonable orders and directions in the conduct of business of his superior officer, relying upon some outside power to sustain him.

To the second invitation, Baer wired shortly:

> Always willing to meet our employees to discuss and adjust
> any grievances. I had hoped that my letter clearly expressed
> our views.

In this impasse, an outside organization, the National
Civic Federation, tried to bring about arbitration, but
failed. On May 8, 1902, Mitchell made a last attempt,
telegraphing to the operators a proposal that the questions at issue be arbitrated by a committee of five persons
to be appointed by the National Civic Federation, and
that in case this proposed solution was unacceptable "a
committee, composed of Archbishop Ireland, Bishop Potter, and one other person whom these two may select, be
authorized to make an investigation. . . ."

In this proposal Baer saw an opening for the exercise
of a talent he had for satire, of a sort. He wrote:

> Anthracite mining is a business and not a religious, senti-
> mental, or academic proposition. The laws organizing [sic] the
> companies I represent in express terms impose the business
> management on the president and directors. I could not if I
> would delegate this business management to even so high and
> respectable a body as the Civic Federation. Nor can I call
> to my aid as experts in the mixed problem of business and
> philanthropy the eminent prelates you have named.[1]

This sentiment about the area between business and
religion was amplified by Baer in a letter he wrote a few
weeks later, after the strike was well under way — a
letter which brought the writer of it, and the whole capitalistic world he reflected, into the focus of the fierce light of
public attention. A citizen of Wilkes-Barre, Pennsylvania, appealing to Baer to end the strike, put his plea
largely on religious grounds. Baer replied:

---

[1] The letters and telegrams from which extracts are here quoted are printed
in full in the report of the Anthracite Coal Strike Commission, Bulletin 46, Department of Labor, May, 1903.

Philadelphia & Reading Railway Company.
President's Office.
Reading Terminal. Philadelphia.   17th July 1902.

My dear Mr. Clark:-

I have your letter of the 16th instant.

I do not know who you are. I see that you are a religious man; but you are evidently biased in favor of the right of the working man to control a business in which he has no other interest than to secure fair wages for the work he does.

I beg of you not to be discouraged. The rights and interests of the laboring man will be protected and cared for - not by the labor agitators, but by the Christian men to whom God in His infinite wisdom has given the control of the property interests of the country, and upon the successful Management of which so much depends.

Do not be discouraged   Pray earnestly that right may triumph, always remembering that the Lord God Omnipotent still reigns, and that His reign is one of law and order, and not of violence and crime.

Yours truly,

Geo. F. Baer

President.

Mr. W. F. Clark,

Wilkes-Barre,

Pennsylvania.

425

I do not know who you are. I see that you are a religious man; but you are evidently biased in favor of the right of the working man to control a business in which he has no other interest than to secure fair wages for the work he does.

I beg of you not to be discouraged. The rights and interests of the laboring man will be protected and cared for — not by the labor agitators, but by the Christian men to whom God in His infinite wisdom has given the control of the property interests of the country, and upon the successful management of which so much depends. Do not be discouraged. Pray earnestly that right may triumph, always remembering that the Lord God Omnipotent still reigns, and that His reign is one of law and order, and not of violence and crime.[1]

This letter got into the hands of the newspapers, was widely reprinted, and became the subject of comment everywhere. The New York *Evening Post* applied to it the mildest adjective — "extraordinary." To the New York *Times* the letter seemed to "verge very close upon unconscious blasphemy." William R. Hearst's New York *American and Journal* observed that "the pious pirate is no new thing. Baer and the relations between a just God and the thieving trusts must be left to the pulpit for adequate treatment."

The pulpit did handle Baer, without gloves, and the clerical press also. Indeed, as between the religious and the lay press it would be difficult to say which displayed the greater indignation, which was stronger in

[1] Among historians there is some doubt as to the authenticity of Baer's letter. It has been reprinted again and again in books dealing with the coal strike and with the relations between capital and labor, in many cases with expressed or implied doubt of its genuineness. Professor Charles R. Lingley, of Dartmouth College, in his "The United States Since the Civil War," quotes a sentence taken from the version reproduced here, while H. T. Peck, in "Twenty Years of the Republic," gives a version in which the word "entrusted" appears in place of the phrase "given the control." The present writer is of the opinion that the letter is genuine. although he has not been able to locate the original. The copy printed here is, in turn, from a photographic copy owned by Reverend J. J. Curran, Rector of St. Mary's Catholic Church, Wilkes-Barre, Pa. The other two letters from Baer to Mitchell here quoted are unquestionably authentic—they appear in the official report of the Coal Commission—and sufficiently suggest Baer's personality. The verisimilitude of the phrases used in all three suggests the probability that the disputed letter must have been genuine.

denunciation. The Chicago *Standard* (Baptist) denounced "the selfish, ignorant cant that this captain of industry mistakes for religion," and added: "This is the sort of thing that makes anarchists." The New York *Churchman* (Protestant Episcopal) said Baer's letter was "a ghastly blasphemy." The Boston *Watchman* (Baptist):

The doctrine of the divine right of kings was bad enough, but not so intolerable as the doctrine of the divine right of pluto-crats to administer things in general with the presumption that what it pleases them to do is the will of God.

II

On May 12, 1902, the entire body of anthracite miners, 147,000, left the mines. Throughout the summer no work was done; in the fall, the coal yards, depleted by the previous winter's consumption and not restocked during the summer, were at famine level. Yards in New York which in other years at this time had an average of two thousand tons in storage now had less than a tenth of that amount. On September 1 the price of anthracite, normally about $5 a ton, was at $14. The poor, buying it by the bucket or the bushel, paid a cent a pound, $20 a ton. Toward the end of September several schools in New York were closed in order to conserve their scanty fuel; as the weather grew colder people bought oil, coke, and gas stoves — poor substitutes for anthracite. In the West, mobs seized coal cars passing through the towns on the railways. By September 30, stocks were practically exhausted; for what little coal there was, $20 a ton was asked. A day later the price in New York jumped to $28 and then to $30 a ton.

President Roosevelt was besought to take notice. Mayor Seth Low, of New York, wired him:

The welfare . . . of the country imperatively demands the immediate resumption of anthracite coal mining. In the name of the City of New York I desire to protest through you. . . .

Similar appeals[1] came from the mayors of Chicago, Detroit, and other cities, from governors, from heads of factories fearful about their fuel supplies — not omitting one appeal that introduced a reason of practical politics. Senator Henry Cabot Lodge, from New England, where

From the Minneapolis "Times."
The nation endorses President Roosevelt's course.

he was looking after the election of Republican Congressmen, sent a Macedonian cry in which the larger questions of the constitutional right of a President to interfere, the difficulty of government seizure and operation of the mines, and the dangers of socialism were decidedly obscured by a squeaky hysteria about what would happen if the voters should have no fire in their homes on election day — in New England the first week in November can be quite cold:

[1] Most of the appeals to Roosevelt took the form of asking that he mediate between strikers and operators. There was, however, a different note, which merely said "down with the strikers."

Tariff revision we can discuss. I do not fear it. But the rise in the price of coal we cannot argue with. It hurts people and they say (this is literal): "We don't care whether you are to blame or not. Coal is going up and the party in power must be punished." By the first week in November if the strike does not stop and coal begin to go down we shall have an overturn. I am no alarmist but the indications now on this alarm me. . . . I believe we should hold the House and come out all right if it was not for the rising price of coal which produces an unreasoning sentiment. Now I do not write this to bother you needlessly but to tell you the very great danger in this region and to ask if there is no pressure to bring to bear on those operators to make some small concession — a small one would do now. We have powerful friends in business. The administration is strong. Can nothing be done — *not in public*[1] of course, I know that is out of the question, but by pressing the operators? The coal business here is getting rapidly worse. Schoolhouses are closing for lack of fuel. Prices are enormous and rising. . . . If no settlement is reached it means political disaster in New England and especially in this State. We shall lose the three close districts which will give the Democrats five, and Gus[2] and George Lawrence will both be in serious peril. . . . You have no power or authority of course — that is the worst of it. Is there anything we can appear to do?[3]

Lodge was regarded by Roosevelt as an intimate friend. If he had been anything else, he would probably have received a pretty blistering reply. As it was, Roosevelt explained in very plain words why he could not do anything "not in public," why he could not use secret political pressure of the kind Hanna had used in 1900:

. . . One of the great troubles in dealing with the operators is that their avowed determination in connection with the present matter is to do away with what they regard as the damage done to them by submitting to interference for political reasons in 1900. From the outset they have said that they are never going to submit again to having their laborers given a triumph over them for political purposes. . . . Unfortunately

[1] The italics are Lodge's own.
[2] Augustus Gardner, Republican candidate for Representative in Congress, and son-in-law of Senator Lodge.
[3] Letters from Senator Lodge to Roosevelt, September 22 and 27, 1902.

the strength of my public position before the country is also its weakness. I am genuinely independent of the big monied men in all matters where I think the interests of the public are concerned, and probably I am the first President of recent times of whom this could be truthfully said. I think it right and desirable that this should be true of the President. But where I do not grant any favors to these big monied men which I do not think the country requires that they should have, it is out of the question for me to expect them to grant favors to me in return. I can make no private or special appeal to them, and I am at my wits' end how to proceed. I shall consult Root in the matter.[1]

III

On October 1, 1902, Roosevelt invited the operators and the miners' leaders to go to Washington on October 3, to consult with him for the purpose of trying to reach a settlement. From the conservative newspapers a storm arose. The New York *Sun* said the President's action was "extraordinary," "unprecedented," and "dangerous." Further:

The President says that there are three parties concerned in the coal situation: the United Mine Workers, the operators, and the public. Has the President reflected upon the significance of this utterance? What the President says implies that he ignores the Constitution. The President denies any consideration to the non-union laborers, to the men who want to go to work; yet under the Constitution there is no more sacred right guaranteed to a free people than the right of contract, the right of the free man to sell his labor as he pleases.

The New York *Journal of Commerce* scolded:

The President's course . . . magnifies before the public eye the importance and power of the unions; casts an unwarrantable stigma upon the position and rights of the operators, and adds a trades-union issue to the many unwelcome politico-economic questions of the hour. It is all petty fussiness, and something more serious. Worse by far than any possible strike is

[1] Letter from Roosevelt to Lodge, September 27, 1902.

Mr. Roosevelt's seemingly uncontrollable penchant for impulsive self-intrusion.

On October 3 both parties arrived in Washington, the operators in an offensively belligerent mood. Roosevelt was plainly on the defensive. He had absolutely no authority over them, and knew it. He was acting with no more power than any leading citizen in private life, and frankly said so as he opened the conference:

I disclaim any right or duty to intervene in this way upon legal grounds or upon any official relation that I bear to the situation; but the urgency and the terrible nature of the catastrophe impending requires me to use whatever influence I personally can to . . . end a situation which has become literally intolerable. With all the earnestness there is in me I ask that there be an immediate resumption of operations in the coal mines in some such way as will, without a day's unnecessary delay, meet the crying needs of the people. I appeal to your patriotism, to the spirit that sinks personal consideration and makes individual sacrifices for the general good.

No sooner had Roosevelt concluded his punctiliously phrased appeal than the miners' leader, John Mitchell, rose. Mitchell's rather romantic personality never appeared to better advantage. His natural distinction of person and manner was accentuated by his affecting the sober garb and the "reversed" collar of the clergyman. In this gathering of strong men, he stood out easily the most intelligently forceful of all, save Roosevelt. Roosevelt remarked in a letter to Hanna written after the conference: "None of them [the operators] appeared to such advantage as Mitchell, whom most of them denounced with such violence and rancor that I felt he did very well to keep his temper." "Between times," he added, "they insulted me."

Mitchell spoke in a loud, clear voice. He did not make the mistake of berating his opponents or of voicing the

complaints of his followers. Had he done that he would
have lost Roosevelt's sympathy. Instead, he made a
proposal which the operators could not ignore without
drawing upon themselves public condemnation. He said:

> I am much pleased, Mr. President, with what you say. We
> are willing that you shall name a tribunal which shall determine
> the issues that have resulted in the strike; and if the gentlemen
> representing the operators will accept the award or decision
> of such a tribunal, the miners will willingly accept it, even if it
> be against our claims.

Baer's face went red. For his side he offered to submit
any special grievance to the decision of the Court of
Common Pleas in the districts where the mines were
situated. He was standing rigidly by the attitude he had
kept from the beginning — he was determined to keep
it a quarrel between *his* mines and *his* men. One of
the lawyers the operators brought with them read a long
prepared argument which told President Roosevelt his
true duty was to instruct his Attorney-General to bring
suit to dissolve the miners' union as a violator of the Sherman Anti-Trust law. The operators evidently intended to
rouse the President to an outburst of anger and thereby
put him in the wrong; but he kept his temper perfectly,[1]
as did also the labor leaders throughout. The tone of the
operators was one of studied insolence toward the President, and of animosity toward the miners' leaders. They
intimated that Roosevelt had failed in his duty; that he
should long since have broken the strike by the employment of the regular army; and that the responsibility for
the existing situation rested largely upon him. They said
the Government was "a contemptible failure if it can
secure the lives and property and comfort of the people

---

[1] One newspaper account, however, said the President spoke very sharply to
the operators. He was quoted as having remarked to a friend afterward: "There
was only one person there who bore himself like a gentleman, and it wasn't I!"
The exception is supposed to have been Mitchell.

only by compromising with the violators of law and the instigators of violence and crime." Baer, in his remarks to the President, referred to the "crimes inaugurated by the United Mine Workers, over whom John Mitchell, whom you invited to meet you, is chief," and told the President "the duty of the hour is not to waste time negotiating with the fomenters of this anarchy." "Are you asking us to deal with a set of outlaws?" one of the operators, John Markle, inquired of the President; and the other operators commonly spoke of the members of the union as criminals and anarchists. The operators were quoted by a New York *Sun* reporter as saying, after the conference, that they regarded the President's action as "a grand-stand play," and an "intrusion upon a situation that in no wise concerned him."

That evening Roosevelt wrote to Hanna:

> Well, I have tried and failed. I feel downhearted. . . . But I am glad I tried, anyhow. I should have hated to feel that I had failed to make any effort. What my next move will be I cannot yet say.

IV

Fate, and the overreaching arrogance of the operators, supplied Roosevelt with the next move. The newspapers of the morning after the conference, carrying the story of failure and of the intransigence of the operators to a country already angry, inspired a letter to Roosevelt from literally the last man he could have expected to hear from. Grover Cleveland wrote:

> I read this morning . . . the newspaper account. I am so surprised and stirred up by the position taken by the contestants. I am especially disturbed and vexed by the tone and substance of the operators' deliverances.

Cleveland went on to suggest a plan, a rather impractical one, that the miners and operators make a truce long enough to mine sufficient coal to meet the country's most pressing needs, "the parties to the quarrel, after such necessities are met, to take up the fight again where they

From a photograph by Underwood & Underwood.

Grover Cleveland, his son Richard, and Ricky on the steps of their home, Westland, Princeton, New Jersey.

left off, without prejudice if they desire. . . . I know there is nothing philosophical or consistent in all this. If you pardon my presumption in thus writing you, I promise never to do it again."

But it was not the merits of Cleveland's plan that was important. It was the fact he had written — and particularly the fact he had shown himself critical of the operators. When Roosevelt, acknowledging the letter, began, "Your letter was a real help and comfort to me," he was understating his emotions. Cleveland was the one man the capitalists and "intimate friends of the Constitution" were relying on. The chief text of the criticisms of Roosevelt, the example constantly cited to him by conservatives as the one he ought to follow, was what Cleveland had done when he was President, eight years before. Cleveland, in the railroad strike of 1894, had stood on the principle that the only function and the sole authority of the government was limited to keeping order, a function which had the effect of taking the railroads' side by protecting them in their use of strike-breakers. Here, now, in Cleveland's own words, was the reversal of what all the conservatives were saying he stood for, the upsetting of the contrast the conservatives were making between Cleveland as a meticulous observer of constitutional limitations, and Roosevelt as a hot-headed violator of them. Here, in short, was Cleveland upholding Roosevelt in what the conservatives regarded as his unconstitutional and revolutionary course.

Besides, Cleveland was the only living Democratic ex-President. If he did not disapprove what Roosevelt was doing, the whole Democratic party was silenced. Roosevelt need have no fear of political consequences.

Roosevelt, keeping the correspondence with Cleveland confidential, stimulated by an access of strength that could be known to neither the public nor the operators, began, secretly, and in part subtly, the groundwork for a sensational plan.

First, he sent for a general of the regular army. As Roosevelt put it later:[1] "I had to find a man who possessed the necessary good-sense, judgment, and nerve. . . . He was ready in the person of Major-General Schofield,

[1] In his Autobiography.

. . . a fine fellow — a most respectable-looking old boy with side-whiskers and a skull cap, without any of the outward aspect of the conventional military dictator, but in both nerve and judgment he was all right."

To Schofield, Roosevelt revealed his plan and gave contingent instructions which he later summarized:

I would put in [the coal fields] the army. . . . I would instruct [General Schofield] to keep absolute order, taking any steps whatever that were necessary to prevent interference by the strikers or their sympathizers with men who wanted to work. I would also instruct him to dispossess the operators and run the mines as a receiver until I as President might issue further orders. I told [General Schofield] that if I had to make use of him it would be because the crisis was only less serious than that of the Civil War, that the action taken would be practically a war measure, and that if I sent him he must act in a purely military capacity under me as Commander-in-Chief, paying no heed to any authority, judicial or otherwise, except mine.[1]

Roosevelt's final test to determine whether Schofield understood fully what was expected of him was to ask him "if, in case the operators went to court and had a writ served on him, he would do as was done under Lincoln, simply send the writ on to the President."[2]

The general, more and more grave as he realized the portentousness of what was being said to him, answered solemnly that he would. Roosevelt said: "All right, I will send you," and the general made himself and his troops ready to entrain to the coal fields within a half-hour after orders should come from Roosevelt.

This too, Roosevelt kept secret. Particularly did he keep it secret from the man whom he now proceeded to make an unconscious agent in his plan. He sent for Matthew Stanley Quay, Senator from Pennsylvania (where all the anthracite mines were), and Republican boss of

[1] Roosevelt's Autobiography.
[2] "Theodore Roosevelt and His Time," Joseph B. Bishop.

the State. To Quay he broached the possible necessity of sending troops to the mines — Quay, of course, thinking the function of the troops would be merely what had always been the province of federal troops in strikes; namely, to keep order, a service that was, in effect, aid to the operators. Roosevelt asked Quay to arrange with the Governor of Pennsylvania to request Roosevelt to send troops. Quay made no comment or inquiry, merely told Roosevelt he would guarantee that the Governor would request Roosevelt to act the minute Roosevelt asked that the request be made. Roosevelt told Quay he would give him the signal in the shape of a telegram which would read: "The time for the request has come."[1]

Thus mobilized, with Quay ready to have the Governor of Pennsylvania send a request for troops on receipt of the signal, and with General Schofield ready to move within half an hour, Roosevelt proceeded to build up the strongest possible bulwark of public opinion, to make the recalcitrancy of the operators so clear that the country would sustain him in the extremely daring[2] act he planned. Secretly, Roosevelt appointed a committee to investigate the situation and the causes of it, and report to him. If, on the report of such a committee, the operators should still continue to refuse to arbitrate, Roosevelt would be justified, he felt, and would act. To serve on the

---

[1] "Theodore Roosevelt and His Time," Joseph B. Bishop.

[2] This plan of Roosevelt's and the steps he took to be ready to carry it out were told by him in detail, clearly and unequivocally, in his Autobiography. Many wonder whether he really would have put it in effect. David S. Barry, in "Forty Years in Washington," quotes Philander C. Knox, Roosevelt's Attorney-General, as saying that he personally had been consulted by Roosevelt in the matter and had made a report to him in writing to the effect that the President did not possess the power. On receiving the report, Knox said, Roosevelt thanked him and said he would abide by it.

This story may be quite true, and yet mean little. Roosevelt received advice from Knox that a good many projects were of doubtful constitutionality or legality—and then went ahead with them. Lack of precedent had weight with Knox as a lawyer; with Roosevelt it had none. Knox got used to Roosevelt's ignoring his advice and rather admired it. On one occasion when Roosevelt ex-committee he asked Grover Cleveland; Carroll D. Wright, Commissioner of Labor; Marvin Hughitt, president of the Chicago and North Western Railway; Edgar E. Clark, head of the Order of Railway Conductors; and John D. Kernan, of New York.

Just after Roosevelt had secured the consent of these to serve, but before he had made any public announcement, Secretary of War Root took a hand.

v

Root, although the strike was not within his official responsibility, felt deeply that something extremely serious was ahead. With a thoroughness and orderliness characteristic of his mind, he asked for and made a study of the statements made and positions taken by the two opposing sides at the fruitless conference of October 3. From his study, and from his experience in many a tense lawsuit, Root sensed that the difficulty lay in the stage the controversy had reached, the stage where men are made stubborn, more by reluctance to seem to "back down" than by the principle involved. Root went to Roosevelt, told him he thought he saw a possible way by which the thing Roosevelt wanted could be accomplished, without humiliation to anybody, and asked Roosevelt's permission to try his hand at a suggestion for getting out of the impasse. The understanding between Root and Roosevelt was that the former was not committing the

---

pounded a project to Knox, and asked his opinion about the constitutional aspect of it, Knox replied in irony: "Ah, Mr. President, why have such a beautiful action marred by any taint of legality?"

The plan Roosevelt had for handling the coal strike had sufficient analogy to martial law, and to the operation of properties by the federal courts through receivers, to make it less extreme than at first thought it seems. The author of this history, who talked with Roosevelt about the plan more than once, believes Roosevelt would have carried it out. The one condition Roosevelt's spirit could not endure was any situation in which individuals or groups seemed able to defy or ignore the people as a whole and their representative in the White House. Any implication that the government of the United States was helpless before any set of circumstances was always a challenge to Roosevelt and stirred his deepest determination. He could not endure to be dared.

President in any way, but was acting on his individual responsibility.

With Roosevelt's permission, Root wrote a note to J. P. Morgan, asking if he would care to have a talk with him about the situation. Morgan answered by telephone, calling Root at the War Department, and asked him to come to New York, October 11. He suggested that the conference be held on Morgan's yacht, *The Corsair*, anchored in the North River, where reporters would not bother them.

Root found Morgan as willing as himself to see the public aspect of the situation and to try to find a way to end it. (Morgan throughout had never shared the recalcitrancy of the operators; on the contrary, his position had always been one of trying to persuade the operators to arbitrate, but of being resisted, chiefly by Baer.) Root and Morgan, after some discussion, drew up a pencilled memorandum, in which the unwillingness of the operators to arbitrate was reduced to specific unwillingness to arbitrate with Mitchell and the miners' union. This was put upon the grounds that Mitchell was the common head of both the anthracite and the bituminous miners; that anthracite coal was sold in competition with bituminous; that therefore three-fourths of the members of the miners' union — those engaged in bituminous mining — were a rival and competing interest to the industry represented by the anthracite operators; that any increase in wages to anthracite miners would to that extent increase its selling price and put it at a disadvantage as against bituminous. The memorandum omitted practically all the other elements in the dispute and concluded by stating that the operators were willing to arbitrate with the anthracite miners "whether formed in a union or not."

Root, leaving the memorandum with Morgan, returned to Washington. The next day, Sunday, October 12, Morgan had Baer in New York — he came by special train from Philadelphia. "All that Sunday telephones were throbbing through the East as financiers talked to railway chiefs. Monday all met in New York for consultation." Tuesday Morgan telephoned for a special train, went to Washington (accompanied by one of his junior partners, Robert Bacon, a friend and classmate of Roosevelt and bound to him by special ties); called on Root, with him walked to the temporary White House[1] on Jackson Place, and presented to Roosevelt[2] a document signed by the six operators, headed by Baer — a document which when read closely suggests among other things how great may be the difference, often, between the document the public sees and the negotiations and forces that bring it about. The document read, in part:

We suggest a Commission be appointed by the President of the United States (if he is willing to perform that public service) to whom shall be referred all questions at issue between the respective companies and their own employees, whether they belong to a union or not, and the decision of that Commission shall be accepted by us.

The Commission to be constituted as follows:

1. An officer of the engineer corps of either the military or naval service of the United States.

2. An expert mining engineer, experienced in the mining of coal and other minerals and not in any way connected with coal-mining properties, either anthracite or bituminous.

3. One of the judges of the United States Court of the Eastern District of Pennsylvania.

4. A man of prominence eminent as a sociologist.

5. A man who by active participation in mining and selling coal is familiar with the physical and commercial features of the business.

That carefully specified list of five classes from which arbitrators must be chosen is less important for what it

---

[1] The White House was being repaired.

[2] Of this scene Wellman says: "As I saw Morgan walk into the White House with Mr. Root . . . I thought the scene worthy of a place in a drama of American life." This was Morgan's second "journey to Canossa."

includes than for what it excludes. It admitted no person who by any stretch of the imagination could be described as a representative of a labor union. That careful exclusion reflected what was at the very bottom of the operators' hearts, dislike of recognizing the right of labor men to have a union, distaste for admitting equality between labor unions and them. So far as they could they wanted it to appear as if, for them, labor unions did not exist, or at least that they had no place in any sphere so elevated as arbitration. The miners, on the other hand, specified nothing, tried to dictate nothing. They merely told Roosevelt they would like very much to have on the board Bishop Spalding, of the Catholic diocese of Peoria, Illinois, and some one — they did not give any name — representing union labor. They did not ask that he be a member of the miners' union — any organized-labor man would do. They were willing either that the two be added to the operators' five, or included among them.

As the operators' signatures had been obtained by Morgan, Roosevelt had Root, in order to ascertain whether the operators would assent to the miners' wish, telegraph for some member of Morgan's firm to go to Washington. Morgan sent two of his junior partners, George W. Perkins and Robert Bacon. On the night of October 15, in Roosevelt's rooms at the White House, they spent a hectic three hours, from ten till one, with the telephone open to the offices of Morgan and Baer.

Roosevelt said he thought the comparatively slight suggestion the miners had made should be deferred to. Bacon and Perkins hurried to the telephone. From New York they were given binding orders not to permit an organized-labor man to be added to the operators' list of arbitrators. Roosevelt argued and coaxed. It would be ridiculous, he urged, to appoint a board to arbitrate a labor dispute that had no labor man on it. Perkins and

Bacon were willing; they were younger men than Morgan and Baer, and less flinty in their attitude toward labor than most of their older colleagues among the magnates of banking and industry; besides, they genuinely admired Roosevelt, had affection for him personally, and respect for his rank. Bacon and Perkins poured Roosevelt's arguments and exhortations into the telephone, but all they got from New York was an unrelenting refusal to permit labor to be officially represented on the board. Roosevelt felt almost as sorry for them as he was vexed with their superiors and troubled about the success of the negotiations. In a letter to Lodge he described them as "literally almost crazy. . . . They grew more and more hysterical."

At length, after hours of high-voltage discussion, at about midnight, it dawned on Roosevelt what was in the operators' minds. The operators were not willing that anybody *described as a labor man* should be added to the list of specified classes. "They did not mind my appointing any man, whether a labor man or not, so long as he was not appointed *as* a labor man, or *as* a representative of labor. They did not object to my exercising any latitude I chose in the appointments so long as they were made under the headings they had given."

The words, including the italicized *as*'s are Roosevelt's.[1] He added:

I shall never forget the mixture of relief and amusement I felt when I thoroughly grasped the fact that while they would heroically submit to anarchy rather than have Tweedledum, yet if I would call it Tweedledee they would accept it with rapture; it gave me an illuminating glimpse into one corner of the mighty brains of these "captains of industry." In order to carry the great and vital point and secure agreement by both parties, all that was necessary for me to do was to commit a technical and nominal absurdity with a solemn face. This I gladly did. I announced at once that I accepted the terms.

[1] "Theodore Roosevelt—An Autobiography."

Thereupon Roosevelt conducted, so to speak, one of the most rapid courses in higher education that ever raised the scholastic standing of an humble and modest man. Among his appointees to the Arbitration Commission was one upon whom he conferred the honorary degree of "eminent sociologist," a gentleman who up to that time had been known only as Grand Chief of the Order of Railway Conductors, E. E. Clark.[1]

In giving out the list for publication, Roosevelt let the public in on the joke, so far as he could, by adding after Clark's name a parenthetical explanation that he had been appointed

as a sociologist — the President assuming that for the purposes of such a Commission, the term sociologist means a man who has thought and studied deeply on social questions and has practically applied his knowledge.

But "the relief of the whole country was so great that the sudden appearance of the head of the Order of Railway Conductors as an 'eminent sociologist' merely furnished material for puzzled comment on the part of the press."[2]

To Finley Peter Dunne ("Mr. Dooley"), Roosevelt, writing as one humorist to another, told of the enjoyment he had got from the fight:

I feel like throwing up my hands and going to the circus; but as that is not possible I think I shall try a turkey shoot or bear hunt or something of the kind instead. Nothing that you have ever written can begin to approach in screaming comedy the inside of the last few conferences before I appointed the strike commission, and especially the complicated manœuvres by which, weaving in and out among the tender susceptibilities of the operators and the miners, I finally succeeded in reconciling both to the appointment of the president of the labor union as an "eminent sociologist."

[1] He added later, on his own account, Bishop John L. Spalding, to whom the operators did not object, and Carroll D. Wright.
[2] "Theodore Roosevelt—An Autobiography."

Comment on the President's success was carried on in superlatives. Only his inveterate critics and the operators saw in the situation anything not deserving praise. Walter Wellman, writing in the *Review of Reviews* for November, 1902, said of the settlement that it was "the greatest event affecting the relations of capital and labor in the history of America." Foreign newspapers joined in the chorus of approval, the London *Times* saying:[1]

> In a most quiet and unobtrusive manner the President has done a very big and entirely new thing. We are witnessing not merely the ending of the coal strike, but the definite entry of a powerful government upon a novel sphere of operation. . . . [Roosevelt's] personal prestige and reputation . . . will be immeasurably enhanced when the American people grasp the far larger issues involved in his striking departure from precedent. Let the Americans stick to their President and strengthen his hands. If there is any living man who can show them the way out of the dangers threatening them, that man is Mr. Roosevelt.

In this chorus of world-wide acclaim came a piping note from Senator Lodge:

> It is a very great public service you have rendered, and I rejoice in it more than I can express. It has had a great effect already in this State. The tide turned in our favor as soon as the settlement was known. I was speaking in the western part of the State and I could see the change go on, as the spirits of our people went up, and I think we have every reason to believe that we shall elect our governor by a good large majority, and elect twelve Congressmen, all by reduced majorities, but still with a gain of three seats.[2]

[1] The London *Times's* comment included understanding of the possible deeper and future significance of Roosevelt's action. One of the tests, not necessarily infallible or complete, of the place that such a man as Roosevelt should be given in history, is whether innovations introduced by him have become permanent, have crystallized into institutional practice. Roosevelt set a precedent for Presidents to take cognizance of coal strikes. The precedent was followed in practically every coal strike until the one in 1926-27, when President Coolidge kept his hands off. In the quarter-century that passed between the coal strike of 1902 and the year 1927, it cannot be said that any measurable progress had been made, either in England or in America, toward formulating means for settling strikes through official governmental action.

[2] Letter from Henry C. Lodge to Theodore Roosevelt, October 20, 1902.

On October 23 the miners resumed work.[1] On November 10 Roosevelt went on a bear hunt[2] in Mississippi.

Roosevelt, ten years later, fixed October, 1902, and the settlement of the coal strike as the time he "struck his own note" about big business. Lawrence F. Abbott had written in a newspaper article a sentence fixing November, 1904, the month Roosevelt was elected President in his own right, as the time "he began to shape the government upon the policies, in contradistinction to those of McKinley, which have now become historically associated

[1] The miners made the following four demands when the Arbitration Commission met:

(1) An increase of 20 per cent in wages.

(2) A reduction in the workday from 10 to 8 hours.

(3) The adoption of a weight system for piecework.

(4) The formulation of a working agreement between the mine operators and the United Mine Workers to fix wage rates and to adjust grievances.

The awards granted by the Commission were as follows:

(1) A retroactive increase of 10 per cent in wage rates for contract miners; no increase for the others, who numbered two-thirds of the personnel, but they were paid at the same rate for nine hours that they had previously received for ten.

(2) A reduction in the workday to 9 hours.

(3) The old system of payment should be retained.

(4) A working agreement between the miners and the operators was proposed, but without recognition of the United Mine Workers' Union.

Thomas Kennedy, secretary-treasurer of the United Mine Workers of America, who has read the proof of this chapter, calls attention to the fact that the award of a retroactive 10 per cent increase of wages applied only until the commission ended its work; and says that an additional important award was the creation of the Anthracite Board of Conciliation to settle grievances.

[2] While he was in camp near Smedes, Miss., a newspaper dispatch described him as refusing to shoot a small bear that had been brought into camp for him to kill. The cartoonist of the Washington *Post*, Clifford K. Berryman, pictured the incident. For one reason or another, whimsical or symbolic, the public saw in the bear episode a quality that it pleased to associate with Roosevelt's personality. The "Teddy-bear," beginning with Berryman's original cartoon, was repeated thousands of times and printed literally thousands of millions of times; in countless variations, pictorial and verbal, prose and verse; on the stage and in political debate; in satire or in humorous friendliness. Toy-makers took advantage of its vogue; it became more common in the hands of children than the woolly lamb. For Republican conventions, and meetings associated with Roosevelt, the "Teddy-bear" became the standard decoration, more in evidence than the eagle and only less usual than the Stars and Stripes.

Cartoon by Berryman, drawn in 1902, which started a Teddy-bear vogue lasting as
long as Roosevelt lived. The original is in the National Press Club
at Washington. (See foot-note, p. 445.)

with his administration." On the margin of the newspaper
clipping Roosevelt wrote: "No, the mere force of events
had made me strike absolutely my own note by October,
1902, when I settled the coal strike and started the trust-
control campaign."

25

WALL STREET TRIES TO GET RID OF ROOSEVELT

Hanna, in a Preliminary Skirmish, Acts—with Strange In-
caution—As If Roosevelt Were a Pawn. The Pawn Takes a
Hand in the Game, with Ensuing Devastation to Hanna.
Roosevelt's Nomination Becomes Inevitable. Whereupon
Wall Street Determines to Make Use of the Democratic
Party to Displace Roosevelt. After the Democratic Candi-
date for President Sends a "Gold Telegram," Wall Street
Surveys Its Alternatives and Decides It Is Better, on the
Whole, to Accept "Theodore, with All Thy Faults—."

ROOSEVELT's forceful intervention in the coal strike, his
initiation of the suit to dissolve the Northern Securities
Company; his proposals, in messages to Congress, of
legislation to regulate the trusts; his frequent trips about
the country, during which at almost every stop of his
train he told of plans for bringing the trusts under control
— all had justified the worst fears the big business interests had felt when Roosevelt, through the accident of an
assassin's bullet, had been projected into the White House.
They determined to get him out of it, and to substitute,
for the ensuing term, their hearts' desire, Mark Hanna.

Hanna, knowing politics better than Wall Street did,
understanding Roosevelt's rapidly growing strength with
the people, did not believe it possible to displace him.
But Hanna did believe it was possible to strengthen his
own position with relation to Roosevelt, and the authority
of the party organization over him. Roosevelt had got into
the White House through fate, without thanks to anybody; to continue there, he must be nominated on his own
account — and nomination must come through the party

machinery. Hanna, as National Chairman, having control of the machinery, thought he could manage it in such a way as to make the nomination seem to go to Roosevelt as a favor, and put Roosevelt under obligation. Hanna, therefore, was pleased with the movement to nominate himself, which would give him the opportunity later to abdicate in Roosevelt's favor. Moreover, the movement was flattering to Hanna — the editorials in the conservative press, the fund raised to "put him over," the public declarations of important business and political leaders, all had the effect of heightening Hanna's prestige, and prestige was the thing that Hanna, since McKinley's death, had missed sadly and needed mightily. Moreover, there was always the possibility that he might really get the nomination — in a year much can happen in politics.

But before the plans to nominate Hanna had had time to more than formulate themselves nebulously, the conflict between him and Roosevelt was precipitated by an incident in a local feud in the State which Hanna represented in the Senate, Ohio.

The other, and senior, Senator from Ohio was Joseph B. Foraker. Foraker loved Roosevelt's policies no more than Hanna did — indeed, Foraker was destined a few years later to go down to political oblivion as the climax of a mortal conflict with Roosevelt. Foraker was even more faithful to the big business interests than Hanna. At the moment, however, Foraker's major passion was jealousy of Hanna; between the two there was rivalry in the Senate, rivalry for standing with the great corporations, and rivalry for control of the local Republican organization in Ohio.

Foraker, more alert than Hanna, more watchful to take such tricks as fate provided, seeing an opportunity to use Roosevelt's popularity to advance his own interests, determined to seize the credit for being the first Ohio

Republican leader to climb aboard the Roosevelt band-wagon.

In late May, 1903, Foraker gave out a statement that began by oiling Roosevelt with unctuous phrases — "Roosevelt had made a good President . . . alert, aggressive, and brilliant, successful, best known and most popular man in the United States." That, like the opening of many a public interview, was merely of the nature of preliminary platitude. The real point of Foraker's statement had to do with an action he proposed should be taken by the Ohio Republican State Convention scheduled for June, 1903. His allusion to that, also, called for another instalment of explanatory introduction. He knew it would be regarded as unusual and even premature for the Ohio State Convention of 1903 to take an action looking to the presidential nomination of 1904, and that it ought properly to be the privilege of the following year's convention to express Ohio's judgment about the succession to Roosevelt. But, said Foraker, "many States declared last year in favor of him; nearly all the northern States will make similar declaration this year." Consequently, Foraker concluded: "I do not know of any reason why Ohio should not also declare for him. I think it would be very wise for the Republicans of Ohio at the approaching State convention to declare their intention to support Roosevelt next year as our candidate for the Presidency." [1]

That statement was designed (a) to give Foraker, as against Hanna, credit for being the original Roosevelt man in Ohio; (b) to secure for Foraker the friendliness of all the Roosevelt following in Ohio; and (c) to give Foraker the prestige of originating the policy of the Ohio Republican convention. Further than that, the interview was certain to force a show-down about Hanna's relation to the

[1] "Notes of a Busy Life," Joseph B. Foraker.

presidential nomination. Hanna would be compelled to say whether he was or was not a candidate. If he chose the former, he would thenceforth have against him the growing Roosevelt strength and might lose not only the nomination for the Presidency but his Senate seat as well; if he chose the latter, he would become definitely a less potent figure in national politics. All the cards were in Foraker's hands and he played them with superb political shrewdness.

Foraker's move threw Hanna into a rage — and in rage he acted. If Foraker did "not know of any reason why Ohio should not declare for Roosevelt," Hanna did. Certainly Hanna saw a reason why Ohio should not adopt so important a policy on an initiative coming from his rival, Foraker. Hanna could not afford the spectacle of Foraker directing the policy of their common State on so material a point. Whatever was to be done by Ohio, Hanna thought, should be decided by him. He was the big man in Ohio Republican politics; he was Ohio's big man in the nation.

Hanna, choosing the second of the alternatives open to him, gave out a counter-statement, saying:

I am not, and will not be, a candidate for the presidential nomination. [But] on account of my position as chairman of the Republican National Committee, I am supposed to have a vital interest in the results in Ohio. It would be presumed that I might have some influence as to the policy or action of the State convention this year in national affairs.

Hanna's statement then went on to give reasons — rather lame ones — why the Republicans in Ohio should not commit themselves on the presidential nomination a year ahead of time.

Hanna, having acted in rage, reflected in panic. His interview was not on the street an hour before it occurred to him to think of how it might read to one who, as between him and Foraker, had no interest in either — but who had a decided interest in the controversy in which he was being used as, so to speak, the battle-ground. Hanna suddenly realized that to Roosevelt the reasons he had given, for opposing endorsement of Roosevelt's candidacy, might not seem so ingenuous as he hoped they would seem to Ohio Republicans. Hurriedly, Hanna telegraphed to Roosevelt:[1]

The issue which has been forced upon me in the matter of our State Convention this year endorsing you for the Republican nomination next year has come in a way which makes it necessary for me to oppose such a resolution. When you know all the facts I am sure you will approve my course.

Hanna was so uneasy that he felt it was desirable to provide Roosevelt promptly with "all the facts." Within the same busy forty-eight hours of his reading the Foraker statement, giving out his own, and sending his telegram, he wrote Roosevelt a letter. It was utterly artless. Hanna had not a particle of subtlety in his nature, nor was he capable of carefully arranging his words and sentences so as to create a desired atmosphere — it is doubtful if Hanna ever rewrote any letter — what he had to say, he said. His curiously disjointed letter to Roosevelt, with its irrelevant underscorings, reflected exactly the things that were in his mind: confidence that what he had done had been necessary and inevitable; uneasiness lest Roosevelt might not understand; dislike of having to explain; the wish to appear to take Roosevelt's approval for granted; a desire to placate Roosevelt by dragging into the letter some things designed to make Roosevelt feel good. He began by saying that he had been entirely ignorant of what was going on until Foraker's statement "came out in the papers." Then

[1] May 23, 1903. Roosevelt was in Seattle, on a Western trip.

I at once expressed my disapproval for the following reasons.
. . . It places me in an embarrassing position as Chairman of
the National Committee; and last but not *least* it is meant to be
unfriendly toward me. You know the past history of several
things of kindred nature so I will not dwell on the motives which
are the real incentive to this action, only that I shall oppose the
resolution and you may feel sure without anything but the
best of motives and in what I consider your best *interests*. I
am hearing from all over the country. There is but one opinion,
that this is an attempt to put me in a false position and to
your injury. ¶I almost committed an "impulsive" act myself
by stating in my interview to the Associated Press (copy enclosed) that I felt sure you would not approve — (under the
circumstances). It is not necessary to hesitate between good
and bad judgment when the motives are *known*. I spent a few
days in New York last week and remembered your suggestion
to me. There is need of missionary work there. But with this
embarrassment thrust upon me will make me a useless article.
Our convention comes the 2nd and 3rd of June, and promises
to be a hot *time*.

Hanna was to learn quickly that Roosevelt was not
leaving his "best interests" to the protection of Hanna;
that Roosevelt was fully capable of caring for his own
interests, and vigilantly resourceful in taking advantage
of the "breaks in the game." With Hanna's telegram
before him, and without waiting for the letter with "all
the facts," Roosevelt wrote out a reply which he dispatched to Hanna, at the same time giving out a summary
of it to the newspapers. The reply was at once an answer
to Hanna and, in effect, an announcement, the first, of
his own candidacy — and additionally and importantly
useful to Roosevelt as setting up in the public mind a
sense of contrast and antagonism between himself and
Hanna, who was popularly looked upon as the symbol of
the trusts:

Hon. M. A. HANNA,
   Cleveland, Ohio.
                    Seattle, Wash., May 25, 1903.

Your telegram received. I have not asked any man for his
support. I have had nothing whatever to do with raising this

issue. Inasmuch as it has been raised of course those who favor my administration and my nomination will favor endorsing both and those who do not will oppose.

THEODORE ROOSEVELT.

Hanna, outmanœuvred in one way by Foraker and in another by Roosevelt, his prestige dwindled to a miniature of what it had once been, accepted the situation with what philosophy he could muster. It was a complete and irrevocable surrender. His decision he telegraphed to Roosevelt:

Your telegram of the 25th. In view of the sentiment expressed I shall not oppose the endorsement of your administration and candidacy by our State Convention. I have given the substance of this to the Associated Press.

Roosevelt, in the leisure of several days later,[1] wrote Hanna a long letter, in which frank truth is mingled with the forgivable disingenuousness of politeness, in just about the proportions of the degree to which Hanna's predicament was his own fault, and the degree to which Roosevelt had taken advantage of Hanna's predicament in order to get an advantage for himself:

Ogden, Utah, May 29, 1903.

I do not think you appreciated the exact effect that your interview had in the country at large. It was everywhere accepted as the first open attack upon me, and it gave heart . . . to my opponents. The mischievous effect was instantly visible. The general belief was that this was not your move, save indirectly; that it was really an attack by the so-called Wall Street forces on me, to which you had been led to give a reluctant acquiescence. My view was that you of course had an absolute right to be a candidate yourself, but that if you were not one you would be doing me and the Republican party serious harm by fighting and very probably beating the proposition to endorse me by the Ohio Convention. ¶ After thinking the matter carefully over I became sure that I had to take a definite stand myself. I hated to do it because you have shown

[1] May 29, 1903.

such broad generosity and straightforwardness in all your dealings with me that it was peculiarly painful to me to be put, even temporarily, in a position of seeming antagonism to you. No one but a really big man — a man above all petty considerations — could have treated me as you have treated me during the year and a half since President McKinley's death. I have consulted you and relied on your judgment more than has been the case with any other man.

Roosevelt, writing confidentially to Senator Lodge, May 27, 1903, could be more candid:

I . . . decided that the time had come to stop shilly-shallying, and let Hanna know definitely that I did not intend to assume the position, at least passively, of a suppliant to whom he might give the nomination as a boon. I rather expected Hanna to fight, but made up my mind that it was better to have a fight in the open at once than to run the risk of being knifed secretly. I am pleased at the outcome as it simplifies things all around, for in my judgment Hanna was my only formidable opponent so far as the nomination is concerned. The whole incident has entirely revived me. I was feeling jaded and tired. The trip has been very severe and I have gotten so I [could] not sleep well, which always tells on one. But this last business gave me a new and vivid interest in life.[1]

Lodge, replying to Roosevelt, gave him a bit of Washington gossip: "Foraker almost wept with joy when he read your statement."

After the excitement was all over, the New York *Commercial Advertiser* summed up the net results in an editorial written in a style that has since unfortunately gone out of fashion:

Senator Hanna, with really marvellous agility, considering his years and his rheumatic afflictions, stepped to his seat on the Roosevelt band-wagon yesterday, . . . remarking as he settled into his place that he was uncommonly glad to join the company, and should have done so before had he known that

[1] From "Selections from the Correspondence of Theodore Roosevelt and Henry Cabot Lodge."

the band was about to begin to play and the procession to move. ¶ The seats on the band-wagon are now all filled, and the company is a cheerful and smiling one as the wheels begin to go round. Behind shrubbery and lying in gulleys along the line of march there are discernible a few sour-visaged persons with mud balls and squirt guns in their hands who are threatening various kinds of disaster to the wagon and are saying to one another: "You just wait! We'll upset the thing yet!" But they have little faith in their own predictions, and will be extremely careful about getting themselves in front of the vehicle.[1]

Any lingering hope of nominating Hanna that Wall Street retained was dissipated by the death of the latter four months before the convention, February 15, 1904.

The big business interests and the conservative press accepted the inevitable.[2] The New York *Sun*,[3] six weeks before the convention, proposed the Republican party platform should be:

WHEREAS Theodore Roosevelt is the national Republican party, be it

---

[1] Another newspaper, the Pittsburgh *Leader*, told the story in verse:

> Up in the treetop triumphantly sat
>   Old Mark Hanna.
> Says he, "there's a winner right under my hat
>   Old Mark Hanna.
> Let no would-be President get in my way
> For the State of Ohio will do what I say,
> I've a grip on the boys and they've got to obey
>   Old Mark Hanna." . . .
>
> Just then came a message designed to distress
>   Old Mark Hanna.
> By Teddy 'twas sent. He alone, could suppress
>   Old Mark Hanna.
> He said: "I am onto your infamous plot
> And you'd better let up or I'll show you what's what."
> These terrible words overpow'red on the spot
>   Old Mark Hanna.
>
> Very like thirty cents is that former grand duke
>   Old Mark Hanna. . . .

[2] Roosevelt's nomination, on June 23, was unanimous.

[3] On May 4, 1904.

RESOLVED, That we emphatically endorse and affirm Theodore Roosevelt.

Whatever Theodore Roosevelt thinks, says, does, or wants is right.

Roosevelt and Stir 'Em Up! Now and Forever; One and Inseparable!

II

If the big business interests were now to prevent Roosevelt's continuation in the Presidency, they must do it through the Democrats. Many of them turned to that alternative. The Democratic party, after Bryan's two successive and cumulatively disastrous defeats, was now in control of the New York and other Eastern conservative "Safe-and-Saners" — available for Wall Street to use as an instrument to get rid of Roosevelt. The "Safe-and-Saners" were going to nominate a thoroughly conservative New York judge, Alton B. Parker. Bryan, belligerent to the last ditch, adopted a strategy of having the convention write a platform which should include a free-silver plank, which Parker could not run on, and which would compel him to decline the nomination. Bryan made his fight in the committee on resolutions and was beaten, 35 to 15. The convention unanimously adopted a platform silent on currency, and nominated[1] Parker.

Immediately, through the convention ran a rumor that Parker had sent a telegram refusing the nomination unless the party platform should specifically endorse the gold standard. Instantly, "excitement was intense. Men, even seasoned veterans, were running around in circles." The presiding officer, Champ Clark, of Missouri, to prolong the proceedings, ordered the band to play continuously. The Bryan Democrats of the West and South were enraged. Tillman, of South Carolina, felt he and the

---

[1] With 658 votes to 200 for William R. Hearst, and 107 scattering.

others of his faction
had been, as Champ
Clark told, "deceived,
seduced, maltreated,
and hornswoggled; he
was swearing and shed-
ding floods of tears by
turns; he had lost his
handkerchief and used
his shirt-sleeve to wipe
off his tears and other
effluvia." Tillman
threatened to withdraw
the vote of the eighteen
delegates from South
Carolina, which would
have reduced Parker's
vote below the two-
thirds required by the
rules, and would have
made Parker's title to
the nomination doubt-
ful at least.

From a photograph by Harris & Ewing.

Senator Tillman and his daughter. Senator
Tillman was commonly known as "Pitch-
fork" Tillman, due to a phrase he used in
describing what he would do to Grover
Cleveland. In his later years in the Senate
he mellowed much, and when he was dying
asked that Senator Lodge, of Massachusetts,
speak at his obituary services. To most
Southerners Senator Lodge was anathema,
because of his long advocacy of the "Force
bill" for the presence of Federal soldiers at
the elections in southern States to protect
the negro in his right of suffrage.

The violence was
stimulated by the pub-
lication in a local St.
Louis newspaper of the
alleged telegram, read-
ing:

Senator E. W. Car-
mack, Tennessee delega-
tion: The Gold Standard
is established by law and I cannot accept the nomination unless
that plank is contained in the platform.

Culberson, of Texas, arose, with the newspaper in his

hand, and said: "Mr. Chairman, for reasons which are obvious to all the delegates here, it seems to me we ought not to proceed to nominate a candidate for Vice-President at this time. I therefore move that the convention take a recess. [Cries of "Why?"] I think the delegates understand what I mean. . . . We want to know, before a candidate for Vice-President is nominated, who will be the nominee of this convention for President. I therefore move the convention take a recess until 8:30 to-night." "Taking that recess," wrote the chairman of the convention, Champ Clark, "probably prevented a riot."

During the recess, the Missouri delegation determined to introduce a resolution to rescind the nomination, and arranged with the chairman, Champ Clark, for the necessary parliamentary procedure. The projected action became known and intensified the excitement. Finally some one got the telegram Parker had actually sent. It read:

Hon. W. F. Sheehan,   Esopus, N. Y., July 9, 1904.
   Hotel Jefferson, St. Louis, Mo.
   I regard the Gold Standard as firmly and irrevocably established, and shall act accordingly if the action of the convention to-day shall be ratified by the people. As the platform is silent on the subject, my view should be made known to the convention, and if it is proved to be unsatisfactory to the majority, I request you to decline the nomination for me at once, so that another may be nominated before adjournment.
                                    Alton B. Parker.

After furious debate, the convention voted to reply to Parker as follows:

The platform adopted by this convention is silent upon the question of the monetary standard, because it is not regarded by us as a possible issue in this campaign, and only campaign issues are mentioned in the platform. Therefore, there is nothing in the views expressed by you in the telegram just received which would preclude a man entertaining them from accepting a nomination on said platform.

III

In the ensuing campaign between Parker and Roosevelt, the business interests that hated the latter followed a course reflected by the outstanding journalistic exponent of them. The New York *Sun* had begun its treatment of Roosevelt when he became President by flattering assumption that his great good-sense and solid character would of course cause him to follow the steps of McKinley and to abide faithfully by the orthodox principles of the Republican party, including the party's protective guardianship of the interests of business. When Roosevelt compelled the coal operators to arbitrate the strike of 1902, and when he started suit against the Northern Securities Company, *The Sun* attacked him with a

The Sun.

THURSDAY, AUGUST 11, 1904.

Entered at the Post Office at New York as Second-Class Mail Matter.

THEODORE! with all thy faults——

One of our contemporaries says that the only place in Africa bearing the name of ⸻NLEY is Stanley Pool in the Congo State. ⸻ quite accurate, for 900 miles ⸻ngo is the lower end of a falls that have ⸻ since

trenchant force rarely exceeded in political controversy. As the question of Roosevelt's renomination by the Republicans approached, *The Sun* demanded that it be denied him, and that the standard be given to Mark Hanna. When Roosevelt's nomination became inevitable, *The Sun* continued protesting.

After Roosevelt was nominated, and after the Democrats had nominated Parker, *The Sun*, and the financial interests it represented, surveyed the alternatives. Their emotions clamored that they oppose Roosevelt; their intellects told them that while Parker personally was a satisfactory conservative, it was still clear that fully half the Democratic party had the attitude of Bryan toward big business. In this dilemma, *The Sun*, after five weeks' reflection, printed one of the briefest editorials that ever expressed a great newspaper's position in a campaign, a compact triumph of the qualities of intellect and humor that caused *The Sun* to be universally admired, even by those who most strongly disagreed with it. *The Sun's* announcement of its choice read simply:

Theodore! with all thy faults ——

As the campaign went one, *The Sun* explained its conversion in later editorials:

We prefer the impulsive candidate of the party of conservatism to the conservative candidate of the party which the business interests regard as permanently and dangerously impulsive.

The campaign ended in victory for Roosevelt by an unprecedented majority, the Democrats carrying not one State north of the Mason and Dixon line, and not all those south of it, the most disastrous defeat suffered by any major party since the 1872 campaign of Horace Greeley. Missouri[1] went Republican for the first time since Civil War and Reconstruction days.

IV

Roosevelt, elected, said to Mrs. Roosevelt: "I am no longer a political accident." To the newspapers he gave out a memorable statement designed to assure the public that his Presidency would be influenced by no consideration of his personal political fortunes, but that his actions

[1] The news that Missouri had gone Republican came to the office of the Chicago *Tribune* about five o'clock. Within two hours John T. McCutcheon drew a cartoon that became famous, "The Mysterious Stranger." See page 461.

would be determined on principle, and could be judged on merit:

> I am deeply sensible of the honor done me by the American people in thus expressing their confidence in what I have done and have tried to do. I appreciate to the full the solemn re-

"The Mysterious Stranger," a famous cartoon by John McCutcheon, published by the Chicago *Tribune*, November 10, 1904, the day after the election returns showed Missouri had gone Republican.

> sponsibility this confidence imposes upon me, and I shall do all that in my power lies not to forfeit it. On the 4th of March next I shall have served three and one-half years, and this three and one-half years constitutes my first term. The wise custom which limits the President to two terms regards the substance and not the form. Under no circumstances will I be a candidate for or accept another nomination.

26

THE SUPREME COURT REVERSES
ITSELF

By Declaring the Northern Securities Company Illegal, the
Supreme Court Puts New Life into the Sherman Anti-
Trust Law, and Vindicates Roosevelt. Appraisals, Friendly
and Unfriendly, of One of His Outstanding Achievements.

I

THE suit initiated by Roosevelt against the Northern
Securities merger, after two years in the lower Federal
Courts, reached final decision by the Supreme Court of the
United States on March 14, 1904. To the Court it was a
clear question, whether it should or should not reverse
itself. By its decision in the Knight case nine years before, it had said in effect that a trust organized in the form
of a holding-company was not a violation of the Sherman
Anti-Trust law. Under the protection of that decision,
substantially all the existing trusts in the country, and
many new ones, had organized themselves in the holding-
company form. Now the Court was asked to declare
illegal a holding-company similar to the Knight one.
"The parallel," said Justice White, "between the two
cases [the Knight case and the Northern Securities case]
is complete."

The Court, by five to four, reversed itself, declared the
Northern Securities Company illegal. "This combination," said Justice Harlan,

is . . . a trust, a combination in restraint of commerce. No
scheme or device could more certainly come within the words
of the act, "combination in the form of trust or otherwise,"
or could more effectively and certainly suppress free competition.

The action was sensational in all respects — as a reversal of itself by the Supreme Court of the United States, in its effect on corporate industry, in its assertion that as between business and government, government is supreme. Roosevelt can be pardoned for the markedly triumphant tone of his comment:

From a photograph by Henry Miller.

Supreme Court Justice John M. Harlan, who in his decision ordering the dissolution of the Northern Securities Company held that "no scheme could more effectively and certainly suppress free competition."

This decision [the preceding decision, in the Knight case] I caused to be annulled by the court that had rendered it. . . . The Northern Securities suit is one of the great achievements of my administration. I look back upon it with pride, for through it we emphasized the fact that the most powerful men in this country were held to accountability before the law. It was necessary to reverse the Knight case in the interests of the people against monopoly and privilege, just as it had been necessary to reverse the Dred Scott case in the interests of the people against slavery and privilege. The success of the Northern Securities case definitely established the power of the government to deal with all great corporations. We had gained the power.[1]

This estimate by Roosevelt was no higher than that of others, who were disinterested and competent to make expert appraisal. "In my judgment," said a historian of American finance, Alexander Dana Noyes,[2] "the overthrow of the Northern Securities combination was the

[1] These sentences are taken partly from a statement made by Roosevelt in 1904, a few months after the decision; partly from his autobiography written nine years later.
[2] In "Forty Years of American Finance."

most positive achievement of the Roosevelt administration in the field of corporation finance."

This commentator within the world of finance itself put his approbation, not merely on the ground of protection of the people from monopoly, but on that of benefit to sound finance and sound organization of industry: "The interest of investors, of the financial markets themselves, would have been placed in the most serious jeopardy had that merger been upheld. For the promoters of the Northern Securities Company were travelling on a path of capital inflation which logically had no end except in eventual exhaustion of credit and general bankruptcy."[1]

Of all the approval of Roosevelt's action, of all the exalted appraisals put upon its importance, the most convincing — because of the source — came from the Democratic New York *World*, which put its commendation in the form of frank admission:

It is just as well to record some plain truths, however unpleasant or surprising. . . . The first [energetic] effort to enforce the [anti-trust] law was made by Theodore Roosevelt, a Republican President. The first Attorney-General to vigorously prosecute offenders and to test the law was a Republican Attorney-General, Philander C. Knox. The decision of the Supreme Court of the United States, given as a finality from which there is no appeal, upholding the law as perfectly constitutional and absolutely impregnable in every respect, as *The World* for twelve years constantly insisted, was due to five

[1] For this strong assertion, Noyes had good reasons. The Northern Securities type of holding-corporation, if sustained, "might"—these are the words of Justice Brewer in the decision—"be extended until a single corporation whose stock was owned by three or four parties would be in practical control . . . of the whole transportation business of the country." Actually, some of the promoters of the Northern Securities Company, in particular Harriman, were proceeding in that direction, pyramiding holding-company on holding-company; buying control of railroad A, using its credit to borrow money with which to buy railroad B, and so on. Harriman testified in a hearing before the Interstate Commerce Commission that if the law would let him alone he would "spread not only over the Pacific Coast, but over the Atlantic. . . . I would go on as long as I live."

judges, every one of whom is a Republican. Under these circumstances it does not seem probable that the Democrats can make great capital in seeking to monopolize the anti-trust issue.

"The United States," *The World* said on another occasion, "was probably never nearer to a social revolution than it was when Theodore Roosevelt became President." The change Roosevelt wrought was expressed by the owner of *The World*, Joseph Pulitzer, in words that may not be improved, in a summary of Roosevelt's achievements which carries conviction not only by the discriminating quality that is obvious in its phrasing, but also by the background and position of the man who uttered it. Pulitzer was a Democrat, the owner of the leading Democratic paper in the country; he had, besides, personal reasons for not liking Roosevelt. He devoted every resource of an almost abnormal intellectual energy to understanding the spirit of America and knowing the quality of its public men; and in his present judgment he was writing with peculiar privacy and intimacy, in the form of a personal letter of instruction to the editor of his paper, Frank Cobb, to whom he said: "There is too much nagging Roosevelt. Support him on main line — no hypercriticism of his minor faults":

If Roosevelt had never done anything else, and if he had committed a hundred times more mistakes, and if he were one hundred times more impulsive, changeable, unpresidential in dignity, loud and vociferating in manner and speech — . . . if he had done nothing else except to start the great machinery of the government and the most powerful force and majesty of the law in the direction of prosecuting these great offenders, he would be entitled to the greatest credit for the greatest service to the nation. This one initiative impulse and persevering instinct must be held as offsetting a hundred wrong impulses of a minor character. The greatest breeder of discontent and socialism is lack of confidence in the justice of the law, popular belief that the law is one thing for the rich and another for the poor.

Pulitzer's judgment concluded with five words that have the brevity and compact truth of an inscription such as almost might appear on Roosevelt's monument:

He has subjugated Wall Street.

The World, amplifying the spirit of its owner's private

After Roosevelt's victory over the Northern Securities Company in 1904, the Minneapolis *Journal* cartoonist pictured the trusts as ready to "eat out of his hand," an assumption that was premature.

judgment, picking out Roosevelt's concrete crowning act, said on the day following his death:

By his procedure in the Northern Securities case he succeeded in demonstrating that the country had laws under which the multiplication of trusts could be curbed, that the highest court of the nation would sustain these laws, and that the government of the United States was not at the mercy of Wall Street and organized capital. This having been demonstrated, the trust question came to answer itself under the steady pressure of public opinion.[1]

II

"History," said Henry Adams,[2] "is a tangled skein that one may take up at any point, and break when one has revealed enough" — a dictum designed less to help the reader than to excuse the writer for stopping where he chooses, the latter being the one who is permitted to interpret "enough."

In the present history, the several chapters ending with this one tell with reasonable completeness, or at least to a point of sufficient finality, one of Roosevelt's outstanding achievements — his demonstration that no group is more powerful than the government; his ending, by this demonstration, of one of the causes of the long surge of outcry against the trusts — the feeling that they were above the law. The same chapters explain the rise of the trusts and follow them through the successive phases they had reached about 1904.

Where to go from here is a problem of which the embarrassment lies in the multitude of possible answers. If the aim were a complete history either of the trusts or of Roosevelt, and that only, the appropriate next chapter would be an account of the use Roosevelt now made of the Northern Securities decision — the suits he began against the Standard Oil Company, the beef trust, the tobacco trust, and some others — the actions which constituted his answer to the New York *World's* "Now what

[1] The quotations from Pulitzer are detached from two letters sent by him to Cobb in March and August, 1907. The order of some of the sentences is rearranged. The quotation from *The World* editorial is from a summing up of Roosevelt's career on January 7, 1919.
[2] In the "Education of Henry Adams."

are you going to do next!"; to the Hartford *Times's* demand that he bring "a thousand or more suits at once,"
and to the New York *Times's* assertion that "nothing
. . . can now restrain the administration from letting
loose all the dogs of war upon the guilty restrainers of
trade." These suits, resisted by the ablest lawyers the
trusts could find, were contested step by step, for years.
The proceedings revealed practices justifying the popular
suspicion and alarm about the trusts, and brought from
the courts condemnation practically as severe as had been
uttered by any radical, whether poet or politician.

If the discussion of trusts in this volume were ideally
complete, it would include the later phases of the attitude
of the government toward them, especially the policy
adopted by Woodrow Wilson's Democratic administration. If the discussion were ideally balanced, as well as
complete, it would include some other aspects of the trusts,
and some sequels. It would tell the destiny of the two
largest fortunes that arose out of the trust era, the stupendous benefactions through which Andrew Carnegie
and John D. Rockefeller gave ironic answer to the fear,
widely entertained about 1900, that the fortunes made
through the trusts would multiply cumulatively, and become the foundation of a hereditary plutocratic caste in
America. A balanced discussion would include certain enrichments of the average man which came partially as an
accompaniment of the organization of industry into large
units; would explain the subsiding of acute alarm about
them, the failure of some early apprehensions about them
to materialize, the partial tolerance of them that accompanied the economic well-being of America during the
nineteen-twenties.

If the aim of the present volume were confined to picturing the career of Roosevelt, it would pass from his

achievement in the courts, to his achievements in legislation, beginning with his successful pressing, in the
1905–6 session of Congress, of the bill giving the Federal

From "Puck," September 21, 1904.

"I rather like that imported affair."

During the campaign of 1904, the Democrats charged Roosevelt with having
ambitions to be a Cæsar."

Government the power, in effect, to make railroad rates.
To describe at this point the fight Roosevelt made for the
Hepburn Railroad Rate bill, would achieve dramatic
unity, for in that fight Roosevelt's antagonist was Foraker
of Ohio, who made 86 speeches against the bill; who called
part of it "revolutionary" and "contrary to the spirit

of our institutions," and called another part of it, tautolog-
ically, "a cheat, a humbug, and a fraud"; who carried his
fight to the end, voting against the bill as the only Republican, and one of only three Senators — for which he was
canonized by the New York *Sun*: "The Republican who
voted 'No!' . . . deserves the praise due the man tena-
cious of his purpose. The Muckrake pack have yapped
and snapped at 'the railroad lawyer.' "

However, the present volume being one of a series whose
aggregate purpose is to tell the story of the average man in
America, the conditions of that scope and aim — in some
senses an amplification, in others a limitation — dictate
postponement of the railroad legislation, as well as the
later phases of trusts, and use of the remainder of this
volume for some other experiences of the average man
during this period.

27

THE CRUSADE FOR PURE FOOD

A Popular Novel Causes the Public to Pay Startled Attention to One of Its Sources of Food. The Book Becomes a "Best Seller," but the Author Finds a Flaw in His Pleasure. President Roosevelt Reads Some Magazine Articles and Becomes "All Act." A Long-Sustained Campaign against Food Adulteration Comes to a Climax. From Old to New in American Food Habits. Spring-Houses, Butter-Making, the Village Bakery, Drovers, "Preserving Time," and Other Details of an Older and Simpler Era in America. The Passing of the Old-Time Butcher. Women, Becoming Incensed at Abuses by Food Manufacturers, Conduct a Crusade and Win a Victory, Thereby Learning, among Other Lessons, That the Liquor Interests Are Not Invincible. From Which, Indirectly, Other Results Follow. Roosevelt Practises "Executive Usurpation" at the Expense of Congress, Which Becomes Indignant — but Passes the Bills He Demands. The Natural History of a Reform Movement That Succeeded. Together with Some Piquant Sequels.

I

In 1906, Upton Sinclair, a young man devoted to romantic philosophy, realistic literature, and experimental socialism, finished a novel,[1] named it "The Jungle," carried the manuscript to five different publishers who rejected it, decided to print it as he[2] could, and asked his friend, fellow Socialist, and fellow author, Jack London, to write the announcement. London, seeing the novel as what the author meant it to be, described it as an appeal for socialism, a protest against "wage slavery," and wrote:

[1] A Socialist periodical, *The Appeal to Reason*, financed Sinclair with $500, upon which he lived for seven weeks among the stock-yards workers.

[2] Subsequently, it was published by Doubleday, Page & Co., became the best-selling book in the United States for a year, was translated into seventeen languages—and then went out of print for ten years, when Sinclair took back the plates himself and tried to revive it.

CIRCULATE "THE JUNGLE"

Dear Comrades: . . . The book we have been waiting for these many years! It will open countless ears that have been deaf to Socialism. It will make thousands of converts to our cause. It depicts what our country really is, the home of oppression and injustice, a nightmare of misery, an inferno of suffering, a human hell, a jungle of wild beasts. ¶And take notice and remember, comrades, this book is straight proletarian. It is written by an intellectual proletarian, for the proletarian. It is to be published by a proletarian publishing house. It is to be read by the proletariat. What "Uncle Tom's Cabin" did for the black slaves "The Jungle" has a large chance to do for the white slaves of to-day.

London's most troubling apprehension was that the book might encounter a "conspiracy of silence" on the part of "capitalism," by which he meant merely that he feared it might not be read; that it might make no more noise and get no more circulation than is the usual and normal fate of more than ninety-nine new books out of every hundred. Hence he warned his Socialist comrades:

Remember, this book must go out in the face of the enemy. . . . The most dangerous treatment it will receive is that of silence. For that is the way of capitalism. Comrades, do not forget the conspiracy of silence. Silence is the deadliest danger this book has to face.

"The Jungle" was one of the earliest examples of Tolstoyan pessimism and other Russian influences on American fiction, and, as a novel, was measurably comparable to the best of its Slavic models. It told the epic tragedy of Jurgis, a Lithuanian peasant who saw in his native village one of the posters with which American industrial corporations and steamship companies lured immigrants to America. Jurgis came to Chicago, and got a job in the stock-yards — which Sinclair called "Packingtown," a name that had been used locally, and which "The Jungle" caused to become familiar nationally and to endure for several years. In Packingtown, the immigrant came into contact with about every evil that American industry and politics contained. He had to pay graft to get his job, and more to keep it; he lived in a lodging-house where the keeper "would rent the same bed to double shifts of men, one working every day and using it at night, the other working by night and using it by day"; he was cheated by the real-estate man who sold him a house on the instalment plan under a contract the Lithuanian could not read; he and his family were infected by hideous diseases, and by moral ulcers as well, from the conditions under which they toiled; he was "speeded up" beyond his strength by "pace-makers"; he found the company he worked for had secret mains through which they stole water from the city; he saw his neighbors used as pawns and victims of the worst practices of municipal politics; he was blackmailed into paying high prices for adulterated beer because "the saloon-keeper 'stood in' with all the big politicians in the district"; he went through the familiar experiences of being "laid off," of striking, and of being "blacklisted"; he was persecuted by "spotters"; he lost his savings through a bank failure; when an intolerable grievance led him to "beat up" the foreman over him, he found the company "stood in" with the courts, and he was sent to jail unjustly. Hardly a solitary American influence, institution, or individual that this immigrant-laborer met, failed to cheat him, exploit[1] him, brutalize him.

Not only was Jurgis the victim of constant tragedy.

[1] One, who at the author's request has read the proofs of this chapter in a spirit of defending the packers, makes the point that much of the exploitation of immigrants was committed by fellow countrymen of themselves, who, having preceded them to America by a few years, used what knowledge they had picked up of American ways and institutions, to take advantage of "greenhorns." This is true, and applies to the whole subject of immigration. But it is only a partial and slight defense of the industrial system with which the immigrant came in contact.

Every human being that had any important part in the book was a tragedy. And not only the human beings. The animals were portrayed by Sinclair as tragedies. As one result, the workmanship of the book was like the picture it aimed to convey of the stock-yards, a welter of the terribly grim, together with some other things that Sinclair meant to be terribly grim, but which to the average American reader were almost comically trivial. In the spirit of his Russian models, Sinclair, giving souls to the unhappy pigs, wrote:

One could not stand and watch very long without becoming philosophical, without beginning to deal in symbols and similes, and to hear the hog-squeal of the universe. Was it permitted to believe that there was nowhere upon the earth, or above the earth, a heaven for hogs, where they were requited for all this suffering? Each one of these hogs was a separate creature. Some were white hogs, some were black; some were brown, some were spotted; some were old, some were young; some were long and lean, some were monstrous. And each of them had an individuality of his own, a will of his own, a hope and a heart, a desire; each was full of self-confidence, of self-impor-tance, and a sense of dignity. And trusting and strong in faith he had gone about his business, the while a black shadow hung over him and a horrid Fate waited in his pathway. Now sud-denly it had swooped upon him, and had seized him by the leg. Relentless, remorseless it was; all his protests, his screams, were nothing to it; it did its cruel will with him, as if his wishes, his feelings, had simply no existence at all; it cut his throat and watched him gasp out his life. And now was one to believe that there was nowhere a god of hogs, to whom this hog-personality was precious, to whom these hog-squeals and agonies had a meaning? Who would take this hog into his arms and comfort him, reward him for his work well done, and show him the meaning of his sacrifice?

The squeals of the pigs, as their throats were slit, seemed to Sinclair a symphony of tragedy:

A most terrifying shriek . . . followed by another, louder and yet more agonizing — for once started upon that journey the hog never came back — at the top of the wheel he was shunted off upon a trolley, and went sailing down the room. And meantime another was swinging up, and then another, and another, until there was a double line of them, each dangling by a foot and kicking in frenzy — and squealing. The uproar was appalling; one feared there was too much sound for the room to hold — that the walls must give way or the ceiling crack. There were high squeals and low squeals, grunts, and wails of agony.

One wondered, as one read, just what did this particular detail of Packingtown prove. A pig, one felt, would have squealed just as loudly, would have been just as reluctant to be killed by an old-time individual butcher in a sylvan village, as by a trust in Chicago; and was otherwise indifferent to the economic and social aspects of the ceremony. As for the reader to whose sympathies Sinclair appealed, it was rather common knowledge that the initial step in the process of providing bacon for breakfast is accompanied by sounds dissonant to sensitive ears.

But let no one think "The Jungle" was a book to smile at. As a picture of America taking peasants from the fields of Europe and throwing them into the crucible of American industry, like ore or any other raw material; as the reality of what idealism called the "melting-pot," [1] "The Jungle" was a not too greatly exaggerated bit of truth about American industrial life as it was at that time — a "Jungle" could have been written about the coal mines, the steel-mills, and many other industries.

Sinclair's vagarious excitability always left the reader of his books uncertain how far the author's intention was art, and how far propaganda. So far as Sinclair had in mind propaganda for reform, he meant his book to show the process by which workers became, and in Sinclair's judgment ought to become, Socialists.

[1] Authorship of this phrase was commonly attributed to Israel Zangwill. Americans, at the time, were pleased with this conception of their country.

But all this passed over the public's head. The public ignored the tragedy of Jurgis the man, neglected the sociological jeremiad, was unmoved by the plea and propaganda for socialism. Sinclair's picture of the sausage-making machines, for example, was meant by him to make readers feel sad about the number of hand-workers displaced. But what most impressed the public was something unappetizing about the stuffing process: "There was a sort of spout, a stream of sausage-meat would be shot out . . . a wriggling snake of sausage of incredible length."

What the public took hold of avidly and excitedly were some adventitious allusions to the food they were buying and eating; casual passages which Sinclair intended as mere bits of local color, as minor in the whole picture as the squeals of the pigs; off-hand details which vivified the impression made upon some of the more sensitive senses by the modern mass manufacture of food. One was the stock-yards smell,[1] which Sinclair described quite mildly:

a strange pungent odor, that you caught in whiffs; you could literally taste it as well as smell it — you could take hold of it, almost, and examine it at your leisure . . . an elemental odor, raw and crude; it was rich, almost rancid, sensual and strong.

That was the most innocuous of Sinclair's bits of description. It, alone, would have made no commotion. The stock-yards smell was an old story; newspapers had made jokes about it for years. But Sinclair went farther.

He pictured a meat inspector, a government official, so agreeably engaged in chatting with a visitor about the deadliness of the dangers inherent in eating tubercular

---

[1] An official of one of the packing companies, who has read this chapter, makes the point that the "stock-yards smell" was due not to conditions attending the preparation of food, but to the fertilizer and glue factories near by. By 1927, he wrote, the larger packing-houses had eliminated disagreeable odors from the processes of preparing food.

pork, that he let a dozen carcasses pass him without testing them. Another inspector, more meticulously conscientious, had proposed, as a means of saving frugal packers from temptation, that tubercular carcasses be

From a photograph by Underwood & Underwood.
A sausage-making machine.

treated with an injection of kerosene — and had been dropped from the government's inspection service, quickly and mysteriously — an incident not only raising disagreeable doubts about the wholesomeness of the meat every one was eating, but implying that the packers had a political pull which enabled them to get rid of overconscientious inspectors.

"There was said to be two thousand dollars a week hush-money from hogs that had died of cholera on the trains," and which "were . . . hauled away to a place in Indiana where they made a fancy grade of lard." Old cattle, and diseased ones, made into canned beef. "Potted chicken" made of "tripe, the fat of pork, beef suet, hearts of beef, and waste-ends of veal."

Devilled ham . . . made out of the waste-ends of smoked beef that were too small to be sliced by the machines; and also tripe dyed with chemicals so that it would not show white.

Old rancid butter "oxidized" by a forced-air process, to take away the odor, rechurned with skim-milk, and sold in the cities. A good part of what the public buys for lamb and mutton is really goat's flesh! . . . The rats were nuisances; the packers would put poisoned bread out for them; they would die, and then rats, bread, and meat would go into the hoppers together. . . . Men worked in the tank-rooms, full of steam, in some of which there were open vats near the level of the floor . . . [when] they fell into the vats, sometimes they would be overlooked for days, till all but the bones of them had gone out to the world as Durham's Pure Leaf Lard.[1]

The passages giving these bits of local color in the Odyssey of Jurgis, as he worked his tragic way through Packingtown, were not more than eight pages in the 308

---

[1] In order that the reader of this volume may escape the error, practically universal, of classifying Sinclair and his "Jungle" with the "Muckrakers" who made much history during this period, it should be understood that "The Jungle" was a novel, fiction; and that these charges about conditions in the stock-yards did not purport to have any more than the loose standard of accuracy that fiction demands for local color and background. Moreover, Sinclair as artist was so submerged by Sinclair as propagandist, that accuracy about background was even less compelling on him than on artists who are artists wholly. As fiction, the charges in "The Jungle" are to be taken as faithful to the broad picture, the impression. Sinclair gave many of them as portions of the offhand conversation of stock-yard workers among themselves. He did not pretend to have seen these things, nor to have verified them, nor to have taken them from official records. There was truth in them, but not necessarily literal truth.

The "Muckrakers"—Lincoln Steffens, Miss Ida Tarbell, Ray Stannard Baker, and others—were utterly different from Sinclair in their methods. They put out their product as *fact*, and asked the public to accept it and test it as such. The Muckrakers spent months of investigation before printing a brief article of five or six thousand words. They investigated everything, confirmed everything. (Samuel S. McClure, who was editor of *McClure's Magazine* when that periodical

of "The Jungle"; but it was those eight pages the public seized upon.

For appreciation of his larger purpose, his artistic and social objective, Sinclair had to accept what came to him from a few high-brow critics and radicals in America, and some abroad, such as Winston Churchill, then prominent as an English writer, later as a cabinet member, who wrote:

This terrible book . . . pierces the thickest skull and most leathery heart. It enables those who sometimes think, to understand. It is possible this far-reaching book may come to be a factor in far-reaching events. The issue between capital and labor is far more clearly cut to-day [in America] than in other communities or in any other age.

Sinclair, seeing no increase in the Socialist vote in America, seeing the social revolution no nearer, seeing only an immense commotion about pork and beef, showed a flaw in his gratitude for the enormous fame the book brought him. In editions subsequent to the first, he inserted a foreword, in which he accepted the judgment of those literary critics who had compared "The Jungle"

was the pioneer and the best of the muckraking publications, verifies my own recollection that a single magazine article by Lincoln Steffens or Miss Tarbell often represented six months of investigation and upward of three thousand dollars of expense, aside from the writer's salary.) The Muckrakers took their material from what they themselves saw, or from sworn testimony in lawsuits or in legislative investigations. They made it a point to talk with everybody who had important, first-hand information. Almost always they discussed their material with the man accused, or the head of the corporation they were investigating. Since most of the articles and books written by the Muckrakers would have been libellous if incorrect, the manuscripts were almost always subjected to scrutiny by lawyers.

The fictional character of Sinclair's "Jungle" bothered President Roosevelt when he came to use it as the basis of a demand for pure-food legislation. While there was abundant truth in the "Jungle" (and more in some conditions Sinclair did not mention) to justify the legislation, it was embarrassing to be unable to find proof for some details of Sinclair's charges.

For the public, the impressionistic impression, so to speak, that Sinclair conveyed was as much as was needed; the public made no meticulous inquiry into details, but sensed strongly that there was something rotten in Packingtown, literally.

with several classics of social reform; and naïvely confirmed it as his own. Sinclair's foreword to the latest edition of "The Jungle" avers:

"The Jungle" belongs with books like Harriet Beecher Stowe's "Uncle Tom's Cabin," Charles Dickens's "Oliver Twist," which have influenced legislation and helped to improve the conditions of the lowly.

But Sinclair, speaking of himself, complained that he had wished to appeal to the hearts of the people, but had only succeeded in reaching their stomachs:

I had not been nearly so interested in the "condemned meat" as in something else, the inferno of exploitation. I realized with bitterness that I had been made a "celebrity," not because the public cared anything about the workers, but simply because the public did not want to eat tubercular beef.

The disappointed author started a co-operative boarding-house in New Jersey, called "Helicon Hall" [1] (the name led to some ribald puns) in which the boarders were supposed to take turns at the dish-washing. The boarding-house failed to co-operate, conspicuously; and Sinclair joined an "individualist-anarchist single-tax" [2] colony at Arden, Delaware. Later, he lived near Los Angeles, California, where he ran for Congress on the Socialist ticket, and spent his later career as writer of pamphlets and books

---

[1] Mr. Sinclair, who has been kind enough to read the proofs of this chapter, wrote me July 29, 1927, that Helicon Hall was not a co-operative boarding-house: "We employed professional people to do the housework; the difference was that we did not treat them as social inferiors." Other points in this chapter he corrects or modifies by saying that in 1927 "The Jungle" was still being sold in a fairly successful way; that while he was living at the stock-yards he "had the company and the backing of Adolphe Smith, a representative of the London *Lancet,* who was probably the world's greatest authority on slaughter-houses; he was there to study Packingtown; he gave me the benefit of his expert knowledge, and on this account I considered and still consider that my report of conditions was as carefully prepared and documented as the work of any of the Muckrakers. . . . I have no desire to hide behind the screen of fiction. I believed every word that I wrote. I could not bring legal proofs for some of it, but things may be true in spite of that."

[2] This is Sinclair's own characterization, in a letter to the author.

(none of them attaining the fame of "The Jungle") expressing acute dissatisfaction with the way the world was run.

For the effect "The Jungle" had on the average American, hygienic rather than spiritual or social, we can rely on that incomparably astute exponent of the typical American point of view, "Mr. Dooley":

Dear, oh dear, I haven't been able to ate annything more nourishin' thin a cucumber in a week. . . . A little while ago no wan cud square away at a beefsteak with betther grace thin mesilf. To-day th' wurrud resthrant makes me green in th' face. How did it all come about? A young fellow wrote a book. Th' divvle take him f'r writin' it. Hogan says it's a grand book. It's wan iv th' gr-reatest books he iver r-read. It almost made him commit suicide. The hero got a fancy job poling food products out iv a catch-basin, an' was promoted to scrapin' pure leaf lard off th' flure iv th' glue facthry. Th' villain fell into a lard-tank an' was not seen again ontil he turrned up at a fash'nable resthrant in New York. Ye'll see be this that 'tis a sweetly sintimintal little volume, to be r-read durin' Lent. I see be th' publishers' announcements that 'tis th' gr-reatest lithry hog-killin' in a peryod iv gin'ral lithry culture. If ye want to rayjooce ye'er butcher's bills buy "The Jungle." It shud be taken between meals, an' is especially ricomminded to maiden ladies contimplatin' their first ocean voyage.

To the packers, "Mr. Dooley" recommended counterpropaganda, in the shape of novels as a side-line to hams and beef:

Well, sir, th' packers arr-re gettin' r-ready to protect thimsilves again' "The Jungle." It's on'y lately that these here gin'rous souls have give much attintion to lithrachoor. Th' on'y pens they felt an inthrest in was those that resthrained th' hectic cow. If they had a blind man in th' Health Departmint, a few competint frinds on th' Fedhral bench, an' Farmer Bill Lorimer[1] to protect th' cattle inthrests iv th' Gr-reat West,

[1] Then United States Senator from Illinois, later expelled on charges of excessive expenditure in connection with his election by the Legislature.

they cared not who made th' novels iv our counthry. But Hogan says they'll have to add a novel facthry to their plant, an' in a few months ye'll be able to buy wan iv Nels Morris's pop-lar series warranted to be fr'm rale life, like th' pressed corned-beet.

This anticipation of what the packers would do to overcome the effect of "The Jungle" had the prescience of the prophet and philosopher that "Mr. Dooley" was. To the packers "The Jungle" came as a proof, peculiarly convincing and peculiarly painful, of several ancient adages, including the two which say that troubles never come singly, and that it never rains but it pours. Seventeen of the heads of the beef industry had recently fallen into a form of trouble with the Federal Government which included serious menace of jail, on the charge that they had combined into a monopoly. In defending themselves against that charge, the packers, distracted souls, were already using all their resources of lawyers and press-agents, at the moment when they were hit by the storm aroused by "The Jungle." Gallantly they stiffened their legal and literary sinews for the extra effort the situation called for. The best-known of the packers, J. Ogden Armour, wrote a series of articles for the *Saturday Evening Post*. (Sinclair charged that the hard-pressed Mr. Armour had saved himself the labor of actually writing the articles by employing a literary hack.) A well-known publicist of the day, Elbert Hubbard, who had begun his writing career as a radical iconoclast and ended it as a composer of laudatory panegyrics about big business, wrote a defense of the packers, in which he said "The Jungle" was "a libel and an insult to intelligence." This the packers put into plate-matter for newspapers, and also mailed out a million copies throughout the country. These efforts they supplemented with the leverage of widespread newspaper advertising.

But much more than the effects of "The Jungle" entered into the storm that arose throughout the country. The things Sinclair suggested with his bits of impressionistic painting about beef were paralleled by conditions known with exactness about the large-scale preparation of other foods. "The Jungle," indeed, was merely the final, spectacular, fictionistic climax to a long agitation that had been carried on in solid and convincing ways by patient investigators, food chemists in the employ of the State and Federal Governments, journalists of the exact-minded "Muckraker" type, leaders of women's clubs, and other reformers and altruists.

II

During the quarter-century preceding Theodore Roosevelt's accession to the Presidency in 1901, a revolution had taken place in the food habits of the American people. Prior to about 1875, food, excepting imported spices, condiments, stimulants, and a few fruits, had been produced and marketed mainly by farmers and small one-man businesses or partnerships. Most families had a cow or two, and those that had none bought their milk from a farmer-neighbor and had it delivered, still warm from the morning or evening milking, by one of the farmer's half-grown sons. The fruits and vegetables consumed were mainly such as were produced during the summer on adjacent farms and carried to town in the farmer's market-wagon. In the villages and towns there were bakeries, each an economic unit in itself, in which the wife "tended store" and handed out bread and "rusks," literally hot from the oven, to neighbor-customers whom she called by their first names. In the larger shops of the cities the baker employed one or more assistants, who were called journeyman bakers. From every one the

old-time baker had the regard paid to an honest neighbor,[1] his business carried on under the eyes of all.

"The day before Christmas." One of the series of drawings by John McCutcheon,
cartoonist of the Chicago *Tribune*, depicting average American life before the
nation had changed from predominantly rural to predominantly urban.

Such attempts as were made to preserve food by cooling
or otherwise were confined to the farmer or the housewife.
One of the earliest devices in America was the "spring-

[1] From the boys of the village he had more. They included his place of business in the ritual of their days, and on fixed afternoons, especially Fridays, would
ebb away from the swimming-hole or the game of marbles, to drift toward the
bakery, knowing that at a certain hour its basement windows would be a source
not only of solid nourishment to the corporeal body, but also of ethereal aromas
stimulating to the imagination; scents as exalting to the nostrils as poetry to the
ear; scents associated with Cathay and Malabar, Kanadu and Khubla Khan;
scents of cinnamon, ginger, cloves, and spice; scents no less potent for uplifting

house" that was a feature of many of the farms in the older-settled part of the country. To say that a man built a spring-house as soon as he had finished his dwelling, is to seem to give importance to the institution, but actually underrates it. The site of the spring was the first thing to which the pioneer gave attention: a spring on that side of a hill which was in the lee of the prevailing winds, combining nearness to water with the minimum of winter cold, determined the site of every early farmhouse whose owner was guided either by his own common sense or the traditions of his kind.

The first improvement made to the spring was merely to hollow out the earth with a shovel. (As late as the 1880's there were families[1] to whom that sort of spring

---

pleasure than the cadences of Tennyson and De Quincey. The boys knew, too, that an ostentation of readiness to do errands, if displayed at hours aptly selected, would be followed by such an immediacy of reward as to cause the chore and the reward to merge into a single experience, a delectable whole. To carry under one's arm a package of fresh rusks, the heavy, sweetish scent still steaming from the processes of baking hardly yet completed, was but little less a pleasure than to sink one's teeth softly into the thick, dark, almost viscous ginger-cake that the baker gave as payment in advance for the errand. It was the kind of chore, too, that was a service to two people, the baker and his customer, and consequently led sometimes to duplication of reward; if you were particularly polite to the woman to whom you delivered the package; and if you improvised those postures and facial gestures that convey the impression of a smiling and willing youth with approved Sunday-school traits; and if you made yourself just a little conversational, lingering long enough to speak of the fine weather and to suggest reluctance to leave so nice a lady too abruptly — it sometimes happened — at least it happened often enough to give to the experience the stimulating element of a gambling chance—that the housewife would unwrap the package before your eyes and would detach one of the rusks in the spirit partly of a reward for a specific service, but more largely of a sign of approval of a good boy. One watched the unwrapping and the detachment of the rusk with some suspense, agreeably exciting, for while all of them were good, the corner ones, baked on two sides, were decidedly the best.

[1] When water was only to be had by carrying it from a spring, always some distance and sometimes through rain or snow, there was meaning in the ancient adage, "Never throw out the dirty water 'til the clean comes in." To some degree, another adage accompanied it, "Waste not, want not." A good many old precepts disappeared before modern invention and changed ways of life; and with the precepts went traits of character related to them. By 1925 probably half the children in the United States, those who lived in the cities, had never known what it was to carry water, nor any way of procuring it except by turning a tap. To them it was difficult to think of water as a thing that should be conserved, or could be wasted.

was the only water supply, though by that time the more prosperous of the farmers had built new houses, with wells and pumps, leaving the original house and the spring with it, to laborers or tenants.) The next improvement

When water had to be pumped by hand there was point to the saying, "Never throw out the dirty water 'til the clean comes in."

was to build a circular wall around the spring — that had no more purpose than merely to keep the dirt from falling in. In time, a little house was built around the spring, usually of masonry, its floor a platform of flat stones called flagstones, around which the water from the spring was led to spread out so as to form a rectangle of pools, in which sat the pans of milk, the butter, and such other articles as lent themselves to the brief preservation this primitive form of refrigeration would provide, awaiting the day, rarely more than a week away, when they would be either consumed by the farmer, or taken to town to sell. The spring-house was one of the points of a farmer's pride. On hot summer days he frankly exulted in its coolness, liked to enjoy and display to others the physical luxury of it, believed and boasted that its water was colder than that of any neighbor.

By 1927, most of the old spring-houses had become tumbled ruins. For the purposes of keeping milk cool, and of churning, they were displaced first by local "creameries" to which the farmer took his fresh milk each day, and later by the early morning "milk-train," headed cityward on the near-by railroad. With the coming of the creamery as an organized industry, and mechanical substitutes for the household art of butter-making, many farmers' wives forgot the use of such old-time implements as the "skimmer," a thin dish of metal shaped like a saucer, designed to skim off and hold the thick cream while the thinner milk dripped out through holes in the bottom; the butter-ladle, a small slab of smooth wood with a handle, used to "work" the butter to a desired consistency; and the butter "mould" which imparted to the product embossed designs of acorns, or other similitudes pleasing to the eye.

With the spring-house, as an early device for the preservation of food, stood the cellar. Sometimes there was a vault, merely a large pit dug into the earth close by the house, walled and covered. Usually, in the Northern part of the country, each farm had its ice-house, also a pit in the ground, in which was stored ice cut from a near-by stream, the slabs covered with sawdust. For cities, the ice-supply was cut from the rivers — until very recently one could see the immense wooden ice-houses along the banks of the Hudson above New York, or along the Delaware and Schuylkill near Philadelphia. For cities on the

coast and in the South, these near-by supplies were supplemented with ice from Maine, cut in the streams during
the winter, stored there, and shipped in schooners during
the summer.[1]

An old-time spring-house, near West Chester, Pennsylvania, 1927.

In the era of these primitive devices for cooling, diet
was limited. An orange was a luxury most rare. Up to
about 1880, until refrigerator cars came into common use,
a child who had eaten more than one orange in a whole
year was likely to be above the average in economic
status and in good luck. Fresh vegetables were limited to
the brief season of their ripening. No one living more
than a day's travel from the ocean ever thought of having

[1] It was the destruction of one of these schooners that led to an early device
for artificial cooling; a physician in a Florida town, whose wife was sick, waiting
in vain for the schooner that was to bring the town's supply of Maine ice, found
that he could reduce the temperature of the sick-room by setting a vessel of am-
monia on the top of a step-ladder and letting it drip.

oysters or any other variety of sea-food. Fresh beef was available on the farms for only the few days following the annual beef-killing, though of course a farmer who was extravagant, and all town-dwellers, could buy at the

Courtesy of the Frigidaire Company.

An up-to-date electric refrigerator and kitchen-cabinet for use in modern homes where space is limited.

butcher shops, where beef was slaughtered once a week or oftener.

Lacking means of preserving food by coolness, every advantage was taken of the means of preserving the substance, though at the expense of much of the savor, by desiccation. Meat and fish were sometimes dried and salted or were preserved by pickling in brine. Nearly every kind of fruit — apples, apricots, peaches, plums, raisins — was dried in the sun by arts that every house-wife knew. Their substance was saved, enough to make them "filling" to the hungry; but their savor, and especially their aroma, escaped in nimbuses of fragrance that gave an added delight to the autumn air.

A more glamorous method of preserving food, especially fruits, was the old-time housewife's art of making jellies and "preserves," a technic inherited as the accumulated lore of generations. Knowing nothing of the science of chemistry, she knew perfectly the art of cooking to just the point where, if she stopped there, the product would achieve the desired condition of preservation that was expressed by a verb, "to jell." Security against infection by dirt from outside was achieved by a scum that hardened on the top, and by a cover of unbleached yellow muslin tied tightly around the top with string. About the 1860's came a patented vessel, still called, in deference to the ancient traditions, a "fruit-jar," though it was not earthenware but glass, accompanied by a circular strip of rubber to put between jar and cover and insure more perfect sealing; a type very widely used was "Mason's." It sent the old-time earthen "jar" and "crock" into cellars and attics, from which forty or fifty years later, about 1920, they began to come back, now in the dignified, or at least dandified, rôle of *objets d'art*, antiques commanding prices of five and ten dollars from women whose mothers had bought them as utilitarian objects for the same number of cents.[1]

"Preserving time," hard as the work was, and hot, and demanding continuity for long hours, was[2] nevertheless

[1] So great was the effect of mass manufacture, so quickly did styles change in every line, and so great became the vogue of collecting antiques, that articles were sold as antiques in the cities almost before they had passed out of daily use in the rural districts.

[2] A competent authority warns me against unqualified use of the past tense, in speaking of household jelly-making and preserving. While it has been abandoned by great numbers of city women, and has diminished in proportion to the population, probably as much of it was done in 1927 as in 1890. For the continued practice of the art, much credit is due the schools of household economics in Western universities, which have at once improved the art and made it familiar to the younger generation of women.

regarded as a pleasure by the old-time housewife, probably one of the outstanding delights of her year. Persons
who were children then remember preserving time as a
period when women hummed or sang as they stirred the
pots, bustled about cheerfully — as far as possible from
consciousness of feeling drudgery. Modern women of the
cities, who never did it, and whose very nature, almost,
has been changed by their environment, think of preserving as they think of the similarly gone old-time sewing,
as something that must have been arduous. One doubts
if that is the way it appears in retrospect to women who
did it. Their reflections about the moderns would probably take the form of wonder how any woman could prefer
to spend an autumn afternoon at bridge, watching the
spots and the similitudes of royal figures on shifting cards;
or gazing at antic aperies on a silver screen in a dark and
crowded room — rather than picking apples and pears
from the low-hanging orchard boughs, carrying them in
their aprons to the house, peeling them, stewing them;
and then enjoying the sense of accomplishment on pouring
the completed work into the jars; setting jars and bottles
on a window-ledge where their colors glowed against the
autumn sun, distilled essences of the orchard. Later,
from the depths of the kitchen closet, their rich amber
would reflect the cheerful winter fire.

The mood of it went with the time of year; it came, of
course, with the ripening fruit, and the preserving process
added its contributions to the orchard scents that filled the
atmosphere. In the air was the first hint of autumn coming, and with preserving went the assurance of provision
against it. The work conveyed a kind of moral satisfaction, fulfilled ancient adages, copy-book maxims, and
Bible precepts about thrift, providing for the future,
reaping as one soweth. It made one feel kin to the bee,
who buzzed about, a steady guest at the process. There

was self-satisfaction, too, satisfaction to the ego; the pleasure of feeling "This I have done, and it is good" — a sense of satisfaction that went with the old-time individual industry, and disappeared with it (that emotion could rarely attend the system of division of labor and piece-work); a kind of satisfaction that made the housewife a kin to the artist, sharer of his joy of creating and completing. That was a satisfaction not only for the day the preserves were finally cooled and put away; it was renewed at every opening of the closet door. In winter, between opening a jar of one's own preserves, and opening one packed in Chicago, there was many a spiritual parasang.[1]

For meat, the villages and towns relied on local butchers who bought their cattle and pigs from near-by farmers, and slaughtered them in their local slaughter-houses, all one-man, or one-man-and-a-helper institutions. They had pride of calling, these old-time butchers — no driven, sweat-shop Jurgises, they. With the pride of vocation went a bit of the artist. They had a secret of carving through the white and marbled fat to the crimson tissues of the muscles, and of arranging folds and petals in the similitude of flowers — roses, chrysanthemums, peonies. Sometimes they achieved the draftsmanship of designs — panels, arabesques, even portraits. It was their pride, too, to have an appearance becoming to their calling, to have a portliness of body and a healthy ruddiness of countenance such as would suggest a testimonial to the excellence of the meat they sold. Once a year, usually

---

[1] A university teacher who has read the proofs of this chapter says that "developments in canning fruits and vegetables are a part of industrialization, just as much as the displacement of other household arts, like weaving, by manufactured goods. There are heart-burnings in all the steps in industrialization. Sometimes it has gone too far; sometimes it has been badly done, but the basis of it lies in our mechanistic civilization, and this you ought to point out."

Washington's birthday, the butchers made a ceremony of "beef-show day," when they stood, a noble sight, in spotless white smocks reaching from head to heels, topped off with glittering high silk hats,[1] against a background of an immense beef hung from the meat-rack. Because they had pride of calling in themselves, they had individuality in the minds of their customers. Patrons bought, not chops, but Watson's chops, or Miller's, feeling, not that Watson cut his meat in any unique way, but that the meat had the dependability of Watson, the character he had to have to keep his standing in his community.

Between these old-time individual butcher-shops, and the modern packing-houses, comparisons seriously invidious to the former were made by the packers, in the course of the publicity campaign they conducted when "The Jungle" compelled them to turn their ingenuity in preservation and renovation to renovating their own reputations. Some of these comparisons were enabled to be true by the fact that with the passing of years research had discovered relations of cause and effect between disease and conditions[2] of food-supply, which had formerly been unknown to the butchers or to any one else, and invention had perfected sanitary devices that likewise had been unknown in the earlier period. But about the individual butcher there was one outstanding and sufficient safeguard. He looked across his counter into the eyes of customers who knew him, who had known his father before him, whose children went to school with his children. He had to hold up his head in his own community.

[1] These details were recalled in 1927 by some elderly persons as having prevailed at Wilmington, Delaware, in the 1870's and 1880's.

[2] One of the disadvantages attending the old-time purveying of meat was noted on the margin of my proofs by R. W. Dunlap, Assistant Secretary of the United States Department of Agriculture: "Up to about 1895 meat was hauled about the dusty streets and roads by horses or mules, and peddled to farmers and folks in small villages."

The woman who patronized an old-time butcher bought her meat as J. Pierpont Morgan said he loaned money, "on character."

For the meat supply of large cities there was an additional agency, the drover. He was a picturesque character who for much of each year led a caravan kind of life, travelling, usually on horseback or by wagon, as far as two or three hundred miles from the city, among the back-country farmers. From them he bought cattle and pigs,[1] a few at a time, adding them to his "drove," which he herded along the roads toward the city, with many an urging cry of "Ho!" and "Hi!"; and, at the cross-roads, with much expletive eloquence at the inherent disposition of cattle (and especially pigs) to take the wrong turning; with much galloping forward and backward along the side of the drove; and with many irritated reflections, not repressed, about the precautious doubt of pigs as they consider the security of frail wooden bridges they are urged to cross. (A porcine trait that most unjustly is called perversity or stubbornness, but which ought to be respected as laudable prudence and conservatism.) At night the drover usually stopped at one of the old inns[2] that dotted the country every few miles.

The objective of the drover was usually a farm within

---

[1] Some elderly persons who have read the proofs of this passage about the old-time drovers raise doubts about hogs having been taken to the city in droves "on the hoof." I am confident that in many parts of America they frequently were. In England, a century or so ago, geese and turkeys were driven up to London in flocks, by drovers whose practice was to drive them first through tar, and then through sand, to provide their feet with a protection for the journey.

[2] In 1927, an old-time drover named Thomas W. Phillips, living at Atglen, Pa., recalled an aspect of these inns which I had never before seen mentioned. He said there were three separate kinds, often located close by each other: those that provided rooms and beds for drovers whose status in life, as marked by the weight of their leathern money-bags, was proportioned to such luxuries; those in which the hired-man or apprentice slept on the floor of the big bar-room; and those which had big yards or fields in which the cattle could be penned over night.

a half-day's drive of the city, which was his home and business headquarters; or he had an arrangement with some farmer similarly situated. On this farm, the cattle and pigs were rested after their journey, and fattened, and were then delivered "on the hoof" to the city butchers and slaughter-houses, in such numbers as the market, from time to time, demanded.

The fattening, according to common legend, sometimes involved a delicate art. According to a cynical tradition, the process included a manipulation of the appetites of the cattle which would cause them to become very thirsty, and therefore to consume much water, which, on the scales of the butcher a few hours later, would weigh as much as food which would have cost more. A steer with his thirst sufficiently stimulated by prolonged restraint from water, and then given salt, could readily drink an amount of water equal to five per cent of his weight. To keep the cattle from water for several days, and then, during the last few hours before delivering them at the slaughter-house, to drive them past an ample and inviting stream, was a presumed practice which provided at once some of the prosperity of the drovers and much of the humor of the time. An analogical echo of one of these jokes is extant to-day, though hardly a person among those who repeat the familiar allusion, or take advantage of the practice, knows the origin of the phrase. A famous drover of those days was named Daniel Drew. With money made in his droving, Drew went into Wall Street, and, surveying the processes of money-making which he found in his new arena, was reminded of the advantage of watering stock before delivering it to the consumer. "Watered stock," just disappearing from the patois of the cattle business, became universally familiar in the terminology of corporation finance.

One other relic has been left in the world of finance

by a business that has wholly disappeared.[1] In many cities, including New York,[2] a "Drovers' Bank," or a "Farmers and Drovers' Bank" is valued for its age and old-time traditions by a generation of patrons who have no curiosity about the origin of the name.

III

The drover, as an incident in the supply of meat to larger cities, as the middleman between the city consumer and farmers who lived one or two hundred miles away, was the beginning of anonymity in the business of purveying food. He came into existence with the earliest development of cities, which meant distance between the producer of food and the consumer of it. Quickly, as the cities[3] grew larger and larger, and as modern industry

[1] The drover whom I used to see driving cattle in the direction of Philadelphia, along the country roads of Chester County, Pennsylvania, died in the early 1880's. I never saw one later. By 1890, I doubt if there was an active one left in the whole country.

[2] When I wrote the first draft of this manuscript, this allusion to New York was correct. By the time I corrected the proofs, the landmark had disappeared, one more relic gone of an occupation already extinct, its memories surviving only in the nomenclature of banks. On May 9, 1927, the Comptroller of Currency, Mr. Joseph W. McIntosh, informed me that the "National Butchers and Drovers' Bank of the City of New York" disappeared nine months before, on September 18, 1926, by merger with the Irving Bank-Columbia Trust Co. The cities which still had national banks containing the word "Drovers" as of May 5, 1927, were (other cities and towns may have state banks with "Drovers" in their names):

> Baltimore, Drovers and Mechanics' Bank.
> Philadelphia, Drovers and Mechanics' Bank.
> York, Penna., Drovers and Mechanics' Bank.
> Chicago, Drovers' Deposit Bank.
> Kansas City, Drovers' Bank.
> Marion, Kans., Farmers and Drovers' Bank.

[3] The problem of purity in food supply, like many of the most troublesome questions that arose in America, was caused by or associated with increase of population, and the particular way the increase was distributed. As cities grew larger, problems were bound to arise in food supply. Doctor Alonzo E. Taylor, of the Food Research Institute of Stanford University, points out that the problem of sanitation in respect to foodstuffs, from the moment of origin to the moment of consumption, increases in even greater proportion than increase of population. Without pretending to accuracy, one might put it, let us say, that as population doubles, the problem of sanitation of food quadruples.

developed, the whole operation of food-supply was to become impersonal; quickly there was to be not merely one middleman or two — the business was to become a chain, intricately linked.

It was a decade or so after the Civil War that the old-time, simple, unorganized, one-man purveying of food began to give way to an overpowering new philosophy that was getting into business generally — bigness[1] in operations, bigness in the number of workers employed, bigness in profits. The mechanism for it was supplied or made possible by the railroads; the motive was supplied by the zest for profits. The railroads made it practicable at once to collect the raw materials over a large territory and to supply customers over a territory equally extended. When the expansion reached its height, it could happen that a steer might be bought near a little village, be shipped several hundred miles to Chicago, be butchered there, and then be shipped back as dressed meat to be bought by the same man who raised the steer — passing, in the process, through the hands of scores of men who had no acquaintance with each other and no sense of responsibility toward the others in the chain — and who, especially, had no sense of personal relation to the consumer, or responsibility to him.[2]

In this process of immense expansion, the more enterprising among the small establishments doubled, quadrupled, multiplied to a hundred times the size of the old-

---

[1] Not only into business. "Bigger and bigger" became a slogan of aspiration in almost every field of American life—by no means omitting the colleges and churches. A variation of it said "Bigger and better," a phrase in which the charm of alliteration put a spell on the ear and the eye, dulling them—as is usually the intent of slogans—to the point where the brain did not think nor discriminate, did not understand that what was "bigger" might not necessarily be "better"; that "bigger" is not necessarily more desirable than smaller.

[2] In the earlier era, "much of the food consumed was produced in the home or in the immediate neighborhood of the home, so that consumers knew where and how it was made, of what it was composed, by whom it was handled, and whether or not it was kept under sanitary conditions. As the manufacture of food was transferred to the factory, and shipped for longer and longer distances, it became

time business units. The less aggressive, and those less endowed with imagination, succumbed. So did those whose consciences or temperaments made them disinclined to sell a product unless it had been made by their own hands, or under their own eyes. All who had any defect in adaptability to the new order in its raw early stages, succumbed. In the meat-packing business, the growth of the big went on until, in 1905, about thirty years after the tendency began, seventeen men, composing the heads of five corporations, were indicted by the Federal Government as having monopolized the meat business of the country.

The new order of business was insatiable in its reaching out for means of aggrandizement. Any new idea that promised to increase sales, reduce costs, and multiply profits was eagerly seized. The promoter, the banker, the lawyer, were drawn into its service — not omitting, as we shall see later on, the politician and the lobbyist; the advertising man and the expert accountant; the inventor and the chemist — especially, in the food business, the chemist.

The shipment of food over long distances, the selling of it many months or even more than a year after it had been prepared, involved preservation. Some of the arts of overcoming distance and time, which the philosophy of bigness required of the chemist and of the inventor, were legitimate. They developed and perfected the art of refrigeration, and the results of that constitute one of the most conspicuous of those enrichments that have come to

---

increasingly difficult for consumers to know much about the food they bought. At the present time (1926) few city consumers have any personal knowledge of the methods of production, manufacture, and handling of the food they eat; and a larger and larger proportion of food now consumed on the farms is purchased at the grocery."—R. W. Dunlap, Assistant Secretary of Agriculture, before the American Grocery Manufacturers' Association, October 7, 1926.

the average man in our times. Refrigeration, including the refrigerator car, with other inventions, brought to the average man by 1925 such an abundance and variety of food, such a freedom from limitations of season, time

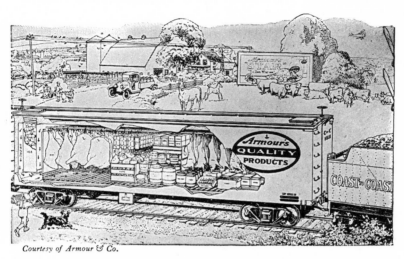

Courtesy of Armour & Co.

Sketch showing the ingenious economy of space in refrigerator cars.

or distance, as enabled him to smile at the notion of Lucullus being an epicurean.

After artificial refrigeration, refrigerator cars, and cold storage, and after the mass organization of food-purveying that accompanied them, an average man, even a poor man, might eat meals including oranges from California or Florida, lemons from Sicily, olives from Italy, new potatoes from Bermuda, bananas from Central America, grapefruit from the Isle of Pines, and fresh meats and fish from hundreds of miles away.

The chemists and inventors employed by the big food purveying organizations devised ingenious containers of glass, tin, and paper or oiled paper, by which food of many varieties could be packed or preserved in large quantities, could be shipped great distances and marketed conveniently. These containers — indeed, the whole system of selling by the package — insured cleanliness in transit and cleanliness in retail stores. If there were impurities in some of the food purveyed by some corporations — and we shall see there were — it was solely the

Interior of a chain grocery store, 1925. One of the benefits brought by large-scale manufacturing and distribution in the food industry is cleanliness. With foods packed in sealed containers at the factory there is little chance for the contamination that was possible when they were retailed from barrels and bins.

impurities that went in at the time of packing. Once goods were sealed into their containers of tin, glass, and paper, they were marketed under conditions more conducive to public health than had formerly been the case; were secure against contaminations sometimes associated with keeping goods in bulk, as they were kept and sold in the old-time stores — bins with only a hinged lid, bins of sugar, of beans, of coffee; barrels, usually with the top off, containing fish or meat in brine.

One other advantage came with organized business, its inventors and chemists. Drugs could be shipped from every quarter of the world, their volatile oils preserved for an indefinite time by air-tight packing. Before that, the medical resources of the old-time home had consisted of a very small number of "store-bought" drugs, a paper package of dried leaves of senna, a few lumps of alum, a few more of camphor, perhaps a bottle of turpentine. The greater reliance of the family was on home-gathered herbs — bone-set, pennyroyal, St. Johnswort — plucked in the autumn along the weedy edges of the fields, and hung in dry wisps from the attic rafters, where they imparted a pungent fragrance to the upper rooms of the house; mustard seeds, sassafras roots. Access to a greater variety of drugs, and more intelligent use of them were made possible by invention and chemistry, though these benefactions were destined to be attended by evils, as we shall see.

IV

Some of the services of the inventor and chemist to bigness were definitely not services to the public. Refrigeration was asked to do more than its stage of development at that time was able to do. Presently the chemist was solicited to do by his arts what ice could not do.[1] More accurately, the chemist was asked to do what nature meant never should be done. The chemist was asked not merely to eke out nature, not merely to adapt nature; he was asked to make an impossible bridge between nature and the new philosophy of bigness; he was asked to cheat, deliberately and flagrantly. In the case of some products of nature, fruits, vegetables, or what not,

---

[1] Representatives of a large packing-house, to whom the proofs of this chapter were submitted, note that "chemists were brought into the packing industry not to adulterate meats, but to maintain standards of quality through chemical control, and to develop by-product utilization."

the chemist was asked to, and actually did, devise artificial substitutes. In 1906, *Current Literature* made a summary of the opinion of medical periodicals — if there was exaggeration in it, that was due to an easily understandable indignation:

The commercial importance of analytical chemistry now is due mainly to the unscrupulousness with which it subserves the purpose of the adulterators of food, drink, and medicine. . . . The resources of chemical science are mainly ransacked to provide cheaper and artificial substitutes for natural products.[1]

The chemist suggested substances which, added to foods, prevented their too early decomposition, and coloring matters which concealed decomposition that had already taken place; and still other substances possessing the magic property of restoring foods, already deteriorated, to a deceiving simulation of freshness. Stale, rancid, soiled, and unsalable butter, in various degrees of putrefaction, was made over and sold for fresh. Eggs, which the passage of time had made a little more than mellow, and which for that reason had been theretofore unusable;

---

[1] A chemist in the employ of manufacturers of food, to whom I showed the proofs of this chapter, objected strongly to this quotation on the ground that it does injustice to the profession of chemists. It is to be borne in mind that the condition described is of the year the quotation was originally printed, 1906. Any assertion that uses the word "mainly" is apt to be based on loose information, and is difficult to prove. The judgment of the author of this book, based on knowledge at the time and on investigations for this volume, is that much evil was practised by chemists in the food and drug business; what proportion those engaged in vicious practices bore to the profession as a whole, is impossible to say. Even in 1927, one found among chemists employed by food manufacturers a point-of-view which, in effect, defended adulteration, provided it was not, in the chemist's judgment, fraudulent; or provided the adulterant was not, in the chemist's judgment, harmful to health. The moral aspect of misbranding, the ignoring of the right of the buyer to get what he pays for, and to know what he is buying, seemed to have, in the minds of many chemists in the food industry, less weight than it has with the public.

If the profession of chemistry is sensitive about the charge made by the medical profession in 1906 as to chemists in the employ of food and drug manufacturers, they can accept more than corresponding credit for the work done by chemists in the employ of State governments. No work more devoted or more intelligent was ever done in the public interest.

eggs which would have ruined the reputation of any old-time grocer selling them to an old-time housewife whose senses were experienced in recognizing the more advanced phases of nature — such eggs, in the new impersonality of big business, its complexities and the secrecies of its chemistry, were deodorized with formaldehyde, became a standard commodity of commerce, and were sold in enormous quantities for cake-making. In the earlier period of the use of cold storage,[1] the word "fresh" when used in connection with eggs as well as meat, conveyed no

[1] What are the proper limits of cold storage, as practised in modern food-purveying, what is the point at which its use becomes deleterious, has always been a subject of dispute. When Senator Weldon B. Heyburn, of Idaho, was leading the fight for the Pure Food bill in 1906 he expressed the distaste of a man who lived where cattle were the chief product, but was asked to eat refrigerated beef coming from packing-houses two thousand miles away; and his distaste also for some of the economic and social aspects of the modern system of food-purveying.

"I know of an instance where a carcass of choice meat of exceptionally fine appearance from one of the big packing-houses in Chicago was sent to a camp of workmen. It was packed cold, solid, almost frozen, and it put about eighty men in the hospital inside of twenty-four hours, because it had been in cold storage for over two years. . . . I have no sympathy for the cold-storage system. I broke it up in a city in which I lived by persuading the community to patronize only the meat dealer who bought his cattle in the country in which he lived and slaughtered them and prepared the meat in a cleanly way and handed it over his counter free from these objectionable features. We built up a prosperous dealer in meat, who bought our own cattle from our own ranches and our own farmers and sold it to the community. I believe the best condition in the cattle business exists when every farm has its little bunch of fat cattle and sends them to market with about an inch or an inch and a half of fat on the ribs, fresh killed and cool, and prepared for consumption. It distributes the business locally throughout the country. Who is benefited by this great concentration of capital, this concentration of what they call enterprise in the city of Chicago? It had better be distributed among a thousand farmers and a thousand communities in the country."

Part of Senator Heyburn's statement should be read with the qualification that he was speaking as of that time. That the art of refrigeration has progressed, and that the practice is more guarded, is believed, in 1927, by every one familiar with the subject. There is still, however, difference of opinion among experts about the permissible limits of its use. One expert whom I have consulted makes a distinction between "frozen meat" and "chilled" meat, saying the latter is preferable. "Freezing ruptures the walls of the cells; when they are thawed out, a confluence results, enzymes are set free, the flesh tends to soften and turns a dark color; frozen meat must be consumed promptly after being thawed out; experiences with frozen meat have raised a prejudice against refrigeration which should not apply to chilled meat." On the other hand, representatives of a large packing-house, whom I consulted during the writing of this chapter, assure me that "chilled meats can be kept for only short periods of time; frozen meats, properly handled, will keep for a very long period."

necessary guarantee of nearness in time to the living animal. Apples, of which the succulence, in their pristine stage, had proved over-alluring to some of the smaller invertebrates; and other apples in a condition that represented too great a zeal for conservation, were made into a jelly which, mixed with flavoring substances derived by chemistry from coal tar, appeared on the market labelled "currant," "blackberry," "plum jam," "pure apple butter."

Before a meeting of the National Association of State Dairy and Food Departments, at St. Louis in 1904, Professor Edwin F. Ladd, Food Commissioner of North Dakota,[1] told of experiences he had had in analyzing foods:

More than 90 per cent of the local meat-markets in the State were using chemical preservatives, and in nearly every butcher shop could be found a bottle of "Freezem," "Preservaline" or "Iceine." . . . In the dried beef, in the smoked meats, in the canned bacon, in the canned chipped beef, boracic acid or borates is a common ingredient.

The adulteration did not stop with meats, said Professor Ladd, but included almost every variety of food:

Of cocoas and chocolates examined, about 70 per cent have been found adulterated. . . . Ninety per cent of the so-called French peas we have taken up in North Dakota were found to contain copper salts. Of all the canned mushrooms, 85 per cent were found bleached by sulphites. There was but one brand of catsup which was pure. Many catsups were made from the waste products from canners — pulp, skins, ripe tomatoes, green tomatoes, starch paste, coal-tar colors, chemical preservatives, usually benzoate of soda or salicylic acid.

Antiseptic chemicals were used to preserve food longer than it could be preserved wholesomely, or to arrest decomposition at the point to which it had gone when the food was preserved. The Year Book of the United States

[1] He was later United States Senator.

Bureau of Chemistry for 1900 reported analyses of 152 "patent preservatives" then in the market, many of them "guaranteed to keep meat, fish, poultry, etc., for any length of time without ice." Other chemicals were used to give a color to foods out of which the natural color had passed, or to give a brilliancy of color that unaided nature never attempted. Another form of fraud consisted of substituting cheaper or inferior goods for goods of better quality, or goods sold under another name. If all the farms in Ohio had maple orchards, in the opinion of the Ohio Dairy and Food Commissioner, they probably could not supply the so-called maple sugar sold in that State. If every square foot of land in Vermont were covered with maple trees, they could hardly produce all that was sold throughout the country as "Pure Vermont Maple Syrup." Professor Ladd, at the St. Louis meeting of 1904, reported that,

> while potted chicken and potted turkey are common products, I have never yet found a can in the State which really contained in determinable quantity either chicken or turkey.

Chemicals, or adulterants, or substitutes, came to appear in much of the food that average persons ate. At the annual meeting of the National Association of State Dairy and Food Departments at St. Paul in 1903, a report on "The Use of Coloring Matter and Antiseptics in Food Products" was read by the State Analyst of South Dakota, James H. Shepard, to whom training in chemistry had given a bent for austere truth, as well as a convincing way of setting out proof. That extraneous substances appeared in most of the articles in common use for food, he took for granted — to his audience of food officials, that did not need proof. What he was intent on showing was the aggregate of such substances absorbed in a day by the average person, and the effect of such an aggregate on the human body. This was his answer to some food manufacturers who, unable to conceal their use of chemicals or other adulterants, claimed the amount in the portion for a single meal was so small as to be harmless.

"In order," said Professor Shepard, "to bring this matter out more forcibly, I have prepared a menu for one day such as any family in the United States might possibly use, and I am not sure but the working man in our cities would be quite likely to use it." Professor Shepard's menu, omitting the few articles not commonly adulterated, such as potatoes, was:

Breakfast
Sausage, coal-tar dye and borax.
Bread, alum.
Butter, coal-tar dye.
Canned cherries, coal-tar dye and salicylic acid.
Pancakes, alum.
Syrup, sodium sulphite.
   This gives eight doses of chemicals and dyes for breakfast.

Dinner
Tomato soup, coal-tar dye and benzoic acid.
Cabbage and corned beef, saltpetre.
Canned scallops, sulphurous acid and formaldehyde.
Canned peas, salicylic acid.
Catsup, coal-tar dye and benzoic acid.
Vinegar, coal-tar dye.
Bread and butter, alum and coal-tar dye.
Mince pie, boracic acid.
Pickles, copperas, sodium sulphite, and salicylic acid.
Lemon ice cream, methyl alcohol.
   This gives sixteen doses for dinner.

Supper
Bread and butter, alum and coal-tar dye.
Canned beef, borax.
Canned peaches, sodium sulphite, coal-tar dye and salicylic acid.
Pickles, copperas, sodium sulphite, and formaldehyde.
Catsup, coal-tar dye and benzoic acid.

Lemon cake, alum.
Baked pork and beans, formaldehyde.
Vinegar, coal-tar dye.
Currant jelly, coal-tar dye and salicylic acid.
Cheese, coal-tar dye.
This gives sixteen doses for supper.

"According to this menu," said Professor Shepard, "the unconscious and unwilling patient gets forty doses of chemicals and colors per day."

On a table in the House of Representatives, when the Pure Food bill came up for discussion in 1906, were displayed several hundred food samples — bottles, cans, and cartons purchased at grocery stores throughout the country.[1] Attached to each was an analysis made by chemists of State and municipal health and food bureaus. A few among them were:

Maple syrup. Adulterated with a large percentage of cane syrup.
Honey. Largely glucose and bugs.
Plum preserves. Very largely adulterated with glucose, colored with a coal-tar dye.
Pineapple jelly. Made up largely of glucose and preserved with benzoic acid.
Olive oil. This is a sample of oil claimed to have been made in France; largely cotton-seed oil and sesame oil.
Extract of lemon. Purely an artificial product.
Apple-cider extract. Prepared from ethers and alcohol.
Carbonated soda water. Artificially colored with coal-tar dye.
Alfalfa seed. Picked out of raspberry jam.
Filler for cayenne pepper. Ground wood and corn meal.
Mustard filler. Wheat flour and turmeric.

The extent of the adulteration of food, of the use of chemicals and artificial dyes, as set out in official statements supported by carefully attested analyses, was so

[1] The display was assembled by a chemist of the United States Bureau of Chemistry.

great as to be practically universal.[1] In Congress,[2] James R. Mann read a "partial list" filling a page of *The Congressional Record*, from which the following few are taken:

Milk. Colored with annatto, axo colors, and caramel; preserved by formaldehyde, boric acid, borax.

Coffee. Colored with Scheele's green, iron oxide, yellow ochre, chrome yellow, burnt umber, Venetian red, turmeric, Prussian blue, indigo; adulterated with roasted peas, beans, wheàt, rye, oats, chicory, brown bread, pilot bread, charcoal, red slate, bark, date stones.

Butter. Colored with carrot juice; adulterated with oleomargarine, renovated butter; preserved with borax, boric acid, formaldehyde, salicylic acid, sulphurous acid.

In the annual report of the Department of Foods of Massachusetts for 1906, analyses were printed showing that "evaporated cream" sold by three of the best-known manufacturers in the United States was "ordinary milk, evaporated to about one-half its volume; in no sense are they cream."

It was not that American merchants and manufacturers were especially vicious or dishonest. They had as high an average of uprightness as any other class. Human nature had not suddenly changed. The trouble had its roots in the evolution that had taken place in business, the substitution of the corporation for the individual, and the injection of distance and middlemen between producer and consumer. That evolution had done away with checks which, operating between man and man, had stiffened the standards of indigenous human nature. The corporation threw about business a cloak of impersonality behind which practices could be carried on which

[1] In the Senate, January 23, 1906, Senator McCumber said the American people were annually paying three billion dollars for adulterated and misbranded foods.

[2] June 21, 1906.

under the older system would have brought odium to their perpetrators, which enabled men who wanted to be dishonest, to be so, and to put their honest competitors under a disadvantage. There was no way for the consumer to differentiate between good and bad merchandise. There was no Federal law to compel manufacturers to use only wholesome materials in their food products, or to prepare them with a decent regard for the health of the public. Nor was there any way by which consumers could distinguish between honest manufacturers and others. This condition was insidiously demoralizing to business and brought about a general lowering of standards. Wholesome, properly prepared food products were subjected to commercial disadvantage by counterfeits, selling more cheaply. Conscientious manufacturers found it difficult if not impossible to compete with their less ethical business rivals, and were driven in self-defense to emulate their meretricious trade practices. Many manufacturers gave sympathetic support to the movement for a pure food law, so far as they could do so without incurring too much animosity from others in their trades.

Of the whiskey manufactured in the United States, just about five per cent was pure, in the sense that the Federal Government was willing so to label it. It would be inaccurate and unfair to say that all of the other 95 per cent was adulterated, in the common meaning of that word. This 95 per cent was divided between "blended" whiskey and "rectified" whiskey. Blended whiskey was composed of two or more pure straight whiskies, and nothing else. Rectified whiskey was made up of straight pure whiskey adulterated with neutral spirits and other substances.

The proofs of the adulteration of whiskey were as numerous, and as chemically attested, as in the case of food. However, we may short-cut repetition, and escape the dreariness of chemical symbols, by reprinting a demonstration which composed one of the most vivid and convincing speeches ever made in Congress; it came from Congressman (later Senator) Augustus O. Stanley, of Kentucky, on June 23, 1906:

I want to say this, that I have no objection to a man blending two kinds of whiskey, but I do object to his making any kind of whiskey "while you wait." Here is a quart of alcohol [holding it up]. It will eat the intestines out of a coyote. It will make a howling dervish out of an anchorite. It will make a rabbit spit in a bulldog's face. It is pure alcohol, and under the skill of the rectifier he will put in a little coloring matter and then a little bead oil [illustrating]. I drop that in it. Then I get a little essence of Bourbon whiskey, and there is no connoisseur in this House who can tell that hellish concoction from the genuine article; and that is what I denounce. [Applause.] I say that the coloring matter is not harmful; I say that the caramels are not harmful; but I say that the body, the stock, of the whiskey I made is rank alcohol, and when it gets into a man it is pure hell. [Applause.][1]

Along with the rest went the adulteration of drugs; the sale of medicines under false, misleading, or incomplete labels; the use, without restrictions, in patent medicines, of opium, morphine, cocaine, laudanum, and alcohol; the preposterously false and cruelly misleading curative qualities claimed. These patent medicines were sold in every drug store in the land, and in many rural general stores. It was an immense traffic; in 1900, the

[1] Competent and disinterested chemists who have read the proofs of this statement say that (1) blended whiskey is no more harmful than pure whiskey, and is as legitimate a manufactured product as pure whiskey, and that (2) rectified or synthetic whiskey (the kind described by Congressman Stanley) if composed of pure grain alcohol and caramel or other harmless ingredients, and diluted with an equal volume of water, is no more harmful than blended or pure whiskey. (Some rectified whiskeys contained ingredients not to be described as harmless, and were sold under labels grossly false.) Chemists, in making this statement, ignore the element of fraud, of the right of the consumer to get what he pays for, and to be told on the label exactly what is in the bottle.

total volume of business was $59,611,355. The patent-medicine manufacturers comprised, at that time, the largest single user of advertising space in newspapers.[1] Farmers living remote from physicians; and, in the towns and cities, persons of modest means to whom a physician's fee was an item to be considered, used patent medicines as practically the sole remedy for every kind of sickness.

In the patent-medicine business, the essential art was not medicine, nor chemistry. The fundamental genius for it was psychological. It consisted of skill in playing on the credulity of the simple-minded and the trusting. The patent-medicine man and the quack doctor were hang-overs from primitive man's belief in magic, descendants of the "medicine man" of the American Indians, and the "conjure" and "voodoo" doctors of African savages, who persuaded people to believe diseases could be cured by irrelevant specifics — a stick or a root from the forest, incantations, the finger-nail of your enemy, "hair of the dog that bit you." They were atavistic "throw-backs" to the time when man was not able to reason, or at least did not reason in this field — remaining in a time when knowledge of the relation between cause and effect, the nature of disease, its source, prevention, and cure, had been brought to the status of a science.

The patent-medicine manufacturers made an art of describing the symptoms of diseases in such a way as to terrorize the reader of their pamphlets and advertisements into believing he had one or more of the ailments they pretended to cure; and in describing their cure-alls in terms to convey the conviction of hope. Some of the largest solicited the public, especially women, to write to the eminent physician whom they represented to be the

---

[1] This statement may be doubtful. Local department stores were just coming, about 1900, to be large advertisers. Patent-medicine manufacturers were undoubtedly the largest national advertisers.

head of the concern, and whom they often referred to in a manner meant to suggest vast experience and inspire confidence, "Old Doctor ———." The patent-medicine business was the one in which the modern device of adaptable "form-letters" was developed. The letters of the sick, of the hypochondriac, and of the sympathy-seeking, rarely reached the eye of any doctor, but went to great staffs of clerks and stenographers, who gave them just enough attention to classify them as having to do with "cancer," or "consumption," or whatever the ailment might be, and then typed the standardized form of reply, usually beginning unctuously with "Dear Friend." The letters from the "suckers" were saved and became an important part of the stock in trade of many quacks. When the concern to whom the letter had been originally directed had sold as much medicine to the patient as his credulity would absorb, his letter and others, made up into bundles of thousands, were sold as "prospects" to other concerns.

The secrets of the patent-medicine business were made known to the public by a series of exposures conducted by Edward W. Bok in his widely circulated *Ladies' Home Journal* in 1904-5; and by a similar series written by Samuel Hopkins Adams and others in *Collier's Weekly* in 1905.[1] Bok — moved by discovering the extent to which his women readers medicated themselves by mail, dosed themselves and their children with dubious concoctions, and wrote trustingly intimate letters to concerns that made them articles of commerce — dug to the roots of the whole system. He reproduced an advertisement of Lydia E. Pinkham's Vegetable Compound, which said:

Mrs. Pinkham, in her laboratory at Lynn, Mass., is able to do more for the ailing women of America than the family

---

[1] These, like most of the exposures of frauds that led to the subsequent reform, preceded Sinclair's "Jungle."

physician. Any woman, therefore, is responsible for her own suffering who will not take the trouble to write to Mrs. Pinkham for advice.

Alongside this benevolent invitation Bok printed the photograph of a tombstone in Pine Grove Cemetery at Lynn, the picture large enough to show the lettering which recited the death of Lydia E. Pinkham twenty-two years before.[1] Bok reproduced the label of Mrs. Winslow's Soothing Syrup, a medicine for quieting the fret of teething babies, as it was sold in America — and alongside it the label of the same medicine as sold in England, the two being identical except that the English label, under the requirements of the British law, informed mothers that "This preparation, containing, among other valuable ingredients, a small amount of morphine, is, in accordance with the Pharmacy Act, hereby labelled 'Poison'."[2]

This illustrated Bok's objective, and the objective of the whole crusade for the truthful labelling of medicine, food, and liquor; namely, that there should be a law in America requiring that the bottle, carton, or package should bear a label stating exactly what drugs and chemicals were in the medicine; and what chemicals, coloring matter or preservatives had been added to the food. Bok printed chemical analyses of twenty-seven widely advertised patent medicines — very surprising the contents of some were; and argued for a law which should require the analysis to be printed on the label of every bottle of patent medicine sold to the American public.

The *Collier's Weekly* articles by Samuel Hopkins Adams, under the frank title "The Great American

[1] Samuel Hopkins Adams wrote: "There is a Mrs. Pinkham, widow of the son of Lydia E. Pinkham. The great majority of the gulls who 'write to Mrs. Pinkham' suppose themselves to be addressing Lydia E. Pinkham."

[2] Later, the makers of this remedy published their formula on the label in America, as well as in England. An addition to this foot-note is suggested by Samuel Hopkins Adams: "Because they had to; but they soon dropped out the morphine content rather than label it."

Fraud," discussed the curative claims — as compared with the chemical analyses — of scores of patent medicines. Peruna, which purported to cure a good many things — Adams thought the only thing it would really and infallibly cure was acute thirst for alcoholic liquor in

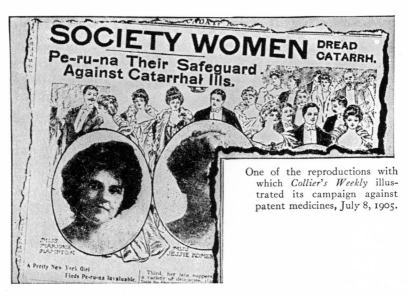

One of the reproductions with which *Collier's Weekly* illustrated its campaign against patent medicines, July 8, 1905.

Prohibition territory; he reprinted an order forbidding Peruna on Indian reservations, issued by an official who wanted to carry out the government's benevolent purpose of saving its wards from intoxication.

Another of the facsimile reproductions, with which Adams illustrated how forceful pictorial journalism can be, was of the verdict of a coroner's inquest into the death of a two-year-old child at Cincinnati, October 30, 1905, reading:

Deceased came to her death from the poisonous effects of opium, the result of drinking the contents of a bottle of Doctor Bull's Cough Syrup.

It would be conducive to the safety of the public at large if it were required by law that all proprietary remedies containing poisonous drugs be labelled with a caution, or better still, with a formula showing the dangerous ingredients and the proper antidotes. Had the bottle been so labelled in this instance, the life of this child could probably have been saved.

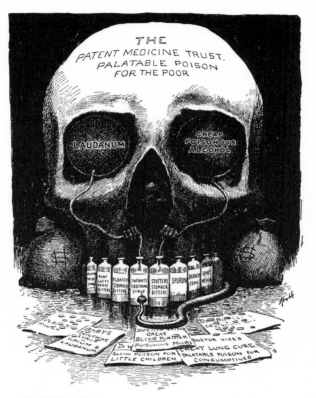

From "Collier's," June 3, 1905.

One of the series of drawings that accompanied Samuel Hopkins Adams's articles for *Collier's* on "The Great American Fraud." The patent-medicine business was not a trust; but at that time "trust" was a brick hurled by cartoonists, editors, and clergymen at any businesses they regarded as undesirable.

To each of the patent medicines Adams paid what he deemed to be its just deserts. Some contained dangerous drugs; some were no worse than innocuous. To some, whose principal content was alcohol, Adams even con-

ceded what virtue was supposed, in pre-Prohibition days,
to lie in a small dose of tonic or bitters, plus the psychological virtue of permitting earnestly naïve temperance
folks to drink a little liquor under the comforting and
harmless delusion that they were not violating their total-
abstinence pledges, but merely taking medicine. Some
patent medicines made utterly impossible claims to curative properties; some were more restrained. Adams analyzed and discussed, among others: "Dr. King's New
Discovery for Consumption — Greatest Discovery of the
Nineteenth Century"; and "Dr. Kline's Great Nerve
Restorer — Fits Permanently Cured"; and "Shiloh's
Consumption Cure — the Cure That Is Guaranteed
. . . " and "Warner's Safe Cure — Does Your Back
Ache? It's Your Kidneys"; and "Swamp-Root — Thou-
sands Have Kidney Trouble and Don't Know It"; and
"Wine of Cardui — Take Cardui and You Will Soon Be
Well"; and "Hydrozone — Positive Preventive of Yellow
Fever."

In addition, Adams probed his penetrating lance under
the secret formulas of "the opium-containing soothing
syrups, which stunt or kill helpless infants; the consumption cures, perhaps the most devilish of all, in that
they destroy hope where hope is struggling against bitter
odds for existence; the headache powders which enslave
so insidiously that the victim is ignorant of his own fate;
the catarrh powders which breed cocaine slaves." Four
widely advertised "catarrh powders" were picked out
by Adams as "the ones most in demand." "All of them,"
he wrote, "are cocaine; the other ingredients are unimportant."

v

The suspicion that something very wrong was going on
in food, drink, and medicines, the resentment against it,
and the effort to overcome it, began with the farmers.

Farmers made butter, which came from cows. Beef packers manufactured oleomargarine, which came from cows also, though not via the lacteal teats. Oleomargarine was just as good as butter; but many of the makers, as if they had some native preference for indirection, wanted to sell oleo not as oleo but as butter. Oleo, naturally almost as white as lard, was colored with dyes so as to give to the consumer an exceptionally vivid suggestion of cows grazing in sunny fields of buttercups.[1]

The farmers, in order to protect themselves, in the States where they were politically powerful, brought about the institution of departments of agriculture in the State governments, with chemists and law officers whose business it was to ferret out and pursue imitations of butter, as well as adulterated butter. This function led naturally to an official and minatory curiosity about other adulterated or artificially colored food products, and substitutes for food products, and ultimately about drugs and medicines. By 1900 several States had official departments of food and drugs, devoted to analyzing products on sale in the State. Some of these officials were very able and very energetic; one of the best was Edwin F. Ladd, State Chemist of North Dakota, later United States Senator from the same State.

This farmer movement was the beginning of food analysis in the United States — of food analysis, that is, by public officials and in the interest of the public. The State chemists were, so to speak, counter-chemists, devoting themselves to unearthing the practices of those chemists who had sold themselves into the service of the food adulterators. The State chemists, and the little

---

[1] The farmers had the incentive of outraged honesty, but also a selfish motive. They wanted, not merely to prevent oleo from being sold as butter, but to outlaw oleo; wanted to keep the age-old monopoly of butter as the only thing that goes with bread to make one of the most familiar phrases in folk language. With that purpose the farmers tried, and to some extent succeeded, in getting laws that not only forbade the artificial coloring of oleo, but put a special and heavy tax on it.

staffs they built up around them, had several especially pregnant effects; they developed a technic of food
analysis, of discovering adulteration and identifying the
adulterants; they induced State legislatures to enlarge
the pure food statutes to include all kinds of food, in
addition to butter, and secured increasing appropriations
for enforcement; they caused the formation of local,
municipal boards of health, and the passage of city
ordinances requiring higher standards of purity, especially
for milk. By all their activities they stimulated popular
interest in sanitation.

In 1898, the official chemists of as many States as had
then adopted the institution formed the National Association of State Dairy and Food Departments, which
thereafter held annual meetings. Robert McDowell Allen,
of Kentucky, was elected secretary of the Association in
1902. He developed a zeal for purity in food, accompanied by exceptional skill in the arts of publicity and
politics necessary to combat the food-manufacturing interests, who, up to that time, had been all-powerful.

One of the earliest results of the organization of the
State chemists into a national association, with annual
meetings, was realization that they must have, in addition to their State laws, a national one. Under the Federal
Constitution, the shipment of food from one State into
another could be controlled adequately and practicably
only by a Federal law. Moreover, the State laws varied
greatly in the standards they set up. There was essential
unfairness to the manufacturers of food in having different
requirements in different States. The need of a national
law, uniform throughout the country, was imperative.

One of the earliest of the State chemists, one of the
first men to take an interest in food sanitation, and
easily the outstanding figure in the crusade for pure food,

was Doctor Harvey Washington Wiley, a very mountain among men, a lion among fighters. He had graduated from Hanover (Indiana) College in 1867 at the age of 22; had taken his A.M. degree in 1870; his M.D. at Indiana Medical College in 1871; his B.S. at Harvard in 1873, meantime teaching Latin, Greek, and chemistry in several colleges. In 1874, when Purdue University, Indiana, was founded, Doctor Wiley was appointed its first chemist, and later was made State chemist of Indiana. In 1883, he was appointed chief chemist of the Department of Agriculture[1] at Washington. There he remained until 1912, a period of twenty-nine years, at once the major portion of his mature life, and the whole period of the fight for pure food in the United States.

Wiley, watching with the eye of an expert the metamorphosis of the food industries of the country, saw clearly the evils and abuses that accompanied the change. Endowed by nature with a capacity for passionate indignation, having the spiritual zeal of a crusader and the physique to endure hard fighting,[2] he dedicated himself to waging war on the evils and to this end launched out on a campaign of public education. Let the consumers once become fully aware of what the food manufacturers were doing, he reasoned, and there would surely follow an irresistible demand for a statutory corrective.[3] Wiley

[1] Among his activities and avocations, Doctor Wiley wrote "Songs of Agricultural Chemists" in 1892, "Principles and Practice of Agricultural Chemistry" (three volumes) between 1894 and 1897, and hundreds of government bulletins and scientific papers.

[2] With all his endurance and courage, Wiley had moments that tried his spirit. Not only had he to fight the massed enemies in front; back of him, in the Department of Agriculture, was a spirit, partly of contentment with what is, partly of the political power of the manufacturers he attacked, which at all times made Wiley's position difficult, and frequently menaced his hold on the office that gave him most of his leverage. Once, when I opened the door of his office, he turned his head and glowering eyes toward me, looked at me silently a moment, then raised both his hands and said: "Last night in my closet I prayed for help."

[3] The same idea was used in other fields by Commissioner Garfield, Senator Beveridge, President Roosevelt, and Woodrow Wilson, who gave it the familiar names "publicity" and "pitiless publicity."

brought to his task of popular education an unusual array
of talents. He could write and speak interestingly and
authoritatively. He was convincing and persuasive. He,
better than any one else, knew the intimate details of the
partnership that had come into being between the pre-
served-food manufacturer and the commercial chemist —
and the harmful effects it was having on the digestive
organs of the American people. And he, better than any
one else knew how to tell about it. As time went on,
there arose a demand for his services as a lecturer. On
the platform the forcefulness and originality of his utterances gained from the impressiveness of his appearance:
his large head capping the pedestal of broad shoulders and
immense chest, his salient nose shaped like the bow of an
ice-breaker, and his piercing eyes, compelled attention.
He had a keen instinct for the dramatic. In 1903, he
caught and held the attention of the entire country
through the so-called "poison-squad" experiments, in
which he fed volunteers, from the employees of his bureau,
foods containing preservatives, with the object of determining whether or not they were injurious to health —
an episode which caused Doctor Wiley to be called, jeeringly or affectionately, according to the point-of-view,
"Old Borax."

Wiley came to have increasingly the confidence of the
public, as, indeed, of all who wanted pure-food legislation. He was frequently called on for technical advice
by Congress and by the pure-food workers. With the
jeopardized private interests, however, and with the press
and politicians who were friendly to them or otherwise
skeptical about the need of reform, Wiley was anathema.
The New York *Sun* bestowed on him the title "chief
janitor and policeman of the people's insides."

Hardly any man in the United States, excepting only
Roosevelt himself, had a larger or more powerful group

of enemies than Wiley. In time, it came to be said of
him, as is usually said of crusaders, that he was extreme.
The adjective caused no abatement of Wiley's crusading
belligerency. He gave as good as he got. When some of
his proposals were resisted by a powerful Congressman
from New York State, James S. Sherman (later Vice-
President in the administration of Taft), Wiley pointed
out that the Congressman was himself a canner, and
called him "Short-weight Jim." Manufacturers who used
chemicals the harmfulness of which was as yet unproved;
those who used a comparatively small percentage of
dubious preservatives; those who claimed, as many then
did, that it was impossible to preserve foods without
chemicals; those who said there was no harm in making
food more alluring by the use of dyes — all fought Wiley,
in the press so far as they had access to it, through associations of chemists where they could, through the use
of political influence with Congress and with Doctor
Wiley's superiors and associates in the Department of
Agriculture. All of which the grim old doctor met with
his Puritan challenge: "Tell the truth on the label and
let the consumer judge for himself."

Wiley, on one of his trips through the country, speaking
before the Village Improvement Association of Cranford,
New Jersey, stirred a latent crusading zeal in one of the
members, Miss Alice Lakey, who became a leading spirit
in the reform. She infected the New Jersey State Federation of Women's Clubs, and later the General Federation of Women's Clubs and the National Consumers'
League.[1]

---

[1] The forces for reform were further augmented by accretions from among the
food manufacturers themselves. From every standpoint it was to the advantage
of the better class among these to have the dangerous and dishonest practices of
their unscrupulous competitors curbed. The pure-food movement as a whole was
criss-crossed with intricate motives entertained by various groups of food manufacturers.

Miss Lakey was moved by one of the most dynamic of forces, the indignation of a woman against evils practised, as the adulteration of food partly was, for profit at the expense of the health and happiness of children. She, becoming, so to speak, Doctor Wiley's apostle among the women, procured an exhibit of impure or otherwise adulterated foods, with which she lectured up and down the land, transforming the suspicious disquiet of the women into outraged resentment and strenuous action.

The women of the country were ripe for the crusade. Enough of them had lived through the transition from home and village food-industry, to large-scale corporation food-industry, to know the taste, odor, and sight of pure products of nature; and to recognize that in what they were now obliged to buy, and what they could not avoid feeding to their children, there were elements new and mysterious, and therefore disquieting. These women, by the support they gave Doctor Wiley, by the pressure they brought upon Congress — without votes, without ever thinking they needed votes, did a work greater than anything that women accomplished or attempted during the eight years after women got the suffrage in 1919.

The groups fighting for the Pure Food law staged, at the St. Louis Exposition of 1904, one of the most effective bits of propaganda ever achieved, for pure food or for any other purpose.

A large space had been allotted there to manufacturers of preserved foods, who put on display practically every brand and variety of canned and bottled goods manufactured in the United States. The pure-food workers, chiefly from the Association of State Food and Dairy Departments, secured from the Exposition officials permission to open a booth near by. Then the State chemists of Illinois, Massachusetts, Michigan, Ohio, Kentucky,

North Carolina, Minnesota, Utah, Oregon, Connecticut, South Dakota, and Nebraska[1] set to work. They took samples of well-known artificially colored foods. From each they extracted the dye. With the extracted colors, they dyed pieces of wool and silk. To each bit of cloth they attached a properly attested chemist's certificate, explaining the nature of the dye, and giving the name of the food sample from which it had been taken. Then they shipped the whole exhibit to the pure-food booth at the St. Louis Exposition.

When the exposition opened, visitors by the thousands filed by the beautifully arranged display of the food manufacturers — and then paused at the pure-food booth. Here they saw duplicated many of the cans and bottles on view in the food manufacturers' booth, each having a placard naming the deleterious substances used in its coloring and preservation. On a table, in a brilliantly hued lay-out, were the silk and woollen cloths that had been colored with dyes extracted from the foods. The subtle purpose was that the passer-by would reason that silk and wool are animal tissues, that a human being's intestines are animal tissues also, and that a dye which would bring a brilliant green, or carmine, or yellow to wool and silk, might, when swallowed in food, bring the same color to the passer-by's insides.

The passer-by was moved to reflect that a color might be agreeable and harmless when used where it could be seen, on one of the detachable ornaments of the outer periphery of the human organism, as on a necktie, for example; but that the same color, when used on the

---

[1] This list, as well as some other details of this episode, was given me in 1927 by R. M. Allen, who in 1904 had been secretary of the Association of State Chemists. Though Mr. Allen modestly refrains from saying so, I suspect he had much to do with the stratagem. He was one of the outstanding leaders in the fight for a pure food law, and possessed, among his other qualities, an instinct for politics and publicity that is not necessarily included in the equipment of a chemist.

lining of one's insides, was at best useless from the point
of view of ornamentation, and at the worst might have
adverse effects on one's health.

As it happened, many Americans had an exceptional
familiarity with the tints of the viscera, and a concern
about them not shared by the non-medical laity of other
nations, for the reason that some fifteen or twenty years
before there had been introduced into many of the public
schools a new branch of learning, physiology. The science
was imparted through vividly illustrated text-books and
colored charts, of which the purpose was not merely to
teach hygiene in the broadest sense, but particularly to
inculcate the desirability of total abstinence from alcoholic liquors; to which end the illustrations included a
colorful profusion of pictures of portions of the human
anatomy which, but for the laudable design of promoting
total abstinence, would have been, in the normal American attitude about the less obvious organs of the human
body, decorously concealed from youth, rather than
pressed upon their consciousness. Many of the pictures
in the physiology text-books were in pairs, in the "before
and after" manner. The "before" pictures showed the
normal coloration of the mechanism for metabolism. The
"after-taking" pictures showed the coloration of the same
organs and tissues as they would be when transformed by
the consumption of specified quantities of alcoholic liquor.
Since the impression meant to be made by the "after-
taking" pictures was designed to be one of restraint, it
followed that the colors in which the "after-taking" results were pictured had such a vividness and variegation
as would have been, but for this detail of American education, unfamiliar to all except those who chanced to
have made, because of their vocations or otherwise,
unusual adventures into the farther reaches of the spec-
troscope.

The result of familiarity with the tinting of the viscera thus brought about, and the concern about it that had been implanted, was that many Americans felt an acute disquiet about any departure from the conventional in the coloring of the internal organs. In short, the average American examined that display in the aisles of the St. Louis Exposition with intentness and minuteness, and passed on with a readiness to listen favorably to any agitator who thought Congress ought to do something about the use of artificial coloring in food. Not only were great masses of average folks impressed. "Congressmen and Senators," R. M. Allen wrote me in 1927, "State legislators, delegations from women's clubs, newspaper and magazine writers and editors flocked to the exhibit. Some of the food manufacturers considered getting injunctions against us and against the management of the fair, but decided this would only increase public interest. Toward the close of the fair one of my associates in the direction of the exhibit said: 'It has kindled a fire of public interest which no power on earth will be able to put out.'"

VI

The earliest fruit of the workers for national pure-food legislation was a bill sponsored by Senators Porter J. McCumber, of North Dakota, and Weldon B. Heyburn, of Idaho, reported November 11, 1902, requiring that:

Compounds, combinations, imitations, blends, shall be labelled, branded or tagged so as to show the character of contents thereof.

This, or an equivalent bill, passed the House on two different occasions, but in the Senate,[1]

---

[1] At that time, the Senate, still elected by State legislatures, was called the citadel of "the interests," a fact which formed part of the demand for direct election by the people that was adopted in 1913.

by the manipulation of appropriation and other bills, especially by those who have been opposed to this proposed law,
we have been unable to secure a vote in four years.[1]

The repeated shelving of the Pure Food bill became a
jibe, and the jibe had its own effect on public opinion.
Life[2] put it:

> "Who is that shabby-looking, patched-up individual trying
> to get on the floor of the House?" asks the Legislative Enact-
> ment of the Appropriation Schedule.
> "That?" answers the Appropriation Schedule. "O, that's
> old Pure Food Bill. When he first came here he looked pretty
> good, but now he has been knocked around and changed so
> much that his former friends don't know him at all. In a minute
> you'll see him thrown out bodily again."

The reasons for the prolonged failure of the Pure Food
bill were akin to the reasons Roosevelt found it difficult
to force through the Railroad Rate bill. The Republicans,
who were in control of Congress, were the party of "big
business." The Republican party, nationally and locally,
went hand-in-hand with big business nationally and
locally. From big business the Republicans got most of
their campaign contributions. On big business most of
the Republican Senators and Members, and practically
all the more powerful ones, depended for re-election.
Many Senators were heads of big businesses, such as
Hanna of iron and Elkins of coal; or lawyers for big
business, such as Depew for railroads, and Foraker for the
Standard Oil Company. Food manufacturing, meat packing, and liquor manufacturing bulked large in big business;
in addition, by a fraternal custom of one for all, they could

---

[1] Senator Porter W. McCumber, *Congressional Record*, December 12, 1905.
Twenty-one years later Senator McCumber wrote: "As a young Senator, I labored
under great disadvantages. The Steering Committee was against my bill. The
older Senators, who knew how to do things, and who came from sections where
much of the materials manufactured under false names were produced, were
steadfast in their zeal to prevent consideration."
[2] February 15, 1906.

call on coal, iron, textiles, and the railroads for help. Some of the businesses affected by the Pure Food bill, like the liquor manufacturers, maintained nation-wide organizations, which, with their affiliations, reached into the election precincts and took a direct hand in the election of friendly Congressmen and the defeat of unfriendly ones. Their organizations were headed at Washington by lobbies, closely knit and ably captained.

One organization, the National Wholesale Liquor Dealers' Association, in a report to its members, made an incautious brag. The boast fell into the hands of R. M. Allen, was copied by him and sent to each Senator, was read in the debates, was printed in *The Congressional Record* and in some newspapers, and became, by a familiar boomerang effect, a powerful agency for the Pure Food law, frightening some Congressional henchmen of the liquor interests, or, by its illumination to the public, releasing others from subservience:

NATIONAL WHOLESALE LIQUOR DEALERS' ASSOCIATION OF
AMERICA

To the Wholesale Wine and Spirit Trade.

GENTLEMEN:—We are to-day mailing you . . . the argument of our General Counsel, Mr. W. M. Hough, against the discriminating features of the Heyburn Pure Food bill. This, together with his arguments against the Hepburn-Dolliver Prohibition bill, exhibits a small part of the work of this Association which has prevented these measures from becoming laws at the last two sessions of Congress.

We wish to impress upon you the important fact that the two Hepburn bills have not been finally disposed of.

(Signed)   DAVID STAUBER,
                                         Secretary.

Many of the pure-food leaders in Congress were willing to endorse the claim of their enemy, the Liquor Dealers' Association, that it was the most powerful and effective enemy of the bill. Congressman James R. Mann, of Illinois, however, who led the fight for the bill in the House, thought, because of a special reason, the most effective opponents of the pure-food legislation were the patent-medicine makers, and their trade organization, "The Proprietary Association of America." Congressman Mann said:

The Proprietary Medicine Association is a powerful organization, because it is the greatest advertiser that there is in the papers of the country. Some of the officials of the Proprietary Medicine Association are endeavoring, and have been endeavoring for some time past, in every way possible to prevent this provision that the contents of prepared foods and patent medicines should be stated on the label.

Congressman Slayden, of Texas, agreed with Mann:

It is notorious, Mr. Chairman, that the opposition to this measure is largely controlled, inspired, and directed by a tremendous lobby representing the manufacturers of so-called "patent or proprietary medicine`." . . . It is evident, Mr. Chairman, to every man who has studied the course of this legislation that there has been somewhere back in the dark a tremendous power which has been able to stay the hands of the reformer time and time again, when the people were demanding protection to their health and their bodies and their minds and seemed on the point of getting it. Somewhere back of it all there has been a power that seemed irresistible.[1]

The Proprietary Medicine Association, like the Wholesale Liquor Dealers' Association, was the victim of an exposure, based, like that of the liquor dealers, on an incautious boast of power, which fell into the hands of *Collier's Weekly*. *Collier's*, having got hold of the minutes of a meeting of the Proprietary Association of America, in which the patent-medicine men discussed ways and means of preventing adverse legislation, printed part of a speech made by the Association's president, F. J. Cheney, manufacturer of "Hall's Catarrh Cure." Cheney ex-

---

[1] *Congressional Record*, June 22, 1906.

plained that he had used in his business, for two years, "a plan whereby we will have no difficulty whatever." Cheney's idea was "to shift the responsibility," by inserting in his advertising contracts with some fifteen thousand newspapers a clause reading:

It is mutually agreed that this contract is void if any law is passed in your State prohibiting the manufacture or sale of proprietary medicines.

With this clause in effect, Cheney's procedure, whenever patent-medicine legislation was introduced, was to wire or write to each paper in the State, warning it that should this legislation pass

it will force us to discontinue advertising in your State. Your prompt attention regarding this bill, we believe, would be of mutual benefit. We would respectfully refer you to the contract we have with you.

Collier's printed a similar, but stronger, clause from the contract of C. I. Hood & Co., manufacturers of Hood's Sarsaparilla, beginning: "In case national or State legislation shall be enacted adverse to the manufacture or sale of proprietary medicines. . . ." It printed another, of the manufacturer of Ayer's Sarsaparilla, bolder yet:

In case any matter detrimental to the J. C. Ayer Company's interests is permitted to appear in the reading columns or elsewhere of this paper. . . .

Collier's cited cases in which these contracts had been invoked, in which newspapers had protested against proposed action by the legislatures, and in which legislation had been prevented. It mentioned some other papers that had declined. (To one of which *Collier's*[1]

---

[1] This exposure by *Collier's* (which it entitled "The Patent Medicine Conspiracy Against the Freedom of the Press") led the *World's Work* magazine to say in May, 1906:

"The most degrading and extraordinary muzzling of the press that has perhaps

was indebted for some of the original documents it reproduced.)

VII

In February, 1905, a committee[1] of six from the organized workers for pure food, headed by Robert M.
Allen, Secretary of the National Association of State
Dairy and Food Depatments, called on President Roosevelt. One of the six carried in his mind for twenty years,
as his most vivid recollection of the event, an irrelevant
detail. As they completed their plea to Roosevelt to
help them get a pure-food law, an old colored man standing in the office, said: "Amen, I hopes you get that law."

Roosevelt was sympathetic, promised to look into the
need for the law and told them to come back in the fall.
During the summer he talked with Doctor Wiley, with
Doctor Ira Remsen, of Johns Hopkins, and with his personal physician, an exceptionally wise man, Doctor Samuel W. Lambert. In November, 1905, when the committee[2] called again, Roosevelt told them, as recounted
by Robert M. Allen in 1927:

I, of course, want to be the first to make my message to
Congress public, but I am going to trust you and tell you that
it will contain a recommendation for a law to stop interstate
traffic in adulterated foods and drugs. But it will take more

---

ever occurred in the United States is . . . at the hands of the manufacturers of
patent medicines. It is impossible to speak with patience about this nefarious
business or about this degradation of many public journals through their advertising patronage."

It should be added that after the pure-food fight got before Congress, some of
the leading newspapers in the largest cities of the country gave powerful help to
the reform.

[1] Consisting, in addition to Allen, of Miss Alice Lakey; Horace Ankeny, pure
food commissioner of Ohio; J. B. Noble, commissioner of Connecticut; A. B.
Fallinger of the national organization of retail grocers; and Sebastian Mueller, of
the H. J. Heinz Company, of Pittsburgh.

[2] On this occasion the committee included Doctor Charles A. L. Reed, former
president of the American Medical Association, then chairman of its National
Legislative Council.

than my recommendation to get the law passed, for I understand that there is some very stubborn opposition.

Roosevelt in his annual message, delivered to Congress December 5, 1905, fulfilled his promise in three brief, forceful sentences:

I recommend that a law be enacted to regulate interstate commerce in misbranded and adulterated foods, drinks, and drugs. Such law would protect legitimate manufacture and commerce, and would tend to secure the health and welfare of the consuming public. Traffic in foodstuffs which have been debased or adulterated so as to injure health or to deceive purchasers should be forbidden.

That month, December, 1905, the bill was reintroduced by Senator Heyburn, of Idaho. This time, with the powerful friend in the White House, and with the support of the sentiment that had been built up, the bill could no longer be headed off by mere obstruction. The Republican leader, Nelson W. Aldrich, of Rhode Island, had to fight in the open, an extremely unusual experience, for his art of leadership lay partly in his minute knowledge of the political and business affiliations of the Senators — his knowledge of what strings to pull; partly in the power to command Republican Senators which went with his official position as leader; and partly in his skill in parliamentary procedure. Because he had those stronger leverages of power — and also because he was one of the least eloquent of Senators — Aldrich rarely made speeches. Now, he broke his rule of silence, the action being partly justified by the fact that as a wholesale grocer (among other large interests) he had expert knowledge of the subject-matter. He based his argument,[1] however, not on the private interest of food purveyors, but on public interest — the "liberty of the people":

[1] *Congressional Record*, December 13, 1905.

Is there anything in the existing condition that makes it the duty of Congress to put the liberty of all the people of the United States in jeopardy ? . . . Are we going to take up the question as to what a man shall eat and what a man shall drink, and put him under severe penalties if he is eating or drinking something different from what the chemists of the Agricultural Department think desirable ?

Senator Nelson W. Aldrich (February, 1905), who argued that the Pure Food law was a curtailment of liberty.

That specious fallacy was too glaring to escape exposure. The Pure Food bill put no regulation on any consumer; all its regulations were on makers and sellers. The only prohibitions in the bill were few: against selling diseased meat, or decomposed food, or dangerously adulterated food. The bulk of the provisions of the bill did not prohibit the sale of anything, but merely demanded that the label should truthfully describe the contents, a regulation which, far from limiting the consumer's freedom, enlarged it. As Senator McCumber replied:

On the contrary, it is the purpose of the bill that a man may determine for himself what he will eat and what he will not eat. It is the purpose of the bill that he may go into the markets and when he pays for what he asks for that he shall get it, and not get some poisonous substance in lieu thereof, for the benefit of some particular individuals who desire to make a little money out of the sale of these poisonous articles which are imposed on the public.

Clear as that logic was, it did not prevent Senator Spooner, of Wisconsin, from repeating Aldrich's argument, saying: "the bill needs revamping in the interest of the liberty of the citizen." Senator Platt, of Connecticut — oblivious to the irony of the fact that pure food bills had knocked for years at the Senate door, and that for four years Senator Heyburn had sought to get consideration of this particular bill — demanded more time, saying it was "an imperfect and ill-conceived bill," which might hurt "the little fellow," perhaps some "poor, hardworking woman — I for one am not going to pass a bill in a hurry because there is some clamor somewhere that the subject must be attended to."

About the middle of February, 1906, the American Medical Association brought direct pressure on Aldrich. Doctor Charles A. L. Reed, of Cincinnati, Chairman of the Association's Legislative Council, told Aldrich he had back of him some 135,000 physicians, all organized locally into about 2000 county units, each member instructed not only to act himself but to ask his patients and friends to bring pressure on the Senate. Doctor Reed told Aldrich further that he and the members of the American Medical Association were determined to carry this issue of the Pure Food bill into partisan politics if necessary.

The opposition, as respects the Senate, collapsed a few days later, on February 15, 1906. The circumstances were told the author by Ex-Senator Beveridge, of Indiana, in 1927, shortly before his death:

The Senate was in a jam and public feeling had become intense. Aldrich came to me one afternoon and said: "Tell Heyburn if he asks consideration for the Pure Food bill there will be no objection."[1] (Some fight was going on between us and the Old Guard, and this was obviously a manœuvre, to save something else they thought more important; I think perhaps

[1] William Loeb, Jr., who was Roosevelt's private secretary, told me, June 17, 1927, that Roosevelt "made a personal appeal to Aldrich and the latter was persuaded to withdraw his opposition to the passage of the bill, although he did not promise to vote for it."

they counted on killing the Pure Food bill in the House, later, but I cannot recall certainly.) So I went to Heyburn and told him to bring up the Pure Food bill instantly and the Old Guard would not block him. Heyburn could not believe it and said he was tired of being made a fool of by asking useless consideration which he had asked so many times before. However, I insisted, for I never knew Aldrich to promise anything that he did not make good. I told Heyburn there was no time to waste, and to act without any questions. I sat down beside him and told him that I would be responsible. Finally, about the middle of the afternoon, Heyburn got up. . . .

On February 21, 1906, the bill passed the Senate 63 to 4. Aldrich refrained from voting. The four negative votes were cast by Senators Bacon, Bailey, Foster, and Tillman — all Democrats and all from the South; their motive was wholly concern lest the law should turn out to be a new encroachment of the Federal Government on the constitutional powers of the States.

The hurdle of the Senate was now passed, after seventeen years. The bill went to the House and was referred to the appropriate committee. There it slept. And it slept. Furtive obstruction, the chloroform of the lethal committee-room, was now what the bill had to fear. There was not a doubt that, if it came to a vote, it would pass.

In a few weeks the friends of the bill observed a disconcerting sign: the professional lobbyists, carrying their packed grips out of Washington hotels on their way home. They asked a friendly journalist, Henry Beach Needham, to see what he could find out. Needham diplomatically approached one of the Republican leaders of the House, who told him that the business interests affected by the bill were so large, and there would be so much controversial debate on it, that the leaders had decided not to bring the bill out of committee at that session.

VIII

It was at this stage, March, 1906, that one of the re-
percussions of Sinclair's "Jungle," published the preceding month, reached Roosevelt. Whether he picked
the book up in the course of his voracious reading,
whether he took notice of the public clamor about it, or
whether some one called his attention to it, is not of
record. Of what happened when he read it, there has
been published nothing that the historian can regard as
sound testimony — no eye-witness account, no formal
description, no entry in any diary. In the lack of anything more documentary, let us accept the scene "Mr.
Dooley" imagined for the delectation of the public:

It put th' Prisidint in a tur-rble stew. Oh, Lawd, why did I
say that? Think iv — but I mustn't go on. Annyhow, Tiddy
was toying with a light breakfast an' idly turnin' over th'
pages iv th' new book with both hands. Suddenly he rose fr'm
th' table, an' cryin': "I'm pizened," begun throwin' sausages
out iv th' window. Th' ninth wan sthruck Sinitor Biv'ridge on
th' head an' made him a blond. It bounced off, exploded, an'
blew a leg off a secret-service agent, an' th' scatthred fragmints
desthroyed a handsome row iv ol' oak-trees. Sinitor Biv'-
ridge rushed in, thinkin' that th' Prisidint was bein' assas-
synated be his devoted followers in th' Sinit, an' discovered
Tiddy engaged in a hand-to-hand conflict with a potted ham.
Th' Sinitor fr'm Injyanny, with a few well-directed wurruds,
put out th' fuse an' rendered th' missile harmless. Since thin
th' Prisidint, like th' rest iv us, has become a viggytaryan . . .

Roosevelt was disgusted by "The Jungle" in the
sense "Mr. Dooley" implied, but also in the sense that he
regarded Sinclair as having made an overdrawn picture.
The aspect of "The Jungle" that stirred Roosevelt was
its reflection on the United States Government and his
administration of it. There were Government inspectors
in the packing-houses; if bad beef were being sold, the
Government inspection service was at fault. Roosevelt,

though confident the conditions could not be as bad as Sinclair painted them, determined to get the facts. He called "The Jungle" to the attention of Secretary of Agriculture Wilson, whose department was entrusted with meat inspection at the packing-houses. Wilson sent a committee of three officials from his department to Chicago to investigate. With that, Roosevelt for the moment dropped the matter, turning to the Railroad Rate bill, and the other preoccupations of his busy winter. Within a very short time, his attention was called back to the beef-packers.

The publishing firm of Doubleday, Page & Company, at the time Sinclair submitted to them the manuscript of "The Jungle," had taken the precaution, before deciding to publish it, of sending a lawyer to Chicago to determine if conditions at the packing-houses were really as Sinclair pictured them. The lawyer reported that they were, and wrote an article describing what he had seen. This article and two others, one by a former city bacteriologist of Chicago and the other by a physician whose practice was among the stock-yard workers — all three only less sensational than "The Jungle"—the firm decided to publish in the magazine it owned, *The World's Work*, edited by Walter Hines Page. Before printing the articles, the firm sent proofs of them to Roosevelt.

Instantly Roosevelt became "all act." Allegations made in fiction by a writer for whose mind Roosevelt had qualified respect was one thing; allegations made by a serious and responsible magazine were quite different. Roosevelt decided the investigation already initiated by Secretary Wilson was not enough, because those investigators, being from the same department as the meat-inspection service, being, indeed, the men responsible for the administration of the inspection service, might be regarded by the public as insufficiently eager to uncover derelictions of fellow workers and subordinates. Roosevelt determined to have an investigating commission free from any possible suspicion of temptation to make a "whitewashing" report.

In the personnel of the commission Roosevelt now appointed, there was insult to the packers, and to the whole nexus of conservative interests to whom Roosevelt had become anathema. One member, James Bronson Reynolds, was a reformer — his whole occupation was that — a manager of "settlement houses" on the East Side of New York, an "uplifter." The other, Charles P. Neill, also a "settlement worker," was, as United States Labor Commissioner, identified with what in that day was called in some quarters the "rights of the workers." Giving Neill official authority to investigate the property of the packers was a breach of caste, an encouragement to irreverence among the lower orders.

In the early oral report the commission made to Roosevelt, the detail that most disturbed him was the fact that the government label on the prepared products of the packers was being flagrantly misused. The products carried, conspicuously, the legend: "Inspected and passed by the United States Government." Actually, the only inspection done by the Government was confined to the killing-floors, where carcasses were examined and, if found diseased or otherwise unfit, were condemned. No Government inspector saw, or was required by the law to see, the later stages of preparation of products put out with the assurance of the Government's O. K. The Government inspectors saw the killing of the hog, but saw nothing else of the many processes that took place between the killing, and the shipment of "potted ham."

Roosevelt's immediate impulse was to direct that the use of the Government labels be discontinued forthwith.

He realized, however, that this would create a sensation
which, added to the furore already ablaze because of
Sinclair's book and the *World's Work* magazine articles,
would do immense damage to the packers' business, not
only throughout America but in Europe, especially Germany, where the apparent guarantee of the United States
Government was relied upon
to meet official German standards.

*From a photograph by Harris & Ewing,
Washington.*

Senator Albert J. Beveridge, of Indiana, author of the Meat Inspection amendment of 1906.

Roosevelt felt that with the
report of his commission in his
hands, and with the publicity
raging over the charges from
other sources, he could surely
secure the enactment of a law
which would extend Government inspection to all the processes of preparing meat. His
intention was not to make
public the report of his commission, but merely to take
the leaders of Congress into
his confidence, and hurry
through a proper measure.

He had Senator Beveridge of Indiana prepare a carefully worded measure, which was made a rider to the
Agricultural Appropriation bill, became known as the
"Beveridge Amendment," was introduced into the Senate
on May 22, 1906, and three days later, May 25, passed
without debate, without the formality of reference to a
committee, and without a dissenting vote. Only action
by the House remained.

But the packers, panic-stricken by the avalanche of
trouble that had struck them, committed the incredible
folly of fighting the one measure which could rescue them,

which would assure the world that henceforth the Government of the United States would inspect every process of packing and by its stamp guarantee the purity of the products. If they had been calm enough to analyze their emotions, they would have realized their panic was caused less by fear of the Meat Inspection bill than by fear of the publication of the Neill-Reynolds report, now in the President's hands. Roosevelt was quite willing to suppress the report, preferred to suppress it — but only on condition of consent to the passage of the Meat Inspection rider. To the packers and their friends in Congress he said that if they would accept the Beveridge amendment, or if they and their lawyers would in good faith sit down with representatives of the Government and draw up any bill that would extend genuine Government inspection to all departments of the packing-houses, he would, on signing the bill, make a public statement that whatever had been the justification for past criticisms, the new law could be accepted as a guarantee of purity for the future.

But the packers were too frantic to understand where their own interest lay. Sinclair, taking advantage of the new uproar, printed several articles in newspapers repeating and amplifying the charges in "The Jungle." The packers in their desperation had some Western Senators demand that Roosevelt cause his commissioners to issue a public statement saying that some of the worst of Sinclair's charges were unfounded. In their frantic panic the packers wanted to stop everything, quickly. They came on to Washington; they inspired more than a thousand telegrams to Roosevelt protesting against publication of the Neill-Reynolds report; they dragooned the live-stock raisers of the country into supporting them, on the theory that the ruin to the packing-houses was already beginning to back up on the live-stock raisers;

they tried to intimidate Roosevelt's commissioners;
surest sign of all that they had lost their heads, they tried,
through themselves, and their friends in Congress, to
intimidate Roosevelt.

In the House it became apparent that a strong effort
would be made to emasculate the Meat Inspection amendment. It took Roosevelt just one day to realize this.
The report of the commission had been delivered to him
on June 2, 1906. On June 4, he sent to the House a
message strongly urging the passage of the Beveridge
Amendment as it came from the Senate. With it he sent
the first part of the Neill-Reynolds report. The balance
he withheld for use in case the packers and House leaders
continued recalcitrant. Roosevelt's message began:

> This report is of a preliminary nature. I submit it to you
> now because it shows the urgent need of immediate action by
> Congress in the direction of providing a drastic and thoro-
> going [1] inspection by the Federal Government of all stock-
> yards and packing-houses and of their products. . . . The
> conditions shown by even this short inspection to exist in the
> Chicago stock-yards are revolting.

The preliminary report of Roosevelt's commission,
which he sent to Congress with his own message, was such
as ought to have inspired the packers with an ardent
wish never to see, nor have the public see, a more complete one. In part, that portion of the report that Roosevelt sent with his message read:

> Many inside rooms where food is prepared are without win-
> dows, deprived of sunlight, and without direct communication
> with the outside air . . . vaults in which the air rarely changes.
> Usually the workers toil without relief in a humid atmosphere
> heavy with the odors of rotten wood, decayed meats, stinking
> offal, and entrails. The tables on which meat was handled, the
> tubs, and other receptacles were generally of wood, most of
> which were water-soaked and only half cleaned. The privies, as

---

[1] Roosevelt, at this time was practising "simplified spelling," then very new.

a rule, were sections of workrooms, enclosed by thin wooden partitions, ventilating into the workrooms. In a word, we saw meat shovelled from filthy wooden floors, piled on tables rarely washed, pushed from room to room in rotten box carts, in all of which processes it was in the way of gathering dirt, splinters, floor filth, and the expectoration of tuberculous and other diseased workers. Where comment was made to floor superintendents about these matters, it was always the reply that this meat would afterward be cooked, and that this sterilization would prevent any danger from its use. Even this, it may be pointed out in passing, is not wholly true. A very considerable portion of the meat so handled is sent out as smoked products and in the form of sausages, which are prepared to be eaten without being cooked. Some of these meat scraps were dry, leathery, and unfit to be eaten; and in the heap were found pieces of pigskin and even bits of rope strands and other rubbish. Inquiry evoked the frank admission from the man in charge that this was to be ground up and used in making "potted ham."

From Washington the Neill-Reynolds report was telegraphed to the press. Everybody read it. As the standing indictment against the packing industry, it supplanted "The Jungle." Everywhere indignation flamed. The subject was not one the nuances of which could most fittingly be expressed in rhyme, but newspaper versifiers found it inspiring. The New York *Evening Post* parodied a familiar rhyme:

> Mary had a little lamb,
> And when she saw it sicken,
> She shipped it off to Packingtown,
> And now it's labelled chicken.

The packers, having now to face a public excited not merely by a novel but by an official report, adopted several different lines of defense; more accurately, too distracted to adopt any plan, they rushed blunderingly into several different positions, more striking for their simultaneousness than for their consistency. In words, they issued a signed statement assailing the Neill-

Reynolds report and claiming the whole crusade against them was sensationalism unsupported by facts. In deeds,[1] they began a furious clean-up of the packing-houses with squads of carpenters and plumbers, and other species of renovators, not omitting whitewashers. At the same time, they opposed the amendment for inspection on the ground that it was unconstitutional.

The confusion in the minds of the packers was dissipated in a little while by one concrete fact most appealing to them, their sales reports. "The sale of meat and meat products," said one packing-house executive,[2] "has been more than cut in two." Another, speaking before the House Committee on Agriculture, said:

The results have been disastrous. Every country in Europe has taken up the agitation.[3]

[1]Accompanying a communication to tne House Committee on Agriculture, June 8, President Roosevelt sent a letter from Mrs. Mary E. McDowell, director of the University of Chicago Settlement, who had just made visits to several slaughter-houses and described conditions as she found them:

"On every hand there was indication of an almost humorous haste to clean up, repave, and even to plan for future changes. Brand new toilet-rooms, new dressing-rooms, new towels, etc. Swift's and Armour's were both so cleaned up that I was compelled to cheer them on the way by expressing my pleasure at the changes. The sausage girls were moved up-stairs where they could get sunlight. They, too, have dressing-rooms, etc. . . . At Libby's the girls are to be put into a blue calico uniform, which they will buy at half price. They are putting in toilet-rooms which they say are temporary, and that when the building is remodelled they will have these put in a better place. The haste toward reform would have been amusing if it were not so nearly tragic."

[2] Thomas E. Wilson, manager for Nelson Morris & Company, before the House Committee on Agriculture, June 1, 1906.

[3] The effect of the exposures on Europe, not anticipated in America, dismayed many who read the philippics that English newspapers directed at American business while English and other foreign packers made off with the trade that had previously been America's. Senator Henry Cabot Lodge appeared in his familiar rôle of consistent chauvinist, admitting (for American consumption) that the packers were very bad, but refusing to concede that English ways were better. Lodge laid responsibility for the packers' losses at their own door:

"[They] believed that they could defeat this legislation. They saw fit to make an open contest about it. They have got the report published. They have had their debate. They have had it all pulled over in the newspapers, and I wonder now whether they think it has profited them much in the end. I say, Mr. President, and I say it in all seriousness, that those packers in Chicago and those owners of the Standard Oil have done more to advance socialism and anarchism and unrest

Other countries that produce in competition are taking advantage of it. They will get the benefit and we stand the losses. I hate to think what the ultimate results will be. If we are cut out of the foreign trade we will not be able to handle the stock that raisers and farmers send us, and I don't know how we are to avoid a terrible calamity in the western country at least.

The trade losses brought to the packers a receptiveness of mind in which they were willing to listen to those who counselled that the Meat Inspection amendment might have a virtue, that the stamp of the Government on their products would be a certificate of character, much needed as the only thing that could restore public confidence and bring back their lost trade. With this realization by the packers came willingness to accept Government inspection. The prospect was so bright with new hope that it caused them to forget their previous conviction that the amendment was unconstitutional. In their reversed state of mind, their objection on principle to paternalism and to encroachment of Federal jurisdiction on State functions, was obscured by the appreciation of its usefulness to them. What was utilitarian to them could not be populistic. They about-faced and became earnest advocates of an inspection law — not exactly the pending measure, but a modification of it strong enough to still public clamor, while not so drastic as to inconvenience them too greatly.

---

and agitation than all the socialistic agitators who stand to-day between the oceans."

But to criticism coming from England, Senator Lodge replied:

"The methods of the people over in England are different from ours. If anything disagreeable occurs there, they smother it up. They set to work to cure it, but they say as little about it as possible. They try to forget it, and they say, "All is right, and see how bad the French and the Germans and the Americans are." Our way is different. We pull everything out into the open. We make it appear not only as bad as it is, but we make it appear usually ten times worse than it is. We drag all the dirty linen out and shout and shout for fear people will not pay attention to it. On the whole, I think ours, unjust as it often is, is the better way, for I think it shows that there still remains among us a capacity for honest public indignation with wrong.

IX

By the strategy Roosevelt had practised, by the use he had made of "The Jungle" and the Neill-Reynolds report, the legislative situation was now changed. No longer was there any chance of either the Pure Food bill or the Meat Inspection rider being kept chloroformed in the committees until the session ended. Public opinion was too insistent for immediate action. It was fairly certain both bills would be voted on, and equally certain both would pass. The only hope of the opposition was to emasculate them, or otherwise to make them as harmless as possible. For that purpose, as respects the Meat Inspection rider, the packers had a good friend in the chairman of the Committee on Agriculture that had charge of the rider, James W. Wadsworth,[1] of Geneseo, New York. He was a farmer, but hardly the sort of farmer who would be chosen as head of the Committee on Agriculture in any good-faith inspection of horny hands as the certificate of contact with the soil. Wadsworth's family for generations had been land-grandees, owning large acreages near Geneseo. By his associations and by his long service in Congress he had become a main prop of the Republican organization.

Wadsworth, as chairman of the committee in charge of the Meat Inspection rider, conducted his hearings with obvious intent to minimize the reports of conditions in the stock-yards. Almost all the witnesses the committee heard were friendly to the packers, and those who were not were handled without gloves. One witness was Congressman Wharton, Representative from the packing-house district. Everybody was wrong, said Wharton from the depths of a professed intimate knowledge of the stock-yards, who claimed that packing-house methods

---

[1] This was the father of the James W. Wadsworth who later became United States Senator from New York.

were a threat to the health of the workers and of the nation. His testimony, as reported in the New York *Sun*, was that

he had been employed in the packing-houses and knew the conditions there. He had been a worker in what was known as hog-house No. 2. He had worked as a trucker and came into contact with all parts of the establishment. From his personal observations he knew that the conditions of filth and uncleanliness . . . as described did not exist. There might be isolated instances where things were not exactly as they should be, but as a general thing conditions were as clean and wholesome as in the average restaurant, hotel, or home kitchen. That there were offensive odors was natural — one ought not to expect to find a rosebud in a slaughtering-house.

Commissioner Neill was brought before the committee also — but less for the information he could furnish than to hold him up to ridicule, and indirectly to bring discredit upon his report. At times the questions asked of him and the manner in which they were asked by the chairman and several of the committee, elicited reproofs from other committee members. How did he know, Chairman Wadsworth asked Neill, that the men who expectorated on the floor in the packing-houses had tuberculosis, as the Neill-Reynolds report alleged? When Neill, in answer to a question, stated that in many of the rooms there was a "stinking" odor, he was pounced upon by Wadsworth with the demand that he explain what he meant by the word "stinking." Neill's reply was a definition that might well be adopted by the dictionaries. "Well," he said, "when something smells so loud that you can't express it by saying it smells, then you say it stinks." When he said he had seen strands of rope in scraps of meat about to be ground up into "potted ham," Wadsworth asked: "Do you think that rope was put in there intentionally for the purpose of being put in the can with the meat?" Neill replied that he did not know why it was there, whether because of negligence or design, but he was certain it was there and equally certain it should not have been there.

When the hearings of the House Committee had run their course, a vote was taken and the Beveridge amendment was rejected, 9 to 7. A substitute amendment, prepared by Chairman Wadsworth, was reported out by a vote of 11 to 6.

Roosevelt, outraged, wrote Wadsworth a subtly and deliberately provocative letter:

. . . The more closely I investigate your proposed substitute the worse I find it. Almost every change is one for the worse. Perhaps the amendment as you have now drafted it is not quite as bad as it was when you submitted it to me in the first instance, but it is very, very bad. I am sorry to have to say that this strikes me as an amendment which, no matter how unintentionally, is framed so as to minimize the chance of rooting out the evil in the packing business.

Wadsworth wrote his reply while in the first flush of angry resentment:

You are wrong, "very, very wrong," in your estimate of the committee's bill. It is as perfect a piece of legislation to carry into effect your own views on this question as was ever prepared by a committee of Congress. Every member of the committee is absolutely as honest and sincere as yourself in his desire to secure the passage of a rigid meat-inspection bill. They know the meaning of the English language. . . . I regret that you, the President of the United States, should feel justified, by innuendo, at least, in impugning the sincerity and the competency of a committee of the House of Representatives. You have no warrant for it.

The Wadsworth substitute, after being strengthened by the committee, was really not as weak as the President asserted, and Roosevelt himself later changed his view of it. Excepting a few provisions there was little to choose

between it and the original amendment. One contro-
verted point was who should pay the cost of inspection.
The original amendment proposed that this expense be
borne by the packers; the Wadsworth substitute that it
be met by government appropriation.

This question became the subject for wrangling after
the Wadsworth rider passed the House and went to the
Senate. Senator Warren was insistent that the cost of
inspection be paid by the Government. If this were not
done, he said, the packers would pass the cost along to
the cattle-raisers, for whom Senator Warren, as "the
greatest shepherd since Abraham," was solicitous. Some
of Warren's reasoning was picturesque. On June 23,
1906, he said:

We now have in our bill appropriations for investigations
of the white fly and the brown-tailed gnat and the bobtailed
beetle, and the Lord only knows what else, all at the expense
of the United States. Since when, after expending a hundred
thousand dollars or more upon the brown-tailed gnat, is it
wrong to charge the United States a matter of two or three
million dollars for the examination of the immense meat product, which is the greatest industry of the entire line of American industries?

This naïve plea was too much for the sense of humor
of Senator Proctor, of Vermont. Senator Proctor believed
that since the packers had themselves created the conditions that had cost them public confidence in their products, they should bear the cost of whatever Government
action was necessary to rehabilitate them. He said:

It strikes me there is a little weakness in the Senator's comparison between the gypsy moth, the brown-tailed moth, and
beef. The brown-tailed moth comes to us as a sad dispensation
from Providence, while the beef comes from the packers, and
we can hardly hold Providence responsible for the latter.

To both the Meat Inspection rider and the Pure Food
bill, some of the opposition was constitutional and, as

such, intellectually honest (although the phrase "intimate friends of the Constitution" came to be used derisively). All the votes cast against the Pure Food bill on the final roll-call were by Democrats who sympathized with the purpose of the bill, but felt it should be carried out by the States; felt that the National Pure Food bill was an unconstitutional extension of a police power which, they thought, the Federal Government did not have and ought not to have.

Some opposition was on, so to speak, semi-constitutional grounds — resistance to domination of Congress by the Executive branch of the Government. On June 20, 1906, the Washington *Post*, taking up the cudgels for Congress, read the President a lecture, of a sort he was destined to hear often, dealing with the constitutional limitations of his office, an admonition applicable not only to his course about the Meat Inspection amendment and the Pure Food bill, but to some other measures he was advocating:

As a lawgiver the President's position is that of a negative quantity — at least that is what the Constitution says about it — and he can only advise or partially veto. That is all he has got to do with legislation. We hold to the paradox it is better to do the wrong thing the right way than to do the right thing the wrong way — that is to say, it is better that Congress pass a bad law as the result of its own free and independent deliberation than to enact a good law at the dictation of the Executive. . . . To speak the plain truth, Congress has done things it did not want to do, and has left undone things it wanted to do. It has been completely overshadowed in the Government. And was it for this that the Long Parliament fought a king for seven years in the old country?

This opposition to "Presidential dictation" in legislative matters was voiced sincerely by men who sympathized completely with the purposes of the measures Roosevelt was pressing. Congressman Henry, of Texas, mingled earnestness with humor:[1]

---

[1] *Congressional Record*, June 22, 1906, pages 8968–69.

We have reached that period in our history when the President of the United States says, in a letter to a member of this body: "I am willing to accept so and so from Congress"; "We are willing for you to do so and so." And members of this body, who ought to have some independence, abdicate their functions to the Chief Executive. [Applause.] . . . So far as I am concerned, as long as I am a member of this body, when it becomes apparent to me that a bill is in flagrant violation of the Constitution, I intend to keep my oath of office as a Representative of the people. [Applause.] I read a very clever editorial yesterday morning stating that there was a movement in Kansas to elongate one inch the nether extremities of cotton shirts. Now, if under this bill it is constitutional to regulate pure food, it does seem to me that an amendment would be proper and in order providing that cotton shirts going into interstate and foreign commerce shall be extended at least one inch at the nether extremity for the health, comfort, and preservation of the people using them. [Laughter and applause.]

Eventually the Wadsworth substitute, with its provision that the cost of meat inspection be paid by the Government, prevailed in the Senate. The momentum of the Meat Inspection amendment carried with it the Pure Food bill, which, its enemies thought, had been safely chloroformed in the committee. "It was amusing," Robert M. Allen wrote in 1927, "to see the lobbyists come hurrying back from their vacations, to the Raleigh and the Willard."

In the end, the exposures of the packers by Roosevelt's commission, of the wholesale liquor dealers by themselves, of the patent medicines by *The Ladies' Home Journal* and *Collier's*, of food adulteration and food dyeing by Doctor Wiley and State and city food officials — the aggregate of all that worked into the strengthening of Roosevelt's hand, and was invincible.

The Pure Food bill passed the House, June 23, 1906, 240 to 17, the 17 negative votes being cast by Democrats whose opposition to the bill was based on the Democratic principle of States' rights. It went to conference, was

passed again by both Houses, was signed by President
Roosevelt June 20, and on January 1, 1907, went into
effect.

The Wadsworth substitute Meat Inspection amendment, with some changes to meet Roosevelt's wishes,

Congressman James W. Wadsworth, who opposed Roosevelt's Meat Inspection
measure and, as a result, lost his seat in Congress. The photograph
was printed in *Leslie's Weekly*, April 20, 1905.

passed the House after a brief debate and without a roll-
call on June 19; was agreed to by the Senate; was signed
by the President June 30; and went into effect July 1, 1906.

X

There were several sequels, reflections, and conclusions.
Organized women had learned that organized liquor is
not invincible. The liquor interests had met their first
important defeat. Partly because of incautious boasting
of their power, they broke their own backs. Once defeated, they were weakened permanently. "I have often
thought," R. M. Allen wrote in 1927, "in the light of

subsequent events, that this defeat hastened the independence of Congress toward the Prohibition question. If that interest had supported a strict bill against adulteration and misbranding of liquors and then supported its enforcement, they would probably have gained enough public sentiment to have successfully postponed national Prohibition."

Another conclusion was in the words of Walter H. Page, editor of *World's Work*. It was, he said, having in mind the passage of both the Railroad Rate bill and the Pure Food and Meat Inspection measures, the most "ferocious, . . . the most loquacious, one of the most industrious, and at times one of the most exciting sessions of recent years. A stimulating breeze was blowing over the national government all through the session."

The "stimulating breeze" was Roosevelt.

A sequel, comparatively unimportant in itself but pregnant as a sign, was the later career of Congressman Wadsworth. By his resistance to the Meat Inspection rider, he was "in bad" with Roosevelt. Because of being in bad with Roosevelt, he was in bad with the public. In the strong Republican district that he had represented almost continuously since 1881, he was defeated, in the next election, by an independent Republican, who, after being nominated by the Democrats, adopted a cow as his emblem, plastered the district with posters of her, and on election day rode into Congress on her back.

This defeat, of one of the strongest and most highly placed of the "Old Guard" Republican leaders in the House, was more than an incidental casualty. In its implications, sinister to Roosevelt's opponents in Congress, it constituted a mark in the elevation of the President's power — led to recognition that a Congressman or Senator who resisted legislation advocated by Roosevelt ran the risk of loss of confidence by his own constituents.

The lesson was learned by others, and Roosevelt in later sessions of Congress did not hesitate to make use of it.

Wadsworth never came back to public life. Six months after his defeat, in May, 1907, having been further offended by Roosevelt in the matter of the removal from office of the Collector of Internal Revenue at Rochester, he delivered a thoughtful, well-considered judgment:

The whole thing stamps the President as unreliable, a faker, and a humbug. For years he has indulged in lofty sentiments, and violates them all for the sake of satisfying his petty spite. . . . Thank God, he can't fool all the people all the time, and the country is fast awakening to the real character of this bloody hero of Kettle Hill.[1]

[1] The desire of an author to acknowledge his indebtedness to those who help him is attended by an inevitable impediment. The finished work usually includes views and versions of events which some of those who aided would hesitate to indorse. This is especially true in the treatment of a subject as controversial as the Pure Food law and its passage. With this explanation, the author wishes to express gratitude to many persons who have read the proofs of this chapter in one or another of the evolutions through which it passed, or who otherwise aided in trying to make the narrative accurate. Among them are several whose part in the events is told in the chapter, including Upton Sinclair, Doctor Harvey W. Wiley, Robert M. Allen, Miss Alice Lakey, Charles P. Neill, ex-Senator Porter J. McCumber, Samuel Hopkins Adams. Others are Doctor Charles A. L. Reed, ex-President of the American Medical Association; Doctor Alonzo E. Taylor, Director of the Food Research Institute, Leland Stanford University; William Loeb, Jr., formerly Secretary to President Roosevelt; F. J. Gardner and A. T. Kearney, of Swift and Company; Sebastian Mueller, of Heinz & Co.; Remick W. Dunlap, formerly Dairy and Food Commissioner of Ohio; ex-Congressmen Victor Murdock and Swager Sherley.

28

THE AIRPLANE EMERGES

Man Learns to Fly, but Has Difficulty in Realizing It. A
Scientist, Over-Confident about the Ultimateness of Things
as They Are, Assures the World that Human Flight Cannot
Be. Another Scientist, Believing It Can Be, Tries to Make It
an Actuality, but Fails Spectacularly, Thereby Deepening
the Average Man's Conviction that Flight by Man Is Impossible. Whereupon Two Young Men Not Then Classified as
Scientists, Though Entitled to Be, Proceed to Fly.

I

ABOUT the time of the turn of the century, the most alert
and authoritative of the popular magazines in America
was *McClure's*. Its policy expressed itself in a serious
effort to say the last word, and, in another sense, the final
word, on current developments in all fields. *McClure's*,
wishing to give its readers the most unimpeachable
thought on the possibility of human flight, procured an
article from Simon Newcomb, Ph.D., LL.D. Newcomb
was a scientist of the best standing. He had been professor of mathematics at the United States Naval Academy and at Johns Hopkins University, had been editor
of the *American Journal of Mathematics*, had supervised
the erection of the Lick Observatory telescope, had made
important discoveries in the field of the velocity of light,
had been given honors by many distinguished scientific
societies of the world and by American universities and
by Oxford, Cambridge, and Dublin.[1]

[1] The author is under obligation to many persons who have been kind enough
to read the proofs of this chapter at one stage or another of the evolution through
which it has passed, including Orville Wright, Katharine Wright Haskell, Secretary of Commerce Hoover, Vilhjalmur Stefansson, General Frank Lahm, General

Newcomb's article, in the September, 1901, issue of *McClure's*, reveals the distinguished mathematician divided between two emotions: irritation that aviation should be taken seriously by sensible persons, and patience in the purpose of making his readers see, as clearly as he did, how futile the notion was. He seemed determined to explain in an A B C manner the fundamental and eternal reasons from which even the unerudite reader could make the inevitable deduction. He gave his article the title: "Is the Airplane Coming?" and introduced his answer with an allusion amusing to read in the light of his own fate, as it is now seen:

If I should answer no, I should be at once charged with setting limits to the powers of invention, and have held before my eyes, as a warning example, the names of more than one philosopher who has declared things impossible which were afterward brought to pass.[1] Instead of answering yes or no, I shall ask the reader to bear with me. . . ."

Professor Newcomb did not quite say "no"; rather he said "no" in a manner meant to carry greater conviction than that small word could:

No builder of air castles for the amusement and benefit of humanity could have failed to include a flying-machine among the productions of his imagination. The desire to fly like a bird is inborn in our race, and we can no more be expected to abandon the idea than the ancient mathematician could have been

William Mitchell, General Mason M. Patrick, Colonel Roy C. Kirtland, Colonel B. D. Foulois, Major H. H. Arnold, Major W. C. Sherman, Paul Henderson, Grover Loening, Griffith Brewer, Arthur Ruhl, Byron Newton, James H. Hare, William E. Hoster, and George Rothwell Brown.

[1] A classic instance of philosophic short-sightedness, of the sort that Newcomb here derides, was Lactantius, who in the fourth century sought to cast ridicule upon the theory of antipodes, saying:

"Is there any one so foolish as to believe that there are antipodes with their feet opposite to ours, people who walk with their heels upward and their heads hanging down? That there is a part of the world in which all things are topsy-turvy: where the trees grow with their branches downward, and where it rains, hails, and snows upward?"

expected to give up the problem of squaring the circle. . . .
As the case stands, the first successful flyer will be the handiwork of a watchmaker and will carry nothing heavier than
an insect.[1]

Farther on Professor Newcomb's suppressed impatience
burst through his inhibitions for a moment and betrayed
him into a more nearly explicit negation:

The example of the bird does not prove that man can fly. . . .
Imagine the proud possessor of the aeroplane darting through
the air at a speed of several hundred feet per second! It is the
speed alone that sustains him. How is he ever going to stop?

Finally, Professor Newcomb lost entirely, for a careless
moment, the pose of making an open-minded inquiry, and
came out with a statement positive enough to assure him
a place among those skeptical philosophers he derided because they had set limits to man's inventiveness:

I have shown that the construction of an aerial vehicle which
could carry even a single man from place to place at pleasure
requires the discovery of some new metal or some new force.

In this confidence of negation, Professor Newcomb was
supported by the Engineer-in-Chief of the United States
Navy, Rear Admiral Melville, who in *The North American
Review* for December, 1901, wrote that he was convinced,
after a consideration of the physical and mechanical facts
involved, that there was no basis for optimism as to the

---

[1] Professor Newcomb patiently amplified his reasoning in an article in *The
Outlook* in 1903:

"Suppose that an inventor succeeds, as well he may, in making a machine
which would go into a watch-case, yet complete in all its parts, able to fly around
the room. It may carry a button, but nothing heavier. Elated by his success, he
makes one on the same model twice as large in every dimension. . . . The result
is that his machine is eight times as heavy as before. But the sustaining surface
is only four times as great. As compared with the smaller machine, its ratio of
effectiveness is reduced to one-half. Quite likely the most effective flying-machine
would be one carried by a vast number of little birds. If the watchmaker can make
a machine which will fly through the room with a button, then by combining ten
thousand such machines he may be able to carry a man. But how shall the combined forces be supplied?"

success of the dirigible balloon or the flying-machine, either for commercial transportation or in war. "A calm survey," he said, "of certain natural phenomena, leads the engineer to pronounce all confident prophecies at this time for future success as wholly unwarranted if not absurd."

Those articles reflected the magazines and newspapers as they were when they wished to be benevolently elementary in instructing their readers against fallacy. Ordinarily when editors alluded to the flying-machine they made gibes about it, treated it as a useful addition to the "mother-in-law" and "There were two Irishmen" jokes — stock subjects for standard humor. To dismiss aviation with the damnation of jeers was orthodox. *Puck*, a periodical genially confident of the ultimateness of things as they are, printed on October 19, 1904:[1]

"When," inquired his friend, more for the sake of asking than for the answer, "will you wing — I believe that is the correct term — your first flight?"

"Just as soon," replied the flying-machine inventor, "as I can get the" — And, yet, it has been said that lunatics have no sense of humor — "laws of gravitation repealed."

Newspapers occasionally published articles or fiction stories that dealt with the coming day of the flying-machine in the spirit of a kind of semi-serious pseudo-science; of the Jules Verne sort — perpetual motion, rain-making, pits dug through to China, messages from Mars, and visitors from outer space. Aviation was regarded as kin to these, a legitimate field for interesting fantasy.

This was the prevailing attitude of the printed word, in the popular sense, toward aviation. It had the effect of confirming the average man's age-long conviction that

[1] The printing of this joke, as late as October, 1904, illustrates the incredulity of the public toward aviation, its sheer inability to accept flight as among human possibilities. Actually, human flight had been accomplished ten months before, and the event had been recorded in newspapers.

human flight belonged in the world of fable, increased his disbelief in the possibility of it.

II

Langley's Attempt and Failure

There was a scientist, of the highest standing, Professor Samuel P. Langley, Secretary of the Smithsonian Institution, who believed human flight was possible, who spent the major part of his mature lifetime trying to make it an actuality — and had the tragic fate of deepening in a spectacular way the average man's conviction that human flight could never be.

Langley — born at Roxbury, Massachusetts, in 1834; educated at Boston and in Europe; astronomical assistant at Harvard College Observatory in 1865; assistant professor of mathematics in the U. S. Naval Academy in 1866; director of the Allegheny Observatory at Pittsburgh for twenty years; secretary of the Smithsonian Institution[1] at Washington from 1887 on — Langley, during the 1880's, devoted himself to working out mathematical tables of wind pressures. In the early 1890's, he made several small model airplanes, the earlier ones having their propellers driven by twisted rubber bands, and the later ones having motors of compressed air, carbonic acid gas, and steam.

On May 6, 1896, one of Langley's models, weighing about 26 pounds, having wings measuring 14 feet from tip to tip, and equipped with a miniature steam-engine, was set going on the banks of the Potomac River at Washington.[2] It sustained itself in the air about a minute and a

[1] Langley was the inventor of the bolometer, an instrument capable of detecting changes of temperature less than one hundred-millionth of a degree Centigrade, and the discoverer of an extension of the invisible infra-red rays.

[2] Without any one in it, of course, and carrying no weight but its own. Of these early experiments of Langley, Alexander Graham Bell (inventor of the telephone) said in 1913: "In 1896, the success of Langley's aerodrome model convinced the world that motor-driven flying-machines of the heavier-than-air type were really practicable." Doctor Bell may have been convinced, but the world certainly was not.

half and travelled a distance of about half a mile, dropping gently into the river when the fuel and water in the tiny engine were exhausted. Later the same year, on November 28, 1896, a similar model travelled about three-fourths of a mile at a speed of thirty miles an hour.

This success with a model was regarded by Langley as a definite demonstration that flight with a motor-driven machine was practicable. He regarded it also as the completion and culmination of his work; being 62 years old and having many other interests to engage his time, he wished to leave to others the carrying on of the further development of aviation.

But the United States War Department had been impressed. The Board of Ordnance and Fortifications urged Langley to attempt a machine capable of carrying a man. Langley consented, reluctantly. With a subsidy of $50,000 from the Board, with the support and help of the Army, with the backing of the Smithsonian, with the confidence of so much of the scientific world [1] as believed aviation

---

[1] Doctor Langley was encouraged and assisted in his experiments by his friend, Alexander Graham Bell, inventor of the telephone. The writer of this history took dinner with the two men at Bell's summer home at Baddeck, Nova Scotia, on September 6, 1901. (During the dinner news came of the shooting of President McKinley.) Doctor Langley and Doctor Bell had not long before engaged in one of the most curious experiments ever attempted by two quite serious gentlemen over fifty, both gray-whiskered and with reputations in fields of solemn gravity. One of them had stood on the porch holding a kitten by the feet, legs upward, and dropped it over and over again to a pillow on the grass a few feet below, while the other serious gentleman took observations. The purpose was to discover just how a kitten rights itself in falling and lands on its feet. These experiments, together with some others Bell carried on with tetrahedral kites, had been designed to make progress toward a beginning in practical aviation. At dinner that night Doctor Bell emphasized the assertion that man would make no real progress toward aviation through experiments with balloons—balloons were mere diversion. He said the only hope of aviation lay in the possibility that some one might learn how to get a heavier-than-air machine to rise, and how to control it in the air. Turning to Doctor Langley, but looking at me, Doctor Bell said: "You and I won't live to see it, Professor, but this young man will see the day when men will pick up a thousand pounds of brick and fly off in the air with it." My own reaction to that assertion, I refrained from uttering, but to myself I said: "That is all right; that old gentleman has a right to talk. He invented the telephone and that gives him a license. All the same, I know he is talking plain nonsense."

Doctor Bell, living until August 2, 1922, saw much that he had predicted.

possible at all, Langley with an assistant, Charles M. Manly, built an engine really remarkable, considering the state, at that time, of progress in internal-combustion engines. Weighing but 124 pounds, it developed under

Charles M. Manly and Samuel P. Langley.

test 52.4 horse-power, a record best understood when it is realized that Europe and America had been scoured for a 12 horse-power engine weighing in the neighborhood of 100 pounds, and none had been found. This engine Langley and Manly placed in a man-size airplane having two sets of wings placed tandem fashion — a replica of the early smaller models in every respect save the engine.

Delay followed delay, but on October 7, 1903, seven years after the Board of Ordnance and Fortifications had made its appropriation, preparations were complete for the first trial flight.

The scene was at Widewater, Virginia,[1] at a point where the Potomac River broadens out into a kind of bay some four miles wide. In this spacious background, about a mile from the Maryland side of the river, were set up paraphernalia as novel as the expected event. For a parent-ship, Doctor Langley had built a huge, long, ark-like house-boat; on its top, from stern to bow, was a runway of two rails seventy feet long; on the runway, at the stern, backed tightly against coiled springs, was what Langley called a "catapult car" designed to hurl the airplane into space.[2] Atop the "catapult car" rested the airplane itself.

About what happened that day,[3] so far as it had to do with the scientific and expert mechanical aspects of the experiment, there was disagreement at the time. Manly, who was in the airplane, seemed not to have been able to follow the rapidity of the events with sufficient calmness of observation. Langley, the inventor, who was not present, had a theory about what had happened differing from Manly's. The airplane, as well as parts of the catapult car and the runway, was so damaged as to make post-mortems uncertain in their findings. (Out of the vagueness of it all arose disputes about priority of invention, complications about patents, lawsuits; and rival allocations of credit for making the first flyable airplane, which blazed into acuteness as late as 1925.)

---

[1] About thirty miles southeast of Washington.

[2] Throughout all his thought and experiment, Doctor Langley held to the principle that the airplane must be thrust into the air, must be given an initial velocity, by some power outside itself.

[3] October 7, 1903.

But as to how it looked to a wholly disinterested and very much uninitiated outsider, there is vivid evidence in the narrative of a reporter, George Rothwell Brown:

At noon it was realized the crucial moment was at hand. . . . Mr. Manly, wearing a pair of light trousers, canvas shoes, a

The Langley airplane, the instant after launching, October 7, 1903, Widewater, Virginia.

life-preserver, and a pair of automobile glasses, climbed into the car. Two tugs, each with a portion of the Smithsonian force on board, were stationed at a distance from the ark. Manly started the naphtha engine. When all was ready, [he] nodded his head to a helper, who fired a sky-rocket warning to the photographers on the Virginia beach to be on the qui vive. The serious work of the experiment was about to begin.

A few yards from the house-boat were the boats of the reporters, who for three months had been stationed at Widewater. The newspaper men waved their hands. Manly looked down and smiled. Then his face hardened as he braced himself for the flight, which might have in store for him fame or death. The propeller wheels, a foot from his head, whirred around him 1000 times to the minute. A man forward fired two sky-rockets. There came an answering "toot, toot," from the tugs. A mechanic stooped, cut the cable holding the catapult; there was a roaring, grinding noise — and the Langley airship tumbled over the edge of the house-boat and disappeared in the river, sixty feet below. It simply slid into the water like a handful of mortar.[1]

The whole country yelled. It was a day of triumph for every faithful defender of the immutability of what is. Practically every head-line and news story seemed to reflect smug satisfaction in the proof that man's age-long conviction about the impossibility of human flight was still sound and right; seemed almost savagely gratified that an impious professor questioning the law of gravity had been so sensationally rebuked and humiliated. The news stories seemed to reflect, too, the suspicion, partly condescending, partly truculent, of laymen against scientists, an attitude commoner then than now. The stories actually seemed to gloat in affirmation and repeated reaffirmation of the unqualified completeness of the failure. The head-lines of the Washington *Post* read:

BUZZARD A WRECK

LANGLEY'S HOPES DASHED

Costly Contrivance Utterly Unable to Take Wing — The Navigator Escapes with a Ducking and Has the Shapeless Mass of Steel and Cloth Stored Away.

In emphasizing the conclusiveness of the failure, the Washington *Post* said:

The experiment resulted in a total and admitted failure. The elaborate construction of "wings," designed after those of the buzzard, collapsed with the first weight put upon them. It was demonstrated that the "flying-machine," over which a force of government-paid scientists has been working for ten

[1] The Washington, D. C. *Post*, October 8, 1903. Condensed and slightly paraphrased.

years, . . . was as incapable of flight as a dancing-pavilion floor. Confronted by a defeat so evident, the experts did not attempt to explain away their failure. They just threw up their hands. The once pretty and artistic-looking airship was little more than a bedraggled pile of torn rags and kindling-wood, with an apparent value of a dollar. Its ruination was complete.

This note of almost eager emphasis on the finality of the failure, the suggestion of pleased satisfaction, of skepticism justified, ran through all the accounts.[1] The Washington *Star's* head-lines proclaimed : "Airship Fails to Fly — Professor Langley's Machine Goes to River Bottom." The New York *Herald's* captions said: "Costly Airplane Wreck — Travels Only as Far as Catapult Sends It — Inventor a Disappointed Spectator." The New York *Sun* added a touch of impishness:

LANGLEY'S AERODROME SWOOPS INTO POTOMAC
AND DUCKS PROFESSOR MANLY

AERODROME DID A FLIPFLOP

Then Turned Its Nose Up, and Went Into the Potomac. Mr. Manly Had a Bath with It.

At Langley's second and final failure, December 8, 1903, the jeering became a kind of triumphant ecstacy of ironic flouting. It was as if an impudent invader of man's mental status quo had been repulsed, and the defenders were celebrating. One account said:

The scientists, hardened by reverses, did not seem to care who saw them, and sailed down the river, the once sacred airship perched on the pinnacle peak in a don't-worry fashion. The rest of the Smithsonian staff, the stuffers of birds and rabbits, climbed to the top of the Smithsonian tower with telescopes and field-glasses and watched. . . .

In tune with the head-lines and news articles, but more finished in their acidity, were the editorials. The Washington *Post* of October 8, 1903, said:

[1] There were two attempts, both disastrous—one October 7, the other December 8, 1903. The head-lines here quoted refer, some to one, some to the other.

It is not too much to say that the Langley flying-machine has fulfilled the fondest expectations of its critics.

Those who have watched its career during the past ten or twelve weeks may now point proudly to forecasts that have been opulently realized. . . . The "buzzard" flew exactly as far as its initial impetus compelled it to fly and not a hair's breadth farther. With the exhaustion of that impetus it fell into the water with all the rude directness of an unsupported brickbat. Any stout boy of fifteen toughening winters could have skimmed an oyster shell much farther, and that without months of expensive preparation or any of the august accessories of government fleets, appliances, and retinues. The buzzard is a di-dapper, and that is all there is about it.

Its radiant wings were draggled, its intricate and tender bowels were dishevelled. Eight years of almost inspired labor and some $70,000 of real money are now evaporating with the moisture in which their fruits were plunged. Nothing save the time and money has been lost. Above all things, the principle survives — triumphant, immortal, unassailable. What if the machine fell down like a tenement-house, at least it was constructed like a carrion crow.

The Washington *Star's* editorial comment combined an elucidation of scientific principle, a demonstration of impregnable logic, and a concluding witticism, probative and persuasive:[1]

THE BUZZARD

Of course there is still hope. Hope, indeed, springs eternal in the breast of the seeker for the secret of human flight. But if once a perfect launching device can be secured there will remain the test of the machine itself, which as yet is unproved. Then there will yet remain the even more important question of alighting. It is one thing to leap off a building and to hold the body in the position demanded by theory and insure a safe descent, but it is another thing to manage to hit the ground with sufficient gentleness. It was an Irish hod-carrier who declared that he was never hurt by falling off a scaffold. It was the bringing up at the bottom that broke his ribs.

The Boston *Globe* barbed its arrow with assumed naïveté:

---

[1] December 9, 1903. Condensed.

Perhaps if Professor Langley had only thought to launch his airship bottom-side up, it would have gone into the air instead of down into the water.

A "colyumnist" of the day most wittily combined two topics much in the current news; with one stone, so to

A sardonic cartoon by Berryman, of the Washington *Post*, December 9, 1903, the day after the second failure of the Langley airplane.

speak, he hit the Langley bird that did not soar — and the cost of living that did: "If Professor Langley had only thought to hitch his airship to the price of beef!"

On December 10, 1903, an editorial in a Washington newspaper turned to an aspect of the failure more pertinent to forevisioned statesmanship:

There seems to be but one or two more words to say about the Langley flying-machine, and they should relate exclusively to its status as a source of expenditure by the government. We note Professor Langley's renewed assurances of confidence and high consideration, which we are quite willing to regard as creditable to his sentimental side. Professor Manly also, we understand, is willing to try it again under reasonable conditions of salvage. All this is their own affair, and *The Post* would be the last to discourage such engaging zeal. As we see this matter, however, the government should promptly sever its relations with an experiment which has involved a very large outlay of the public money without disclosing a single ground for hope. . . . In the past we have paid our respects to the humorous aspects of the Langley flying-machine, its repeated and disastrous failures, the absurd atmosphere of secrecy in which it was enveloped, and the extensive pageantry that attended its various manifestations. It now seems to us, however, that the time is ripe for a really serious appraisement of the so-called aeroplane and for a withdrawal by the government from all further participation in its financial and scientific calamities.

This sentiment about expense and government endorsement was shared within Congress by the contemporary watch-dogs of the Treasury. On January 24, 1904, Congressman James M. Robinson, of Indiana, said: "Here is $100,000 of the people's money wasted on this scientific aerial navigation experiment because some man, perchance a professor wandering in his dreams, was able to impress the [military] officers that his aerial scheme had some utility." [1]

Langley, on the day after the second failure, December 8, 1903, was quoted by the Washington *Post* as saying:

---

[1] As I write this, Mr. Robinson, now an ex-Congressman, is still living. On May 27, 1926, I wrote him at his home in Los Angeles to verify the quotation above. He replied: "Acknowledging the courtesy and care of yourself and desire for accuracy—the extract cited is correct. I had satisfaction, in common with Hemenway, of Indiana, and Hitchcock, of Nebraska, in getting after a few of the fads in appropriations of that time. Living as I now do near the Douglas airplane factory, and saddling over the Clover airplane field at Santa Monica daily, I might considerably revise my original notion."

"The accident was a most peculiar one and I am at a complete loss to tell how it was brought about. . . . I am positive that the trouble lay with the launching apparatus and not with the machine itself, but what caused it I have not been able to find out."

However Langley the scientist may have remained confident about aviation, Langley the man was desperately hurt, hurt to the point of physical illness,[1] by the tornado of ridicule. It came from high and low. One specimen which, because of the elevation of its source, is worth reviving for posterity came from Ambrose Bierce:

I don't know how much larger Professor Langley's machine is than its flying model was — about large enough, I think, to require an atmosphere a little denser than the intelligence of one scientist and not quite so dense as that of two.

The author of that was a scholar, an important figure in American literature, known particularly for distinction of style. If Ambrose Bierce could write like that about Langley, what could the lesser lights of the newspapers do ? They did it, a-plenty.

[1] When he died, two years later (February 27, 1906), it was commonly said his end was hastened by humiliation.

Eight years after his death, and eleven years after the Langley plane had failed, after the ridicule had died down, and after the Wrights had made aviation successful, Langley's associates in the Smithsonian Institution, rather pathetically, resurrected the ruined machine, brushed the dust off its broken wings, made some changes in it, fitted it with a new and more powerful engine, arranged with an aviator to fly it—and then set it up in the Smithsonian Institution with a unique placard saying in part, "first . . . airplane . . . capable of . . . flight." As an act of sentimental loyalty to their departed chief, one likes to record it. As a precedent for scientific institutions and museums generally, it had a tendency to blur the facts of history. It was remarked, with a permissible latitude of ironic analogy, that the precedent, if widely followed, would entail a doubling, at least, of the space of museums, which would need to accommodate not only the actual "firsts" of history, but the potential firsts; including replicas not only of the first ships that crossed the ocean, but also of the rather numerous ships "capable" of crossing it; paintings not only of Columbus, but also of the not inconsiderable number of men who might be regarded by devoted partisans as "capable" of discovering America. Some scientists, who believed Langley's plane in its original form was not capable of flight, and others who felt the act of Langley's associates tended to impair the honor due the Wrights, have used harsh words in deploring it.

By the newspaper accounts of Langley's failure, by the editorial jeers about it, by the quips in comic periodicals and the skits in the vaudeville theatres, the struggling new science Langley had striven so earnestly to advance was discredited; and the skeptical multitudes were given spectacular confirmation of their conviction that human flight could not be, flattering approval for their steadfastness of belief that what has not been, cannot be.

III

Orville and Wilbur Wright

We leap, as the old-fashioned melodramatists used to say, nine days, short December days. Langley's final failure had taken place December 8, 1903. By one of the most ironic coincidences ever staged by the "twin imposters," there occurred on December 17, 1903, the culmination of the experiments of two men who, in every detail of their background and nearly every material circumstance attending their efforts, were as far removed from Langley as if the contrast had been deliberately arranged by some cosmic deity in an exceptionally sardonic mood. Where Langley was known to the whole world as one of its foremost scientists, Orville and Wilbur Wright were known merely as practical mechanics[1] — in the very limited circle where they were known at all. Where Langley had the prestige of a great scientific institution, the Smithsonian, the Wrights had only the background of a bicycle shop. Where Langley had the backing of a United States Government subsidy of $50,000, the Wrights had only the resources of a small manufacturing and repair business. Langley's work had been carried on under the observation of learned societies and the United States Army, and had

---

[1] This phrase, while it fits the popular understanding of the Wrights, calls for decided modifications in view of their extraordinary scientific work.

been watched by newspapers and magazines;[1] the total number of persons who had seen or heard about any part of what the Wrights had been doing for five years was probably less than a hundred, a few helpers and friends, and casual callers at their shop. The final trials of the Langley machine had taken place under the fierce glare of the mechanisms for publicity concentrated at the nation's capital, and had been followed by practically every newspaper reader in the United States and many in Europe; the test by the Wrights of their machine took place at one of the most inaccessible spots in America, without a newspaper man present, nor any one else except the Wrights themselves and a few coast-guards. Between the pageant-attended, publicity-charged atmosphere of Washington on December 8, 1903 — and the remote sand dunes of Kitty Hawk, North Carolina, on December 17, the literal difference was nine days in time and two hundred miles in space; by all the attending circumstances, including the outcome, the difference was immeasurable.

Wilbur Wright was born eight miles east of Newcastle, Indiana, April 16, 1867; Orville at Dayton, Ohio, August 19, 1871. Wilbur's four years of greater age gave him, in the younger brother's eyes, a natural leadership for which he was qualified by an innate trait of initiative, a disposition to ignore accepted ways and go his own. This trait caused Wilbur to break a family tradition which was an expression of the cultural viewpoint of their father, a well-to-do bishop of the United Brethren Church,[2] that all

---

[1] It is by no means meant to imply that Langley sought the publicity. On the contrary, he had the modesty and reticence of a scholar. But the novelty of his experiments and the scene of them (at Washington), the association of the Army with them, together with Langley's public position, made minute and wide-spread publicity inevitable.

[2] The broad-minded bishop-father, happily, rated his sons' bent toward individual judgment and decision above his own preference that they follow a course within the orthodox meaning of "intellectual." "Bishop Wright originally intended Wilbur to follow in his footsteps and enter the Church."

the children should be given a college training. Two older brothers, Reuchlin and Lorin, and a sister, Katharine, youngest of the family, were sent to college; but Wilbur on leaving high school stepped immediately into the practical world. Orville followed him four years later.

The first joint venture of the brothers was a local

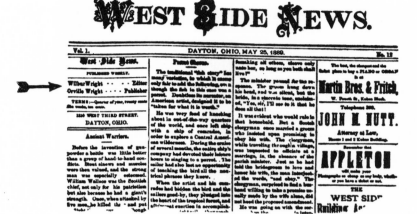

The first joint enterprise of the Wright brothers as youths was *The West Side News*, printed on a press invented and built by Orville Wright.

weekly paper. As late as 1927, older residents of Dayton could still point out an unimposing brick building bearing a faded wooden signboard reading "West Side News"; and could still recall a scene of the year 1889 — Wilbur Wright lying flat on the roof, clutching the feet of Orville, who, hanging head downward, fastened the sign in place. The faded files of *The West Side News*, and two other journalistic ventures of the years between 1889 and 1895, *The Evening Item* and *Snapshots*, reveal not ordinary neighborhood sheets but journals that included treatment of general subjects, publishers whose interests ranged from machines to intellectual abstractions. Orville made every part of the printing-press, except the bed, which being of iron had to be cast in a foundry. A visiting foreman-printer of a more orthodox make of press, having a slightly alarmed curiosity about printers who seemed independent of press manufacturers, once spent an hour of concentration lying on his back beneath Orville's machine, and arose with remarks to the effect that he had thought he knew all about printing-presses, but he'd "be hanged" if he could understand what made the Wright press go.[1]

The Wrights gave up their newspaper and printing business partly because their temperaments included an eagerness to explore the untried, and a lack of zest for repetition of the familiar. When the "safety" bicycle craze of the nineties swept over America, they set themselves up as manufacturers, repairers, and retailers of the new machines. They built two models, the Wright Special and the Van Cleve, the former selling at the low price of $18. Their output was small, never exceeding 100 machines a year, all sold locally. They also invented and manufactured a wheel-hub having a reserve set of bearings, and a coaster-brake.

This little bicycle shop was the cradle of the newest art in the world and was, besides, its laboratory and its banker. It was kept going until the owners had definitely achieved aviation. In it the Wrights made their scientific experiments during such intervals as could be snatched from the bicycle jobs. For years all their expenses were met from its modest profits.

One evening, in the summer of 1896, Wilbur Wright, reading a newspaper after his day in the shop, chanced upon an account of the death of a German engineer, Otto

---

[1] An essential aspect of the Wrights was their natural mechanical ingenuity supplemented by resourcefulness forced upon them by slenderness of means. At Kitty Hawk, when they could not afford seven dollars for a stove, they made one from an empty carbide can.

Lilienthal, who had been killed by the fall of a "glider."[1]
Orville was at home convalescing from an attack of ty-
phoid fever. Wilbur kept the newspaper and showed it
to his brother after Orville had completely recovered. By
the impression that chance newspaper article made on
two minds intellectually curious and inclined toward experiment, the Wrights were drawn into that web, of
which an earlier experimenter had written:[2]

If there be a domineering, tyrant thought, it is the conception
that the problem of flight may be solved by man. When once
this idea has invaded the brain it possesses it exclusively. It
is then a haunting thought, a walking nightmare, impossible to
cast off. If now we consider the pitying contempt with which
such a line of research is appreciated, we may somewhat conceive the unhappy lot of the poor investigator whose soul is
thus possessed.

The Wrights found in their bishop-father's library
Marey's "Animal Mechanism." After they had read
that, they wrote to the Smithsonian Institution at Washington and received some pamphlets, together with advice
about what books to buy.[3]

A fair summary of what the Wrights could assay, from
the existing literature of aeronautics, of past progress
toward solving human flight, if set down roughly chrono-
logically, would begin with the Greek legend of Icarus,
who fell into the sea when the wax fastenings of his wings
were melted by the sun. About 400 B. C., Archytas of
Tarantum built a wooden mechanical bird. About the

[1] At this point it is well to make the technical terminology of this narrative clear.
A "glider" was a set of wings on a frame — it had no motive-power. All the
Wrights' experiments during their first three years were with gliders. When later
they added an engine and propellers, the machine became an "airplane."

[2] Louis Pierre Mouillard, in "The Empire of the Air," 1881.

[3] They read "The Empire of the Air," by Louis Pierre Mouillard; "Experiments
in Aero-Dynamics," and "Story of Experiments in Mechanical Flight," by Samuel P. Langley; "Experiments in Soaring," by Otto Lilienthal; "Progress in Flying-Machines," by Octave Chanute. They sent for and received *The Aeronautical
Annuals* for 1895, 1896, and 1897, published by James Means, of Boston, an aviation enthusiast, experimenter, and inventor.

time Columbus was discovering America, Leonardo da Vinci drew the designs for a flying-machine to be driven by flapping wings. (Fortunately for several other arts, da Vinci's interest in flying came to an end before it reached the experimental stage.) In 1783, the Montgolfier brothers, Frenchmen, with Benjamin Franklin an interested spectator, made the first balloon ascension in a bag made of paper, filled with air heated and expanded by burning straw. While the War of 1812 was going on, an Englishman, Sir George Cayley, made tiny airplanes and built the first glider, which would, he wrote, bear a man up "so strongly as scarcely to allow him to touch the ground, and would frequently lift him up and carry him several yards together." In 1842, another Englishman, W. S. Henson, designed and patented a twin-propeller, steam-driven monoplane which was an advance over everything of the past, but which we know could not have flown safely for the reasons that it lacked sufficient power and had no provision for lateral stabilizing. John Stringfellow, an Englishman, made a steam-driven model, which he flew in June, 1848, in a disused lace factory at Chard, Somerset, England, and again at Cremorne Gardens, London. After 1860, inventors in many lands occupied themselves with aviation, some building machines which they proposed to propel by steam or gasoline engines, and others making gliders. In the eighties and nineties, Otto Lilienthal made hundreds of gliding flights, and had built a power machine when an accident caused his death in 1896. In the same year, at Washington, Professor Samuel P. Langley flew a small model airplane (described on page 557). In 1899, Percy Pilcher, an English aviation enthusiast, was killed while gliding. During the nineties Octave Chanute[1] improved on Lilienthal's

[1] Chanute was born in Paris in 1832, and came to this country in 1838, living in Louisiana. He built the Missouri River bridge at Kansas City in 1867, and laid out the Chicago stock-yards.

glider, and his assistants, Herring, Avery, and several others, made many flights.

Of what all this amounted to in actual accomplishment, of all the progress that had been made in aviation up to the time the Wrights began, there is an authoritative statement in Nelson's Encyclopedia:

> The experiments antecedent to the Wrights . . . . did not attain practical[1] results. Just how much each of them contributed toward the final success it is hard to say. Most of them made valuable additions to the knowledge of the science, but all mixed the practicable with the impracticable in such a way as to make it risky to adopt their conceptions as the basis of actual flight.

Another way of expressing the existing state of knowledge of aviation at the time the Wrights began their glider experiments is in the words of Octave Chanute, the engineer, who, with one other, had experimented most in aviation, and was the most optimistic of all about it. "Flying-machines," Chanute said, "will be gradually evolved *within one or two generations*, but the evolution will be costly and slow." [2]

---

[1] Partisans of Professor Langley claim the word "practical" in this quotation from Nelson's Encyclopedia does not do justice to Langley's 1896 success with a model. The quotation is indisputably accurate as respects flight by man.

[2] *The Independent*, October 22, 1900.

The Assistant Secretary of the Navy for Aeronautics, Edward P. Warner, disagrees with Chanute and with the conviction of the author on this point. He wrote (February 18, 1927):

"I do not think that, in the light of our present knowledge, it is possible to stand by the statement that flight would have been delayed for at least a generation without the Wrights. Others both here and abroad were close on the track and I think it is almost certain that there would have been successful flight by 1907 or 1908 in any event."

The author knows of no experimenter in America, apart from the Wrights, whose work gave promise that he would solve the problem of flight. As late as 1908, after the United States Army invited bids for the construction of an airplane, the only airplane presented was the Wrights'. Two other Americans who had entered bids failed to present machines for the trials and forfeited their deposit money. In Europe, the only country interested in aviation was France, and the interest there is directly traceable to the Wrights through Chanute. England and Germany were apathetic, following the deaths of Pilcher and Lilienthal.

The Wrights, reading the literature they had collected, discussing it, finding analogies for some of the principles in their own experience as bicycle experts, arrived at conclusions characteristic of original minds, minds accustomed through their daily work to test theory by practice. They observed that the aeronautical enthusiasts fell into two groups. One gave chief attention to machines equipped with power, the other to gliders. The Wrights chose to align themselves with the second group, "partly," wrote Wilbur Wright, "from impatience at the wasteful extravagance of mounting delicate and costly machinery on wings which no one knew how to manage."

Having decided that soaring in a glider should be the immediate step, they reached another conclusion equally characteristic of their instinct for reality. The essential need was practice. The reason, as it seemed to them, why the problem had remained so long unsolved, was that

no one had been able to obtain any adequate practice. We figured that Lilienthal in five years of time had spent only about five hours in actual gliding through the air. . . . It would not be considered at all safe for a bicycle rider to attempt to ride through a crowded city street after only five hours' practice, spread out in bits of ten seconds each over a period of five years. We thought that if some method could be found by which it would be possible to practise by the hour instead of by the second there would be hope.

The problem, itself, Wilbur Wright put in terms easily understandable:

The[1] person who merely watches the flight of a bird [supposes] the bird has nothing to think of but the flapping of its wings. [In fact] this is a very small part of its mental labor. To even mention all the things the bird must constantly keep in mind in order to fly securely would take a considerable part of the evening. If I take this piece of paper, and after placing it parallel with the ground, quickly let it fall, it will not settle

[1] Wilbur Wright, before the Western Society of Engineers, September 18, 1901.

steadily down as a staid, sensible piece of paper ought to do, but it insists on contravening every recognized rule of decorum, turning over and darting hither and thither in the most erratic manner, much after the style of an untrained horse. Yet this is the style of steed that men must learn to manage. Now, there are two ways of learning how to ride a fractious horse: One is to get on him and learn by actual practice how each motion and trick may be best met; the other is to sit on a fence and watch the beast a while, and then retire to the house and at leisure figure out the best way of overcoming his jumps and kicks. The latter system is the safer, but the former, on the whole, turns out the larger proportion of good riders. It is very much the same in learning to ride[1] a flying-machine; if you are looking for perfect safety, you will do well to sit on a fence and watch the birds; but if you really wish to learn, you must mount a machine and become acquainted with its tricks by actual trial.

In scientific terms, the problem of remaining safely afloat in the air consists in causing the centre of gravity to coincide with the centre of pressure. But in actual practice, as Wilbur Wright put it, there is "an almost boundless incompatibility of temper which prevents their remaining peaceably together for a single instant, so that the operator, who in this case acts as peacemaker, often suffers injury to himself while attempting to bring them together."

While the Wrights were pondering over this problem, in 1899, it happened that one evening Orville went with his sister to the home of some friends, Wilbur remaining at

---

[1] The achievement of the Wrights is usually described as the invention of the airplane; a separate achievement, equally important, was their learning the physical art of flying. Senator Hiram Bingham, himself an aviator, having read the proofs of this chapter, wrote me, February 2, 1927:

"Had any one been able to construct a 'Spad' or a Sopwith 'Snipe,' which you will remember were two of the best military planes flying over the front at the end of the War — had any one been able to build such a machine from his scientific knowledge and inventive genius, and constructed such a plane in all its perfection, and if this had been the first plane ever built, no one would have been able to fly it. No one ever learned to fly first on an advanced type of plane. Whoever would have been foolhardy enough to have attempted such a flight would have been killed."

the shop. Business was slack and Wilbur to pass the time idly picked up an empty cardboard box which had been left on the counter by a customer who had bought an inner-tube for his bicycle. This box was oblong in shape and not dissimilar in outline to the bi-plane glider the brothers were planning to build. Wilbur noticed he could twist the box between his hands, distorting its surfaces. Holding it before him, he observed that with slight exertion he could warp it so that simultaneously the surface on the right side forward had a downward inclination, and that on the left side forward an upward inclination. The idea occurred to him, could not the surfaces of a glider be warped in the same manner, thus achieving a method for lateral balancing based on the application of varying vertical wind pressures on either wing as desired ? Keeping on an even keel had been the problem that had defeated all previous experimenters. It was the greatest of all the problems to be solved before man could fly. Did the twisted tire-box give the clue to its solution ? [1]

When Orville returned he found Wilbur sketching a system for warping the glider wings in the manner suggested by the tire-box. The idea was explained to Orville; he thought it good; and a discussion began which lasted until far into the night.

---

[1] The reader can easily visualize that twisted carton. He can easily understand Wilbur Wright's description of the problem of aviation in terms of a bird flying. He can grasp the statement of it in terms of centre of gravity and centre of pressure, but he may have difficulty in deciphering the achievement when it is tortured into terminology satisfactory to the tautological exactions of the Patent Office:

". . . to move the forward corner of the lateral edges of the aeroplane on one side of the machine either above or below the normal planes of the aeroplanes, a reverse movement of the forward corners of the lateral margins on the other side of the machine occurring simultaneously. During this operation each aeroplane is twisted or distorted around a line extending centrally across the same from the middle of one lateral margin to the middle of the other lateral margin, the twist due to the moving of the lateral margins to different angles extending across each aeroplane from side to side, so that each aeroplane-surface is given a helicoidal warp or twist. . . ."

And so on, for several hundred words of Patent Office circumlocution.

That forgotten evening in a humdrum bicycle shop in a quiet Dayton street, when two earnest men became excited over a twisted cardboard box, marks, more than any other event, the moment when the secret of flight was discovered. It is a mile-stone in history, aviation's equivalent to Newton's observation of the falling apple.[1]

Up to now (1899) the brothers had spent little money except for books. Many a time they would have liked to build a glider in order to settle a disputed point by actual experiment, but always they had had to consider cost: to build any sort of glider and experiment with it meant an expensive trip to some other locality, because at Dayton the terrain was too level and the winds too light.

With the wing-warping idea that had come to them from the carboard box, the Wrights again felt the urge to build a glider to test out the new principle. But again, as before, caution, and the meagreness of their resources, prevailed over enthusiasm. They contented themselves with building a model having hinged joints, pulleys, and controlling wires, with which they clarified and modified their cardboard-box inspiration.

A year later, in the summer of 1900, they built their first large glider, incorporating in it the best ideas that had come from their years of reading and discussing, including their own wing-warping principle. (It was made

---

[1] Orville Wright, who has read the proofs of this chapter, believes that too much stress "is laid upon the importance of the discovery of our particular mechanical device for setting the wings at different angles of incidence to secure lateral balance." He wrote: "This furnishes an episode dramatic beyond its importance. It was one of our few discoveries made purely by accident of observation rather than as a result of study. It was not the revelation of a basic principle—it was merely a better mechanical embodiment of a basic principle which we had already discussed for several months. The basic idea was the adjustment of the wings on the right and left sides to different angles so as to secure different lifts on the opposite wings. Our first design embodying this idea was structurally weak. The incident which you describe was the discovery of a stronger mechanical structure. This basic idea is used in all airplanes today, but this mechanical device on which you lay so much stress has been used but little by others."

of light, strong wood, the wings covered with tough muslin, of the brand known as "Pride of the West.") For vertical control, it had projecting a few feet in front a small horizontal plane which could be moved up or down at will.

While the glider was taking shape in their hands, the Wrights wrote to the Weather Bureau at Washington, asking where in the United States they could find the best conditions for gliding experiments; that is, a combination of hilly country with fairly constant winds of rather high velocity. They did not say in their specifications that the hills should be of such a material as to do the minimum of damage to a falling structure of wood and cloth or to a falling man; but doubtless they were pleased when their correspondence with the Weather Bureau, and later with a North Carolina postmaster, resulted in the suggestion of Kitty Hawk, a region of rolling hills, but hills made of sand, dunes built up by the strong winds blowing steadily from the sea.

To Kitty Hawk the brothers went in September of 1900, the journey occupying a week's time. To their dismay they found that at that season the winds did not blow strongly enough to support a glider with a man aboard. Characteristically making the best of the means at hand, they flew the glider as a kite, manipulating the controls from the ground.

That first season at Kitty Hawk (1900) was disappointing. The hours and hours of practice they had hoped to obtain finally dwindled down to about two minutes. But they acquired one assurance. While their new wing-warping device for lateral stability did not solve the problem completely, it nevertheless worked sufficiently well to give them reason to believe that with modification it would do what they hoped.

This encouragement, however, was more than balanced

by a distrust that began to undermine their confidence in the mathematical tables on which they had based their calculations of wind-pressures and "drift." These tables had been worked out by others before the Wrights became interested in aviation; on their accuracy depended all progress that could be achieved by anybody. According to the Lilienthal tables, then regarded as the best — they had been tested and accepted by Langley[1] — the Wright glider, having an area of 165 square feet, should have been supported in the air at an angle of 3 degrees to the horizontal in a wind blowing 21 miles an hour; actually its angle was nearer 20 degrees.

The Wrights, returning to the bicycle shop at Dayton,[2] built another glider corresponding in wing camber exactly to that used by Lilienthal in the experiments from which he derived his tables, and a year later, in the fall of 1901, went again to Kitty Hawk.

This glider, like the first, did not behave as it should have if the Lilienthal tables were correct. After being launched, it would "nose" down to earth and could be kept in flight only by setting the elevation rudder at the extreme upward angle. It was clear the mathematical tables — the calculations upon which all progress in aviation rested — were faulty.

The Wrights returned to Dayton utterly discouraged, especially Wilbur. "Nobody will fly," he said, "for a thousand years" — an extreme of pessimism out of which

---

[1] Orville Wright wrote me March 14, 1927:

"Wilbur and I always held Langley in high respect—which respect we continued to hold after the discovery of the inaccuracies in his work in aerodynamics. For one of his standing in the scientific world to allow his name to be associated with an art held in utter disrepute by the scientific world, showed a courage and firmness of character much to be admired. He risked an established reputation, when even success could have added but little lustre to it."

[2] The Wrights gave their first glider to Captain and Mrs. Tate, at whose home they had stopped on arriving at Kitty Hawk, and Mrs. Tate used the fabric of the wings to make dresses for her two young children.

the family laughed him to the extent of reducing his estimate to fifty years.

"We saw," the brothers wrote later,[1] "that the calculations upon which all flying-machines had been based
were unreliable, and that all were simply groping in the
dark. Having set out with absolute faith in the existing
scientific data, we were driven to doubt one thing after
another, till finally, after two years of experiment, we cast
it all aside. . . . Truth and error were everywhere so
intimately mixed as to be undistinguishable."

Here were two men who had left high school at seventeen, who had had little experience in the theory of mathematics, who for six years had relied on Lilienthal's tables
of pressures and "drift" and head resistances as they had
relied on the multiplication table. What faced them now
was no less than the job of working out new tables —
doing the scientific part of aviation from the ground up.
The task was one for trained mathematicians — indeed
trained mathematicians had already done it, and done it
wrong.

The job would not have dismayed them too much, had
they not been obliged to take their personal circumstances
into account. Up to this time they had regarded their
experimenting as a diversion; now it began to be a serious
matter. Further progress was highly problematical and
could only be attained by experimenting on an ambitious
scale. For their expenses they had to rely on the bicycle
business. To continue their experiments on the scale now
necessary meant a greater drain on their resources, at all
times scanty. It meant also their absence from Dayton
for months on end, during which their business must
suffer.[2] The Wrights came very near dropping aviation
after they returned from Kitty Hawk in 1901.

[1] A joint article in *The Century Magazine*, September, 1908.

[2] "It was not the cost in money that embarrassed us—our laboratory experiments were inexpensive—it was the cost in time. We found this scientific re-

But they were, as Mouillard put it, in the web of "a domineering, tyrant thought . . . impossible to cast off." There was a quality in the spirit of the Wrights that made them susceptible to that kind of tyrant.

In the winter of 1901-1902, in their Dayton shop, they built an ingenious wind-tunnel, designed to give results free from the errors in measurements and calculations of their predecessors. Under the necessity of learning the mathematical part of aviation from the rudiments up, they made preliminary measurements of many different-shaped surfaces, and, later, systematic measurements of standard surfaces, so varied in design as to bring out the underlying causes of differences in pressures.

By the fall of 1902 they had tables of their own making. Again they went to Kitty Hawk, and now, for the first time, the glider performed according to calculations. In September and October (1902) nearly 1000 flights were made, several covering distances of over 600 feet. Some, made against a wind of 36 miles an hour, proved the effectiveness of the new device for control.

The Wrights had now reached substantially the end of the glider phase of their progress. They had carried out the programme they had laid out years before, to learn to fly by getting on a glider and flying. In the course of that, they had of necessity done what they had never anticipated being obliged to do, had dismissed the entire accumulation of scientific data, had explored the scientific basis of aviation from the ground up, and had written it anew. They had found by scientific experiments what elements were needed to give a glider the maximum of lifting power and how to manœuvre it in flight. They had learned —

search so interesting that we gave to it not only our leisure time in the evenings, but too much of our time in the day, to the neglect of our business."—Orville Wright, in a letter to the author, 1927.

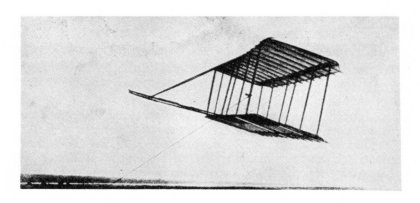

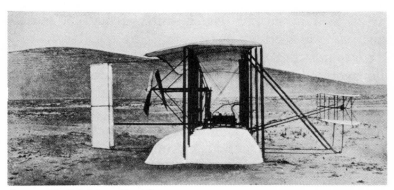

The first Wright glider, being flown as a kite, Kitty Hawk, North Carolina, 1900.

One of the later Wright gliders in flight.

The Wright airplane that made the first flight in history, December 17, 1903.

and this was most important — the personal, physical art of flying, what to do in the air as a swimmer learns what to do in water. The physical agility they had acquired was described by a witness:

Something went amiss. The glider wavered, stopped, and plunged downward. As she struck the ground a round ball of hands, arms, and legs rolled along the sand. Then the ball unwound itself and Orville Wright, arising, put a handkerchief to his badly scratched face and walked slowly back to appraise the damage. Later on there were more accidents, more sandpapering of the Wright chin. Once the glider turned turtle, and on numerous occasions it darted downward when it was supposed to soar aloft. Whatever the occasion, you could look for one thing: In case of accident a round ball would roll neatly along the ground and when it stopped Orville Wright would stand up, scratched and bruised, but always calm, dignified, and unemotional.

That the Wrights, in their joint study and experiment, accomplished more than the aggregate of all their predecessors, is accounted for chiefly by a factor in their association which is so unique, so distant from anything with which the average man is familiar, that one cannot assume it will dawn upon the reader unless attention is called to it.

It was not that the Wrights, being two, had an advantage over lone workers. That, to be sure, was a contributing element in their success. Other men working alone had learned some of the secrets of flight, but their knowledge had been snuffed out when, as frequently happened, they succumbed to the risks that are inseparable from experimentation. Had one of the Wrights been killed, there would have been no loss to the sum of the world's knowledge of flight; the surviving brother could have carried on with at least a chance to succeed.

Nor was the sentimental aspect of the brothers' relations of fundamental importance in their success. Their affection for each other did not differ from what is frequent between brother and brother and between close friends.

It was something else. Historians of aviation have sensed it but have not expressed it in words nor seen the importance it had. To put it as Griffith Brewer does is not enough:[1]

Only the wonderful combination of these two brothers who devoted their lives together for this common object . . . made the discovery of the art of flying possible.

That touches but does not bring out the unique element that had most to do with the Wrights' success. That was an intellectual kinship that grew up between them — more than a kinship, a twinship — more even than a twinship, a unity.

From early youth the Wrights had the same tastes, the same interests, the same likes and dislikes. They worked together, lived together, played together. A bond of this kind between brothers is usually dissolved at adolescence, by separation in high school or college, by marriage and the earning of a living. In the case of the Wrights it was never broken.

Always where one was found the other was not far away. Usually they were together, working silently or engaged in discussion. Strangers meeting Wilbur Wright spoke of him as taciturn. At a banquet in France, in 1908, on being urged to speak, he said that flying, not speech-making, was his business; he did not "wish to emulate the parrot, the bird that talks most and flies least." But Wilbur's reticence vanished when he was with Orville. Orville was a constant challenge to him, and he to Orville. Each felt the urge to express himself, to expound his views,

[1] Griffith Brewer, an English authority on aeronautics and close personal friend and associate of the Wrights, lecturing before the British Aeronautical Society, June 16, 1916.

to dissect the opinions of the other. When their discussions had to do with mechanical flight, all that was needed to start a three or four hour argument was for one brother to express an opinion or cite an authority. That was the signal for the other to take the other side. If the issue had to do with natural laws, out would come the books on physics and mathematics, the slide rules, the tables of logarithms.

Many who knew the Wrights, or observed them, commented on their propensity for argument. Griffith Brewer mentioned it in the lecture in which he described his first meeting with the brothers in France, in 1909:

It soon became obvious how suited they were to thrash out the many intricate problems which continually arose. Nothing was ever taken for granted until proved by themselves in actual practice. In the arguments, if one brother took one view, the other took the opposite as a matter of course, and the subject was thrashed to pieces until a mutually acceptable result remained.

Similar testimony is given by Colonel B. D. Foulois,[1] one of the United States Government representatives with the Wrights during the 1908 and 1909 tests of the machine bought by the Army, who said he had

never seen a more harmonious human working-unit. Orville was the more reflective. To him Wilbur would expound his theories and ideas. Orville would assort, discard, and both would argue. Although ideas perhaps coincided, they would nevertheless examine them, drop out some, and later pick up the ends and parts and reassociate them as though there had been no difference of opinion whatever. Both knew instinctively what parts contributed to gaining their ultimate end.

One can imagine what those never-ending debates extending over a lifetime did to two minds, both resourceful, both with high capacity to surround and digest facts, and

[1] Quoted by Oscar Cesare, New York *Times*, September 27, 1925.

both endowed with a rugged intellectual honesty that discountenanced the support of a contention for mere argument's sake. Never did a discussion drop from the intellectual to the emotional plane, disintegrate into mere

From a photograph by E. F. Bigelow.
Wilbur and Orville Wright, sitting on the rear porch of their Dayton home, in 1910.

squabbling. No matter with what intensity the brothers argued, they never resorted to unfair tactics or to ridicule. They had no liking for a victory not won on merits. Indeed, there was no question of victory between them, nor of advantage. The two, working toward decision, were as one man making up his mind.

From their constant association throughout more hours of the day than human beings are together ordinarily; from their continuing presence together under the same sets of circumstances, a curious phenomenon developed: the associative thinking of both came to be identical. Their trains of thought ran on parallel tracks and their automatic reactions became the same. Again and again it happened that, having spent an evening discussing a problem, they would appear at breakfast next morning with identical solutions. Frequently, when the brothers were near each other in the bicycle shop or elsewhere, both at the same moment would start singing the chorus of the same popular song; or, again, both would break a silence by uttering the same remark.[1] As the years went on and these coincidences became more frequent, the brothers' curiosity was stirred. After some characteristically impersonal analysis, they decided their lifelong association must have brought their minds into a state of synchronization, so that events occurring in their vicinity had identical reflexes in their minds and led to identical mental and physical reactions. Almost their minds became as one, and their muscles responded as to the same brain. In any emergency each brother knew just what the other would do. More accurately, they did not go through any process of "knowing." Each acted instinctively and automatically as if the other were himself. In a crisis, if Wilbur happened to be in the machine and Orville on the ground, Orville sensed instinctively what Wilbur would do to avert disaster; and Orville automatically applied the compensatory motion. On other occasions, the man on one side of the glider realized intuitively,

---

[1] Byron Newton, who got to know the brothers well in the years following his reporting of their flights at Kitty Hawk in May, 1908, writes me: "There was an amusing side to the plurality or oneness of their brotherly association. When asked to have a drink or cigar either one would answer: 'No, thank you, we don't drink.'"

without watching, what the man on the other side would do in any contingency. Indeed, not only did each know what would be the next action of the other; each could anticipate what the other would do several steps in advance. That was important, in the difficult business of men balancing themselves on big gliders in the wind, in the period when methods of control were not known, and were being explored.

This quality of the Wrights, in a curious way, ran counter to a law of matter, and enabled them to triumph over matter. Mathematical law affirms that the whole is equal to the sum of the parts; that one and one make two, and never more. But this particular union of the Wrights brought an element outside of and above calculations of quantity.

For two men to co-operate toward an intellectual end is not unusual; in modern research laboratories as many as a score of men work together toward a single invention. But the Wrights were not merely two workers. They were not two at all; they were parts of one; they were, in effect, one Wright raised to an nth power, which is a different thing and much greater.[1]

This twinship, multiplied, was the unique feature of the Wrights. Through it they invented the airplane, as neither of them alone would have. Through it they brought flight to the world at least a generation before it would have come but for them.

In 1903, the Wrights were ready for the final stage, the application of power to their glider, the construction of a

---

[1] Mrs. Katharine Wright Haskell, sister of Orville and Wilbur Wright, after reading the proofs of this chapter, wrote me: "My brothers grew into a rather unique relation that did truly mean one raised to the nth power. It was remarkable. I noticed instances of the kind you speak of over and over. And their voices were so alike that I was one day startled to hear Orville speaking over the telephone so like Will that it was hard to realize that Wilbur was gone." (Wilbur Wright died May 30, 1912.)

power-driven airplane. Little time was lost deciding the engine must be of the internal-combustion type, but when they applied to automobile manufacturers and other makers of gasoline engines, they found no one willing to contract to provide them with the sort of engine they re-

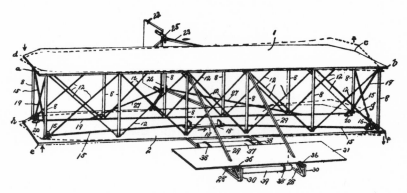

Orville and Wilbur Wright made their first patent application on March 23, 1903. This drawing, which accompanied their application, illustrated the working of the wing-warping device for lateral stability, and, together with the specifications which they prepared themselves, sufficiently answers the belittling phrase often applied to them—"just practical mechanics."

quired. Thrown on their own resources, they built the engine themselves.[1]

Building an engine gave them less trouble than building a propeller. The average man looks upon the propeller of an airplane as little more than a gracefully turned piece of wood. He thinks of it in terms of Heppelwhite carving. He does not realize that every line and curve represents not a wood artisan's sense of beauty, but the minutely

---

[1] That is one illustration of their resourcefulness. Some other experimenters had given as much time, care, and study to the engine as they had to all the other problems to be solved. (Building the engine for the Langley airplane bankrupted one manufacturer and the engine itself was the chief reason why, although work on the plane was begun in 1896, it was not ready for trial until 1903.) The Wrights knew from their calculations exactly how much power was needed to lift their machine into the air and how much weight could be carried in flight. For their purpose all that was needed was a rudely built engine of relatively small power in proportion to its weight. Their calculations in this, as in other details of their work, turned out in practice to be correct.

calculated resultant of almost infinitely intricate formulas, the product of days and weeks of study and labor by scientists, engineers, draftsmen, and skilled mechanics. Structurally, the propeller does not give the impression of great strength, yet it must live up to the strain of an engine having the energy in some cases of five hundred horses.

Of the original work that went into the first Wright propeller, the brothers wrote:[1]

Our tables made the designing of the wings an easy matter, and as screw-propellers are simply wings travelling in a spiral course, we anticipated no trouble from this source. We had thought of getting the theory of the screw-propeller from the marine engineers, and then, by applying our tables of air-pressures to their formulas, of designing air-propellers suitable for our purpose. But the marine engineers possessed only empirical formulas. It seemed necessary to obtain such a thorough understanding of the theory as would enable us to design it from calculations alone, a problem [which] became more complex the longer we studied it. With the machine moving forward, the air flying backward, the propellers turning sidewise, and nothing standing still, it seemed impossible to find a starting-point from which to trace the various simultaneous reactions. Contemplation of it was confusing. After long arguments we often found ourselves in the ludicrous position of each having been converted to the other's side, with no more agreement than when the discussion began. It was not till several months had passed that the various reactions began to untangle themselves. . . . Our first propellers, built entirely from calculation, gave in useful work 66 per cent of the power expended, about one-third more than had been secured by Maxim or Langley.

On Wednesday, September 23, 1903, the Wrights, with their glider, their engine, and their propellers, left Dayton for Kitty Hawk — their fourth trip. Arriving there, they began fitting their engine and propellers to their plane. They were ready on December 17, 1903. That was nine

[1] *The Century Magazine*, September, 1908.

days after Langley had made his final spectacular failure at Washington, and after the newspapers had flooded the country with the conviction of conclusive proof that human flight could not be.

Of what happened at Kill Devil Hill that day, there was a newspaper account in a local paper which a fair number of readers must have seen, but which practically none took in.

An employee of the business office of a paper in Norfolk, Virginia, the *Virginian-Pilot*, H. P. Moore, heard from a friend in the local railroad freight office that a barrel of oysters had been shipped from there to somebody named "Wright" at Kitty Hawk. Moore, coupling this with stories of a year before that two men named Wright had been flying a "box-shaped kite" at Kitty Hawk, scented a situation which he thought the news department of the paper should know about. He told the managing editor, Keville Glennan, and the two set in motion such leads as occurred to them. Among other things they took advantage of the friendly relations that alert newspapermen always maintain with telegraph operators, and found that a message had passed through Norfolk from Kitty Hawk to Bishop Wright[1] at Dayton, Ohio, which included the words, as Mr. Moore recalled them years later, "First successful flight to-day with motor. All well and happy."[2] Out of this and similar fragments, Moore and Glennan constructed the story that appeared in the Norfolk *Virginian-Pilot* on December 18, 1903. It bore a seven-column head, which fulfilled the function of attracting attention somewhat more successfully than it conformed to strict accuracy:

[1] Father of the Wright brothers.
[2] Mrs. Katharine Wright Haskell in 1927 recalled this message as reading: "Success. Four flights to-day. Longest 852 feet. 59 seconds. Home Christmas." "Certainly nothing about 'well and happy,'" she added.

FLYING MACHINE SOARS 3 MILES IN TEETH OF HIGH
WIND OVER SAND HILLS AND WAVES AT KITTY HAWK
ON CAROLINA COAST

NO BALLOON ATTACHED TO AID IT

The story underneath made up in picturesqueness what it lacked in statistical accuracy of detail, difficult to ac-

A historic newspaper article. Original account of the earliest human flight in all time. From the Norfolk, Va., *Virginian-Pilot*, Dec. 18, 1903.

quire late at night at a point 68 miles from the scene. One regrets that even with the spread that knowledge of airplanes had reached in 1927, some of the public will fail to find in this narrative some of the particular kinds of interest that all aviators assuredly will:

The problem of aerial navigation without the use of a balloon has been solved. *The Virginian-Pilot* is able to state authoritatively the nature of [the] invention, its principle, and its chief dimensions. . . . Wilber [sic] Wright, the chief inventor, sat in the operator's car. The big box began to move slowly at first. The machine slowly began to go higher and higher until finally it soared sixty feet above the ground. Maintaining this height by the action of the underwheel, the forward speed of the huge affair increased until a velocity of eight miles an hour was attained.

Steadily it pursued its way, first tacking to port,[1] then to starboard, and then driving straight ahead. "It is a success," declared Orville Wright to the crowd on the beach after the first mile had been covered. But the inventor waited. Not until he had accomplished three miles,[2] putting the machine through all sorts of manœuvres en route, was he satisfied. Then he selected a suitable place to land, and, gracefully circling, drew his invention slowly to the earth, where it settled, like some big bird, in the chosen spot.

"Eureka," he cried, as did the alchemist of old.[3]

Of this account, printed in the local Norfolk *Virginian-Pilot*, condensed versions were sent by its authors to newspapers in New York and some other cities. Such metropolitan papers as printed[4] it at all, did so inconspicuously. Its atmosphere of unreality, the palpable evidence that it was a second-hand account by some one who had not seen what he described, caused managing editors to classify it not as first-page news, but as fifth-page fantasy of the sort they were accustomed to receive from out-of-the-way spots. Possibly also managing editors may have been moved by a realization, or more probably unconsciously influenced by the fact, that for them the situation presented difficulties; newspapers which on December 9, 1903, the day after Langley's failure, had told the world that aviation was not, and could not be — could not consistently explain on December 18 that aviation was.

For an account of the first flight ever made by man in a power-driven plane, more technical if less picturesque

---

[1] A nautical vocabulary was natural to Norfolk reporters.

[2] The longest of the four flights made that day was actually 852 feet, less than a quarter of a mile. The degree of discrepancy, about 1700 per cent, is not far from the average under similar stimuli to reportorial imagination.

[3] Among the early experiences recalled to Orville Wright, in 1927, in the course of reading the proofs of this chapter, none brought livelier fun than the calling back of this first newspaper story of his achievement. Of all the men in the world, about the last to cry "Eureka!" would have been Wilbur Wright.

[4] Moore recalled, in 1926, that they "raked down" $170 for their night's work.

than the one in the Norfolk *Virginian-Pilot*, we may turn
to Orville Wright himself:[1]

During the night of December 16, 1903, a strong cold wind
blew from the north. When we arose on the morning of the
17th, the puddles of water, which had been standing about camp
since the recent rains, were covered with ice. The wind had a
velocity of 22 to 27 miles an hour. We thought it would die
down before long, but when ten o'clock arrived, and the wind
was as brisk as ever, we decided that we had better get the
machine out. . . .

Wilbur, having used his turn in the unsuccessful attempt on
the 14th, the right to the first trial now belonged to me. Wilbur
ran at the side, holding the wing to balance it on the track. The
machine, facing a 27-mile wind, started very slowly. Wilbur
was able to stay with it till it lifted from the track after a
forty-foot run.

The course of the flight up and down was exceedingly erratic. The control of the front rudder was difficult. As a
result the machine would rise suddenly to about ten feet, and
then as suddenly dart for the ground. A sudden dart when
a little over 120 feet from the point at which it rose into the air,
ended the flight. This flight lasted only 12 seconds, but it was
nevertheless the first in the history of the world in which a machine carrying a man had raised itself by its own power into the
air in full flight, had sailed forward without reduction of speed,
and had finally landed at a point as high as that from which it
started.

Wilbur started the fourth and last flight at just 12 o'clock.
The first few hundred feet were up and down as before, but by
the time three hundred feet had been covered, the machine
was under much better control. The course for the next four
or five hundred feet had but little undulation. However, when
out about eight hundred feet the machine began pitching again,
and, in one of its darts downward, struck the ground. The
distance over the ground was measured and found to be 852
feet; the time of the flight 59 seconds.

The Wright brothers dismantled their machine, packed
it in "two boxes and a barrel," and returned to Dayton.
They had invented the flying-machine indisputably.
Otherwise their fortunes were such as to give them the

---

[1] "How We Made the First Flight," an article in *Flying*, December, 1913.

concern familiar to inventors. Their bicycle business had become less remunerative — bicycle shops, like livery stables, were beginning to feel the presence of curious new establishments which the public was learning to call "garages."

To raise funds to develop their invention, the Wrights sold a farm in Iowa that had been given them by their father. Since, with their power plane, they no longer needed the strong winds and steep dunes of Kitty Hawk to assist them in getting off the ground, they secured permission to conduct their experiments in an unused field belonging to Torrence Huffman eight miles out of Dayton. Putting up a crude shack to serve as workshop and hangar, they set to work gaining practice in controlling the machine in straight flights and in learning how to guide it to right and left.

This latter, on its face, seems simple, but the brothers found it otherwise. Projecting to the rear of the airplane was a vertical rudder, and seemingly all that was necessary to change the direction of flight was to deflect this rudder to one side or the other. But doing this had the effect of causing the machine to fall into a dangerous side slip. With inexhaustible patience the brothers studied and experimented, risking their lives every time the machine left the ground, and finally settled upon a method of turning copied after the flight of birds. By means of wires and guides the vertical rudder was connected to the lever which controlled the warping of the wings. A thrust on the lever then caused the wings to warp and the rudder to deflect simultaneously.

Thereafter the Wrights, within one week during the fall of 1904, were able to make two more landmarks. On September 15 Orville made the first turn in the air and on September 20 Wilbur made the first complete circle.

A year later they achieved another landmark when, on

October 4, 1905, Orville Wright made the first of several flights lasting over half an hour.[1]

News of these half-hour flights filtered through scientific and Army channels to France, where an almost hysterical interest in aviation had sprung up. The French could not believe the reports of the Wright flights. A member of the French Aero Club, Captain Ferber, wrote to the brothers for corroboration. When it was given to him he replied saying there "was not a man in all France who believed they had done what they claimed." The Frenchmen appealed to F. S. Lahm, an American living in Paris, to find out the truth about the Wrights. Lahm cabled to his brother-in-law, Henry M. Weaver, in Chicago, December[1], 1905:

> Verify what Wright brothers claim, necessary go Dayton, prompt response cable.

Weaver went to Dayton, saw Orville Wright, and, on December 6, 1905, wrote to Lahm in France:

> Mr. D. Beard lives across the Springfield road from the experimental field, and to him Mr. Wright took me first. I found him an intelligent man of about 60. He told me of the work which had gone on under his eye for so long a time, and assured me absolutely there was no question as to the flights. He had often observed them, and particularly knew of the series ending October 5th of this year. We next called on Farmer Stauffer, living half a mile farther up the road. He was a typical American farmer, with jolly face, and voluble. He rents the farm which includes the field where the flights were made. On October 5th he was cutting corn in the next field east, which is higher ground. When he noticed the aero-

[1] The dates, distances, and other details of the 1905 flights were as follows:

Date	Distance	Time	Cause of Stopping	Pilot
Sept. 26	11⅛ miles	18 m. 9 s.	Exhaustion of fuel	W. W.
Sept. 29	12 miles	19 m. 55 s.	Exhaustion of fuel	O. W.
Sept. 30	....	17 m. 15 s.	Hot bearing	O. W.
Oct. 3	15¼ miles	25 m. 5 s.	Hot bearing	O. W.
Oct. 4	20¾ miles	33 m. 17 s.	Hot bearing	O. W.
Oct. 5	24⅛ miles	38 m. 3 s.	Exhaustion of fuel	W. W.

plane had started on its flight he remarked to his helper: "Well, the boys are at it again," and kept on cutting corn, at the same time keeping an eye on the great white form rushing about its course. "I just kept on shocking corn," he continued, "until I got down to the fence, and the durned thing was still going round. I thought it never would stop."

Weaver's letter, read at a meeting of the French Aero Club, caused almost a riot among the members.

IV

The World Refuses to Believe

The Wrights had flown, again and again; had remained in the air as much as thirty-eight minutes and covered as great a distance as twenty-four miles. But the world did not know it, refused to believe anybody who said it had happened, and remained unaware of it until more than four years after the first flight occurred.

The explanation lay partly in the circumstances of the Wrights' flights: the lack of publicity about their experiments, the absence of reporters when their flights were made, the fact that just before their first flight the world had been flooded with accounts of the spectacular failure of Langley; the fact that newspapers which, on December 8, 1903, had described Langley's failure as proof of the impossibility of flight, could not readily eight days later convince the world if they tried, nor even themselves, that human flight had actually taken place.

But to a much greater extent, the explanation lay in the fixed state of mind of the average man about aviation — an incredulity so great that to resurrect it now, after it has so completely gone, to recreate for the reader of to-day the attitude of the average man prior to 1908, is one of the major difficulties of the writing of this history.

So firmly embedded in man's deepest consciousness was his conviction of the impossibility of human flight, that hardly any printed account could convince him it had actually been accomplished. The experience of believing had to wait, for each man, until he actually looked up with his own eyes and saw an airplane flying. Only then did he get the sensation of conviction, the thrill. It is a reasonable summary of historical fact to say that man in the mass never took in the accomplishment of human flight. The experience of awareness came to men one by one, to each as he saw it for himself.[1] Men did not merely say, just as an expression of truculent doubt: "I will believe it when I see it." Such a mood would have seemed to concede that flight might be possible, that there might be differences of opinion about it, and legitimate debate. And the actual mood was that for man to fly in the air was as inconceivable as for water to run up-hill. Indeed, a simile that had become firmly embedded in the common speech, which expressed the apotheosis of impossibility, was to say of a man who projected some action: "He can no more do that than he can fly." The impossibility of flight was looked upon as one of the fixed and eternal facts of nature, like gravity and the succession of the seasons. The non-existence of flight was in the same category as the existence of God.

It seems reasonable to suppose that man took on this negative conviction, that he could not fly, very early in the

[1] In this view, Orville Wright agrees. In 1925 he wrote me:
"You ask why it was that the public took so little notice of our 1903 flights and not until 1908 awoke to the fact that human flight had actually been accomplished. I think this was mainly due to the fact that human flight was generally looked upon as an impossibility, and that scarcely any one believed in it until he actually saw it with his own eyes. Only a few, probably less than a dozen, saw the first flights, of 1903. In 1904 and 1905 the number of witnesses was increased to a hundred or two; in 1908, to thousands. Hundreds of people have told me that they saw the first real demonstration of mechanical flight. But as hardly any two of these had seen the same flight, I have come to the conclusion that almost no one ever really believed who had not himself actually seen a flight. It amuses me that practically every one now thinks he has always believed in its possibility and that many think that before 1903 they had predicted its early accomplishment! At the time, we couldn't find a half-dozen such. This inability to believe without seeing probably accounts for the slowness of the general public to become interested, and also for the fact that to-day, after twenty years have passed to dull the edge of the novelty of it, the interest in aviation is greater than it ever has been before."

race's history — almost as early as he took on the positive
conviction that he could walk. One can visualize the
experiences through which the acceptance of the limitation was forced upon him. The occasions must have been
frequent with primitive man when he wished himself
away from where he was, quickly. Countless times a hairy,
skin-clad progenitor of civilized man, running at top
speed from the claws of a wild beast or the war clubs of a
marauding tribe, must have wished his next frantic leap
would carry him into the air. The power to fly must have
seemed to him the sure escape from whatever menaced
him — merely to run must have been a reluctantly
accepted compromise between his need for escape and his
means for it. Whenever he was threatened by danger, by
pestilence or famine; whenever his course was blocked by
mountain, desert, or stream, he must have thought of
flight as the most desired of powers. He must have given
much time to thoughtful longing for something that
should be the equivalent of wings, before he turned to
devising a cart, or constructing a raft, or training an
animal to bear him on its back. These must have seemed
half-way substitutes, sadly incomplete in their sufficiency
to man's need; must have come only with the accompaniment of permanent acceptance that flight could not
be. Neanderthals sunning themselves at their cave-
mouths, and, at a later stage, shepherds on the hillsides,
must have gazed at the eagles winging their secure ways
and wondered why other creatures had a power that man
lacked. That sort of speculation, long pursued by many
men, must have been, in the aggregate, one of the greatest of man's contemplations.

Man, having first thought of flight as a practicable
reality, having experienced a myriad of impulses to attempt it, and having always failed — man then took on
failure as a mental habit, accepted impossibility as the

true reality. He took flight, first, out of the category
of the practicable; then out of the category of aspiration.
Finally he placed it in the category of the permanently
impossible — about the only other impossibility ranking
with it was eternal youth. Man put the negation of the
possibility of flight at the very bottom of his store of
certainties, along with his other earliest realities like the
sun and the seasons. Thereafter, his chief use of the idea
came to be as a figure of speech to picture the utterly unattainable. "Oh, had I the wings of a dove!" meant, not
the expression of a longing, but the typical expression of
an unescapable despair, the most vivid imaginable picture
of the cannot-be.

Having put the impossibility among his permanent
realities, he put the possibility among his permanent
fantasies. For man to have the equivalent of wings
came to be the chief of his fancies, the most familiar of
the mental toys with which his imagination played. He
wove fairy-stories about it, made it the base of a myth
about a magic carpet, associated it with miracles. He
came to use it as the symbol of escape, both from physical
danger or distress and from spiritual sorrow; made it
the first of his wishes for the supernatural, the means of
attaining the most desired of conditions. When he thought
of Heaven, he located it where it could only be reached by
flight. When he peopled Paradise with angels, the one
physical characteristic with which he marked them off
from himself was wings.

Now, in the early years of the twentieth century, man
was asked to transfer flight from his fantasies to his
realities. The suggestion that he uproot this from his
oldest stock of immutabilities — that he believe flight
is — was as disconcerting as to ask him to believe that
death is not.

A person blind from birth, who has accepted blindness

as a permanent state, who has built about himself a
world in which blindness is a basic condition, and to
whom, in his maturity, sight has come — that is the
classic example of surprise to the human mind. The
experience of a world which had accepted the impossibility of flight, and now saw flight, was not dissimilar.

Awareness by the world that human flight had actually
been accomplished did not come until 1908, when the
Wrights again went to Kitty Hawk for another series of
flights.

v

The World Becomes Aware

In the wide-spread web which collects news where it
happens, and the intricate mechanism that delivers it to
the reader in his paper, there is a figure, called, in the terminology of the craft, a "string" man, a query man.[1]

The string man is the farthest outpost of the organization. He operates in the outer fringes of the net where
news does not happen with regularity or certainty, in little
towns where employment of a salaried correspondent is
not justified, in out-of-the-way corners of the world, remote mining camps, lighthouse stations on the coast —
places where months may pass without anything of news
value developing, but where news, when it does "break,"
may have potentialities of high importance. To take care
of such events, it is the custom of the great newspapers
and news-gathering agencies to maintain a relation with
some local man, whose duty it is to send them promptly
a brief skeleton dispatch about any occurrence which in
his judgment calls for attention from headquarters, and to
"query" whether they want further details.

---

[1] So called because he cuts from the newspaper the items he has contributed,
pastes them on a long strip of paper similar to a newspaper column, and is paid
according to the length of his "string." Some string men cover local events.

The string man is an interest-provoking figure, one of the free lances of his world. He is apt to be adventurous by temperament, preferring chance rather than steadiness of work and income, deliberately following a career in which the opportunities are uncertain and not anticipatable. He is kin to the prospector who "wild-cats" for minerals where minerals have never been found. He belongs to the glamorous tribe of chance-takers, pioneers, soldiers of fortune — spirits whose lives are not shadowed by the gray walls of a rut; whose adventures, when portrayed on the stage or in a novel, charm with their romance.

In the year 1908, one of these lone sentinels of the press, D. Bruce Salley, covered a beat beginning at Norfolk, Virginia, and stretching south for a hundred miles along the deeply indented coast-line of Virginia and North Carolina. Salley had a roving assignment from the Norfolk *Landmark* to wander up and down this lonely region of drifting sand-dunes in quest of maritime news; and in addition had the usual query man's relation to outside newspapers, including the New York *Herald*, to which he sent dispatches dealing with shipwrecks and other local events having sufficient national importance to justify the attention of the metropolitan press.

From Salley, on the evening of May 6, 1908, about the hour when the Broadway theatres were filling and the staffs of the New York papers were gathering for their work, came a telegram saying that at Kitty Hawk, North Carolina, two brothers named Wright had flown almost a thousand feet at a height sixty feet above the ground in a flying-machine without a balloon attachment.

To the managing editors, whose function it is to pass instant judgment upon the probable news value of the query man's information, to determine how much weight shall be given to it, and to decide whether it is sufficiently important to call for subsequent treatment by reporters dispatched from the home office — to them, the reports from North Carolina presented a problem serious and delicate.[1]

Aviation, to managing editors, was vexation. Hardly a week passed without its report or "tip" about an inventor, usually in some remote part of the world, who had a wonderful new idea for overcoming gravitation, or who had built, or was going to build, a machine that would fly. As none of these stories, so far as the managing editors knew, had ever been convincingly substantiated; as, indeed, scores of them when run down had turned out to be hoaxes, or attempts to deceive, or the impractical dreams of irresponsible visionaries, the whole subject of aviation had fallen into the category called, by the editor of the Cleveland *Leader* who had received one of Salley's queries, "wild-cat stuff." [2] From Europe,[3] during two years prior to 1908, had come accounts of some short airplane flights, but American editors had not regarded them as convincing. Rumors had come to the newspaper offices about the flights already made by the Wrights, but the editors had not credited them. Altogether, the mood of American managing editors was one of extreme scepticism.

To managing editors walking their careful tight-rope between not being misled by irresponsible rumors, and not missing authentic news, the reports from North Caro-

---

[1] There is no dispute that it was Salley who sent out the first eye-witness dispatch describing the 1908 flights. Editors of papers other than those which Salley served picked up the news instantly, and had to settle the same quandary — what to do about it.

[2] The Cleveland paper, indignant at Salley's dispatch, refused to pay the telegraph tolls on it, and sent him a sharp message to "cut out the wild-cat stuff," to which Salley replied: "Am not in habit of filing such matter; good story to-day; Wrights make new records."

[3] November 12, 1906, Santos-Dumont, a Brazilian living in Paris, remained in the air twenty-one seconds. October 26, 1907, Henry Farman remained in the air fifty-two seconds at Paris.

lina presented one more opportunity to be damned if they did and damned if they didn't. Should they print the story without first verifying it, their reward might be unbelief and ridicule. On the other hand, they had to consider the possibility that Salley might be right, in which event, if they should let pass the opportunity to treat the report with the conspicuousness it deserved, their position would be even more unhappy.

These editorial dubieties lasted less time than it takes to tell them. The decision reached was midway between caution and daring, closer to the former than to the latter. One can read the editors' mood in the yellowed pages of the New York *Herald* for May 7, 1908. Salley's flying-machine story is on the first page, but not at the top of a column. It occupies a position less prominent than two other dispatches — "Republicans to Push Currency Bill" and "Deposed Emperor of Korea to Be Exiled to Japan." In head-lines it is on a parity with three other front-page stories: one about a retired sea-captain who "possesses a formula by which one may live a hundred years"; one about Andrew Carnegie giving $200,000 to the General Society of Mechanics and Tradesmen, and one bearing the caption: "Negro Beats and Robs Aged Couple."

This cautious restraint in the printing of Salley's dispatch was one side of the policy usual with newspapers in such cases; the other side was the prompt dispatching of one of *The Herald's* own staff correspondents, Byron R. Newton, to the scene. On the way south Newton was joined by William Hoster, of the New York *American*, Arthur Ruhl, of *Collier's Weekly*, James H. Hare, a news photographer for *Collier's*, and a representative of the London *Daily Mail*, which, in the ownership of Lord Northcliffe, was paying close attention to aviation.

These correspondents two days later descended upon

Salley in somewhat the mood of generals summoned from the comforts of staff headquarters by an outlying sentinel with information he deems important. If the sentinel's report proves correct, he will be given approval touched with condescension; otherwise he will hear extremely unpleasant remarks about his credulity, veracity, sobriety, and other traits of intelligence and character.

The New York correspondents found Salley confidently exultant. He had stumbled on his scoop, he said, while out prospecting for maritime news, through some life-savers who had told him they were helping the Wrights. Believing that the brothers objected to visitors, Salley had not gone near their camp but had watched them through field glasses while perched in a tree some distance away. Twice each day, he said, he had seen the Wrights, assisted by life-savers, start the machine down a runway on the ocean side of Kill Devil Hill, largest of the dunes. On gaining momentum the machine would rise into the air, sometimes to a height of fifty or sixty feet, and after circling about would settle gently back to earth.

One of the New York correspondents, writing of it later, said that Salley's story sounded like a not very plausible bit of romancing. He asked Salley if the Wrights flew on windy days.

"They do," Salley replied. "They went up the other day when the wind was blowing so hard it almost shook me out of my tree. I could hardly keep my glasses on them."

The correspondent of the New York *Herald*, Byron R. Newton, whether moved by skepticism of his own about Salley's veracity, or by consciousness of the public's skepticism about the whole subject of flying, decided to practise safety first, by using in his early dispatches a phrase of disavowal, "according to Salley." His first story, filed shortly after his arrival and printed in *The Herald* May 9, read: "The aeroplane of the Wright brothers was flown almost at will over the sand dunes at Kill Devil Hill to-day . . . according to D. Bruce Salley, a spectator. He says . . . "

This dispatch was tucked away in an obscure corner of one of the inside pages of *The Herald* — clearly the editor was a skeptic. Next day, May 10, *The Herald* lapsed into silence, its first page devoted to Charles E. Hughes running for Governor of New York; President Roosevelt's young son, Quentin,[1] playing in a baseball game at Washington; Admiral Robley D. Evans, giving up command of the Atlantic Fleet; the New York police parade; a Korean insurrection against Japan; a sucide; and a divorce. May 11, *The Herald* was again silent, but on this day down among the sand dunes of North Carolina events were transpiring which would leave no room for further skepticism about human flight.

Of what happened at Kill Devil Hill, on May 11, 1908, there is an excellent description by *The Herald* correspondent, told in retrospect fifteen years later. Newton's occasional exuberance of language is safely within the proportions of the spur to the imagination that the event was.

The[2] assignment directed me to "get to Kill Devil Hill at any cost and tell the true story that will settle the question about the Wright brothers once and for all."

I covered the assignment. I got to Kill Devil Hill. I told the true story, but when that story went out to the world it was like a chapter of daring fiction.

To reach the Kill Devil country was a three days' journey.

[1] Youngest child of Theodore Roosevelt. Ten years later, July 17, 1918, he was killed while heading a combat flight of American airplanes over the German lines in France.

[2] Condensed and slightly paraphrased from an article in the New York *World*, December 16, 1923.

From Elizabeth City, N. C., we had to skirt the Dismal Swamp, and then by means of a one-lung motor-boat go down through Pamlico, Albemarle, and Roanoke Sounds, landing finally at the quaint little hamlet of Manteo, on Roanoke Island. There are few places in the United States so cut off from the modern world. In this little settlement the sound of a locomotive has never been heard. At that time automobiles were as unknown there as Noah's Ark.

First we sent out a scout to see if any arrangement could be made to observe the experiments openly. It was a tedious day's journey, and the scout returned reporting that immediately upon his appearance the Wrights had drawn their machine into the shed, locked the doors, and courteously but promptly escorted him to his boat, with the positive declaration that their experiments would not be seen by any human eye except their squad of assistants which included a few of the life-saving crew from Kitty Hawk station.[1] Therefore, it was a case of ambush and secret observation. Accordingly, we equipped ourselves with necessary supplies, food, water, blankets, etc., organized our little expedition of five men and started out the next morning.

Lying between the Atlantic and the chain of sounds, is a

[1] On this point, the secrecy alleged to have been practised by the Wright brothers, and the necessity of concealment by the correspondents, there is much disagreement of recollection. William E. Hoster, writing to the author March 5, 1927, agrees in large part with Newton's account, saying:

"We were compelled to make our headquarters in a little inn on Manteo Island and journey over every morning at daybreak in an open launch across Pamlico Sound, and then walk about ten miles over sand dunes to a small clump of trees half a mile from the Wright brothers, where we established our camp. A considerable portion of this ten miles had to be made on our hands and knees—otherwise we would have been visible to the Wright brothers. It was from this clump of bushes, lying flat on our stomachs and watching through field glasses, that we saw what turned out to be the first maintained flight. . . ."

Arthur Ruhl wrote the author, February 21, 1927:

"I don't recall any 'camp,' as Byron Newton's story describes it. We all went over from Manteo to the land side of the strip of land on which the Wrights were flying and walked through the woods and crept through the underbrush until we were within sight of them. I recall that two of us walked over and chatted with the Wrights after our first view of the flight. Either then or afterward they told me they had known from the life-savers that we had come over from Manteo, so that all our elaborate stealth was scarcely justified."

James H. Hare, in a letter, February 15, 1927, uses the phrase "we lay in ambush."

Orville Wright, in a letter to the author June 28, 1927, said:

"We had work to do and did not want to be bothered by newspaper men, but as to closing doors and escorting any one away, that is pure fiction. Salley came over to camp on May 5th according to our note-book."

narrow strip of land, from a half mile to several miles in width, one of the wildest and most inaccessible stretches on the continent. For the greater part it is covered by enormous sand dunes, constantly changing in form and oftentimes reaching an altitude of 300 feet, and frequently completely covering tall pines and whole sections of forest. Interspersed among the sand dunes are many ponds and patches of dense jungle, infested with wild cattle, hogs, and turkeys, and literally squirming with moccasins, rattlers, blacksnakes and an abundance of jiggers, mosquitoes, and other pestiferous things.[1] Under the cover of one of the jungle patches we made our camp. It was on the edge of the open sand field where the Wrights were operating and about a mile distant. From our hiding-place we could observe every movement through our glasses. For two days we remained in our hiding-place.

Over at the little camp of the Wrights there was constant activity. Each morning, long before sunrise, they had their machine out and continued tinkering at it till nightfall. Now and again the propellers would start and, feverishly, we watched them flashing in the gleaming sunlight, but the machine did not rise. The machine had no wheels, but was equipped with wooden skids, or runners, and received its initial momentum by being placed on a small truck which ran on a monorail until sufficient velocity was gained to leave the ground.

On the third morning our vigil had become very irksome. We were standing in a group debating whether we should

[1] The zoological details of this story of Newton's are questioned. One of Newton's companions, James H. Hare, the photographer, after reading the proofs of this chapter, wrote, with an apparent conviction of the superiority of the photographic mind to the literary one: "I fail to remember those 'herds of wild hogs and cattle, etc., etc.' that stampeded at sight of the terrifying monster. But then of course I have not the qualities of imagination to see the literary aspects of a story."

Another of the correspondents, Arthur Ruhl, wrote: "I don't recall any snakes, and the 'jungle' was simply sand, pines, and scrub. But there were plenty of ticks."

Yet another of the party, William E. Hoster, wrote: "Illustrating the perils undergone by the devoted representatives of the press in their self-sacrificing pursuit of the festive news item, I recall that our sole source of drinking water was a small stream which trickled through to the rear of our camp. I was on my knees lapping up some water, I think on the morning of the day when the flight was accomplished, when Newton let loose a yell, hurled me to one side, and when I had gotten to my feet again, I discovered that he had dispatched a big copperhead snake which had come up to share the water with me."

Residents of the vicinity of Kitty Hawk who have read the proofs of this chapter, especially A. W. Drinkwater, the telegraph operator who transmitted the stories, are emphatic in denying the number and malevolence of snakes and other unappreciated fauna in that neighborhood.

withdraw quietly to Manteo and denounce the Wrights as fakirs, or march militantly over to their camp and have the satisfaction of stating what we thought of them — and at that moment something happened.

At other times when the propellers were in motion, they had given forth a sound quite like the clacking of a grain reaper, but now we heard that sound increasing with a sharper stac-

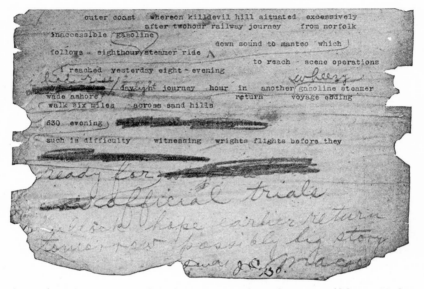

A page from the manuscript of the first newspaper dispatch sent out of Manteo, N. C., about the Wright brothers' flight of May 6, 1908.

cato, and as we looked we saw the machine glide swiftly along the monorail and across the white sand, saw men racing along by its side, heard their shouts and then we saw the machine rise majestically into the air, its white wings flashing and glistening in the morning sun. On it sped at an altitude about fifty feet from the ground. I have never experienced another moment with like sensations. It was like standing in the presence of some overpowering calamity. I recall the one utterance that escaped our lips; Jimmie Hare, in his richest Cockney flavor, merely said: "My Gawd!"[1]

[1] James Hare, always called "Jimmy," one of the pioneers of news photography, was for a generation among those present at about every spot in the world where important news was happening. His birthplace had given him a London accent which his sense of fun and his camaraderie led him to accentuate.

On sped the great white craft straight toward one of the high sand dunes. Then to our bewildering amazement we saw the wings on one side warping slightly, saw the operator pulling at the levers and the craft heeled over slightly, turned in a graceful curve and came straight toward where we were hiding. It passed almost directly over us, but so completely were we all absorbed that only two of us opened the shutters of our cameras, and it chanced to be my good fortune to make a good snap and to get the first photograph[1] of an airplane in actual flight.

No wonder that we were paralyzed and dumb with the wonder of it all. It was something that few mortals had believed to be within the scope of possibility. Again and again the machine wheeled about over our heads and as it came closer on the second circuit we were still further amazed to discover that two men were in it. They were Wilbur Wright and a mechanic.[2]

There was something weird, almost uncanny, about the whole thing. Here on this lonely beach was being performed the greatest act of the ages, but there were no spectators and no applause save the booming of the surf and the startled cries of the sea birds. Often, as the machine buzzed along above the sand plains, herds of wild hogs and cattle were frightened from their grazing grounds and scurried away for the jungle, where they would remain for hours looking timidly out from their hiding-places. Flocks of gulls and crows, screaming and chattering, darted and circled about the machine as if resentful of this unwelcome trespasser in their hitherto exclusive realm. There was something about the picture that appealed to one's poetic instincts — the desolation, the solitude, the dreary expanse of sand and ocean and in the centre of the melancholy picture two solitary men performing one of the world's greatest wonders.

For several hours the flights continued, but they were not of long duration. After circling about for a few minutes the machine would alight and men would come up and tinker about it for a time and then off again. Finally we saw the machine glide away behind one of the big sand mountains, heard the clatter of its propellers suddenly stop, saw the men running across the sand, but we knew no more than that. Then it was a race back to Manteo to get the big story out to the world and

---

[1] Mr. Newton is in error on this point. On page 583 is reproduced a photograph of the first flight the Wrights ever made.

[2] The mechanic's name, Orville Wright says, was Charles Furnas.

that was difficult,[1] indeed, because the only telegraphic communication between Roanoke Island and the mainland was a line maintained by the United States Weather Bureau. Another problem was to determine how to write the story. We knew that the flying-machine had made the speed of a fast rail-

Courtesy of the United States Signal Corps.

The first seaplane, "The Loon," being tried out by its constructor, Glenn Curtiss, in December, 1908. It was not until 1911 that the pontoon attachment was perfected and the first flight from water made. In the summer of 1908, "The Loon," as an airplane without pontoons, won the Scientific American trophy at what is believed to have been the first successful publicly announced flight in America.

road train, but in those days no one would believe that. We had seen it soar over the tops of the sand mountains and turn corners as gracefully as a sailing-yacht, but no one would be-

[1] It was difficult, and was made more complex by an attempt of the London *Daily Mail* correspondent to practise an old device for "keeping the wire." Mr. Alpheus W. Drinkwater, who was and still is (in 1927) in charge of the Weather Bureau Station at Manteo, writes me that on the evening of May 11 the first reporter to appear in his office was the London *Daily Mail* man:

"Mr. McGowan immediately filed about seven or eight hundred words which he had written coming over on the boat. By the time I had finished this, all the other reporters had arrived and were preparing their copy. It was then that McGowan marked a page in a magazine and told me to send it while he prepared more copy. Mr. Salley and Mr. Newton did not say anything, but neither had a pleased

lieve that either. So we toned down the story somewhat and even at that we were accused of flagrant faking.[1]

In looking back at a dairy I kept, I find, written at Manteo May 14, 1908, this entry:

"Some day when the world has had time to understand the great achievements of these modest, obscure men, scientists and historians will dig up the fragments and civilization will erect a great monument[2] there."

---

look. Mr. Hoster said enough for all the rest, and had it not been for the cool heads of Mr. Newton and Mr. Salley some one would have got hurt. After a few minutes I arranged matters satisfactorily to all by explaining that my office belonged to the government and not to a commercial telegraph company, and that my official closing hour was four-thirty. I was willing to do them a favor in sending their dispatches after hours, but I would do so only on condition that thirty minutes of my time should be allotted to each man, and that the one who was first one night should be last the next. Everything went smoothly from then on. Mrs. Drinkwater, Mr. Salley, and I sent out some thirty-eight thousand words during the week the reporters were here.

[1] Newton's dispatch in the New York *Herald* May 12, 1908, said the Wrights had flown "two and seven-sixteenths miles, the distance being computed by the telegraph poles of the U. S. Weather Bureau. . . . Imagine a noisy reaper flying through the air with a rising and falling motion similar to that of a bird. . . ." On May 13: "Correspondents from all sections, including the London papers, are arriving here." On May 14: "With the ease and swiftness of a huge eagle, the Wright brothers' aeroplane made a flight of three miles at ten o'clock this morning. . . . There is no longer any ground for questioning the performance of the men and their wonderful machine."

Arthur Ruhl, concluding the account he wrote for *Collier's Weekly*, May 30, 1908, wrote:

"Then, bedraggled and very sunburned, we tramped up to the little weather bureau and informed the world, waiting on the other side of various sounds and continents and oceans, that it was all right, the rumors true. and there was no doubt that a man could fly."

[2] In 1927, Congress took steps to erect a monument.

29

1904

January 21. The body of James Smithson arrived in America from Genoa, where it had lain for eighty-four years, since his death in 1820. Smithson, an English scientist, natural son of the Duke of Northumberland, although he had never been in America, left over $500,000 "to found at Washington, under the name of the Smithsonian Institution, an establishment for the increase and diffusion of knowledge among men." The legacy had been brought to America in 1834 in one hundred and five bags, each containing one thousand sovereigns.

February 5. Diplomatic negotiations between Russia and Japan were broken off. On February 10, formal declarations of war were made. The war occupied much of America's attention until it ended, September 5, 1905, with arbitration brought about by President Roosevelt.

March 3. The New York newspapers reported a meeting of the Rainy Day Club, organized for the serious purpose of giving mutual moral support to women who had begun to wear the "rainy day skirt," which, in its shortest form, reached the shoe-tops. The club was addressed by Charles R. Lamb, vice-president of the National Sculptors' Society, who urged the wearing of the skirt not only on rainy days, but on any and every occasion. "The short skirt," he said, "is the symbol of the emancipation of women."

In November, *Life* printed a joke which, when included in the present volume, encountered mystification on the part of stenographers and proof-readers, leading to the necessity of explaining that (a) in 1904, silk stockings were an unusual and costly luxury; and (b) at that time the skirts worn by women concealed the stockings, except on rainy days when it was permissible to raise the skirts a few

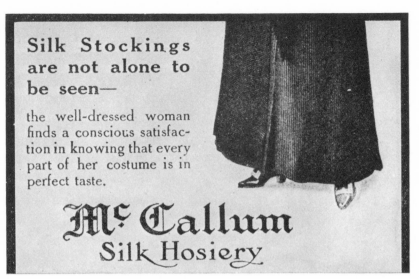

Silk Stockings
are not alone to
be seen—

the well-dressed woman
finds a conscious satisfaction in knowing that every
part of her costume is in
perfect taste.

Mc Callum
Silk Hosiery

A McCallum advertisement in 1904.

A McCallum advertisement in 1927.

McCallum's slogan, "You just know she wears them," was kept up until a time when
there wasn't any doubt about it.

inches from the wet pavement. With this elucidation, the joke should be understandable to a generation in which knee-length skirts and silk stockings are both universal. The more savant will recognize that the difference between the generation to which this joke was clear, and the one to which it was not, was far more than one of manners and style; it was economic and social:

William G. McAdoo and party at the top of the shaft on the New York shore, after having walked through the first Hudson River Tunnel from New Jersey to New York, March 11, 1904.

MADGE: "So you spent that five-dollar gold piece? You told me you were saving it for a rainy day."

DOLLY: "So I was. I bought a pair of silk stockings with it."

March 11. An impressive achievement of a man who later became important in politics was described by the New York *Tribune* of the following day:

A few minutes before noon yesterday, the shield from the Jersey end of the Morton Street tunnel touched that from the New York end, and the dreams and intermittent toil of thirty years were completed. A minute later, William G. McAdoo, president of the New York and New Jersey Railroad, builder of the tunnel, stepped out into the Morton Street shaft and was the first man to cross the North River on dry land.

March. The unusually cold winter of 1903-04 gave New York eighty days of sleighing in Central Park. The mean temperature in New York was 26½ degrees, lower

This photograph was printed in *Leslie's Weekly*, March 30, 1905, under the caption "A statesman automobilist, Senator Depew, of New York, en route to the Capitol at Washington in his horseless carriage."

by 5⅓ degrees than any winter since the establishment of the Weather Bureau.

April 5. Chicago voted overwhelmingly in favor of municipal ownership of street-railways. The vote on one plan which authorized the municipality to construct, own, operate, and lease street-railways, was 152,434 in favor and 30,104 against. The plan was never carried into effect.

April 23. The Rev. Thomas B. Gregory, writing in

the New York *American*, protested against the suggestion that Kansas City send a number of its girls to participate in a "beauty show" at the St. Louis Exposition:

Imagine a really refined and innocent young girl sitting upon a platform at a great exposition to be gazed at and ogled and

Photograph by S. E. Wright in "Leslie's Weekly," April 20, 1905.

Mayor-elect Dunne, of Chicago, and his family, at the time when President Roosevelt called approving attention to large families.

discussed and commented upon by the great mixed multitude. . . . No truly refined young girl would submit to such a thing. The bare thought of it would drive her mad. She would rather die than be subjected to such vulgar publicity.

May 2. The New York *Tribune* asked: "How many generations must come and go before we get automobiles of artistic and graceful lines? Most of the self-motors on

our streets are monsters of ugli-
ness. Why cannot these chariots
be put together so that they will
make at least some approach to
symmetry?"

May 3. Under the auspices of
the League of American Wheelmen,
five thousand cyclists gathered at
Boston, listened to an address by
General Nelson A. Miles, and made
a run through the park system.

May 9. "Cy" Young, pitcher
of the Boston American League
team, shut out Philadelphia without allowing a man to reach first
base, a feat achieved only twice
before in major-league baseball
history.

May 15. A Lackawanna Railroad newspaper advertisement —
one of a series that attracted so
much attention as to become almost current literature — showed
a passenger locomotive engineer

Advertisement from *Puck*,
February 10, 1904.

conversing with a young woman in "spotless white," the
famous "Miss Phœbe Snow." The accompanying verse
read:

> Miss Snow draws near
> The cab, to cheer
> The level-headed
> Engineer,
> Whose watchful sight
> Makes safe her flight
> Upon the Road
> Of Anthracite.

May 18. The Western Union Telegraph Company ordered its employees not to accept for transmission over its wires news from race-tracks to "pool-rooms." This ended a familiar institution of city life.

A cozy seat
A dainty treat
Makes Phoebe's
happiness complete
With linen white
And silver bright
Upon the road
of Anthracite

Lackawanna
Railroad

Courtesy of the Delaware, Lackawanna & Western Railroad Company.

One of the famous "Phœbe Snow" advertisements of the Lackawanna Railroad.

May 23. German, French, Belgian, and Dutch steamship companies announced a cut in steerage rates, to $10, to compete with English lines carrying immigrants to America.

June 12. For the first[1] time, a layman, Doctor Woodrow Wilson, delivered the baccalaureate sermon at Princeton, a striking step in a transition of influence and emphasis in American colleges and universities — from clergymen to lay scholars, including scientists; and later to men with talent for administration.

June 16. The steamship *General Slocum* burned, in New York harbor, with a loss of about 900.

June 19. Forty-six Mergenthaler typesetting machines were ordered by the Government Printing Office, to supersede the laborious hand-set method.

[1] So far as the more accessible records show.

July. 382,000 acres of government land in the Rose-bud Reservation, South Dakota, were opened to settlement in 160-acre lots, the last large government grant

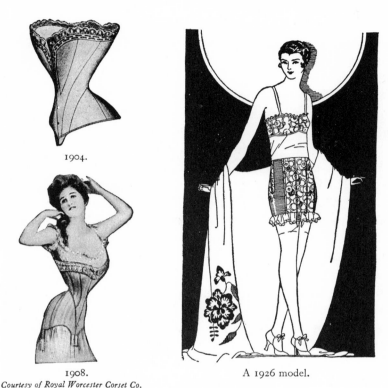

1904.

1908.
Courtesy of Royal Worcester Corset Co.

A 1926 model.

A cycle of styles in women's corsets.

to settlers. One railroad, the Chicago & North Western, carried more than 30,000 people to the opening.

August. At Mulberry and Bleecker streets, New York, where intemperance was supposed to be especially great, the "Subway Tavern" was established by leaders in reform. It sold the same liquors as other saloons, but, said the manager, "only the purest." It was dedicated by Bishop Henry C. Potter, of the Protestant Episcopal

Church, who led in singing, "Praise God from whom all blessings flow," and made an address saying the Tavern was "in many respects the greatest social movement New York has ever known." The Tavern was intended to be a clean, wholesome place, where every influence would discourage rather than induce drunkenness. The religious press was almost a unit in criticizing Bishop Potter, one editor saying, "A man can get drunk at the Bishop's bar just as quickly as at any other."

September 9. New York City's first mounted police went on duty.

September 16. At the meeting of the Dressmakers' Protective Association in New York it was predicted that "corsets will always stay straight-front as long as we shall live."

September 28. New York City newspapers recorded that a policeman had halted an automobile in which a woman was smoking a cigarette, saying, "You can't do that on Fifth Avenue." The woman was arrested.

December 5. On the assembling of Congress, attention was called to the impending retirement, after 29 years' service, of Senator Cockerill, of Missouri, who would take with him into retirement the last pair of cowhide boots worn in the Senate.

The Bookman for January, 1905, listed the "best sellers" of 1904 in the following order:

1. "The Crossing," by Winston Churchill.........913 points
2. "The Little Shepherd of Kingdom Come," by John Fox, Jr............................866 "
3. "Rebecca of Sunnybrook Farm," by Mrs. Kate Douglas Wiggin.........................718 "
4. "The Deliverance," by Ellen Glasgow.........648 "
5. "Sir Mortimer," by Mary Johnston...........524 "
6. "In the Bishop's Carriage," by Miriam Michelsen 419 "
7. "The Silent Places," by Stewart Edward White.400 "
8. "My Friend Prospero," by Henry Harland.....348 "

Other books popular or important during 1904 were "The Wings of the Morning," by Louis Tracy; "The Sea Wolf," by Jack London; "The Heart of Rome," by F. Marion Crawford; "The Memoirs of a Baby," one of several delightful books about children, written by Josephine Daskam (later Josephine Daskam Bacon); "Gordon Keith," by Thomas Nelson Page; "Rulers of

From "Leslie's Weekly," March 31, 1904.

Instruction to the long-skirted women of 1904 about "right and wrong ways of entering a 'motor-wagon.'"

Kings," by Gertrude Atherton; "The Cost," by David Graham Phillips; "Cherry," by Booth Tarkington; "Old Gorgon Graham," by George Horace Lorimer. "Beverly of Graustark," by George Barr McCutcheon, continued to be widely read. "Colonel Carter's Christmas," by F. Hopkinson Smith, was popular as another chapter in the life of one of the most lovable characters ever created by an American author. 1904 was the year of Joseph C. Lincoln's "Cap'n Eri," earliest of a series of Cape Cod stories that delighted a large portion of the reading public of America for more than twenty years.

Among books other than fiction, Booker T. Washington's "Working With the Hands" was a sequel to "Up

From Slavery," both being autobiographical narratives of the life of a remarkable negro.

Francis E. Leupp wrote a biography of Theodore Roosevelt from the point of view of a Washington correspondent, and Jacob A. Riis one from the point of view of a New York newspaper reporter and social reformer. Miss Ida M. Tarbell's "History of the Standard Oil Company" was a feature of what was called at the time "The Literature of Exposure." In the same field Lincoln Steffens's magazine articles about municipal corruption were collected and published as "The Shame of the Cities." Albert J. Beveridge's "The Russian Advance" appeared in 1904.

"The Limerick Up-To-Date Book," by Ethel Watts Mumford, included,

> There was an old man of Tarrentum
> Who sat on his false teeth and bent 'em;
>   When asked what he'd lost,
>   And what they had cost,
> He replied, "I don't know, I just rent 'em."

During the early months of 1904, Richard Mansfield played in "Ivan the Terrible," a personification of sinister wickedness and pathetic misery. Maude Adams toured in "The Pretty Sister of José," not one of her happiest parts. James K. Hackett played in "The Fortunes of the King," Mrs. Fiske in "Leah Kleschna," Ethel Barrymore in "Sunday." J. M. Barrie's "Little Mary" was played in America for the first time on January 4, 1904; much of the talk it gave rise to centred about its title, a euphemism still used by Victorian English society to avoid calling an indispensable organ for the digestion of food by its right name. The play itself did not live up to the interest excited by the whimsy of its title.

Annie Russell played in "Mice and Men"; Virginia Harned in "The Light that Lies in Woman's Eyes";

Margaret Anglin in "The Eternal Feminine"; Blanche Walsh in "The Kreutzer Sonata." Mme. Réjane toured several American cities in French plays; for playing "Sapho" she encountered the usual criticism. Wilton Lackaye played in a dramatization of Frank Norris's "The Pit"; the audiences were attracted chiefly by an elaborate grain-exchange scene with a frenzied mob of brokers. Rose Stahl appeared in "The Chorus Lady." A New York revival of "The Two Orphans" caused a *Bookman* contributor to designate it as "probably the most perfect specimen of pure melodrama ever put together; it illustrates the undoubted fact that a play as a play may be immensely successful without possessing the slightest literary merit whatsoever." Two famous comedians, Weber and Fields, after their performance on January 30, 1904, ended a combination that had entertained New York for a decade and went each his separate way.

The Theatre Magazine for 1904 said "the great successes of the year" had been: "The County Chairman," "The Other Girl," "The Girl from Kay's," "Sweet Kitty Bellairs," "Raffles," and "Her Own Way." Also successful were: "The Dictator," "The Secret of Polichinelle," "The Yankee Consul," "The Virginian," William Gillette in "The Admirable Crichton," Eleanor Robson in Israel Zangwill's "Merely Mary Ann," "The Man from Blankleys," "The Proud Prince," Ada Rehan and Otis Skinner in "The Taming of the Shrew" and "The Merchant of Venice," and Arnold Daly in "Candida."[1]

In the autumn of 1904, Henry Miller played in "Joseph Entangled," William H. Crane in "Business Is Business," Mrs. Fiske in "Hedda Gabler," Amelia Bingham in "The

[1] Walter Prichard Eaton wrote: "You should state that Arnold Daly's performance of 'Candida,' in 1904, really started the modern appreciation of Shaw in America."

Climbers"; Charles Wyndham and Mary Moore in "David Garrick." Nance O'Neil played in "Fires of St. John" and "Hedda Gabler." Nat Goodwin in "The Usurper" was a cowboy millionaire translated to aristocratic romance and a poodle-haunted tower.

"Mrs. Wiggs of the Cabbage Patch" opened September 3, 1904, with a cast which included Miss Mabel Taliaferro as "Lovey Mary" and Will T. Hodge as "Mr. Stubbins of Bagdad Junction." Leo Ditrichstein played in "Are You a Mason?" and Della Fox in "The West Point Cadet." Edna May played in "The School Girl," James K. Hackett in "The Fortunes of the King," Arnold Daly in "The Man of Destiny," Mrs. Patrick Campbell in "The Sorceress."

Caruso in 1904.

John Drew appeared in a farcical romance, "The Duke of Killicrankie." Herbert Kelcey and Effie Shannon played in "Taps." Mrs. Fiske revived "Becky Sharp." William Faversham played his fourth season in "Letty." George Ade's "The College Widow" was described as a "pictorial comedy." Ade's "County Chairman" resumed, after having already run 237 performances. Yet another Ade production was "The Sho-Gun." E. H. Sothern and Julia Marlowe played "Romeo and Juliet" and "Much Ado About Nothing." May Irwin's vehicle for robust humor was

"Mrs. Black Is Back." Cecilia Loftus played Zangwill's "The Serio-Comic Governess." Lillian Russell appeared in "Lady Teazle," a musical version of Sheridan's "The School for Scandal."

Denman Thompson in "The Old Homestead."

Denman Thompson played in "The Old Homestead," still.

A landmark was the appearance, on October 23, 1904, of Mrs. G. H. Gilbert, announced as "her farewell to the stage," in "Granny," written for the occasion by Clyde Fitch. A pandemonium of affectionate demonstration

arose when Mrs. Gilbert recited the rhymed epilogue
Fitch had written for her:

Dear friends in front, the curtain must not fall
Until a grateful woman says good-by to all. . . .
Dear days! so many too, red-lettered ones, and gold!
The curtain falls on all of them — I'm eighty-three years old.

During 1904, an Italian tenor, described as "heir to
Jean de Rezke in the affections of America," Signor
Enrico Caruso, completed his first season in America,
begun the preceding autumn.

A much-emphasized incident of the musical year was
the production of Wagner's "Parsifal," first given in New
York on Christmas eve of the preceding year, 1903. A
critic, W. J. Henderson, suggested that New York was
as much interested in Kundry's kiss, lasting forty-five
seconds, as in the reproduction of the Lord's Supper —
"the latter lugged in by Wagner to awe pious minds." A
woman writer, Eleanor Franklin, said the performance
was "profanity, sacrilege, blasphemy, and a gigantic outrage."

1904 was the year of two vogues that President Roosevelt helped bring about: "jiu-jitsu," an art of self-defense
in which the President was instructed by a Japanese who
went regularly to the White House; and the "simple life,"
started by a French author and clergyman, Charles
Wagner, whom Roosevelt invited to dine. Another fad
was "Fletcherism," started by an Englishman who "finds
satisfaction and profit in chewing his food very fine."
Two new phrases for American diplomacy were current:
"shirt-sleeves," meant to describe Secretary of State John
Hay's directness; and "hair-trigger," meant to lampoon
Roosevelt's promptness and forcefulness.

In women's fashions, the lingerie shirt-waist, said a
New York newspaper, "will reign supreme this summer."

The spring models were described as the essence of daintiness, made of sheer white muslin and mull, lace-trimmed and fancy, with many frills; "the shirt-waist in all its charming variations has come to stay forever." The vogue of veils was still on the increase. The "renaissance sleeve" was a new name for its more humble predecessor and equivalent, the "leg of mutton." A fashion dispatch from Paris to the New York *Tribune* said that "gowns, even for young girls, are complicated with ruchings, pleats, shirrings, and all manner of handwork." *Judge*, on September 24, published a complaint in verse against the current styles of feminine hair-dressing:

From "The Theatre Magazine," June, 1904.

Julia Marlowe in her runabout.

From "The Theatre Magazine," June, 1904.

Virginia Harned with Miss Louise Drew in an electric Victoria.

> She's taken a fancy to fix her hair
> In a sort of a strange "sky-scraper" affair.

Topics that ran through the news with the manner of novelty included the growth of divorce, woman suffrage,

and instalment buying, especially of diamond rings. . . .
A régime of "mild enforcement" in New York under
Chief of Police William S. Devery was described by the
phrase, "the lid is off." . . . The Louisiana Purchase
Exposition at St. Louis ran through the summer. . . .
On June 4, a New York race-track "book-maker" was

*From "The Ladies' Home Jour-
nal" of May, 1904.*

*From "The Ladies' Home Jour-
nal" of April, 1927.*

*From "The Ladies' Home Jour-
nal" of January, 1902.*

A cycle of styles for children.

murdered; his companion, Nan Patterson, became the
star of a sensational murder trial. . . . "Cigarette cou-
pons" came into use as a selling device, adopted by chain
tobacco stores, then also new; "trading stamps" had
existed a little longer. . . . Architects said the day of
the piazza was past, its place taken by the "enclosed
porch." . . . Phrases treated as new were "brain-fag,"
"rakish derby," "get-rich-quick." "Travelogues" was a
word used by Burton Holmes to distinguish his illustrated
lectures. . . . "Black-hand" letters . . . the "kissing-

bug" . . . much deploring of the influence of a new variation of light music, "ragtime." . . . "Golf vests" for
men, red or green with silk sleeves. . . . Cassie Chad-
wick, a Cleveland woman, induced some important bank-

Buick car in 1904.

ers to lend her immense sums on the basis of the relationship she claimed to have to distinguished public men, and
the mysterious contents of a safe-deposit box that turned
out to be mythical. . . . The outstanding popular song
was "Bedelia."

That the year was regarded as good was suggested by
the poetical summing up of *Judge* for December 10:

> Good old year of nineteen-four!
> Every one had goods in store —
> Wheat galore, a dollar up,
> Lots to eat and lots to sup.
> None abroad is mad at us;
> Naught at home to cause a fuss —
> May the year ahead give more
> Of the brand of nineteen-four!

30

1905

February 15.   General Lew Wallace died. His novel "Ben Hur," published in 1880, was still selling strongly. The sale of more than 1,000,000 copies of it, together with royalties from the drama based on it, had brought Lew Wallace greater financial returns than had been received by any other author of his generation in America. His other books, less well-known, were "The Fair God" and "The Prince of India." Wallace had been variously soldier, lawyer, legislator, and diplomat.

February 22.   Doctor William Osler initiated a characteristic American whirlwind of controversy and objurgation, ameliorated by occasional zephyrs of satire and humor. Osler was the leading member of the medical faculty of Johns Hopkins University, and was delivering a valedictory before leaving to become Regius Professor of Medicine at Oxford. He said: "I have two fixed ideas . . . the comparative uselessness of men above forty, [and that a very large proportion of the evils of the world] may be traced to sexagenarians." He went on with a facetious allusion to "the admirable scheme" of a suppositious college into which, at sixty, men retired for a period of contemplation before a peaceful departure by chloroform. The following day, newspapers throughout the country carried such headlines as: "Osler Recommends Chloroform at Sixty."

The word "Oslerize" passed into the current tongue with connotations divided between oppobrium and mirth. Wagon-loads of letters were delivered to Osler's home in Baltimore. He was deeply pained at the failure of the public to distinguish between the serious and the jocular in his address.

February. A survey by a clergyman revealed that there were one hundred fifty-seven religious sects in the United

Advertisement from *Leslie's Weekly*, May 11, 1905.

States. Among them were the Schwenkfeldians, the River Brethren, the Six-Principle Baptists, the Old Two-Seed-in-the-Spirit Predestinarian, the United Zion's Children, the Social Brethren, the Christadelphians, the Life and Advent Union.

February. A statue of Frances E. Willard — the first of a woman — was placed in Statuary Hall in the National Capitol.

March 1. Battle flags captured from the Confederate armies, which had been in the custody of the War Department at Washington since the Civil War, were returned to the Southern States.

This episode was a landmark, a measure of the time required for the subsiding of passions aroused by war. For attempting it eighteen years earlier, in 1887, Grover Cleveland, then President, had been denounced as a "non-combatant" who "did not think of the blood and torture of battle."

From "Leslie's Weekly," February 1, 1906.

Edith, daughter of Secretary of War Elihu Root, in 1905.

March 22. Congregational ministers of New England protested against the acceptance of $100,000 for foreign mission work from John D. Rockefeller, on the ground that the Standard Oil Company stood "before the public under indictments for methods which are socially destructive."

March 25. Maurice Barrymore, actor, and one of the famous wits of the day, died. He made a place for himself in the affections of American theatregoers as leading man for Mrs. Langtry and Mme. Modjeska; and, just before his final illness, as Rawdon Crawley in Mrs. Fiske's performance of "Becky Sharp." The fame he had in his own right was perpetuated by his daughter Ethel, and his sons John and Lionel.

March. An over-confident prediction was made by Chauncey M. Depew, in a speech before the Transportation Club in New York:

Within ten years the steam locomotive of to-day will be seen in the museum for the inspection of the antiquarian, and we will be able to proceed over the rails by means of electricity at a rate of seventy-five miles an hour.

April 23. Joseph Jefferson died. Considering everything, including the length of his tenure on the stage, he

Photograph by Earle, in "Leslie's Weekly."
New York mounted policeman training his horse not to fear automobiles.

was probably the foremost actor in the affections of the American people. His stage career paralleled more than two-thirds of all our national history. Born in Philadelphia, in 1829, the son, grandson, and great-grandson of actors, he played at the age of four, in Washington, D. C., as the miniature of one of the most familiar indigenous American stage characters — carried upon the stage blacked up, and introduced by T. D. Rice, one of the fathers of American minstrelsy, with the lines:

> Oh ladies and gentlemen, I'd have for you to know,
> I've got a little darky here that jumps Jim Crow.

As a youth Jefferson followed the American army to Matamoras in the Mexican War in 1846. He made his first hit as Doctor Pangloss in "The Heir-at-Law" in 1857; and played Asa Trenchard to the elder Sothern's Lord Dundreary in 1858. With daring audacity he staged "The Octoroon," and in it played Salem Scudder at a

From the Albert Davis Collection.

Joseph Jefferson as Rip Van Winkle.

time when the country was at white heat about slaves. During the last forty years of his life he occasionally played Bob Acres in "The Rivals," but toward the end identified himself completely with America's outstanding folk-lore character, Rip van Winkle. For its unique position as an American classic, "Rip van Winkle" is indebted as much to Joseph Jefferson as to Washington Irving, for Jefferson not only made it familiar but introduced new touches into the stage version, which he first wrote for himself and later persuaded Dion Boucicault to help him reconstruct. With his gun, his tattered clothes, his twenty years of beard, the background of gnomes rolling kegs of schnapps in the mountain twilight, the village tippler's timidly deferential attempts to placate a shrewish wife, and his bewildered efforts, after his twenty-year sleep, to comprehend an altered world — Jefferson planted the memory of his gentle, whimsical personality deep in the affections of practically two centuries of Americans: older persons who had seen the beginning of the 1800's, and children who may live — and remember Joseph Jefferson — until near the end of the 1900's. Some of the mellow hold that Jefferson had on America's affections arose from his long comradeship with Grover Cleveland, with whom he used to go fishing at Buzzard's Bay, Massachusetts.

April 24. Will Rogers, described in the newspapers, either by mistake or by press agent's license, as a "full-blooded Cherokee Indian" (actually one-eighth Indian), was the feature of the opening of the horse show at Madison Square Garden. It was claimed that Rogers was the only man in the world who could lasso both rider and horse at the same time with two different ropes.

April. Grover Cleveland in an article in *The Ladies' Home Journal* advised women not to join clubs, except those with "purposes of charity, religious enterprise, or intellectual improvement. . . . Her best and safest club is her home." In the October number he wrote that "sensible and responsible women do not want to vote. The relative positions to be assumed by man and woman in the working out of our civilization were assigned long ago by a higher intelligence than ours."

May 20. Geraldine Farrar, American soprano of the Berlin Opera House, made her first public appearance in Paris in the part of Marguerite. A critic cabled: "Her voice is pure and clear, her methods are simple, and, what is rare, she can act."

Courtesy of the Remington Typewriter Company.

"Typewriter" of early 1900's.   "Typist" of 1925.

The "blind" typewriting machine, and "typewriting in sight."

May 31. For the first time in a Memorial Day parade in New York the headquarters colors were not carried by Grand Army veterans. The aged men found themselves obliged to pass this portion of their ceremony over to younger arms. In 1904, 2000 veterans had been in line; in 1905, only 1500.

May. Extra long hatpins, designed to hold in place the broad sailor hats in vogue this year, were on sale. *Life* printed this:

HUSBAND: (house-hunting) Do you think, dear, we can get our piano through this door?

WIFE: I wasn't thinking so much of the piano as I was of my new hat.[1]

---

[1] The survival until 1905 of another freak vogue in women's styles was reflected in the following item among the news in the Rochester *Union and Advertiser*:

"A woman who was waiting for a train in a Minneapolis railroad station yesterday lost her bustle, in which was five hundred dollars."

May. Bathing costumes for women at Narragansett were "of soft twill foulard, dark blue or black, made with skirt, long sleeves and high neck, and worn with a narrow linen collar. With this is worn a sunbonnet, and often gloves, the stockings and shoes being as dainty as

Photograph by Brown Bros. in "Leslie's Weekly," June 8, 1905.

American women golfers who competed in the Englishwomen's Golf Championship Tournament at Cromer, Scotland.

those for ordinary house wear. Veils, of thin red gauze, are also advocated by some to protect the complexion."

June 1. The Lewis and Clark Exposition opened at Portland, Ore.

June 7. The highest price ever paid so far for land in New York was recorded with the sale, by the estate of Benjamin D. Silliman, of the corner at Wall Street and Broadway, known as No. 1 Wall Street, containing 1250 square feet, for $700,000. Since the old four-story building was to be removed, the land value was $558.65 a square foot. A current story about the plot related that a prospective purchaser had put his offer thus: "You said you wanted $5 gold-pieces put all over that plot, and I am here to give them to you." Whereupon the owner explained he had meant the gold-pieces should be placed on their edges.[1]

June 11. The Pennsylvania Railroad inaugurated "the fastest long-distance train in the world," eighteen hours, each way, between Chicago and New York. At Mentor, Ohio, four days later, June 15, the eastbound complement of the train suffered a minor accident. On June 18, the New York Central met the Pennsylvania's challenge, and inaugurated an eighteen-hour train of its own, the "Twentieth Century Limited." Twenty-five thousand people gathered to see the first departure of this train from Chicago. Near LaPorte, Ind., it travelled a measured mile in forty seconds. On the third day of the new schedule, June 21, the eastbound "Twentieth Century Limited" also had a wreck, in which nineteen lives were lost. A day later the New York Central lengthened its schedule to nineteen hours, but on June 26 it was announced that speed had not been the cause of the accident and the eighteen-hour schedule was resumed. This action was necessary, said the president of the New York Central, in order that his road should be able to compete with the Pennsylvania.[2]

July 24. The body of John Paul Jones, discovered in a built-over Paris cemetery by Ambassador Horace

---

[1] The highest-priced land ever sold, I was informed by Joseph P. Day in 1926, was the corner of Wall and Nassau Streets, bought by the Bankers' Trust Company, December 31, 1909, for $1,150,000. Omitting the building, which was removed, the price was $622.29 for each of the 1848 square feet.

[2] Fast railroad time between Chicago and New York began with the World's Fair of 1893, when, for 180 days, the New York Central ran an "Exposition Flyer" in twenty hours. In June, 1902, both the Pennsylvania and the New York Central roads inaugurated a regular twenty-hour service. In June, 1905, the Pennsylvania Railroad announced an eighteen-hour train, and in a trial run, on June 6, 1905, actually made the trip in seventeen hours. Later, in the interest of safety and economy, both roads abandoned the eighteen-hour schedule and returned to the twenty-hour one.

Porter after a six-year search, and convoyed to the United States by a fleet of American warships, was landed at Annapolis for burial in the grounds of the Naval Academy.

August 27.   Yellow fever, which for several months had been epidemic in New Orleans, leaped the State boundaries. Along the Mississippi River, towns and cities were instituting vigilance committees to patrol the river day and night, and Governor Vardaman, of Mississippi, ordered out the militia to guard his State line against the entrance of yellow fever refugees.

October 23.   The New York *Tribune* received information from Paris on coming styles in women's dress:

"Jilted," a picture of the times, in *Judge*, July 22, 1905.

"The Directory style, adroitly combined with the high Empire waist, modernized by trimmings of rare lace and costly fur, is now definitely adopted for the coming season. The skirts are little short of revolutionary. Not since the days of the Directory have they applied such searching sculptural indiscretion to the female outline. Young and willowy women favor the new style. Dowagers hope it won't last."

New Fitted Petticoat

The "ANNA HELD"

As advertised in *The Theatre Magazine*. This type of petticoat was fashionable in 1905 and for several years thereafter. "The sensation of the Fashion World. Clinging closely to the form from the waist over the hips and down to the deep flounce without a pucker, it presents an ideally smooth surface upon which the closest fitting gown of to-day's fashion will hang without a wrinkle. And yet—here's the genius of it—*it positively does not bind*, all through a clever trick in the making. Best quality silk taffeta, black and all colors. Cut circular, fastens at the back with glove snaps, has deep flounce fashioned in various styles. All leading department stores in the United States sell the 'Anna Held' Fitted Petticoat."

November 8. A milestone in transportation was recorded in an advertisement of the Chicago & North Western Railway: "The new Overland Limited, electric-lighted daily train from Chicago to California." Reading-lamps were placed in each berth.

November 28. Directors of the Chicago, Milwaukee & St. Paul Railway Company formally authorized the extension of the road from the Missouri River to the Pacific Coast, at an estimated cost of sixty million dollars. This was the last great trunk line to be built.

December 14. The New York *Tribune* published a note on women's styles for the year:

The new skirts are so wide that at first glance they seem to require artificial means to hold them out. Petticoats now measure more than eight yards around the feet and the skirt must be of corresponding width. Both petticoat and circular skirt fit closely around the hips and have the fulness at the back in becoming inverted pleats. All skirts touch

An "outing suit" of 1905.

A sports frock of 1927.

Afternoon dress of 1905—of 1927.

the ground on all sides and boast a short train in the back. evening dresses, of course, have much longer trains than the street dresses, and many of these are elaborately beaded and embroidered.

Two of the popular books of 1905, Mrs. Humphry Ward's "The Marriage of William Ashe," and Edith Wharton's "The House of Mirth," were said by a Chicago minister to be "revelations of the degeneracy in what is falsely called 'the higher circles' or the 'favored classes.'" Mrs. Wharton's book, he said, revealed the "coarse phases of wealth — the 'newly rich,' the gambling, speculating, globe-trotting representatives of gold"; and Mrs. Ward's "the realms of culture, where poets, diplomats, lords, and cabinet officers move . . . the vulgarity of cigarette-smoking women and lecherous, champagne-sipping men."

On January 14 Thomas Dixon's "The Clansman" made its appearance in an edition of 50,000 copies, and three days later Owen Johnson's "In the Name of Liberty," a story of the French Revolution. Among "best sellers" for the year were: "The Masquerader," Katherine Cecil Thurston; "The Prodigal Son," Hall Caine; "The Affair at the Inn," and "Rose of the River," Kate Douglas Wiggin; "Beverly of Graustark," George Barr McCutcheon; "The Truants," A. E. W. Mason; "Nancy Stair," Elinor Macartney Lane; "The Millionaire Baby," Anna Katherine Green; "The Conquest of Canaan," Booth Tarkington; "The Secret Woman," **Eden Phillpotts**; "The Sea Wolf," Jack London; "The Garden of Allah," Robert Hichens; "The Princess Passes," C. N. and A. M. Williamson; "The Two Captains," Cyrus Townsend Brady; "Paradise," Alice Brown; "The Coming of the Tide," Margaret Sherwood; "The Man on the Box," Harold McGrath. Ralph Connor's "The Prospector" was described as a novel of "muscular Christian-

From "The Theatre Magazine," December, 1904.
Ethel Barrymore in "Sunday."

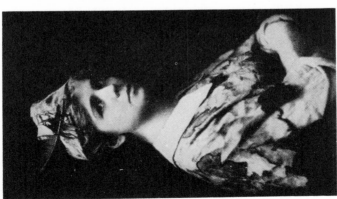

From "The Theatre Magazine," February, 1905.
Lillian Russell, in 1905.

Maude Adams as Peter Pan, in 1905.

645

ity."   Among books not fiction, two of the most note-
worthy were J. T. Hobhouse's "Democracy and Reaction," and Frederick Howe's "The City the Hope of
Democracy."   Robert Hunter's "Poverty" went into a
new edition.

In the early months of 1905, Maude Adams played in
"The Little Minister," pre-
ceded by a one-act play entitled "'Op o' Me Thumb,"
to audiences "nightly dis-
solving in salty tears."   On
April 17, at the Academy of
Music, Blanche Bates gave
the one thousandth per-
formance of Yo San in "The
Darling of the Gods."   Lawrence D'Orsay completed in
May his nine hundredth
performance of "The Earl
of Pawtucket."   "Trilby,"
Paul M. Potter's stage version of Du Maurier's novel,

From the Albert Davis Collection.

David Warfield in "The Music Master."

was revived on May 9, with
Wilton Lackaye as Sven-
gali.   David Warfield had
a spectacular success in "The Music Master," which
had held over from the fall of 1904 — William Winter
spoke of him as "the rising star of eccentric comedy,"
and of his performance as "deeply pathetic as an emblem
of heroism and paternal affection piquant with involun-
tary humor."   Richard Mansfield, then generally conceded to be the greatest American actor, played "Beau
Brummel," "Richard III, "Doctor Jekyll and Mister
Hyde," Shylock, and other rôles.   Forbes Robertson
played "Hamlet" — there was general unanimity of

judgment that he was at that time "the only Hamlet of
the modern world." Viola Allen played "The Winter's
Tale" and "Twelfth Night" with a superfluity of scenery
that caused John Corbin to call it "Shakespeare in
Chromo." "Florodora" was back in New York after
being played in practically every town in the United
States. William Gillette revived "Sherlock Holmes";

From "The Theatre Magazine," February, 1905.
The classic attitudes of Isadora Duncan in her Greek barefoot dances.

Edward Terry played the sentimental "Sweet Lav-
ender"; Ada Rehan in "The School for Scandal";
Robert Edeson in "Strongheart"; Mrs. Leslie Carter in
a tragedy called "Adrea"; Margaret Illington in Augustus Thomas's "Mrs. Leffingwell's Boots"; E. S. Willard
in "The Professor's Love Story"; George M. Cohan in
"Little Johnny Jones"; Williams and Walker in "In
Dahomey," including the "Jonah Man" song. Arnold
Daly played in Shaw's "You Never Can Tell." A new
pun appeared, "Ibscene."

George Bernard Shaw's play, "Mrs. Warren's Profession," was suppressed by the police after its first performance, October 31. "It is revolting in theme," said
the New York *Sun*, and *The Evening Post* termed it "per-

vading poison" placed on the stage with "cynical effrontery."

Maude Adams, in a suit of boyish buckskins, playing "Peter Pan," asked "Do you believe in fairies?" "There were not many children there," said John Corbin; "it was an audience of grown-ups — a typical New York first-night audience — but under the spell of the sweet Barrie fancy, the impish Barrie laugh, the half-mocking Barrie melodramatics, it had become just so many little children; at the sound of Peter's plea it arose and shouted, 'Yes!'" (This run of "Peter Pan" lasted from November 6, 1903, to June 9, 1906.) Sarah Bernhardt played "Magda," "Sapho," "Phèdre," and several others, including, of course, "La Dame aux Camélias" — a play so disliked by actors (other than the star) that Frank Craven was moved to write a verse about it:

> What piece do we all know by heart?
> Camille.
> What piece contains but one good part?
> Camille.
> If damned plays should run a race,
> East Lynne might give it quite a chase.
> But which would finish in first place?
> Camille.

Robert Loraine played in "Man and Superman." Nat Goodwin in "Beauty and the Barge." An all-star company performed "The Sporting Duchess," described as "the greatest English melodrama ever produced." James K. Hackett and Mary Mannering performed "The Walls of Jericho." Chauncey Olcott played "Edmund Burke"; Henry E. Dixey "The Man on the Box"; Arnold Daly in Shaw's "John Bull's Other Island" and "Mrs. Warren's Profession"; Sothern and Marlowe in "The Merchant of Venice," and other Shakespearian plays; Olga Nethersole in "The Labyrinth." William Faversham played "The Squaw Man"; Blanche Bates played "The Girl of the Golden West"; the Ben Greet players gave "Macbeth." George Ade's comedy, "The Bad Samaritan," had for its hero a man of fifty-eight who refused to take seriously Doctor Osler's theory about what to do with elderly men. *Puck*, in September, predicted that "the most important dramatic event of the present century will be the permanent withdrawal from the stage of 'Uncle Tom's Cabin' " — by 1927, it had not yet happened.

INDEX

Abbott, Lawrence F., 445.
Ackerman, John J., 74 (*f.n.*).
Acropolis, 52.
Actors—
  Adams, Maude, 624, 646, 648.
  Ade, George, 626.
  Allen, Viola, 647.
  Anglin, Margaret, 625.
  Barrymore, Ethel, 624, 634.
  Barrymore, John, 634.
  Barrymore, Lionel, 634.
  Barrymore, Maurice, 634.
  Bates, Blanche, 646, 649.
  Ben Greet players, 649.
  Bernhardt, Sarah, 648.
  Bingham, Amelia, 625.
  Campbell, Mrs. Patrick, 626.
  Carter, Mrs. Leslie, 647.
  Caruso, Enrico, 628.
  Cohan, George M., 647.
  Crane, William H., 625.
  Craven, Frank, 648.
  Daly, Arnold, 625, 626, 647, 648.
  Ditrichstein, Leo, 626.
  Dixey, Henry E., 648.
  D'Orsay, Lawrence, 646.
  Drew, John, 626.
  Edeson, Robert, 647.
  Farrar, Geraldine, 638.
  Faversham, William, 626, 648.
  Fiske, Mrs. Minnie Maddern, 624, 626.
  Fox, Della, 626.
  Gilbert, Mrs. G. H., 627.
  Gillette, William, 625, 647.
  Gilmore, Kittie, 183.
  Goodwin, Nat, 626, 648.
  Hackett, James K., 624, 626, 648.
  Harned, Virginia, 624.
  Hodge, Will T., 626.
  Illington, Margaret, 647.
  Irwin, May, 626.
  Jefferson, Joseph, 635.
  Kelcey, Herbert, 626.
  Lackaye, Wilton, 625, 646.
  Langtry, Lillian, 634.
  Loftus, Cecilia, 627.
  Loraine, Robert, 648.
  Mannering, Mary, 648.
  Mansfield, Richard, 624, 646.
  Marlowe, Julia, 626.
  May, Edna, 626.
  Miller, Henry, 625.
  Modjeska, Mme., 634.
  Moore, Mary, 626.
  Nethersole, Olga, 648.
  Olcott, Chauncey, 648.
  O'Neil, Nance, 626.
  Rehan, Ada, 625, 647.
  Réjane, Mme., 625.
  Rice, T. D., 635.
  Robertson, Forbes, 646.
  Robson, Eleanor, 625.
  Rogers, Will, 637.
  Russell, Annie, 624.
  Russell, Lillian, 627.
  Shannon, Effie, 626.
  Skinner, Otis, 625.
  Sothern, E. H., 626.
  Sothern and Marlowe, 648.
  Stahl, Rose, 625.
  Taliaferro, Mabel, 626.
  Terry, Edward, 647.
  Thompson, Denman, 627.
  Walsh, Blanch, 625.
  Warfield, David, 646.
  Weber and Fields, 625.
  Willard, E. S., 647.
  Williams and Walker, 647.
  Wyndham, Charles, 626.
Adams, F. A., 253 (*f.n.*).
Adams, Henry, 49, 192, 467.
Adams, Maude, 624, 646, 648.
Adams, Samuel Hopkins, 512, 513, 515, 516, 552 (*f.n.*).
Ade, George, 626.
Advertising, medium of culture, 1 (*f.n.*).
Aeronautics, literature of, 572.
"Aggregated capital," 327.
Agricultural implements, manufacture of, 263, 264.
Airplane engines, 590–591.
Airplane, first successful flight of, 593, 594, 595.
Albright, Mrs. J. H., 79 (*f.n.*).
Albums, autograph, 148–153.
Aldrich, Nelson W., 531.
Aldrich, Thomas Bailey, 117.
Alexander ("How Big Was Alexander?"), 41.
"All Bound Round with a Woollen String," 180.
Allen, Ethan, 55.
Allen, Robert McDowell, 518, 523

651